THE ENGLISH CIVIL WAR

OSPREY
PUBLISHING

DEDICATION

To Robin and Simon
and in memory of Anna

NICK LIPSCOMBE

THE ENGLISH CIVIL WAR

AN ATLAS AND CONCISE HISTORY OF THE WARS OF THE THREE KINGDOMS
1639–51

OSPREY PUBLISHING
Bloomsbury Publishing Plc
Kemp House, Chawley Park, Cumnor Hill, Oxford OX2 9PH, UK
1385 Broadway, 5th Floor, New York, NY 10018, USA
E-mail: info@ospreypublishing.com
www.ospreypublishing.com

OSPREY is a trademark of Osprey Publishing Ltd

First published in Great Britain in 2020

A catalogue record for this book is available from the British Library.

ISBN: HB 9781472829726; ePDF 9781472847164; XML 9781472829719

20 21 22 23 24   10 9 8 7 6 5 4 3 2 1

Maps by www.bounford.com
Originated by PDQ Digital Media Solutions, Bungay, UK
Printed and bound in China by RR Donnelley Asia Printing Solutions Limited

Osprey Publishing supports the Woodland Trust, the UK's leading woodland conservation charity.

To find out more about our authors and books visit **www.ospreypublishing.com**. Here you will find extracts, author interviews, details of forthcoming events and the option to sign up for our newsletter.

CONTENTS

CONTENTS

FOREWORD

I am delighted to be able to pen the forward to this unique and important study. Since the end of the English Civil Wars (the name by which they are popularly known, although the subtitle wisely emphasises that they stretched across three kingdoms) historians have continued to debate the nature of the conflict itself. Was it a class war? Was it a revolution? And, most importantly perhaps, are the long-term implications of any significance today? Over the centuries which have followed, there has been much interest not only in the political elements but also in the personalities of the conflict and the places which it affected.

The war took many forms and involved many places. Research has recently emphasised the high death toll of this extended and bitter struggle, on the battlefield and through disease and social dislocation. Thanks to the National Civil War Centre at Newark, a pivotal town in the conflict, and the many iconic battlefield sites which the Battlefields Trust is honoured to help protect, interpret and publicise, we can both commemorate and try to understand this key period in our national, if not international, history.

Curiously, a serious venture to map the conflict in its entirety has never been attempted before. A glance at the bibliography and content of this work is a good indicator of the enormity of the project and, perhaps, provides the explanation for this gap.

In 2017, Nick Lipscombe approached Howard Simmons, my predecessor as chair of The Battlefields Trust, to gauge his views and solicit his support for this atlas project. Howard, well aware of Nick's award-winning *Peninsular War Atlas and Concise History* (Oxford, 2010), was only too willing to agree and to offer help. The Battlefields Trust is a registered charity dedicated to preserving, promoting and interpreting Britain's battlefield sites. It is this latter point that is central to this important project: the advancement of battlefield survey and archaeology has provided new evidence, confirming or changing historical perspectives on battles and sieges in this and other historical periods. Nick's work has embraced that evidence and, in some cases with Trust members, has taken it a step further. He has also provided a link with national and regional mapping to the many battles and sieges, some of which have never been mapped before.

The result is this most magnificent atlas of the Wars of the Three Kingdoms. It is the most ground-breaking piece of work on the wars for decades. On behalf of the Battlefields Trust, our thanks to Nick for this excellent book, which we hope will stimulate further interest in the Wars and inspire visits to the key sites.

Emeritus Professor Anne Curry
Chair of the Battlefields Trust, March 2020.

PREFACE

The Magna Carta, or Great Charter of 1215, was intended to re-balance the power between the king and his subjects, and between the king and his barons. In other words, it was about sovereignty. Eight hundred years after the signing of Magna Carta, the United Kingdom finds itself embroiled in another struggle for sovereignty; this time with the European Union. Sandwiched between these two tumultuous events, was another more brutal struggle for the nation's sovereignty, the Civil Wars that raked the Three Kingdoms[1] in the 1640s during the reign of Charles I. Mark Twain purportedly said that 'history might not repeat itself but it sure does rhyme' and this, it seems, is the case for the nation's periodic struggle for rule.

This *Atlas and Concise History of the Wars of the Three Kingdoms* concentrates primarily on the military aspects of the wars and provides political (including social and religious) detail in order to better understand the developing political process as a part of an armed negotiation and subsequent military action. Although military campaigns were an extension of the political process, the latter changed and escalated over time, necessitating renewed legitimization and a move to more active warfare. The military campaigns from the Bishops' Wars in the late 1630s to the final conquest of Ireland in 1652 have never been mapped in their entirety before. Self-evidently, the maps form the mainstay of the work. To that end, I have utilized the same format I used to map the Peninsular War.[2] This proved to be popular and has considerable advantages as the reader is able to connect the text directly to the relevant map. However, it does have the hindrance of restricting the amount of text available to describe a particular battle or incident. My greatest challenge, therefore, was deciding what to leave out rather than what to include.

Mapping battles, sieges and events that took place nearly 400 years ago has been a challenge; particularly for the smaller, or lesser known, military engagements. Official military maps did exist but these were mainly prepared for defence against invasion, fortification of the northern border with Scotland and naval dockyards and depots. In the wake of the wars in England (but not Wales) only the major battles were mapped and recorded. In Scotland, the mapping concentrated on the rebellion and its subjugation, while in Ireland the mapping tended to concentrate on Protestant colonialization and the subjugation of the Catholic Irish. For most of the Civil War encounters there is a good idea of the general area of the battle or event. Sieges were, by their very nature, easier to locate, but even here there were challenges as to the locations of siege batteries and exact sites of attacks. Since 1990, battlefield archaeology has enabled us to determine more precise locations, deployments, events and even the outcomes of battles. Historic England's Register of Historic Battlefields identifies 46 important English battlefields, of which 22 relate to the English Civil War. The Historic Environment Scotland Inventory of Historic Battlefields consists of 43 battles, of which nine relate to the Wars of the Three Kingdoms. No such register appears to exist for Ireland, making the task of mapping events there more complicated. Recent archaeological work and discoveries on some of the civil war battlefields enabled me to fine-tune certain battles and adjust others. I have tried to use the most up-to-date information to depict these actions, and the help I have received in this regard has been invaluable. However, battlefield archaeology does not provide all the answers and needs to be interpreted with care and a good understanding of weapon characteristics, ballistics and tactics. At Winceby, for example, a recent study confirmed that the battle did not take place at the hitherto accepted location. Equally, however, it did not determine (as it was limited geographically) where the battle did actually take place.[3] Similarly, at Cheriton, a number of finds that were lifted from the battlefield between 1974 and 1990 were not properly processed and documented, leading to speculation and doubt.[4]

Even when we are sure of where a battle was fought, it remains a challenge to piece together the sequence of events. Very few individuals had timepieces, so time is a relative concept in battles of the era. Maps were virtually non-existent. Units did not keep war diaries and much of what individuals recorded in their journals and memoirs was hearsay gleaned subsequently around campfires. Nevertheless, the amount of primary source material available is surprisingly abundant. A glimpse at the extensive bibliography to this work bears testament to this. I have tried to weave some of the more poignant and colourful of these accounts into the stories. In so doing, it has been remembered that such accounts were often prejudiced, particularly those that cover the struggles in Ireland. In conclusion, therefore, this work is far from the panacea, but I hope that it provides a unique and perhaps long-overdue detailed map study into the military events of the Wars of the Three Kingdoms.

This project would not have been possible without an extraordinary amount of help from so many. The venture has been undertaken in conjunction with the Battlefields Trust, the National Civil War Centre, Newark, and the Scottish Battlefields Trust. I am deeply indebted to Howard Simmons, the (former) Chairman of the Battlefields Trust, who warmly embraced the concept of an atlas covering the wars in the mid-17th century. His support, and that of the other trustees, has been a significant driver. Sir Jon Day and Michael Rayner provided an invaluable conduit between myself and the expertise within the Trust, for which I am deeply grateful. Two members of the Trust deserve particular thanks. The first is Simon Marsh, whose depth of knowledge, expertise and enthusiasm has been vital. The second is Gary Chilcott, who helped me with the tricky but fascinating battlefield at Cheriton and went on to produce the majority of Orders of Battle that feature in the extensive appendices. Other members of the Trust who deserve mention and praise include Professor Anne Curry, Phil Steele, Julian Humphrys, Adrian Webb, Chris Scott, Don Smith, Len Davis, Tony Spicer, Alan Turton, Gregg Archer and, finally, Stephen Ede-Borrett. At the National Civil War Centre, I am indebted to Kevin

---

1 England, Scotland and Ireland – Wales at that time being considered part of England.

2 Lipscombe, N. J., *The Peninsular War Atlas* (Oxford, 2010).

3 Weston, S., *Lincolnshire's lost Battlefield? A Battlefield Survey of the Battle of Winceby, 1643* (York University, 2013).

4 Klaxton, K. M., *The Archaeology of an English Civil War Battlefield. What can the analysis of small finds contribute to the understanding of the Battle of Cheriton?* (York University, 2017).

Winter, Glyn Hughes and Carol King. I was pleased that the Scottish Battlefields Trust was also keen to participate and I am grateful to its Director, Arran Johnston, for checking the accuracy of the maps of the Scottish battles. Sir John Day was also a huge help in deciphering and assisting in some of the lesser-known and recorded battles in Ireland.

In addition, I would like to recognize the help and guidance provided by Professor Jeremy Black, Professor Charles Esdaile, Professor Peter Gaunt, Professor Martyn Bennet, Professor Peter Wilson, Stephen Bull and Chris Wardle. On the ground I have been assisted across the country by Peter Burton and Martin Marix-Evans at Naseby; Nick Allen and Nick Haynes at Cropredy; Captain Tom Bunting (the Station Staff Officer at BAD Kineton) at Edgehill; Richard Shaw (Battle of Worcester Society) at Worcester and Powick; Martin Fiennes (and the Saye and Sele family) at Broughton Castle; Derek Lester at Chalgrove; and Dr Keith Lawrence and Paul Topham at Nantwich. I am also grateful to Arthur Haselrigg (3rd Baron Hazelrigg), Bob Eddlestone, Andrew and Judith Sumnall, Elias Kupfermann, Nigel and Sally Branston, Phil Philo, David Garner and all the staff at the Bodleian and British Libraries.

I owe huge appreciation to Richard Sullivan and Marcus Cowper at Osprey Publishing for having the continuing confidence in me and in agreeing to undertake a work of this nature and magnitude. I have greatly enjoyed working alongside Russell Butcher who co-ordinated the work. To the cartographers, Trevor Bounford and Denise Bee I owe particular thanks. In redrawing all my maps, they have gone well beyond the call of duty and assisted in a number of areas from their own research and diligence. My final thanks are reserved for a special few. To my wife, Ina, for her help with the proofreading and her unswerving support on our many ventures across the country in search of answers, understanding and confirmation. To Sarah and Robin King, who have proofread all my books and who stepped up to the plate once again to undertake this not inconsiderable task, I am, as ever, very grateful. My final thanks are for Professor Anne Curry, the current Chair of the Battlefields Trust, who very kindly agreed to write the foreword.

Nick Lipscombe
Oxford, March 2020

CHRONOLOGY – THE WARS OF THE THREE KINGDOMS, 1639–52

The following abbreviations are used throughout the chronology: Royalist (R); Parliamentarian (P); Covenanter (C); Irish (I).

1609: Plantation of Ulster and the movement of Protestants onto confiscated Irish land.

1611: King James Bible published.

27 March 1625: James I dies and Charles I accedes to the throne.

1 May 1625: Charles I marries Henrietta Maria, a French, Bourbon, Roman Catholic princess.

1626: Parliament dismisses George Villiers, 1st Duke of Buckingham from command of English forces in Europe; a furious Charles I dismisses Parliament.

October 1627: English forces under Buckingham defeated at La Rochelle, France.

1628: Charles recalls Parliament; Parliament draws up Petition of Right which Charles reluctantly accepts.

23 August 1628: Buckingham assassinated in Portsmouth by John Felton.

1629: Charles dismisses Parliament and does not call it again until 1640, thus commencing the Personal Rule.

1633: William Laud appointed Archbishop of Canterbury.

23 July 1637: Charles attempts to impose Anglican services on the Presbyterian Church of Scotland; Jenny Geddes sparks a riot which leads to the National Covenant.

23 July 1637: New Scottish prayer-book causes a riot in Edinburgh.

12 June 1638: Conclusion of John Hampden's trial for non-payment of Ship Money.

1639–40 THE BISHOPS' WARS

1639

27 February: Charles issues denunciation of the Covenanters, accusing them of trying to overthrow him.

13 March: The Marquis of Huntly musters Royalist forces in north-east Scotland.

27 March: Charles departs for York and despatches the Marquis of Hamilton (R) to Yarmouth to assemble a transport fleet.

7 April: Charles instructs Hamilton (R) to act against the Scottish 'rebels'.

20 May: The Covenanter army begins assembling at Duns on the Scottish–English border.

30 May: Charles joins his army at Berwick.

1 June: The Earl of Arundel (R) crosses border and reads out the King's proclamation at Duns.

3 June: The Earl of Holland's (R) cavalry advances to drive Scots out of Kelso; finding themselves outnumbered, they retreat.

5 June: Charles agrees to negotiate with the Scots.

18 June: Treaty of Berwick signed. Earl of Montrose (C) bombards Viscount Aboyne's forces defending the Brig o' Dee outside Aberdeen.

20 June: Scottish army withdraws from Duns and disbands.

5 December: Failed negotiations lead Charles to regard war with Scotland as unavoidable and he calls Parliament to demand finance.

1640

19 March: Irish Parliament meets in Dublin and agrees to recruit an army of 9,000 to serve the King.

13 April: The first meeting of the Short Parliament, at which Charles demands finance to continue the war against Scotland. MPs voice their concern about the legality of the dissolution of Parliament in 1629.

17 April: John Pym attacks the King's policies in a two-hour speech, and the House of Commons refuses to grant any money.

24 April: Charles appeals to the House of Lords for support against the Commons' motion.

25 April: The House of Lords support the King, insisting that money should be granted.

5 May: Charles dissolves the Short Parliament.

11 May: Riots in London in protest at the dissolution.

12 May: Negotiations for a Spanish loan to Charles break down; in desperation, the King permits Henrietta Maria to approach the Pope's emissary for a loan from the Vatican.

Late May: The Covenanters besiege the King's forces within Edinburgh Castle.

2 June: The Scottish Parliament meets against the King's wishes.

Early July: The Covenanter army begins to muster.

July: The Earl of Stafford assembles the Irish army (R) at Carrickfergus in preparation for invading Scotland.

End of July: Covenanter army assembles at Duns.

3 August: Scottish decide to mount a pre-emptive invasion of England.

20 August: Covenanter army crosses the River Tweed. Charles leaves London for York.

28 August: Battle of Newburn Ford; Lord Conway (R) fails to prevent the Covenanters crossing the River Tyne, forcing the English army to withdraw from Newcastle towards Durham.

30 August: Covenanters march into Newcastle unopposed.

15 September: Charles's forces within Edinburgh Castle (Patrick Ruthven) surrender.

2 October: Treaty negotiations begin at Ripon.

26 October: Charles forced to sign the Treaty of Ripon, signalling an end to the Bishops' War. Scots occupy Northumberland until the final settlement is ratified by the English Parliament.

3 November: First meeting of the Long Parliament.

11 November: Impeachment of Lord Strafford commences: he had advised the King to use an Irish army against England.

7 December: House of Commons declares Ship Money to be illegal.

11 December: The Root and Branch Petition (abolition of episcopacy) submitted to the Long Parliament.

18 December: Archbishop Laud impeached for high treason.

1641

5 February: House of Lords passes the Triennial Bill.

13 February: House of Commons petitions for the disbandment of Strafford's Irish army.

15 February: Charles gives his assent to the Triennial Bill.

19 April: The House of Commons declares Strafford a traitor.

2 May: Charles sends a force to the Tower of London to try to release Strafford.

12 May: Strafford beheaded on Tower Hill.

22 June: Charles gives his assent to a bill to abolish tonnage and poundage.

25 June: Charles dismisses Count Rossetti, the papal envoy.

5 July: Parliament abolishes the Courts of High Commission, the Star Chamber and the Councils of Wales and The North.

10 August: Charles signs Treaty of London with Scottish Commissioners.

17 August: Charles ceremoniously enters the Scottish Parliament.

21 August: The Army of the Covenant leaves Newcastle and disbands at Leith a week later.

August: The Root and Branch Bill (end to episcopacy) rejected by the Long Parliament.

October: Outbreak of rebellion in Ireland in the Ulster plantation.

23 October: Plot to seize Dublin Castle betrayed.

26 October: Armagh captured by Irish insurgents.

28 October: Charles appeals to the Scottish Parliament for an army to crush the Irish uprising. The Covenanters distrust the King and request consent of the English Parliament before intervening.

31 October: Dundalk captured by Irish insurgents.

13 November: Charles ennobles a number of leading Covenanters and appoints them to the Scottish Privy Council.

17 November: Charles dissolves the Scottish Parliament.

21 November: Irish insurgents besiege Drogheda.

30 November: Publication of the 'Proceedings of Parliament'; effectively the first public newspaper. It marks the beginning of the English press.

30 November: Siege of Wicklow Castle relieved by Charles Coote (R).

1 December: The Grand Remonstrance is presented to the King.

December: The Irish uprising spreads to Roscommon, Mayo, Sligo, Kilkenny and Tipperary.

23 December: Charles gives a conciliatory reply to the Grand Remonstrance.

30 December: Sir Simon Harcourt (R) arrives in Dublin at the head of an army of 1,100.

FIRST ENGLISH CIVIL WAR

1642

January: The Irish uprising spreads to Antrim, Limerick and Clare.

4 January: Charles unsuccessfully attempts to personally arrest the Five Members (John Pym, John Hampden, Denzil Holles, Sir Arthur Haselrig and William Strode) on the floor of the House of Commons.

10 January: Charles and his family leave Whitehall for Hampton Court; two days later they go to Windsor Castle.

11 January: The Long Parliament appoints Sir John Hotham (P) governor of Hull, with orders not to deliver its magazine without Parliament's authority. Battle of Swords: Coote (R) defeats the insurgents near Dublin.

12 January: Parliament orders Goring (P) to hold Portsmouth against any demands made by Charles.

19 January: Parliament orders the raising of two new regiments of the London trained bands.

31 January: Hotham (P) secures arsenal at Hull for Parliament.

1–3 February: Ormond (R) burns Newcastle (Ireland) and recaptures Naas in County Kildare.

5 February: The bishops of the Church of England are excluded from the House of Lords by the Bishops Exclusion Act.

20 February: Irish insurgents attack Drogheda.

21 February: Colonel Monck and Sir Richard Grenville (R) arrive in Dublin with 1,500 foot and 500 horse.

23 February: Henrietta Maria goes to the Netherlands with Princess Mary and the crown jewels, in order to raise troops and supplies for the Royalist cause.

27 February: Charles rejects the Militia Bill: designed to give power over the Militia to Parliament.

5 March: Long Parliament passes the Militia Ordinance as Charles would not assent to the Bill. Parliament now has control of the trained bands.

10 March: Ormond (R) raises the siege of Drogheda.

15 March: Ralph Hopton (R) released from the Tower; Earl of Warwick (P) appointed Admiral of the Fleet (against Charles's wishes); Hotham (P) arrives in Hull as governor.

19 March: Charles enters York and establishes his Court. The town of Galway declares for the insurgents.

15 April: Battle of Kilrush; Ormond (R) defeats insurgents under Mountgarrett (I).

23 April: Hotham (P) refuses Charles entrance to Kingston upon Hull.

27 April: Monro (C) advances into Armagh.

End April: The siege of Cork is lifted. Muskerry (I) besieges Limerick Castle. Coote (R) captures Philipstown and Trim.

17 May: Charles orders the Law Courts to move to York; despite Parliament declaring the move illegal, the Great Seal is sent to the city.

20 May: Charles forms a body of Lifeguards to protect him under the command of Sir Thomas Byron (R).

30 May: The arsenal at Hull is transported by ship to London.

3 June: Charles summons a meeting of the gentry at Heworth Moor outside York.

18 June: Charles rejects the Nineteen Propositions: requiring him to give up control of the Militia and the right to appoint ministers.

21 June: Battle of Glemaquin: Stewart's Lagan army defeats O'Neill's (I) insurgents to secure Donegal and north-west Ulster.

20 June: Magazines at Preston, Warrington and Liverpool secured for the Royalists.

21 June: Muskerry and Barry (I) capture Limerick.

5 July: Parliament appoints the Committee of Safety, consisting of five peers and ten MPs.

12 July: Parliament resolves to raise an army. Earl of Essex (P) commissioned as Captain-General.

July: Charles unsuccessfully besieges Hull.

July and August: Numerous military appointments for both the Royalist and Parliamentarian armies are made.

2 August: Colonel Goring (R) declares Portsmouth for the King; a week later Warwick (P) arrives with five warships to blockade the port.

4 August: Earl of Leven (C) arrives in Ulster to command the Covenanter army against the insurgents.

8 August: Earl of Northampton (R) seizes the magazine and artillery at Banbury for the Royalists and marches to Warwick.

12 August: Royalist Mayor of London (Gurney) arrested and detained in the Tower. Parliamentarians capture Portsbridge near Portsmouth.

15 August: Cromwell (P) seizes the magazine at Cambridge. Prince Rupert and Prince Maurice (R) land at Tynemouth and move to join Charles.

21 August: Dover Castle surprised and taken by the Parliamentarians.

22 August: Charles raises his standard at Nottingham and the **war officially commences**.

23 August: Skirmish at Southam; Brooke (P) drives back Northampton's forces (R) and is able to lift the siege of Warwick.

4 September: Goring (R) holds a council of war and surrenders Portsmouth to Sir William Waller (P).

9 September: Essex (P) leaves London and marches towards the King's forces at Nottingham.

14 September: Lord Saye and Sele (P) occupies Oxford.

19 September: Charles issues Wellington Declaration, promising to defend the established church and govern according to the laws of the land.

23 September: Battle of Powick Bridge: Prince Rupert (R) routs Essex's (P) advance guard.

24 September: Earl of Derby (R) besieges Manchester.

29 September: Yorkshire Treaty of Neutrality signed, but repudiated by Parliament on 4 October.

October: The Irish Catholic Confederation was formed after an assembly at Kilkenny. Derby (R) abandons siege of Manchester.

4 October: Hotham (P) captures Cawood Castle.

17 October: Charles reaches Birmingham; the townsfolk seize the King's carriages containing the royal plate. Skirmish at King's Norton.

23 October: Battle of Edgehill, Charles's (R) and Essex's (P) armies meet and both claim a victory.

29 October: Charles enters Oxford in triumph.

1 November: Skirmish at Aylesbury (Battle of Holman's Bridge); Rupert (R) attacks the Parliamentarian garrison at Aylesbury. It is unclear if/when this action took place, and whether Rupert was involved.

7 November: Rupert (R) summons Windsor Castle to surrender; Venn (P) refuses.

12 November: Skirmish at Brentford: Rupert (R) attacks a small Parliamentarian force.

13 November: Battle of Turnham Green; Essex (P) faces Charles's (R) army; the latter chose to withdraw.

18 November: Hopton (R) besieges Exeter.

21 November: Hopton (R) driven away from Exeter towards Tavistock.

1 December: Earl of Newcastle (R) defeats Yorkshire Parliamentarians under Hotham (P) at Piercebridge and crosses the River Tees.

3 December: Newcastle (R) enters York.

5 December: Wilmot (R) storms and captures Marlborough.

6 December: Newcastle (R) defeats Fairfax (P) at Tadcaster and secures Pontefract.

13 December: Lord Grandison (R) surrenders Winchester to Waller (P).

18 December: Henderson (R) occupies Newark.

23 December: Lambert (P) besieges Skipton Castle.

1643

6 January: Earl of Stamford (P) arrives in Exeter to assume command of the Parliamentarian forces in Devon.

7 January: Rupert (R) launches unsuccessful attack on Cirencester.

13 January: General Preston (R) besieges Bir Castle in King's County, Ireland.

16 January: Skirmish at Guisborough: Cholmley (R) attacks Slingsby (P).

18 January: Hopton (R) appointed commander of the Royalist Western Army.

19 January: Battle of Braddock Down; Ruthven (P) defeated by Hopton (R).

22 January: Hopton and Lord Mohun (R) storm and capture Saltash.

26 January: Preston (R) captures Fort Falkland in King's County, Ireland.

27 January: Newcastle (R) withdraws to York with the Royalist northern army.

28 January: The Long Parliament sends commissioners to negotiate the Treaty of Oxford (unsuccessful). William Brereton (P) defeats Aston (R) at Nantwich, which he fortifies and holds as the headquarters of Parliament's forces in Cheshire.

1 February: Skirmish at Yarm; Royalists recapture the town.

2 February: Rupert (R) storms and captures Cirencester.

3 February: Charles presents his counterproposals at Oxford, calling for peace.

9 February: Seaton (P) storms and captures Preston.

16 February: Derby (R) driven back from attacking Bolton.

19 February: Parliamentarian forces seize Lancaster.

20 February: Lord Herbert (R) advances from south Wales towards Gloucester and defeats Berrow (P) at Coleford.

21 February: General Chudleigh (P) defeats the Royalists at Modbury and relieves siege of Plymouth.

22 February: Rupert (R) tries to intercept Waller's (P) advance guard as it moves west from London.

24 February: Parliament passes an Ordinance for raising money for the maintenance of the Parliamentarian army.

28 February: General Ballard's (P) forces attack Newark but are repulsed.

3 March: Waller (P) occupies Winchester.

7 March: Rupert (R) tries to capture Bristol, but the plot fails and he is forced to withdraw.

11 March: Ormond (R) besieges Ross in County Wexford, but he abandons the siege three days later.

13 March: First Battle of Middlewich; Brereton (P) defeats Aston (R).

14 March: Cromwell (P) seizes Lowestoft.

18 March: Battle of Ross; Ormond (R) defeats Preston (I) and the Leinster Confederates when they try to block the former's withdrawal to Dublin.

19 March: Battle of Hopton Heath; Northampton (R) defeats Brereton (P) and Gell (P). Northampton is killed in action and Rupert assumes command of the Royalist army in the Midlands.

20 March: Derby (R) captures Preston and Lancashire; Blackburn also surrenders to the Royalists.

21 March: Waller (P) storms Malmesbury and Cromwell (P) occupies King's Lynn.

23 March: Newcastle (R) and Henderson (R) capture Grantham.

24 March: Waller surprises Lord Herbert's Welsh Royalists at Highnam, near Gloucester.

26 March: Rupert (R) recaptures Malmesbury.

30 March: Battle of Seacroft Moor; Goring (R) routs Fairfax (P) as he withdraws from Tadcaster.

2 April: Newcastle (R) recaptures Wakefield.

3 April: Battle of Camp Hill; Rupert (R) storms Birmingham. Brereton (P) attacks Derby's Headquarters (R) at Warrington.

4 April: Waller (P) captures Monmouth and Chepstow the following day.

10 April: Rupert (R) besieges Lichfield.

11 April: Battle of Ancaster Heath; Willoughby (P) defeated by Cavendish (R).

13 April: Battle of Ripple Field; Maurice (R) blocks Waller's (P) advance towards Worcester. Earl of Castlehaven defeats a British detachment under Crawford marching to raise the siege of Ballinakill.

16 April: Commencement of siege of Reading by Essex (P) and an army of 19,000.

20 April: Derby (R) defeated by Shuttleworth (P), giving control of Lanarkshire to Parliamentarian forces. Derby escapes to the Isle of Man.

21 April: Lichfield surrenders to Rupert (R).

25 April: Battle of Sourton Down; Hopton (R) surprised and routed by Chudleigh (P). Waller (P) takes Hereford.

26 April: Reading surrenders to Essex (P).

28 April: Crowland captured by Parliamentarian forces.

6 May: Newcastle (R) recaptures Sheffield. Action at Middleton Cheney; Northampton (R) thwarts an attempt by the Parliamentarians to capture Banbury Castle.

8 May: Lady Arundel (R) surrenders Wardour Castle to Hungerford (P).

16 May: Battle of Stratton; Hopton (R) defeats Stamford (P).

18 May: Waller (P) abandons Hereford, due to lack of men, and returns to Gloucester.

20 May: Parliamentarian forces begin to besiege Manchester.

21 May: Fairfax (P) storms and captures Wakefield against heavy odds, but is unable to garrison the town and withdraws to Leeds.

23 May: The House of Commons impeaches Henrietta Maria for high treason, having brought arms and ammunition into the country.

27 May: Norris (R) surrenders Warrington to Parliamentarian forces.

29 May: Waller's (P) attack on Worcester fails and he withdraws, returning to Gloucester.

31 May: Earl of Antrim (R) taken prisoner by Covenanter forces in Ulster; his captured correspondence reveals the plan for a Royalist uprising in Scotland supported by an Irish Catholic army.

4 June: Hopton's army (R) links up with Maurice (R) and the Marquis of Hereford (R) in Somerset; they establish garrisons at Taunton, Bridgwater and Duncaster Castle, and then move on Wells and Bath.

4 June: Castlehaven (I) defeats Sir Charles Vavasour (R) at Cloghlea, County Cork.

8 June: Waller (P) occupies Bath.

16 June: Long Parliament passes the Licensing Order, designed to institute publishing censorship.

18 June: Battle of Chalgrove Field: Rupert (R) conducts a raid outside Oxford; John Hampden (P) killed in the skirmish.

22 June: Newcastle (R) resumes operations in Yorkshire.

28 June: Essex (P) tenders his resignation after his leadership is criticized.

30 June: Battle of Adwalton Moor; Newcastle (R) defeats Fairfax (P).

1 July: First meeting of the Westminster Assembly of Divines set up to reform English Church.

3 July: Newcastle (R) occupies Bradford after Fairfax (P) escapes; Lady Ann Fairfax taken prisoner.

4 July: Battle of Burton Bridge; Tyldesley (R) launches a cavalry charge across the bridge to secure passage for a Royalist relief convoy.

5 July: Battle of Lansdown (or Lansdowne); Waller (P) narrowly defeated by Royalist Western Army under Hopton (R).

10 July: Waller (P) pursues Hopton (R) and besieges Devizes.

13 July: Battle of Roundway Down; Maurice, Wilmot and Byron (R) inflict heavy defeat on Waller (P).

18 July: Brereton (P) probes Chester but withdraws after two days.

20 July: Battle of Gainsborough; Willoughby (P) captures the town.

24 July: On the recommendation of John Pym's committee, Parliament agrees to pay the arrears for Essex's army, to reinforce his cavalry and to raise more recruits.

26 July: Storming of Bristol; Fiennes (P) surrenders to Rupert (R).

28 July: Cromwell and Sir John Meldrum (P) defeat Cavendish at Gainsborough but cannot hold the town as Newcastle (R) approaches.

30 July: Willoughby (P) surrenders Gainsborough to Newcastle (R).

4 August: Capel (R) attacks Nantwich, but the attack fails. Erle (P) abandons the siege of Corfe Castle.

7 August: Irish insurgent leader O'Neill (I) defeats Lord Moore at Portlester.

10 August: Charles begins siege of Gloucester. Earl of Manchester appointed to command the Eastern Association army.

17 August: Church of Scotland ratifies the Solemn League and Covenant.

23 August: Manchester (P) begins the siege of King's Lynn.

30 August: Brereton (P) captures Eccleshall Castle.

2 September: Newcastle (R) commences the siege of Hull. Barnstaple surrenders to Maurice (R).

4 September: Stamford (P) surrenders Exeter to Maurice (R).

5 September: Essex (P) arrives at Prestbury Hill and forces Charles (R) to lift the siege of Gloucester.

11 September: Brereton and Sir Thomas Myddleton (P) seize Wem and establish a garrison.

15 September: The Cessation of Arms signed for Charles by the Marquis of Ormond (R) and Lord Mountgarret (I) for the Confederates; a one-year ceasefire allowing English troops in Irish garrisons to return to England to fight for the Royalists. Royalists commence siege of Plymouth.

16 September: King's Lynn surrenders to Manchester (P).

18 September: Skirmish at Aldbourne Chase.

20 September: First Battle of Newbury; Essex (P) engages Charles's (R) force: the latter withdraws, enabling Essex to move towards London.

25 September: Long Parliament and the Westminster Assembly ratify the Solemn League and Covenant. Under the terms of the deal with Scotland, the Committee of Safety is superseded by the Committee of Both Kingdoms.

29 September: Charles (R) resolves to form two new armies. Lord Hopton is appointed commander of a new Western Army to advance on London through Wiltshire and Hampshire; Lord Byron is appointed commander of a new army in Cheshire to regain Lancashire and assist the Earl of Newcastle in Yorkshire. Both armies to be reinforced by troops returning from Ireland.

30 September: Scottish troops occupy Berwick.

Early October: William Ogle (R) captures Winchester by surprise attack.

3 October: Astley (R) reoccupies Reading.

6 October: Maurice (R) captures Dartmouth in a surprise attack.

9 October: Manchester, Fairfax and Cromwell (P) besiege Bolingbroke Castle.

11 October: Battle of Winceby; Cromwell and Fairfax (P) rout Henderson (R). Meldrum (P) attacks the Royalist siege works at Hull.

12 October: Newcastle (R) abandons the siege of Hull.

15 October: Dyve (R) captures Newport Pagnell.

17 October: Capel (R) attempts to recapture Wem, but his force is decisively beaten by Brereton (P) at Lee Bridge while trying to escape.
20 October: Lincoln surrenders to Manchester (P).
30 October: Essex (P) recaptures Newport Pagnell and moves to capture St Albans.
November: Alasdair MacColla (R) raids the Western Isles of Scotland and captures Colonsay.
10 November: Ravenscroft (R) surrenders Hawarden Castle to Brereton (P).
12 November: Waller's (P) second attempt on Basing House fails. Brereton (P) captures Flint Castle.
16 November: The arrival of Royalist regiments under General Erneley (R) from Ireland drives Brereton (P) back in north Wales.
December: More Royalist regiments arrive from Ireland and land in north-west.
7 December: Parliamentarian force in Hawarden Castle surrenders to Erneley (R).
9 December: Arundel Castle surrenders to Hopton (R).
11 December: Richard Norton (P) attacks Royalist garrison at Romsey.
13 December: Waller (P) storms the Royalist garrison at Alton. Steele (P) surrenders Beeston Castle (Cheshire) to Byron (R).
20 December: Gainsborough surrenders to Meldrum (P). Waller (P) attacks Arundel.
22 December: Royalists abandon siege of Plymouth.
26 December: Second Battle of Middlewich; Brereton (P) defeated by Byron (R).

1644

4 January: Parliamentarian forces begin bombardment of Arundel Castle, which surrenders to Waller (P) two days later.
10 January: Byron (R) besieges Nantwich.
19 January: The Scots under Leven (C) march south and join Parliament's army, threatening York.
20 January: Charles commissions Earl of Antrim (R) to raise an army of 10,000 soldiers for service in England and 3,000 for service in Scotland.
25 January: Battle of Nantwich; Fairfax and Brereton (P) defeat Byron (R) and raise the siege.
28 January: Earls of Antrim (R) and Montrose (R) sign a formal agreement whereby Montrose will raise Royalist forces in Scotland and declare for the King; Antrim will undertake to raise forces in Ireland and the Western Isles and invade north-west.
2 February: Newcastle (R) occupies Newcastle hours before the Scottish army (C) appear to the north of the city.
3 February: Leven (C) demands the surrender of Newcastle which is rejected; Leven's men storm the outworks to the north-east.
10 February: Parliamentarian cavalry from Hull rout Royalists at Kilham then raid Bridlington.
20 February: The same group of Parliamentarian cavalry from Hull raid Whitby.
22 February: Laugharne (P) in conjunction with Swanley's (P) naval squadron, cross from Milford Haven to attack the Royalist fort at Pill near Pembroke, which surrenders two days later.
26 February: Laugharne (P) captures Roche Castle.
4 March: Leven (C) occupies Sunderland. Lambert's (P) cavalry capture Tadcaster. Rupert (R) defeats Mytton (P) at Market Drayton.
6 March: Meldrum (P) commences the siege of the Royalist stronghold of Newark. He attempts to storm the place two days later.

9 March: Laugharne (P) captures Tenby.
10 March: Carew Castle surrenders to Poyer (P); only Pembroke Castle remains in Royalist hands.
13 March: Hopton Castle surrenders to Woodhouse (R).
20 March: Covenanters storm and capture the fort at South Shields.
21 March: Rupert (R) relieves the siege of Newark.
24 March: The armies of Leven (C) and Newcastle (R) meet north of Sunderland but do not commit to battle. Marquis of Huntly (R) occupies Aberdeen.
27 March: Hopton and Ruthven (R) occupy Alresford.
29 March: Battle of Cheriton; Waller (P) defeats Hopton and Ruthven (R). Parliament's first decisive victory of the war.
Early April: Waller (P) storms and captures Winchester but Royalists maintain the castle. Waller's (P) troops capture Salisbury, Andover, Bishop's Waltham and then seize Christchurch (Dorset).
11 April: Lord Fairfax, Thomas Fairfax, Lambert and Meldrum (P) join forces to storm and capture Selby.
15 April: Montrose (R) occupies Dumfries.
18 April: Newcastle (R) occupies York.
23 April: Leven (C) and Fairfax (P) besiege York. Maurice (R) commences the siege of Lyme Regis.
2 May: Marquis of Argyll (C) recaptures Aberdeen.
6 May: Manchester (P) captures Lincoln.
10 May: Montrose (R) attacks the Covenanters at Morpeth; the town surrenders.
14 May: Monro (C) seizes Belfast.
24 May: Malmesbury surrenders to Massey (P).
25 May: Rupert (R) captures Stockport.
28 May: Storming of Bolton by Rupert (R); so-called 'Bolton Massacre'.
29 May: Montrose (R) captures Morpeth Castle from Covenanters.
2 June: Waller (P) seizes Newbridge and secures crossing over the Thames above and below Oxford.
5 June: Bombardment of York commences.
9 June: Waller (P) captures Sudeley Castle in Gloucestershire and Purefoy (P) captures Compton House in Warwickshire.
11 June: Rupert (R) captures Liverpool after a five-day bombardment. All of Lancashire (except Manchester) under Royalist control.
12 June: Gage (R) captures Boarstall House near Aylesbury.
23 June: Denbigh and Mytton (P) capture Oswestry.
29 June: Battle of Cropredy Bridge; Waller (P) inflicts a defeat on the Royalist rearguard but mutinous Parliamentarian army begins to desert in large numbers.
1 July: The siege of York is lifted.
2 July: Battle of Marston Moor; the combined forces of Fairfax, Manchester (P) and Leven (C) inflict a decisive defeat on Rupert and Newcastle (R), thereby ending Royalist influence in the north of England.
3 July: Myddleton (P) defeats Royalist cavalry under Marrow (R) attempting to recapture Oswestry.
4 July: The allies resume the siege of York. Rupert (R) withdraws west to the Welsh border while Montrose (R) withdraws north to the Scottish border.
8 July: Blake (P) captures Taunton.
16 July: Glemham (R) surrenders York to Fairfax (P).
23 July: Grenville (R) abandons siege of Plymouth as Essex (P) advances towards Tavistock.
25 July: Rupert and Byron (R) occupy Chester.
3 August: Grenville (R) occupies Tregony in an attempt to block Essex (P) from the west.

4 August: Massey (P) defeats Mynne (R) at Redmarley, exposing Herefordshire to Massey's raids. Myddleton and Mytton (P) raid Welshpool and rout a Royalist cavalry unit.

7 August–2 September: Battle of Lostwithiel; Charles (R) traps Essex's (P) army at Lostwithiel and a stand-off ensues.

7 August: Gage (R) attacks Waller's headquarters at Abingdon.

11 August: Grenville (R) drives Essex's (P) cavalry out of Bodmin and advances to Respryn Bridge, where he makes contact with the King.

12 August: Leven (C) resumes siege of Newcastle.

14 August: Middleton (P) defeated at Bridgwater.

22 August: Gerard (R) captures Haverfordwest.

26 August: Brereton (P) attacks Langdale (R) at Malpas in Cheshire and drives Royalists into north Wales.

1 September: Battle of Tippermuir; Montrose (R) routs Elcho's Covenanters and occupies Perth.

2 September: Skippon (P) surrenders the Parliamentarian infantry at Lostwithiel.

5 September: Myddleton (P) captures Montgomery Castle.

8 September: Erneley and Vaughan (R) launch a surprise attack on Myddleton (P) at Montgomery, forcing the latter to retreat to Oswestry.

12 September: Gage (R) drives the Parliamentarian forces out of Basingstoke.

13 September: Battle of Aberdeen; Montrose (R) defeats Balfour's Covenanters.

18 September: Battle of Montgomery; Byron (R) attempts to recapture Montgomery Castle but fails, leaving the Parliamentarians in control of central Wales.

23 September: Parliamentarians reoccupy Basingstoke and resume siege of Basing House.

29 September: Horton (P) resumes siege of Donnington Castle.

2 October: Myddleton (P) captures Powis Castle.

18 October: Goring (R) drives Waller's (P) army from Andover; the King's army subsequently occupies the town. Horton (P) abandons siege of Donnington Castle.

19 October: The Covenanters storm and capture Newcastle. Myddleton (P) captures Ruthin.

24 October: The Long Parliament passes the Ordinance of no quarter to Irish soldiers in England.

25 October: Northampton (R) relieves the siege of Banbury Castle.

27 October: Second Battle of Newbury; combined armies of Parliament inflict a tactical defeat on the Royalists, but fail to gain any strategic advantage. Tynemouth Castle surrenders to the Covenanters.

1 November: Royalists surrender Liverpool to Meldrum (P).

3 November: Royalists surrender Laugharne Castle in Pembrokeshire.

4 November: Long Parliament sends Propositions of Uxbridge to the King at Oxford.

9 November: Charles and Rupert (R) relieve Donnington Castle.

19 November: Norton (P) abandons siege of Basing House.

22 November: Crossland (R) surrenders Helmsley Castle to Fairfax (P).

8 December: Myddleton (P) storms and captures Abbey-Cwm-Hir in Radnorshire.

19 December: Parliamentarians and Covenanters besiege Pontefract Castle in Yorkshire. Self-Denying Ordinance passed by the House of Commons.

20 December: Fairfax (P) captures Knaresborough Castle.

21 December: Laugharne (P) captures Cardigan but Slaughter (R) retains control of the castle until 29 December when it is captured.

1645

3 January: Ludlow (P) routed at Salisbury by Sir Marmaduke Langdale (R).

6 January: Parliament agrees to the creation of the New Model Army.

10 January: Archbishop Laud executed on Tower Hill.

11 January: Rupert (R) attacks Abingdon but is repulsed.

15 January: Goring (R) attacks Christchurch, Dorset, but is repulsed.

20 January: Preston (I) besieges Duncannon Fort in County Wexford.

27 January: Brereton (P) tries to capture Chester but is repulsed.

2 February: Battle of Inverlochy; Montrose (R) defeats Duncan Campbell of Auchinbreck, destroying the power of the Campbells in the Highlands.

20 February: Maurice (R) outmanoeuvres Brereton (P) and relieves the siege of Chester.

22 February: Meldrum (P) captures town of Scarborough but Royalist defenders hold out in the castle.

23 February: Mytton (P) captures Shrewsbury.

25 February: Langdale (R) routs Rossiter's (P) force at Market Harborough and marches towards Newark.

28 February: Dyve (R) driven from Weymouth.

1 March: Langdale (R) defeats Lambert (P) at Wentbridge and temporarily lifts first siege of Pontefract.

8 March: Cromwell (P) captures Hillesdon House.

19 March: Duncannon Fort, County Wexford surrenders to Preston (I).

21 March: Parliamentarians commence second siege of Pontefract.

April: 1,400 Scottish soldiers leave Ulster to counter the threat from the Earl of Montrose (R).

4 April: Montrose (R) storms Dundee then evades Baillie's Covenanter army and escapes to Highlands.

22 April: Rupert (R) drives Massey's (P) forces out of Ledbury.

23 April: The Long Parliament passes the Self-Denying Ordinance. Siege of Taunton reinstated by Berkeley and Grenville (R). Gerard (R) defeats Laugharne (P) at Newcastle Emlyn.

24 April: Cromwell (P) defeats Northampton (R) near Islip and crosses River Cherwell.

25 April: Gerard (R) captures Picton Castle.

26 April: Cromwell (P) defeats Vaughan (R) at Bampton.

29 April: Cromwell's (P) summons for surrender of Faringdon Castle is rejected. Gerard (R) recaptures Carew Castle.

May: Clubman risings gathering momentum across south of England.

8 May: Blake (P) repels a Royalist assault on Taunton.

9 May: Battle of Auldearn; Montrose (R) defeats Hurry (C).

18 May: Brereton (P) abandons sieges of Chester and Hawarden Castle as Charles's (R) army moves north.

26 May: Massey (P) storms and captures Evesham, cutting Royalist lines of communication between Oxford and Worcester.

30 May: Rupert (R) storms Leicester.

1 June: Galvanized by the fall of Leicester, Parliament orders the New Model Army to march against Charles (R).

5 June: Fairfax (P) abandons the siege of Oxford and marches north.

9 June: Massey (P) defeats Lunsford (R) near Ludlow.

14 June: Battle of Naseby: New Model Army inflicts decisive defeat on Charles and Rupert; most of the Royalist artillery and stores captured.

18 June: Leicester surrenders to Fairfax (P).

28 June: Carlisle surrenders to Covenanters.

29 June: Goring (R) abandons siege of Taunton.

July: Publication of the King's papers captured at Naseby.

2 July: Battle of Alford; Montrose (R) defeats Baillie (C).

8 July: Massey (P) defeats Porter (R) at Isle Moor, Somerset.

10 July: Battle of Langport: Fairfax (P) routs Goring (R).

21 July: Pontefract Castle surrenders to Poyntz's (P) Northern Association army. Fairfax (P) storms Bridgwater in Somerset and captures the eastern quarter of the town, which surrenders two days later.

23 July: The Covenanters storm Canon Frome in Herefordshire.

25 July: Scarborough Castle surrenders to Poyntz (P).

31 July: Bath captured in a surprise attack by Colonel Okey (P).

1 August: Battle of Colby Moor; Laugharne (P) defeats Stradling (R) near Haverfordwest.

2 August: Fairfax (P) besieges Sherborne Castle, Dorset.

5 August: Laugharne (P) storms and captures the Royalist garrison at Haverfordwest.

15 August: Battle of Kilsyth; Montrose (R) defeats Baillie (C). Dyve (R) surrenders Sherborne Castle to Fairfax (P).

16 August: Montrose (R) occupies Glasgow.

17 August: Sir Robert Stewart and the Lagan army rout Irish cavalry (I) near Sligo.

23 August: Fairfax (P) commences siege of Bristol.

1 September: Leven (C) receives news of Montrose's (R) successes in Scotland. Leven (C) abandons the siege of Hereford and marches north.

5 September: Carew Castle in Pembrokeshire surrenders to Laugharne (P).

11 September: Rupert (R) surrenders Bristol to Fairfax (P).

13 September: Battle of Philiphaugh; Leslie (C) defeats Montrose (R).

14 September: Dalbier (P) begins bombarding Basing House.

20 September: Jones (P) storms the outer defences of Chester and bombards main city walls. Picton Castle in Pembrokeshire surrenders to Laugharne (P) after a 20-day siege.

21 September: Cromwell (P) occupies Devizes in Wiltshire and besieges the castle, which surrenders the next day.

24 September: Battle of Rowton Heath; Poyntz (P) defeats the King's cavalry under Sir Marmaduke Langdale (R). Lacock House in Wiltshire surrenders to Pickering (P).

26 September: Lucas (R) surrenders Berkeley Castle to Rainsborough (P).

28 September: Cromwell (P) enters the city of Winchester and summons Winchester Castle to surrender.

5 October: Winchester Castle surrenders to Cromwell (P).

8 October: Town of Sligo captured by Coote (P) in co-operation with the Lagan army.

10 October: Chepstow surrenders to Morgan (P).

12 October: Laugharne (P) occupies Carmarthen.

14 October: Cromwell's (P) army storms and sacks Basing House.

15 October: Digby and Langdale (R) defeat Parliamentarian infantry at Sherburn-in-Elmet, but are subsequently routed by Copley's (P) cavalry.

17 October: Fairfax (P) advances to Tiverton in Devon, captures the town and bombards the castle.

24 October: Final defeat of the Northern Horse by Sir Richard Browne (P) on Carlisle Sands. Digby and Langdale (R) escape to the Isle of Man.

25 October: Monmouth surrenders to Morgan (P).

1 November: At Denbigh, Colonel Jones (P) defeats Vaughan (R), who was marching for the relief of Chester.

3 November: Royalist outpost at Shelford Manor near Newark stormed by Poyntz (P) and the Northern Association army; the defenders are massacred.

4 November: Royalist garrison at Wiverton Hall near Newark surrenders to Poyntz (P).

6 November: Beeston Castle and Bolton Castle surrender to the Parliamentarians.

15 November: Final siege of Skipton Castle by Thornton (P) begins.

27 November: Leven (C) joins Poyntz (P) to besiege Newark.

2 December: Montrose (R) besieges Inverness.

18 December: Morgan and Birch (P) capture Hereford for Parliament in a surprise attack.

21 December: Mallory (R) surrenders Skipton Castle to Thornton (P).

1646

3 January: The Covenanters reoccupy Aberdeen.

9 January: Cromwell (P) routs Lord Wentworth's (R) troops in a surprise attack at Bovey Tracey in Devon.

12 January: Royalists abandon the siege of Plymouth.

18 January: Fairfax (P) storms and captures Dartmouth and surrounding outposts.

26 January: Powderham Castle surrenders to Fairfax (P), completing his encirclement of Exeter.

3 February: Byron (R) surrenders Chester to Brereton (P) after a 136-day siege.

10 February: Hopton (R) occupies Torrington in north Devon. Fairfax (P) marches north to intercept him.

16 February: Battle of Torrington; Fairfax (P) defeats Hopton (R), who withdraws into Cornwall.

18–20 February: Laugharne (P) defeats Royalist forces besieging Cardiff.

27 February: Corfe Castle in Dorset surrenders to the Parliamentarians.

9 March: Brereton (P) captures Lichfield city and begins a siege of 'the Close'.

14 March: Hopton (R) surrenders to Fairfax (P) at Truro.

Mid-March: Hawarden Castle surrenders to Parliament.

17 March: Parliamentarians besiege Pendennis Castle in Cornwall.

21 March: Battle of Stow-on-the-Wold; Lord Astley (R) defeated by Brereton (P) at the last pitched battle of the First Civil War.

1 April: Boys (R) surrenders Donnington Castle to Dalbier (P).

8 April: Ruthin Castle surrenders to Mytton (P).

13 April: Siege of Exeter ends with the surrender of Royalist garrison. Fairfax (P) occupies Exeter, then marches for Barnstaple.

14 April: Whitley (R) surrenders Aberystwyth in Cardiganshire to Powell (P) after a siege of several months.

20 April: Barnstaple surrenders to Fairfax (P). Dunster Castle in Somerset surrenders to Blake (P).

23 April: St Michael's Mount in Cornwall surrenders to Hammond (P).

26 April: Bridgnorth Castle captured by Parliament.

27 April: King Charles flees from Oxford disguised as a servant as the New Model Army approaches the city.

29 April: After raising a new force in the Highlands, Montrose (R) besieges Inverness but is driven off by Middleton (C).

3 May: Oxford besieged by Fairfax (P) and the New Model Army.

5 May: Charles surrenders to a Scottish army at Southwell, Nottinghamshire.

6 May: Newark falls to the Parliamentarians.

9 May: Banbury Castle near Oxford surrenders to Whalley (P).

21 May: Parliamentarians besiege Worcester.

5 June: Battle of Benburb; Irish Confederates under O'Neill (I) defeat Monro (C).

11 June: Charles writes to both Houses attempting to open peace negotiations directly with Parliament. He is obliged by the Scots to order the Marquis of Ormond to abandon his negotiations with the Irish Confederates, though he is aware that a treaty has already been concluded.

14 June: Anglesey surrenders to Welsh Parliamentarians.

15 June: Charles renews his order for Montrose (R) to disband his forces in Scotland, but Montrose demands guarantees from the Covenanters for the safety of his men.

24 June: Surrender of Oxford ends the English Civil War. Prince Rupert and Prince Maurice leave the country under terms. James, Duke of York, a prisoner of Parliament.

10 July: Lichfield Close surrenders to Brereton (P). Roscommon Castle surrenders to Irish Confederates commanded by Preston (I).

12 July: Bunratty Castle in County Clare surrenders to the Irish Confederates.

22 July: Siege of Worcester ends with surrender of Royalist garrison.

27 July: Wallingford Castle surrenders to Fairfax (P).

30 July: Proclamation of the First Ormond Peace in Dublin. Montrose (R) disbands his forces at Rattray near Blairgowrie. Parliamentary commissioners arrive in Newcastle to negotiate with the King.

31 July: Goodrich Castle surrenders to Parliament.

17 August: Pendennis Castle in Cornwall surrenders to Parliament.

19 August: Raglan Castle surrenders to Parliament.

24 August: Flint Castle in north Wales surrenders to Parliament.

7 October: Parliament votes that the New Model Army be kept in pay for another six months.

9 October: Long Parliament passes the Ordinance for the abolishing of Archbishops and Bishops in England and Wales and for settling their lands and possessions upon Trustees for the use of the Commonwealth.

12 October: Parliament asks the Marquis of Ormond (R) to step down as Lord Lieutenant of Ireland; he orders the destruction of all crops, mills and bridges within an 8-mile radius of Dublin.

22 October: Disbandment of Parliament's Western Association Army.

26 October: Denbigh Castle in north Wales surrenders to Parliament.

18 November: Conway Castle in Wales surrenders to Parliament.

15 December: Final details of the payment and withdrawal from England of the Scottish army agreed between Parliament and the Scottish commissioners. Scotland to receive a total of £400,000.

31 December: The Lords and Commons agree that the King should be taken to Holmby House in Northamptonshire while the English and Scottish Parliaments discuss how to proceed.

1647

19 January: Holt Castle surrenders to Parliament.

26 January: Parliamentary commissioners arrive in Newcastle to take charge of the King.

6 February: Ormond (R) offers to surrender his office as lord lieutenant of Ireland to the English Parliament. Parliament orders the demolition of selected fortifications throughout England.

12 February: The last of the Scottish regiments leave English soil.

4 March: The House of Lords votes against continuing to raise taxes to pay the army.

10 March: General Leslie (C) marches north against Royalists still in arms in Scotland.

13 March: Harlech Castle, the last Royalist stronghold in Wales, surrenders to Parliament.

17 March: Fairfax (P) orders the New Model Army to stay at least 25 miles outside London.

21 March: A deputation of Parliamentary commissioners meets Fairfax (P) and senior officers at Saffron Walden in Essex to discuss plans for disbandment and the formation of a new army to go to Ireland.

22 March: Army officers refuse to volunteer for service in Ireland without assurances from Parliament regarding: settlement of arrears; indemnity from prosecution for past service; details of which regiments are to remain in England; who is to command in Ireland.

9 April: Colonel Michael Jones (P) appointed governor of Dublin and commander of Parliamentarian forces in Leinster.

10 April: Confederate Leinster army marches into County Carlow; Preston (I) storms and captures Carlow Castle.

16 May: 223 officers sign a Representation of the Army, setting out army grievances for presentation to Parliament.

18 May: The King's letter of 12 May read in Parliament. Presbyterian MPs and Scottish commissioners accept his offer as a basis for a settlement. Despite the Representation of the Army, the Presbyterians continue to plan the disbandment of the army without settlement of grievances.

21 May: Cromwell (P) delivers the report of the military commissioners to Parliament, reassuring MPs that the soldiers will remain loyal if fairly treated.

24 May: Argyll and Leslie (C) join forces to defeat MacColla (R) at Rhunahoarine Point in Kintyre. MacColla flees to Ireland; his followers are massacred.

28 May: Mutiny of Colonel Rainsborough's (P) regiment at Portsmouth. Agitators direct the mutineers to march for Oxford to secure the army's artillery train.

29 May: Fairfax (P) calls for a General Council of the Army, which draws up the Solemn Engagement, stating that the army will not disband until satisfactory arrangements have been made and that a general rendezvous of the army be held at Newmarket.

31 May: Parliament orders the army artillery train to be removed from Oxford to London. Cromwell (P) orders Cornet George Joyce (a junior officer in Fairfax's Horse) to ride to Oxford in order to safeguard the train of artillery for the army, and then to take a body of 500 horse to Holmby House and secure the King against any attempt by the Presbyterians to remove him to Scotland.

3 June: Joyce (P), with a troop of New Model Army cavalry, seizes the King from his Parliamentarian guards at Holdenby House and places him in the 'protective custody' of the New Model Army.

4–5 June: At a rendezvous on Kentford Heath near Newmarket the officers and men of the New Model Army give their assent to the Solemn Engagement

7 June: Parliamentarian force of 2,000 troops under Jones (P) lands near Dublin.

10 June: General Rendezvous of the New Model Army on Triploe Heath near Cambridge. The Council of the Army rejects Parliament's latest terms. A letter signed by Fairfax, Cromwell, Ireton (P) and ten other officers is sent to the City authorities outlining the soldiers' grievances. The Army marches to Royston.

12 June: The New Model Army marches from Royston towards London. The Militia Committee orders the trained bands to mobilize, but only the Westminster regiment turns out in strength.

19 June: The Marquis of Ormond (R) surrenders Dublin to Jones (P).

15 July: Preston (I) captures the fortress of Naas near Dublin for the Confederates.

17 July: George Monck (P) appointed commander of all Parliament's forces in Ulster with the exception of Monro's Covenanters.

23 July: Preston (I) captures the fortress of Maynooth for the Confederates then besieges Trim, in preparation for an attack on Dublin.

28 July: The Marquis of Ormond (R) surrenders the lord lieutenancy of Ireland to Parliamentary commissioners at Dublin and sets sail for England.

29 July: The army marches for London.

1 August: General Council of the Army offers the Heads of Proposals. Jones (P) marches out of Dublin against Preston's (I) Confederates.

4 August: Supporters of the army open the city gates; four regiments occupy Southwark. Fairfax receives a letter from the City announcing its intention to submit. Jones (P) joins with forces commanded by Sir Henry Tichborne (P), Parliamentarian governor of Drogheda, and Colonel Moore (P) from Dundalk.

6 August: The army marches to Westminster. The Lord Mayor and aldermen welcome Fairfax (P) at Hyde Park; the Common Council greets him at Charing Cross.

7 August: In a deliberate show of strength, the army marches through London on the way to its new headquarters at Croydon.

8 August: Battle of Dungan's Hill; Jones (P) defeats Preston (I) and the Confederate Leinster army. Siege of Trim lifted; the forts at Naas and Maynooth recovered for Parliament.

5 September: George Monck (P) arrives at Dublin to take command of Parliamentarian forces in Ulster.

9 September: Army Council discusses terms for the King's restoration.

21 September: Publication of the first issue of the Royalist news book *Mercurius Pragmaticus*.

2 October: Jones (P) marches from Dublin against the Confederates; he joins Monck (P) to form a combined Parliamentarian army in Ireland of 6,000 foot and 1,600 horse. During October, Jones's campaigns against O'Neill (I) clear northern Leinster of Confederate strongholds.

6 October: The Army Council resolves to open new negotiations with the King, offering him more lenient terms than those offered by Parliament.

7 October: Jones (R) storms Portlester; garrison massacred.

11 October: Charles refuses to negotiate with the army; the Royal council is dismissed.

28 October: Beginning of the Putney Debates under the presidency of Cromwell. The Council of the Army meets in Putney church to discuss *The Case of the Armie and the Agreement of the People*.

6 November: Parliament resolves to force its Propositions on the King without negotiation.

9 November: New Army Council appointed, consisting of officers only. Three separate smaller army reviews to be held; anxious to maintain army discipline, Fairfax (P) requests that Church lands be sold to provide for the soldiers' pay.

11 November: Charles escapes from Hampton Court.

13 November: Charles arrives on the Isle of Wight and stays at Carisbrooke Castle. Battle of Knocknanuss; Lord Inchiquin (P) defeats the Confederate army of Viscount Taaffe (I) in Munster.

14 November: Fairfax (P) and Council of Officers submit The Army Remonstrance outlining its intention of abandoning negotiations with Charles and to bring him to trial as an enemy of the people.

15 November: At Corkbush Field, near Ware, Hertfordshire, two regiments threaten to mutiny. Fairfax and Cromwell (P) personally confront the troops; three ringleaders arrested. Private Richard Arnold shot as an example.

24 November: Cromwell (P) turns against the King when a letter is intercepted in which Charles tells the Queen his plans to negotiate with the Scottish Presbyterians rather than the army (the 'saddle letter').

15 December: Charles sends the Scottish commissioners a draft of the terms he is now willing to accept.

26 December: Charles signs the Engagement with the Scottish commissioners.

SECOND ENGLISH CIVIL WAR

1648

3 January: House of Commons passes the Vote of No Addresses, by which no more approaches are to be made to the King because of his secret negotiations with the Scots.

End February: Colonel Barry (R) lands at Cork with instructions from the Marquis of Ormond to open negotiations for an alliance between Royalists in Ireland and Confederates.

Mid-March: Lord Saye and Sele (P) attends the King at Carisbrooke Castle and tries to persuade him to come to terms with Parliament.

23 March: Colonel Poyer (R) declares for the King at Pembroke in south Wales.

3 April: Lord Inchiquin (R) declares for the King and for an alliance with the Irish Confederates and the Scots.

9 April: Poyer (R) marches to Carmarthen to rendezvous with Colonel Powell (R); their combined force estimated at between 3,000 and 4,000 men.

17 April: Colonel Horton (P) arrives at Neath to enforce the disbandment of Parliamentarian troops in south Wales.

28 April: Sir Marmaduke Langdale (R) occupies Berwick for the King, intending to hold it until the arrival of the Scottish army. Sir Philip Musgrave (R) takes Carlisle for the King, opening a route into England for the Scots.

1 May: News reaches the Army Council of War at Windsor that Fleming (P) has been killed by Royalist insurgents in south Wales. Fairfax sends Cromwell with two regiments of horse and three of foot to join Horton (P) in putting down the rebellion; Waller (P) sent to secure Cornwall.

4 May: Duke of Hamilton (C) appointed commander of the Scottish army to invade England; levy of the Engager army begins.

8 May: Battle of St Fagans; Royalist insurgents under Laugharne (R) routed by Horton (P). Remnants of the Royalist army retreat into Pembroke Castle.

20 May: The Inchiquin Truce: a cessation of hostilities signed between Lord Inchiquin (R) and the Confederate Supreme Council at Kilkenny.

25 May: Ewer (P) takes Chepstow Castle by storm.

27 May: Archbishop Rinuccini excommunicates all supporters of the Inchiquin Truce. O'Neill (I) declares for Rinuccini, but Irish leaders Clanricarde, Preston and Taafe (I) support the Supreme Council. The divisions preclude any possibility of help for the Royalists from Ireland.

1 June: Battle of Maidstone; Fairfax (P) defeats the Kent Royalists.

4 June: Cromwell's (P) attempt to storm Pembroke Castle repulsed.

5 June: Dover Castle surrenders to Rich (P). Colonel John Morrice (R) seizes Pontefract Castle in Yorkshire and declares for the King.

12 June: Skirmish on Mauchline Moor; anti-Engager insurgents dispersed by Middleton and the Earl of Callendar (R).

13 June: Fairfax's (P) attempt to storm Colchester repulsed by Sir Charles Lucas (R); a siege ensues.

24 June: Cromwell's (P) second attempt to storm Pembroke Castle repulsed.

1 July: Lilburne (P) captures 400 Royalists under Sir Richard Tempest (R) in a surprise attack at Cartington in Northumberland.

6 July: Earl of Holland (R) attempts to secure Reigate Castle but is resisted by Lord Monson (P).

8 July: The Duke of Hamilton's (C) Engager army crosses the border into England. Hamilton marches to join forces with Langdale's (R) Royalists at Carlisle.

11 July: Laugharne and Poyer (R) surrender Pembroke Castle to Cromwell (P).

12 July: Walmer Castle surrenders to Colonel Rich (P).

14 July: Fairfax's (P) troops seize the Hythe, Colchester's harbour on the River Colne. Skirmish at Penrith between Lambert's (P) rearguard and Engager (C) cavalry.

16 July: Cromwell (P) departs Pembroke and marches for the north.

17 July: The Scots (C) attack Lambert's (P) headquarters at Appleby; he withdraws across the Pennines to Barnard Castle in Durham, awaiting the arrival of Cromwell (P).

22 July: The Prince of Wales's (R) fleet arrives off Yarmouth in Norfolk, but local magistrates supported by a small body of troops prevent him from landing.

31 July: Appleby Castle in Westmorland surrenders to the Scots (C).

13 August: Cromwell and Lambert (P) join forces at Wetherby near York; they advance across the Pennines in pursuit of Hamilton (C).

14 August: A landing force from the Prince of Wales's (R) fleet attempts to lift the siege of Deal but is driven back by Rich (P).

17 August: Battle of Preston; Cromwell (P) defeats Langdale (R) and occupies Preston while the Engager army (C) withdraws south towards Wigan.

19 August: Battle of Winwick Pass; final defeat of Hamilton's (C) Scottish army.

25 August: Hamilton (C) surrenders to Lambert and Grey (P) at Uttoxeter in Staffordshire. Deal Castle in Kent surrenders to Rich (P).

27 August: Colchester surrenders to Fairfax (P). He occupies the city the next day.

30 August: The Royalist and Parliamentarian fleets manoeuvre in the Thames estuary but are driven apart by bad weather. The Prince of Wales (R) sails for the Netherlands the next day.

5 September: Leven (C) secures Edinburgh Castle. Sandown Castle in Kent surrenders to Rich (P).

16 September: Monck (P) secures Belfast, Carrickfergus and Coleraine against Scottish supporters of the Engagement in Ulster. Monro (C) sent as a prisoner to England.

19 September: Earl of Warwick's (P) fleet arrives in the Netherlands to blockade the Royalist fleet in Helvoetsluys harbour. Warwick tries to persuade the crews to desert and return to Parliament.

21 September: Cromwell (P) crosses the River Tweed and advances into Scotland.

3 October: Ormond (R) lands at Cork as the King's Lord Lieutenant in Ireland with instructions to encourage the alliance between Lord Inchiquin (R) and the Confederates in the interests of forming a united Royalist party in Ireland.

14 October: Cromwell (P) at Carlisle, from where he marches into Yorkshire and sets up his quarters at Knottingley, intending to enforce the submission of Pontefract and Scarborough – the only castles still holding out for the King.

10 November: Henry Ireton (P) introduces the Army Remonstrance to the General Council of the Army, calling for the purging of Parliament and the trial of the King. Fairfax (P) and a majority of Council members oppose the Remonstrance.

18 November: The General Council of the Army at St Albans adopts the Army Remonstrance.

25 November: Colonel Ewer (P) sent to relieve Colonel Hammond (P) of his charge of the King at Carisbrooke.

1 December: Fairfax (P) orders Charles (R) to be moved from the Isle of Wight to Hurst Castle.

2 December: The army marches into London.

6 December: Pride's Purge, when troops under Colonel Thomas Pride (P) remove opponents of Oliver Cromwell (P) from Parliament by force of arms resulting in the Rump Parliament.

23 December: Charles (R) arrives at Windsor Castle. Riots in support of the King break out in the town and are violently suppressed by soldiers.

28 December: First reading in Parliament of an ordinance instituting a special court for the trial of the King.

1649

1 January: An ordinance passed by the House of Commons proposing a special court for Charles's trial.

2 January: House of Lords rejects the ordinance for the King's trial.

4 January: Rump Parliament declares itself supreme authority in the land, with powers to pass laws without the consent of the King or the House of Lords.

15 January: 'An Agreement of the People of England' presented to the Rump Parliament.

17 January: The Second Ormond Peace: Ormond (R) concludes a treaty with the Irish Confederates to raise 18,000 troops for the King in exchange for toleration for Catholics and constitutional reform in Ireland.

20 January: Opening of the King's trial; Charles refuses to recognize the legal authority of the High Court.

21 January: Prince Rupert's (R) squadron of seven warships sails from Helvoetsluys in the Netherlands for Kinsale in southern Ireland.

27 January: Charles's death warrant signed.

30 January: Charles I executed by beheading at Whitehall.

2 February: Parliament resolves to strengthen the Navy against the threat from Prince Rupert's (R) fleet and Irish privateers by sending 30 warships and 40 armed merchantmen to sea.

5 February: Eldest son of Charles I, Charles, Prince of Wales, proclaimed 'King of Great Britain, France and Ireland' by the Scottish Parliament.

7 February: Rump Parliament votes to abolish the English monarchy and the House of Lords.

9 February: Publication of *Eikon Basilike*, allegedly written by Charles I.

14 February: Rump Parliament creates the English Council of State.

17 February: Charles II (R) renews Ormond's (R) commission as Lord Lieutenant of Ireland.

Mid-February: The Scottish Presbytery of Belfast denounces the execution of King Charles and encourages the Ulster Scots to refuse to cooperate with the Parliamentarian commanders Monck and Coote. Charles II proclaimed King of Great Britain, France and Ireland by Hugh, Viscount Montgomery and other Irish Royalists at Newtownards in Ulster.

22 February: Charles II (R) appoints Montrose (R) his Captain General in Scotland.

26 February: Ormond (R) sends representatives to persuade O'Neill (I) to join the Royalist alliance but O'Neill will only consider doing so if six counties in Ulster are restored to the native Irish.

14 March: Jones (P) replies to Ormond, rejecting his authority as Lord Lieutenant of Ireland and refusing to surrender Dublin.

15 March: Council of State nominates Cromwell (P) to command the army to be sent to Ireland.

17 March: Rump passes an Act abolishing the monarchy.

19 March: Rump abolishes the House of Lords.

24 March: Morrice (R) finally surrenders Pontefract Castle to Lambert (P) after a nine-month siege.

28 March: Arrest and imprisonment of Leveller leaders.

Late March: Parliamentarian garrison at Londonderry besieged by the Lagan Army of Ulster.

8 May: Battle of Balvenie; Ker (C) routs Pluscardine's (R) rebels, bringing the Royalist uprising in the Highlands to an end. O'Neill (I) and Monck (P) sign a three-month cessation of hostilities at Dundalk.

14 May: Cromwell and Fairfax (P) suppress Leveller mutineers at Bedford.

15 May: Ormond (R) sends Inchiquin (R) and Castlehaven (R) north from Kilkenny to clear the way for a Royalist advance on Dublin.

16 May: Inchiquin (R) captures Leix Castle in Queen's County.

19 May: England declared a Commonwealth.

21 May: Castlehaven (R) captures Athy in County Kildare from O'Neill's (I) garrison.

1 June: Ormond (R) musters 14,000 men near Clogrennan near Carlow and prepares his campaign against the Parliamentarian garrisons in Leinster.

19 June: Ormond's (R) army arrives at Finglas on the northern outskirts of Dublin and prepares to blockade the city.

22 June: Charles II arrives at Brussels in the Spanish Netherlands to negotiate for help from Spain. He is rejected by the Archduke Leopold, on the orders of King Philip.

28 June: Charles II sends Sir Robert Meynell to Rome to seek help from the Pope.

Early July: Monro (C) joins the Lagan army besieging Londonderry with 2,000 Ulster Scots.

9 July: The Marquis of Clanricarde (I) captures Sligo in Connacht.

11 July: Drogheda surrenders to Inchiquin (R).

24 July: Monck (P) surrenders Dundalk to Inchiquin (R) after most of the garrison defect.

28 July: Ormond's (R) troops storm and capture Rathfarnham Castle near Dublin.

2 August: Jones (P) recaptures Baggotrath Castle and goes on to inflict a decisive defeat on Ormond's (R) coalition army at the battle of Rathmines.

12 August: Ormond (R) succeeds in getting O'Neill (I) to join the Royalists against the Parliamentarians.

15 August: Cromwell (P) arrives in Dublin with 35 ships. Henry Ireton (P) sets sail for Ireland with a second force which joins Cromwell at Dublin a week later.

10 September: Cromwell (P) storms and captures Drogheda; many of the garrison put to the sword.

15 September: Coote (P) captures Coleraine; the garrison is put to the sword. Venables (P) occupies Dundalk, which the Royalists have abandoned.

17 September: Charles II lands at Jersey, hoping to move from there to lead the Royalists in Ireland.

21 September: Carlingford surrenders to Venables (P). The next day he occupies Newry.

27 September: Venables (P) occupies Lisburn and marches to invest Belfast.

28 September: Arklow Castle surrenders to Cromwell (P).

29 September: Ferns Castle surrenders to Cromwell (P).

30 September: Belfast surrenders to Colonel Venables (P) and Enniscorthy, in County Wexford, surrenders to Cromwell (P).

October: First publication of *Eikonoklastes* by John Milton; a rebuttal of *Eikon Basilike*.

2 October: Jones (P) captures Fort Rosslare guarding Wexford harbour, enabling Parliamentarian fleet to land siege artillery.

11 October: Sinnott (I) surrenders Wexford Castle to Cromwell (P); storming and massacre of the garrison.

19 October: Sir Lucas Taaffe (I) surrenders New Ross to Cromwell (P).

20 October: O'Neill (I) agrees to join Ormond (R) against Cromwell.

2 November: Colonel Dalziel (C) signs articles of surrender at Carrickfergus, agreeing to deliver the town and castle on 13 December.

6 December: Coote and Venables (P) defeat forces under Montgomery and Monro (C) at Lisnestrain near Lisburn.

13 December: Coote (P) occupies Carrickfergus. All of Ulster under Parliamentarian control except Charlemont and Enniskillen.

1650–1660 THE (ENGLISH) INTERREGNUM

1650

11 January: House of Commons requests Cromwell's (P) return from Ireland to deal with the situation in Scotland; Cromwell ignores the request until he has secured Ireland.

31 January: Cromwell (P) captures Kilbeheney Castle in County Limerick.

2 February: Cromwell (P) captures Rehill Castle in County Tipperary.

3 February: Cromwell (P) advances to Fethard Castle in County Tipperary, which surrenders without resistance.

4 February: Cashel Castle surrenders to Cromwell (P) without resistance.

8 February: Callan surrenders to Reynolds (P) after the execution of captured soldiers.

10 February: Ireton (P) storms and captures Ardfinnan Castle.

24 February: Cahir Castle in County Tipperary surrenders to Cromwell (P).

27 February: Kiltinan Castle in County Tipperary bombarded into submission by Cromwell (P).

1 March: Ballisonan Castle near Carlow surrenders to Hewson (P). Royalists abandon garrisons at Athy and Maryborough (Portaloise).

3 March: Hewson (P) advances to capture Castledermot.

21 March: Gowran Castle surrenders to Cromwell (P).

27 March: Sir Walter Butler (R) surrenders Kilkenny to Cromwell (P).

Late March: Lord Broghill and Henry Cromwell (P) defeat Lord Inchiquin's (R) forces near Mallow in County Cork.

21 April: Dunbeath Castle surrenders to Hurry (P).

27 April: Battle of Carbisdale; Strachan (C) defeats Montrose (R).

1 May: Treaty of Breda signed between Charles II and the Scottish Covenanters.

10 May: Lord Broghill (P) defeats an Irish relief force marching for Clonmel at Macroom in County Cork.

11 May: Carrigadrohid Castle near Macroom surrenders to Broghill (P).

16 May: Cromwell (P) storms Clonmel.

17 May: The Mayor of Clonmel surrenders to Cromwell (P).

27 May: Cromwell (P) concludes conquest of Ireland and returns to England leaving Ireton (P) in command.

2 June: Charles II sets sail for Scotland without having agreed to the Covenanters' new demands.

18 June: Reinforced by regiments of the New Model Army, Coote (P) advances to attack the Ulster Confederates.

21 June: Battle of Scarriffhollis; Coote (P) defeats the last Confederate field army, under the command of Heber MacMohan, Bishop of Clogher (I).

23 June: Charles II lands in Speymouth, Scotland, and signs the Solemn League and Covenant.

26 June: Fairfax (P) resigns as commander-in-chief of the Commonwealth army. Cromwell (P) appointed in his place.

28 June: Cromwell (P) marches for Scotland with 16,000 men.

11 July: Parliament passes a new Militia Act. Property holders to contribute proportionately to defence costs. Lords-lieutenant of counties to be replaced by commissioners appointed by Parliament or the Council of State.

13 July: Inchiquin's (R) forces in County Kerry defeated by Colonel Robert Phayre's (P) cavalry.

22 July: Cromwell (P) crosses the border into Scotland.

29 July: Cromwell (P) advances towards the defensive lines around Edinburgh but cannot draw the Scots out into the open.

31 July: Scottish lancers under Colonel Montgomery (C) attack Cromwell's (P) camp at Musselburgh.

6 August: Preston (I) surrenders Waterford to Ireton (P).

12 August: Duncannon Fort near Waterford surrenders to Ireton (P).

14 August: O'Neill (I) surrenders Charlemont Fort in Ulster to Coote (P).

24 August: Cromwell (P) storms and captures Red Hall, a fortified house commanding the crossing of the Water of Leith.

1 September: Cromwell (P) falls back to Dunbar.

3 September: Battle of Dunbar; Cromwell (P) routs the Scots. Leslie (C) retreats to Stirling; Committee of Estates abandons Edinburgh for Stirling.

4 September: Lambert (P) occupies the city of Edinburgh but Walter Dundas (C) refuses to surrender Edinburgh Castle.

5 October: Colonel Montgomery (C) finds Charles taking refuge in a shepherd's hut in the mountains. The King agrees to accompany him back to Perth.

25 October: Colonel Axtell (P) defeats the Marquis of Clanricarde's (I) forces at Meelick Island on the River Shannon.

1 December: Lambert (P) defeats Colonel Ker (C) and the Western Association army at Hamilton.

1651

1 January: Charles II crowned King of Scots at Scone.

23 February: Tantallon Castle surrenders to Monck (P).

9 March: Arrest of John Birkenhead and other conspirators at Greenock; capture of correspondence regarding plans for widespread Royalist insurrection in England.

29 March: Arrest of Royalist conspirator Tom Coke. In exchange for his life, Coke reveals full details of Royalist plans and names the leaders of the conspiracy in England. Widespread arrests follow.

23 May: Sir John Grenville (R) agrees to surrender the Isles of Scilly after General-at-Sea Robert Blake (P) offers generous terms.

18 June: Lord Dillon (I) surrenders Athlone to Coote (P).

12 July: The Battle of Knocknaclashy; Lord Broghill (P) routs Viscount Muskerry's (I) Irish relief force marching for Limerick.

20 July: Battle of Inverkeithing; Lambert (P) defeats Sir John Brown (C).

24 July: Monck (P) captures Inchgarvie in Fife.

29 July: Monck (P) captures Burntisland, securing Cromwell's (P) base of operations in Fife.

2 August: Perth surrenders to Cromwell's (P) summons.

6 August: Monck (P) arrives at Stirling; town surrenders but castle continues to resist for another eight days.

16 August: Skirmish at Warrington Bridge. Combined force of Lambert and Harrison (P) withdraws before the Royalist advance.

25 August: Battle of Wigan Lane; Derby (R) and the Lancashire Royalists routed at Wigan by a regiment of horse under Lilburne (P).

28 August: Battle of Upton; Lambert (P) captures Upton Bridge on the outskirts of Worcester, allowing Cromwell's (P) army to operate on both banks of the River Severn.

1 September: Monck (P) storms Dundee; his troops massacre up to 800 soldiers of the garrison and plunder the town.

3 September: Battle of Worcester; Cromwell (P) defeats Charles II (R) and the Scots (C). The last major battle of the Wars.

6 September: Charles II spends the day hiding in the Royal Oak in the woodlands surrounding Boscobel House.

7 September: Aberdeen occupied by English troops.

15 October: Charles II sails for France from Shoreham, near Brighton, in Captain Tattershall's coal boat the *Surprise*.

16 October: Charles II lands in Normandy.

19 October: Charles II joins Henrietta Maria and James, Duke of York, in exile in Paris.

25 October: Royalist garrison at Mount Orgueil on Jersey surrenders to Colonel Heane (P).

26 October: Limerick surrenders to Ireton (P).

31 October: Royalist garrison on the Isle of Man surrenders to Duckenfield (P).

10 December: Cromwell (P) summons a conference of army officers and lawyer MPs to discuss the settlement of the nation.

1652

13 March: Colonel O'Dwyer (I) surrenders Irish forces in Tipperary and Waterford.

12 May: Preston (I) surrenders Galway to Coote (P).

1652–1654 First Anglo-Dutch War, fought entirely at sea between the navies of the Commonwealth of England and the United Provinces of the Netherlands. It resulted from trade disputes; the English navy prevailed, forcing the Dutch to accept an English monopoly on trade with England and her colonies.

20 April 1653: Rump Parliament disbanded by Oliver Cromwell.

18 December 1653: Cromwell installed as Lord Protector.

1653–58 THE PROTECTORATE

3 September 1654: First Protectorate Parliament assembles (dissolved 22 January 1655).

25 March 1655: Battle of the Severn fought in the Province of Maryland; won by a Puritan force fighting under a Commonwealth flag, which defeated a Royalist force fighting for Lord Baltimore.

17 September 1656: Second Protectorate Parliament assembles until 26 June 1657.

23 February 1657: Oliver Cromwell offered the crown.

13 April 1657: Oliver Cromwell declines the crown.

3 September 1658: Death of Oliver Cromwell.

1658–59 THE PROTECTORATE UNDER RICHARD CROMWELL

7 May 1659: Rump Parliament restored by Richard Cromwell after coercion by army officers.

25 May 1659: Richard Cromwell delivers a formal letter resigning the position of Lord Protector.

13 October 1659: Army dissolves Rump Parliament.

1660 THE ENGLISH RESTORATION

30 January 1660: Charles II proclaimed King of England.

March 1660: Convention Parliament elected.

4 April 1660: Charles II issues the Declaration of Breda, making known the conditions of his acceptance of the crown of England.

25 April 1660: Convention Parliament assembles for the first time.

29 May 1660: Charles II arrives in London; the English monarchy is restored.

July 1660: Richard Cromwell leaves England for France, where he goes by a variety of pseudonyms, including 'John Clarke'.

29 December 1660: Convention Parliament disbanded by Charles II.

23 April 1661: Coronation of Charles II at Westminster Abbey.

30 January 1661: On the twelfth anniversary of the beheading of Charles I, the exhumed remains of Oliver Cromwell are posthumously executed (Cromwell's severed head displayed on a pole outside Westminster Hall until 1685).

LEGEND TO MAPS

PHYSICAL FEATURES

 Contour (height in feet)

 River (arrow shows direction of flow)

 Marsh/bog

 Woodland

 Hedge

 Enclosed land (this would have been heavily subdivided, but rarely recorded in detail)

 Road

 Bridge

 Track

 Ditch/dyke

 County border

 National border

○ Town (neutral)

 Church

MILITARY SYMBOLS

 Royalist force (represented by royal blue)

 Parliamentarian force (represented by red)

Covenanter/Engager force (represented by sky blue)

Scottish Royalist force (represented by royal blue)

Irish Royalist force (represented by royal blue)

Irish rebel force (represented by green)

Battle or skirmish

Neutral castle or fort (represented by grey)

Castle (Irish)

Siege of castle or fort (inner castle in colour of garrison; outer roundel in colour of besieging forces)

● Town (Royalist)

◉ Siege of city/town (inner dot in colour of defenders; outer circle in colour of besieging forces)

Sconce/fortified position

Fortified line

Earth fortifications

 Siege line/trench line (Parliamentarian)

 Sap line (Parliamentarian)

Bridge of boats

Barricade

Ship/naval force (Parliamentarian)

Baggage train (Covenanter)

Siege or garrison artillery (Parliamentarian)

Field artillery (Royalist)

▲ Bivouac area (Royalist)

Movement (Parliamentarian)

Attack (Covenanter)

Withdrawal (Parliamentarian)

UNIT SYMBOLS

Pike formation (Royalist)

Musket formation (Parliamentarian)

Cavalry (Irish)

Dragoons (Royalist)

 Dragoons or musketeers deployed (Parliamentarian)

AUTHOR'S NOTE

Where the information boxes on the maps contain a number in brackets, corresponding notes can be found in the Notes to Maps section on page 327.

INTRODUCTION – ORIGINS OF CONFLICT

The bravest are surely those who have the clearest vision of what is before them, glory and danger alike, and yet notwithstanding, go out to meet it.

Thucydides (471–400 BC)

It is not unreasonable to suggest that any single-issue explanation of the causes, origins and/or significance of the English Civil War can ever be adequate. As a study, it is a many-headed monster attached to the same body. In fairness, the debate as to its origins has never abated; in fact, it has morphed, largely because historians reinterpret, quite rightly, the old based on the new. But this has not resulted in consensus – far from it. Even the title of the war has been subject to challenge as new and contrasting theories continue to emerge.

The 17th-century post-war interpretations tended to be shaped by the freshness of the trauma. Bulstrode Whitelocke, a lawyer, one of Cromwell's advisors, and the Lord Keeper of the Great Seal of England, suggested the nation had stumbled into conflict: 'It is strange to note how we have insensibly slid into the beginning of a civil war by one unexpected accident after another.'[1] Other early English accounts were rather simplistic, or driven by personal circumstance in pointing the finger of culpability. Lord Clarendon (Edward Hyde) blamed the King's opponents; Lucy Hutchinson, the wife of a prominent Parliamentarian who died in prison (under Charles II), considered it a struggle between priestcraft and tyranny; Thomas May, a Parliamentary secretary, was unequivocal in his blame of the monarch and his close personal advisors; while Thomas Hobbes blamed mankind, which he considered to be obsessed with society's need of authority.[2] Contemporary accounts from Scotland and Ireland are less balanced in their blameworthiness. Other than official papers, the memoirs of the Marquis of Montrose on the one hand, and the letters of Robert Baillie on the other, provide the case for and against (respectively) Charles's cause north of the border,[3] while a collection of letters and seminal documents put together by John Gilbert for the Irish Archaeology and Celtic Society, in the latter part of the 19th century, gives a good contemporary insight into the struggle from the perspective of the Irish 'rebels'.[4] At this stage, however, there was no attempt to place the conflict into a multinational context.

Another contemporary view was provided by James Harrington, an English political theorist and advocate of republicanism. He looked at the longer-term reasons, namely that feudalism was on the wane while the middling classes were on the wax. As such, he threw a socio-economic cause into the mix, widening the debate in terms of foundation and time. Thus, four pillars were established, one at each corner of the debate. As Peter Gaunt summarized in his first-rate short work on the wars, 'these key variables – long-term or short-term, political and constitutional (including

religion) or socio-economic – provide a matrix into which most subsequent interpretations can be placed'.[5]

Curiously, however, during the 18th century the debate did not advance with anything like the same intensity of the subsequent two centuries. The issue over James II's suitability to the English crown led to divisions and the emergence of two political groups: the Whigs, who opposed the idea, and the Tories, their Royalist opponents. In short, the Whigs proposed Parliamentary primacy over the monarch, while the Tories supported the idea of monarchical primacy (but not necessarily absolutism) in the constitutional process. It was, in a way, an echo of the divide between Parliamentarian and Royalist that had led to war in the first instance. Then, following the Glorious Revolution of 1688–89, the Whig view triumphed and their explanation of history began to mature. This 'Whig interpretation' was seen as a combined struggle of political and constitutional liberty and a secular and religious revolution. It provided the descriptive basis of the civil struggles for the 19th-century historian Thomas Babington Macaulay, published in his defining and highly readable five-volume work, *History of England*. His *magnum opus* endorsed the classic Whig statement and demonstrated those (consequent) virtues with examples of Parliamentary government that had developed in Britain (and America). Macaulay's work was followed 30 years later by Samuel Rawson Gardiner's tomes covering the period leading to the Civil War, the war itself and the subsequent period of the Commonwealth and Protectorate.[6] Once again, this is undeniably a great work, but the problem is that neither author made an attempt to consider the struggle as anything other than one of political liberty and religious evolution. Indeed, Gardiner's statement that 'on the whole, the nobility and the gentry took the side of the King, while the townsmen and the yeomanry took the side of Parliament' could not have been more deliberately misleading.[7]

At the end of the Victorian period socio-economic historians were laying the foundations of scientific economic history, which led to a number of reappraisals and new interpretations of the Civil War, along class and commercial lines. In 1887 Karl Marx argued, in *Das Kapital*, that the appropriation and exploitation of the land by a feudal aristocracy resulted in the rise of the English bourgeoisie commercial class, who were acting out of their own interest to acquire political power.[8] He made the distinction that the bourgeoisie class of English 'gentry' were not part of the nobility and that the Civil War was, therefore, a class struggle. This argument was developed by Richard Tawney in his work *Religion and the Rise of Capitalism* in 1926 and again in an article for the *Economic History Review* entitled

---

1 Cobbett, *Parliamentary History of England*, vol. II, p. 1415.
2 Hyde, *Great Rebellion*; Hutchinson, *Life of Colonel Hutchinson*; May, *History of Parliament of England*; Hobbes, *Causes of the Civil Wars*.
3 Wishart, *The Memoirs of James Graham Marquis of Montrose*; Laing, *Letters and Journals of Robert Baillie*.
4 Gilbert, *Affairs in Ireland*.

5 Gaunt, *The English Civil Wars*.
6 Gardiner, *Accession of James I*, *Great Civil War* and *Commonwealth and Protectorate*.
7 Gardiner, *Great Civil War*, vol. I., p. 11.
8 Marx, *Capital*, vol. I., pp. 676–8.

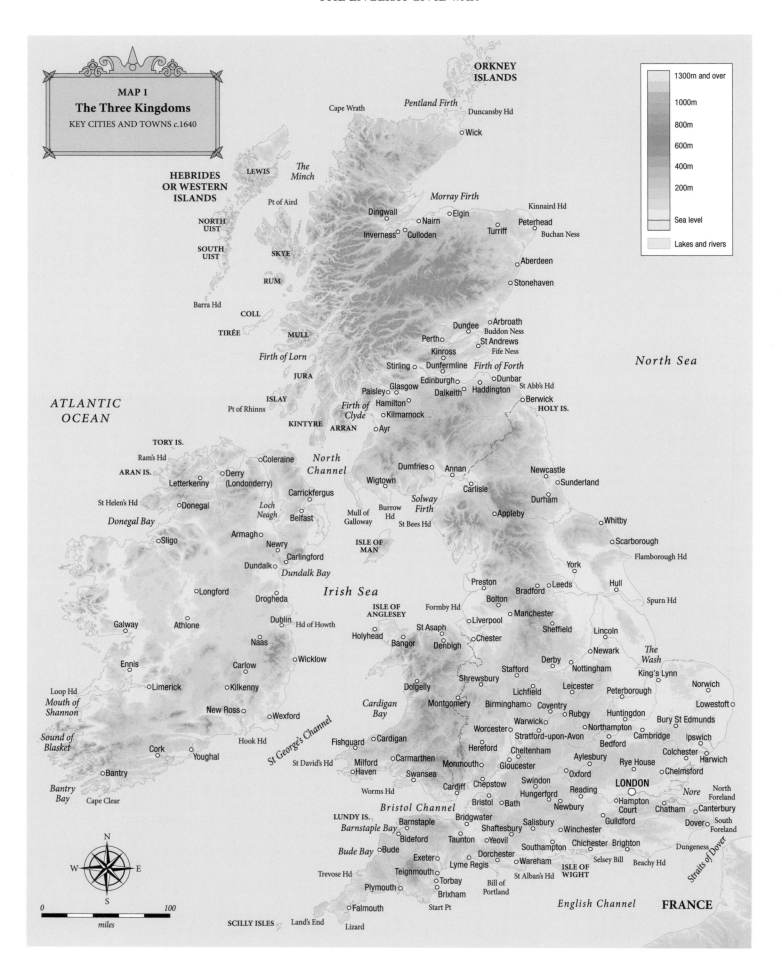

MAP 1

The Three Kingdoms

KEY CITIES AND TOWNS *c.*1640

ORKNEY
ISLANDS

1300m and over
1000m
800m
600m
400m
200m
Sea level

Lakes and rivers

Pentland Firth
Cape Wrath
Duncansby Hd
Wick

HEBRIDES
OR WESTERN
ISLANDS

LEWIS
The Minch

Pt of Aird

Morray Firth
Kinnaird Hd
Dingwall
Nairn   Elgin   Peterhead
NORTH
UIST
Inverness   Culloden   Turriff   Buchan Ness

SOUTH
UIST
SKYE   Aberdeen

RUM   Stonehaven

Barra Hd
COLL

TIRÉE
MULL   Dundee   Arbroath
Buddon Ness
Perth   St Andrews
JURA   Kinross   Fife Ness
Firth of Lorn   Stirling   Dunfermline   *Firth of Forth*

North Sea

ISLAY   Edinburgh   Dunbar
Paisley   Glasgow   Dalkeith   Haddington   St Abb's Hd
Pt of Rhinns   Hamilton   Berwick
*Firth of
Clyde*   Kilmarnock   HOLY IS.
KINTYRE   ARRAN   Ayr

*ATLANTIC
OCEAN*

TORY IS.
Ram's Hd   *North
Channel*   Dumfries   Annan   Newcastle
ARAN IS.   Coleraine   Wigtown   Carlisle   Sunderland
Letterkenny   Derry
(Londonderry)   Durham
St Helen's Hd   Carrickfergus   Mull of   Burrow   *Solway   Appleby
Donegal   *Loch   Galloway   Hd   Firth*   Whitby
Donegal Bay   Neagh*   Belfast   St Bees Hd   Scarborough
Sligo   Armagh   Flamborough Hd
Newry   ISLE OF
MAN   York
Carlingford   Preston   Leeds   Hull
Longford   Dundalk   *Irish Sea*   Bradford   Spurn Hd
Drogheda   ISLE OF   Formby Hd   Bolton   Manchester
ANGLESEY   Liverpool   Sheffield   Lincoln
Galway   Athlone   Dublin   Hd of Howth   St Asaph   Chester   Newark   *The
Holyhead   Bangor   Derby   Wash*
Naas   Denbigh   Stafford   Nottingham   King's Lynn
Ennis   Carlow   Wicklow   Shrewsbury   Lichfield   Leicester   Peterborough   Norwich
Limerick   Kilkenny   Dolgelly   Birmingham   Coventry   Rugby   Huntingdon   Lowestoft
Loop Hd   Montgomery   Warwick   Northampton   Bury St Edmunds
*Mouth of   New Ross   *Cardigan   Worcester   Stratford-upon-Avon   Bedford   Cambridge   Ipswich
Shannon*   Wexford   Bay*   Hereford   Cheltenham   Colchester   Harwich
*Sound of   Fishguard   Cardigan   Aylesbury   Rye House   Chelmsford
Blasket*   Cork   Hook Hd   Carmarthen   Monmouth   Gloucester   Oxford
Youghal   St David's Hd   Milford   Swansea   Cardiff   Chepstow   Swindon   Reading   **LONDON**   *Nore*   North
Bantry   Haven   Hungerford   Hampton   Foreland
*Bantry   Worms Hd   Bristol   Bath   Newbury   Court   Chatham   Canterbury
Bay*   Cape Clear   *Bristol Channel*   Bridgwater   Salisbury   Winchester   Guildford   Dover   South
LUNDY IS.   Barnstaple   Shaftesbury   Chichester   Brighton   Foreland
Barnstaple Bay   Bideford   Taunton   Yeovil   Southampton   Selsey Bill   Beachy Hd   Dungeness
Bude Bay   Bude   Exeter   Dorchester   Wareham   ISLE OF   *Straits of Dover*
Trevose Hd   Teignmouth   Lyme Regis   St Alban's Hd   WIGHT
Plymouth   Torbay   Bill of   *English Channel*   **FRANCE**
SCILLY ISLES   Land's End   Brixham   Portland
Lizard   Start Pt   Falmouth

N
W   E
S

0   100
miles

'The Gentry Take the Power to Which Their Economic Success Entitles Them'.[9] Hugh Trevor-Roper in his 1957 work *The Social Causes of the Great Rebellion*, endorsed this change in the socio-economic balance of power. But it was Christopher Hill's work, at much the same time, that hijacked the 17th-century struggle, labelling it a 'bourgeois revolution'. His work and viewpoint were quickly dubbed the 'Marxist interpretation' and published as a Marxist textbook.[10] Hill sought to equate the 'English Bourgeois Revolution' with the revolution in France in 1789 and that in Russia in 1917. Clearly such comparisons are awkward, but that is not to suggest that the Marxist interpretation does not have some merit, particularly when it is considered in parallel with the growth of radical groups such as the Levellers, Diggers and Ranters (see glossary for definitions). Nevertheless, the consensus view of the utility of Marxist ideology to the Civil War in 17th-century England remains sceptical. There is, however, general consensus that the Marxist interpretation 'over-estimated both the influence and the revolutionary ideology of the radicals, thereby inflating the Civil Wars into a revolution that… England never had'.[11] Despite this, the Whig view and Marxist socio-economic interpretations are both useful. They serve to highlight the emergence of modern liberalism on the one hand, and the growth of a middling-class and capitalist organizations on the other.

During the mid-20th century, a number of revisionist historians returned to the traditional themes of a political, constitutional and religious struggle. Some even resurrected the theory that the principal participants of historic events are agents of a process of which they themselves are totally unaware. Yet others returned to the short-term theme encompassing the problems associated with the running of the state and the church during the reign of Charles I, stemming largely, but not exclusively, from the King's personality and inflexibility. Nevertheless, in many late 19th- and early 20th-century accounts of the war, the socio-economic causes are never far away. Winston Churchill, in his *History of the English-Speaking Peoples*, wrote that 'underlying the apparently clear-cut constitutional issue was a religious and class conflict'.[12] This vision of the wars as David rising up against Goliath pervades, but it was simply not the case. In the English Civil War, brother fought against brother, and father against son. It was not a struggle pitting peasant against aristocrat, as was the case in France in 1789 or Russia in 1917. While some historians have concentrated on the problems at the nation's core, others have taken a bottom-up approach by analysing the four interlocking causes (political, constitutional, religious and socio-economic) from a provincial or county starting point. This approach is considered by late 19th- and 20th-century historians to be closer to the coalface.

However, the research conducted on county histories has found no clear-cut connection of a class conflict.[13] It is accepted that some working-class men rose in the ranks of the Parliamentarian army and navy, while none did in the Royalist ranks. It is vitally important to recognize that the war would not have taken place at all if the governing classes had not been deeply divided.[14] Men from the same social background, with comparable economic interests and similar political and religious ideals, found themselves in opposite forces. Peter Young and Richard Holmes summed it up impeccably:

> Just as the war itself originated in a multiplicity of causes, so the nation was divided along a series of irregular jagged lines which defy simple interpretation in clear-cut social, religious, geographical or economic terms. It was in no sense a class war, a conflict between nobility and commoners or even between Court and Parliament.[15]

Other historians have suggested that the wars resulted from an economic crisis, but this does not pass closer scrutiny. By the end of the 16th century high levels of inflation were back under control and both wages and rents had increased, albeit not by as much as the price of food. Lawrence Stone wrote about a 'crisis in the aristocracy' caused by a combination of inflation and static rents; his work concentrates on the longer-term causes of, *inter alia*, financial instability.[16] However, it is difficult to support or reject Stone's work as a key driver, or set of drivers, which ignited the struggle. Leaving aside the financial issues with the monarchy, there is some economic traction with regard to the counties. Maurice Ashley writes:

> In the poorer parts of England and Wales the gentry, for the most part, fought for Charles I. Indeed, the mixed farming (unenclosed or 'champion') areas such as Kent, Norfolk and Suffolk were extremely wealthy regions where the Parliamentarians were the strongest, whereas in the mainly pastoral districts, such as Cheshire and Lancashire, the south-western shires and much of Wales, the inhabitants on the whole were loyal to the King.[17]

This provincial angle is an important one. John Morrill, in his fascinating work *The Revolt of the Provinces, Conservatives and Radicals in the English Civil War 1630–1650*, examines the growth of the county as a coherent political and social community in the early 17th century. He argues that the generalizations that stem from the Whig or Marxist views are incomplete, that the definitions of 'court' (in particular) and 'country' are unclear, and that the impact and influence of the county have been underplayed and misunderstood.[18] Other revisionist historians, such as Anthony Fletcher and Conrad Russell, elevated this county angle and suggest that the pressures and influences of the three separate kingdoms was a key driver in destabilizing the situation and contributing to war.[19]

Seventeenth-century England (including Wales) formed just one part of a 'composite monarchy' of the three Stuart kingdoms. The Stuarts were the first dynasty to unite all three kingdoms under a single crown. Charles I considered the struggle to be a single war, and he certainly had no qualms about deploying forces and resources from one kingdom to try to resolve matters in another. In 1644, for example, there were English and Scottish troops in Ireland, Scottish and Irish troops in England, and Irish (but not English) troops in Scotland. England's position within that multiple polity, while not one of *primus inter pares*, was especially influential. However, this helps little in unravelling the nature and causes of the conflict, which were confusing, convoluted and changed during the 12-year struggle. Even the

---

9   Tawney, *Religion and the Rise of Capitalism* and *Economic History Review* article, reprinted in Taylor, *Origins*, pp. 32–42.
10 Hill, *English Revolution*.
11 Anderson, *Civil Wars*, p. 21. See also Parry, *The English Civil War and After*, and Ashton, *The Civil War and the Class Struggle*, pp. 97–102.
12 Churchill, *English-Speaking*, vol. II, p. 185.
13 Ashley, *Civil War*, p. 16.
14 Ollard, *War without an Enemy*, p. 12.
15 Young & Holmes, *English Civil War*, p. 27.
16 Stone, *Causes of the English Revolution*.
17 Ashley, op. cit., p. 8.
18 Morrill, *Revolt of the Provinces* pp. 13–51.
19 Fletcher, *Outbreak of the Civil War* and Russell, *Causes of the English Civil War*.

MAP 2
The Three Kingdoms
COUNTY BOUNDARIES *c.*1640

ORKNEY

CAITHNESS

SUTHERLAND

ROSS

NAIRN-SHIRE
ELGIN-SHIRE
BANFF-SHIRE

INVERNESS-SHIRE

ABERDEENSHIRE

KINCARDINESHIRE

FORFARSHIRE

PERTHSHIRE

FIFESHIRE
KINROSSSHIRE
CLACKMANNANSHIRE

ARGYLLSHIRE

STIRLING-SHIRE
HADDINGTON

DUMBARTONSHIRE

RENFREW-SHIRE
EDINBURGH
BERWICKSHIRE

LANARK-SHIRE
PEEBLES-SHIRE
SELKIRKSHIRE

AYRSHIRE
ROXBURGH-SHIRE

DUMFRIESSHIRE
NORTHUMBERLAND

KIRKCUDBRIGHT-SHIRE

WIGTOWNSHIRE

CUMBERLAND
DURHAM

COLERAINE
ANTRIM

TYRCONNEL

ULSTER

TYRONE

ISLE OF MAN

WESTMORELAND

FERMANAGH
DOWN
ARMAGH

SLIGO
MONAGHAN

CONNAUGHT
LEITRIM
CAVAN

YORKSHIRE

MAYO
ROSCOMMON
LOUTH

LONGFORD

WESTMEATH
MEATH

GALWAY

LEINSTER

FLINTSHIRE
LANCASHIRE

LINCOLNSHIRE

KING'S COUNTY
DUBLIN

ANGLESEY
DENBIGH-SHIRE
CHESHIRE
DERBYSHIRE

KILDARE

CAERNARFONSHIRE
NOTTINGHAM-SHIRE

QUEEN'S COUNTY
WICKLOW

RUTLAND

CLARE

MERIONETH-SHIRE
STAFFORD-SHIRE
LEICESTER-SHIRE

CARLOW

NORFOLK

LIMERICK
KILKENNY
MONTGOMERYSHIRE
SHROP-SHIRE

TIPPERARY
WARWICK-SHIRE

MUNSTER
WEXFORD
1
3

2
SUFFOLK

KERRY
CORK
WATERFORD
CARDIGANSHIRE
RADNOR-SHIRE
WORCESTER-SHIRE
4

PEMBROKESHIRE
HEREFORD-SHIRE
6
5
7
ESSEX

CARMARTHEN-SHIRE
GLOUCESTER-SHIRE

BRECKNOCKSHIRE
GLAMORGAN-SHIRE
8
LONDON

MONMOUTHSHIRE
BERKSHIRE

WILTSHIRE
SURREY
KENT

SOMERSET
HAMPSHIRE
SUSSEX

ISLE OF WIGHT

DEVON
DORSET

CORNWALL

1 HUNTINGDONSHIRE
2 NORTHAMPTONSHIRE
3 CAMBRIDGESHIRE
4 BEDFORDSHIRE
5 BUCKINGHAMSHIRE
6 OXFORDSHIRE
7 HERTFORDSHIRE
8 MIDDLESEX

N
W   E
S

0   100
miles

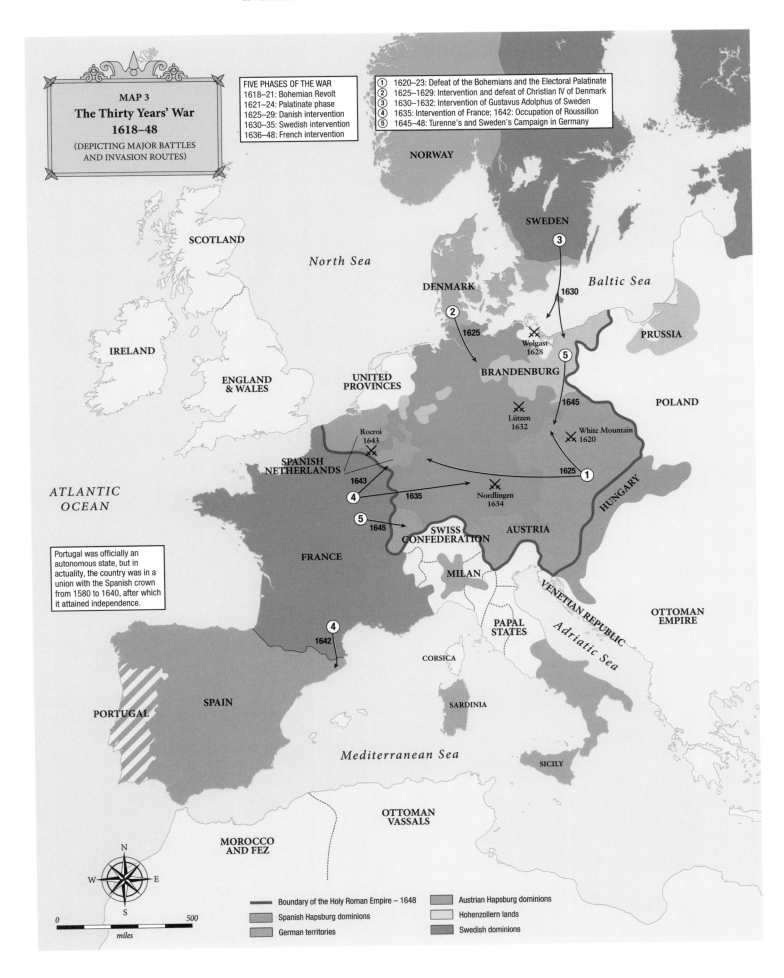

MAP 3
**The Thirty Years' War
1618–48**
(DEPICTING MAJOR BATTLES
AND INVASION ROUTES)

FIVE PHASES OF THE WAR
1618–21: Bohemian Revolt
1621–24: Palatinate phase
1625–29: Danish intervention
1630–35: Swedish intervention
1636–48: French intervention

① 1620–23: Defeat of the Bohemians and the Electoral Palatinate
② 1625–1629: Intervention and defeat of Christian IV of Denmark
③ 1630–1632: Intervention of Gustavus Adolphus of Sweden
④ 1635: Intervention of France; 1642: Occupation of Roussillon
⑤ 1645–48: Turenne's and Sweden's Campaign in Germany

NORWAY

SWEDEN

SCOTLAND

North Sea

Baltic Sea

DENMARK

③
1630

②
1625

PRUSSIA

IRELAND

Wolgast
1628

BRANDENBURG

⑤

ENGLAND
& WALES

UNITED
PROVINCES

POLAND

1645

Lützen
1632

Rocroi
1643

White Mountain
1620

*ATLANTIC
OCEAN*

SPANISH
NETHERLANDS

1643

1625
①

HUNGARY

④
1635

Nordlingen
1634

⑤
1645

SWISS
CONFEDERATION

AUSTRIA

Portugal was officially an
autonomous state, but in
actuality, the country was in a
union with the Spanish crown
from 1580 to 1640, after which
it attained independence.

FRANCE

MILAN

VENETIAN REPUBLIC

*Adriatic
Sea*

OTTOMAN
EMPIRE

PAPAL
STATES

④
1642

CORSICA

PORTUGAL

SPAIN

SARDINIA

Mediterranean Sea

SICILY

OTTOMAN
VASSALS

MOROCCO
AND FEZ

N
W   E
S

0   500
miles

Boundary of the Holy Roman Empire – 1648
Spanish Hapsburg dominions
German territories
Austrian Hapsburg dominions
Hohenzollern lands
Swedish dominions

outcome is in dispute. The Restoration of Charles II in 1660 unbuttoned much of what the Parliamentarians had fought for in the 1640s. Thirty years later, the Glorious Revolution ended the Stuart line, but not the Jacobite struggle, suggesting that the civil wars were never really fought to conclusion.

As the nature and causes of these wars have been extensively debated over the last 350 years, so has the search for a more suitable title. In that time, the struggles have been known as 'the Great Rebellion', 'the Puritan Rebellion', 'the Cause', 'the English Revolution' and, more recently, 'the British Civil Wars'. However, in the mid-17th century, Scotland was an independent country and Ireland effectively an English colony, so the 'British' tag is unsatisfactory. Perhaps the best solution, and the term seemingly preferred by many historians today, is 'the Wars of the Three Kingdoms'.[20] However, even this fails to represent the impact and effect of the bloody religious wars on the Continent that raged throughout this period. It is important, therefore, to view the Wars of the Three Kingdoms as a peripheral part of the Thirty Years' War. The Spanish Hapsburgs, the French Bourbons and (to a lesser extent) the Dutch Republic, were active participants in the Wars of the Three Kingdoms, their ambassadors promising (but seldom delivering) financial aid and military support.[21]

One particular area that has received scant exposure in the plethora of books and papers on the subject of the wars is that of the print revolution and press censorship. The collapse of censorship and explosion of print is not so much a cause as a driver. Nevertheless, it is a factor that cannot be ignored. The explosion of cheap print brought news and shaped opinions, one way or the other, to a far wider audience. 'This print revolution had a profound impact on *who* was affected by the civil wars and *how* the revolution was experienced by the ordinary citizens.'[22] It also had a profound effect upon the political practice, although it is important to acknowledge that the majority of publications addressed religious issues and, in particular, the control and management of the church. Nevertheless, the primary impact and influence on citizens, in the early to mid-17th century, can be readily compared with that of the internet revolution in the late 20th century. It took the debate outside capitals to the counties and, in so doing, transformed political culture, broadening it both socially and geographically. It is hard to imagine how the Covenanters' movement in Scotland, or the appeal for popular support with the Grand Remonstrance[23] in England, would have been successful without the persuasive power of print.

Therefore, the very title 'The English Civil War' is both confusing and, in many respects, a misnomer. It is unhelpful and ultimately detrimental to detach the Irish and Scottish wars from the complex chain of events in England (and Wales) between 1639 and 1651. Of course, it also depends on where, to coin John Kenyon's words, 'you set the stone rolling': 1558, on the accession of Elizabeth I; 1603, on the accession of James I; or perhaps 23 July 1637, when Jenny Gedes threw her stool at the dean of St Giles, Edinburgh?[24] Ollard sums it up well: 'As the kaleidoscope is jarred by the succession of events, the groupings change their pattern.'[25] Two distinct patterns emerge: the decades leading up to 1638 and the period from 1638 to 1642. The former resulted in war in Scotland, and the latter encompassed rebellion in Ireland and ultimately civil war in England.

20 Even this does not take into account Wales, but since 1284 it formed part of the Kingdom of England.
21 Kenyon & Ohlmeyer, *Military History*, p. xx.
22 Peacey, *Revolution in Print*, p. 10.
23 The Grand Remonstrance was drawn up in late summer 1641 to give renewed impetus to political change in light of the King's apparent conciliation, which some felt had drawn a veil over the matter of sufficient and long-lasting alteration.
24 Kenyon & Ohlmeyer, op. cit., p. xxiii.
25 Ollard, op. cit., p. 12.

CIVIL WAR ARMIES, FIGHTING COMPONENTS AND THEIR TACTICS

THE FIRST STANDING ARMY

The term 'revolution' is bandied about quite freely by historians. It certainly enjoys more than a cameo role in describing events in British 17th-century history. The continued development of weaponry and a considerable evolution in battlefield tactics created the perfect ingredients for regime change and led Michael Roberts to categorize the period between 1560 and 1660 as a 'military revolution'.[1] Jeremy Black, however, deliberates that this military revolution started earlier and finished much later,[2] while Geoffrey Parker has reservations about the basis of Roberts' arguments, and considers the military advances to have been more evolutionary than revolutionary.[3] In support of Roberts, there is no doubt that armies were much larger in this period and, more significantly perhaps, they began to come under state control. A factor that changed their emphasis and led, among other things, to increased proficiency. However, if this military revolution evolved gradually for the larger armies on the European Continent, then in the case of Britain's military development, it was more of an ignition at the period's close. 'The history of the Civil War is the history of the evolution of an efficient army out of a chaos', wrote Charles Firth in his excellent work *Cromwell's Army*.[4] And so it was, more or less, although it must be recognized that the Wars of the Three Kingdoms have no meaningful place in the evolution of military strategy.

One of James I's early decisions, on accession in 1603, was to end the long war between England and Spain that had dragged on during the twilight years of Elizabethan reign. The English military structure was dismantled; only the guards and garrisons of the forts remained in pay and on establishment. The Militia Acts of 1558 were repealed and the government ceased to hold militia musters, or authorize training for several years.[5] Even by its own standards the militia became decadent. Despite this, James found that he could ramp up the militia during a crisis, such as following the Gunpowder Treason Plot of 1605 and in times of national emergency. Although this policy satisfied the King's immediate requirements, it completely missed the point that the two indispensable requirements for an effective fighting force are expenditure on up-to-date equipment, and continuous training. For reasons of countering a real threat from outside the country, the trained bands of the coastal counties were on a better footing than those of inland counties, but the modernization of the force in general lagged behind the curve. Furthermore, the reluctance of the country gentry to breed war horses, and to practise military equestrian manoeuvres, virtually brought the horse bands to extinction.[6]

The outbreak of the Thirty Years' War in 1618 altered the dynamics, but to an impoverished monarch like James, estimates of £2 million to raise and transport an army of 30,000, and £900,000 a year to maintain them, were simply unaffordable.[7] In order to try to get around this financial obstacle, James authorized the raising of English and Scottish regiments for foreign service. They were funded by the country who employed them and, in turn, they provided a pool of war-experienced officers and men. The accession of Charles I in 1625 rekindled an aspiration for military involvement on the Continent. But there was little desire by central or local governments to adequately fund an army, or to address the underlying malaise within the militia. Charles's attempts to influence the outcome of the Continental wars, with operations against Cadiz in 1625, and La Rochelle two years later, were nothing short of national military humiliations. The huge and fruitless loss of life, and the appalling sight of the wounded and diseased soldiers and sailors on their return, was a key catalyst for Parliament's 1628 Petition of Rights, which fundamentally restricted the sovereign's constitutional liberties with regard to the use of the nation's citizens in time of war. During the period of Charles's personal rule (1629–40), attempts (by him) to reform the militia continued to be met with opposition from numerous factions. Yet money and military power remained inexorably linked, and, as the King had no funds available to pay for an army or to reorganize and modernize the militia, both he and the nation remained exposed and vulnerable. Matters came to a head during the Bishops' Wars (see chapter 2), when Charles needed to raise an army to counter the Scottish invasion. The northern trained bands were mobilized but the outcome was yet more humiliation. Fundamentally disobedient, as well as being poorly trained, equipped, supplied and led, the results of 40 years of military mismanagement were all too apparent.

Within two years, relations between Crown and Parliament had collapsed and armed force was deemed necessary to decide the constitutional impasse. From a standing start, both sides now needed to create great war machines comparable to those that had, and were, laying waste to great swathes of the Continent. Each side sought to defend their political position by taking control of the country's existing military resources. For the King, the mechanism was in place for him to muster an army under the terms of the Commission of Array. For Parliament, no such apparatus existed and so they chose to take control of county militias through ordinance, namely legislation passed by Parliament that does not have the royal assent necessary to make it statute.[8] Parliament, however, had one major advantage: they controlled London, which included not only the most capable of the trained bands in the country but also the machinery of government, and with it, the control of the Office of the Lord High Admiral and the Board of Ordnance. Hence, the other great commercial cities and ports were almost exclusively supportive of the Parliamentarian cause. Charles underestimated these advantages and was slow off the mark. Parliament, conversely, nominated

---

1 Roberts, *Military Revolution.*
2 Black, *A Military Revolution?*
3 Parker, *The Military Revolution: Military Innovation and the Rise of the West.*
4 Firth, *Cromwell's Army*, p. 1.
5 Manning, *An Apprenticeship in Arms*, p. 136.
6 The trained bands were local militia regiments organized on a county basis and controlled by the lords-lieutenant who were expected to appoint professional soldiers to drill the militia and teach them to use the pike and musket. The horse bands were the equestrian/cavalry equivalent.

---

7 Barnett, *Britain and Her Army*, p. 61.
8 Braddick, *War and Politics*, p. 2 (online source).

Robert Devereux, the Earl of Essex, a professional soldier with considerable experience from both the Thirty Years' War and Sir Edward Cecil's ill-fated expedition against Cadiz. A swift and enthusiastic execution of the Militia Ordinance, during the summer of 1642, energized the Parliamentarian war effort and helped fill the ranks of Essex's army and, in particular, the reserve army under the Earl of Warwick raised in October 1642.[9]

In very simplistic terms, the King controlled Wales and the west, while Parliament controlled London, the south-east and the east. However, it would be wholly wrong to conclude that the process of county allegiance to faction was smooth and uniform.[10] Furthermore, both the King and Parliament soon discovered that neither held ultimate authority when it came to calling out the militia. To complicate matters further, when county militias did muster they demonstrated little desire to leave their home areas. Both sides, therefore, had to resort to recruiting additional volunteers. The King chose to do this by offering royal commissions to any man who agreed to raise a regiment in support of the crown. As it turned out, it was a policy that was to lead to disorganization within the Royalist ranks, as every new regiment denied replacements for existing regiments, creating an army of company-strength regiments.[11]

At the outbreak of civil war on 22 August 1642, the two armies were, on paper at least, numerically balanced, although the Royalists enjoyed more officers in senior positions who had previous military experience. Not surprisingly, the early engagements failed to deliver a decisive victory. In 1644, prompted by this military stalemate, as well as a significant crisis with and between its senior military commanders, Parliament chose to reform its forces through the Self-Denying Ordinance and the 'new modelling' of the army. Samuel Gardiner, in his renowned history of the war, wrote that 'a standing army would bring with it many dangers, but the King was already less dependent on local organizations than Parliament was, and unless Parliament could secure its mastery over local associations, it must be content to succumb in the struggle which it had invented.'[12] In the end it was the dubious performance of Parliament's armies in the autumn of 1644, and the in-fighting between many of its generals, that drove reform. The concept had been laid before the House of Commons by one of Parliament's military commanders, Sir William Waller, in June 1644 with the words, 'Till you have an army merely your own, that you may command, it is impossible to do anything of importance.'[13] Cromwell, one of the main protagonists for change and a spearhead of the internecine struggle, tied the purge of some of its general officers to the creation of this new army. During the highly charged debate on the issue in the House of Commons on 9 December 1644, Cromwell delivered a form of ultimatum: '... I do conceive if the Army be not put into another method, and the War more vigorously prosecuted, the People can bear the War no longer, and will enforce you to a dishonourable peace'.[14] What set this new model army apart from its predecessor was its regular organization and national (rather than regional) focus and reach.

The new army consisted of 12 infantry regiments, each divided into ten companies of 110 men apiece. The cavalry consisted of 11 regiments, each containing six troops of 100 men. The dragoons were not regimented but divided into ten separate troops, each 100 strong. According to Lieutenant General Hammond's account, the artillery train consisted of four demi-culverins, four long sakers and 20 ordinary sakers. The accuracy of this is unclear as the train was supplied with two demi-culverins and eight sakers in April 1645, with another saker and three drakes being subsequently sent up to Windsor for the army.[15] The artillery train was provided with two regiments of infantry and two companies of firelocks (infantry with flintlock in preference to matchlock muskets), which were used for the purposes of protection during escort only.[16] When the New Model Army took to the field in May 1645, it was understrength, but the following month it inflicted the first decisive defeat of the war on Charles's forces at Naseby. From that point forward the writing was on the wall.

FIGHTING COMPONENTS

For some military historians, the military revolution took place much earlier than the century leading up to the English Civil War. They argue that this revolution took place in the century after gunpowder arrived in Europe, at the start of the 14th century.[17] Indeed, the English army had used gunpowder artillery for the first time in the field as early as 1346 against the French at the Battle of Crecy. However, its use was limited and its practicality open to debate. It was not until the mid-16th century that the effectiveness of gunpowder artillery and portable firearms began to make a significant impact on the conduct of war.[18] Nevertheless, the advent of gunpowder did not alter the three fighting components on the field of battle, the infantry, the cavalry and the (field) artillery; it merely redefined their roles and transformed combined tactics accordingly.[19]

A 17th-century army, therefore, retained the three fighting components. There were two quite different types of infantry – musketeers and pikemen. The introduction of firearms had increased the importance of the infantryman, but that evolution was slow and developed in tandem with the ever-increasing efficiency of the infantry musket itself. Most musketeers were armed with a matchlock rather than a flintlock musket, mainly for reasons of cost.[20] A trained soldier could load and fire every 30 seconds, although in the heat of battle, a minute was a more realistic time. The musketeer carried two kinds of powder, a fine powder for the priming charge and a coarser powder for the propellant charge. A number (normally about 12) of pre-prepared quantities of propellant powder were held in leather or wooden tubes and slung from a belt, or bandolier, worn over the left shoulder. The other infantrymen were known as pikemen; they wore a combe-cap, an armour corslet (back and breast) and tassets and carried an 18-foot-long (5½-metre) pike (but in practice it was a good deal shorter, for practical reasons). Before the end of the civil wars the corslet and tassets had been abandoned for the purpose of greater mobility and comfort on longer campaigns. Pikemen considered themselves a cut above the average musketeer, as their weapon and customs were ancient. Charles Firth, in his

9   Holmes, *Eastern Association*, p. 35.

10 Ibid., p. 34.

11 Barnett, op. cit., p. 80.

12 Gardiner, *Great Civil War*, vol. 2, p. 5.

13 Ibid., p. 5. See also Firth, *Cromwell's Army*, chapter III.

14 Carlyle, *Cromwell's Letters*, vol. I, p. 176.

15 National Archives SP28/145 f.60r.

16 Fortescue, *History of the British Army*, vol. I, pp. 214–16. There were three types of firelock: the flintlock, the snaphaunce and the wheel-lock.

17 Gunpowder was invented in China in the ninth century; it was first documented there two centuries later and then spread to Europe via the Muslim world and India.

18 The last battle on English soil, where the longbow was used as a principal weapon, was at Flodden Field as late as 1513.

19 In stating this, it is assumed that the Greeks deployed the first artillery with the field ballista; heavier catapults and trebuchets were really used for sieges and were not, therefore, like subsequent siege guns, part of the fighting component.

20 Tallett, *War and Society*, p. 2.

Name	Calibre (inches/mm)	Length (feet/cm)	Weight of Gun (lb/kg)	Weight of Shot (lb/kg)	Team Horses/Men
Siege Guns					
Cannon of 8	8/203	8/244	8,000/3,629	63/28.6	16/90
Cannon of 7	7/178	10/305	7,000/3,175	47/21.3	12/70
Demi-Cannon	6/152	12/366	6,000/2,722	27/12.3	10/60
Field Guns					
Culverin	5/127	11/335	4,000/1,814	15/6.8	8/50
Demi-Culverin	4.5/114	10/305	3,600/1,633	9/4.1	7/36
Saker	3.5/89	10.5/320	1,500/680	5.25/2.4	5/24
Saker – Drake	3.5/89	5.25/160	1,200/544	5.25/2.4	5/24
Minion	3/76	8/244	1,500/680	4/1.8	4/20
Falcon	2.75/70	6/183	700/318	2.25/1	2/16
Falconet	2/51	4/122	420/191	1.25/0.6	1/10[1]
Robinet	1.25/32	3/91	120/54	0.75/0.3	1/8
Source: An amalgam of Firth, Hogg, Haythornthwaite and Henry.[2]					

1: The figures of horses and men for the Falconet and Robinet are guestimates.

2: Firth, ibid., pp. 147–63; Hogg, *English Artillery*, pp. 28–9; Haythornthwaite, *Illustrated Military History*, p. 53; Henry, *Civil War Artillery*, p. 9.

excellent work on armies and tactics of the era, suggested that 'adventurous gentlemen who enlisted to see the wars preferred to trail a pike'.[21] Indeed, a letter in 1632 from General von Wallenstein to his colonels argued that in any infantry clash the pikemen decided the issue and he chided his officers for equipping their weakest, least-trained men with the weapon.[22]

Nevertheless, over time, the inevitable superiority of the musket began to tell. Pikemen were mainly used to protect the musketeers from cavalry attack and for storming the breach during sieges. On the battlefield, they adopted a more open formation, with about a yard between pikemen, thereby giving enough space for the artillerymen and/or musketeers to retreat through the pike formation for shelter. At the end of the 16th century, there were two pikemen to one musketeer, but by the end of the Wars of the Three Kingdoms (and across Europe) there were two musketeers to one pikeman. In time, the infantry developed a movement from line to square to protect themselves from cavalry and this was accelerated by the introduction of the bayonet. On the Continent, the French seem to have been using a makeshift bayonet from 1647, although there are earlier 17th-century references to long knives called 'bayonets'. William Barriffe, in his 1661 edition of his drill book, talks about unscrewing forks (meaning the staff from the musket rest) and inserting them in musket barrels.[23] However, a designed plug bayonet was not in use by British troops until the late 1660s. Within a few years the socket bayonet had been developed and the pikeman's days were numbered.

The growth in importance and effectiveness of infantry and artillery (who provided battlefield firepower) also led, over time, to a decrease in cavalry. There were a number of reasons for this. Cavalry were fearfully expensive; the horses were particularly susceptible to gunshot and less effective against well-drilled infantry. As a result, and due to a national shortage of mounts, by 1645 the infantry in the Parliamentarian forces outnumbered the horse by two to one.[24] Nevertheless, if the cavalry could get among a body of infantry, whose formation had been broken, the consequences were devastating. There were two types of cavalry: the heavy cuirassiers, clad entirely in armour, and the lighter harquebusiers (arquebusiers), who had only a helmet, breastplate and heavy buff leather coat. The lancers, and cavalry equipped with a light horseman's staff, had all but disappeared in England in the years leading up to the wars, although some remained in Scottish cavalry regiments. It was not long before the cuirassiers were also redundant, their full suit of armour proving too cumbersome for protracted campaigning and too expensive for mass production. The cuirassier was designed for shock action, charging against the enemy formations, whereas the harquebusiers were used for reconnaissance, pickets (outpost duty) and skirmishing. However, with the demise of the heavy cuirassier, the harquebusier was used increasingly in direct action. There was no standard equipment for cavalrymen, but it was generally accepted that a harquebusier was armed with a carbine or harquebus, a sword, a pair of saddle pistols and, in some cases, a poll axe.[25] Finally, there was another mounted soldier, a dragoon, who was really a horsed infantryman able to move at speed to different parts of the battlefield and then dismount. They were a cheap source of mounted troops, as their horses were inferior to those of the cavalry and, as such, both sides raised large numbers relatively quickly. They wore no armour and, it would appear, were not issued with buff coats but the infantry redcoat and a hat rather than helmet.[26]

There were three types of artillery: field guns, siege guns (including heavy mortars) and garrison or coastal guns. There was a bewildering array of ordnance and the terminology is confusing, but the table above provides

21 Firth, op. cit., p. 71.

22 Tallett, op. cit., p. 27.

23 Barriffe, *Military Discipline*, p. 145. According to Simon Marsh, Barriffe also makes reference to the practice of making the musket rest have more of a pointed end seemingly so it could be used as a 'Swedish feather' – effectively a stake that was carried by musketeers to place before them as a defence against cavalry.

24 Tallett, op. cit., p. 29.

25 Barriffe, op. cit., 116–17.

26 Ibid., pp. 124–5.

a summary of the types and sizes of guns. 'Cannon' derives from the Latin *canna*, a reed or tube, 'culverin' from the Latin *culubrinus*, snake-like, and 'saker' from the Arabic *saqr*, a species of falcon. The majority of these guns and mortars were cast in bronze and the majority fired iron balls.

The Board of Ordnance was responsible for the supply and upkeep of military stores, including all guns, mortars and munitions, and the necessary gunpowder, to both the navy and the army, in that order (for reasons of national defence). There were no standing artillery units at the time of the civil war. The Board also had responsibility for providing small arms (pistols, muskets, harquebusiers and carbines) to the infantry and cavalry and providing the means for maintenance and repairs. The original Board had been set up around 1406 as the 'designated keeper of the matters ordnance' within the Tower of London. During Henry VIII's reign (1491–1547) the organization was placed on a more official footing within the (White) Tower, while the Office of the Armoury and Royal Arsenal moved to the Royal Dockyard at Greenwich. At the outbreak of the civil war, arsenals existed at the Tower of London, Upnor Castle (Medway) and at Chatham, Hull and Portsmouth dockyards as well as Edinburgh and Dublin castles. Within months of the commencement of the war, Parliament held all the key arsenals in England, as well as most of the foundries.[27] Consequently, in late 1642, when Charles moved his capital and military headquarters to Oxford, he established, with mixed results, a foundry at Frewin Hall (Brasenose College) and two powder mills at Osney, so he would not have to rely entirely on foreign imports.[28]

TACTICS

There was no shortage of military manuals at the start of the 17th century. The need to train and educate the militia, and subsequently the untrained civilian volunteers, provided a burgeoning market. Charles Carlton, in his admirable work, states that 35 appeared in the seven years between 1634 and 1641.[29] Most of them were concerned with discipline, mustering, victualing, paying, moving and motivating an army. A lesser number provided tactical information and drill movements for the use of the musket and pike. Some, like John Cruso's work and the anonymous work entitled *Pallas Artnata*, were the operating bibles for the cavalry.[30] However, as prolific and extensive (and indeed complicated) as this plethora of manuals was, none were written to cover combined-arms tactics and integration. That is to state that the three fighting components were not trained to fight together; instead, their training was specific to their arm, and the business of combined-arms warfare was, therefore, constrained to the views and decisions of the commanders on the day of battle. This is all the more noteworthy when juxtaposed against the achievements of Maurice of Nassau and (particularly) Gustavus Adolphus, who were experimenting with combined-arms groupings and operations using light guns in a mobile fashion in support of advancing infantry and cavalry, or the placing of musketeers in support of the cavalry during a charge.[31] There is scant evidence of similar doctrinal combined-arms use of artillery during the Wars of the Three Kingdoms, and while there are examples of infantry being placed in support of the cavalry, known as 'interlining' or 'commanded musketeers', this appeared to be the exception rather than the rule. The Parliamentarians tried it at Edgehill with limited success, while Prince Rupert, who had experience of combined-arms tactics on the Continent, used the tactic more frequently, most notably at Marston Moor and Naseby.

There were a number of treatises on the use of artillery published prior to and during the war. These focussed on the use of artillery during sieges and paid little attention to the use of artillery on the battlefield.[32] Despite this, the gunners knew their trade and the capabilities and limitations of their equipment. There were standard words of command for swabbing, loading and firing the gun. Firing tables were compiled so that the weight of propellant, elevation and ranges were recorded. Guns were organized into batteries with a 'gentleman of the ordnance' responsible for each battery.[33] There was no standard gun crew *per se*, but a gun team would consist of an experienced gunner, a couple of matrosses (semi-skilled gunners) and a number of labourers to move the gun and the ammunition. European armies were experimenting with the movement of lighter guns (falcons, falconets and robinets) in support of infantry and cavalry, but there is very little evidence that this tactic was used doctrinally during the Wars of the Three Kingdoms.[34] Even Colonel Wumbrandt's much-hyped 90-pound leather gun, designed for lightness and mobility, and much used by the Swedes in the Polish campaigns of the 1620s, proved unreliable and was eventually withdrawn.[35]

Artillery pieces, once deployed, generally remained static and were only ordered to move at the end of battle or to execute a retreat. It is unclear whether guns were allocated and designated as regimental guns at this time – that is, under the protection and command of allocated infantry battalions/regiments.[36] Overall command of the artillery lay with the General of the Ordnance at army level, and how he delegated and deployed the field artillery was unclear. It may well be that he dispersed it across the frontage, in between regimental gaps, giving the appearance of regimental guns. To ease resupply and to fit in with the deployment of the rest of the army, guns tended to be deployed in groups or, more likely, pairs of guns. The heavier guns tended to be on the flanks and slightly set back,[37] although the European approach was to have a large battery of heavier guns in front of the infantry and regimental pieces deployed with each battalion. Their positions were, for fairly obvious reasons, in front of the infantry but might be deployed behind on high ground, as was the case at Newburn Ford with the Covenanter guns, and at Edgehill with some of the Royalist guns.

The effective range of the guns depended upon a whole series of factors, but a suitable yardstick is 1,000 yards.[38] As such, they had a far greater reach than the infantry and were accordingly brought to bear early in the battle,

27 The Tower of London had very little by way of arms at the outbreak of the war, having supplied the armies in Ireland and the Bishops' Wars.
28 Henry, ibid., p. 5.
29 Carlton, *Going to the Wars*, pp. 71–2.
30 Cruso, *Militarie Instructions for the Cavallrie*, is an English treatise on the use of the single rapier and the sword, anonymously published in 1639. The author is listed as 'G. A.' and it is widely believed to be Gideon Ashwell, a fellow of King's College Cambridge. It should not be confused with *Pallas Armata – military essayes of the Ancient Grecian, Roman and modern art of war*, written in the years 1670 and 1671 by James Turner and published in 1683.
31 Firth, op. cit., p. 147. The battles at Leipzig 1631 and Lützen 1632.
32 Norton, *Of the Art of Great Artillery, The Gunner and The Gunner's Dialogue*; Nye, *Art of Gunnery*; Ward, *Anima'dversions of Warre*.
33 Marsh, *Train of Artillery*, p. 8.
34 Hogg, op. cit., p. 40. First recorded use of English artillery as a mobile weapon is at Blenheim in 1704.
35 Tallett, op. cit., p. 33.
36 Ibid., p. 242. Hogg records that the first evidence of battalion guns does not emerge until 1686.
37 Ibid., p. 222.
38 Effective range was a relative concept but it was more applicable than maximum range, for at the latter the effectiveness of the projectile would be negligible.

in order to disrupt and demoralize the tightly packed enemy formations. It was hoped that this bombardment would provoke the enemy to attack and/or to move his troops out of effective range. However, there is little evidence, in eyewitness accounts or battle reports, of the effectiveness of artillery on civil war battlefields. Sergeant Henry Foster's account at the First Battle of Newbury is a rare example: 'The enemy's cannon did play most against the red Regiment of Trained Bands; they did some execution amongst us at first, and were somewhat dreadful when men's bowels and brains flew in our faces; but blessed be God that gave us courage, so that we kept our ground, and after a while feared them not.'[39]

There are, perhaps, four reasons why artillery did not have a huge impact during civil war encounters. Firstly, guns were expensive and needed highly skilled operatives: both were in short supply. Secondly, they tended to be deployed individually or in pairs – it is not until Dunbar in 1650 that we see massed artillery deployment. Thirdly, they had a slow rate of fire; Eldred in *The Gunner's Glasse* of 1646 states that the average rate of fire was eight shots an hour (one every seven and a half minutes) and after 40 shots the piece had to cool for an hour.[40] Eldred is almost certainly referring to heavier guns, like a cannon of 7 or 8 or a demi-cannon; the rates of fire for the medium and small field guns would be far quicker, at about one round every two to three minutes. British gunners served the gun from a leather bucket filled with gunpowder placed behind the ordnance. This was both slower and most unwelcome to the adjacent infantry and cavalry. It was not long before they adopted the Continental system of paper cartridges made using a special former and then filled with powder.[41] The Swedes had already perfected the use of pre-prepared charge bags, particularly for their lighter guns. Fourthly and finally, the only projectile widely available was round shot, and given the long reload times, this was not hugely effective against infantry or cavalry advancing and/or in the attack. It is puzzling why more use was not made of canister or grape shot – rather confusingly called 'case' at this time. The first officially recorded use was in 1450. The inventory of ordnance supplied to Essex's army identified some 'cases of tin' for different types of ordnance. However, in the gunners' defence, there was clear evidence that case/canister caused considerable damage to the guns' barrels. It is not an overgeneralization to state that the true worth of the artillery during the Wars of the Three Kingdoms was not realized on civil war battlefields but with their use at the numerous sieges.

Cavalry tactics changed considerably during the wars. The demise of the heavier cuirassiers transferred the task of direct cavalry action to the harquebusiers. This decision was also driven by a need to make a clear distinction between the cavalry and the dragoons. It should be noted that this policy was reversed during Cromwell's Irish campaigns of 1649–50, where large-scale cavalry on cavalry actions was almost non-existent. In the run-up to the civil wars, the rapid evolution of battlefield tactics, and the almost simultaneous demise of the cuirassier, caused understandable confusion with regard to the role and tactics of the cavalry. The Dutch system of deploying five or six ranks deep had been superseded by the Swedish method of deploying and advancing three ranks deep. The Swedish system also ensured a greater frontage than the Dutch style for the same number of horses, which led to Dutch-style deployments being enveloped by the Swedish system. However, the Dutch system provided the ability to counter-march so that a caracole could be performed, with the front-rank

firing and then withdrawing to the rear to reload, as the next rank came up. This required space between troops to allow the withdrawal to the rear, and those gaps could be exploited by the Swedish-style attack. Edgehill was a case in point. In this manner, Gustavus Adolphus taught his troopers to withhold their fire when they charged, to charge at a more rapid pace, and to always charge home,[42] in so doing capitalizing on the shock effect of cavalry. A recent study by historian Gavin Robinson, in an article for the *Journal of Military History*, has examined the possibility that the shock was a physical collision instead of, or in addition to, the psychological effect of cavalry charging home. That is, that cavalry crashed into each other at the climax of the charge.[43] He concludes that it is difficult to prove or disprove, as the available evidence is ambiguous and because the cavalry drill books of the period are not a reliable guide to execution of tactics in the field.

At the start of the wars there is little doubt that the Royalists (generally) adopted the Swedish style and the Parliamentarians the Dutch style, but by 1645 they were all working, to a greater or lesser extent, on the former. However, the removal of armour and a greater reliance on firearms over the sword and sabre had led (on the Continent) to the German Reiters adopting the pistol as their main weapon, with rank after rank riding up and firing until a breach in the wall of pikes had been formed which, swords drawn, they then exploited. There is evidence that Prince Rupert adopted a reversal of this tactic at Edgehill. Richard Bulstrode, a Royalist cavalry officer, recorded in his memoirs:

> Prince Rupert passed from one wing to the other giving positive orders to the horse, to march as close as possible, keeping their ranks with sword in hand, to receive the enemy's shot without firing either carbine or pistol till we broke in amongst the enemy, and then to make use of our firearms as need should require; which order was punctually observed.[44]

Cavalry charges are possibly the most misunderstood and misrepresented of all battlefield manoeuvres. The word 'Charge!' conjures to the mind the movement of a vast body of horse at the gallop across the battlefield. The reality was, in point of fact, very different. To maintain a semblance of order, with knees and stirrups locked, the formation would begin at a trot, increase to a fast trot, and finally (but not always) reach a canter. Rarely would the formation reach the gallop. As Firth wrote, 'repeatedly we hear of charges made at "a full trot", or, as Cromwell terms it, "a pretty round trot".'[45] The increased use of, and reliance upon, firearms in cavalry attacks inevitably led to a more measured advance towards enemy lines. Rupert's frequent cavalry charges are in contrast to the steadier pace adopted by the Parliamentarian cavalry, and while the former may have created surprise, there is little doubt that Cromwell was able to gather his cavalry for a second charge, while Rupert, generally, could not. The tactics adopted by both sides for the use of their dragoons are more uniform. Dragoons had a number of tasks, including providing pickets, holding key points like bridges, lining hedges or holding enclosures, and providing dismounted musketeers to support regular cavalry. They were equipped with a shorter musket and a short sword and used drummers, not buglers, to communicate orders on the battlefield.

39 Foster, *True and Exact Relation* – British Library.
40 Rogers, *Artillery*, p. 45.
41 Marsh, op. cit., p. 12.
42 Ibid., p. 131.
43 Robinson, *Equine Battering Rams*, p. 720.
44 Firth, op. cit., p. 133, citing Bulstrode, *Memoirs and Reflections*, p. 81.
45 Ibid., p. 142.

Infantry tactics witnessed the greatest change, with the 'pike and shot' era in its final throes. Infantry units were organized in regiments commanded by a colonel, subdivided into a number of companies commanded by captains. On paper at least, the largest regiments should have been 1,200 strong, with a colonel's company of 200 men, a lieutenant colonel's company of 160 men, a (sergeant) major's company with 140 men, and seven captain's companies each of 100 men. However, in practice there could be any number of companies and each would be fortunate to muster more than 30 men apiece.[46] Indeed the whole business of the size, composition and nomenclature of subunits, units and formations is very difficult to tie down and an attempt to dovetail this with modern terminology is almost meaningless. In addition, the tactics of pike and shot, combined (or otherwise) with artillery and cavalry, are equally confusing. In view of the fact that communications were very slow on civil war battlefields, the initial deployment of the army, to meet and counter 'every' eventuality, was supremely important. In simplistic terms, by the early 17th century there were two systems: the Dutch (Maurice of Nassau) and the Swedish (Gustavus Adolphus) – see the diagram opposite (symbols as per Legend to Maps).

The Dutch system had been defined and refined by three members of the house of Nassau: William Louis, Count of Nassau and stadtholder in Friesland; his brother John; and Maurice, son of William of Orange, who held various stadholderships and served as captain-general of the Dutch forces in Flanders and Brabant.[47] They devised a system whereby the musketeers would deploy in six ranks; the first rank would fire and counter-march to the rear to reload, while the second rank marched forward and fired before they counter-marched, and so on. This provided the basis of a continuous volley fire. In addition, the infantry was spread out in a more linear fashion so as to maximize their firepower and minimize the effects of incoming artillery fire. This tactic was, however, not without drawbacks for it reduced the psychological reassurance from tightly knit formations under fire and increased the possibility of men breaking and running to the rear. Training, discipline and words or signals of command were deemed essential to overcome this shortcoming, and in 1607 a drill book was produced by Jacob de Gheyn, *Wapenhandelinghe van Roers Musquetten ende Spiessen* (The Exercise of Arms for Calivers, Muskets, and Pikes), which provided the basis for the Dutch system that predominated during the Thirty Years' War.

In addition to the Dutch and Swedish systems, a new German doctrine had been adopted by the 1640s. It was, to all intents and purposes, a composite of the Danish and Swedish systems and it was this German style that was to became the model increasingly used by both sides during the Wars of the Three Kingdoms.[48] At Edgehill (1642) the Royalists deployed using the Swedish style, while the Parliamentarians were closer to the German system; there is no surviving plan of the Parliamentarian deployment.[49] At Marston Moor (1644) the Royalists adopted the German style, as did the New Model Army at Naseby in 1645.

In the advance or attack, the infantry would either keep up a steady constant fire or hold their fire until well within musket range before delivering a huge simultaneous volley and falling on the enemy pikemen and musketeers. The constant rate of fire was maintained using the counter-march system. The advance would be undertaken by both pikemen and musketeers. The musketeers would then use the butt-end of the weapon once it had been discharged. If the final charge was successful, the second line or reserve was deployed to continue the attack, while the front line fell back and rallied behind the second line, where they would reload and form the new reserve. Commanded musketeers could also be withdrawn from the formation to form a separate body in order to deploy in support of the cavalry, to strengthen the wings, to line hedges or to occupy buildings, often in support of or in conjunction with dragoons. They might also have been used to form a skirmish line in front of the main body, although the tactic and use of large-scale skirmish lines was not utilized widely throughout the wars.

46 Reid, *King's Armies*, p. 16.
47 Tallett, op. cit., p. 24.
48 Roberts, *Pike and Shot*, p. 6.
49 Ibid., p. 60.

DUTCH SYSTEM (TRIPLE ORDER BATTLE)

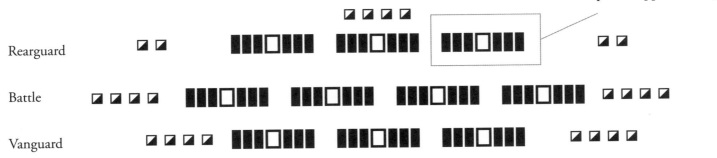

Battalion of 500 men –
shot to pike at approximately 2:1.

Rearguard

Battle

Vanguard

The central pike block was drawn up in ranks of between five and ten men and the flanking musketeers were drawn up between eight and 12 men.

ENEMY

The front rank would fire a volley, then turn about and march to the rear down the intervals between the files to reload their weapons. The second rank would then step up and fire and this would continue for as long as the ammunition lasted.

SWEDISH SYSTEM (BRIGADED DIAMOND)

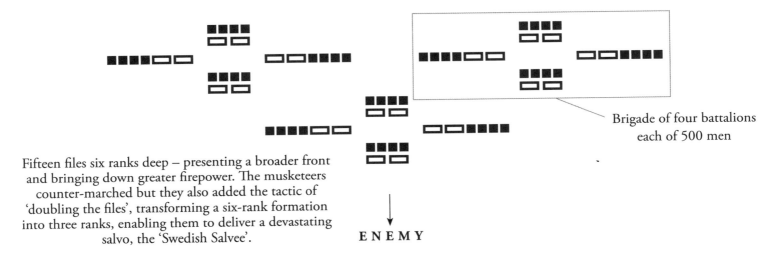

Brigade of four battalions
each of 500 men

Fifteen files six ranks deep – presenting a broader front and bringing down greater firepower. The musketeers counter-marched but they also added the tactic of 'doubling the files', transforming a six-rank formation into three ranks, enabling them to deliver a devastating salvo, the 'Swedish Salvee'.

ENEMY

GERMAN SYSTEM (CHEQUERBOARD)

Brigade of four battalions,
each of 500 men.

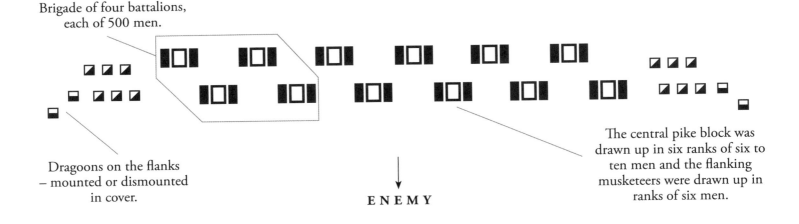

Dragoons on the flanks
– mounted or dismounted
in cover.

ENEMY

The central pike block was drawn up in six ranks of six to ten men and the flanking musketeers were drawn up in ranks of six men.

CHAPTER 1

THE EARLY STUARTS AND THE DIVINE RIGHT OF KINGS, 1603–37

PART 1: FROM THE END OF THE MIDDLE AGES TO THE STUARTS

During the reign of Henry VII (1485–1509), the decline of feudalism gathered speed as the King set about dividing and undermining the power of the nobility and dismembering the so-called 'bastard feudalism'. He also set about restoring the fortunes of an effectively bankrupt exchequer. James Harrington, in his highly controversial work *The Commonwealth of Oceana*, stressed the corollary of this socio-economic change during this period:

> This did mightily concern the might and manhood of the Kingdom, and in effect amortize a great part of the Lands to the hold and possession of the Yeomanry or middle People, who living not in a servil or indigent fashion, were much unlink'd from dependence upon their Lords, and living in a free and plentiful manner, became a more excellent infantry; but such a one upon which the Lords had so little Power, that from henceforth they may be computed to have bin disarm'd.[1]

The pace of socio-economic change under Henry VII was significant, but it palled into insignificance when compared to the transformation during the reign of his son, Henry VIII (r. 1509–47). Under feudalism the King was answerable to the Pope. Henry VIII's decision to break with Rome led to the establishment of the Church of England and the Dissolution of the Monasteries. It was the final 'nail in the coffin' for feudalism but it had far wider consequences. In 1534 the Act of Supremacy made Henry VIII (and subsequent monarchs) the supreme head, on earth, of the Church of England. It made that power enforceable by Act of Parliament and, as such, increased the authority of both the monarch and the executive. Two years later, the Dissolution of the Monasteries led to a massive transfer of wealth into the hands of the laity. This, in turn, led to the gradual sale and redistribution of church property and lands, and with it, the creation of a far larger and wealthier class of gentry.

But Henry VIII was no supporter of Lutheranism; his early vision for the Church of England was more in line with Catholic teachings. He continued to uphold transubstantiation and demanded clerical celibacy. Despite instituting some Protestant measures, Henry sided with Rome on key issues of doctrine and practice. But the events he set in motion would not permit England to return to the past. During the reign of his son, Edward VI (1547–53), England turned staunchly Protestant. After a brief and bloody return to Catholicism under Mary I (1553–58), his daughter Elizabeth I (1558–1603) set England on a permanently Protestant course. Differing interpretations of the Bible led to division and disagreement,

requiring supreme direction from none other than the monarch. In 1559 the Elizabethan Settlement sought to establish a peaceful coexistence between the established Catholic and developing Protestant ideas and ideals. In short, it set out to establish, or at least defend, the concept of a 'broad church', to balance those in favour of a 'High Church' sympathetic to a considerable degree with Catholicism, and a 'Low Church' more aligned to Calvinism.[2] In Scotland and Ireland the situation was different again. In the former the Presbyterian establishment was split by supporters of Episcopalianism (advocating government of a church by bishops) and the anti-Episcopalians, as well as by a strong Catholic element within the Highlands. In Ireland, the Catholic majority resented, for political as well as religious reasons, the Presbyterian minority in Ulster.

Such complex arrangements were an obvious catalyst for friction. Yet it was the Church of England that, by the early 1600s, demonstrated greater stability and sense of purpose through a balanced and tolerant attitude towards Catholicism. This middle way arguably spared the nation the horrors of religious conflict that were poised to ravage Europe for 30 long years.[3] Nevertheless, external influences emanating from that international struggle, and internal pressures from the more radical elements of both Protestants and Catholics, led to constant change. In England and Scotland anti-Catholic feeling, which had been mounting throughout the reign of Elizabeth I, generated the formation of a group of ultra-Protestants, known derogatively as 'Puritans', who demanded greater change and purification of Catholic practices. 'To Puritans, the Reformation had not gone far enough. To Anglicans it had gone, or threatened to go too far.'[4] The Puritans turned to their supporters in the English Parliament in an attempt to introduce a Presbyterian system, whereby control would be in the hands of the parish ministers chosen by their congregations and not in the hands of the bishops appointed by the crown. Such a system (Calvinism) had been established in Scotland by John Knox in 1568, but Elizabeth was not to be swayed. On James's succession in 1603, he elected to maintain the status quo and thus Puritanism was checked but not eradicated.[5] But anti-Catholicism and the Puritan cause were reignited in 1605, when Robert Catesby and a group of Catholics made a failed attempt to assassinate the King in the Gunpowder Treason Plot.

PART 2: THE REIGN OF JAMES I, 1603–25

It is not irrational to propose that James's insensitive handling of religious issues, in all his 'Three Kingdoms', laid the 'spiritual' foundations for future conflict. When he succeeded to the throne in 1603 the royal treasury was bare. This severely curtailed any foreign policy ambitions. At this time, thanks principally to Magna Carta, money was the business of Parliament,

---

1 Harrington, *Commonwealth of Oceana*, p. 69.

2 Davies, *The Isles*, p. 559. Note the term 'Anglican' did not come into general use until after 1660.

3 Worden, *English Civil Wars*, p. 9.

4 Ibid., p. 11. Worden also gives an excellent summary of the Puritan ideals and beliefs.

5 Anderson, *Civil Wars*, pp. 2–3.

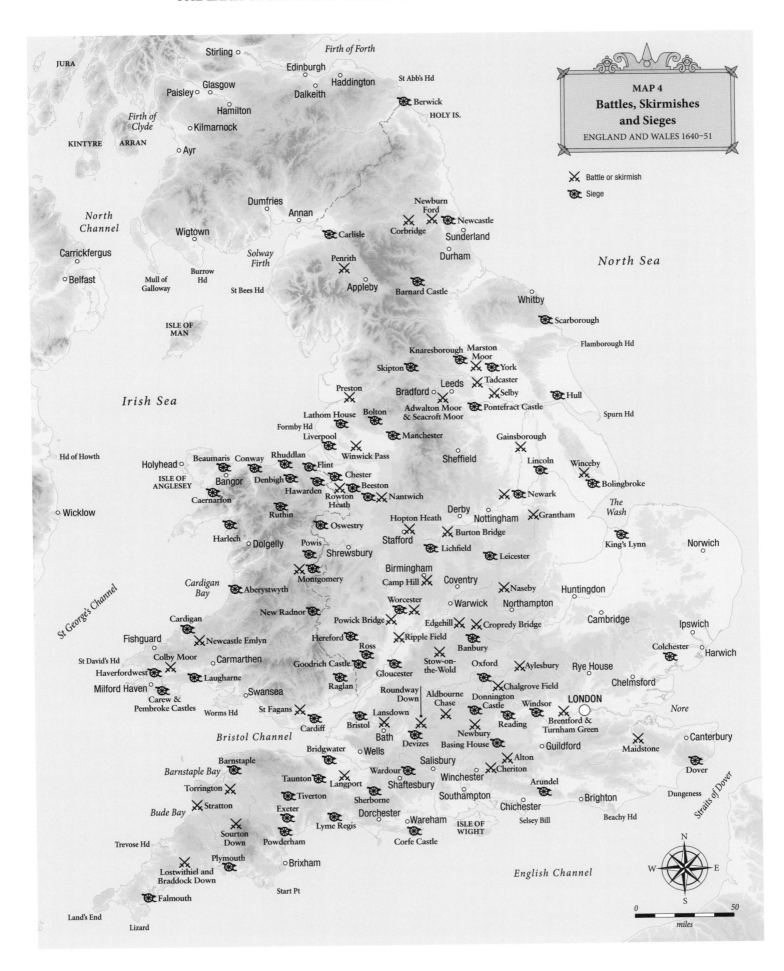

MAP 4
Battles, Skirmishes and Sieges
ENGLAND AND WALES 1640–51

✗ Battle or skirmish

⚙ Siege

JURA

Stirling

Firth of Forth

Edinburgh

Glasgow
Paisley
Haddington
Dalkeith

St Abb's Hd

Berwick

HOLY IS.

Firth of Clyde
Hamilton

KINTYRE ARRAN
Kilmarnock

Ayr

Dumfries
Annan

North Channel

Wigtown

Newburn Ford
Corbridge Newcastle
Sunderland

Carlisle

North Sea

Carrickfergus

Belfast

Mull of Galloway
Burrow Hd
St Bees Hd

Solway Firth

Penrith

Appleby

Durham

Barnard Castle

Whitby

ISLE OF MAN

Scarborough

Flamborough Hd

Knaresborough Marston Moor
Skipton York

Irish Sea

Preston
Bradford Leeds Tadcaster
Selby Hull

Spurn Hd

Lathom House Bolton
Formby Hd
Liverpool

Adwalton Moor & Seacroft Moor

Pontefract Castle

Hd of Howth

Holyhead
Beaumaris Conway Rhuddlan
Flint

Manchester
Gainsborough

Winwick Pass

Sheffield

Lincoln Winceby

ISLE OF ANGLESEY
Bangor Denbigh
Chester
Beeston

Bolingbroke

Caernarfon
Hawarden
Rowton Heath Nantwich

Newark

The Wash

Wicklow

Ruthin

Derby
Nottingham
Grantham

Harlech Dolgelly Powis Oswestry
Shrewsbury

Hopton Heath

Stafford Burton Bridge
Lichfield
Leicester

King's Lynn

Norwich

Birmingham
Camp Hill Coventry
Naseby Huntingdon

Cardigan Bay
Montgomery
Aberystwyth

Worcester
Warwick Northampton

Cambridge

Ipswich

Cardigan
New Radnor

Powick Bridge
Edgehill Cropredy Bridge
Colchester Harwich

Fishguard
Newcastle Emlyn
Hereford
Ross Ripple Field
Banbury

St David's Hd
Colby Moor
Carmarthen
Goodrich Castle
Stow-on-the-Wold
Oxford Aylesbury Rye House
Chelmsford

Haverfordwest
Laugharne
Raglan
Gloucester
Chalgrove Field

Milford Haven
Swansea
Roundway Down
Aldbourne Chase
Donnington Castle Windsor LONDON

Nore

Carew & Pembroke Castles
Worms Hd
St Fagans
Lansdown
Newbury Reading
Brentford & Turnham Green

Bristol Channel
Cardiff Bristol
Bath Devizes Basing House Guildford

Canterbury

Maidstone

Bridgwater Wells
Salisbury
Alton
Cheriton
Dover

Barnstaple
Wardour Winchester
Arundel

Barnstaple Bay
Taunton Langport
Shaftesbury
Southampton Chichester Brighton

Torrington
Tiverton
Sherborne

Dungeness

Exeter
Dorchester
Selsey Bill
Beachy Hd

Bude Bay
Stratton
Lyme Regis
Wareham
ISLE OF WIGHT

Straits of Dover

Sourton Down
Powderham
Corfe Castle

English Channel

Trevose Hd

Plymouth
Brixham

Lostwithiel and Braddock Down

Start Pt

Falmouth

Land's End

Lizard

N
W E
S

0   50
miles

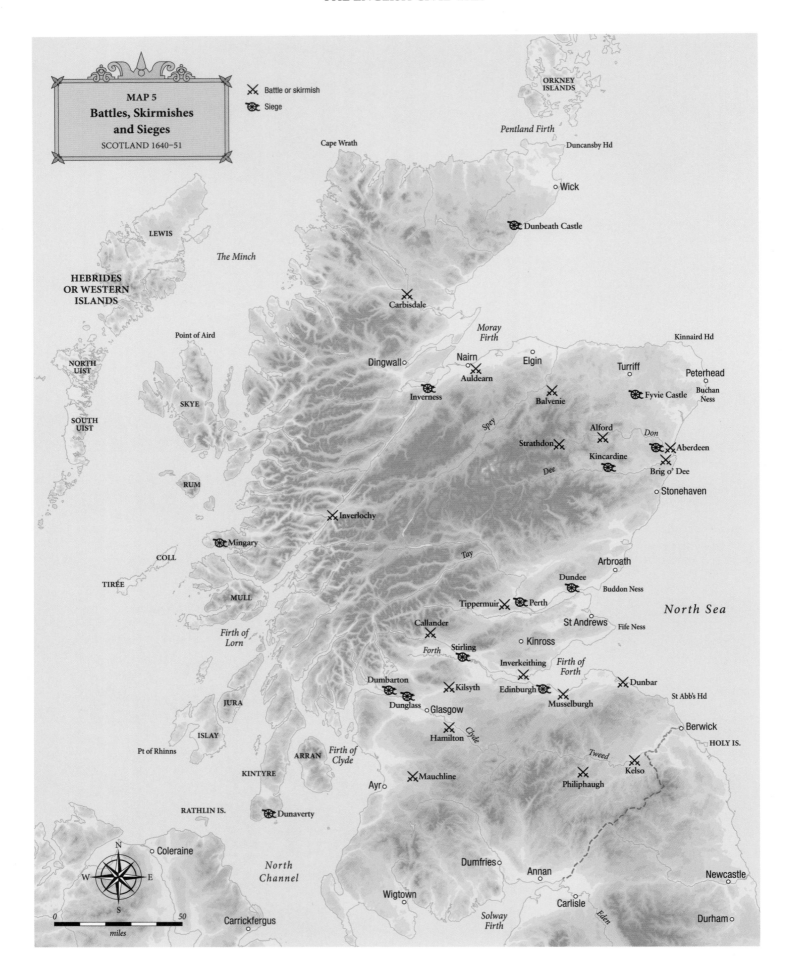

MAP 5
**Battles, Skirmishes
and Sieges**
SCOTLAND 1640–51

⚔ Battle or skirmish
⚙ Siege

ORKNEY
ISLANDS

Pentland Firth

Cape Wrath

Duncansby Hd

○ Wick

⚙ Dunbeath Castle

LEWIS

The Minch

HEBRIDES
OR WESTERN
ISLANDS

⚔ Carbisdale

*Moray
Firth*

Kinnaird Hd

Point of Aird

Dingwall ○

Nairn ○

⚔ Auldearn

Elgin ○

Turriff ○

Peterhead ○

NORTH
UIST

SKYE

⚙ Inverness

Balvenie ⚔

⚙ Fyvie Castle

Buchan
Ness

Spey

SOUTH
UIST

Alford ⚔

Don

Strathdon ⚔

⚔ Aberdeen

RUM

Kincardine ⚙

Dee

Brig o' Dee

○ Stonehaven

COLL

⚔ Inverlochy

⚙ Mingary

TIREE

Tay

Arbroath ○

Dundee
⚙

Buddon Ness

MULL

Tippermuir ⚔ ⚙ Perth

St Andrews ○

Fife Ness

*Firth of
Lorn*

Callander
⚔

Forth

Kinross ○

North Sea

Stirling ⚙

Inverkeithing ⚔

*Firth of
Forth*

JURA

Dumbarton
⚔

⚔ Kilsyth

Edinburgh ⚙ ⚔

⚔ Dunbar

St Abb's Hd

⚙ Dunglass

Musselburgh ⚔

Glasgow ○

ISLAY

Clyde

Berwick ○

Pt of Rhinns

ARRAN

*Firth of
Clyde*

Hamilton ⚔

HOLY IS.

Tweed

KINTYRE

⚔ Mauchline

Kelso ⚔

RATHLIN IS.

Ayr ○

Philiphaugh ⚔

⚙ Dunaverty

N

○ Coleraine

*North
Channel*

Dumfries ○

Annan ○

Newcastle ○

W — E

Wigtown ○

Carlisle ○

S

Eden

Durham ○

Carrickfergus ○

*Solway
Firth*

0   50
miles

while foreign policy and wars were firmly in the domain of kings.[6] However, Parliament was an occasional body summoned at the will of the monarch; its role was threefold: to vote taxes and, as a result, release funds for national and foreign projects (i.e. war or national defences); to consider and propose legislation; and, finally, to offer counsel to the crown.[7] Despite Magna Carta, the monarch still had some forms of raising revenue through feudal taxes, but for James, having inherited debts and with high inflation, he was compelled to summon Parliament in April 1614. He promised reform with the one hand, while demanding revenue with the other. Parliament began to realize the enormity of their power and a fierce row broke out between the Lords and Commons over Parliamentary privilege. For a monarch like James Stuart, who believed passionately about the divine right of kings and absolutism, such behaviour was intolerable. In the end, having secured no additional funding, he dissolved Parliament. The battle of wills between crown and Parliament had been set in motion.

In 1618 matters escalated when the Thirty Years' War broke out between the Catholic Holy Roman Emperor and some of his German Protestant states. It soon developed into a pan-European power struggle for Continental hegemony. The defeat of the Protestants, at the Battle of White Mountain (modern-day Prague) in 1620, drove the Elector Palatine and his wife from Bohemia and into exile in Holland. The Elector was James's son-in-law, married to his oldest daughter Elizabeth. Immediately there were demonstrations in England; the populace demanded action against the Catholic coalition, placing James between two equally undesirable alternatives. In 1621, with no room to manoeuvre, James recalled Parliament in order to release funds for a war in support of Continental Protestantism. However, Parliament had other ideas. They had long been aware of James's intentions of securing the Infanta, sister of the Spanish King Philip IV, to be the wife of Charles, the Prince of Wales. Although it would cement an alliance with Catholic Spain at a time of military vulnerability, and promise a large dowry that would ease the royal finances, it was a dangerous game. It would inevitably complicate relations with Rome, and such overt support to Catholicism would incite considerable discontent at home and play into the hands of the Puritans. The Anglicans and Puritans within Parliament were divided on the issue. The former were more predisposed to consider the Continental Protestant differences rather than their similarities, and sought to separate religion from foreign policy. They were less inclined to get embroiled in a foreign struggle than the Puritans, who wanted to be loyal to their faith and to their country. It was, ironically, a rare moment of common ground between the King and Puritans.[8] That aside, James was apoplectic with rage with Parliament, who had ignored royal prerogative and meddled in affairs of State. Parliament responded by issuing a formal 'protestation'. James tore the said protestation from the book with his own hand, dissolved the assembly and ordered the arrest of the trouble-makers. It was a pivotal moment. It poisoned relations between the King and Parliament on the one hand, and exposed the nation's military impotence on the other.

In 1622, the Thirty Years' War entered its second phase, known as the Palatinate Phase (see map 3). Conflict intensified, drawing in Catholic Spain, which despatched an army from the Spanish Netherlands in support of the Holy Roman Emperor. The concept of large Catholic armies operating within northern Europe was far too close to home for comfort. James, with his hands tied by a lack of funds, was still keen to pursue the marriage of the Prince of Wales to the Spanish Infanta in the hope that this alliance would persuade the Spanish Hapsburgs to abandon their alliance with the Austrian branch of the family and, *ipso facto*, result in the restoration of his son-in-law to the throne of Bohemia. However, the whole affair was a fiasco. The Infanta was decidedly averse to the idea and the Spanish King Philip imposed impossible conditions. But matters were not helped by the inept handling of the negotiations by James's favourite minister, the Duke of Buckingham.[9] In the end, the affair seriously damaged both James's and Charles's reputations and, to make matters worse, news arrived that the Elector Palatine had been stripped of his title by the Holy Roman Emperor.

By 1624, James was growing ill; he recalled Parliament for what was to be his last time. Members of Parliament and peers debated the nation's involvement in the Thirty Years' War, as well as tackling a backlog of legislation (none had been enacted since 1610). The outcome was the enactment of 73 acts, the highest number in any single session since the reign of Henry VIII. The most significant was the Monopolies Act, which put a stop to the practice of the crown selling monopoly licenses; it was yet another snub at royal prerogative.[10]

PART 3: CHARLES I, ACCESSION TO CONFLICT, 1625–38

James died in March 1625, but some months beforehand, Charles had already assumed *de facto* control of the Three Kingdoms. On his accession, Charles inherited a principally Catholic Ireland, a predominantly Calvinist Scotland and an English Church beset with post-Reformation problems and prejudices. These structural flaws required a monarch of considerable stature. In 1612, at the age of 18, the heir-apparent Henry had died of typhoid and, thereby, robbed the nation of a future monarch who might have risen to the challenge and succeeded. Charles was a humourless man, lacking in self-confidence. Historian Blair Worden merits him with three characteristics, which were not calamitous on their own but in cocktail they were fatal: the first, that he had contentious policies which he pursued with contentious methods; the second, that he was devoid of political judgement; and finally, that he was untrustworthy.[11] It is worth adding that Buckingham's relationship with Charles, although not sexual like that with his father, was extremely close. He was his constant companion and advisor; the younger Charles was both influenced and moulded by Buckingham's often questionable counsel.

Since childhood, Charles had been immersed in a deep understanding of the sanctity and obligation of the monarch. 'The king was the keystone in the arch of government which held together a rigid social system.'[12] His

---

6 Magna Carta is a charter signed by King John at Runnymede, near Windsor, on 15 June 1215. Drafted by the Archbishop of Canterbury to make peace between the unpopular King and a group of rebel barons, it promised the protection of church rights, protection for the barons from illegal imprisonment, access to swift justice, limitations on feudal payments to the crown, and established that the crown could not levy or collect any taxes. This latter clause did not take into account feudal taxes, which were omitted, being unfamiliar at the time of drafting.

7 Worden, op. cit., p. 16.

8 Ibid., p. 13.

9 Born George Villiers in 1592, he had caught the eye of the King in 1614 at a hunt and quickly rose through the ranks of nobility, being made a duke in 1623. The personal relationship of Buckingham to James is much debated but it is fairly certain that the two were lovers.

10 It also provided the first copyright and patent law in English history.

11 Worden, op. cit., p. 7.

12 Kenyon & Ohlmeyer, *Military History*, p. 3.

father had been an absolute believer in the divine right of kings; the idea that he was God's direct representative on earth. In his *Basilikon Doron* (Royal Gift), a trilogy on the treatise on government written in 1599 by James for his sons, he is quite clear on the matter of divine appointment:

> Therefore (my Sonne) first of all things, learne to know and love that God, whom-to ye have a double obligation; first, for that he made you a man; and next, for that he made you a little GOD to sit on his Throne, and rule over other men. Remember, that as in dignitie he hath erected you above others, so ought ye in thankfulnesse towards him, goe as farre beyond all others.[13]

Peter Rubens' ceiling paintings in Banqueting House, commissioned by Charles in 1629, are a powerful statement of the Stuarts' belief in that divine right. Charles grasped and embraced, with his core, this fatherly guidance. However, he missed, or at best confused, the part in the second book of *Basilikon Doron*, that his son should be a good king, as opposed to a 'tyrant', by establishing and executing laws as well as governing with justice and equality. If we are to believe that *Eikon Basilike* (Royal Portrait) was indeed penned by Charles's hand, then it provides evidence that Charles, in his final months, realized his failings with regard to just and equal government. John Milton's response, *Eikonoklastes* (Icon Breaker), published in 1649, is an attempt to justify Charles's execution and to counter *Eikon Basilike*, based upon the premise that Charles had effectively lost the plot, powered through a misguided belief of his divine status. It is interesting, therefore, that Milton's work failed to reverse *Eikon Basilike* or to change public opinion. For Charles's admission of failure allows us, not unreasonably, to paint a picture of a man who wanted to do well but lacked the wherewithal to do so. He was, undoubtedly, badly served by his counsellors; but while this may have been a cause for conflict, it was indisputably his duplicity that ultimately led to his execution.

Had Charles made the prerogative courts (the Star Chamber, the Court of the Exchequer and Court of the Chancery) more respectful of the law, and exerted greater control over the autonomy of justices of the peace (gentry in the countryside and aldermen in the cities) he might have nurtured public support.[14] The small local courts, run by these justices of the peace, were the coalface of justice to the King's subjects. They were empowered to try all crimes, except treason, or crimes committed by the King's servants (the latter were tried by the King's judges at one of the prerogative courts). The King controlled the appointment of judges but he could not control the operation of the law.[15] The common courts were well known for their corruption, high costs and delay, but any hope that the Court of Chancery would provide remedy had long since been abandoned. The Court of the Star Chamber was the most powerful of the prerogative courts; it was, in effect, the King's inner council. It had been set up in the reign of Henry VII to defend subjects against the rich and powerful, to protect David from Goliath, but over time it morphed from David's

protective sling to Goliath's establishment sword. Certainly Charles, and his ministers, used it to silence critics of the court, church or Privy Council.[16]

In 1624, still smarting from the rebuff by the Spanish king for the hand of his sister, Charles agreed on an approach to Catholic France for the hand of Princess Henrietta Maria, the sister of Louis XIII. Once again Buckingham's hand was firmly on the tiller and, once again, there were numerous religious caveats within the deal, designed to strengthen Catholicism and the rights of the English Roman Catholics. Early negotiations looked like stalling, in much the same way as those in Spain, until on Charles's accession, a secret guarantee was secured for the freedom of worship of English Catholics and for Henrietta Maria's capacity to exercise her faith, should she become queen. Christopher Hibbert, in his biography of Charles I, wrote that 'She was to have her own chapels and chaplains in every royal palace; she would be accompanied to England by a bishop and twenty-eight priests; all her private attendants were to be French and Catholic.'[17] If that was not potentially contentious enough to the Protestant establishment, it was news of Buckingham's promise to help Cardinal Richelieu (Louis XIII's chief minister) in the reduction of the Huguenot stronghold of La Rochelle that was greeted with considerable and open hostility when news of it broke.

Charles's first Parliament in 1625, which sought funding for a war with Spain, the very war Parliament had angled for the previous year, was dissolved in uproar when the members turned on Buckingham for his conduct in the affair. Parliament only agreed to the release of funds to the crown, known as 'Tunnage' and 'Poundage' (duties on imports and exports), for a single year.[18] Charles responded, quite shrewdly, by elevating a number of the 'trouble-makers' to positions as sheriffs, who were *ipso facto* ineligible for membership of the Commons. The following year, with the war against Spain now ongoing, and a naval dispute with France also threatening war, Charles was compelled to call Parliament again. He demanded his rights to Tunnage and Poundage indefinitely and for a 'donation' to help fund the war. John Eliot, a Cornish squire and former friend of Buckingham, found himself, in the absence of other leaders of the opposition who had been removed by elevation to sheriffs, the leader of the House. He demanded an immediate inquiry into the disastrous 1625 Cádiz expedition (by English and Dutch forces) and made an open and daring attack upon Buckingham himself. In rage, Charles ordered Eliot's arrest and, in order to protect his friend, dissolved Parliament. He had secured neither funding nor resolution and cut his lifeline.[19]

Charles decided to levy duties for Tunnage and Poundage independent of Parliament's wishes. He cited royal prerogative and ordered subscriptions for a forced loan to furnish additional revenue. In 1627 in a *cause célèbre* the King won a moral victory, in what is known as the 'Five Knights' Case', when the judges ruled that a group of dissenters, who had refused to pay the loan, had been imprisoned legitimately. It was a minor triumph and one which had forced the crown to justify its action in the courts. However, to make matters worse, Buckingham had completely bungled the expedition to La Rochelle in support of the Huguenots; it had been a costly failure and

13 James I, *Basilikon Doron or His Majesties Instrvctions To His Dearest Sonne, Henry the Prince*. From the British Library online collection.
14 Davies, op. cit., p. 576 lists 11 prerogative courts: the Court of Chancery, Court of Requests, Court of the Privy Council, Court of the Star Chamber, Council of the North, Council in Wales, Council of the West, Court of the Castle Chamber, Court of the Duchy of Lancaster, Court of the County Palatine of Chester and the Court of Stannaries. Some of these, however, were administrative bodies rather than prerogative courts.
15 Wedgwood, *King's Peace*, p. 140.
16 This privy council, which should have been the central government was, in fact, no more than a council of courtiers chosen by Charles from his friends and servants for their servility and sycophancy.
17 Hibbert, *Charles I*, p. 87.
18 These funds were traditionally voted to each monarch for life; their withholding was a clear statement of intent and a flexing of Parliament's muscles.
19 Eliot was sent to the Tower but his fellow MPs demanded his release, along with his Parliamentary colleague Sir Dudley Digges, and refused to continue business until they were freed.

a national embarrassment. In 1628, when Parliament was called again, its members were seething with discontent. Both houses responded quickly by issuing a formal Petition of Right, drawn up to question the current, and to limit the future, royal prerogative. Its principal author was Edward Coke, a former Speaker of the Commons and rival to Francis Bacon, a noted defender of royal prerogative. Buoyed by their apparent success, Parliament went further and declared it illegal for taxes to be collected without Parliamentary consent, stated that arbitrary imprisonment was illegal, and that the billeting of soldiers in private dwellings and the application of martial law to civilians were prohibited. Parliament did, however, agree to grant the King Tunnage and Poundage for another year and, surprisingly perhaps, avoided debate and criticism of Buckingham's handling of the La Rochelle fiasco.

Four weeks later, during Parliament's summer adjournment, John Felton, a disgruntled and discharged naval officer, took matters into his own hands and assassinated Buckingham. Charles was bereft at the loss of his close confidant and beloved first minister. Convinced that Eliot was behind the assassination, the King was bent on revenge. Buckingham's assassination had removed a problem, but Parliament was well aware that he was a symptom and not the cause. For the first time, criticism of the King's ministers took second stage to direct criticism of the King himself. Within days Charles decided to prorogue Parliament, but when the message reached the House of Commons, angry members held the Speaker to the chair and passed three resolutions proposed by Eliot. Charles responded by dissolving Parliament and having the ringleaders arrested and imprisoned in the Tower; he did not recall Parliament again until 1640.[20]

During this period, known as 'Personal Rule', the mood was changing not only within Parliament but throughout the country as a whole. The fundamentalist Puritan line of a godly commonwealth was the view of a minority, but cloaked with a suspicion and hatred of Catholic (or Popish) practices and intentions, it became a patriotic platform with a comprehensive reach and rallying power.[21] Extreme anti-Catholic texts from northern Europe had long since been received in the country, but now they were published in large numbers, distributed freely and read in the open.[22] Charles and his overtly Catholic Queen were an easy target for Puritanical denunciation, while Catholic triumphs on the Continent, in the Thirty Years' War, fuelled the hyperbole of a fifth-column poised to return England back to Catholicism. In the 1630s a number of key events at home and abroad had effectively disassembled the compromise of religious tolerance and a broad church in England.

With no Parliament, there was no money, and with no money there was no possibility of a foreign war. Immediately after the dissolution of Parliament in 1628, Charles had sought and secured peace with both France and Spain. The following year, the Thirty Years' War entered its fourth phase. Wallenstein's victories over the Danish army of Christian IV led to a short-lived peace and enticed Sweden to enter the war. The Swedish King, Gustavus Adolphus, was concerned at the proximity of Catholic forces and the growing power of the Holy Roman Empire. He was also keen to secure economic influence over the German states in and around the Baltic Sea. From 1630 to 1634 Swedish-led armies drove back the Catholic forces and

regained much of the lost territory and, in so doing, established Gustavus Adolphus as the 'Lion of the North', the figurehead for Continental Protestantism.[23] Many English Puritans, and other English and Scottish Protestant groups, believed this was their destiny and that Charles had shied from his vocation. Furthermore, his decision to allow Spanish ships to use English ports en route to the European war was a clear enough indicator of exactly where his true sympathies lay.

It is debateable whether Charles would have got embroiled in the European wars, even if he had been financially able so to do. What is more certain is that he intended, without Parliament, to govern his Three Kingdoms on the model of Continental absolutism. In 1633, he made two key appointments in support of that policy. The first was Thomas Wentworth, who was to run Charles's government in Ireland, and the second was William Laud, who became Archbishop of Canterbury. Laud had been Bishop of London since 1626; his vision was to restore the church and clergy to a pre-Reformation standing, through the strengthening of ceremonialist aspects of worship, establishing uniformity and upholding episcopal regulation. He had long since wanted to purge the Church of England of Calvinist elements and, to him, Puritans were particularly loathsome. He was no theologian, but he did find the concept of predestination implausible and was therefore branded an Arminian but, in reality, he was less interested in the minutia of salvation and damnation than in the enforcement of religious uniformity and eradication of misguided Protestant minorities. Despite his desire to revive Catholic-style High Church ceremony, he was not a supporter of Rome and he was only too aware of the damage that the Catholics at court were doing to the public perception of 'Popery'. In view of the delicate religious nature of post-Reformation England, even non-Puritans were surprised and alarmed by Laud's approach, and Charles's tacit support of it. But it was not just the laity who had cause for concern, for Laud was hell-bent on recovering much of the church lands and property that had been sold off after the Dissolution of the Monasteries. This set him on a similarly dangerous collision course with the enlarged gentry.

Since the Middle Ages, the crown's principal source of income was derived from lands of royal domain or demesne, and by the start of the 17th century most of these had been sold. By Charles's reign, the income from rents (about £25,000) had fallen to about a third of that enjoyed by his father.[24] But Charles was determined never to have to call Parliament again and, in order to achieve that, he needed financial emancipation. He tasked his financial advisors to dig deep in their search for new sources of income. The King's principal advisor, William Noy, revived a number of medieval practices to satisfy his master's quest. His targets were the Forest Laws, Ship Money and the granting of monopolies. He demonstrated ingenuity by circumventing a legal challenge to the latter by replacing monopoly with patent. Noy also proposed the licensing of new corporations and, in so doing, encouraged a commercial struggle between existing and new companies.[25] However, many of the new 'middling class' were incensed when, in 1634, Charles decided to levy 'Ship Money'. Ship Money was an Elizabethan tax levied on seaports and coastal counties to fund the Royal Navy, naval defences and the building of new ships, in crisis and war.

20 A total of nine MPs were arrested; six were released on making peace with the King but three, including Eliot, were imprisoned at the monarch's pleasure. Eliot was to die three years later at the age of 40, further exacerbating the situation between Parliament and the nation's monarch.

21 Worden, op. cit., p. 21.

22 Davies, op. cit., pp. 560–1.

23 A role they had until the Swedish Empire came to an end in 1721.

24 Wedgwood, op. cit., p. 153.

25 Ibid., pp. 159–62 for a good account of the struggle between two patentees for the manufacture and supply of salt and a similar battle between a soap company granted (sole) permission to manufacture soap using vegetable oil.

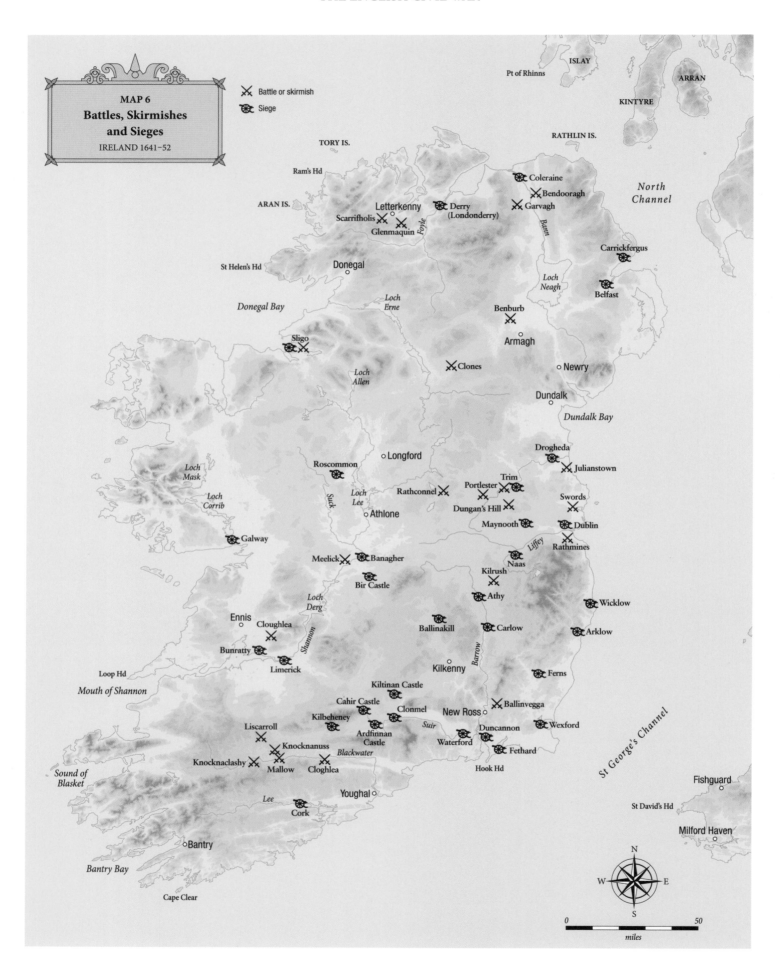

MAP 6
**Battles, Skirmishes
and Sieges**
IRELAND 1641–52

⚔ Battle or skirmish

⚙ Siege

ISLAY

Pt of Rhinns

ARRAN

KINTYRE

*North
Channel*

TORY IS.

RATHLIN IS.

Ram's Hd

Coleraine

Bendooragh

ARAN IS.

Letterkenny

Derry
(Londonderry)

Garvagh

Scarrifholis

Carrickfergus

Glenmaquin

Foyle

Bann

St Helen's Hd

Donegal

*Loch
Neagh*

Belfast

Donegal Bay

*Loch
Erne*

Benburb

Armagh

Sligo

*Loch
Allen*

Clones

Newry

Dundalk

Dundalk Bay

Drogheda

*Loch
Mask*

Roscommon

Longford

Julianstown

*Loch
Corrib*

*Loch
Lee*

Rathconnel

Portlester

Trim

Swords

Suck

Athlone

Dungan's Hill

Maynooth

Dublin

Galway

Liffey

Rathmines

Meelick

Banagher

Naas

Bir Castle

Kilrush

Ennis

Athy

Wicklow

Cloughlea

*Loch
Derg*

Ballinakill

Carlow

Arklow

Bunratty

Kilkenny

Ferns

Shannon

Limerick

Loop Hd

Kiltinan Castle

Mouth of Shannon

Cahir Castle

Ballinvegga

Clonmel

Kilbeheney

New Ross

Liscarroll

Ardfinnan
Castle

Duncannon

Wexford

Knocknanuss

Suir

Knocknaclashy

Blackwater

Mallow

Cloghlea

Waterford

Fethard

*Sound of
Blasket*

Hook Hd

Fishguard

Lee

Youghal

St David's Hd

Cork

Milford Haven

Bantry

St George's Channel

Bantry Bay

Cape Clear

N

W   E

S

0   50

miles

In 1635, realizing he had untapped a vital source of revenue, Charles decided to increase the levy to inland counties as well. By 1636 it was a regular form of revenue and was being used to finance other government 'expenses'.

It was not long before the King's right to collect a maritime tax in peacetime and in inland counties was legally challenged. The Buckinghamshire landowner and entrepreneur John Hampden refused to pay the 20 shillings assessed on his land in Stoke Mandeville. He had been a Member of Parliament since 1621 and was no stranger to confrontation with the crown and the King's advisors. He had refused to pay the forced loan in 1626 and had shared the gatehouse gaol at Westminster Abbey with John Eliot. Eliot's death in the Tower in 1632 infuriated the Parliamentarians, and Hampden was waiting for another opportunity to question the King's motives and authority; the levying of Ship Money provided that chance.[26] The court sat in November 1637 and delivered their judgement three months later. The verdict was a narrow victory for the King, with seven of the 12 judges finding in his favour, while five found for the defendant. As such, it was a moral victory for Charles's opponents, but more significantly it provided the catalyst to unite large swathes of provincial gentry against the King and his court, not because they objected per se to the payment of Ship Money but because it led to a breakdown of peace and order within local communities.[27] This altered the dynamics of unrest.

By the late 1630s it was no longer accurate to describe the struggle as one between court and country, where the latter was the political class and ruling order. During the years of personal rule Charles and his ministers were operating in new ground, but their policies eroded local tradition and convention. In France and Spain there was no power base at the local level, but in England the system of primogeniture provided for the first-born male but required his brothers to earn their living elsewhere. Intermarriage, and social interaction between peers and gentry, and gentry and the new middling and mercantile classes, empowered the provinces, thereby ensuring there were no classes to divide.[28] Provincial communities reacted by paralysing local government; they fiercely contested the seats in the elections of 1640 and their manifestos were not so much about national issues and royal policy as much as the effect that those issues and that policy had on their local communities. It was a powerful banner and it struck a chord.

Thomas Wentworth had been one of the trouble-makers in Charles's first Parliament of 1625. He had been moved sideways to become the sheriff of Yorkshire. Like Hampden, he refused to pay forced loans and was imprisoned in 1627 for six months. Once released he took up his seat at the 1628 Parliament and argued for a more moderate version of the Petition of Right, but lost influence and standing among his peers when Eliot and Coke succeeded in carrying through more radical versions. After Buckingham's assassination, Wentworth declared loyalty to Charles and he was made Viscount Wentworth and appointed lord-president of the Council of the North. Charles never forgot Wentworth's early infidelities and never really trusted him. Nevertheless, Wentworth quickly established himself as a forceful and adroit operator and, in May 1629, was appointed to the Privy Council. In 1632, Wentworth was 'elevated' Lord Deputy of Ireland; it was a difficult appointment but Wentworth was up for the challenge and he took up the post in mid-1633.

IRELAND AND SCOTLAND

Ireland had come under the English crown in the middle of the 12th century following the Norman invasion by Henry II. He, and successive monarchs, ruled Ireland as a feudal fief. Numerous English monarchs contemplated campaigns to achieve full conquest, but they lacked both the funds and the resources. At the start of the 16th century, English interest was maintained by an English-speaking elite – the product of old English families of Norman extraction, who practised Catholicism but remained loyal to the crown. In 1530 a number of Protestant settlers were sent to Ireland and they confiscated vast tracts of land from the native Irish and gradually replaced Ireland's colonial elite. Following the suppression by English troops of two rebellions, known as the Desmond Rebellions of 1569 and 1579, 'plantation'[29] won wider acceptance as a policy of control. The English victory over the Gaelic Irish chieftains Hugh O'Neill of Tír Eoghain, Hugh Roe O'Donnell of Tír Chonaill and their allies in the (Irish) Nine Years' War (1594–1603), led to their escape in what is termed the 'Flight of the Earls', and to the Plantation of Ulster. Charles did not have any overt ambitions for Ireland; despite being its sovereign, he had never set foot in the country, nor did he have any intention of so doing. Wentworth's mandate, therefore, was threefold: to govern the country without any interest other than that of the crown; to extend control by continuing and expanding the policy of plantation; and to enforce religious conformity with the Church of England as purported by his close ally Archbishop Laud.[30] He knew only too well that the Irish would not embrace Protestantism and he therefore set about securing the kingdom by Protestant expansion. At every turn, Wentworth questioned the legitimacy of land title, a policy that brought him into confrontation with established Catholics and Protestants alike and drove them into the hands of the King's adversaries in England and the Covenanters in Scotland.

When Charles inherited the throne, Scotland was both orderly and loyal to the crown. His father had not forgotten his Scottish roots but Charles was an absentee monarch who, in less than 13 years, had managed to unite the majority of the Scottish nation against him. The Scottish royal institution was very different from the English court that James inherited from the Tudors. The Scottish king was very much a 'first among equals' with his nobility; it was a system that lacked the formality and flattery of the English court. Charles acted as if unaware of these major differences. He chose to ignore the Scottish ways, preferring instead to embrace the English system and even enhance it by moving towards the more extreme French and Spanish court culture. Scotland was about one-fifth the population size of England and Wales at this time: one million Scots and five million English and Welsh. But they had almost the same number of nobles as existed in England: 105 in Scotland and 121 in England.[31] The Scottish nobles believed, as tradition had it, that they had a right to share power with their King. The Scottish feudal system had struggled with an absentee monarch under James VI (James I of England), but with Charles they inherited an absentee monarch who exhibited aloofness and disdain to boot, and this was simply too much.

The Presbyterian Kirk, set up in 1567, when Mary Queen of Scots abdicated was, by 1630, the established church in Scotland and referred to

---

26 Eliot had been imprisoned for opposing the crown on numerous occasions. Charles was determined to punish Eliot as he considered him responsible for Buckingham's death. In early 1632 Eliot developed consumption, but his petition to take leave in the country was rejected by Charles. He died on 27 November 1632.

27 Morrill, *Revolt of the Provinces*, pp. 25–9.

28 Worden, op. cit., p. 17.

29 The Plantation of Ulster was the organized colonization (plantation) of Ulster by people from Scotland and England.

30 Kenyon & Ohlmeyer, op. cit., p. 14.

31 Stevenson, *Scottish Revolution*, p. 18. James had supported the nomination of a number of new nobles during his reign.

as such. Its doctrine was based on extreme Calvinism and its ministers were elected by their own congregations, while discipline was entrusted to lay elders. One of James's greatest successes in Scotland had been the establishment of royal control over the Kirk and the integration of bishops within the church government. As such, the Church of Scotland combined elements of Episcopacy and Presbyterianism and this worked well, until Charles decided to elevate the former at the expense of the latter.[32] The bishops were some of the most trusted of Charles's Scottish advisors; in 1634 he made them justices of the peace, and two years later, elevated many of them to the Scottish exchequer at the expense of positions hitherto held by nobles. Charles, determined to have religious uniformity in England and Scotland, took the process one step further and ordered the preparation of a modified English prayer-book. The book was to be imposed on the Kirk, which, in his opinion (and with some justification), lacked a regulated and standardized form of worship. Laud rose to the challenge, no doubt delighted at the chance to impose his will on the errant Church of Scotland. On 23 July 1637, attempts to read the prayer-book in Edinburgh for the first time resulted in riots which quickly spread across Scotland. Charles has seriously miscalculated the repercussions of trying to force such a measure on the Kirk and the Scottish nation. He had underestimated the strength of Scottish nationalism, and the influence of the Kirk, who did not view him as the supreme governor of their faith as he was to the Church in England. The country's nobles united with the Kirk's ministers and they rose, in one voice, in violent opposition.

Charles was baffled at the news of rioting in Edinburgh and rather predictably ordered the (Scottish) Privy Council to punish the ringleaders. This body was not dissimilar to its English counterpart; however, there was one fundamental difference. In England the King was (often) present at meetings and had his hand on the tiller, while in Scotland they were acting on direction from a distant ruler. The Council and its members were in an impossible position: duty bound to support the King, yet for many their sympathies lay with their countrymen. The stand-off continued throughout the rest of 1637. Charles continued to underestimate the depth of discontent and the precariousness of the situation. Laud was outraged and, not surprisingly, he encouraged Charles to take a strong hand, maintaining that any laxity would hearten the Puritans in England and in Westminster in particular. John Stewart, Earl of Traquair, the Lord Treasurer in Scotland, travelled to London to warn the King that if he wanted to impose the new book on Scotland, he had better support the enforcement with 40,000 men at arms. Traquair was sent back north of the border with a flea in his ear and bearing the King's written response. Events were beginning to spiral out of control.

Let all who live in the land tremble,
For the day of the LORD is coming.
It is close at hand –
A day of darkness and gloom,
A day of clouds and blackness,
Like dawn spreading across the mountains
A large and mighty army comes,
Such as never was in ancient times
Nor ever will be in ages to come.

Joel 2:1–2

---

32 Ibid., p. 23.

CHAPTER 2
THE BISHOPS' WARS, 1639-40

Throughout the 1630s animosity and disillusionment grew in Scotland, exacerbated by administrative decay, economic hardship, an absentee monarch and religious mayhem. However, any suggestion, even as late as 1637, that the nation was on the brink of war or, God forbid, revolution, was considered absurd. Yet within months, following the attempted introduction of the new English prayer-book, petitions gave way to open meetings of discontent, many chaired and attended by Scottish nobles. The King's intransigence on the subject, and his open and continued disdain for their repeated petitions, led the Scots to raise more unofficial councils and to the founding of the 'Tables'.[1] In mid-February 1638 Traquair returned from consultations with Charles, bearing his uncompromising rejoinder and potent proclamation. These threats were a serious miscalculation. The previous month a committee in Edinburgh had agreed to 'the renewing of the old Covenant for religion'.[2] The new National Covenant was signed at Greyfriars Kirk on 28 February. It called, among other things, for an immediate withdrawal of the prayer-book and the replacement of rule by bishops. In fact, the Covenant was much more than that; it was, to all intents and purposes, a revolutionary manifesto that was very skilfully drafted so as to avoid allegations of treason, but it was also written in such a way as to appeal to and evoke popular support. It ends with a declaration of loyalty to God and the King; the latter only if he upheld the people's right to worship as they saw fit. It was signed in February by the great and good across Scotland; the 'Covenanters', as they became known, celebrated 'that glorious marriage day of the kingdom with God'.

Charles was not used to having his authority questioned and realized that his supremacy in Scotland had been usurped; his Scottish Privy Council was, to all intents and purposes, powerless. Charles decided to send James, Third Marquis of Hamilton and 'one of their own', north as a royal emissary in an attempt to convince his Scottish subjects of the error of their ways and, in so doing, give them a second chance. Hamilton took with him two new proclamations, but these were merely reiterations on the same theme. Hamilton had also been empowered to raise an army – a clear indicator that Charles was prepared to settle the issue by force if necessary. A few days before Hamilton arrived in Edinburgh the Covenanters had refused permission for a ship, docked at Leith, to unload its cargo of munitions destined for Edinburgh Castle. Events were beginning to spiral out of control. In fact, Hamilton had received notification while at Berwick (en route to Edinburgh) that the Covenanters would not entertain the vague concessions he was bearing. Before he entered Scotland, he wrote to the King, urging the early assembly of an English army. Hamilton's mission had become an exercise to buy time for that army to assemble, and by July 1638, both King and Covenanters were arming openly.

Mustering an English army was no easy task. Attempts to improve the regional militias had been sporadic during the Stuarts' reign and the burden of costs as contentious as Ship Money. The programme to reequip them with better weapons had, however, enjoyed greater success, and this accounts for the eagerness of both sides to seize and secure the nation's armouries in 1642. Charles called for the mobilization of the northern counties' militia (or trained bands) and requested an additional special levy of 6,000 men. Results were less than satisfactory; many of the northern tenants-in-chief and trained bands' officials had some sympathy with Scottish grievances. Despite this, by March 1639 Charles had an army, on paper at least, of 20,000 men. However, the quality of the troops was decidedly dubious and, lacking any funds to pay for mercenaries in order to strengthen the force, Charles called upon his Irish lords to make up the numbers. Randal MacDonnell, Second Earl of Antrim, answered the call, rallying the Irish families in Ulster.[3] Antrim was ordered to raise 5,000 men but he boasted of mobilizing twice that number; however, he lacked officers to train and lead the new recruits. His plan to entice experienced soldiers from Irish families fighting on the continent was strongly opposed by Wentworth, who agreed to provide 100 drill sergeants from the King's army and some old soldiers to command.

Charles retained some control in Scotland, as not all the barons, lairds and ministers had signed the National Covenant. This support was largely constrained to the north-east, where the Marquis of Huntly swore allegiance to the crown and maintained a force of a few thousand Royalist supporters. Most significantly, however, Charles also controlled the Royal Navy, and this, coupled with the fact that 'loyal garrisons' maintained control within Edinburgh and Dumbarton castles, provided him the basis of a plan. Charles's grand strategy was to attack Scotland on three fronts as well as from within. Hamilton was to sail up the east coast with 5,000 men and link up with Huntly and then march south to Edinburgh; while Antrim, with as many as 10,000 men from Ulster, would land in Argyll using Dumbarton Castle and the Isle of Arran as bases before fanning out into the interior. Finally, Charles's army of 20,000 would move north and cross the border into Scotland and approach the capital from the south.

The Covenanters drew inspiration that theirs was a just and holy cause for nationalistic as well as religious reasons and that failure, for the ringleaders at very least, would be fatal. Strong motivators indeed. The Covenanters' problem was a lack of trained commanders; the clans had trained reserves of manpower but their methods and tactics were antiquated and, as the soldiers only spoke Gaelic, their employability was limited. There were, however, many Scottish officers serving on the Continent, and the Covenanters were quick to realize the importance of these men to their struggle.[4] One such officer was Alexander Leslie, a field marshal in the Swedish army, who returned home and held titular command of the

---

1 'Tables' were informal meetings used to avoid the impression that these gatherings usurped government. They became the instruments through which the Covenanters governed the country.

2 Stevenson, *Scottish Revolution*, p. 82.

3 Kenyon & Ohlmeyer, *Military History*, p. xx.

4 Stevenson, op. cit., p. 131.

Covenanter forces.[5] Under his guidance the forces adopted the Swedish model of recruiting, in which the country was divided, more or less, into quarters and a mass levy introduced, evoking an encouraging and patriotic response. Costs were borne across the parishes on a pro rata basis. Leslie structured the force in a doctrinally conventional method with three musketeers to two pikemen and manned the artillery with regular gunners to service and transport the ordnance. The morale and discipline of the force were fostered and maintained, and copies of 'The Articles and Ordinances of War' were distributed. This far-sighted document outlined the behaviour expected and allowed by the soldiers with regard to their enemy, their comrades and civilians.[6] It formed the basis of a similar document, 'Laws and Ordinances of War established for the better conduct of the Army', issued for the New Model Army some years later.

Like so many military plans, Charles's grand strategy was undone long before the various components were in place. In February 1639 the Covenanters struck the first blow with the seizure of Inverness town and castle, thereby securing the arms and ammunition stored there. Huntly responded by moving armed horsemen on a Covenanters' meeting at Turriff a week later, but promptly withdrew when it was clear that, despite being outnumbered, they were up for a fight. Huntly's timidity prompted Leslie and James Graham, the Fifth Earl of Montrose, to move the combined north-eastern Covenanter armies up to capture Aberdeen. They were unopposed and entered Aberdeen in March, capturing Huntly in the process. He was taken to Edinburgh. The same month Covenanter forces captured the castles at Dunglass and Tantallon, but it was the capture a few days later, of Edinburgh Castle and that at Dumbarton, which disrupted, but did not derail, Charles's plan. The Covenanters also made preparations to secure the south-western coastline and the coastal area leading to the Firth of Forth, where it was clear Hamilton's amphibious force would now divert, having lost Huntly's support in the north-east.

Hamilton left Yarmouth in April and anchored off Leith on 1 May. He had no immediate intention of landing but was instead waiting for the King's army to approach from the south and for the publication of the latest of the King's proclamations. The latter offered widespread pardon but nothing of any substance to convince the Covenanters to reconsider. Meanwhile Charles arrived at York on 30 March and was somewhat disenchanted both in the size of his army (he had hoped for 30,000) and the quality and expertise of the troops. Furthermore, he had received news that Antrim's force of 10,000 was, through insensitivity towards clan allegiance, destined never to leave Ireland. Charles ordered Wentworth to make good the numbers by coming over with a force from the Irish army. Wentworth pleaded with the King, asking him to wait, as his forces were not ready. Furthermore, in an attempt to strengthen his argument, he urged caution, using inside information and intelligence to sketch the depth and strength of the Covenanter armies. Charles was nonplussed, and on 30 May he was with his army at Birks (3 miles west of Berwick). It was the first army he had ever commanded in the field.

Leslie had begun concentrating Covenanter forces in the Scottish borders as early as April and had ordered them not to advance closer than 10 miles of the border as per the royal injunction. But on 25 April some of the English troops entered Scotland and read out the King's proclamation at Duns. The Covenanters took this as a violation and promptly moved

forces further south. One such group was stationed in Kelso and, on 3 June, Charles sent just over 3,000 men to drive them out. The English force quickly found themselves outnumbered and in danger of being cut off and withdrew in haste. Their arrival back in Birks was a bitter blow to Charles and a sharp lesson on the use of force. The corresponding collapse in morale was instantaneous across the English army and when Leslie moved nearly 20,000 men to Duns on 5 June, Charles lost his nerve. The Scots sent an entreaty to negotiate and Charles wasted little time in agreeing. The King and Covenanter nobles signed the Treaty of Berwick on 18 June. The agreement underscored a return to the *status quo ante bellum*; the two armies were to disband, work was halted on all fortifications, all castles belonging to the King would be restored and all Royalist prisoners freed.[7] Furthermore, Charles agreed to summon a general assembly in Edinburgh to discuss the matter of ecclesiastical vicissitudes. Neither side was naïve enough to believe that the articles contained in the treaty would provide the basis for lasting settlement. However, for now, the relief that armed conflict had been averted was palpable.

Despite Charles's more apparent problems, things had not gone that smoothly for the Covenanters and the movement of a large force to Duns by Leslie had been, largely, a bluff.[8] Nevertheless, when the Scots commissioners arrived back at Edinburgh they were not warmly received; the handing back of Edinburgh Castle was an unadulterated symbol of capitulation and many of the nobles were accused of treachery. In July, preliminary negotiations between the King and the Covenanters did not progress well, and in the end, Charles decided not to attend the assembly in Edinburgh in person but decided to send Traquair as his representative. Traquair, who was between a rock and a hard place, made a bit of a hash of negotiations and, as a result, they became long and drawn out. By November Charles had instructed Traquair to prorogue the Scottish Parliament until June 1640, convinced that the motives of the Covenanters, and Puritans for that matter, were political and not religious. Despite his earlier military rebuke, he was determined to bring the matter to a close by force.

Charles once again turned to his Lord Deputy in Ireland for help. Wentworth was summoned home and became the King's closest advisor on matters of war (while retaining a hand on the tiller in Ireland). In January the following year he was created the Earl of Strafford. Strafford embraced his new appointment with zeal and all but ordered Parliament to raise funds in order to finance the war effort. However, Scotland was not the King's sole concern; events there and on the Continent were about to collide and expose both England's weaknesses and its divisions. The Covenanters' anti-Episcopalian stance had fired up the English Puritans but there was an even greater cause for concern. The death of the Protestant standard-bearer Bernard of Saxe-Weimar at Breisach created a power vacuum which the Elector Palatine was keen to fill. In order to achieve this, he needed his uncle Charles's moral and military support, neither of which Charles was willing to provide, particularly while the matter of Scotland remained unresolved. To make matters worse, Bernard's victory at Breisach had prevented Spanish troops from moving from the Hapsburg dominions in southern Germany to the Spanish Netherlands (see Map 3). Following some high-level diplomatic exchanges Charles had agreed that Spain could, firstly, count on English neutrality, and secondly, use contracted English shipping to move the Spanish forces. It was a decision that, not surprisingly, infuriated both

5   Kenyon & Ohlmeyer, op. cit., p. 47. King Charles created him Earl of Leven and
    Lord Balgonie in October 1641.
6   Ibid., p. 46.

7   The following day, unaware of the peace negotiations, Huntly's son (the
    Duke of Aboyne), at the head of the Gordons, was defeated by Montrose at the
    Brig O'Dee, enabling the Covenanters to capture Aberdeen.
8   Stevenson, op. cit., pp. 145–51.

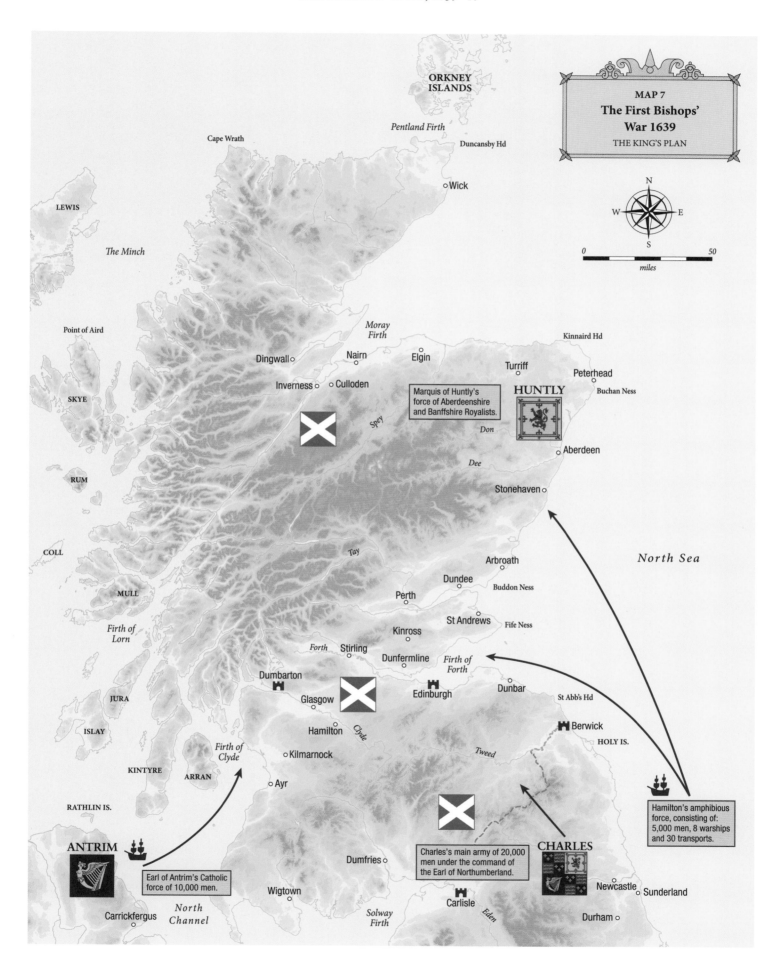

ORKNEY
ISLANDS

Pentland Firth

Cape Wrath

Duncansby Hd

○ Wick

MAP 7
**The First Bishops'
War 1639**
THE KING'S PLAN

N
W E
S

0   50
miles

LEWIS

The Minch

Point of Aird

*Moray
Firth*

Kinnaird Hd

Dingwall ○   Nairn ○   Elgin ○   Turriff ○   Peterhead ○

SKYE   Inverness ○   ○ Culloden   **HUNTLY**   Buchan Ness

Marquis of Huntly's
force of Aberdeenshire
and Banffshire Royalists.

Spey   *Don*

RUM   *Dee*   ○ Aberdeen

○ Stonehaven

COLL   *Tay*   *North Sea*

MULL   Arbroath ○

                                                              Dundee ○   Buddon Ness

*Firth of
Lorn*   Perth ○

                                                    St Andrews ○   Fife Ness
                                              Kinross ○
JURA   *Forth* Stirling ○
                                        Dunfermline ○   *Firth of
                              Dumbarton ▣   Forth*
ISLAY   Glasgow ○   Dunbar ○   St Abb's Hd

                              Hamilton ○   *Clyde*   Edinburgh ▣

KINTYRE   ARRAN   ○ Kilmarnock   *Tweed*   ▣ Berwick
                                                                        HOLY IS.
RATHLIN IS.   ○ Ayr

ANTRIM ⛵   Charles's main army of 20,000   **CHARLES**
                                                    men under the command of
Earl of Antrim's Catholic   the Earl of Northumberland.
force of 10,000 men.

Hamilton's amphibious
force, consisting of:
5,000 men, 8 warships
and 30 transports.

                    Dumfries ○   Newcastle ○ ○ Sunderland

Carrickfergus ○   Wigtown ○   Carlisle ▣
                                                                        Durham ○
*North
Channel*   *Solway
                              Firth*   *Eden*

49

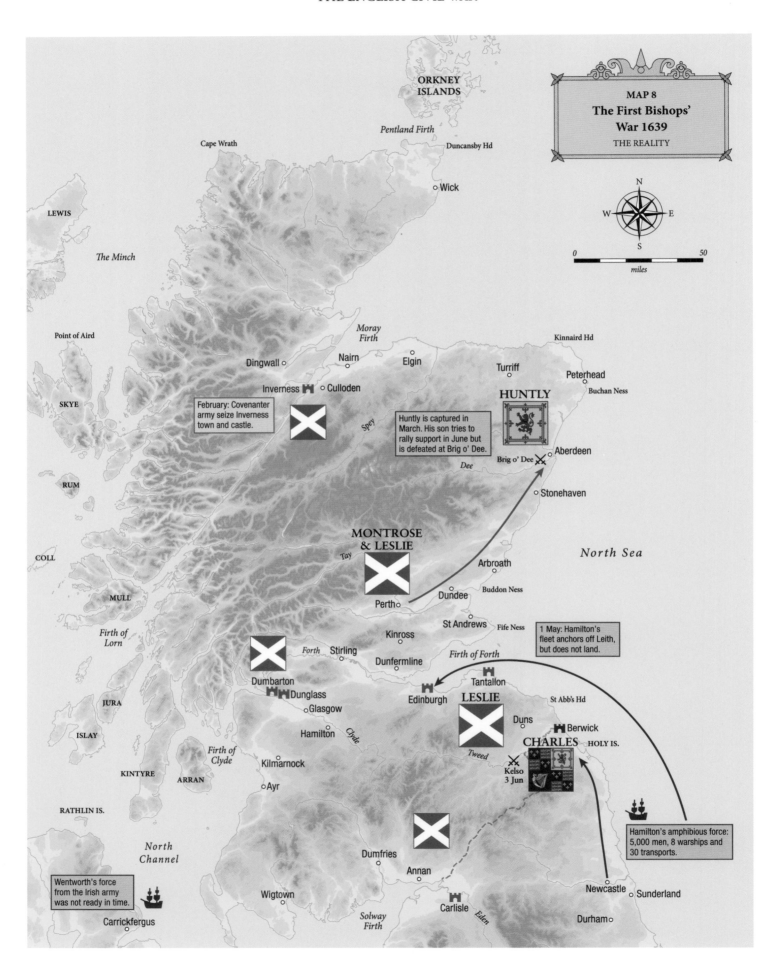

MAP 8
**The First Bishops'
War 1639**
THE REALITY

ORKNEY
ISLANDS

Pentland Firth

Cape Wrath

Duncansby Hd

Wick

LEWIS

The Minch

*Moray
Firth*

Kinnaird Hd

Dingwall

Nairn

Elgin

Turriff

Peterhead

SKYE

Inverness

Culloden

Buchan Ness

HUNTLY

February: Covenanter
army seize Inverness
town and castle.

Spey

Huntly is captured in
March. His son tries to
rally support in June but
is defeated at Brig o' Dee.

Aberdeen

Brig o' Dee

Dee

RUM

Stonehaven

COLL

North Sea

**MONTROSE
& LESLIE**

Tay

Arbroath

MULL

Perth

Dundee

Buddon Ness

Kinross

St Andrews

Fife Ness

1 May: Hamilton's
fleet anchors off Leith,
but does not land.

*Firth of
Lorn*

Forth

Stirling

Dunfermline

Firth of Forth

Dumbarton

Dunglass

Tantallon

Edinburgh

LESLIE

St Abb's Hd

JURA

Glasgow

Duns

Berwick

Hamilton

CHARLES

HOLY IS.

ISLAY

Clyde

Kilmarnock

*Firth of
Clyde*

Tweed

KINTYRE

ARRAN

Kelso
3 Jun

RATHLIN IS.

Ayr

*North
Channel*

Dumfries

Hamilton's amphibious force:
5,000 men, 8 warships and
30 transports.

Wentworth's force
from the Irish army
was not ready in time.

Annan

Wigtown

Newcastle

Sunderland

Carlisle

Eden

Durham

Carrickfergus

*Solway
Firth*

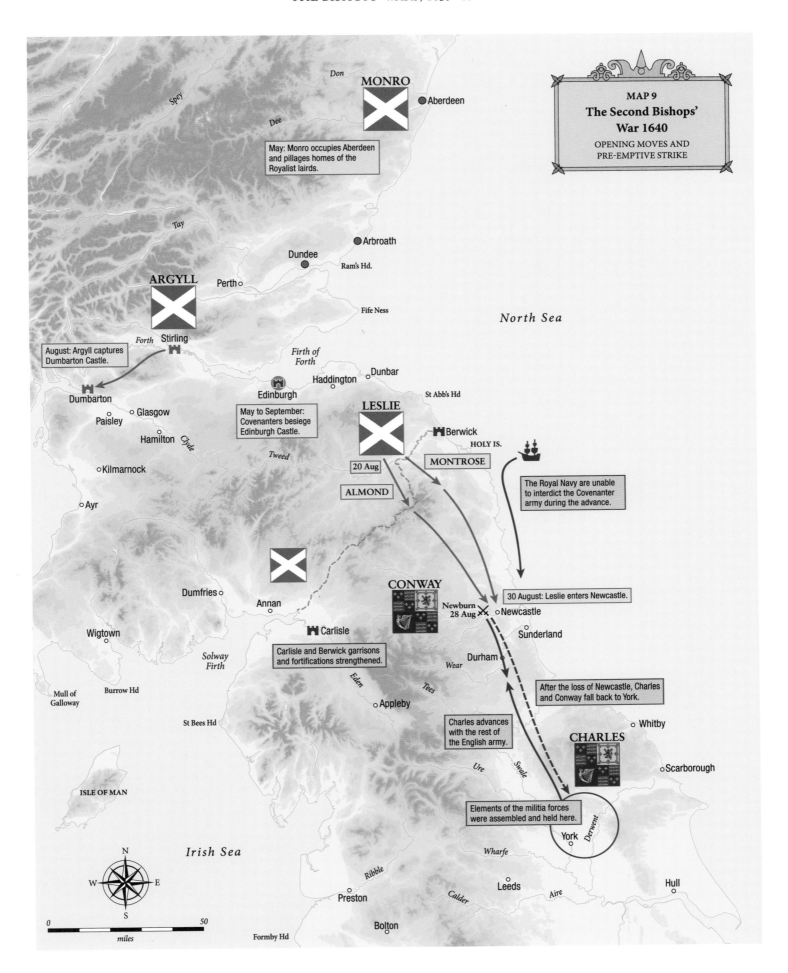

MAP 9
**The Second Bishops'
War 1640**
OPENING MOVES AND
PRE-EMPTIVE STRIKE

MONRO

May: Monro occupies Aberdeen
and pillages homes of the
Royalist lairds.

Aberdeen

Don

Spey

Dee

Tay

Arbroath

Dundee

Ram's Hd.

ARGYLL

Perth

Stirling

Forth

August: Argyll captures
Dumbarton Castle.

Dumbarton

Glasgow

Paisley

Hamilton

Clyde

Kilmarnock

Tweed

Ayr

North Sea

Firth of
Forth

Fife Ness

Dunbar

Haddington

Edinburgh

St Abb's Hd.

LESLIE

Berwick

HOLY IS.

MONTROSE

May to September:
Covenanters besiege
Edinburgh Castle.

20 Aug

ALMOND

The Royal Navy are unable
to interdict the Covenanter
army during the advance.

Dumfries

Annan

Carlisle

CONWAY

Newburn
28 Aug

30 August: Leslie enters Newcastle.

Newcastle

Wigtown

Solway
Firth

Carlisle and Berwick garrisons
and fortifications strengthened.

Sunderland

Durham

Wear

Mull of
Galloway

Burrow Hd

Eden

Tees

Appleby

After the loss of Newcastle, Charles
and Conway fall back to York.

St Bees Hd

Charles advances
with the rest of
the English army.

Whitby

CHARLES

ISLE OF MAN

Ure

Swale

Scarborough

Elements of the militia forces
were assembled and held here.

York

Derwent

Irish Sea

Wharfe

N
W   E
S

Ribble

Calder

Aire

Hull

0   50

miles

Preston

Leeds

Bolton

Formby Hd

the Dutch and the Protestants in England. The whole debacle culminated in a naval battle off the Kent coast during which a large Spanish fleet in neutral English waters was destroyed by Admiral Tromp's Dutch fleet.[9] It did little for Charles's domestic and international standing.

Early in March 1640 Strafford left for Ireland with the King's authority to raise an army of 8,000 foot and 1,000 horse. With debts incurred from paying the forces raised to fight (what was dubbed) the first Bishops' War, and with the payment of Ship Money all but ceased, Charles had no option but to recall Parliament for the first time in 11 years. They met on 13 April 1640 and agreed to vote huge sums in the form of 12 subsidies, but first their grievances were to be heard and addressed.[10] Charles, despite his desperation for funding, was furious at this presumptuous approach to government and, after three weeks, he tired of the charade and dissolved the 'Short Parliament'. Charles attempted to secure funds from Philip IV of Spain, and when that failed, he agreed to allow his Queen to approach the Pope's emissary on the possibility of a loan from the Vatican. To worsen matters, the trust between the King and the gentry, the very men required to raise the militia forces, was at breaking point. Wholesale desertion began among the newly levied troops; they became disorderly and, in some cases, whole units mutinied and even murdered their Catholic officers.

Percy Algernon, Earl of Northumberland, had been appointed commander-in-chief of the English army. Great plans were discussed to man and equip an army of 35,000 foot and 3,000 horse. Offers were made to English (and Scottish) mercenaries fighting abroad in order to strengthen the leadership, and elaborate plans to fortify and strengthen the fortresses at Carlisle, Berwick and Newcastle were drawn up. However, all these elaborate plans relied on more than Strafford's enthusiasm to become reality. While Charles continued to try to fund his war machine, the militia army was ordered to concentrate in central Yorkshire. A large force of about 12,000 was deployed to Newcastle and Berwick and command of the forward army was vested in Lord Conway, who established his headquarters in the former city. He spent his meagre resources fortifying Berwick and had none to spare when it came to Newcastle.[11] His failure to gather accurate intelligence as to the strengths, dispositions and intentions of the Covenanter forces was significant, but it was his rather contemptuous and decidedly over-confident reports that were about to completely wrongfoot the monarch.

North of the border, as early as spring 1640, the Covenanters had returned to a war-footing. In May, Monro occupied Aberdeen, while the following month Argyll mustered a force of about 5,000 and set about clearing Royalist sympathizers in central Scotland.[12] Under the guidance of Leslie, units began besieging Edinburgh Castle and masking the fortress at Berwick while he gathered a vast army of about 20,000 foot, 2,000 horse and over 60 pieces of artillery. Aware of the disorder and deficiencies of the English army to the south, Leslie defied the agreement and on 20 August, leaving a strong garrison at Edinburgh to his rear, he masked the fort at Berwick and sent Lord Montrose over the River Tweed at Coldstream, while Lord Almond was to cross at Kelso. The same day, concerned that the tone of

Conway's reports had changed, Charles left London and headed north. Strafford, who was in London at the time, but who had fallen ill, did not follow him for some days.[13]

Leslie's army marched on two inland routes (preventing the Royal Navy monitoring or impeding their progress) directly towards Newcastle. The march to the Tyne took seven days, during which time the Berwick garrison failed to orchestrate any meaningful sorties against Leslie's left flank. Leslie's aim was to cross the Tyne at the fords at Newburn, about 4 miles upstream from Newcastle. Conway decided to block their advance using the River Tyne as the barrier. On 24 August he deployed west to the fords at Newburn with 3,000 foot, 2,000 horse and a single battery of eight guns. He left the majority of his force, about 7,500 men, to guard the unprepared but important city (it was, among other things, the source of London's coal). On the south bank of the Tyne opposite Newburn, he reinforced the two sconces and waited for the arrival of the Scots and English reinforcements, hoping that the latter would outpace the former. The balance of the English army was making desperately slow progress from York, and Charles was a couple of days behind them with a rearguard.

Early on 28 August the first of Leslie's troops arrived on the heights above the two fords. Montrose pushed the cavalry out to the flanks and Alexander Hamilton (commanding the artillery) established a number of guns on the higher ground by the church. 'Leslie battered Conway's entrenchments till his raw infantry left their guns and ran, and the Scottish horse and foot crossed the ford with little resistance from the English cavalry.'[14] In the mid-afternoon, the first wave of dragoons and foot soldiers waded the two fords, supported by heavy artillery fire from the north bank. They drove away the Royalist cavalry and quickly overwhelmed the two small sconces. Harry Wilmot, commanding a cavalry detachment, charged the Scots as they tried to establish a bridgehead on the south bank, but the Scottish discipline held and, as every minute passed, their numbers were augmented. The balance of English cavalry then fled, trampling down their unfortunate infantry in the process. Had it not been for the quick thinking of Lieutenant Colonel George Monck, who deployed and directed the few artillery guns to keep back the by now rampant Scots, the English losses would have been far greater. Monck's biographer wrote:

> ... at Newborn [sic], after the Scots pressed hard upon his Quarters, with very few Men, and less ammunition, he so lined the Hedges with his Firelocks, and brought off the Ordnance with that Bravery and Conduct, that none of all the Scotch regiments had the Courage or Confidence to impede his Retreat.[15]

By early evening (and the turn of the tide) about half the Covenanter force was across the Tyne and on the south bank; Conway pulled back in haste and, after a brief consultation with Sir Jacob Astley (the Sergeant-Major-General of the army), decided to abandon Newcastle and head south with all speed.

The next day the Covenanter armies moved east towards Newcastle, along the north and south banks, and were astonished to find it free of English troops. On 30 August Leslie entered the city and made good use of the plentiful provisions to resupply his army, and he called forward

9 Wedgwood, *The King's Peace*, pp. 289–90, 298–301.

10 A reinvestigation into the Hampden case; an enquiry into the imprisonment of Strode, Valentine, Holles and Eliot; and an investigation into the legality of the Speaker breaking up the last Parliament against their will.

11 Kenyon & Ohlmeyer, op. cit., p. 24.

12 There is evidence that the Covenanting party was coming apart; Montrose began to quarrel with Argyll and this fuelled inter-clan rivalry.

13 Strafford, at 47, was worn out, tormented by kidney stones and suffering constant gout. Wedgwood, op. cit., p. 345.

14 Firth, *Cromwell's Army*, p. 148.

15 Skinner, *General Monk*, p. 18.

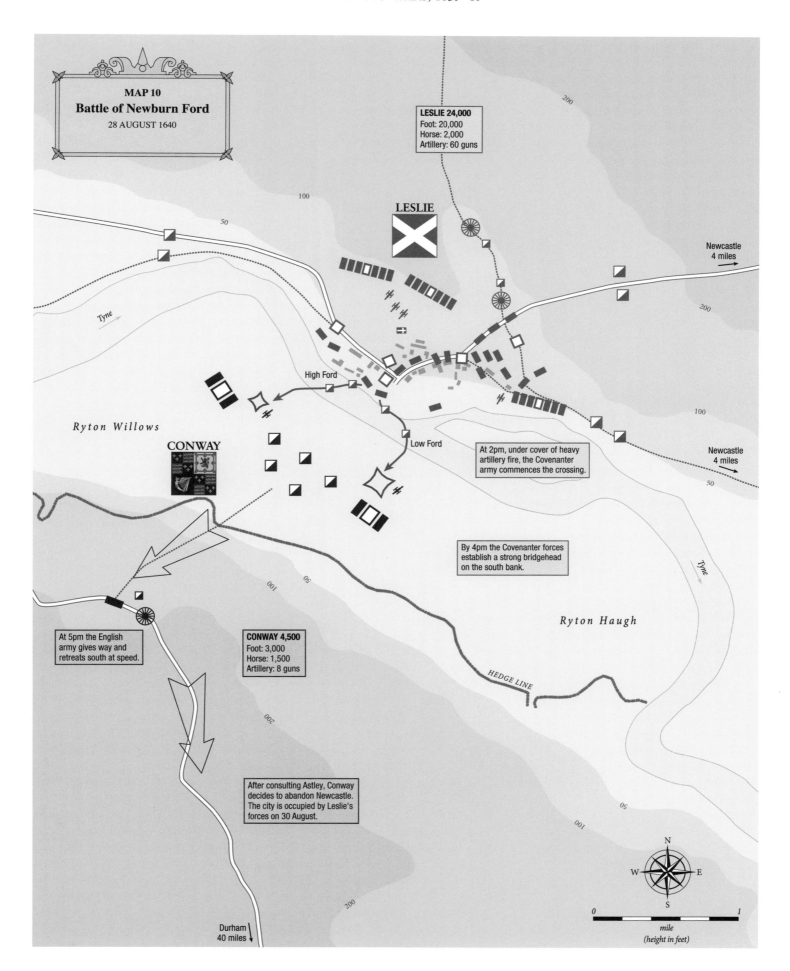

MAP 10

Battle of Newburn Ford

28 AUGUST 1640

LESLIE 24,000
Foot: 20,000
Horse: 2,000
Artillery: 60 guns

LESLIE

Newcastle
4 miles

200

100

50

Tyne

High Ford

Ryton Willows

CONWAY

Low Ford

Newcastle
4 miles

100

50

At 2pm, under cover of heavy artillery fire, the Covenanter army commences the crossing.

By 4pm the Covenanter forces establish a strong bridgehead on the south bank.

Ryton Haugh

Tyne

At 5pm the English army gives way and retreats south at speed.

CONWAY 4,500
Foot: 3,000
Horse: 1,500
Artillery: 8 guns

HEDGE LINE

100

50

200

50

100

After consulting Astley, Conway decides to abandon Newcastle. The city is occupied by Leslie's forces on 30 August.

200

N
W   E
S

0   1
mile
(height in feet)

Durham
40 miles

reserves from Edinburgh.[16] Charles fell back to York and was joined by Strafford on 4 September; later that day Leslie's demands arrived. Once again Charles played for time – it was to become his trademark. However, when the Great Council of Peerage met at York on 24 September, it was clear that England was not behind him. It must have been a bitter blow. The Council urged another truce with Scotland and, in the same breath, advised the recall of the Westminster Parliament. Negotiations opened at Ripon on 2 October and the Covenanters immediately wrongfooted the King by insisting that the talks were purely to discuss a cessation of hostilities and that the details of any subsequent peace treaty would be decided after the English Parliament had met to discuss them. The significance of this rebuff knocked the stuffing out of the King. To make matters worse, if that was possible, the Scots were demanding that the English had to pay £850 a day to quarter the Scottish troops until those peace negotiations were concluded. Charles had been backed into a corner: he had no military response, his Irish army was still months away, and his Council Peers had advised him to accept the terms and recall Parliament. Black days for the Stuart monarchy.

When Parliament assembled, on 3 November 1640, no one could have guessed that it would remain in session until April 1653, thereby receiving the designation the 'Long Parliament'. The mood in the Lords and Commons was both, unsurprisingly, hostile and volatile. Mismanagement of government, an assault on Parliamentary rights, the 11-year gap that constituted 'personal rule', a Scottish army on English soil, and the threat of an Irish Catholic army that might follow, was enough to unite Charles's opponents from all sides of the divide. Nevertheless, there was no hint that rebellion, or worse still civil war, was in the air. The Scots had to be placated, the King's army had to be disbanded, the King's advisors had to be removed, the church had to be reformed and the sins of the past had to be cleansed. Strafford and Laud were charged and imprisoned in the Tower, the former on a charge of 'high misdemeanours' and the latter for 'high treason'.

The collapse of Charles's authority led to a power vacuum. Able and powerful men were quick to fill the void, the Earls of Bedford and Warwick in the Lords and John Pym in the Commons, the latter supported by a number of authoritative accomplices; this cross-house Parliamentary group was known as the 'Junto'. The presence of the Scottish army was a double-edged sword and the Junto used it to hold the King to ransom. Over the next six months, Charles signed Strafford's death warrant, abolished the Star Chamber and High Commission and sanctioned the Triennial Bill, by which a period of no more than three years should elapse without recall of Parliament.[17] However, this was not enough for the Junto who distrusted, with some good reason, Charles's intentions and wanted to strip him of his remaining power and reduce him to a mere signatory. The people began to take the law into their own hands, energized by a sense of awareness of their own power, and encouraged to do so by many in the Junto. The violence was directed against those identified by the Junto as enemies of Parliament and Protestantism. England had begun the slide to civil conflict. However, as it turned out, the first outbreak of violence erupted across the water in one of Charles's other kingdoms – Ireland.

16 Conway removed the heavier guns by road to Durham and had the powder taken off by ship.

17 Strafford's trial opened on 22 March 1641, with Pym leading the prosecution. Strafford defended himself so ably that his alleged treason could not be proved. When it looked as if he might be acquitted, Pym and his supporters resorted to a bill of attainder. After anguished hesitation, King Charles gave way to the clamour for Strafford's execution and gave his consent to the bill. To great popular rejoicing, Strafford was beheaded on Tower Hill on 12 May 1641.

CHAPTER 3
REBELLION IN IRELAND, 1640–42

Wentworth had made many enemies in Ireland, and when the Irish Parliament was recalled in March 1640, they wasted little time in condemning him and his administration in Dublin.[1] However, in the end it was Strafford's fall and not his rule which led to crisis. Two interwoven plots were to ignite rebellion and ultimately drive England to civil war. According to an account related by the Earl of Antrim, the King had insisted that 'those eight thousand men, raised by the Earl of Strafford in Ireland, should be continued without disbanding, and that they should be made up to twenty thousand, and that they should be armed out of the store in Dublin and employed against the parliament'.[2] There is no direct evidence that Charles was planning to use a Catholic army in England, but the fact that he was wholeheartedly prepared to use a Scottish one makes it a distinct possibility. However, once Strafford had been executed (by beheading on Tower Hill on 12 May 1641), and the situation had shifted marginally in the King's favour, he gave orders for the Irish army to disband. It did so in name, but not in reality.

Scattered groups remained under their officers, many waiting for transport to France or Spain in order to fight on foreign service. The seeds of discontent in Ireland from years of social, religious and economic uncertainty and instability, coupled with the ethnic bigotry of 'plantation' and the collapse of Strafford's administration, created the tinderbox, ripe for ignition. The King's defeat at Newburn, his financial difficulties, the sheer presence of an Irish army and offers of help to the Irish from Cardinal Richelieu, in their hour of need, provided the spark.[3] Priests circulated among the soldiers beseeching them to stay in Ireland and preaching that they would be able to 'conduct God's work soon enough'. These troops dispersed to the countryside and trained more in their image. The 'wild Irish' harboured a deep sense of wrong within their isle, and the chieftains now planned, recruited and prepared.

Meanwhile, the English Parliament was preoccupied with the King, Scotland and the entirely unsatisfactory matter of Scottish troops on English soil at the nation's expense. As such they were ostensibly unsighted on events bubbling under in Ireland. Sir Phelim O'Neill, Colonel Hugh MacMahon, Lord Macguire and Rory O'More, and many others, hatched plans to capture the strongholds in the north of Ireland and orchestrate the overthrow of the plantation of Ulster.[4] These Catholic leaders justified their crusade among the people on the premise that the dominance of Puritanism among members of the English Parliament would be rigidly enforced in Ireland, and result in a fundamentalist drive to eradicate Catholicism altogether. It was a powerful call to arms.[5]

When the rebellion broke in Ulster on 22 October 1641 it took many in the Protestant establishment by complete surprise. The insurgents captured the castles at Dungannon and Montjoy by ruse, but their attempt to capture the strategically important castle at Dublin on 23 October eluded them. O'Neill then turned his attention to the castles, fortified houses and towns in Armagh and Monaghan; both counties were quickly overwhelmed by the insurgents. The counties of Cavan and Fermanagh were similarly engulfed, but with less success, while the movement spread from Ulster into Leinster. The insurgents moved south and fought against the government forces in County Wicklow, south of Dublin, and invested the fortress at Drogheda. When surprise had run its course, the northern counties in Ulster quickly and efficiently mobilized in their collective defence. Belfast was secured and the defence of Tyrone was similarly successful thanks, in the main, to the deployment of the Lagan Force.[6] However, by the end of the year the uprising had spread to much of the country, and by early 1642 the remaining counties were either overrun or in a state of emergency. Much has been written about the atrocities committed by both sides – by Catholics during the initial uprising and by Protestants in those areas where the uprising was subsequently 'contained'. Most of these stories have been exaggerated. Far more people, on both sides of the divide, died through starvation and disease than through insurgency or counter-insurgency actions.[7]

The Protestant response within Ireland came from three sources: from within the country, from troops sent from England and from a Covenanter force sent over from Scotland. Within Ireland the Protestant community rallied quickly and raised troops to supplement the elements of the Irish army that had not been turned. In late 1641 this force was over 2,000 foot and 1,000 horse and rose considerably over the coming months. James Butler, the Earl of Ormond, was the commander-in-chief of the government forces. He had moved with haste to Dublin at the outbreak of hostilities, from where he coordinated the government's response. Reinforcements arrived from England in late 1641, and more in February 1642, enabling Ormond to take the offensive. However, it was the arrival of a large Scottish Covenanter army in April 1642, under the command of Major General Robert Monro, that enabled the Protestants to clear much of east Ulster by the summer of 1642. The initial force was 2,500 men but this was constantly reinforced throughout the year, and by the beginning of 1643 this force numbered 11,371 officers and men.[8] The King, having made peace with the Covenanters and secured them as allies, now considered their use in England, once the problems in Ireland had been resolved. It was a dangerous red line.

It is difficult to state with any accuracy the size of the Irish insurgent forces. Certainly, O'Neill's force was many thousand and enjoyed success in the opening insurrection and at the Battle of Julianstown in November 1641, where he ambushed a relief force destined for Drogheda. But at much

---

1   Kenyon & Ohlmeyer, *Military History*, p. 29. Indeed, they provided evidence against Strafford at his trial at Westminster.

2   Ibid., p. 29.

3   Hamilton, *Irish Rebellion*, chapter XII.

4   Ibid., p. 29.

5   Hamilton suggests a less patriotic driver – that many of the ringleaders were heavily in debt and missed the 'olden days' when they could levy rates on the country – and attributes their financial difficulties to English rule rather than their financial extravagance. Hamilton, op. cit., chapter X.

6   A Protestant force raised by Sir Robert Stewart on hearing of the rising. Hamilton, op. cit., chapter XIX.

7   Kenyon & Ohlmeyer, op. cit., p. 74.

8   Ibid, p. 48.

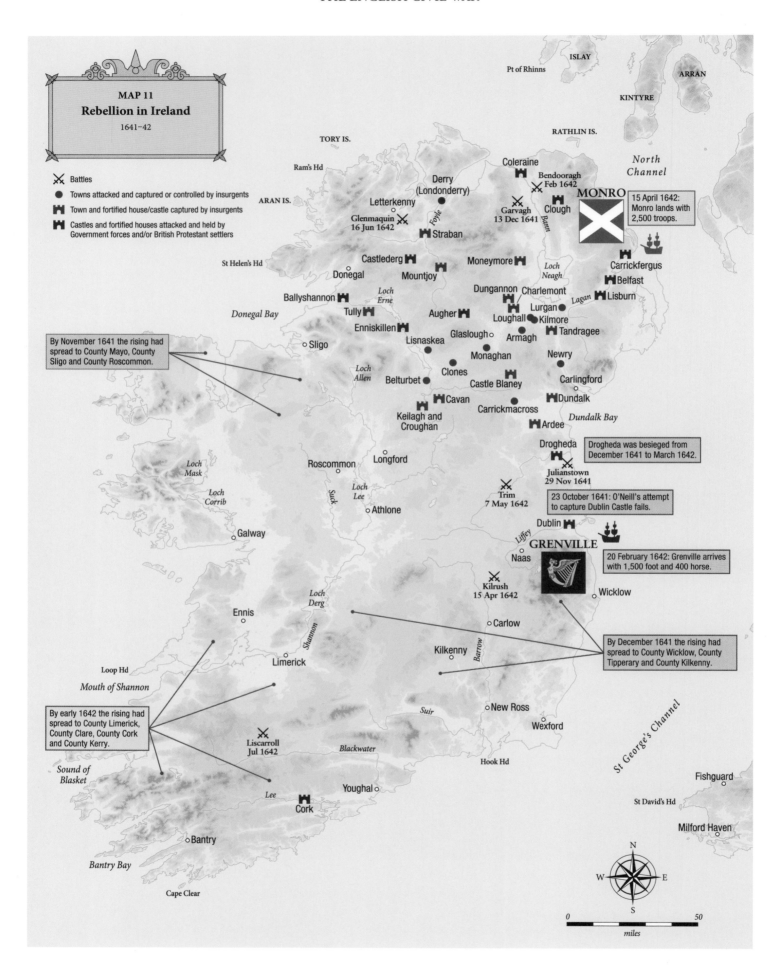

MAP 11
Rebellion in Ireland
1641–42

✕ Battles

● Towns attacked and captured or controlled by insurgents

🏰 Town and fortified house/castle captured by insurgents

🏰 Castles and fortified houses attacked and held by
Government forces and/or British Protestant settlers

ISLAY

Pt of Rhinns

ARRAN

KINTYRE

TORY IS.

RATHLIN IS.

North
Channel

Ram's Hd

Coleraine

Bendooragh
Feb 1642

MONRO

ARAN IS.

Letterkenny

Derry
(Londonderry)

Garvagh
13 Dec 1641

Clough

15 April 1642:
Monro lands with
2,500 troops.

St Helen's Hd

Glenmaquin
16 Jun 1642

Foyle

Straban

Castlederg

Moneymore

Loch
Neagh

Carrickfergus

Donegal

Mountjoy

Dungannon

Charlemont

Belfast

Ballyshannon

Loch
Erne

Augher

Loughall

Lagan

Lisburn

Lurgan

Donegal Bay

Tully

Kilmore

Enniskillen

Glaslough

Tandragee

Lisnaskea

Armagh

Newry

Sligo

Monaghan

By November 1641 the rising had
spread to County Mayo, County
Sligo and County Roscommon.

Loch
Allen

Belturbet

Clones

Castle Blaney

Carlingford

Cavan

Carrickmacross

Dundalk

Keilagh and
Croughan

Ardee

Dundalk Bay

Longford

Roscommon

Loch
Mask

Longford

Drogheda

Drogheda was besieged from
December 1641 to March 1642.

Loch
Corrib

Suck

Loch
Lee

Julianstown
29 Nov 1641

Athlone

Trim
7 May 1642

23 October 1641: O'Neill's attempt
to capture Dublin Castle fails.

Galway

Dublin

GRENVILLE

Liffey

Naas

20 February 1642: Grenville arrives
with 1,500 foot and 400 horse.

Ennis

Loch
Derg

Kilrush
15 Apr 1642

Wicklow

Shannon

Loop Hd

Carlow

Mouth of Shannon

Limerick

Kilkenny

Barrow

By December 1641 the rising had
spread to County Wicklow, County
Tipperary and County Kilkenny.

By early 1642 the rising had
spread to County Limerick,
County Clare, County Cork
and County Kerry.

Liscarroll
Jul 1642

Suir

New Ross

Blackwater

Wexford

Hook Hd

St George's Channel

Youghal

Fishguard

Lee

St David's Hd

Cork

Milford Haven

Sound of
Blasket

Bantry

Bantry Bay

Cape Clear

N

W   E

S

0   50
miles

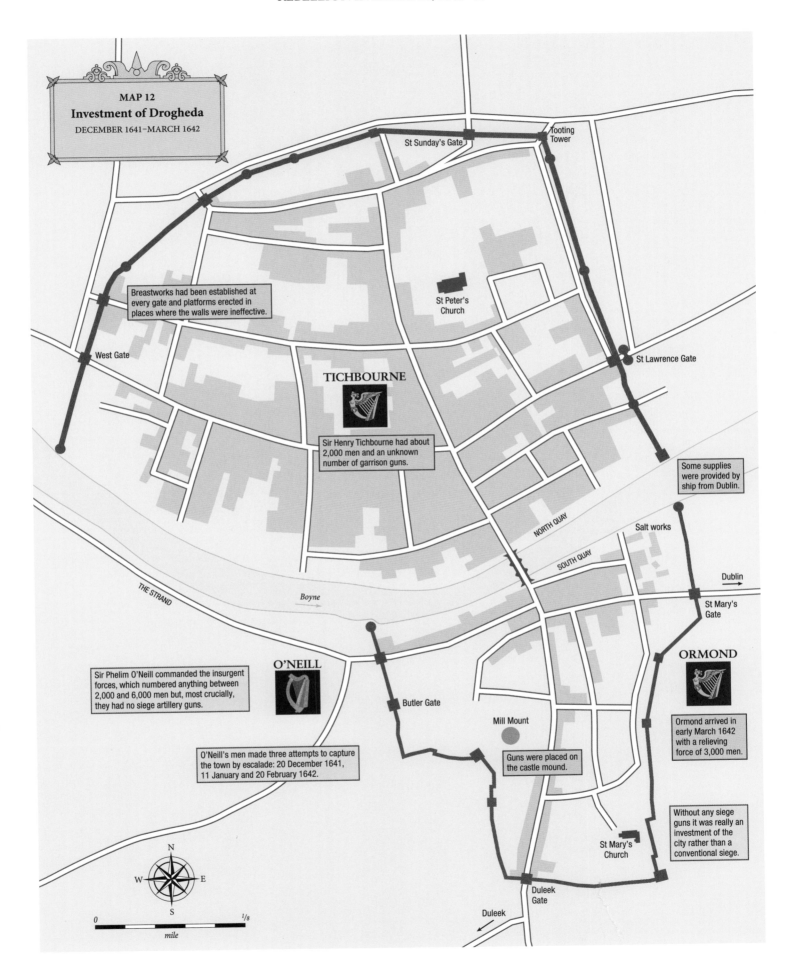

MAP 12
Investment of Drogheda
DECEMBER 1641–MARCH 1642

St Sunday's Gate

Tooting Tower

Breastworks had been established at every gate and platforms erected in places where the walls were ineffective.

St Peter's Church

West Gate

St Lawrence Gate

TICHBOURNE

Sir Henry Tichbourne had about 2,000 men and an unknown number of garrison guns.

Some supplies were provided by ship from Dublin.

NORTH QUAY

Salt works

SOUTH QUAY

Dublin

THE STRAND

Boyne

St Mary's Gate

O'NEILL

Sir Phelim O'Neill commanded the insurgent forces, which numbered anything between 2,000 and 6,000 men but, most crucially, they had no siege artillery guns.

Butler Gate

Mill Mount

ORMOND

Ormond arrived in early March 1642 with a relieving force of 3,000 men.

O'Neill's men made three attempts to capture the town by escalade: 20 December 1641, 11 January and 20 February 1642.

Guns were placed on the castle mound.

Without any siege guns it was really an investment of the city rather than a conventional siege.

St Mary's Church

N
W   E
S

Duleek Gate

Duleek

0   1/8
mile

the same time as this brief victory, the momentum of the rebellion had begun to wane. O'Neill was finally defeated by the Lagan Force, under Sir Robert and Sir William Stewart, at the Battle of Glenmaquin on 16 June 1642. Around Dublin, Ormond's two key lieutenants, Sir Charles Coote and Sir Henry Tichbourne, began to turn the tide. Coote routed the Irish south of the city at Swords in January and then gained a significant victory at Kilrush in April, while Tichbourne raised the second siege of Drogheda in March and went on to recapture a number of strongholds in County Louth. In August 1642, in the south-west, Lord Inchiquin defeated the Munster insurgents under Garret Barry, killing over 700 men in what was to be a major setback for the rebels. The anti-Catholic coalition of locally raised Protestant forces, English reinforcements and Monro's Scots was enough to turn the tide, but their ability to completely subdue the country was hampered by a lack of supplies, the creation of the Irish Catholic Confederation and the outbreak of civil war in England in August 1642.

By late 1642 the shortcomings of a sporadic rebellion were becoming more apparent. A Catholic bishop, Nicholas French, approached a number of Irish nobles in an attempt to coordinate efforts.[9] The Irish Catholic Confederation was formed after an assembly at Kilkenny in October 1642. Its aims were similar to those of Phelim O'Neill but the Confederation realized a need to organize the Irish Catholic war effort against the English and Scottish armies and, by so doing, prevent the renewed subjugation of the nation. In reality, the Confederation was an attempt by the Catholic clergy to legitimize the rebellion and to exert some form of control over the Catholic cause. It was not a simple and straightforward task in bringing the disparate rebel groups to heel, but once corralled, the Confederation was a powerful force. As well as providing military focus, they created a council for each province and a national council for Ireland. This provincial government provided a new civil, legal and military administration for Ireland, and vowed to punish crimes by Confederate soldiers and to excommunicate any Catholic caught fighting against the Confederation. They sent agents to France, Spain and Italy in order to gain financial and moral support and, by so doing, they encouraged a number of Irish officers to return home. Four military districts were established: Owen Roe O'Neill took command in Ulster; his rival Thomas Preston assumed leadership of the Leinster army; Garret Barry was named commander in Munster, and John Burke was appointed lieutenant general in Connacht.[10]

Notwithstanding their apparently overt support for the King, the Irish Confederates remained as contemptuous of the King's prerogative as the Scottish Covenanters and the English Parliamentarians. The Irish were clear that the Confederation was a provisional government, 'to consult of an order for their own affairs, till his Majesty's wisdom had settled the present troubles'.[11] Their charter and royal endorsement was known as the 'Proclamation of Dungannon'. This declaration, produced by O'Neill on 24 October 1641, set out the justification for the Catholic uprising and, most significantly, it claimed that the King had signed it personally. By so doing O'Neill made the open suggestion that the King had commanded him to lead Irish Catholics in defence of the Kingdom of Ireland against Protestants who sympathized with Charles's opponents in England's Parliament.[12] This endorsement by the King, almost certainly a cunning sham, was enough to convince the Covenanters of renewed royal duplicity and to create a highly charged atmosphere in Westminster.

---

9   The Irish Catholic nobles included Viscount Gormanston, Viscount Mountgarret and Viscount Muskerry.

10 Meehan, *Confederation of Kilkenny*, p. 44.

11 Ibid., p. 43.

12 There is evidence that the commission was a forgery, the seal attached to it having been taken from another document.

CHAPTER 4
THE ROAD TO CIVIL WAR, 1641–42

News of rebellion in Ireland came as a surprise and shock to Charles and the English and Scottish Parliaments. However, once the surprise had abated, stories of atrocities against Protestants served as an unwelcome distraction for Charles but played directly into the hands of both the Junto and the Covenanters. Pym, not a man to miss an opportunity, capitalized on this manifest and blatant Popish threat, and the King's apparent duplicity, and set about using the tragedy as an attack on what remained of the royal power. For the Covenanters, the use of their army to protect Protestants and restore order gave them a powerful lever in relations with both Charles and the English Parliament. At the start of 1642, therefore, the matters and concerns of the three kingdoms were interwoven and interdependent. In order to understand how and why this was the case it is necessary to run through the extraordinary events of 1641.

Since Newburn Ford (August 1640) Charles had been in a desperate position, with his authority and finances threatened. He had shown considerable conciliation, albeit tinged with the occasional threat, in an apparently despairing attempt to appear assertive. He had agreed to the Triennial Bill in February. He had lost his principal advisors, Strafford and Lord, and suffered the ignominy of signing the former's death warrant in May, an action which energized the Junto to issue a fresh set of power-curtailing initiatives. Ship Money was declared illegal, along with revenue raised through Tonnage and Poundage, leaving the King with few sources of income. The Star Chamber was abolished along with the Court of the High Commission; the latter was an ecclesiastical organ which had spent much of the previous decade instigating Laudian initiatives. In June, Pym introduced the Ten Propositions, designed to increase Parliament's control over the King's advisors, remove Catholics from court and, for reasons of national security, to place the navy and army in 'safer' hands and to overhaul the militia. Charles felt continually backed into a corner and was furious at Parliament's continued appetite for manipulation.

Yet there is evidence that for all the King's concessions he was merely vying for support and playing for time. He made belated attempts to win the support of Robert Devereux, the Earl of Essex, by appointing him to the King's Privy Council and subsequently to Lord Chamberlain, a position which gave him command of all armed forces south of the River Trent. Public opinion, which had reached fever pitch at Strafford's execution, began to swing back in the monarch's favour. The Ten Propositions were an attempt to curtail that slide and a calculated, if somewhat frantic, reaction to the King's carefully thought-out decision to travel to Scotland. It was feared, not without grounds, that Charles's intentions were to gather and rally the (remnants of the) English and (possibly) the Scottish armies and march on Westminster. Parliament were galvanized into paying off the Scots, thereby securing the removal of the Covenanter army from English soil (25 August), and paying arrears to the English army in the north and ordering its disbandment (18 September).

Charles arrived in Scotland in mid-August and pursued a characteristically duplicitous policy of appeasing the Covenanters while attempting to exploit their growing authoritarianism. A plot emerged of a plan to kill the Covenanter nobles, and the Junto seized on this rumour of a royal plot to regain control north of the border through murder and intrigue. It sent shockwaves through Westminster just as Parliament reassembled after their summer recess. With Charles away, and having made inadequate provision for government in his absence, the Junto seized the moment. Pym raised the heat with news of plots north of the border. Were there similar plans for Westminster? Elements of the Ten Propositions were resurrected and he attempted to get rid of the King's supporters in the House of Lords and expel the 13 bishops in situ there. At this moment, news of the Irish rebellion reached Parliament. Its arrival deflated Pym's crusade and gave Charles a badly needed 'get out of jail' card on his return from Scotland. The King proposed the raising of an army of 10,000 to go to Ireland, but Parliament saw through the trickery. The month of December witnessed furious manoeuvring by both sides.

On 1 December, the Grand Remonstrance was issued to the King, having passed the House a month earlier while Charles was still in Scotland. 'Lengthy, prolix, strident and frequently confused it was both a list of demands and a restatement of past grievances, more of a public manifesto than the petition it claimed to be.'[1] Many resented Pym's high-handed tactics within Parliament and a sizeable vote against the Remonstrance indicated growing support for the King. Charles was angry that the manifesto had already been published without a chance to rebuff it behind the scenes, particularly in view of the manifest threat to national security posed by rebellion in Ireland. He responded by discharging the guard of the House of Commons, relinquishing Essex's control of the militia forces, dismissing William Balfour as Lieutenant of the Tower of London and replacing him with the psychotic Colonel Thomas Lunsford.[2] With growing civil unrest in the capital and evidence that Pym intended to impeach the Queen (for her overt and 'dangerous' support of Catholicism) the King decided to act. With evidence, purportedly gleaned from his trip to Scotland, that Pym and his supporters had encouraged the Scots to invade England, Charles decided to indict Pym and four other *treasonous* Members of Parliament; John Hampden, Arthur Haselrig, Denzil Holles and William Strode. The King's attempts to achieve this were, however, frustrated and so, on 4 January 1642, he decided to take the matter into his own hands and arrest the members himself at the head of an armed guard. As it transpired, the members in question had been alerted to the plot and fled the House. Charles blundered into the executive chamber; he had operated outside the law and by so doing he had united the Houses in opposition, ignored Parliamentary privilege, committed a tragic gaffe and set in motion events that were to prove fatal to the nation.

To understand why they were fatal it is important to consider three aspects, which alone were curable but when mixed together, rather like charcoal, sulphur and saltpetre, were highly explosive. The first is religion.

---

1 Royale, *Three Kingdoms*, p. 150.
2 Lunsford's appointment caused uproar and Charles was forced to replace him at the end of the month with John Byron.

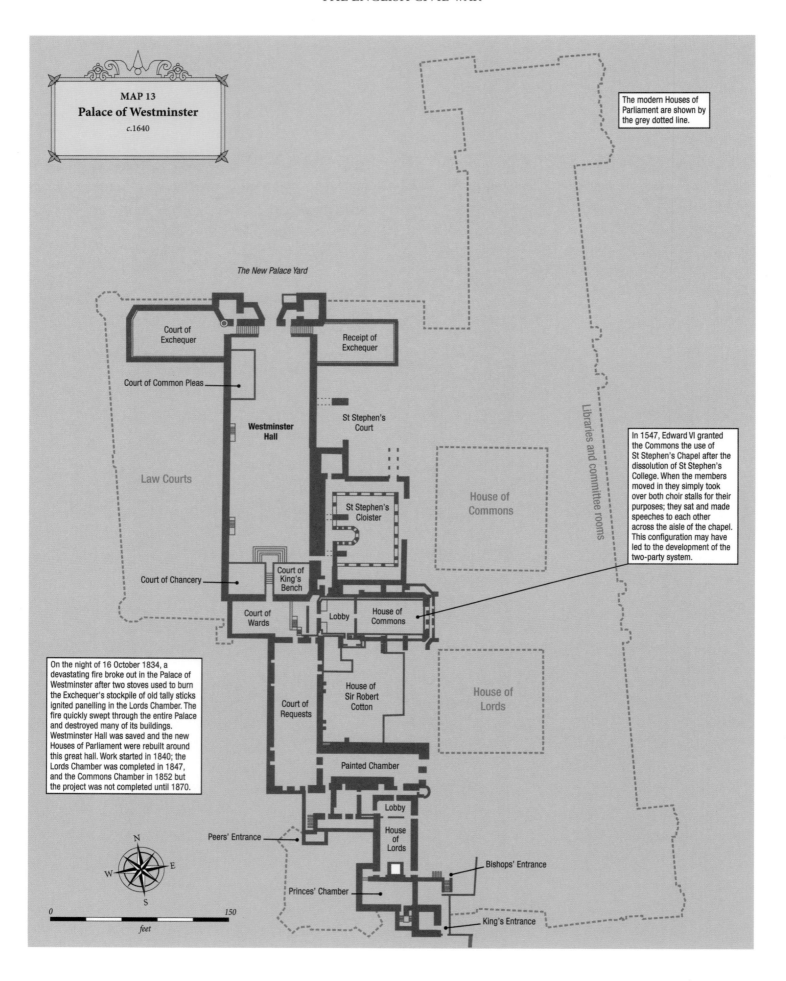

MAP 13
Palace of Westminster
c.1640

The modern Houses of Parliament are shown by the grey dotted line.

The New Palace Yard

Court of Exchequer

Receipt of Exchequer

Court of Common Pleas

St Stephen's Court

Westminster Hall

Law Courts

St Stephen's Cloister

House of Commons

In 1547, Edward VI granted the Commons the use of St Stephen's Chapel after the dissolution of St Stephen's College. When the members moved in they simply took over both choir stalls for their purposes; they sat and made speeches to each other across the aisle of the chapel. This configuration may have led to the development of the two-party system.

Court of Chancery

Court of King's Bench

Court of Wards

Lobby

House of Commons

House of Lords

On the night of 16 October 1834, a devastating fire broke out in the Palace of Westminster after two stoves used to burn the Exchequer's stockpile of old tally sticks ignited panelling in the Lords Chamber. The fire quickly swept through the entire Palace and destroyed many of its buildings. Westminster Hall was saved and the new Houses of Parliament were rebuilt around this great hall. Work started in 1840; the Lords Chamber was completed in 1847, and the Commons Chamber in 1852 but the project was not completed until 1870.

Court of Requests

House of Sir Robert Cotton

Libraries and committee rooms

Painted Chamber

Lobby

House of Lords

Peers' Entrance

Bishops' Entrance

Princes' Chamber

King's Entrance

N
W E
S

0 150
feet

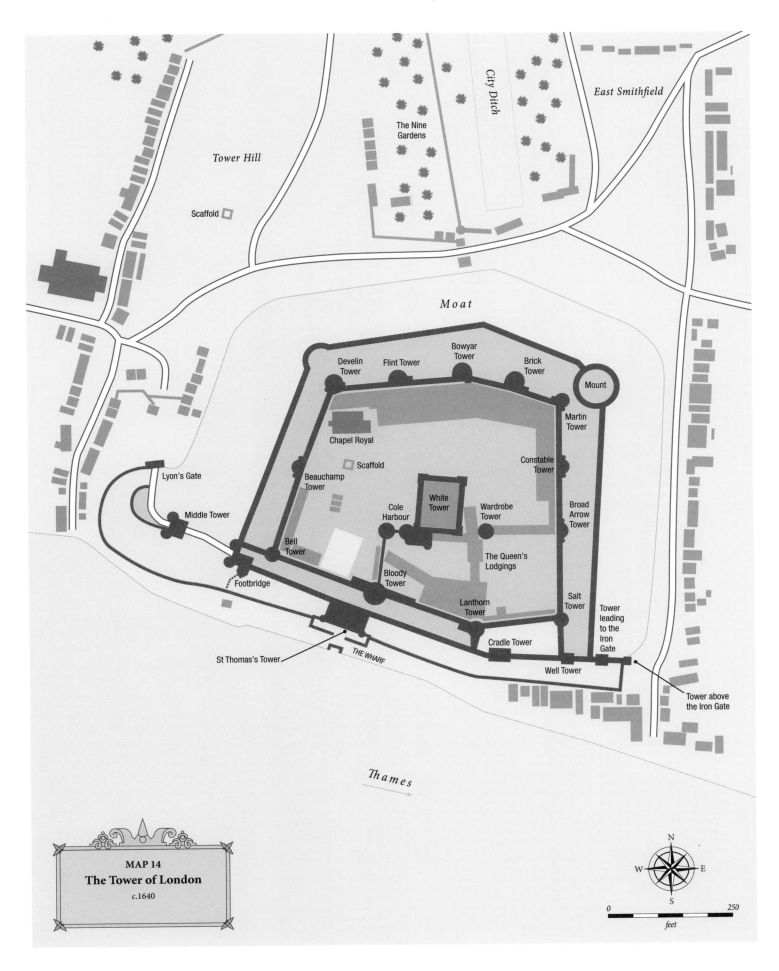

Tower Hill

Scaffold

City Ditch

The Nine
Gardens

East Smithfield

Moat

Develin
Tower

Flint Tower

Bowyar
Tower

Brick
Tower

Mount

Martin
Tower

Chapel Royal

Scaffold

Constable
Tower

Beauchamp
Tower

White
Tower

Wardrobe
Tower

Broad
Arrow
Tower

Lyon's Gate

Cole
Harbour

Middle Tower

Bell
Tower

The Queen's
Lodgings

Bloody
Tower

Footbridge

Lanthorn
Tower

Salt
Tower

Tower
leading
to the
Iron
Gate

Cradle Tower

St Thomas's Tower

THE WHARF

Well Tower

Tower above
the Iron Gate

Thames

MAP 14
The Tower of London
*c.*1640

N
W   E
S

0   250
feet

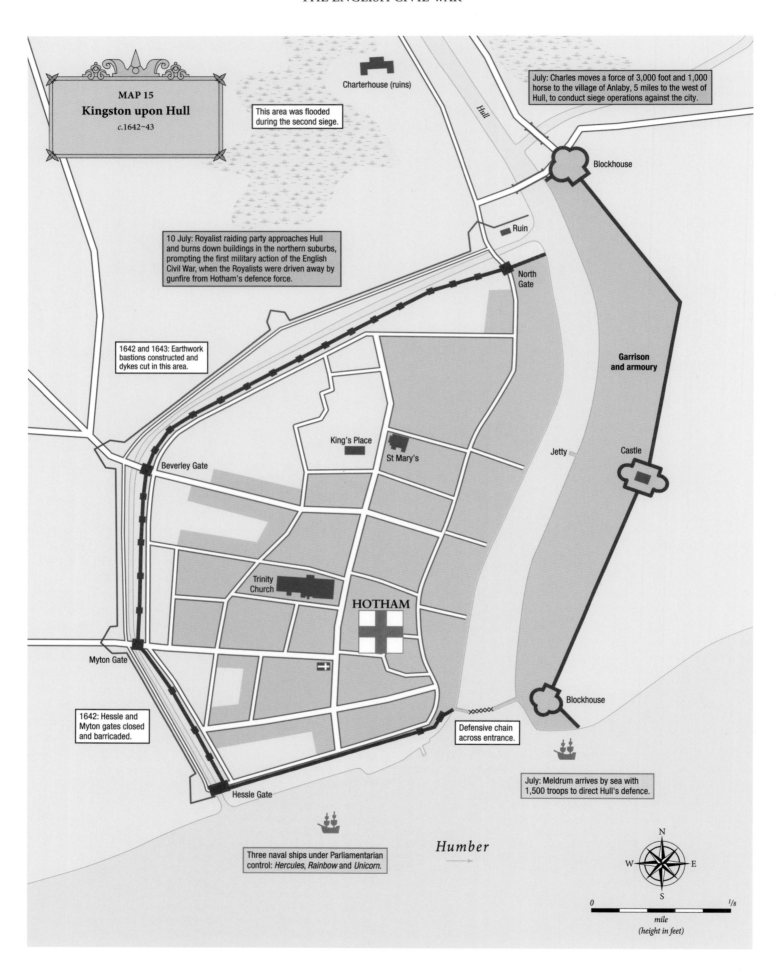

MAP 15

Kingston upon Hull

*c.*1642–43

Charterhouse (ruins)

This area was flooded during the second siege.

July: Charles moves a force of 3,000 foot and 1,000 horse to the village of Anlaby, 5 miles to the west of Hull, to conduct siege operations against the city.

Hull

Blockhouse

Ruin

10 July: Royalist raiding party approaches Hull and burns down buildings in the northern suburbs, prompting the first military action of the English Civil War, when the Royalists were driven away by gunfire from Hotham's defence force.

North Gate

Garrison and armoury

1642 and 1643: Earthwork bastions constructed and dykes cut in this area.

King's Place

St Mary's

Jetty

Castle

Beverley Gate

Trinity Church

HOTHAM

Myton Gate

Blockhouse

1642: Hessle and Myton gates closed and barricaded.

Defensive chain across entrance.

July: Meldrum arrives by sea with 1,500 troops to direct Hull's defence.

Hessle Gate

Humber

Three naval ships under Parliamentarian control: *Hercules*, *Rainbow* and *Unicorn*.

N
W E
S

0   1/8

mile

(height in feet)

Many of Parliament's initiatives encouraged widespread support while others caused deep division. The failure of the Root and Branch Petition, an attempt to abolish the power and structure of the bishops, proved too controversial for many moderates. The fundamentalist nature of Puritanism led to a religious extremism that spiralled out of control and challenged social cohesion. Counter positions in the sectarian debate, including from women (contentious in itself in 17th-century England), threatened to tear the Puritan cause apart and were, consequently, the underlying cause of many of Parliament's initiatives in this pivotal period. The second aspect concerned the publication of the 'Proceedings of Parliament' on 30 November 1641. This was, to all intents and purposes, the beginning of the English national press. Both sides used this new weapon and the print culture, or pamphlet wars, was central to reaching out to a wide audience and influencing key issues. According to historian C. V. Wedgwood, 'The close-printed octavo sheets were passed from hand to hand, were read aloud in ale-houses and brought out to illustrate points of argument, were packed into carriers' carts to keep country readers informed of what went on in the capital.'[3] The final aspect, and connected with and through the first two subject areas, was that of the masses or mob mentality. The rioting of 1640–42 was considerably more violent than hitherto and often political and religious in nature. The people, sensing their new-found strength, borne from disorganized leadership and a challenge to the natural order, began taking the law into their own hands. In London, the key geographic point of friction, the mob was clearly encouraged in its pursuits by many in the Junto – a point supported by the fact that their targets were, in almost every case, enemies of the more orthodox Puritans, those in favour of the Parliamentarian cause, and members of the Junto in particular, namely Catholics, Laudians and Courtiers.[4]

Tensions, which had been simmering in the capital in December, now broke into open hostility and civil disturbance. The House appealed to the city authorities for military help. They responded by sending some of the London trained bands (militia forces) to guard them from the King's guards. A military stand-off ensued and the King had reason to fear for the safety of his family from both Parliament and the London mob. On 10 January, he left for Hampton Court and the following month the Queen was despatched to the Low Countries to raise funds and support for the King's cause. Charles had lost London, the nation's political and economic powerhouse, and with it he suffered his first, and arguably most significant, defeat of the impending war. The slow slide to conflict had begun. It commenced with the struggle for control of the military and naval forces, garrisons, coastal towns and arsenals. Parliament already had the London trained bands, and the great arsenal and stores in the Tower of London, but they reacted with skill and foresight by despatching John Hotham to take over the garrison and arsenal at Hull and by securing the equally significant arsenal at Portsmouth. Most importantly the navy, with the exception of a few officers and vessels, remained under Parliament's control. Charles, as the patron of the Royal Navy, was incensed, especially as the funding raised through Ship Money and put to use by him in furnishing a powerful navy, was now out of his hands and in those of his enemies.

Somewhat farcically, meanwhile, Parliament went about its business as usual and even maintained contact with the King under the auspices that his misdemeanours were the result of 'ill-influence from his ruffians and evil-counsellors'. Charles once again played for time. He agreed to the Bishops' Exclusion Bill (whereby bishops were removed from the Lords) but was not, for one moment, prepared to approve the Militia Bill, which proposed the handing over of command of the militia forces from King to Parliament. The raising of armies was now essential for success in countering the opposition and for the suppression of the Irish rebellion. For the King, the mechanism was in place for him to muster an army under the terms of the Commissions of Array.[5] For Parliament, no such apparatus existed and so they chose to take control of county militias through ordinance, namely legislation passed by Parliament that does not have the royal assent necessary to make it statute. Charles needed a base from which to govern and from where he could deal with the crises in England and Ireland. He headed north via Cambridge, where he heard an oration and tried to muster support. On 19 March, he entered York and established his temporary headquarters.

York was well positioned geographically to maintain contact with the Continent, to open negotiations with the Scots and to orchestrate the seizure of Hull and its arsenal, but despite this it was a poor substitute for London. Meanwhile, the Queen was having some success in raising support on the Continent and was collecting arms and volunteers with the help of Prince Rupert.[6] However, when support was not forthcoming from north of the border, Charles announced a somewhat hare-brained scheme, of proceeding to Ireland to lead the army in putting down the rebels. Most certainly he was contemplating a deal with the Confederates and the uniting of the two forces there for options in England.[7] Another significant blow to his plans was his failure to secure the arsenal and garrison at Hull, where the weapons from his northern army had been stored. Charles had appointed the Earl of Newcastle to the post of governor, but that position was already filled by Parliament's man, John Hotham. He was under clear instructions not to admit the King or any of his supporters. At the end of April, the King decided to make a personal appearance at the city gates, confident that Hotham would acquiesce. He was to be disappointed, but Parliament was taking no chances and in May they ordered the weapons stored there to be transferred to the Tower of London. Conscious of the importance of Hull, Charles managed to squirrel Lord Digby into the place, who eventually beguiled Hotham into yielding. In early July, the King made a show of investing the town, flooding the adjacent fields (see map 15) and erecting batteries, but at the vital hour Hotham appeared to lose his nerve. Parliament, concerned at the governor's questionable resolve, had sent John Meldrum to oversee the security of the key city, thereby undoing any intentions of Hotham to capitulate. Meldrum sallied from the fortress, destroyed the Royalist batteries and drove the investment force from the field.

It was a bitter blow, but Charles did have some successes in the north. Newcastle was seized on 17 June, and the magazines at Preston, Warrington and Liverpool were also in the custody of the King's supporters the same month. Events were now quickly moving towards war. Charles had also succeeded in persuading the Lord Keeper of the Great Seal to join him in York. This placed him at a distinct advantage as his proclamations were, in effect, legal. In response, on 1 June, Parliament had issued their Nineteen Propositions – to all intents and purposes, a demand for the King's unconditional surrender as well as a rehash of the earlier stipulations

---

3   Wedgwood, *The King's War*, p. 38.
4   Miller, *Execution of the King*, pp. 63–4.

5   A commission given by English sovereigns to the gentry to muster and array their inhabitants and to prepare them for war.
6   Prince Rupert was the third son of Charles I's sister Elizabeth, by her marriage to Frederick V, Elector of the Palatinate.
7   Royale, op. cit., p. 162.

within the Ten Propositions. The King's rejection of these proposals was the crossing of the Rubicon. In July Parliament voted to raise an army of 10,000 volunteers and a few days later command was, perhaps inevitably, given to the Earl of Essex. The two armies began to assemble and tensions increased across the country as both sides tried to recruit from the same pool and towns declared for King or Parliament. The two sides began to develop a definite shape but the divisions cannot be simplified along class lines. Most of the peers and greater landowners supported the King, and they brought with them (in many cases but not exclusively) their workers. However, other supporters were found, in large numbers and voluntarily, from the working classes in the major towns and cities. The universities and cathedral cities also sided with the monarchy. The Puritan gentry were exclusively on the side of the Parliamentarians as were religious dissenters; conversely, Catholics supported the King.

A generalization, but one that should be used with caution, is that the Midlands were split, the north and west (including Wales) sided with the King, and the south and east with Parliament. In reality every county, every city and town, and even some households were split in one shape or form under the slogan 'brother against brother and father against son'. Another generalization, but one worthy of mention, is that small, isolated and independent communities tended towards Parliament, while larger communities with mixed farming and communal commitments supported their masters and sided with the monarchy.[8] Recent academics have posited a connection between local economics and topography on one side, and popular culture and political allegiance on the other. However, subdivision along these lines does not fit comfortably across the country. For example, the aristocratic and courtly playground of Northamptonshire was also interwoven with pasture enclosure, owned largely by the new gentry whose sympathies lay preponderantly with Parliament.[9] Finally, it would be incorrect to assume that landowners' tenants blindly joined their masters, the Earls of Northumberland and Huntingdon failing miserably in this regard. The socio-economic background, religious persuasion and geographical influences as to the make-up of the civil war armies have been studied in enormous depth over the years and is beyond the scope of this work. However, one fact remains irrefutable: that the vast majority of the young and middle-aged men who found themselves mobilizing for war in 1642 did so with a mixture of indifference and curiosity.

With the trained bands, Parliament's mobilization was swift and relatively effective. Most of Essex's men came from the London trained bands and from the Surrey and Middlesex militia. At Northampton, more volunteer units joined the Parliamentarian army from the Midlands and East Anglia. There were a number of aristocrats listed among the officers general of the field, a few experienced veterans of the Thirty Years' War as well as some foreign military soldiers of fortune. At the back of the list of the troops of horse was the 43-year-old gentleman of Huntingdon, Oliver Cromwell – not unremarkable as a Member of Parliament but unknown and unfamiliar in terms of military prowess.[10] Charles's army, conversely, took more time to assemble but it also consisted of a number of foreign professionals as well as English and Scottish seasoned soldiers, such as the Catholic Arthur Aston who had served in the Russian, Polish and Swedish armies, and Jacob Astley who had amassed considerable experience fighting in Flanders and Germany during the Thirty Years' War under Christian IV of Denmark and Gustavus Adolphus of Sweden. Undoubtedly his most significant recruit was Prince Rupert, who reached the King at Nottingham on 21 August along with his younger brother Prince Maurice, named after the Dutch Protestant hero Maurice of Nassau who had died in 1625. Both armies had one thing in common: they were ill-trained and ill-prepared for the war on which they were about to embark.

Throughout August both sides continued to capture key installations and facilities. On 8 August, the Earl of Northampton captured the magazine at Banbury and marched to Warwick. Four days later the Parliamentarians captured Portsbridge, near Portsmouth, and closed in on the vital port from land and sea. Cromwell seized the magazine at Cambridge on 15 August, and a week later the Parliamentarians had another significant prize when they stormed and captured Dover Castle. At this stage the Parliamentarian navy was also operating with impunity along the south coast and once they had captured the Isle of Wight, the loss of Portsmouth was only a matter of time. It was to fall in early September and was a considerable loss to the Royalist cause, as it had been earmarked, in Charles's strategic plan, as the main port of disembarkation for troops from France.[11] In early August Charles moved from York, having sent word for a general rendezvous of Royalist forces at Nottingham. With his small force of infantry and horse he wound his way south and was received, with little enthusiasm, at Newark and Leicester before being rebuffed at Coventry. Henceforth, somewhat downcast, he headed directly to Nottingham where, in the driving rain, he raised his Royal Standard on 22 August. The ceremony was somewhat farcical and the Royal Standard did not last the night, succumbing to the high winds, but the intent was unmistakable: he was openly declaring war on those traitors in Parliament who had dared question his divine authority.

Over the coming days, during periods of self-doubt, Charles despatched two delegations to Westminster in order to offer terms. They were both rebuffed.[12] Three days later Essex departed the capital and marched towards the King's forces at Nottingham. His orders were to 'rescue Charles from his evil advisors and bring him back to London'. It was a political mission for a military operation and Essex knew only too well that in order to bring the King back he would have to defeat him in open battle.[13] Many of the Parliamentarian officers were uneasy. They knew what they were doing was both dangerous and treasonable: they had to win; their lives depended upon it. Parliament's force of 6,000 infantry and 4,000 horse was an army in name alone. Disparate groups banded together, lacking cohesion and discipline. As they marched north, through counties largely loyal to their own cause, they plundered houses and committed wilful acts of iconoclasm against artefacts considered Popish. Charles was delighted when he heard the news, considering it a wonderful recruiting tool for his cause. In reality, the Royalists were also indulging in criminal violence against the people and property and, as time went on, attacks on houses of opposition supporters was commonplace, a well-tried and tested weapon of war, particularly civil war. Within months, both armies were forced to improve the internal policing of their forces and to instigate martial law. For now, all Essex and his officers could do was to move the assembly to Northampton, bolster his numbers and shake the whole into a fighting body.

News of the size and movement of the Parliamentarian force prompted Charles to move west to Shrewsbury. This proved to be a more fruitful recruiting ground. Supporters rallied to the monarch in great numbers

8 Ackroyd, *History of England*, vol. III, p. 244.
9 Ashton, *Conservatism and Revolution*, pp. 79, 175, citing, Underdown, *Revel, Riot and Rebellion*.
10 Fortescue, *History of the British Army*, vol. I, p. 200.
11 This was not to happen, as Cardinal Richelieu had refused any requests to help Charles or his Queen.
12 Kenyon, *Civil Wars of England*, p. 34.
13 Royale, op. cit., p. 184.

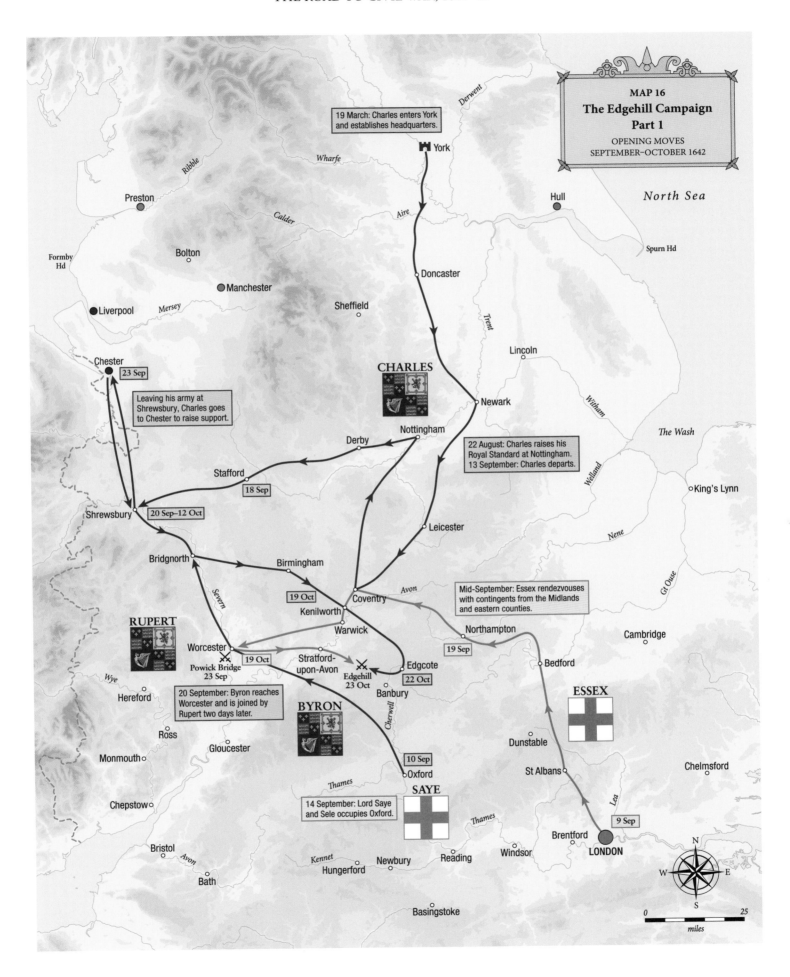

MAP 16

**The Edgehill Campaign
Part 1**

OPENING MOVES
SEPTEMBER–OCTOBER 1642

19 March: Charles enters York
and establishes headquarters.

North Sea

Spurn Hd

Hull

York

Wharfe

Derwent

Ribble

Calder

Aire

Preston

Trent

Doncaster

Bolton

Manchester

Sheffield

Liverpool

Mersey

Lincoln

The Wash

Chester

23 Sep

CHARLES

Newark

Witham

Leaving his army at
Shrewsbury, Charles goes
to Chester to raise support.

Nottingham

Derby

22 August: Charles raises his
Royal Standard at Nottingham.
13 September: Charles departs.

Welland

King's Lynn

Stafford

18 Sep

Nene

Leicester

Shrewsbury

20 Sep–12 Oct

Gt Ouse

Bridgnorth

Birmingham

Avon

Mid-September: Essex rendezvouses
with contingents from the Midlands
and eastern counties.

Severn

19 Oct

Coventry

RUPERT

Kenilworth

Cambridge

Warwick

Northampton

Worcester

19 Oct

19 Sep

Bedford

Powick Bridge
23 Sep

Stratford-
upon-Avon

Edgcote

22 Oct

ESSEX

Wye

Edgehill
23 Oct

Hereford

Banbury

BYRON

Cherwell

Dunstable

Chelmsford

Ross

20 September: Byron reaches
Worcester and is joined by
Rupert two days later.

Gloucester

10 Sep

St Albans

Monmouth

Oxford

Lea

SAYE

Chepstow

Thames

14 September: Lord Saye
and Sele occupies Oxford.

Thames

Brentford

9 Sep

Bristol

Avon

Kennet

Newbury

Reading

Windsor

LONDON

Hungerford

Bath

N

W   E

S

Basingstoke

0   25

miles

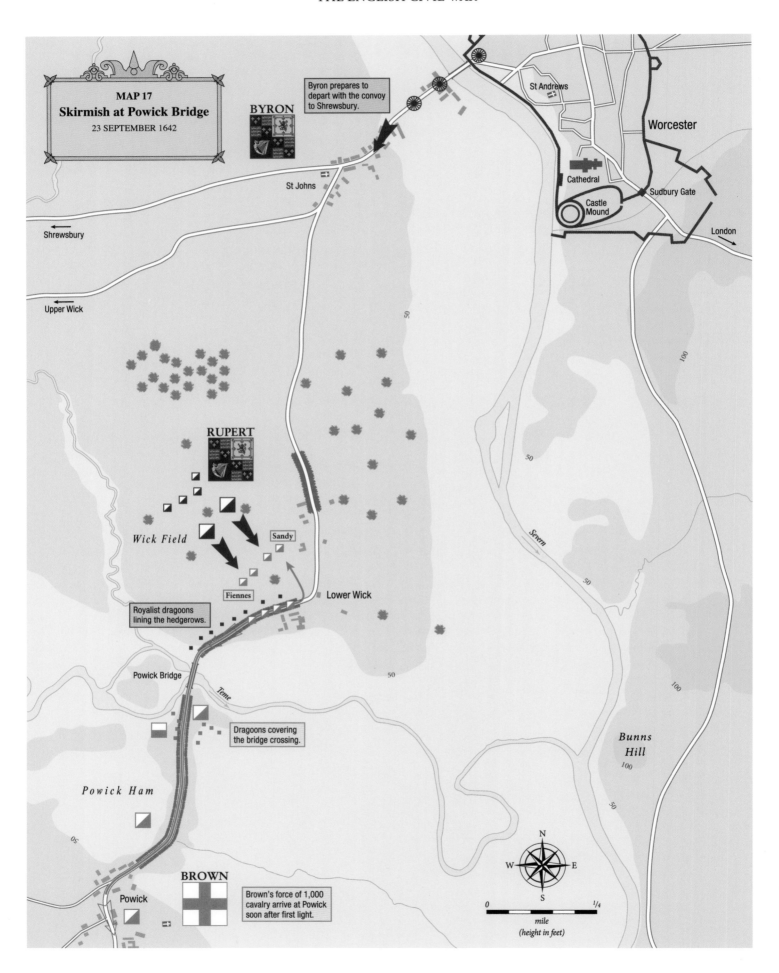

MAP 17

Skirmish at Powick Bridge

23 SEPTEMBER 1642

BYRON

Byron prepares to depart with the convoy to Shrewsbury.

St Johns

Shrewsbury

Upper Wick

Worcester

St Andrews

Cathedral

Castle Mound

Sudbury Gate

London

50

100

50

RUPERT

Wick Field

Sandy

Fiennes

Lower Wick

Royalist dragoons lining the hedgerows.

Severn

50

50

Powick Bridge

Teme

Dragoons covering the bridge crossing.

Powick Ham

50

Bunns Hill

100

100

50

BROWN

Powick

Brown's force of 1,000 cavalry arrive at Powick soon after first light.

N
W E
S

0   1/4

mile

(height in feet)

from Wales, Lancashire, Worcestershire and Shropshire, although the quality of many recruits was questionable.[14] At much the same time, Parliament declared that those opposed to their intentions were 'delinquents whose property would be confiscated'. Designed to force the fence-sitters to act, this proclamation actually provided greater numbers for the Royalist cause, as many landowners flocked to raise forces for the King in the hope that their lives and estates might be protected.[15] Essex moved his army, which now numbered some 14,000, west towards Worcester in an attempt to shadow the King and block any attempt his force might make towards London. With his north flank exposed, Sir John Byron, commanding the Royalist garrison at Oxford, was ordered to abandon the city and to bring with him as much university plate as he could carry, as many students as he could muster, and as many horses as he could procure.

Byron pulled back to Worcester, arriving there on 20 September, and was joined two days later by a cavalry force of about a thousand horse under Rupert's command. However, Worcester's defences were in decay and in no position to withstand an attack. Byron had already elected to evacuate the town if confronted. Essex's army was at Alcester and Colonel Brown, commanding a body of cavalry in the vanguard, proposed an operation to try to capture Worcester by rapid movement of a large body of cavalry, as Captain Nathaniel Fiennes wrote:

> Collonel Brown, who being at Alcester with his Regiment of Dragoones and two Troops of Horse, under the command of Captain Nathaniell, and Captain John Fiennes, he went to my Lord General, and as it should seem suggested to his Excellency that with addition of some more Horse, he might do some service in surrounding the City of Worcester, before his Excellency came thither with his Army, and in keeping all supplies from going into the Town, and those Troops from going out that were already in it.[16]

Brown arrived in front of the city late in the day and tried to force entry at the Sudbury Gate. Having failed to gain entrance he pulled back and crossed the River Severn at Upton, about 8 miles to the south. His plan was to cut off Byron's force which, he anticipated, would evacuate the city by the old bridge over the River Severn on the arrival of Essex's main force from the east.

Brown's Horse began advancing north just before first light and reached Powick soon after dawn. Their southerly movement the previous day had been noticed and the possibility that they might try to advance on the west bank was well known to the Royalist defenders. At some stage during the morning Rupert moved his cavalry in to Wick Field, adjacent to the village of Lower Wick. His intentions are not entirely clear.

However, it is probable that he had deployed to the west bank to cover Byron's imminent withdrawal on the Shrewsbury road and deployed to cover the possibility of Brown's force coming up from the south. Supporting this assessment are the facts that his troopers and their mounts were resting in Wick Field and were not wearing armour.[17] As a precaution, some of the Royalist dragoons had been deployed in the hedges lining the road to the south. Brown had been informed by local Parliamentarian sympathizers that the column was poised to depart and ordered his cavalry to cross the bridge and cut off the large train. Colonel Edwin Sandy's troop crossed first and soon found themselves contained by the narrow lane and were suddenly fired upon by the concealed dragoons in the hedges either side of the track. 'Neither the Rear could be brought up, nor the Van make a Retreat', noted Colonel Edward Massey, the governor of Worcester.[18] Unable to turn, they spurred on their charges and emerged into the relatively open ground of Wick Field.[19]

The Royalists were undoubtedly surprised by the sudden appearance of Sandy's cavalry. The Parliamentarian horse was desperately trying to shake out and prepare to charge. However, Rupert reacted with the speed and awareness of a man far more familiar with the business of the sword. As the Royalist participant and historian the Earl of Clarendon recalled, 'the prince instantly declaring, that he would charge; his brother, the lord Digby, commissary general Wilmot, sir John Byron, sir Lewis Dives, and all those officers and gentlemen, whose troops were not present or ready, put themselves next the prince; the other wearied troops coming in order after them.'[20] The two bodies of cavalry closed at speed, the Royalists with swords in hand while the Parliamentarian troopers waited with loaded carbines and pistols.[21] Nathaniel Fiennes described the moment: 'We let them come up very near to our horses' noses… and then gave fire, and very well to my thinking… but of a sudden we found all the troops on both sides of us melted away, and our rear being carried with them.'[22] The Parliamentarian cavalry fled with the Royalists in pursuit, but the latter were held at the bridge by the dragoons Brown had deployed to cover the crossing. It was a minor engagement in the scheme of what was to come, but the significance of an early Royalist victory was well received by Charles and his men. Losses were no more than 40 or 50 from both sides, but Colonel Sandy was to die of his wounds and Captain Wingate and three Scottish officers were taken prisoner. The fleeing cavalry crossed back across the River Severn at Upton and, in so doing, panicked Essex's lifeguard. They also fled in confusion. Rupert and Byron joined Charles at Shrewsbury and the King now had two options. He could advance back south and engage Essex's army near Worcester, or he could try to give him the slip and march with speed on London. He chose the latter.

---

14 It is strange that no regiments can be directly attributable to the recruits from Worcestershire, Herefordshire and Shropshire in the King's ORBAT at Edgehill; it is assumed that the recruits were enlisted into existing regiments.

15 Ackroyd, op. cit., p. 248.

16 Fiennes, *Skirmish at Worcester.*

17 Willis Bund suggests that Rupert moved with some of his men before this, having heard that there were some Parliamentarians at Powick, *Worcestershire*, p. 42.

18 Corbet, *Gloucester*, p. 28.

19 Willis Bund makes no mention of the concealed dragoons.

20 Clarendon, *History of the Rebellion*, vol. III, p. 235.

21 Rupert had trained the Royalist cavalry in the Swedish style – charging with sword in hand and then reverting to pistols during the pursuit. The Parliamentarians were following the more traditional method of charging, or receiving the charge, by discharging their carbines and pistols and then attacking with the sword. See the chapter 'Civil War Armies'

22 Fiennes, op. cit.

CHAPTER 5

THE CAMPAIGN AND BATTLE OF EDGEHILL, JUNE TO OCTOBER 1642

Oh, Lord! thou knowest how busy I must be this day; if I forget thee, do not thou forget me!

Sir Jacob Astley, at the Battle of Edgehill

Before the King could begin his advance on London he needed to gather more troops. Furthermore, he remained desperately short of funds, and hope that Queen Henrietta Maria would ease the situation with support from the Continent was dealt a blow. The ship *Providence* had landed safely enough in Bridlington in July, but another was blown into Yarmouth and seized by the on-shore Parliamentarian forces, and two other ships were surrendered to Parliament by their own crews.[1] It was not, however, all bad news, for Patrick Ruthven, a professional soldier who had earned his spurs under Gustavus Adolphus, had arrived at Shrewsbury with a handful of experienced Scottish soldiers; and a few days later Thomas Bushell, a skilled engineer, arrived in the town from Wales. He brought with him more good news from across the border. A substantial number of Welsh levies had been recruited for the King's cause. They would take a while to mobilize and plans were made for them to join the King en route. Meanwhile, Essex was entirely content to wait for the King to make the first move. He anticipated a Royalist advance south, down the Severn valley, and established garrisons at Bewdley and Kidderminster in order to screen and counter any such move. He also bolstered the garrisons at Coventry, Warwick and Banbury in order to provide intelligence should the Royalists move through the Midlands. Finally, he made use of the time to better train and organize his main force at Worcester. The affair at Powick Bridge had been a rude reminder of the unproven battle hardiness of his army, and Essex instructed his officers to waste no time 'practising the ceremonious forms of military discipline' and to familiarize the men 'in the rudiments of war'.[2]

Across England acts of vandalism, iconoclasm and violence broke out as both sides jockeyed for position. In London, and the counties of Essex and Kent, Royalist dwellings and churches were targeted by supporters of Parliament. Cornwall had sided with the King but Devon lay in the balance, and both sides mobilized their trained bands. In the north, the Earl of Derby unsuccessfully laid siege to Manchester, while near York, the apparent Royalist stronghold was shaken when Cawood Castle (between York and Selby) was taken for Parliament. In London, the realization that Charles would most likely move to capture the city reenergized efforts to raise more men from within the city, and across the home counties, to replace those men who had marched west with Essex the previous month. London was an unfortified city and there was no time to build defences at this late stage. However, the strength of the city lay in the vigour of its citizens and within days the London trained bands were reporting 8,000 available for muster. Furthermore, the Committee of Safety had instructed the Earl of Warwick to hand over the reins as Admiral of the Fleet and assume command of this force and take responsibility for the vital defence of London.

By the second week of October, the King's army was deemed sufficiently strong to march towards and capture London. Rupert's force was sent as a vanguard, departing Shrewsbury on 10 October. The army followed two days later. Maps were in short supply, and those that did exist were lacking in detail. Instead commanders had to rely on their knowledge and instincts and here the Royalists had a marked advantage, as they knew the terrain far better than many of the Parliamentarian officers.[3] Local guides were also used throughout the war, with mixed results. The speed of advance was, however, painfully slow, allowing cavalry to ride ahead and clear and reconnoitre routes. The long-held perception that 'neither army knew where the other was' is almost certainly not the case.[4] Essex had been receiving continuous reports of the intentions and whereabouts of the King's army from a high-level spy who was Rupert's private secretary.[5] Charles was well aware of the approximate whereabouts of Essex's main body and decided to give it a wide berth. He crossed the River Severn at Bridgnorth, to a rapturous welcome, before pushing on to Wolverhampton, where he was joined by large numbers of the anticipated Welsh levies. The crossing of the River Severn was a clear declaration of intent by the King's army, but Essex wanted confirmation that the entire Royalist army had followed before he gave the order for his army to march east and intercept. On 17 October, the King's army reached Birmingham, where the locals were less welcoming, hurling abuse and seizing the tail-end wagons, some of which were conveying the royal plate. The same day, Rupert skirmished with Parliamentarian cavalry at King's Norton, a few miles south of the city. The next day, news of this encounter arrived at Essex's headquarters near Worcester and he gave immediate orders for his army to march east towards the Parliamentarian base at Warwick.

The Royalists, not wishing to get bogged down, bypassed the strong fortress at Warwick and moved towards Banbury, where they intended to attack the small Parliamentarian force and force the road to London. However, the King's intentions were soon discovered when Captain John Bridges captured a copy of the orders from a Royalist supply train which had ventured too close to Warwick Castle.[6] Essex quickly redirected his army south and issued orders that the next rendezvous was to be at Kineton. On the night of 22 October, the Royalist quarters were widely scattered between Cropredy and Edgcote (about 4 miles north-east of Banbury). Richard Bulstrode, a Royalist cavalry officer, recalled events that night:

---

1 Gardiner, *Great Civil War*, vol. I, p. 37.

2 Wedgwood, *The King's War*, p. 123.

---

3 John Speed's 1610 national survey had little military value.

4 Clarendon, *History of the Rebellion*, vol. II, p. 356.

5 Ellis, *Military Intelligence*, p. 77; Warburton, *Prince Rupert*, vol. II, p. 4. His name was Blake. His letters were in Essex's cabinet, which was captured by the Royalists after the battle. Blake was subsequently tried and hanged in Oxford.

6 It is possible that Essex already had this intelligence from Blake.

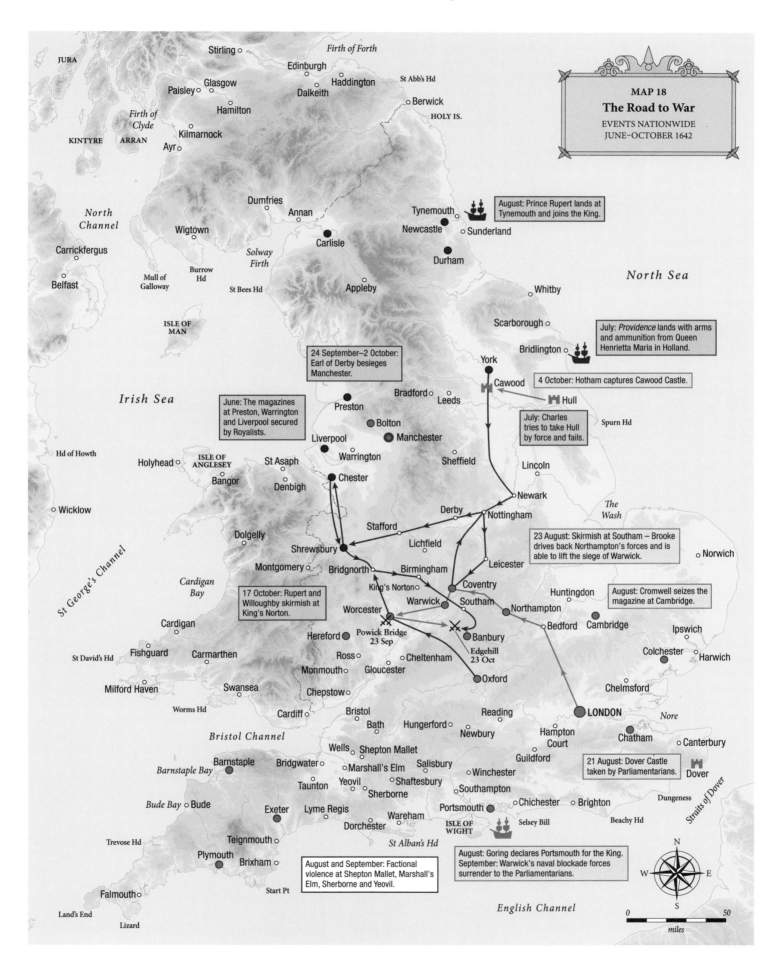

MAP 18
The Road to War
EVENTS NATIONWIDE
JUNE–OCTOBER 1642

August: Prince Rupert lands at Tynemouth and joins the King.

July: *Providence* lands with arms and ammunition from Queen Henrietta Maria in Holland.

24 September–2 October: Earl of Derby besieges Manchester.

4 October: Hotham captures Cawood Castle.

June: The magazines at Preston, Warrington and Liverpool secured by Royalists.

July: Charles tries to take Hull by force and fails.

23 August: Skirmish at Southam – Brooke drives back Northampton's forces and is able to lift the siege of Warwick.

August: Cromwell seizes the magazine at Cambridge.

17 October: Rupert and Willoughby skirmish at King's Norton.

21 August: Dover Castle taken by Parliamentarians.

August: Goring declares Portsmouth for the King. September: Warwick's naval blockade forces surrender to the Parliamentarians.

August and September: Factional violence at Shepton Mallet, Marshall's Elm, Sherborne and Yeovil.

Powick Bridge
23 Sep

Edgehill
23 Oct

0   miles   50

The Prince of Wales's Regiment in which we were, was quartered in two or three Villages under Wormington Hills [Edgehill]. When it was dark, we saw several Fires not far from us, and sending out a Party to see, we were soon informed, that the Earl of Essex was there with his whole Army, and quartered at Keinton, a Market-Town. Whereupon our whole Regiment drew into the fields, and had provisions brought to us from the villages, and we forthwith gave notice to the King and Prince Rupert, and soon after we received Orders to be upon our Guard all night, and to be the next morning by Eight, at the Rendezvous upon Wormington Hills.[7]

Rupert's cavalry were the first troops to assemble on the great hill that the locals called 'Edge Hill'. It commanded views to the west across the Vale of the Red Horse and the village of Kineton, Essex's headquarters. It was 'a faire meadowe land', narrowing as it receded, between some rows of hedges and patches of thick brushwood.[8] Throughout the morning the Royalist troops and artillery wound their way from their bivouac areas towards the hill; the last did not arrive until 2pm. Essex's plan for 23 October had been to march in relief of the small Parliamentarian garrison at Banbury. His army was widely spread, some units as far as 20 miles from Kineton; indeed, many troops of horse were late for the subsequent battle and some did not make it at all. At about 8am, Essex was on his way to church at St Peter's (Kineton) when the alarm was raised. Immediate orders were given for the army to deploy into the open ground east of Kineton and riders were despatched with alacrity to hasten the arrival of John Hampden and the artillery.[9] Charles arrived at the north end of Edgehill, known as Knowle End, at about midday and, as he surveyed the Parliamentarian army deploying in the meadow below, he called for a council of war. Bulstrode sets the scene:

[The council] debated, whether to march towards London, or to march back, and fight the Enemy, who we saw from the Hill, embattelling their Army in the Bottom near Keinton [Kineton]. To march from them was thought dishonourable, as if we feared them, and they would be sure to follow, and give us continual Trouble in our March, when we should not, perhaps find so good Occasion to fight them; and so it was resolved, that we should go down the Hill and attack them.[10]

Rupert began giving the King advice as to how best to organize the army to counter the Parliamentarian forces deploying before them. Rupert proposed the Swedish system, which the Lord General, the Earl of Lindsey, objected to, favouring the simpler German system.[11] Charles opted for the former, prompting Lindsey to inform the King that 'since his Majestie thought him not fitt to perform the office of Commander in Chief, he would serve him as Collonell'.[12] He then went off to command his regiment of foot and

Field Marshal Ruthven was elevated in his stead (see appendix 1 for the details of the two armies). It was an inauspicious start, which speaks volumes about command and control of armies during the civil wars. Throughout the morning, the Parliamentarians continued to deploy. Essex and his officers were able to ride forward into the Vale of the Red Horse and reconnoitre the best positions. He decided to take advantage of the higher ground and the hedges on the flanks to conceal his dismounted dragoons and commanded musketeers. In the centre he adopted the chequerboard deployment with a front and second line favoured by the Germans, with his cavalry deployed on both flanks and his artillery at intervals across his front.[13] His frontage was, however, restricted by enclosed land on both flanks, severely reducing the manoeuvrability for his cavalry. On the left flank, Essex had placed most of the cavalry, a total of 24 troops consisting of more than 1,500 horse, although more may have joined this flank by the time the battle started.[14] Richard Bulstrode, standing on Edgehill, recorded the activity:

The Enemy had all the Morning to draw up their Army, in a great plain Field, which they did to their best advantage, by putting several bodies of Foot with retrenchments and cannon before them, and all their Foot were lined with Horse behind them, with intervals betwixt each body, for their Horse to enter, if need required and upon their right wing were some briars covered with Dragoons, and a little behind, on their left wing, was the Town of Keinton [Kineton], which supplied them with provisions, and where their baggage and carriages were.[15]

The Parliamentarian deployment was over a mile and a half from the bottom of Edgehill and it was immediately apparent that Essex had not deployed his force in order to attack the hill. A subsequent Royalist council of war thereby elected to force the encounter by descending and attacking. It was a strategy not without risk, for the hill was an advantage when held, but a significant obstacle if they were defeated and had to withdraw in haste. The dragoons were the first to descend and they took command of some briars on the Royalist right. They were followed by a vanguard of 600 horse and Dyve's Regiment. The balance then followed and deployed into line of battle using the Swedish diamond formation.[16] It took a considerable amount of time and the King's men were not in position until 2pm. The wind was in their favour; a significant advantage in the era of black powder weapons, where plumes of smoke and battlefield obscuration were a major factor.[17] Commanders on both sides rode up and down the ranks inspiring their men; Charles's rousing speech resulted in a series of loud 'Huzzas', which rippled down the Royalist lines like a Mexican wave. It was enough provocation for Essex to order his artillery to open proceedings, bringing a swift end to the King's inspirational words. The battle had started – it was a little after 2pm.

The cannonade lasted for several minutes (Ludlow recorded that it lasted an hour or thereabouts) and it is clear that the Parliamentarian guns were better sited and had a greater effect.[18] The heavier cannon of the Royalists positioned on the forward slope of 'Bullet Hill' were less effective, as their shot

7 Bulstrode, *Memoirs and Reflections*, pp. 76–7. Richard Bulstrode was a Royalist, while Bulstrode Whitelocke was a Parliamentarian and a one-time Lord Keeper of the Great Seal of England. Rather confusingly, Whitelocke Bulstrode was the second son of Richard Bulstrode.

8 Warburton, *Memoirs of Prince Rupert*, vol. II, p. 12.

9 Hampden's regiment was providing the force protection to the train.

10 Bulstrode, op. cit., p. 79.

11 Most recent publications describe the Parliamentarian deployment as being of the Dutch style the chapter 'Civil War Armies'. This, however, was in three ranks while the German system was two ranks.

12 Young, *Edgehill*, p. 79.

13 No Parliamentary battle plan survives.

14 Kightley, *great battle fought between the Kings army, and His Excellency*. His account of the battle provides this information and indeed his troop was one which arrived late.

15 Bulstrode, op. cit., p. 81.

16 Rupert's engineer, Bernard De Gomme (a Dutchman), drew a map of the deployment after the battle – this survives (Windsor Castle).

17 Kightley, op. cit.

18 Firth, *Memoirs of Edmund Ludlow*, vol. I, p. 47.

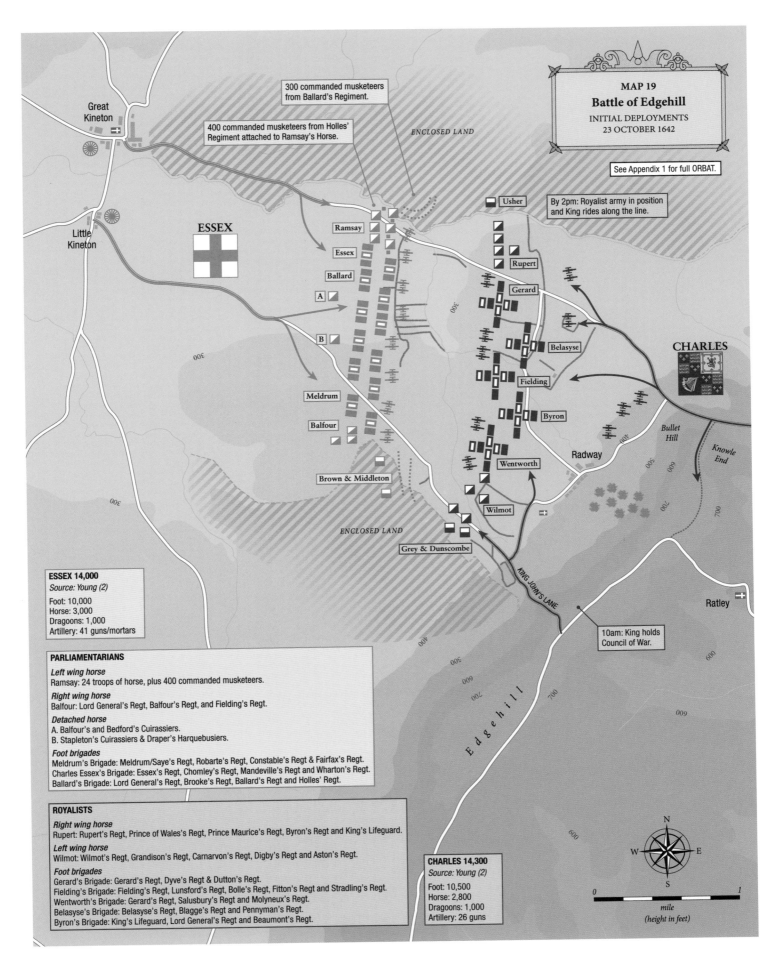

Great
Kineton

Little
Kineton

300 commanded musketeers
from Ballard's Regiment.

400 commanded musketeers from Holles'
Regiment attached to Ramsay's Horse.

ENCLOSED LAND

MAP 19
Battle of Edgehill
INITIAL DEPLOYMENTS
23 OCTOBER 1642

See Appendix 1 for full ORBAT.

Usher

By 2pm: Royalist army in position
and King rides along the line.

ESSEX

Ramsay

Essex

Ballard

Rupert

Gerard

A

B

Belasyse

CHARLES

Fielding

Meldrum

Byron

Balfour

Bullet
Hill

Knowle
End

Wentworth

Radway

Brown & Middleton

Wilmot

Grey & Dunscombe

KING JOHN'S LANE

Ratley

ENCLOSED LAND

10am: King holds
Council of War.

ESSEX 14,000
Source: Young (2)
Foot: 10,000
Horse: 3,000
Dragoons: 1,000
Artillery: 41 guns/mortars

Edgehill

PARLIAMENTARIANS

Left wing horse
Ramsay: 24 troops of horse, plus 400 commanded musketeers.

Right wing horse
Balfour: Lord General's Regt, Balfour's Regt, and Fielding's Regt.

Detached horse
A. Balfour's and Bedford's Cuirassiers.
B. Stapleton's Cuirassiers & Draper's Harquebusiers.

Foot brigades
Meldrum's Brigade: Meldrum/Saye's Regt, Robarte's Regt, Constable's Regt & Fairfax's Regt.
Charles Essex's Brigade: Essex's Regt, Chomley's Regt, Mandeville's Regt and Wharton's Regt.
Ballard's Brigade: Lord General's Regt, Brooke's Regt, Ballard's Regt and Holles' Regt.

ROYALISTS

Right wing horse
Rupert: Rupert's Regt, Prince of Wales's Regt, Prince Maurice's Regt, Byron's Regt and King's Lifeguard.

Left wing horse
Wilmot: Wilmot's Regt, Grandison's Regt, Carnarvon's Regt, Digby's Regt and Aston's Regt.

Foot brigades
Gerard's Brigade: Gerard's Regt, Dyve's Regt & Dutton's Regt.
Fielding's Brigade: Fielding's Regt, Lunsford's Regt, Bolle's Regt, Fitton's Regt and Stradling's Regt.
Wentworth's Brigade: Gerard's Regt, Salusbury's Regt and Molyneux's Regt.
Belasyse's Brigade: Belasyse's Regt, Blagge's Regt and Pennyman's Regt.
Byron's Brigade: King's Lifeguard, Lord General's Regt and Beaumont's Regt.

CHARLES 14,300
Source: Young (2)
Foot: 10,500
Horse: 2,800
Dragoons: 1,000
Artillery: 26 guns

N
W   E
S

0   1

mile
(height in feet)

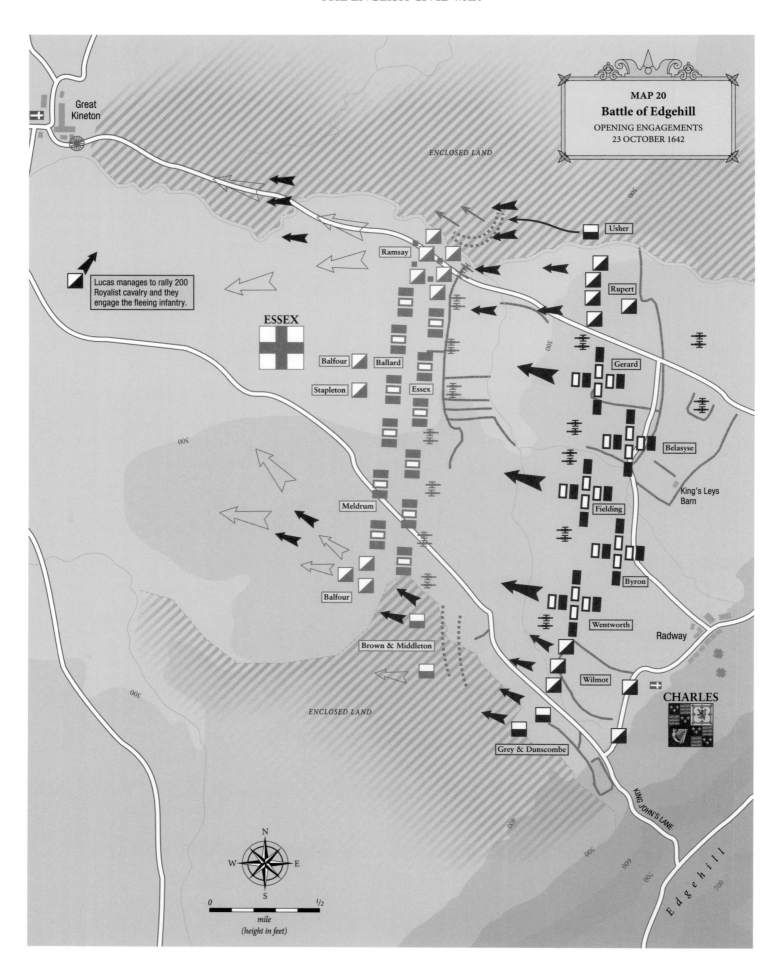

MAP 20
Battle of Edgehill
OPENING ENGAGEMENTS
23 OCTOBER 1642

Great Kineton

ENCLOSED LAND

Usher

Ramsay

Lucas manages to rally 200 Royalist cavalry and they engage the fleeing infantry.

Rupert

ESSEX

Gerard

Balfour   Ballard

Stapleton   Essex

Belasyse

King's Leys Barn

Meldrum

Fielding

Balfour

Byron

Brown & Middleton

Wentworth

Radway

Wilmot

CHARLES

Grey & Dunscombe

ENCLOSED LAND

N
W   E
S

0   ½
mile
(height in feet)

KING JOHN'S LANE

Edgehill

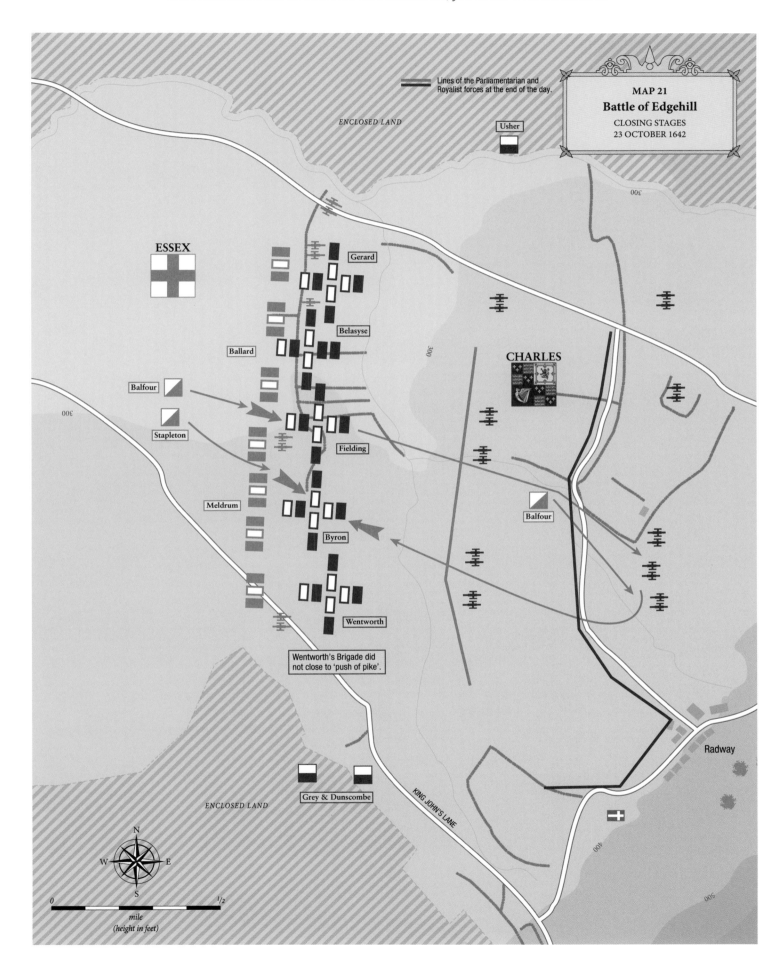

Lines of the Parliamentarian and
Royalist forces at the end of the day.

MAP 21
Battle of Edgehill
CLOSING STAGES
23 OCTOBER 1642

ENCLOSED LAND

Usher

ESSEX

Gerard

Belasyse

Ballard

CHARLES

Balfour

Stapleton

Fielding

Balfour

Meldrum

Byron

Wentworth

Wentworth's Brigade did
not close to 'push of pike'.

Radway

Grey & Dunscombe

ENCLOSED LAND

KING JOHN'S LANE

N
W E
S

0   1/2
mile
(height in feet)

plugged in the ploughed ground rather than ricocheted into the massed formations. On the Royalist right, Usher's Dragoons, under the command of Lieutenant Colonel Henry Washington, advanced as three troops and began a bickering fire with the many commanded musketeers deployed in the hedge lines on the Parliamentarian left. They outflanked the musketeers and succeeded in driving them back. To the south, a comparable fight was ongoing between the Royalist dragoons under Grey and Dunscombe, against the Parliamentarian dragoons of Brown and Wardlawe. The King's men gained a quick and decisive victory, driving Wardlawe's men from the field and forcing Brown's Dragoons back behind Balfour's cavalry. With both flanks cleared of skirmishers the Royalists had set the conditions for their advance.

The Royalist horse on both wings now advanced and then charged the cavalry to their front. In Ramsay's massed cavalry ranks a lone rider spurred his horse towards Rupert's cavalry and announced that Captain Faithfull Fortescue 'had resolved to yield and that the signal should be a shooting of his pistol to the Ground'.[19] Rupert tried to pass the word but it was too late and many of Fortescue's men got their just deserves as they tried to change sides at this critical moment. For Ramsay, the loss of his dragoons on the flank, and Fortescue's contemptible behaviour, did little to steady nerves; before steel clashed they, to a horse and man, beat a hasty retreat. The Parliamentarian left wing collapsed and fled towards Kineton and a number of the Parliamentarian foot were caught up in the panic. They were pursued en masse by the rampant cavaliers. In Kineton, wagons laden with spoils and magazines full of arms were plundered, but the pursuit continued and was only checked by the arrival of Hampden's Regiment en route to the battle.

At the same time, on the Royalist left, Wilmot advanced against Balfour's much smaller cavalry group. The going was far harder as the terrain was interspersed with ditches and hedges. However, the result was more of the same and Balfour's troopers fled with similar determination (along with Fairfax's Foot) and were pursued by Wilmot's rampant cavaliers in much the same fashion. Within minutes the Royalists looked like they had secured victory, but their impetuosity and lack of discipline was to very nearly cost them the battle. For on the north flank, swept up in Rupert's euphoria, the King's Lifeguard of Horse had joined the charge, denying the sovereign his personal bodyguard and a vital cavalry reserve. On the other wing, the two cavalry regiments acting as Wilmot's second line, Lord Digby's and Sir Thomas Aston's, also joined in the chase and subsequent plundering. This left almost no cavalry at all on the Royalist side, a situation that was to have disastrous consequences.[20]

As the Parliamentarians fled the field, Sir Jacob Astley gave the order for the five brigades of Royalist foot to advance. It is unclear whether this was the catalyst which broke the resolve of the (Parliamentarian) Essex Brigade, or whether the majority had already decided the game was up following Ramsay's collapse. Not all ran, that is true, but enough to have led to a complete collapse had it not been for the leadership of Thomas Ballard and the officers in his brigade. They pushed forward and closed the gap with Meldrum's Brigade to their right. Within minutes over 10,000 Royalist foot were engaged with just over 6,000 Parliamentarians. They soon found themselves at push of pike. The outnumbered Roundheads in their plain Dutch order, eight ranks deep, held the initial charge and then, like the allied infantry at Albuera in 1811, refused to give ground. The pikemen

were locked in a fearful struggle, while the musketeers stood-off and continued to pour a volley of fire into the opposing ranks. It was, according to one historian, 'a thing so very extraordinary, that nothing less than so many witnesses as were there present, could make it credible; nor can any other reason be given for it, but the natural courage of English men'.[21]

However, the battle was about to turn. Balfour, having suffered the frustration of watching his cavalry quit the field, realized the opportunity when the entire Royalist cavalry followed in pursuit. He rode to his own troop of cuirassiers in the (centre) reserve of the Parliamentarian line and waited for the Royalist infantry to advance and become embroiled with Meldrum's and Ballard's brigades before ordering two simultaneous charges. Stapleton's cuirassier troop and Draper's harquebusier troop moved forward through the gaps in the foot brigades and charged into Nicholas Byron's Brigade, while the two cuirassier troops under Balfour charged home against Richard Fielding's Brigade in the centre. The sudden appearance of Parliamentarian cavalry was a complete surprise to the Royalists, who assumed that all the cavalry had been driven from the field in the early charges. Furthermore, the Royalist foot were unfamiliar with their drills in Swedish formation to counter horse. Fielding's Brigade bore the brunt of two armour-clad cavalry troops as they bore down on the disorganized infantry. Commanders were killed or taken prisoner and the brigade broke and ran. Balfour's heavy cavalry followed in pursuit, mercilessly cutting down the fleeing infantry until they came up to the main Royalist battery on Bullet Hill. The young princes were nearly captured, having been ordered back to the top of Edgehill by the King only moments earlier. The King was, in fact, behind his infantry and he decided to push forward, concerned to see the men falling back. The Royal Standard, carried by Sir Edmund Verney, was with Byron's Brigade. Byron's men had withstood Stapleton's first charge but now they were attacked by Stapleton a second time, supported by Robartes' and Constable's regiments of foot and, more by luck than judgement, Balfour's cuirassiers from the rear. The brigade broke and the Royal Standard was captured, Verney was killed, and Byron was captured.[22]

On the Royalist right, the Royalist brigade commanders Charles Gerard and John Belasyse had gained some early success against the Parliamentarian infantry on the left. But those gains were undone as the Royalist infantry disintegrated on their left. Their task switched from one of attack to one of self-preservation. Many of them were delighted to see, at this juncture, the return of some of the Royalist cavalry who began to filter back to the battlefield. The returning cavalry were somewhat horrified by the spectacle unfolding before them, having been convinced that the battle was all but over. However, the arrival of Hampden's Regiment served to stem any ardour the cavaliers may have fostered to reignite the contest. The Royalists fell back and the Parliamentarian army moved forward but night brought a close. The Parliamentarian report concluded thus:

> … by this time it grew so dark, and our Powder and Bullet so spent, that it was not held fit we should advance upon them; but there we stood in very good Order; drew up all our Forces, both Horse and Foot; and so stood all that Night upon the Place where the Enemy, before the Fight, had drawn into Battalia, till toward Morning, that the Enemy was gone, and retired up the Hill…[23]

19 Warburton, op. cit., p. 22.
20 Although Sir Charles Lucas had been able to rally about 200 men near to Little Kineton and they began to attack some of the Parliamentary infantry. They were soon embroiled in capturing the infantry from Charles's Essex's Brigade, which was streaming westwards, and so were unable to influence events on the battlefield itself.
21 Clarke, *The Life of James II*, vol. I, p. 12. Note footnote 9 about the Dutch style.
22 It was recaptured by Captain Smith a few minutes later. He was knighted the following day.
23 Parliamentary Report, *Dangerous and bloody fight*, p. 6.

CHAPTER 6
ADVANCE TO LONDON, OCTOBER TO NOVEMBER 1642

Troops from both armies arrived on the field at Edgehill late in the day, but they were too fatigued from their marches to reignite the struggle.[1] Both sides were exhausted and as darkness fell so did the temperature. The Parliamentarians remained on the low ground, while the Royalists huddled at the base of Edgehill and some went up the hillside to light fires to keep warm. An uneasy night followed, interrupted by the haunting sounds of the wounded. A frosty dawn broke to clear blue skies, revealing the horror of the previous day. Neither side had any desire to renew the contest. Essex withdrew his army to the area around the Kineton villages in order to provide them some respite. He sent them back again a few hours later. The two sides deployed in battle formation (battalia) and faced each other for another few hours. Then, with the sun descending in the sky, Essex gave the order to quit the field and began to make preparations to move his army towards Warwick. Bulstrode magnanimously recorded that 'since we retired up the Hill, from whence we came down, and left the *Champ de Battaile* to the Enemy, I think we had no great Reason to brag of a Victory'.[2] Arguably, the Parliamentarians had won the fight, but by withdrawing and leaving the road open to London, they had discarded that victory. The Royalists had secured seven of the Parliamentarian guns and 60 or 70 colours, while losing none of their own artillery and only 16 ensigns/guidons and no standards. Casualties are more difficult to assess as both sides inflated the losses of their enemy, but it is generally accepted that 1,500 men were killed and about 2,000 wounded.

On balance, therefore, the first major battle was a victory for the King. Essex's withdrawal had given Charles an opportunity to move towards and secure London in advance of Parliament's army. Once London was back in Charles's hands it is unlikely that the war could or would continue. With so much at stake it is curious, therefore, that neither side made great haste towards the nation's capital. In fact, both claimed good reason in delaying such a move. Charles argued that he needed a secure base and interim capital of his own. Essex was not hoping to beat the Royalists in a race to London, but to trap them 'between the hammer of his army and the anvil of the strengthened defences of London' under the Earl of Warwick.[3] Prince Rupert's enthusiastic suggestion that he should ride with all the horse, dragoons and 3,000 musketeers and secure London was not, at this stage, in the King's best interest or intentions. Rupert was dismissed as 'being a young man, and naturally passionate [who] might possibly be urg'd in heat of blood to fire the town'.[4] Instead the King was apparently convinced of the need to capture Banbury in the first instance. It fell four days after the battle, without a shot being fired. Lord Saye and Sele's guard made a slightly better job of defending Broughton Castle but, after the arrival of some heavy artillery, they too were forced to surrender. Charles then continued towards Oxford and entered the city in triumph on 29 October. He was not to know as he entered the historic city that it was to serve as his headquarters and principal military base for nearly four years.

In London, news of events at and post Edgehill generated fear but not panic. The House of Lords debated reopening peace negotiations and, two days later, the Commons agreed to the proposal. Essex's army were recovering quickly at Warwick and on 28 October, with intelligence that Charles had not taken the bait, they set off back towards the capital. At Northampton, the army headed south and at St Alban's they picked up the old Roman road and made good time, arriving in London late on 7 November. In hindsight it is clear that Charles had missed his opportunity but in late 1642 that prospect was less apparent. Once settled at Oxford, the King entered five furious days of discussion with his council. The military options were complicated; the Queen was unlikely to garner significant support from the Continent and any movement of arms and munitions from a port to Oxford was fraught with difficulty. His army had recovered after Edgehill but any suggestion that they would remain in and around Oxford during the winter was unlikely; and the suggestion that the King fight to regain his capital from his own people did not sit easily with his hope of being a magnanimous and forgiving ruler. Many in the King's council felt that the divisions in London were such that Charles's mere appearance near the city would be enough to undermine his opponents and that resistance would crumble.[5] Somewhat unsure how to proceed, however, Charles left Oxford with a small entourage on 3 November and was at Reading the next day, which he entered unopposed as the Parliamentarian garrison had been withdrawn the previous day. At Reading, the King received Parliament's offer to treat, which solicited a cool and noncommittal response from the sovereign. Three days later, Rupert tried to capture Windsor Castle with a flying column and some light guns. His attempt failed, despite the bombardment lasting seven hours and causing considerable discomfort to the inhabitants (see map 140). Charles, however, was clearly not in a hurry. His army was short on supplies, and both carts and gunpowder were proving difficult to procure.[6] It was to be another four days before his whole army arrived at Colnbrook (near Windsor). While waiting for them to arrive the King received another Parliamentary delegation offering a proposal. The King asked for time to consider his response and the commissioners returned to London to inform Parliament. That evening, however, Rupert returned with intelligence that large numbers of Parliament's soldiers were deployed to the east, blocking the way into London. Charles felt cheated, and, influenced by Rupert's desire to maintain leverage through force, he agreed to the Royalist army advancing to meet them.

---

1   For the Royalists: the foot regiments of the Earl of Northampton and Earl Rivers. For the Parliamentarians: John Hampden's two regiments of foot, Lord Willoughby's (of Parham) regiment of horse and some guns.

2   Bulstrode, *Memoirs and Reflections*, p. 84.

3   Ellis, *Military Intelligence*, p. 83.

4   Clarke, *The life of James the second*, vol. I., p. 18.

5   Porter & Marsh, *London*, p. 54.

6   Ibid., pp. 58–60.

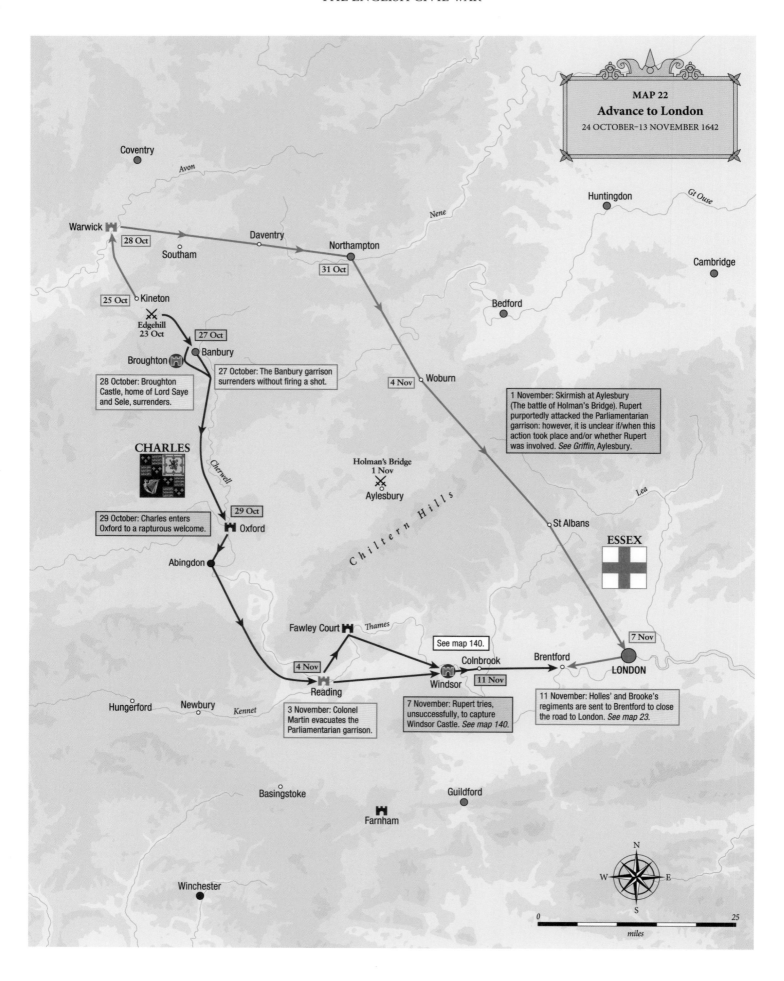

MAP 22
Advance to London
24 OCTOBER–13 NOVEMBER 1642

Coventry

Avon

Huntingdon

Gt Ouse

Nene

Warwick

28 Oct

Southam

Daventry

Northampton

31 Oct

Cambridge

Bedford

25 Oct Kineton

Edgehill
23 Oct

27 Oct

Banbury

Broughton

27 October: The Banbury garrison
surrenders without firing a shot.

28 October: Broughton
Castle, home of Lord Saye
and Sele, surrenders.

4 Nov Woburn

1 November: Skirmish at Aylesbury
(The battle of Holman's Bridge). Rupert
purportedly attacked the Parliamentarian
garrison: however, it is unclear if/when this
action took place and/or whether Rupert
was involved. *See Griffin*, Aylesbury.

CHARLES

Cherwell

Holman's Bridge
1 Nov

Aylesbury

Chiltern Hills

Lea

29 October: Charles enters
Oxford to a rapturous welcome.

29 Oct

Oxford

St Albans

ESSEX

Abingdon

Fawley Court

Thames

See map 140.

Colnbrook

Brentford

7 Nov

LONDON

4 Nov

Windsor

11 Nov

Reading

Hungerford

Newbury

Kennet

3 November: Colonel
Martin evacuates the
Parliamentarian garrison.

7 November: Rupert tries,
unsuccessfully, to capture
Windsor Castle. *See map 140.*

11 November: Holles' and Brooke's
regiments are sent to Brentford to close
the road to London. *See map 23.*

Basingstoke

Guildford

Farnham

Winchester

N

W   E

S

0   25

miles

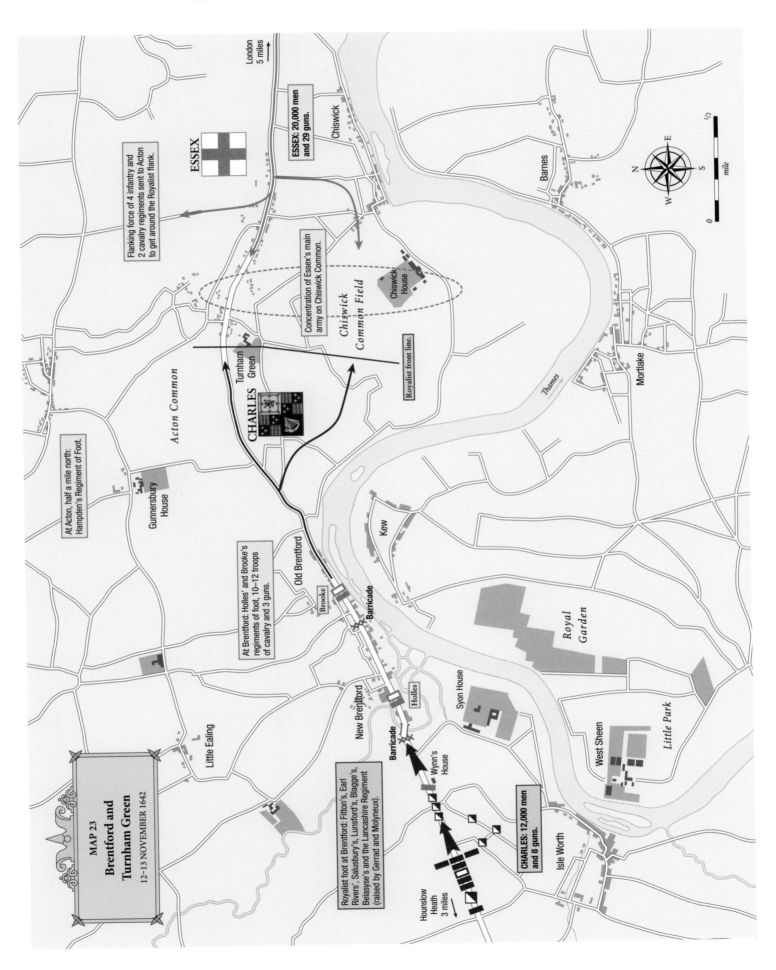

London
5 miles

Flanking force of 4 infantry and 2 cavalry regiments sent to Acton to get around the Royalist flank.

ESSEX: 20,000 men and 29 guns.

ESSEX

Chiswick

Barnes

Concentration of Essex's main army on Chiswick Common.

Chiswick Common Field

Chiswick House

Royalist front line.

Thames

Mortlake

Acton Common

Turnham Green

CHARLES

At Acton, half a mile north: Hampden's Regiment of Foot.

Gunnersbury House

Kew

At Brentford: Holles' and Brooke's regiments of foot, 10–12 troops of cavalry and 3 guns.

Old Brentford

Brooke

Barricade

Royal Garden

Little Ealing

New Brentford

Holles

Syon House

West Sheen

Little Park

Royalist foot at Brentford: Fitton's, Earl Rivers', Salusbury's, Lunsford's, Blagge's, Belasyse's and the Lancashire Regiment (raised by Gerrard and Molyneux).

Barricade

Wynn's House

CHARLES: 12,000 men and 8 guns.

Isle Worth

Hounslow Heath 3 miles

MAP 23
Brentford and Turnham Green
12–13 NOVEMBER 1642

N E
W S

0   mile   ½

The Parliamentarian forces had been arrayed on the two roads into London through Acton and Brentford and at the key bridge across the Thames at Kingston. The Royalist army numbered about 12,000, and on the morning of 12 November it formed up in battle formation on Hounslow Heath ready to receive an attack. Charles had anticipated that the small force at Brentford would have been significantly reinforced during the night. In fact, Parliament had been debating their next step and, not wishing to escalate matters, had agreed upon a cessation of hostilities. However, they had misread the volatility of the situation and the urgent need to communicate their intent. At about 11am the King gave the order for his army to advance. Under cover of a dense fog the army moved east, but as they approached Brentford Edge the size and number of enclosures on either side of the road restricted the movement of the cavalry, leaving the Prince of Wales's Regiment of Horse alone to canter down the London road, supported by about six regiments of foot.[7] Neither of the Parliamentarian commanders, Holles or Brooke, was actually with their regiments (indicating that an attack was entirely unexpected) and the shock caused most of the Parliamentarian cavalry to turn tail for London. Within two hours of fierce fighting the Royalist forces had overcome the barricades and pushed through Brentford. A number of prisoners were taken, along with two drakes.

The sounds of battle drifted east towards the city, causing a combination of panic and anger. Orders were given and the commanders worked throughout the night to concentrate their forces. Hampden had brought most of his regiment down from Acton to assist in the escape of the forces at Brentford, while Essex moved the army that, by a degree of chance, had mustered on Chelsea Field on the morning of 12 November. A number of other men of the London trained bands rallied to the call and some of Ramsay's men were also moved from Kingston, some by boat down the Thames. By dawn on 13 November a force of 20,000 men was drawn up at Turnham Green, the only area of open ground large enough to accommodate an army between Brentford and Hammersmith. In numerical terms, this was close to being the largest ever military confrontation on British soil.[8] The deployment was confined but Essex used his numerical advantage to good effect. His artillery, protected by earthworks, was positioned well forward across the frontage. He also sent a force of four foot regiments (including Hampden's) and two of cavalry round the right flank towards Acton to get in behind the Royalist left. Both sides deployed and faced-off for some considerable time. Indecision within the Parliamentarian senior command, and the continued hope that common sense would prevail and military action be avoided, prompted Essex to withdraw the force sent around to Acton. It was clear, therefore, that the Parliamentarians were not about to open proceedings. Charles, realizing he was heavily outnumbered, now chose to pull back. As Bulstrode recalled, 'finding the Earl of Essex, with his Army, was drawn out upon Turnham Green, with the Trained Bands of the City, and that the Enemy's Army was double to the King's, and that most of our Ammunition was spent, it was therefore thought fit by the Council, that the King should retreat'.[9] The Royalist army was allowed to pull back and was covered by a number of musketeers at Brentford bridge. Charles spent the night at Hampton Court and a few days later was back at Oxford, bringing to an end the Edgehill campaign, and with it, any hope of an early and peaceful resolution to England's crisis.

7 Ibid., p. 74.

8 Ibid., p. 92.
9 Bulstrode, *Memoirs and Reflections*, p. 88.

CHAPTER 7
NATIONWIDE STRUGGLE, DECEMBER 1642 TO MARCH 1643

On 29 November, Charles re-entered Oxford, triggering the start of the city's role as the Royalist capital. The Royalists set about strengthening the city's defences and establishing the monarch's court and his military headquarters. With garrisons in place at Reading, Wallingford and Abingdon (Rupert's cavalry base) a forward line of defences was effectively established around Oxford's rather vulnerable position from its central heartlands in the Welsh Marches (see map 36). Notwithstanding this apparently defensive posture, Charles had every intention of retaining the initiative. His strategic plan was (most likely) to surround London by advancing on the capital on three axes: from his position in the centre, supported by a thrust from the north through the Midlands, and, finally, from the south-west into Kent and into the underbelly of the metropolis.[1] At the same time, he continued to covet foreign support, in part to prevent Parliament gaining from this potentially lucrative source. The Continental powers, meanwhile, were content to wait and to play one side off against the other, in the expectation of diplomatic and/or financial gain in the longer term. In Scotland, the Council appointed by Charles in 1641 refused to help him, while in Ireland the government, which he had refused to recognize, established itself, somewhat ironically given the Scottish position, in his name and stated their loyalty. Politically, therefore, the situation at the end of 1642 was highly volatile and extremely complex.

The King's northern hopes rested on the Earl of Newcastle, who had assumed command of the remnants of the Royalist army in the north from the Earl of Cumberland. The latter was no soldier and more than happy to hand over the reins when Parliamentarian forces in the region began to stir. Lord Ferdinando Fairfax had raised troops from the mill towns around Halifax and Bradford, John Hotham was the garrison commander in Hull, and Hugh Cholmley the garrison commander of Scarborough Castle; together they instigated a plan to combine forces and close in on the Royalist stronghold at York. Newcastle, who had been busy corralling the Royalist elements in County Durham and Northumberland, moved south and dislodged the small Parliamentarian force under John Hotham at Piercebridge, before moving to York to protect the city and meet the threat. He arrived on 3 December and three days later the two forces encountered each other in strength at Tadcaster. Fairfax (who had taken overall command of the force) was outnumbered, dislodged and forced to pull back towards Selby.[2] The next day Newcastle captured the key crossing at Ferrybridge and occupied Pontefract, effectively cutting Fairfax off from his recruiting base and the West Riding towns of Leeds, Bradford, Wakefield and Halifax. Newcastle returned to York, but on 18 December, a smaller Royalist force attacked Bradford and another group, under Sir John Henderson, headed south and captured the

key town of Newark. As the year drew to a close Charles had every reason to be delighted with the progress of his army in the north.

However, three things were about to conspire against Newcastle, altering Royalist fortunes. The first was a significant shortage of arms and powder. The second was the arrival of Queen Henrietta Maria at Bridlington on 22 February, whose wellbeing was now Newcastle's responsibility, along with the large quantity of arms (destined for the Oxford army) she had obtained from the Continent.[3] Thirdly, the skill and generalship of Lord Fairfax's son, Thomas, was about to tip the scales back in favour of the Parliamentarians. 'Black Tom' was an experienced soldier from the Dutch Wars and eager to get on with the task at hand.[4] By the end of December, he had driven the Royalists out of Bradford, forcing them to withdraw to the confines of York. Fairfax continued his offensive in early 1643, recapturing Leeds on 23 January and reopening the links from the West Riding to the garrison at Hull.[5] More bad news for Newcastle was to follow a week later when William Brereton captured Nantwich from Sir Thomas Aston and established the town as his Parliamentarian headquarters in Cheshire. Then, in February, Parliamentarian forces captured Lancaster and Preston and thwarted a serious attempt by Lord Derby to attack Bolton. Perhaps of greater concern to Newcastle was the news that Newark was being attacked by a strong force from Nottingham, Lincolnshire and Derbyshire, led by Thomas Ballard. After two days of fierce fighting around Newark, the skill and determination of Henderson's men, coupled with Ballard's incompetence, were enough to prevent this key town falling into Parliament's hands.[6] Newcastle's relief that communication with the King remained open (and therefore the ability to execute the King's strategic plan) was palpable. The pendulum of changing fortune was to offer more glad tidings when, towards the end of March, news emerged that the Queen had managed to convince Cholmley (at Scarborough) to change sides. However, her attempts to convince John Hotham at Hull, who had also opened communications with the Queen, were less fruitful.[7]

Two components of the King's plan were, therefore, viable, but the third was no more than a pipe dream. The King's aspiration that a Royalist army would rise from the south-west and sweep all before it was hugely over-optimistic. The loyalty displayed to the squires in Cornwall was not replicated in Devon, where attempts to execute the Commission of Array were met with indifference. The large towns and ports of Exeter, Plymouth,

---

1 Gardiner, *Great Civil War*, vol., I., p. 67. There is, however, no material evidence to support Gardiner's claim that this was indeed Charles's strategic plan.

2 Several men had deserted the Parliamentarian army leaving Fairfax just over 1,500 men to face Newcastle's force of 4,500.

3 The latter were under orders to be transported to Oxford without delay.

4 To avoid confusion, the Fairfaxes will be referred to as Lord Fairfax and (Tom) Fairfax.

5 Fairfax, *Short memorials*, p. 15–17.

6 Wood, *Nottinghamshire*, p. 42. It resulted in Ballard's dismissal and his replacement by John Meldrum, a more experienced soldier and the man who had secured Hull for Parliament.

7 Although they planted the seeds and within weeks Hotham was in talks with Newcastle to surrender the key city and port.

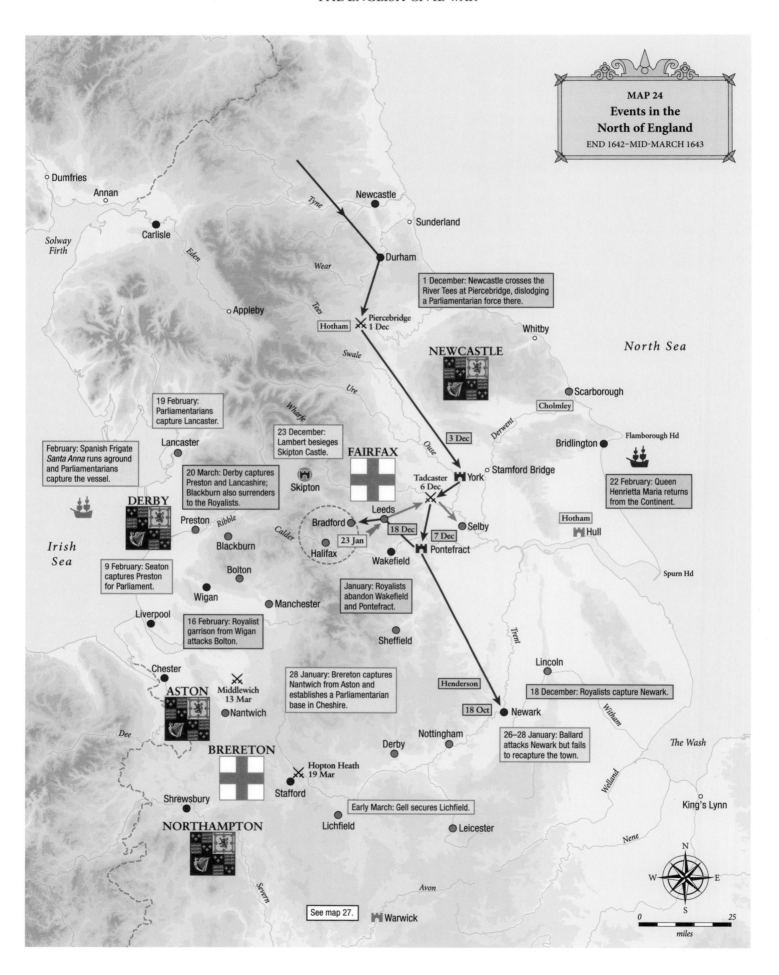

MAP 24

**Events in the
North of England**

END 1642–MID-MARCH 1643

Dumfries

Annan

Newcastle

Sunderland

*Solway
Firth*

Carlisle

Eden

Durham

Wear

Appleby

1 December: Newcastle crosses the
River Tees at Piercebridge, dislodging
a Parliamentarian force there.

Tyne

Tees

Piercebridge
1 Dec

Hotham

Whitby

North Sea

Swale

NEWCASTLE

Scarborough

Cholmley

Ure

19 February:
Parliamentarians
capture Lancaster.

Wharfe

23 December:
Lambert besieges
Skipton Castle.

Ouse

3 Dec

Bridlington

Flamborough Hd

February: Spanish Frigate
Santa Anna runs aground
and Parliamentarians
capture the vessel.

Lancaster

Skipton

FAIRFAX

Tadcaster
6 Dec

York

Stamford Bridge

Derwent

22 February: Queen
Henrietta Maria returns
from the Continent.

20 March: Derby captures
Preston and Lancashire;
Blackburn also surrenders
to the Royalists.

DERBY

Preston

Ribble

Bradford

Leeds

18 Dec

Selby

Hotham

Hull

*Irish
Sea*

Blackburn

Calder

23 Jan

Halifax

7 Dec

Pontefract

Spurn Hd

9 February: Seaton
captures Preston
for Parliament.

Bolton

Wakefield

January: Royalists
abandon Wakefield
and Pontefract.

Wigan

Liverpool

16 February: Royalist
garrison from Wigan
attacks Bolton.

Manchester

Sheffield

Trent

Lincoln

Chester

ASTON

Middlewich
13 Mar

Nantwich

28 January: Brereton captures
Nantwich from Aston and
establishes a Parliamentarian
base in Cheshire.

Henderson

18 December: Royalists capture Newark.

18 Oct

Newark

The Wash

Dee

BRERETON

26–28 January: Ballard
attacks Newark but fails
to recapture the town.

Derby

Nottingham

Witham

Hopton Heath
19 Mar

Shrewsbury

Stafford

Early March: Gell secures Lichfield.

King's Lynn

NORTHAMPTON

Lichfield

Leicester

Nene

Severn

Avon

N

See map 27.

Warwick

W   E

S

0   25

miles

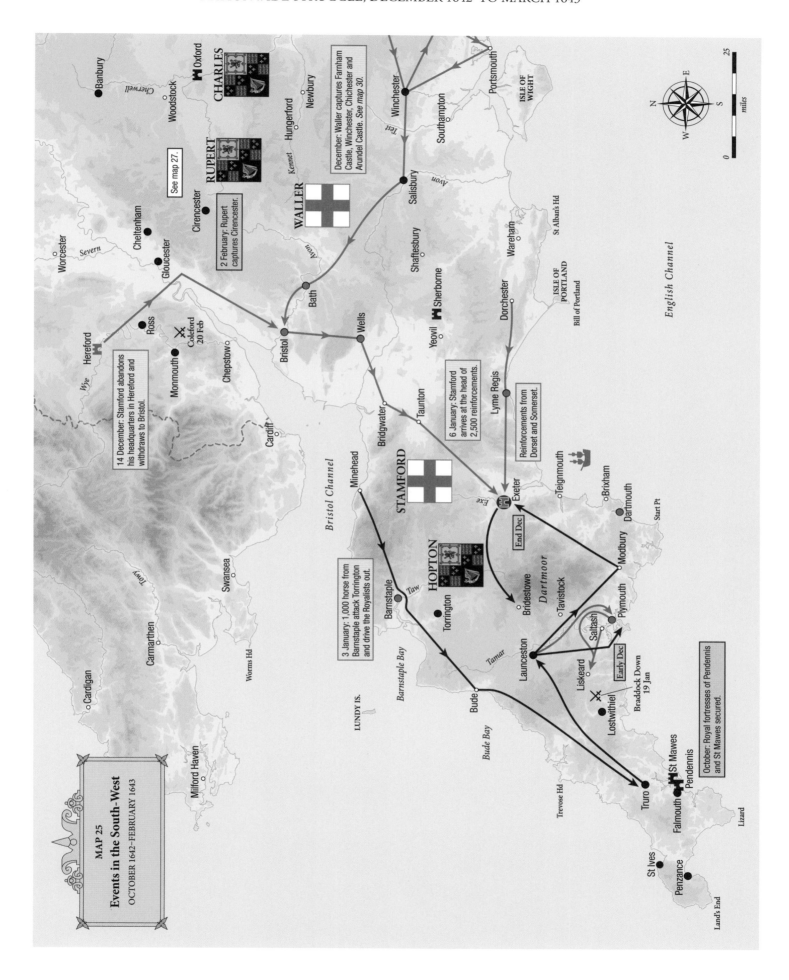

December: Waller captures Farnham
Castle, Winchester, Chichester and
Arundel Castle. *See map 30.*

See map 27.

2 February: Rupert
captures Cirencester.

14 December: Stamford abandons
his headquarters in Hereford and
withdraws to Bristol.

6 January: Stamford
arrives at the head of
2,500 reinforcements.

Reinforcements from
Dorset and Somerset.

End Dec

3 January: 1,000 horse from
Barnstaple attack Torrington
and drive the Royalists out.

Early Dec

Braddock Down
19 Jan

October: Royal fortresses of Pendennis
and St Mawes secured.

MAP 25
Events in the South-West
OCTOBER 1642–FEBRUARY 1643

Barnstaple and Dartmouth had long suffered from royal maladministration and were largely inhabited by Puritan sympathizers.[8] The first clashes had taken place in August and September 1642 (see map 18). They were small affairs, and the early Royalist advantages were quickly reversed by the arrival of the Earl of Bedford and the mobilization of a large Parliamentarian force at Wells. The Marquis of Hertford, the King's man in the region, was forced to take shelter in Sherborne Castle and Bedford wasted little time in surrounding the fortress. Hertford escaped capture, as the execution of the siege lacked both science and direction – a common occurrence during the civil wars. Bedford withdrew to Yeovil and Hertford escaped with his force to Minehead where he intended to embark and join the King in time for Edgehill. However, when only two transports arrived, he took the infantry and artillery and left the cavalry under his second in command, Ralph Hopton. With Bedford summoned north to join Essex's army, both forces had virtually stripped out the soldiery from the south-west.

Hopton made his way to Truro where Richard Buller, the Parliamentarian commander, attempted to arraign Hopton at the Truro Assizes for bringing armed men into the county. Hopton, through some skilled oratory, managed to convince the jury of the obligation of his cause and the consequent justification of his actions. The court found in his favour. They ordered the trained bands to come out for the King, and the town's arms were distributed among them. By early October, therefore, Hopton had managed to cobble together a force of 3,000 and on 15 October the Royalists occupied Launceston, forcing Buller, now hopelessly outnumbered, to flee to Plymouth. Hopton was well aware that the Cornish militia would refuse to move outside Cornwall (for now) and so he set about trying to raise a volunteer army with the intention of marching against the Parliamentarian stronghold at Plymouth. In the interim, the Royal fortress, guarding the mouth of the River Fal, was captured and secured. By November 1642, Hopton's cavalry were raiding across the River Tamar into Devon (the boundary between the two counties) in the hope of securing supplies and recruits, and privateers were running the gauntlet of Parliament's warships, and running stores and munitions to Falmouth and St Ives.

In London, news of Hopton's successes caused considerable concern, and the Committee for Public Safety (responsible for the Parliamentarian war effort nationwide), despite being fully preoccupied with the defence of the capital, authorized the counties of Cornwall and Devon to raise (funded) foot and horse to the tune of 1,000 and 500, respectively. In addition, the Earl of Bedford was to be sent back to the region at the head of a similar number of infantry and cavalry. The recruitment and arrival of this force was, however, to take time, and in early December Hopton was sufficiently strong to move on Plymouth. The garrison commander in Plymouth was a capable and experienced Scottish officer, Colonel William Ruthven, who was more than prepared to take the fight to the Royalists, as he had aptly demonstrated when Hopton's men attacked (and captured) Mount Edgecombe House and the Millbrook on the peninsula to the west of the Tamar estuary.[9] However, Hopton's forces, and resources, were insufficient to mount a realistic siege and he elected to try to recruit more at Modbury by *posse comitatus* (common law conscription). The Devon militia, however, demonstrated little enthusiasm for the King's cause. The gathering was

dispersed when Ruthven led a large body of cavalry to disrupt the meeting and Hopton narrowly escaped being taken prisoner. The Royalist commander decided instead to move against the city of Exeter, which he approached at the end of December. Once again, he was outwitted by Ruthven, who had managed (by land and sea) to get reinforcements into the city. Hopton appealed to the city fathers in an attempt to persuade them, but to no avail. Following a rather abortive attempt to escalade the walls on New Year's Day, Hopton accepted that it was little more than a futile gesture; with supplies running short and morale waning, he decided to head back towards the relative sanctuary of Cornwall.[10] He was harried all the way back by Ruthven, who only broke off the pursuit when Hopton turned and executed a determined rearguard action at Bridestowe. The hopes of Royalist salvation from the south-west remained remote.

On 6 January, the Earl of Stamford arrived at Exeter at the head of at least three regiments of foot (about 2,500 men).[11] These were the long-awaited Parliamentarian reinforcements and it was Stamford's aim to link up with Ruthven's forces at Plymouth and to pursue and destroy the Cornish Royalists. On 13 January, some of Stamford's reinforcements had secured the (new) bridge at Gunnislake and joined forces with Ruthven, who had succeeded in driving out the Royalists from Saltash, where he now crossed the River Tamar. Ruthven concentrated his force at Liskeard and prepared to attack a Royalist force at Lostwithiel. He was, however, unaware that the Royalists had received a large supply of arms and powder purloined from three Parliamentarian ships that had been forced to take shelter in Falmouth. The ships had declared for the King, and their military cargoes were quickly offloaded and distributed to Hopton's force. Significantly, large quantities of money were also offloaded and served to pay all the arrears to Hopton's men, a badly needed and timely incentive.[12] Accordingly fired-up, a Royalist council of war on 18 January at Lostwithiel agreed to advance and engage Ruthven's forces before Stamford's additional reinforcements were in the field.

Early on 19 January the Royalists advanced, and it was not long before the vanguard, consisting mainly of Hopton's Dragoons, were engaged by Ruthven's cavalry on Braddock Down. Ruthven was determined to give battle and had deployed his forces on the eastern side of the hill – although the exact location of the battlefield and the deployment is unclear.[13] Hopton deployed 'the foote in the best order hee could on the west syde of Bradock Downe... and having placed a forlorne of muskettiers in little inclosures that lay before him, and winged all with the few horse and dragoones hee had'.[14] Hopton also had two small guns (minion-drakes, or 2-pounders) that he positioned in the centre and covered from view with some of his cavalry and within 'randome-shott of the enymies bodyes'.[15] As soon as the Royalists were in place Hopton's men were led in prayer. Both sides held higher ground and were separated by a lower ground which fell off to the south. Bevil Grenville was commanding the infantry in the centre and he recalled that 'we saluted each other with bullets', both sides determined to 'keep their ground of advantage and have the other to come over to his prejudice'.[16] However,

---

8 Andriette, *Devon and Exeter*, p. 64.

9 Not to be confused with Patrick Ruthven, who on the eve of the battle of Edgehill, was appointed captain general of the King's armies when the Earl of Lindsey resigned following an argument over deployment of the troops (see chapter 5).

10 Andriette, op. cit., p. 78.

11 Ibid., p. 78.

12 *Mercurius Aulicus*, BL 42:E.246[9].

13 See notes accompanying map 26. Hopton (in *Bellum Civile*) stated that 'the Enymies horse which were already drawn up upon the east side of Bradock Downe at the end of the Lane coming out from Lyskard'. Hopton, in response, 'drew up... on the west side of Braddock Down'.

14 Chadwyck-Healey, *Bellum Civile*, p. 30.

15 Ibid., p. 30.

16 Burne & Young, *Great Civil War*, p. 40.

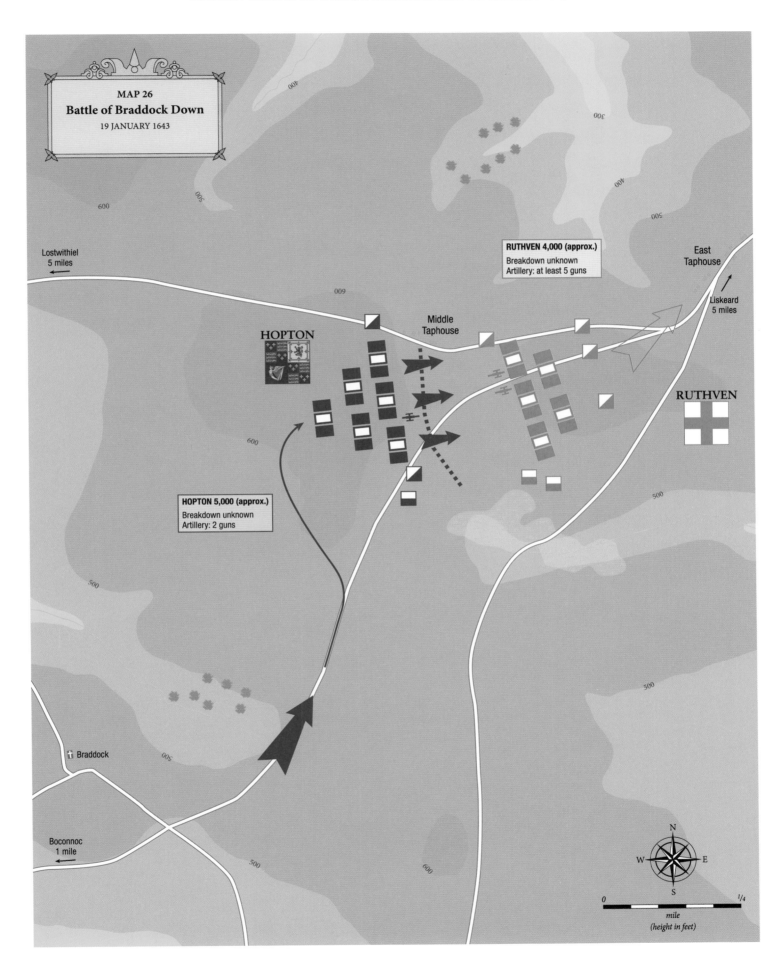

MAP 26
Battle of Braddock Down
19 JANUARY 1643

Lostwithiel
5 miles

RUTHVEN 4,000 (approx.)
Breakdown unknown
Artillery: at least 5 guns

East
Taphouse

Liskeard
5 miles

Middle
Taphouse

HOPTON

RUTHVEN

HOPTON 5,000 (approx.)
Breakdown unknown
Artillery: 2 guns

Braddock

Boconnoc
1 mile

N
W   E
S

0   1/4
mile
(height in feet)

Hopton could see none of the Parliamentarian guns in place and decided to attack. The two small guns were unmasked, fired a couple of salvos and then Grenville led the infantry vanguard in the centre. They came on with great purpose, causing panic among Ruthven's men. The Parliamentarians got off a single volley and then, when the first Roundhead unit broke, they all took to their heels. Any attempt to maintain order was lost as the Royalists pressed them from all sides; the retreat quickly turned to a rout. The Parliamentarians were pursued all the way to Liskeard, where they now had to contend with the townsfolk, who attacked them with all manner of farm implements from the rear.

It was a great victory for the Cornish Royalists. They captured 'twelve hundred and fyftie prisoners most of their coulours all their cannon', which consisted of five cannon, four of which were valuable brass ordnance.[17] The victory also established Sir Ralph Hopton as the undisputed leader of the Cornish Royalists. He did not rest on his laurels and sent a strong column under John Berkeley and Colonel Ashburnham to move against Stamford's force at Launceston, while he advanced with the main force and recaptured Saltash. Stamford fell back towards Tavistock and Ruthven, meanwhile, took shelter inside Plymouth. However, Hopton's force did not have the wherewithal (or the corresponding naval support) to conduct a siege of a fortified city and port like Plymouth. After receiving a check at Chagford on 8 February, and being driven out of Modbury two weeks later (at the cost of 100 dead and the loss of five guns), Hopton fell back to Cornwall. His hopes of a second invasion of Devon had been thwarted for a second time.

Following the King's rather abortive attempt to recapture London, Parliament and the Common Council of the City of London remained split on a future course of action. Requests for the King's return, guaranteeing his protection, along with peace proposals, arrived at Oxford throughout January. The King, in turn, presented counterproposals, calling for a cessation of hostilities and a disbandment of both armies. The Lords accepted the offer but the Members were less optimistic, offering new terms at the end of February. The King batted counterproposals back to London, insisting that naval commanders and garrison commanders be appointed by him. The Commons responded by stating that such a policy would be acceptable, subject to the approval of Parliament. While this seemingly positive dialogue was sustained, both sides continued to strengthen their respective positions by extending their influence (at home and abroad), increasing their forces and setting about trying to create workable chains of command that took into account the geographical spread and ever-increasing provincial nature of the war. In December 1642, inspired by the Royalist association of forces of the northern counties, Parliament passed two ordinances creating, firstly, the Midland Association, combining the military and administrative resources of the counties of Leicester, Derby, Nottingham, Rutland, Northampton, Buckingham, Bedford and Huntingdon, and secondly, the Eastern Association, amalgamating the same in Norfolk, Suffolk, Cambridgeshire, Essex and Hertfordshire. Pym had a burning desire to take this one step further and link the regional associations to form a National Association, along the lines of that adopted by the Covenanters in Scotland. Such an association would clearly enable Parliament to employ forces nationwide, but the concept lacked universal support, particularly at the local/provincial level, and the idea was shelved.[18]

In the centre, Essex was inclined to sit on his hands, allow the process of negotiation to unfold and wait for better weather in the spring before undertaking any major military offensives. But William Waller, who was to become a leading Parliamentarian commander in southern England during the first three years of the war, had other ideas. He swiftly moved to capture Farnham Castle, then sacked Winchester before moving to the south coast, where he captured Arundel and Southsea castles and terrorized Chichester. His victorious run was brought to a halt at the walls of the key naval port of Portsmouth but his exploits earned him the sobriquet 'William the Conqueror' from the people of London. More significantly, his rise to prominence coincided with a structural reshuffle, and made him the ideal candidate to assume command of the new Western Association. It formed in early February and included the counties of Gloucestershire, Wiltshire, Somerset, Worcestershire and Shropshire. Characteristically, Waller wasted no time in moving west to establish his headquarters in Bristol, frightening Salisbury en route for good measure.

The arrival of this credible force presented a very real threat to the Royalist position at Oxford and their supply of 'rough if ready' recruits from Wales. The Royalists, meanwhile, had been busy in the Midlands occupying Lichfield, Stafford and Tamworth. These successes were, however, countered by William Brereton's capture of Nantwich on 28 January, and his defeat of Aston at Middlewich on 13 March. Rubbing salt into the wound, John Gell recaptured Lichfield in early March. With Rupert otherwise engaged screening Essex's forces, the King ordered the Earl of Northampton to go north from his base at Banbury, recapture Lichfield and check the Parliamentarian advance. As the earl approached Lichfield, he received intelligence that Parliamentarian forces, in the guise of Brereton's and Gell's contingents, were moving towards Stafford, and he wasted no time in moving to counter.[19] Leaving most of his foot at Lichfield to continue the siege, Northampton advanced to Stafford where he arranged to rendezvous with Colonel General Henry Hastings and his mounted regiments.[20] Meanwhile, Brereton and Gell had arranged their own rendezvous on Hopton Heath, from where they would advance on Stafford. Gell's forces were the first to arrive; having passed through Weston, they crossed the River Trent and ascended the steep hill to the prearranged heathland. As his men took up their positions, they could see the spires of Stafford to the south-west. Gell deployed his force on the forward slope with his foot positioned behind a low wall that bounded a house in the centre of a walled park. Some dragoons were on their left, dismounted and deployed along the wall on the far side of the road, while yet more dragoons were placed to the right of the foot just inside the walled area. On the far right, the cavalry was arrayed on an open part of the heath. The three heavy guns (probably 9- or 15-pounder culverins) were positioned at the top of the hill just off the road, while the balance of Parliamentarian artillery, consisting of eight drakes (5¼-pounders) were deployed along the wall with the infantry.[21] Brereton's Horse, when they came up, joined the cavalry on the right and the foot did likewise sometime later, extending the line a considerable distance.[22]

Sometime between 11am and midday, Northampton received intelligence that some of the Parliamentarian forces were deploying on the

19 *Mercurius Aulicus*, BL 42:E.247[26] and Lord Compton's battle report (Oxford, 1643).

20 Ibid.

21 Burne & Young, op. cit., pp. 67–8; Young, *Hopton Heath*, pp. 35–6; Royalist battle report, p. 2; Dunrobin Muniments, cited in the English Heritage Battlefield Report, pp. 2–3.

22 I have difficulty with Burne and Young that the line was 1,500 yards in all. Half that length, with the number of troops, is more likely.

17 Chadwyck-Healey, op. cit., p. 30.

18 Holmes, *Eastern Association*, p. 63.

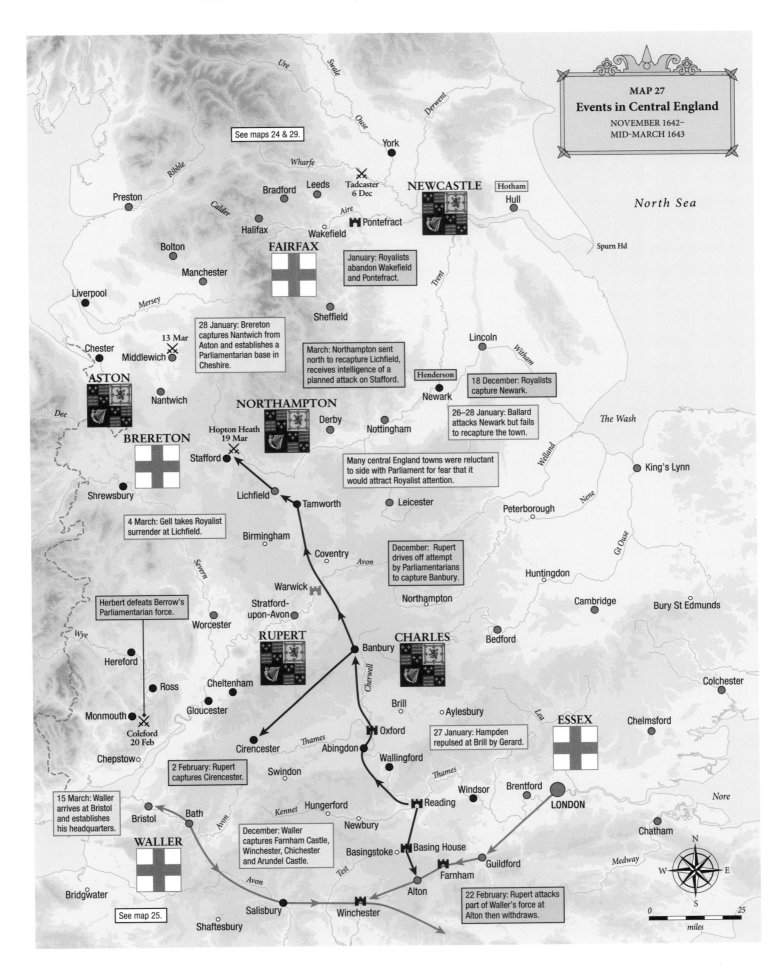

See maps 24 & 29.

MAP 27
Events in Central England
NOVEMBER 1642–
MID-MARCH 1643

North Sea

York

Tadcaster
6 Dec

Bradford   Leeds

NEWCASTLE   Hotham

Hull

Spurn Hd

Preston

Ribble   Wharfe

Aire

Calder

Halifax   Wakefield

Pontefract

January: Royalists
abandon Wakefield
and Pontefract.

Bolton

FAIRFAX

Manchester

Liverpool

Mersey

Sheffield

Trent

13 Mar

Chester

Middlewich

28 January: Brereton
captures Nantwich from
Aston and establishes a
Parliamentarian base in
Cheshire.

March: Northampton sent
north to recapture Lichfield,
receives intelligence of a
planned attack on Stafford.

Lincoln

Witham

ASTON

Nantwich

BRERETON

Dee

Shrewsbury

NORTHAMPTON

Derby

Nottingham

Henderson

Newark

18 December: Royalists
capture Newark.

26–28 January: Ballard
attacks Newark but fails
to recapture the town.

The Wash

King's Lynn

Hopton Heath
19 Mar

Stafford

Lichfield   Tamworth

Leicester

Many central England towns were reluctant
to side with Parliament for fear that it
would attract Royalist attention.

Welland

Nene

Peterborough

4 March: Gell takes Royalist
surrender at Lichfield.

Birmingham

Coventry

Avon

Gt Ouse

Huntingdon

Cambridge   Bury St Edmunds

Herbert defeats Berrow's
Parliamentarian force.

Warwick

Stratford-
upon-Avon

Worcester

December: Rupert
drives off attempt
by Parliamentarians
to capture Banbury.

Northampton

Bedford

Wye

RUPERT

Hereford

Ross

Cheltenham

CHARLES

Banbury

Colchester

Chelmsford

Severn

Monmouth

Coleford
20 Feb

Gloucester

Cirencester

Brill

Cherwell

Aylesbury

Oxford

27 January: Hampden
repulsed at Brill by Gerard.

ESSEX

Chepstow

Thames

Abingdon

Wallingford

Lea

Windsor

Brentford

2 February: Rupert
captures Cirencester.

Swindon

Thames

LONDON

Chatham

15 March: Waller
arrives at Bristol
and establishes
his headquarters.

Bristol   Bath

Avon

Kennet

Hungerford

Newbury

Reading

Nore

WALLER

Basingstoke

Basing House

Guildford

Medway

Bridgwater

Avon

Test

Farnham

Alton

22 February: Rupert attacks
part of Waller's force at
Alton then withdraws.

N
W   E
S

See map 25.

Salisbury

Winchester

0   25

Shaftesbury

miles

December: Waller
captures Farnham Castle,
Winchester, Chichester
and Arundel Castle.

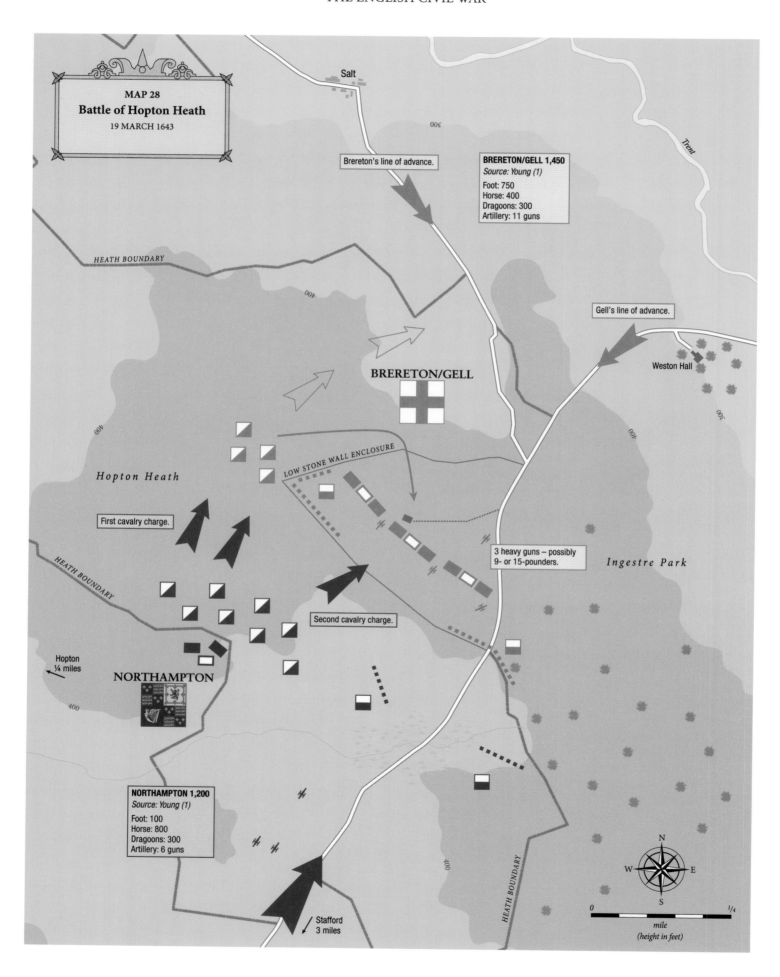

heath. He immediately issued orders for the horse, dragoons and the hundred or so foot, to move up the Weston road.[23] 'As we advanced we discovered Musketeers placed within a walled Close, and some Musketeers and drakes in hedges on our right wing. Against which we sent some of our Musketeers but these being too few to beat them…'.[24] In the interim the Royalist cannon had moved up and a massive 29-pounder demi-cannon came into action and immediately caused destruction and disorder among the Parliamentarian line. An anonymous Royalist participant recorded, 'Att this tyme alsoe wee drew up our Cannon which was one very good piece and did great execucon for the first shott killed six of their men and hurt four and the next made such a lane through them that they had little minde to close agayne.'[25] It would appear that the convex nature of the slope prevented the heavier Parliamentarian guns from hitting the Royalist cavalry as they moved west across the heath, 'for wee were soe nigh that their greate pieces shott over us'.[26] After about half an hour, Northampton, realizing that Brereton's force was not yet up, decided to charge the Parliamentarian lines. It was a dangerous game with only cavalry against a combined force, but he calculated that the deployment of the cavalry separated from the infantry by the walls was a mistake he could exploit. Brereton recalled that it 'was a great disadvantage to us, that both our horse and foote were unhappily disposed of and divided into small bodyes, at such time as the enemie charged us, which was the occasion that the greatest parte of our horse were disordered, and routed, yet very few of them slaine'.[27]

Northampton led the charge personally and was completely successful in driving the majority of Parliamentarian cavalry from the field. A few disorganized troops managed to seek refuge behind the infantry. It was a temporary respite and one they made good use of to reorganize. Meanwhile, Northampton rallied his cavalry and gave orders for a second charge, this time against the wall of infantry behind the low stone walls. A furious fight ensued; the infantry were driven back and the eight drakes overrun and captured, but it was at this point that the tide turned. The sustained musketry fire brought down on the unsupported cavalry began to take its toll. The horses were exhausted and the ground was pitted with rabbit warrens, causing added difficulties for the Royalist horse. In the melee, Northampton was unhorsed, and after slaying a number of foot soldiers, he was offered quarter. If the Royalist account is to be believed he retorted that 'he scorned to take quarter from such base rogues and rebels'.[28] It was at this point that he was despatched with a halberd. Thomas Byron, commanding the Prince of Wales's Horse, launched a third charge that drove the infantry back, but it quickly ran out of momentum. The light was fading and the combatants were exhausted. The order was then given for the Parliamentarian forces to pull back, but as they prepared to do so, about 200 of Brereton's infantry arrived and steadied the line. Both sides then remained motionless on the hilltop a couple of hundred yards apart. During the night, Brereton and Gell decided that there was little to be gained by remaining on the field and gave the order to withdraw. For the Royalists, their commander had been killed but they had captured eight badly needed guns and prevented the fall of Stafford.[29] In their eyes Hopton Heath was an undisputed Royalist victory. Losses are difficult to state with any accuracy. The Parliamentarian losses were relatively low, probably fewer than one hundred, while those of the Royalists were three times that number – a direct result of unsupported cavalry attacking infantry, cavalry and dragoons in a relatively strong position.

---

23 Northampton had left most of his foot at Lichfield and Hastings had none. I estimate that the total Royalist foot was 100–200.

24 Royalist battle report, p. 2.

25 Dunrobin Muniments.

26 Ibid. This gun was purportedly named 'Roaring Meg', but it should not be confused with the great mortar with the same name cast in 1646 for the siege of Goodrich Castle.

27 Stebbing Shaw, *History and antiquities of Staffordshire*, vol. I, p. 54.

28 Royalist battle report, p. 4.

29 The Parliamentarians refused to return Northampton's body, asking, in exchange, for all the artillery, ammunition and prisoners they had lost. Clarendon, *History of the Rebellion*, vol. III, p. 460.

CHAPTER 8

THE NATION DIVIDES, MID-MARCH TO END OF MAY 1643

Concerned for the safety of the key town of Newark, Newcastle despatched his cousin, Charles Cavendish (second son of the Earl of Devonshire) to reinforce the garrison there. Having linked up with Henderson's forces in Newark, the two commanders decided to make a dash for Grantham on 23 March and, having captured the town, they destroyed the fortifications. Stamford was also overrun by the King's sympathizers and the Royalists then marched to the walls of Lincoln. It seemed that the whole of Lincolnshire would soon fall to the King's men. The defection of Cholmley (chapter 7) to the Royalists and the uncertain allegiance of Lord Hotham, in the key city and port of Hull, left Lord Fairfax in an increasingly precarious situation. For now, he remained at Selby with 1,500 men, but at the end of March, feeling isolated, he decided to pull back and join forces with the main Northern Association army in and around Leeds. A few days earlier, in order to cover his father's retreat and screen the Royalist army at York, Tom Fairfax advanced with most of his force towards Sherburne in Elmet. On arrival at the village and 'in order to amuse them more, [they] made an attempt on Tadcaster, where they had three or four hundred men, who presently quit the town and fled to York'.[1] Newcastle immediately despatched George Goring to counter young Fairfax's troublesome movement and to recapture Tadcaster.

Fairfax, on receiving intelligence of Goring's advance, delayed his departure from Tadcaster in the hope of destroying the town's defences. However, Goring's mounted vanguard force of 20 troops of horse moved south with speed. They arrived at one end of the town as the Parliamentarians debouched at the other. Not waiting for the supporting infantry and artillery, which were still some way behind, Goring took about half his mounted cavalry and dragoons (about 800 in all), crossed the river and set off in pursuit. Fairfax was heavily outnumbered in cavalry but was, nevertheless, forced to fight a rearguard action in order to buy time for his infantry to fall back and clear the open ground of Bramham Moor. Fairfax succeeded in getting his men off but they began to lose cohesion as they approached the smaller open space at Seacroft Moor. Fairfax recalled the unfortunate circumstances of the rout that followed:

> Here our men thinking themselves secure, were more careless in keeping order; and whilst their officers were getting them out of houses where they sought for drink, it being an extreme hot day, the enemy got another way as soon as we went into the moor; and when we had almost passed this plain, also, they seeing us in some disorder charged both in the flank and rear.[2]

On this open ground Goring caught and badly mauled Fairfax's men. Two hundred were killed or wounded and another 800 were captured. Tom's

father had, however, managed to make it back to Leeds from Selby with his force intact. Nevertheless, the losses, which they could barely afford, and the unnecessary reversal, were a considerable disappointment and a cause for the concern of the troop morale within the Northern Association. Many of the wives of the 800 prisoners taken by Goring's men implored Lord Fairfax to do something, 'their continual cries and tears, and importunities, compelled us to think of some way to redeem these men'.[3]

In Lancashire, Lord Derby had outwitted the Parliamentarians, and in mid-March had attacked the garrison at Lancaster and then doubled back to attack and recapture Preston, which had been left largely unguarded as the Parliamentarians moved north to assist the garrison at Lancaster. Derby then made a second attempt on Bolton but the garrison was better prepared.[4] The Parliamentarians were, however, determined to regain control of the region and on 1 April they launched a successful attack on the Royalist stronghold at Wigan. Two days later Brereton targeted Derby's headquarters at Warrington but the Royalists sallied out and defeated the Parliamentarians at Stockton Heath. A second attack two days later was also repulsed. The Royalists retained control of the town, and their foothold in Lancashire, but they were cut off and becoming increasingly isolated. Despite this, in mid-April Derby decided to once again take the fight to the Parliamentarians. He moved his headquarters to Preston and advanced towards Whalley Abbey, where he waited for an attack by the Parliamentarian forces under Colonel Shuttleworth. Despite being outnumbered four to one, the Parliamentarians prevailed.[5] It marked the end for the Royalists in Lancashire, Preston was recaptured, and Derby made good his escape to the Isle of Man (where he remained until 1651).

Meanwhile Newcastle, conscious that he needed to open and secure the road south and link up with the Royalist capital at Oxford, now moved to eliminate the threat posed by the Fairfaxes. In early April, he departed York with an army of over 10,000 men and arrived in front of Leeds intent on besieging the city. However, after a couple of days of bombardment he changed his plans. Cognisant of the need to protect his small army and keen not to get embroiled in a lengthy and potentially costly siege, Newcastle was advised and decided upon another plan.[6] He moved to occupy Wakefield and to drive out the small Parliamentarian garrisons at Rotherham and Sheffield. The Fairfaxes were now effectively surrounded in the West Riding enclave but they were under increasing pressure to secure the release of the Parliamentarian soldiers captured following the action at Seacroft Moor. Consequently, during the night of 20 May, Fairfax launched a daring attack with 1,500 foot and horse on the recent Royalist acquisition of Wakefield. Parliamentarian intelligence indicated no more than 600 or 800 men in the town. However,

---

1 Fairfax, *Short memorials*, pp. 23–4.
2 Ibid., pp. 26–7.

3 Ibid., p. 29.
4 Broxap, *Lancashire*, p. 78.
5 Ibid., pp. 81–4.
6 Johnson, *Adwalton Moor*, p. 32. His advisor was a Scot, General James King, a veteran from Continental battles with Gustavus Adolphus, who was a cautious advisor.

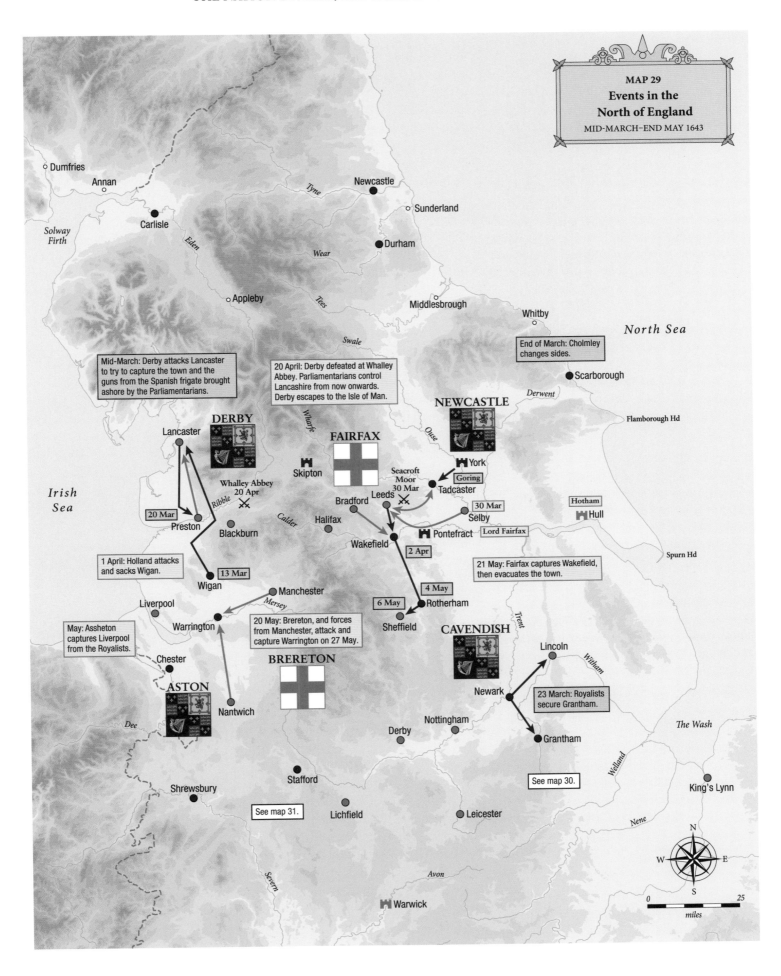

MAP 29

Events in the North of England

MID-MARCH–END MAY 1643

End of March: Cholmley changes sides.

Mid-March: Derby attacks Lancaster to try to capture the town and the guns from the Spanish frigate brought ashore by the Parliamentarians.

20 April: Derby defeated at Whalley Abbey. Parliamentarians control Lancashire from now onwards. Derby escapes to the Isle of Man.

DERBY

NEWCASTLE

FAIRFAX

Skipton

Seacroft Moor 30 Mar

York

Goring

Whalley Abbey 20 Apr

Bradford

Leeds

Tadcaster

30 Mar

Hotham

Hull

20 Mar

Preston

Blackburn

Halifax

Selby

Lord Fairfax

Wakefield

Pontefract

1 April: Holland attacks and sacks Wigan.

2 Apr

21 May: Fairfax captures Wakefield, then evacuates the town.

13 Mar

Wigan

Manchester

4 May

Liverpool

Warrington

6 May

Rotherham

May: Assheton captures Liverpool from the Royalists.

20 May: Brereton, and forces from Manchester, attack and capture Warrington on 27 May.

Sheffield

CAVENDISH

Lincoln

Chester

BRERETON

Newark

23 March: Royalists secure Grantham.

ASTON

Nantwich

Derby

Nottingham

Grantham

King's Lynn

Shrewsbury

Stafford

See map 30.

See map 31.

Lichfield

Leicester

Warwick

0   25

miles

Dumfries

Annan

Newcastle

Sunderland

Carlisle

Durham

Appleby

Middlesbrough

Whitby

North Sea

Scarborough

Flamborough Hd

Spurn Hd

The Wash

Irish Sea

Solway Firth

at the commencement of the attack, it was immediately apparent that this estimate was woefully erroneous. 'They had notice of our coming, and had manned all their works, and set about five hundred Musketeers to line the hedges without the town, which made us now doubt our intelligence, but it was too late.'[7] The struggle was ferocious but the Parliamentarians prevailed and during a Royalist cavalry counter-charge, Goring was taken prisoner. Fairfax continued his account: 'All our men got into the town, the streets were cleared, and many prisoners taken; but the horse got off almost entire.'[8] The Roundheads were amazed to discover that the garrison was more than 3,000 strong and Fairfax thanked God for his victory.

The loss of Wakefield was enough to convince Newcastle to abandon the offensive in the Midlands and he gave the order for his forces to (once again) fall back on York. Despite this, the Fairfaxes' position in West Riding remained precarious and Lord Fairfax appealed to neighbouring Parliamentarian forces for assistance. However, both to the east and west the battle lines were still being decided. To the west, Brereton, supported by Parliamentarian forces from Manchester, had another attempt on Warrington and by 27 May the Royalist stronghold was in Parliament's hands. To the east, the Parliamentarian armies were moving to try to capture the key fortified town of Newark. Assistance, therefore, in West Riding was by no means assured.

It will be recalled that the Eastern Association had been established in December 1642. Until now events in the five eastern counties had been relatively quiet. The key towns were held by Parliament and Royalist support was limited. The Earl of Manchester was in overall command of the Association but the emerging driving force was the Member of Parliament for Cambridge, Oliver Cromwell. As soon as Royalist supporters or sympathies emerged, he was quick to act and extinguish them. The small fishing village of Lowestoft was the first to receive Cromwell's undivided attention, when they declared for the King. Largely, it must be stated, because of the long-standing hostility between its staunchly Roundhead neighbours at Yarmouth.[9] It was a bloodless affair and the town was back in Parliamentarian hands by 14 March, while the ringleaders, including three church ministers, were sent to Cambridge to be severely reprimanded.[10] Cromwell, meanwhile, had been despatched to sort out King's Lynn 'because the malevolents in that town began to raise combustions there'.[11] The principal 'malevolent' was Sir Hammon L'Estrange, the town's governor. Cromwell arrived on 21 March to head up the enquiry. The ultimate fate of the 13 suspects, who were ordered to be sent up to Parliament or imprisoned in Wisbech Castle, is unclear. It seems Cromwell was lenient, on this occasion, as many of them were able to bring about a coup in August 1643 when the town declared for the King (see chapter 10).

It was, in fact, the actions of Henderson and Cavendish in Lincolnshire that were of far greater concern to Manchester and the Eastern Association. Cavendish had captured Grantham and now moved towards Boston, defeating on 11 April a Parliamentarian force of 1,500 men, at Ancaster Heath, under Lord Willoughby of Parham and Captain John Hotham (son of John Hotham in Hull). In early April, in order to counter this Royalist advance, and plausibly, in preparation for a major engagement with Newcastle's Army of the North, Cromwell summoned all the forces from Cambridgeshire, Norfolk and Suffolk and ordered them to collect near Huntingdon. As it transpired, about half these men were subsequently redirected to join Essex's army at Reading, leaving Cromwell just 6,000 men. This 'rump of Eastern Association' would have been hard pressed to hold the Royalist Army of the North, but Cromwell was not a man to be easily intimidated by such a task. On 22 April, he established his headquarters at Peterborough and began planning and preparing.

On 25 April, Cromwell joined forces with Anthony Irby and Miles Hobart, an old Parliamentary colleague, in order to besiege the small town of Crowland. It was an unremarkable event, other than the fact that it was Cromwell's first siege and that the Royalist defender was Captain Cromwell, one of Oliver's cousins. The siege was concluded in three days but there were more pressing matters at hand. The Royalists were clearly preparing to stage an attack on the eastern counties from Newark, and Essex gave orders for Cromwell to rendezvous with John Gell's Nottinghamshire Roundheads at Stamford to secure Lincolnshire. The initiative once again misfired and Cromwell was sent to join forces with Willoughby and Hotham at Sleaford, with the intention of making a pre-emptive strike on Newark. The group rendezvoused near Grantham on 11 May and began unhurried preparations for the advance and attack. The delay, however, allowed the Royalists to gather forces and execute a pre-emptive attack against this Parliamentarian concentration in the early hours of 13 May. Cavendish and Henderson amassed more than a thousand men, including 21 troops of horse and three or four dragoons, and then fell on Lord Willoughby's men in their billets at Belton (about 3 miles north of Grantham).[12] At least 70 were killed and 40 taken prisoner.[13] Later that day the Royalists advanced again and this time engaged Cromwell's 12 troops of horse just north of Grantham. Cromwell recorded, 'after we had stood a little, above musket-shot the one body from the other; and the dragooners had fired on both sides, for the space of half an hour or more; they not advancing towards us, we agreed to charge them'.[14] The Cavaliers were driven from the field, losing over 100 men killed and wounded and over 45 taken prisoner. Cromwell had learned his first lesson in combat. Taking the fight to the enemy can pay disproportionate dividends; 'cavalry battles are seldom won by any other means'.[15]

By mid-March, Waller was firmly established in Bristol at the head of the Western Association and was determined to expand Parliamentarian influence in the area. On 21 March, he stormed Malmesbury and three days later he surprised Lord Herbert's Royalists at Highnam, taking 1,600 prisoners, subsequently securing Gloucester as his prize. Waller's exploits were now a considerable cause for concern to the King, who was beginning to sense the tightening of the Parliamentarian encirclement on his main base in Oxford. Rupert was sent out to recapture Malmesbury, which he achieved by 26 March, before being recalled in order to march to the Midlands to secure the flank of the Queen's convoy from York. Another Royalist force under Prince Maurice was sent west, in Rupert's stead, to counter Waller's advance towards Wales. Maurice, supported by the Royalist infantry brigade commander Lord Grandison, captured Tewkesbury and then advanced across the River Severn by building a pontoon bridge (to the south) while sending part of his force north to cross the bridge at Upton. Maurice's aim was to corner Waller between the rivers Wye and Severn. In the meantime, Waller had occupied Monmouth and captured Chepstow, but he had no intention of fighting a battle with his back to the river and a hostile Wales to his flank. On 11 April, he sent his infantry and

7   Fairfax, op. cit., p. 30.
8   Ibid., p. 34.
9   Ketton-Cremer, *Norfolk in the Civil War*, p. 179.
10 Ibid., p. 182.
11 Ibid., p. 187.

12 Carlyle, *Cromwell's Letters*, vol. I, p. 128.
13 Burne & Young, *Great Civil War*, pp. 57–8.
14 Carlysle, op. cit., p. 129.
15 Burne & Young, op. cit., p. 58.

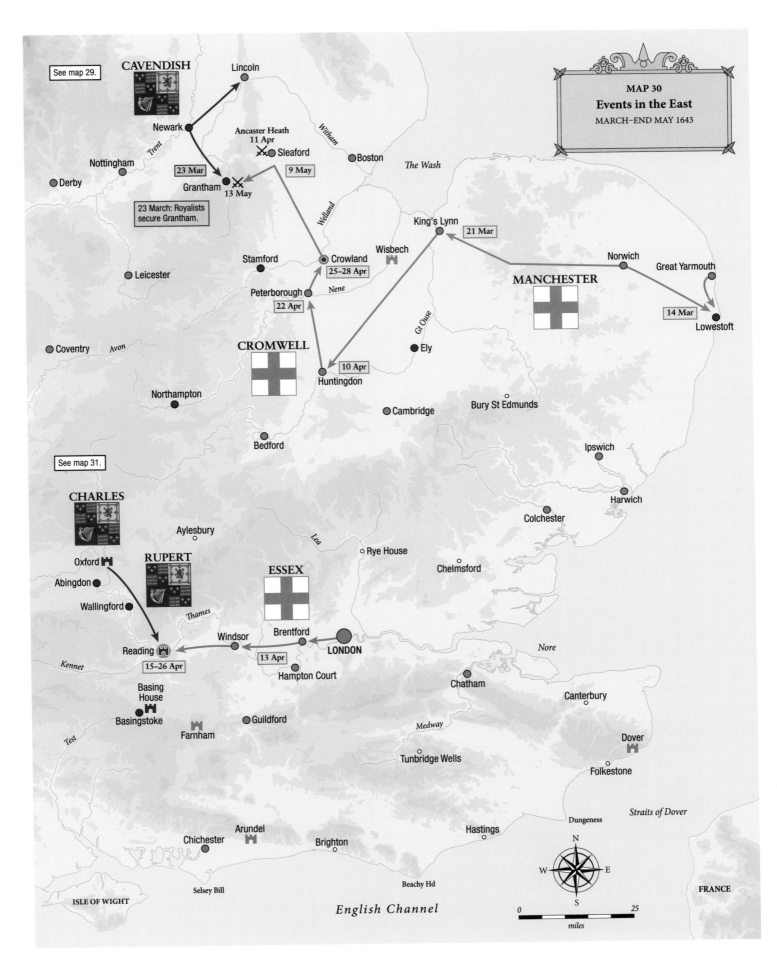

See map 29.

CAVENDISH

Lincoln

Newark

Ancaster Heath
11 Apr

Sleaford

Boston

Witham

The Wash

Nottingham

Derby

Trent

23 Mar

Grantham

13 May

9 May

23 March: Royalists
secure Grantham.

Welland

King's Lynn

21 Mar

Stamford

Crowland

Wisbech

25–28 Apr

MANCHESTER

Norwich

Great Yarmouth

14 Mar

Lowestoft

Leicester

Peterborough

Nene

22 Apr

CROMWELL

Coventry

Avon

Gt Ouse

Ely

Northampton

10 Apr

Huntingdon

Bury St Edmunds

Cambridge

Ipswich

Bedford

See map 31.

Harwich

CHARLES

Aylesbury

Colchester

Rye House

Chelmsford

Oxford

RUPERT

ESSEX

Lea

Abingdon

Wallingford

Thames

Windsor

Brentford

LONDON

Nore

Reading

13 Apr

15–26 Apr

Hampton Court

Kennet

Chatham

Canterbury

Basing
House

Basingstoke

Farnham

Guildford

Medway

Dover

Test

Tunbridge Wells

Folkestone

Dungeness

Straits of Dover

Arundel

Chichester

Brighton

Hastings

N

W   E

S

FRANCE

ISLE OF WIGHT

Selsey Bill

Beachy Hd

English Channel

0   25

miles

MAP 30
Events in the East
MARCH–END MAY 1643

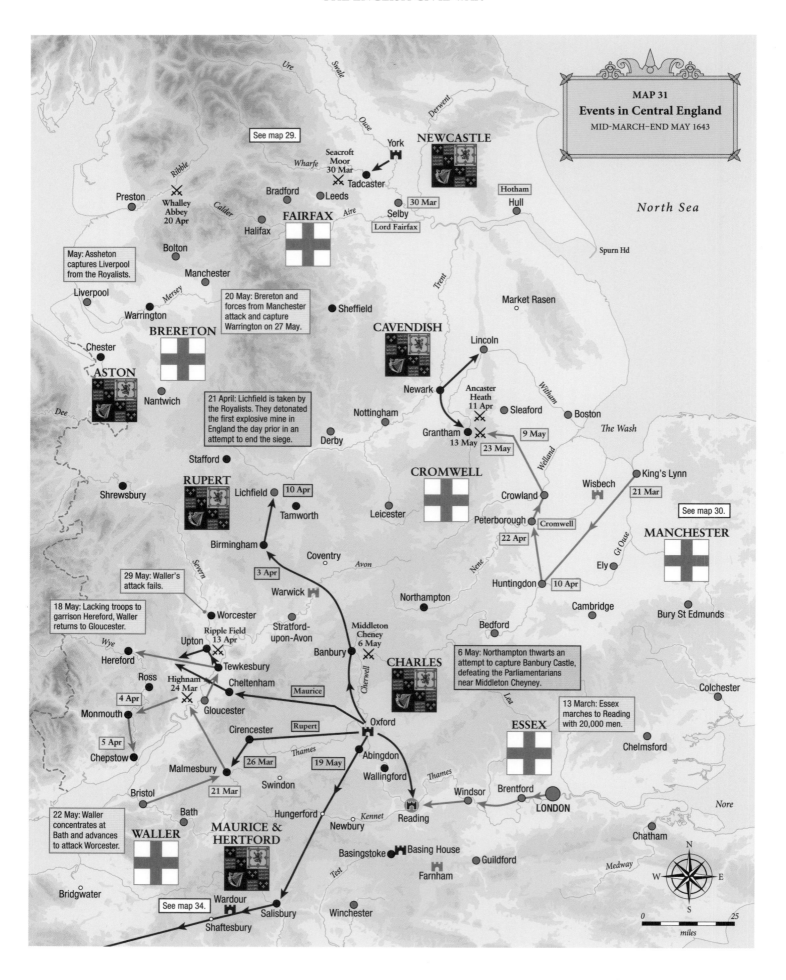

See map 29.

NEWCASTLE

York

Seacroft
Moor
30 Mar
Tadcaster

MAP 31
Events in Central England
MID-MARCH–END MAY 1643

North Sea

Bradford
Leeds
30 Mar
Selby
Hotham
Hull

Preston
Whalley
Abbey
20 Apr

FAIRFAX
Lord Fairfax

Halifax
Bolton

Spurn Hd

May: Assheton
captures Liverpool
from the Royalists.

Manchester

Liverpool
Warrington

20 May: Brereton and
forces from Manchester
attack and capture
Warrington on 27 May.

Sheffield

CAVENDISH

Market Rasen

BRERETON

Chester

ASTON

Nantwich

21 April: Lichfield is taken by
the Royalists. They detonated
the first explosive mine in
England the day prior in an
attempt to end the siege.

Nottingham

Derby

Stafford

RUPERT

Lichfield   10 Apr

Tamworth

Birmingham

Newark

Ancaster
Heath
11 Apr

Lincoln

Sleaford

Grantham
13 May   23 May

9 May

Boston

The Wash

CROMWELL

King's Lynn

Wisbech

21 Mar

Shrewsbury

Crowland

Peterborough   Cromwell

22 Apr

Ely

See map 30.

MANCHESTER

Coventry

Avon

Leicester

Huntingdon   10 Apr

Cambridge

Bury St Edmunds

29 May: Waller's
attack fails.

Warwick

3 Apr

Northampton

Bedford

18 May: Lacking troops to
garrison Hereford, Waller
returns to Gloucester.

Worcester

Ripple Field
13 Apr

Upton

Stratford-
upon-Avon

Middleton
Cheney
6 May

Banbury

CHARLES

6 May: Northampton thwarts an
attempt to capture Banbury Castle,
defeating the Parliamentarians
near Middleton Cheyney.

Colchester

Hereford

Tewkesbury

Ross

Highnam
24 Mar

Cheltenham

Maurice

Chelmsford

4 Apr

Monmouth

Gloucester

Oxford

13 March: Essex
marches to Reading
with 20,000 men.

ESSEX

5 Apr

Chepstow

Cirencester

Rupert

Abingdon

Wallingford

Malmesbury

26 Mar

Thames

19 May

Thames

Windsor

Brentford

LONDON

Bristol

21 Mar

Swindon

22 May: Waller
concentrates at
Bath and advances
to attack Worcester.

Bath

WALLER

Hungerford

Kennet

Newbury

Reading

Chatham

Nore

Medway

MAURICE &
HERTFORD

Basingstoke   Basing House

Guildford

Farnham

Bridgwater

See map 34.

Wardour

Salisbury

Test

Winchester

N
W   E
S

Shaftesbury

0   25

miles

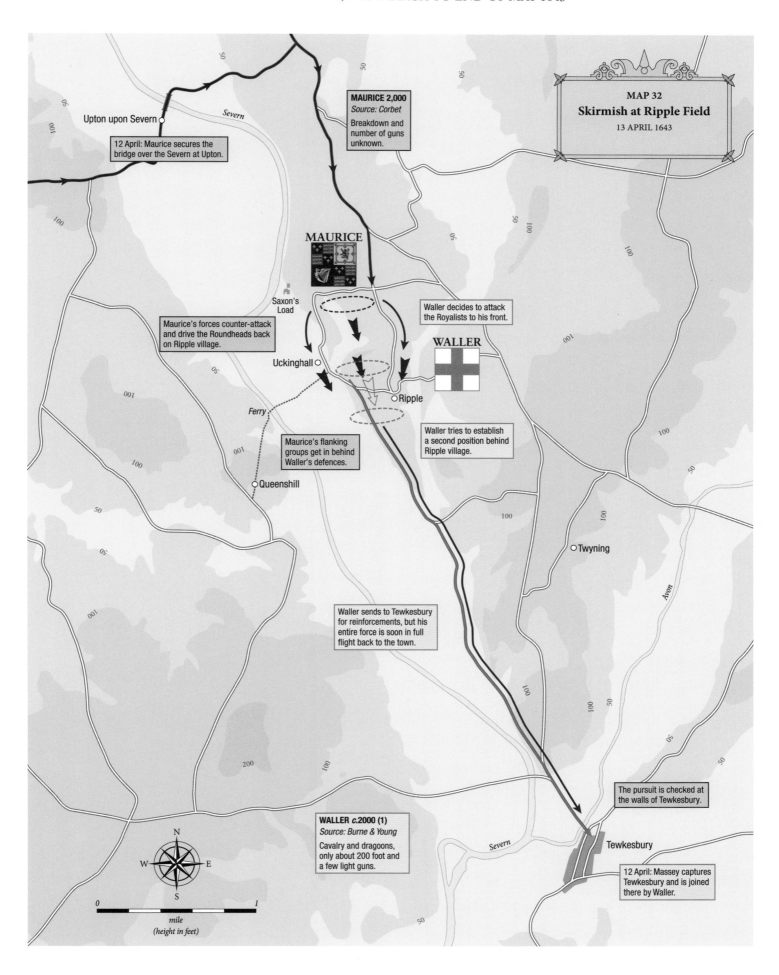

MAP 32
Skirmish at Ripple Field
13 APRIL 1643

MAURICE 2,000
Source: Corbet
Breakdown and number of guns unknown.

12 April: Maurice secures the bridge over the Severn at Upton.

Upton upon Severn

Severn

MAURICE

Saxon's Load

Waller decides to attack the Royalists to his front.

Maurice's forces counter-attack and drive the Roundheads back on Ripple village.

WALLER

Uckinghall

Ripple

Ferry

Maurice's flanking groups get in behind Waller's defences.

Waller tries to establish a second position behind Ripple village.

Queenshill

Twyning

Waller sends to Tewkesbury for reinforcements, but his entire force is soon in full flight back to the town.

Avon

The pursuit is checked at the walls of Tewkesbury.

WALLER c.2000 (1)
Source: Burne & Young
Cavalry and dragoons, only about 200 foot and a few light guns.

N
W   E
S

Severn

Tewkesbury

12 April: Massey captures Tewkesbury and is joined there by Waller.

0   1
mile
(height in feet)

artillery across the Severn estuary, and, after two brief cavalry skirmishes at Newnham and Little Dean, he made it back to the safety of Gloucester. The captured Monmouthshire towns duly returned to Royalist hands.

The newly appointed garrison commander of Gloucester was Colonel Edward Massey, a man who was to stamp his name on the struggles in the region. Wasting no time, he suggested a plan to isolate the Royalist forces.[16] Waller agreed to the proposal and on 12 April he advanced north along the east bank of the Severn towards Tewkesbury. Massey led the vanguard of about 500 men, destroying the Royalist pontoon bridge en route before moving on to capture Tewkesbury. John Corbet, a preacher of God's word from a Gloucester parish, recorded that 'The forlorn hope surprised and slew the sentinel, climbed over the works, and cut down the drawbridge; whereupon both horse and foot rushed in.'[17] Tewkesbury was in Massey's hands, but it was late in the day and his troops were exhausted. Early the next day Waller joined Massey with the balance of 1,500 Parliamentarians and, after a discussion, he decided to send Massey north to try to capture or destroy the bridge at Upton. Soon after Massey departed, Waller received intelligence that Maurice had discovered the previous day that the Royalist bridge south of Tewkesbury had been destroyed and that Maurice had, accordingly, rushed north to secure the key crossing at Upton. Waller followed in the steps of Massey with his force and the two groups linked up a few miles to the north at the small village of Ripple. Meanwhile, Maurice had crossed the River Severn and was probing south.

John Corbet noted that 'The next morning [13 April] Sir William [Waller] advanced towards the Prince, and found him in Ripple Field with his army drawn up, and divided into three bodies, besides the hedges lined with musketeers.'[18] The two forces were numerically balanced, at about 2,000, but Waller had a paucity of foot with only one strong company of Massey's Own, providing fewer than 200 pike and muskets.[19] He brought up some light guns and placed these on a hill, known as 'The Bank', overlooking Ripple Field.[20] Waller tried to get these in action quickly, but their range could not carry to Maurice's troops and it soon became clear that 'having neither shot prepared nor Cannoneers that understood their business' they were of little value.[21] Nevertheless, he decided to attack the motionless Royalists to his front by charging down Ripple Field towards them. Waller's cavalry was swiftly countered and driven back and Waller's initial intentions of making a stand began to evaporate. Conscious that he had a paucity of infantry, that his flanks were vulnerable, and that his only means of retreat was a narrow lane to his back on the road to Tewkesbury, Waller gave the order to fall back. All his musketeers were ordered to line the hedges on the two roads leading to the village, and on the road to Tewkesbury, while his mounted dragoons were to delay the Royalist follow-up. His cavalry was to debouch and establish itself in the fields to the south of the village. His aim was to channel the Royalists down the hedge-lined lanes and, with concentrated musket fire, force them through openings into the fields either side of the road where the Parliamentarian cavalry would charge them.

However, Maurice's flanking groups (particularly that on the right by Uckinghall) were able to disrupt the manoeuvre and attack the musketeers before they had deployed and the cavalry before it got into position. A simultaneous attack in the centre, on the rearguard dragoons, drove them from the field and into the confusion of the tight hedge-lined lanes. Waller sent to Tewkesbury for reinforcements but before the message was received the Parliamentarians were already in full flight. Arthur Haselrig managed to buy some time by getting his cavalry troop to charge the rampant Royalists, but it provided only temporary respite.[22] The Cavaliers pursued the broken Parliamentarians to the walls of Tewkesbury where they checked only when Waller's force was reinforced by men from within the town. It had been a costly defeat for Waller and a salutary lesson. He had lost most of his infantry and a number of his dragoons; it was another example of the superiority of the Royalist cavalry at the early stages of the war. Maurice pulled back to Evesham but his next mission was not long in coming.

Maurice was not alone in being called to assist the King at Reading. Rupert had successfully besieged Lichfield and by 21 April the city was in Royalist hands. A week earlier Essex had marched from Windsor with an army of 19,000 men to besiege the fortified town of Reading. It was a key town, located on the River Thames and at the crossroads of the road west from London to Bristol, and north from Southampton to Oxford and the Midlands.[23] Nevertheless, Charles had resolved to give up the place for lack of guns and powder, but the Royalist governor, Sir Arthur Aston, had other ideas.[24] The town had been fortified from November the previous year with a series of forts, earthworks and ditches. Although they would be of little use against a well-conducted siege and good train of artillery, Aston considered that the defence of the key town was worth a try. Essex's vanguard arrived on 14 April and seized the bridge and redoubt at Caversham, thereby cutting the road to Oxford. Essex sent in a summons for surrender, which was promptly rebuffed. He did not establish a cordon around the town but instead concentrated his force to the west in expectation that he would have to drive off any force sent down from Oxford to raise the siege. The next day the heavy guns were moved (as they arrived) directly into hastily prepared battery positions and the bombardment began. The first real siege of the civil war had begun.

Aston ordered a light gun to be placed in the steeple of St Giles's Church, which was promptly destroyed, along with the steeple, by counter-battery fire.[25] On 18 April the first of the Royalist troops from Oxford arrived, but not on the south bank to the west, on the north bank. Unable to cross Caversham Bridge they made arrangements for about 700 men, and some ammunition, to be sent across the Thames from Sonning (about 3 miles downstream). The crossing was spotted by a Parliamentarian cavalry vedette (sentry), prompting Essex to establish a full cordon the next day as more Parliamentarian troops arrived in the area. The same day, the heavy siege guns advanced to within 250 yards of the west walls and outposts, and the Royalist gunners were running dangerously short of powder and ammunition. Later that day they suffered another blow when Aston was injured by falling masonry. The head wound was so serious that it prevented him from speaking and command was passed to Colonel Richard Fielding.

16 Washburn, *Bibliotheca Gloucestrensis*, p. xxxix.

17 Corbet, *Gloucester*, p. 32.

18 Ibid., p. 33.

19 Burne & Young, op. cit., p. 72.

20 Peter Young, who knew the parish well, called the hill 'Old Nan's Hill', an 18th-century derivative of 'Ordnance Hill', which, almost certainly, evolved as a result of the battle. It is currently known as 'Green's Hill', as it is owned and farmed by the Green family.

21 Corbet, op. cit., p. 33.

22 Haselrig's troop suffered severe losses at Ripple Field. Returning to London, he raised a new regiment of horse, equipped as armoured cuirassiers. They became known as the 'Lobsters' or 'London Lobsters' and formed the heavy cavalry in Waller's army.

23 Barrès-Baker, *The Siege of Reading*, p. 10.

24 Clarendon, *History of the Rebellion*, vol. IV, p. 23. There were only 40 barrels of powder in the place.

25 Barrès-Baker, op. cit., p. 77.

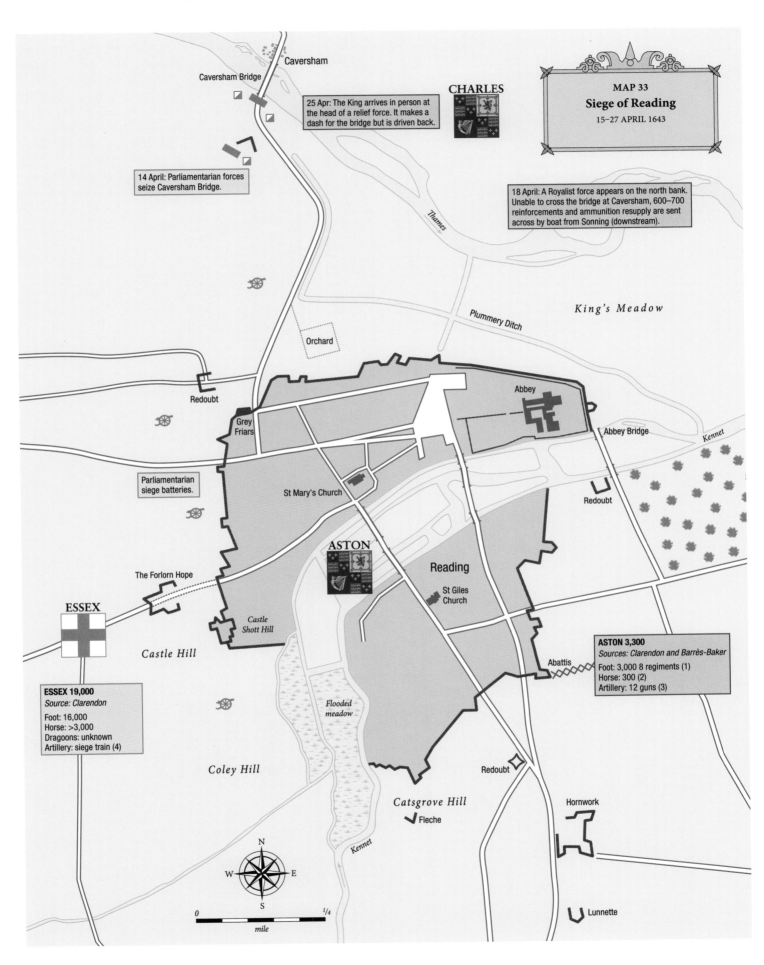

Caversham

Caversham Bridge

CHARLES

25 Apr: The King arrives in person at the head of a relief force. It makes a dash for the bridge but is driven back.

MAP 33
Siege of Reading
15–27 APRIL 1643

14 April: Parliamentarian forces seize Caversham Bridge.

Thames

18 April: A Royalist force appears on the north bank. Unable to cross the bridge at Caversham, 600–700 reinforcements and ammunition resupply are sent across by boat from Sonning (downstream).

King's Meadow

Plummery Ditch

Orchard

Redoubt

Abbey

Grey Friars

Abbey Bridge

Kennet

Parliamentarian siege batteries.

St Mary's Church

Redoubt

ASTON

Reading

The Forlorn Hope

St Giles Church

ESSEX

Castle Shott Hill

ASTON 3,300
Sources: Clarendon and Barrès-Baker
Foot: 3,000 8 regiments (1)
Horse: 300 (2)
Artillery: 12 guns (3)

Abattis

Castle Hill

ESSEX 19,000
Source: Clarendon
Foot: 16,000
Horse: >3,000
Dragoons: unknown
Artillery: siege train (4)

Flooded meadow

Coley Hill

Redoubt

Catsgrove Hill

Hornwork

Fleche

Kennet

N
W   E
S

0   1/4
mile

Lunnette

On 22 April, a man by the name of Flower was ordered to swim across the Thames and inform the garrison that a relief force was on the way. He succeeded in his mission but morale within the town was at breaking point. Charles left Oxford two days later and was joined by Rupert on 25 April on the north bank of the Thames overlooking the besieged town. Together they had an army of nine regiments of foot, over 50 troops of horse and 12 guns.[26] Inside the town, however, the situation seemed hopeless, and despite the fact that they could see the large Royalist force to the north, Fielding opened negotiations. As his white flag fluttered above the ramparts, the Royalists dashed upon the bridge, their artillery firing over their heads. They were quickly picked off by the Parliamentarian infantry on the south bank.[27] Fielding was now caught in a cleft stick by his own making; to have come to their support would have scuppered the truce, but by not so doing he was effectively handing over the town to Parliament. He chose to sit on his hands and the attack failed. Terms were agreed the following day and the fortress was handed over on 27 April. The garrison marched: 'with colours aloft and lighted match, with drums beating and trumpets sounding, horse and foot passed through the ramparts and took the road by Caversham Bridge to Oxford'.[28] The town was then mercilessly plundered by the Parliamentarians, who perceived the release of the garrison to have been a mistake, and it took two days for discipline to be restored. Meanwhile Fielding and his men arrived at Oxford to a muted welcome. Fielding was inevitably court-martialled for surrendering the town and, not surprisingly under the circumstances, sentenced to death.[29]

---

26 Ibid., p. 124.

27 These two infantry regiments were from Colonel Barclay's and Colonel Holborne's regiments. Parliamentary intelligence papers, British Library: Thomason/18:E.100[5].

28 Nash Ford, Internet Site: *Royal Berkshire History*, citing Childs, *The story of the Town of Reading*.

29 He was later reprieved at the last-minute intercession by the Prince of Wales at the prompting of Prince Rupert.

CHAPTER 9
EVENTS IN THE SOUTH-WEST, MARCH TO JUNE 1643

Following Hopton's reverse at Modbury on 21 February, the Cornish Royalists fell back towards their home county and Hopton readily took up the offer of a local truce. Both sides needed breathing space to reorganize and rebuild their forces. The short truce in March was later extended until 22 April. It was one of a number of local initiatives to stand back from the national struggle and followed similar cases in Yorkshire, Cheshire and Dorset.[1] Having witnessed the horrors of civil conflict first hand, many hoped for a successful resolution offered by the newly opened talks between the King and Parliament. While many desired peace, others inevitably used the truce to reequip and rearm. Parliament was critical of these local initiatives, considering them to be derogatory towards their power and authority and counterproductive to ongoing negotiations. As if to emphasize the point, the Parliamentary council of war in Devon used the time to raise three new regiments.

The cessation of hostilities in the region ran out at midnight on 22 April. Earlier in the day Hopton had received intelligence of a Parliamentarian force concentrating at Lifton, a stone's throw from the Tamar and close enough to strike at the Royalist force at Launceston. With Stamford sick of the gout and holed-up at Exeter, command of the Parliamentarian force of 1,500 foot and 200 horse had devolved to James Chudleigh.[2] Chudleigh decided to act immediately after the truce was concluded and early on 23 April he advanced, captured Polson Bridge over the Tamar at first light, and then made best speed towards Launceston in a bid to catch the Royalists off guard. Hopton had ordered a general muster but time was against him. He ordered Grenville's Regiment to occupy a strong defensive position on Beacon Hill, from where he could see Chudleigh's forces advancing towards the feature. At 10am the attack commenced and the Royalists were systematically driven back, hedge by hedge.[3] But as time passed, more and more Royalist reinforcements arrived, which stemmed the flow and turned the tide. Chudleigh was forced into a hasty retreat and was only saved from Hopton's attempt to capture Polson Bridge and cut him off by the timely arrival of Colonel Merrick's Regiment from Plymouth. Chudleigh held off Hopton's counter-attack and withdrew under cover of darkness back through Lifton to Okehampton. His pre-emptive strike had stirred the hornet's nest.

Two days later, Hopton, now fully reinforced to a strength of 3,000 foot, 300 dragoons and 300 horse, and availed of intelligence of considerable unrest among Chudleigh's men at Okehampton, decided to strike.[4] He advanced late in the day with the intention of attacking early on the 26th. Chudleigh got wind of the plan, and despite having a depleted force through the 'neglect and dullness' of his deputy scoutmaster and sergeant major, he

decided to lay an ambush. Marching west with all his cavalry, he deployed his 108 horse into six sections on the slopes of Sourton Down. It was a bold plan and was executed brilliantly. The surprise, when sprung, was enough to cause confusion in the Royalist ranks, which broke and fled. Their charge exhausted, the Royalists rallied and Chudleigh's order to his infantry to advance and seal the victory showed none of the earlier resolve by his horse. Nevertheless, the sight of burning matches in the gorse bushes, left by Chudleigh's men by way of deception, was enough to convince the Royalists that Chudleigh's men had stood their ground. The Parliamentarians grasped their opportunity as they moved back to Okehampton without incident. The Royalists became aware that they had been duped when a tremendous thunderstorm broke overhead, extinguishing the deception. Hopton retreated to Launceston somewhat perplexed at what had just taken place. Such was the relief in the Parliamentarian ranks, however, that word quickly spread that it was God's will and God's work. One anonymous soldier noted:

> ... during the flight of the Cornubians [Cornish] an extraordinary storm of lightning and thunder fell upon them, which lightning singed and burnt the hair of their heads, and fired the gunpowder in their musket pans and bandoliers, which so lamentably scorched and burnt many of their bodies, that they sent for 12 Chyrurgions [surgeons] from Launceston to cure them.[5]

Probably wishful thinking on the part of the Parliamentarian soldier and, whether true or not, Hopton, fired up with indignation, was determined to have another go. However, before he could strike, he received intelligence that more Parliamentarian troops had been moved to the area. Stamford had been apprised of the Royalist plan to link up the forces of Hopton and Maurice and he was determined to stop it. Every available man was mustered for what Stamford considered to be the decisive battle for Cornwall. Stamford headed north with 5,400 foot, 200 horse and 13 guns, and crossed the Cornish border on 15 May destined for Grenville's Royalist force at Stratton. The day prior, the Devon landowner Sir George Chudleigh had been despatched with 1,200 horse in order to make a dash for Bodmin, where the sheriff was holding a *posse comitatus* to raise more troops. Grenville had about 1,200 men at Stratton; the balance of the Royalist forces were spread across the county, with 900 at Liskeard under Lord Mohun, 1,000 at Saltash with Slanning and 700 in Launceston under Trevanion.[6] On 12 May Hopton was at Launceston when he got wind of Stamford's intentions. He gathered his forces and headed north to reinforce Grenville, arriving to the west of Stratton on the evening of 15 May. En route he had left a small force to secure the crossing over the River Neet near Efford House and Mill in Bude.[7]

1 Andriette, *Devon and Exeter*, p. 82, citing Seymour Papers, Devon County Record Office; Coate, *Cornwall in the Great Civil War*, p. 56.
2 Eldest son of (and not to be confused with) George Chudleigh.
3 Coate, op. cit., p. 60.
4 Ibid., p. 62.

5 Anon, *Joyfull newes from Plimouth* (London, 1643).
6 Chadwyck-Healey, *Bellum Civile*, p. 41.
7 Ibid., p. 42. Efford House was also known as Ebbingford House.

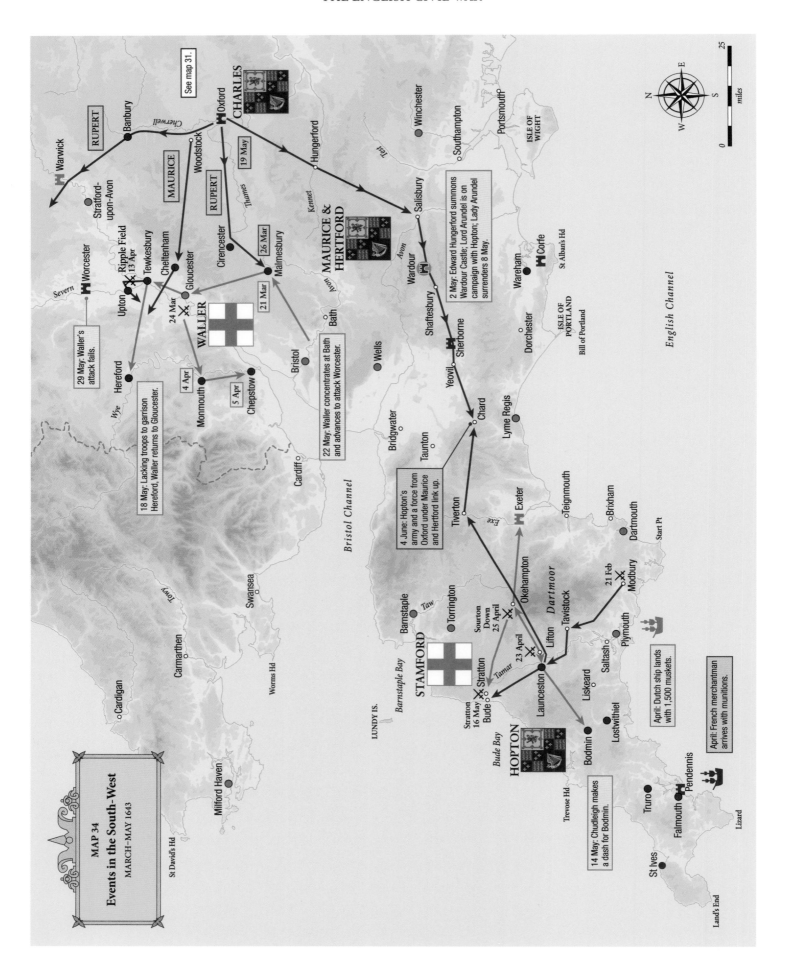

MAP 34
Events in the South-West
MARCH–MAY 1643

See map 31.

RUPERT

MAURICE

RUPERT

MAURICE & HERTFORD

WALLER

STAMFORD

HOPTON

CHARLES

Warwick

Banbury

Stratford-upon-Avon

Cherwell

Woodstock

19 May

Oxford

Hungerford

Kennet

Winchester

Southampton

Portsmouth

ISLE OF WIGHT

Severn

Worcester

Upton

Ripple Field
13 Apr

Tewkesbury

Cheltenham

Gloucester

24 Mar

Cirencester

26 Mar

Thames

Malmesbury

21 Mar

Salisbury

Avon

Wardour

Shaftesbury

Corfe

St Alban's Hd

Wareham

English Channel

Hereford

Wye

Monmouth

4 Apr

5 Apr

Chepstow

Bristol

Bath

Avon

Wells

Sherborne

Yeovil

Dorchester

ISLE OF PORTLAND

BILL OF PORTLAND

2 May: Edward Hungerford summons Wardour Castle; Lord Arundel is on campaign with Hopton; Lady Arundel surrenders 8 May.

29 May: Waller's attack fails.

18 May: Lacking troops to garrison Hereford, Waller returns to Gloucester.

22 May: Waller concentrates at Bath and advances to attack Worcester.

Cardigan

St David's Hd

Milford Haven

Carmarthen

Towy

Swansea

Worms Hd

Cardiff

Bristol Channel

Bridgwater

Taunton

Chard

Lyme Regis

4 June: Hopton's army and a force from Oxford under Maurice and Hertford link up.

Tiverton

Exe

Exeter

Teignmouth

Brixham

Dartmouth

Start Pt

LUNDY IS.

Barnstaple Bay

Barnstaple

Torrington

Taw

Okehampton

Sourton Down
25 April

Dartmoor

Tavistock

21 Feb

Modbury

Plymouth

Lifton

23 April

Launceston

Saltash

Tamar

Liskeard

Bodmin

Lostwithiel

Stratton
16 May

Bude

Bude Bay

Trevose Hd

Truro

Falmouth

Pendennis

St Ives

Lizard

Land's End

April: Dutch ship lands with 1,500 muskets.

April: French merchantman arrives with munitions.

14 May: Chudleigh makes a dash for Bodmin.

N
S
E
W

0   25
miles

98

Stamford arrived in the area the same evening and deployed his force atop a large hill about half a mile to the north-west of Stratton, on which stood an ancient earthwork.[8] It was a strong feature, virtually unassailable from the east, and provided a natural second line of defence if the crest of the hill were overrun.[9] Hopton called an immediate council of war and, despite being outnumbered two to one, they decided to attack early the next morning before George Chudleigh's cavalry arrived to reinforce Stamford's force. The decision was partly predicated on the fact that they had a chronic shortage of rations. Grenville's local knowledge enabled the Royalists to move through the night and be in a position to launch a dawn attack. Hopton divided his force into five groups: four assault groups, each with two guns, and a reserve under John Digby. Hopton, who wrote his memoires in the third person, described what happened next:

> ... Sir Ralph Hopton, undertooke to assault the Enemies Campe upon the south side, next Sir John Berkeley and Sir Bevile Grenvile upon the Avenue next to them upon the left hand, Sir Nicholas Slanning and Coll. Trevanion the next Avenue to that upon the left hand of Sir Thomas Bassett and Coll. Godolphin upon the left hand of all, Mr. John Digby with the horse and dragoones being then about five hundred, stoode upon a Sandy-Common where there was a way leading up to the Enemyes Campe, with order to charge anything that should come downe that way in a body, but els to stand firme in reserve.[10]

The first attack went in at about 5am and the four groups, supported by their light guns, continued the attack for nearly ten hours. By about 3pm the Royalist ammunition was nearly exhausted but Hopton kept this information from his men and decided to make one last push with the pike and sword. The Royalist foot were ordered to hold their fire until they had reached the summit. During this advance, General James Chudleigh (eldest son of George Chudleigh despatched to Bodmin) made a charge at Grenville's Foot. Hopton recalled,

> It fortuned that on that Avenew where Sir Bevile Grenvile advanc'd in the head of his Pikes in the way, And Sir Jo: Berkeley ledd on the muskettiers on each syde of him, Major Generall Chudleigh with a stand of Pikes charg'd Sir Bevile Greenvile so smartliek, that there was some disorder, Sir Bevile Greenvile, in person overthrowen, but being presently relieved by Sir Jo: Berkely and some of his owne officers, hee reenforc'd the charge and there tooke Major Generall Chudleigh prisoner....[11]

It proved the catalyst for the Parliamentarian collapse. The four Royalist groups pushed on all fronts until they united atop the hill, where they turned the captured cannon at the edge of the hill towards the ancient earthwork to finish the job.

Parliamentarian losses were significant, with 300 killed, over 1,700 taken prisoner along with the 13 pieces of ordnance, 70 barrels of powder and a large supply of biscuit and other provisions.[12] Many Parliamentarians escaped but the Royalist pursuit was measured as they were acutely conscious that Chudleigh's Horse had not yet shown itself from the south. Hopton's somewhat unconventional tactics had paid off: he had beaten a numerically superior force established on a highly defendable piece of terrain. In so doing, he secured Cornwall for the King's cause and opened up the possibility of a union of Royalist forces (as per the King's plan) in Somerset. Stamford headed back towards Exeter, amid accusations of bungling and poor generalship. Then, when news came through of James Chudleigh's defection, the blame for this also fell at his feet. Meanwhile, Chudleigh senior had successfully attacked Bodmin but withdrew in haste once news of the Royalist victory at Stratton broke across the county.[13] Hopton tried to intercept the Parliamentarian horse as they withdrew, but they evaded the attempt and slipped back across the Tamar towards Exeter, where a dejected Stamford contemplated the magnitude of the loss at Stratton and the immediate implications for the region and himself.

Hopton advanced into Devon on 21 May and sent a summons to Stamford to surrender Exeter, which was promptly refused. Accepting that the place could only be taken by regular siege, Hopton moved east towards Tiverton and then on to Chard, where, on 4 June, he linked up with a Royalist force under Hertford and Maurice. Their combined numbers amounted to 7,000 men, consisting of 4,000 foot and 2,400 horse. Despite this large force and the Royalist victory in Cornwall, the county of Devon was still far from safe for the King.[14] At much the same time, Parliament was to suffer another, less serious, setback when Waller abandoned Hereford for lack of troops to garrison the place. He withdrew to Gloucester on 18 May and began to arrange for the concentration of his Western Association in and around Bath for another offensive. A few days later he advanced north towards Worcester but, on 29 May, his attempt to capture the city was easily repulsed and he withdrew back to Gloucester, amid rumours of a Royalist cavalry group moving to cut him off.

There can be little doubt that the Parliamentary initiatives would have benefited considerably from more centralized planning and strategic direction. The expanded organization of association armies had some clear advantages to a regionally recruited force but undeniable disadvantages when it came to national cohesion. Essex's power over the generals commanding association armies was vague at best, and rumours that he was resentful of both the Earl of Manchester and William Waller were not altogether unfounded.[15] The fact that Essex's army was fixed at 10,000 men, while Parliament agreed that Manchester's Eastern Association could recruit up to 21,000, was another source of open discontent to Essex.[16] Furthermore, the raising of these new regional association armies was not without its drawbacks and led to some desertion of soldiers from one association to join the ranks of another where, the deserters perceived, the conditions were better. Furthermore, such moves were not without the possibility of personal advancement and financial incentive. The King's army had fewer issues with regard to its chain of command, but it endured similar challenges when it came to filling the ranks thinned by war. Instead of actively recruiting, the King's army was resupplied by creating new regiments. Charles Firth concluded

---

8   The hill bears his name to this day.

9   Coate, op. cit., p. 67.

10 Chadwyck-Healey, op. cit., p. 42.

11 Ibid., p. 43.

12 Ibid., p. 44.

13 George Chudleigh resigned his Commission once his son's defection became known and within a few weeks had followed his example.

14 Andriette, op. cit., p. 88.

15 Wedgwood, *King's War*, p. 199.

16 Firth, *Cromwell's Army*, p. 24.

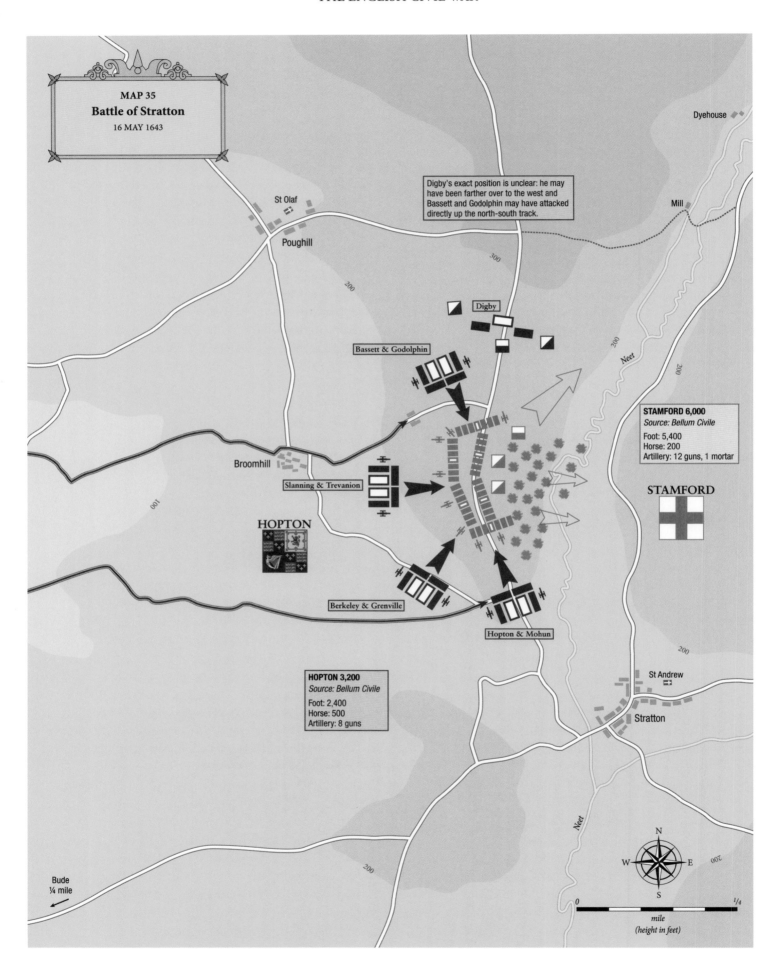

MAP 35
Battle of Stratton
16 MAY 1643

St Olaf

Poughill

Digby's exact position is unclear: he may have been farther over to the west and Bassett and Godolphin may have attacked directly up the north-south track.

Mill

Dyehouse

300

200

Digby

Bassett & Godolphin

Neet

200

200

Broomhill

Slanning & Trevanion

HOPTON

100

STAMFORD 6,000
Source: Bellum Civile
Foot: 5,400
Horse: 200
Artillery: 12 guns, 1 mortar

STAMFORD

Berkeley & Grenville

Hopton & Mohun

HOPTON 3,200
Source: Bellum Civile
Foot: 2,400
Horse: 500
Artillery: 8 guns

St Andrew

200

Stratton

Neet

200

Bude
¼ mile

N
W   E
S

0   1/4
mile
(height in feet)

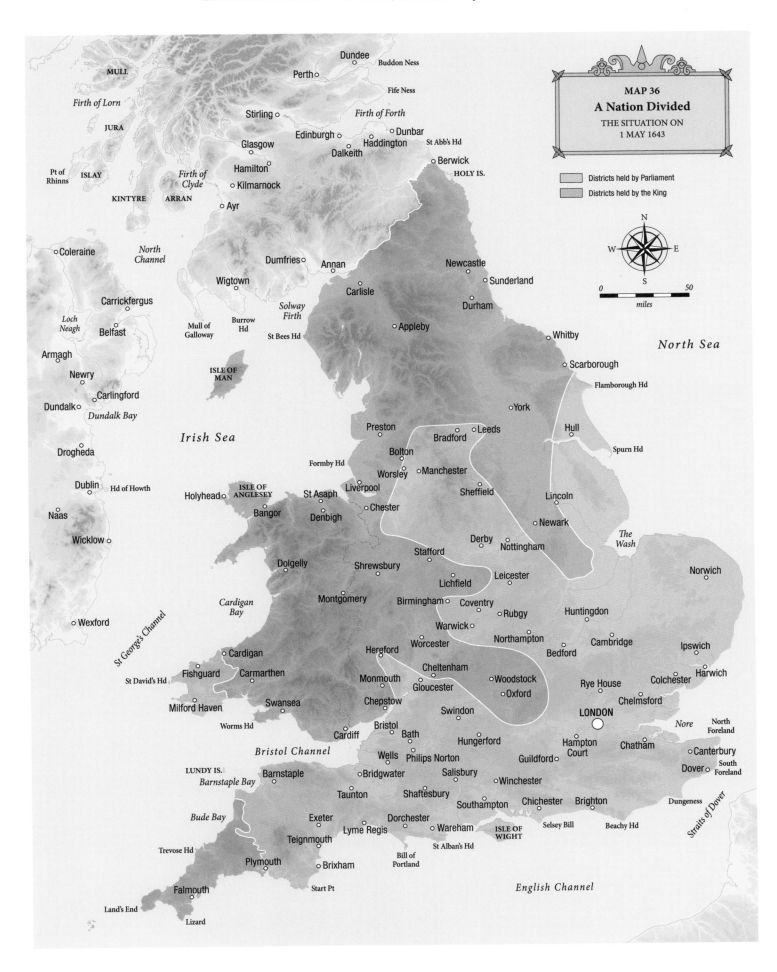

MAP 36

A Nation Divided

THE SITUATION ON
1 MAY 1643

Districts held by Parliament

Districts held by the King

N
W — E
S

0 _____ 50
miles

MULL

Firth of Lorn

JURA

Pt of
Rhinns   ISLAY

KINTYRE   ARRAN

Dundee
Buddon Ness
Perth
Fife Ness

Firth of Forth

Stirling
Edinburgh   Dunbar
Glasgow   Haddington   St Abb's Hd
Dalkeith
Hamilton   Berwick
Kilmarnock   HOLY IS.

Firth of Clyde

Ayr

Coleraine   *North Channel*

Newcastle

Dumfries   Annan
Wigtown   Sunderland
Carlisle   Durham

Solway Firth

Appleby   Whitby   *North Sea*

Carrickfergus   Burrow Hd
Mull of   St Bees Hd
Galloway   Scarborough

Loch Neagh   ISLE OF MAN   Flamborough Hd

Belfast

Armagh   York   Hull
Newry   Spurn Hd
Carlingford   *Irish Sea*   Preston
Dundalk   Leeds
          Bradford
Dundalk Bay   Bolton
          Worsley   Manchester   Lincoln
Drogheda   Liverpool   Sheffield
          ISLE OF   St Asaph   Newark
Dublin   Hd of Howth   ANGLESEY   Chester   *The Wash*
     Holyhead   Bangor   Derby
Naas   Denbigh   Nottingham
Wicklow   Stafford   Norwich
                    Shrewsbury   Leicester
          Dolgelly   Lichfield
                    Montgomery   Birmingham   Coventry
Cardigan Bay   Warwick   Rugby   Huntingdon
Wexford   Worcester   Northampton   Cambridge
               Hereford   Cheltenham   Bedford   Ipswich
St George's Channel   Cardigan   Woodstock   Colchester
          Fishguard   Carmarthen   Monmouth   Gloucester   Oxford   Rye House   Harwich
St David's Hd   Chepstow   Swindon   Chelmsford
     Milford Haven   Swansea   LONDON
Worms Hd   Cardiff   Bristol   Hungerford   Hampton   Chatham
               Bath   Court   *Nore* North Foreland
Bristol Channel   Wells   Philips Norton   Guildford
LUNDY IS.   Bridgwater   Salisbury   Canterbury
Barnstaple Bay   Barnstaple   Winchester   Dover   South Foreland
          Taunton   Shaftesbury
Bude Bay   Chichester   Brighton   Dungeness
     Exeter   Dorchester   Southampton
          Teignmouth   Lyme Regis   Wareham   ISLE OF   Selsey Bill   Beachy Hd
Trevose Hd   St Alban's Hd   WIGHT   *Straits of Dover*
     Plymouth   Bill of Portland
Land's End   Brixham
Falmouth   Start Pt   *English Channel*
Lizard

that 'During 1643 and 1644 the King issued various colonels forty-nine commissions for regiments of foot, and forty for regiments of horse, making up [in theory] a total of 68,000 men.'[17] In reality few of these new regiments employed more than a troop or company in their ranks.

Money was, predictably, an unending problem for both sides. Furthermore, war affected trade and it is not surprising, therefore, that many sought a peaceful and rapid end to the bloodshed. Throughout the spring of 1643 attempts at finding common ground were interspersed with truces and an uneasy quiet between the factions. In March, the Earl of Northumberland arrived at Oxford with Parliament's latest terms, which reiterated its red lines, primarily the abolition of episcopacy, the enforcement of penal laws against Catholics and the punishment of the principal offenders, namely the King's advisors. Charles responded by demanding that all the nation's fortresses be yielded to his army, that all the Parliamentarian forces be disbanded, and that Parliament be transferred outside London to a neutral region, where it could meet without intimidation. Such terms, unacceptable to both sides, were bound to fail. Charles's negotiation for support from Ireland in the guise of the Irish rebels, and from Scotland in the form of a Royalist rising, further played into the hands of Parliament's sceptics. By mid-May the pretence was over and the Parliamentary delegation was ordered to return to London. Three days later Charles rejected the Scottish attempts to rekindle negotiation through their commissioners. The King, buoyed by recent successes in the field and with the imminent arrival of arms and ammunition being transported by his Queen from York, was firm in the belief that the war could be won by a resounding military victory within months.

---

17 Ibid., pp. 25–6.

CHAPTER 10

THE STRUGGLE FOR THE NORTH AND CENTRE, JUNE TO AUGUST 1643

At the beginning of June 1643, the Parliamentarians had little cause for rejoicing. Devon was overrun and Hopton's, Maurice's and Hertford's forces had linked up and were poised to move against Waller at Bath. In the north, the Royalists were growing in strength and Queen Henrietta Maria was ready to head south with a substantial convoy of reinforcements and supplies. Fairfax had abandoned Wakefield after his raid and, although that action had checked Newcastle's offensive, the fact remained that the Parliamentarians were cut off from their garrison at Hull and in a precarious position in the West Riding pocket. Meanwhile, in the centre, since the capture of Reading, Essex had been largely immobile and his army, encamped around Thame and in the Chiltern Hills, was suffering from unprecedented levels of sickness and desertion.

A gathering of Parliamentarian commanders, including Grey, Willoughby, Gell, Hotham and Cromwell, met at Nottingham in early June with the aim of marching in support of Fairfax or intercepting the Queen's convoy (or both), but in the end they failed to agree on any plan. While the commanders talked, their respective forces, numbering between 5,000 and 6,000 men, plundered the local area with impunity. Cromwell was both disillusioned at the lack of collective resolve and furious at the reckless behaviour of the Parliamentarian troops. Colonel Hutchinson, a Parliamentarian officer, recalled that 'Colonel Cromwell, who had likewise had great provocations from him, began to show himself affected with the country's injuries, and the idle waste of such a force, through the inexperience of their chief commander, and the disobedience and irregularities of others.'[1] As it transpired, there was more than idleness and disobedience at play. At Lincoln, young Hotham had been in communication with Newcastle since mid-April. He had proposed that at Hull he and his father had 'found out a way of doing his Majesty real service'.[2] The insinuation was that they would deliver Lincoln and Hull for the King.

The Queen set out from York on 4 June and arrived at Newark on 21 June. She was justifiably concerned, and commanded Newcastle that the Midlands must be cleared of Parliamentarian troops and that Essex's army be contained: 'Have a care that no troop of Essex's army incommodate [sic] us, for I hope that for the rest, we shall be strong enough; for at Nottingham we have had the experience, one of our troops having beaten six of theirs, and made them fly.'[3] She then further delayed her departure with news that Hotham's treachery had been uncovered but that he had escaped, writing, '… you will pardon two day's stop, it is to have Hull and Lincoln. Young Hotham having been put in prison by order of Parliament, escaped, and hath sent to me that he would cast himself into my arms, and that Hull and Lincoln shall be rendered.'[4] Her letter was dated 27 June; the following day orders were issued for the Hothams' arrest, and two days later they were both under arms and

packed off, by sea, to London. The opportunity was lost but the Queen continued her movement towards Oxford on 3 July in buoyant mood:

> I carry with me three thousand foot, thirty companies of horse and dragoons, six pieces of cannon, and two mortars. Harry Jermyn commands the forces which go with me, as colonel of my guards, and Sir Alexander Lesley the foot under him, and Gerard the horse, and Robin Legg the artillery, and her she-majesty, generalissima, and extremely diligent, with one hundred and fifty waggons of baggage to govern, in case of battle.[5]

On 4 July the Royalist cavalry, led by Colonel Thomas Tyldesley, charged across Burton Bridge and drove back the Parliamentarian force under Captain Sanders, and by so doing secured a crossing over the River Trent. The convoy passed the next day, and on 11 July Rupert collected Henrietta Maria at Stratford-upon-Avon. Two days later, the King and Queen were united on the battlefield of Edgehill, and on 14 July they rode, side by side, into Oxford to a tumultuous reception fired by news of great Royalist victories in the west.

Once the Queen had been deposited at Newark, Newcastle was free from his Royal charge and he immediately resumed operations in Yorkshire. He advanced towards Fairfax at Bradford and on 22 July he captured Howley Hall, but then, only 8 miles from Fairfax's small army, he halted. The reasons for the delay are unclear. Perhaps the weather, maybe to rest his men or possibly he was hoping that Fairfax would make the first move. Whatever the reasons, by 30 June, Newcastle had decided he had to act and he moved his force towards Bradford. As it happened, Fairfax had also decided to move towards the Royalist army at much the same time, as he recounted:

> Seeing it impossible to defend ye Towne, but by strength of men, and not above 10 or 12 days provision for so many as were necessary to keep it; we resolved, ye next morning very early with a party of 3000 men, to attempt his whole army as they laid in their quarters, 3 miles off: hoping thereby to put him into some distraction; which could not (by reason of ye unequal number) be done any other way.[6]

However, Fairfax's plan to depart at 4am was undone by General Gyffard's tardiness, which had a whiff of treachery; consequently, it was between 7 and 8am before they finally got under way. Thus, the element of surprise had been lost. What happened next, therefore, was not so much a set piece battle as a meeting engagement.[7]

---

1 Hutchinson, *Life of Colonel Hutchinson*, p. 152.
2 Gardiner, *Great Civil War*, vol. I, p. 141.
3 Everett Green, *Letters of Queen Henrietta Maria*, p. 223.
4 Ibid., p. 221.

5 Ibid., p. 222.
6 Fairfax, *Short memorials*, p. 213.
7 There is debate as to whether Newcastle knew of the Parliamentarian intentions in advance and had his army arrayed and ready. Major Slingsby indicates that both were surprised. Parsons, *Henry Slingsby*, p. 96.

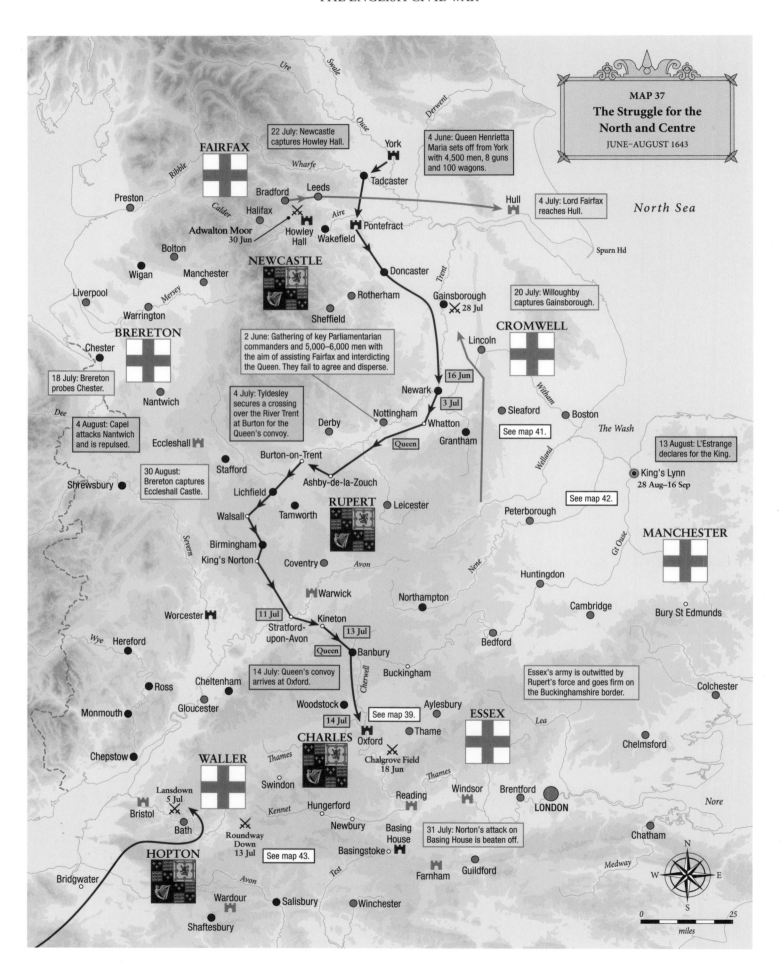

MAP 37

The Struggle for the North and Centre

JUNE–AUGUST 1643

22 July: Newcastle captures Howley Hall.

4 June: Queen Henrietta Maria sets off from York with 4,500 men, 8 guns and 100 wagons.

4 July: Lord Fairfax reaches Hull.

North Sea

FAIRFAX

York

Ure

Swale

Derwent

Wharfe

Bradford

Leeds

Tadcaster

Hull

Preston

Ribble

Halifax

Calder

Aire

Pontefract

Spurn Hd

Adwalton Moor
30 Jun

Howley
Hall

Wakefield

Bolton

Wigan

Manchester

NEWCASTLE

Doncaster

Trent

Gainsborough
28 Jul

20 July: Willoughby captures Gainsborough.

Liverpool

Mersey

Rotherham

CROMWELL

Warrington

Sheffield

Lincoln

BRERETON

2 June: Gathering of key Parliamentarian commanders and 5,000–6,000 men with the aim of assisting Fairfax and interdicting the Queen. They fail to agree and disperse.

Chester

Sleaford

Boston

The Wash

18 July: Brereton probes Chester.

Nantwich

4 July: Tyldesley secures a crossing over the River Trent at Burton for the Queen's convoy.

Newark

16 Jun

3 Jul

Witham

See map 41.

13 August: L'Estrange declares for the King.

Dee

4 August: Capel attacks Nantwich and is repulsed.

Nottingham

Derby

Whatton

Queen

Grantham

Welland

King's Lynn
28 Aug–16 Sep

Eccleshall

Burton-on-Trent

30 August: Brereton captures Eccleshall Castle.

Stafford

Ashby-de-la-Zouch

See map 42.

Shrewsbury

Lichfield

RUPERT

Leicester

Peterborough

MANCHESTER

Walsall

Tamworth

Severn

Birmingham

Coventry

Avon

Nene

Huntingdon

King's Norton

Worcester

Warwick

Northampton

Cambridge

Bury St Edmunds

11 Jul

Kineton

Gt Ouse

Hereford

Stratford-upon-Avon

13 Jul

Bedford

Wye

Queen

Banbury

Essex's army is outwitted by Rupert's force and goes firm on the Buckinghamshire border.

Colchester

14 July: Queen's convoy arrives at Oxford.

Cherwell

Buckingham

Ross

Cheltenham

Woodstock

Aylesbury

ESSEX

Chelmsford

Monmouth

Gloucester

14 Jul

See map 39.

Thame

Lea

Chepstow

WALLER

CHARLES

Oxford

Thames

Lansdown
5 Jul

Thames

Chalgrove Field
18 Jun

Nore

Bristol

Swindon

Windsor

Brentford

Bath

Roundway
Down
13 Jul

Kennet

Hungerford

Reading

LONDON

Chatham

See map 43.

Newbury

Basing
House

31 July: Norton's attack on Basing House is beaten off.

Medway

HOPTON

Avon

Basingstoke

Farnham

Guildford

N

Bridgwater

Wardour

Test

W — E

Salisbury

Winchester

S

Shaftesbury

0   25

miles

The vanguard of Fairfax's force drove back the Royalist forlorn hope at Wisket Hill, consisting of foot, horse and dragoons under the command of Clavering. They retreated under control through the enclosures to their rear and made a stand at a small hill (subsequently named Fairfax Hill). Newcastle arrived to encourage his men to hold the forward position, for he needed time to deploy his main army from the line of march near Adwalton. Captain Mildmay, who was commanding the lead Parliamentarian troops, made a concerted attack on the hill but it failed to dislodge the Royalists. The Parliamentarian forces then fanned out as they emerged from Wisket Hill. Thomas Fairfax recalled, 'I commanded ye right wing with about a 1000 Foot, and 5 Troops of Horse… Major Gen. Gyffard ye left wing, with about ye same number. My Father commanded all in chiefe.'[8] It appears that the Parliamentarians then intended to move on to Hodgson Lane for their final approach to the Royalist Camp near Howley Hall, as this was a more direct route than the Bradford to Wakefield road. This accounts for why the Parliamentarians ceased using the main road as its axis and swung south.

The long-awaited battle between Newcastle's forces and those of the Fairfaxes was now inevitable. Newcastle's officers hurried their army into position behind the enclosed land beyond Adwalton. With the enclosures to his front, limited width and nothing to anchor his wings, it was far from ideal terrain. The Royalist musketeers were commanded forward, leaving the massed pike blocks to form the centre of the Royalist battle line between the enclosed land and Hunger Hill.[9] As more Parliamentarian troops arrived, a second attack captured Fairfax Hill and the Royalist troops fell back to the Royalist battle lines which were now, more or less, formed. From this vantage point the huge advantage the Royalists possessed in cavalry and dragoons became evident and an immediate attack was ordered in the centre in an attempt to capture and hold the enclosures to their front. Fairfax recalled, 'We kept ye enclosure, placing our musketeers in ye hedges in ye moor, which was good advantage to us who had so few horse. There was a gate, or open place to ye Moor, where 5 or 6 might enter a breast. Here they strove to enter, and we to defend…'.[10]

The Roundhead musketeers pushed through the enclosures at the south-east end and forced Newcastle's men back. Some of them sought refuge on Hunger Hill and the Royalist line was withdrawn to the base of the hill. Newcastle realized he had to try to regain the initiative, but his cavalry was going to have difficulty dislodging the Parliamentarians from the hedges and ditches at the edges of the enclosed areas they now occupied. He decided to execute a massed cavalry charge, of about 700 horse, against Fairfax's right wing. 'The horse came downe again and charged us, being about 13 or 14 Troops. We defended o'selves as before, but with much more difficulty, many having gotten in among us; but were beaten off again with losse…'.[11] Fairfax followed up the Royalist retreat with a cavalry charge and came up against their gun line at the base of Hunger Hill. Some elements of the Royalist army began to lose heart. It was about 11am and the Parliamentarians had reason to be content with their progress thus far, but the battle still hung in the balance.

Gifford, on the Parliamentarian left, had advanced with his infantry and cavalry in support of Fairfax during his cavalry attack on the right wing. Gifford's infantry was now in open ground and vulnerable. The battle was about to swing in favour of the Royalists. There is confusion as to who initiated the action that turned the tide. Fairfax wrote, 'One Coll Skirton, a wild and desperate man, desired his Gen. to let him charge once more, with a stand of pikes, with which he broke in upon or men'.[12] While the Royalist newssheet *Mercurius Aulicus* credits Newcastle himself with the gallant deed of instigating a counter-attack by Royalist pikemen.[13] Also unclear is how many Royalist pike formations were involved. However, what is perfectly obvious is that it had an instant effect on the Parliamentarian left wing. Lord Fairfax failed to deploy the reserve in order to stem the flow. Another charge by the Royalist cavalry settled the issue; the Parliamentarian cohesion broken, the force fled from the field, slowly at first, but it soon became a rout.

Royalist sources claimed 2,000 men taken of which 1,500 were prisoners – these figures are, however, far too high and Fairfax's estimate of 60 killed and 300 prisoners is likely to be nearer the mark.[14] The Royalist losses were far lighter, although they included a number of officers. Thomas Fairfax's men had not reached the Bradford road before the Royalist cavalry and so they had to make good their retreat on the Halifax road. By nightfall they had reached Bradford, just as the Royalists arrived from the east and established their heavy batteries. The next day word arrived at Lord Fairfax's headquarters that Hotham had been arrested at Hull. Fairfax left immediately and tried, unsuccessfully, to secure Leeds en route. Thomas Fairfax held out a day longer before escaping without the garrison of 300 men, who were forced to surrender the next day. With Bradford lost, all the other key towns in the West Riding were abandoned. Thomas Fairfax reached Hull on 4 July; his wife and daughter were missing but he was relieved to discover his father within the walls.[15] He was already installed as governor. It had been a frantic week.

Since the capture of Reading at the end of April, Essex's army had done little. Pay was in arrears and discontent began to spread among the rank and file. A lack of suitable rations, contaminated water and overcrowded and unsanitary conditions led to widespread sickness. There was little Essex could do about the lack of money other than appeal to Parliament for the early release of funds, but it was his failure to look at events nationally, and to make a definitive decision, that was to have significant consequences. As Gardiner wrote, 'methodical by nature and by his training in the Dutch service, [Essex] had none of the inspiration of genius or of the daring energy which goes far to supply its place'.[16] During May, Waller was not just hoping but expecting Essex to keep the Royalists occupied by deploying his army between Oxford and Bath. Such a move would have assisted Waller in the west and, most likely, have prevented Maurice and Hertford's move to link up with Hopton's forces in Somerset. Essex, however, was justifiably concerned that such a move would leave the way open to London. Nevertheless, his apparent indecision during the month of May led to widespread discontent as to his suitability to command, both among his colleagues in the field and his political masters in London.

As it transpired, Essex had given orders in late May for his force to move north, cut off Oxford from the Midlands and to intercept and capture the Queen's convoy. But by late May rumours were already

---

8   Fairfax, op. cit., p. 213.

9   Johnson, *Adwalton Moor*, p. 98.

10 Fairfax, op. cit., p. 213.

11 Ibid.

12 Ibid., p. 214. Stuart Reid believes this officer to be Colonel Kirton, who commanded the Earl of Newcastle's Regiment of Foot – Johnson, op. cit., p. 99.

13 *Mercurius Aulicus*, Monday 3 July 1643, BL Thomason/10:E.59[24], p. 350.

14 Ibid., p. 351; Fairfax, op. cit., p. 214.

15 He was to be reunited with both a few days later. His wife had been left within the walls at Bradford but was returned by Newcastle in his personal coach.

16 Gardiner, *Great Civil War*, vol. I., p. 131.

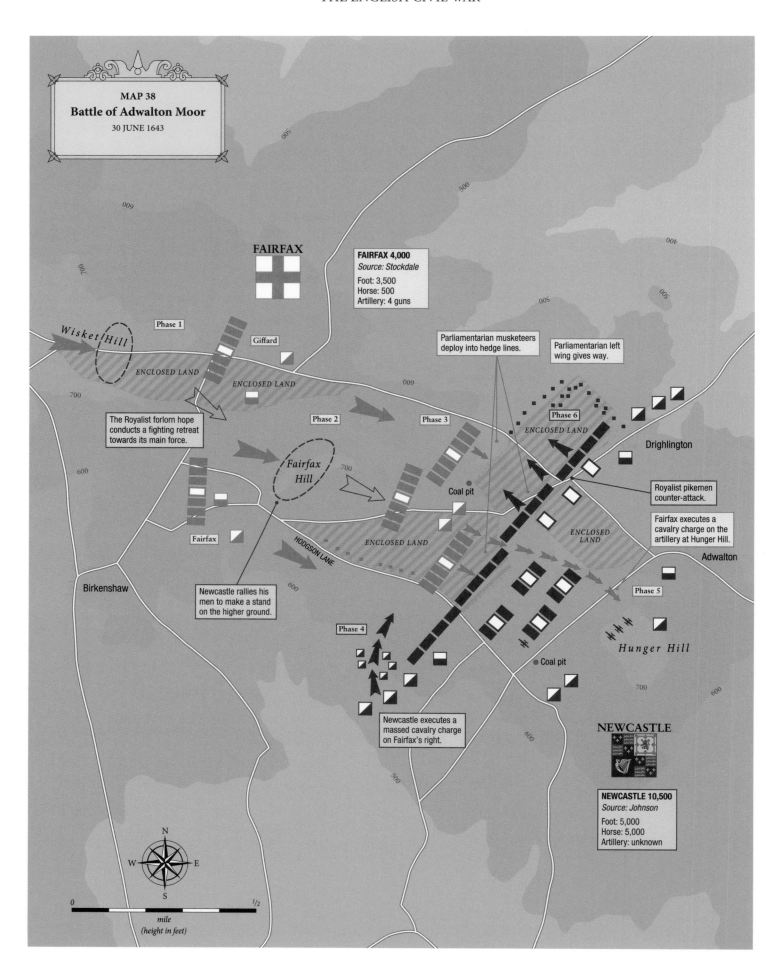

MAP 38
Battle of Adwalton Moor
30 JUNE 1643

Wisket Hill

Phase 1

Giffard

ENCLOSED LAND

ENCLOSED LAND

FAIRFAX

FAIRFAX 4,000
Source: Stockdale
Foot: 3,500
Horse: 500
Artillery: 4 guns

Parliamentarian musketeers
deploy into hedge lines.

Parliamentarian left
wing gives way.

The Royalist forlorn hope
conducts a fighting retreat
towards its main force.

Phase 2

Phase 3

Phase 6

ENCLOSED LAND

Drighlington

*Fairfax
Hill*

Coal pit

Royalist pikemen
counter-attack.

Newcastle rallies his
men to make a stand
on the higher ground.

Fairfax

ENCLOSED LAND

ENCLOSED LAND

Fairfax executes a
cavalry charge on the
artillery at Hunger Hill.

Adwalton

HODGSON LANE

Birkenshaw

Phase 5

Phase 4

Coal pit

Hunger Hill

Newcastle executes a
massed cavalry charge
on Fairfax's right.

NEWCASTLE

NEWCASTLE 10,500
Source: Johnson
Foot: 5,000
Horse: 5,000
Artillery: unknown

N
W   E
S

0   1/2

mile
(height in feet)

circulating in the capital that Essex had passed his sell-by date, as he appeared to be as frightened of fighting the Queen as the King. However, Essex knew that a move towards Oxford could draw the King from the city and that he would need more troops than the 5,000 at his disposal to counter. Accordingly, he issued orders for a concentration of all available Parliamentarian forces in east Oxfordshire. The lukewarm response he received underscored the precariousness of his hold on overall command of the Parliamentarian armies. On 10 June the advance guard of his army marched north and established the headquarters at Thame. While he waited for the reinforcements to arrive, he gave permission for a raid on one of the Royalist outposts at Islip. The raid by 2,500 men found the Royalists waiting and they withdrew without striking a blow. Essex had stirred the hornet's nest, and when Rupert received intelligence from Colonel John Hurry, a Scottish deserter, of the whereabouts and quarters of the Parliamentarian horse and of news of a large pay chest en route to Essex from London, he decided to attack.[17]

Rupert's forces numbered nearly 2,000, three quarters of whom were mounted. Major Will Legge led the forlorn hope of 100 horse and 50 dragoons. Soon after midnight on 18 June he reached the outskirts of Tetsworth, where an alert sentry fired at the approaching body of troops. In less than a minute, the ubiquitous glow of long matches from within the village was enough to convince Rupert to give the place a wide berth. He pushed on down the road towards Postcombe, but before he arrived a Parliamentarian trooper was already raising the alarm at Thame. Several troops of horse were ordered to counter the threat and John Hampden requested permission from Captain Crosse to join his troop. Before they departed Thame, the sounds of battle drifted on the night air. Colonel Herbert Morley's Sussex Regiment of Horse, quartered at Postcombe, were under attack. They saddled up and fled. Rupert then moved on towards Chinnor, where he hoped to intercept the convoy containing the military chest. Inside the village were a couple of hundred dragoons from Samuel Luke's Bedfordshire Regiment. Exhausted from their abortive exploits towards Islip the day prior, the dragoons were caught unprepared, and 50 were killed or wounded and 120 taken prisoner. A Royalist report summed up the action: 'These all weary and new come into the Quarters, were taken sleepers in the Barnes and Houses. Diverse were killed as they bustled up: and others, that upon the Alarme, had already gotten themselves to their Armes.'[18] Rupert lingered near the town. Dawn was approaching and there was no sign of the convoy – in fact the wagon master, alarmed at the sounds of a skirmish in the village, had hidden in a nearby wood.

Somewhat crestfallen and leaving Chinnor in flames, the Royalists turned for home with the Parliamentarian horse hot on their heels. Twice during the chase, the Royalists had to turn and check the advance of the Roundhead cavalry. At about 8.45am the Royalists reached Chalgrove Field where they halted and turned to watch a few of the Roundhead horse and dragoons that had come into view on Golder Hill.[19] Rupert realized he might have to deploy and, if necessary, fight to buy time for his infantry to get clear. He despatched Henry Lunsford's infantry to escort the prisoners and to secure the bridge over the River Thame just west of Stadhampton. At the same time, Wentworth's Dragoons were ordered to

line the hedges on either side of the road heading west and establish an ambush. Rupert waited and watched in Solinger Field (map 40, point A) with his troop of Lifeguards and three regiments of cavalry.[20] Rupert, with his gaze fixed to the east, recorded that 'The Roundhead horse and dragoons were now seen descending Gelder's-hill: they advanced with the more confidence, as they expected every moment to see Essex appearing in Prince Rupert's rear.'[21] The Parliamentarian horse moved towards Rupert's force with purpose and were soon in an area adjacent to them separated by the great hedge, which marked the parish boundary between Chalgrove and Lewknor.[22] Rupert moved west into Sandfield (map 40, point B) and, with a practised eye, watched the majority of enemy horse and dragoons file through the gap in the great hedge, while others moved in reserve near Warpsgrove House.

The dragoons moved towards the Royalist horse, dismounted, and lined another much smaller hedge that ran along the edge of the ancient track known as Upper Marsh Lane. Behind them, the majority of the Parliamentarian horse (about eight cornets) deployed in line. Rupert was not perturbed; he was still planning to pull back and draw the enemy horse into the trap he had set on the Stadhampton road. The Parliamentarians seemed to sense that Rupert was going to continue his westerly movement and, in the hope of delaying their retreat, the dragoons opened fire on the nearest two regiments and dropped a number of riders. Rupert was incensed and exclaimed, 'Yea, this insolency is not to be endured', put his spurs to his horse and leapt the hedge into the midst of the dragoons.[23] Instinctively, about another 15 of his Lifeguards followed and the line of dragoons broke and ran for the lives. More and more Royalist cavalry from Rupert's Regiment and the Lifeguards joined them. The two opposing cavalry groups now faced each other, the Royalists charged, and the whole set about their grisly work. The encounter went on for a considerable time, both sides charging and counter-charging and exchanging sword blows, with exchanges of carbine and pistol in the mix. After several minutes Percy's and O'Neal's regiments (commanding Prince Rupert's Regiment) attacked around their respective flanks. The Parliamentarians realized the game was up, broke and fled through the gap in the hedge. They were pursued by the Royalist cavalry back up Golder Hill. Early in the melee, Hampden, who was to the rear near Warpsgrove House, was struck in the shoulder by two carbine balls.[24] Rupert was aware that his force remained in danger of being cut off on the road back to Oxford by Parliamentarian forces moving further to the west, and reined in his cavalry and called off the pursuit. He pulled back west over the bridge west of Stadhampton, recalled the dragoons, and rested his exhausted force. A short while later he withdrew to Oxford and arrived about 2pm, 'with near two hundred prisoners, seven cornets of horse, and four ensigns of foot, with most of the men he carried from thence; few only having been killed in the action, whereof some were of name'.[25]

<hr/>

17 Hurry, a Scottish mercenary, was to change sides four times. The chest contained £21,000.

18 *Prince Rupert's Late Beating up*, p. 5.

19 There are two good recent papers on the action, both published by Oxoniensia. One by Stevenson and Carter, *Fight at Chalgrove Field*, and the second by Lester and Lester, *Battle of Chalgrove*, the latter is the most useful.

20 Consisting of Prince Rupert's Regiment (commanded by O'Neal), the Prince of Wales's Regiment (commanded by Gamel) and Percy's Regiment of Horse (commanded by Percy); Warburton, *Memoirs of Prince Rupert*, vol. II., p. 204.

21 Warburton, op. cit., pp. 206–7. Gelder's Hill is also recorded as Gilton Hill and Golder Hill.

22 Lester and Lester, op. cit., p. 28, note that a remnant of this hedge still exists on the battlefield; it has a double line of hedges with sufficient space in between for two horses, side by side.

23 *Prince Rupert's Late Beating up*, p. 7.

24 Adair states that he was shot in the back by a cavalier with a double-loaded carbine or pistol. Adair, *John Hampden*, p. 236.

25 Clarendon, *History of the Rebellion*, vol. IV, p. 86.

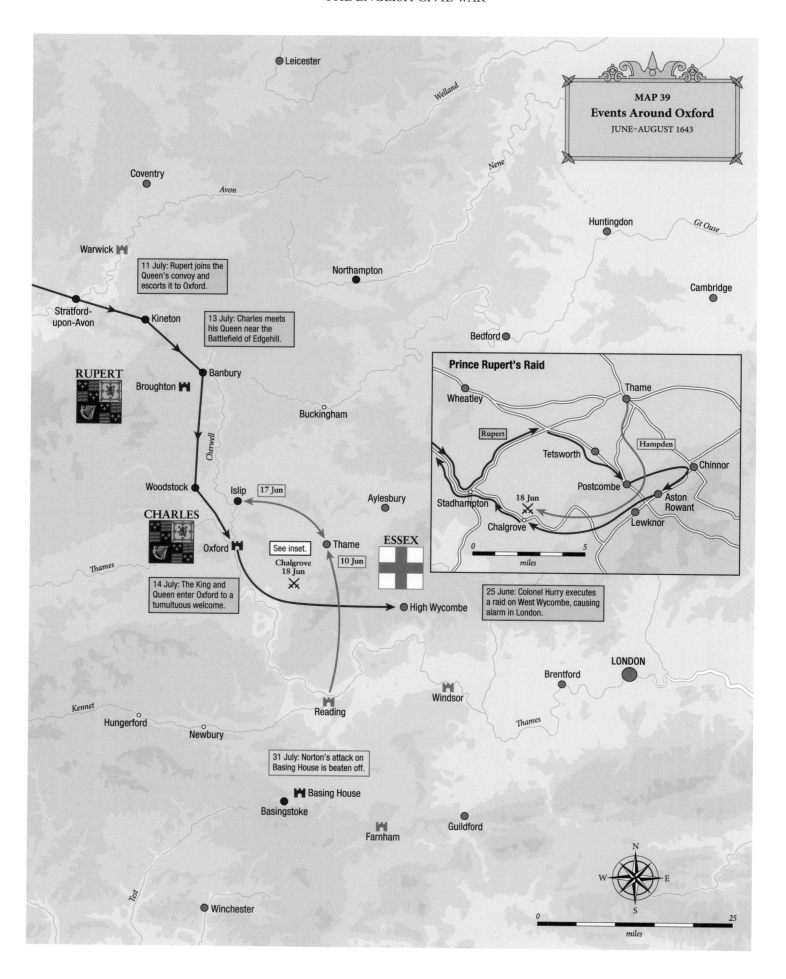

Leicester

Coventry

Avon

Welland

Warwick 🏰

11 July: Rupert joins the
Queen's convoy and
escorts it to Oxford.

Nene

Huntingdon

Gt Ouse

Stratford-
upon-Avon

Kineton

13 July: Charles meets
his Queen near the
Battlefield of Edgehill.

Northampton

Cambridge

RUPERT

Banbury

Broughton 🏰

Bedford

Buckingham

Cherwell

Prince Rupert's Raid

Thame

Wheatley

Rupert

Woodstock

Islip

17 Jun

Aylesbury

Tetsworth

Hampden

Chinnor

CHARLES

Oxford 🏰

See inset.

Thame

10 Jun

ESSEX

Stadhampton

Postcombe

Aston
Rowant

18 Jun

Thames

Chalgrove
18 Jun
⚔

Lewknor

Chalgrove

14 July: The King and
Queen enter Oxford to a
tumultuous welcome.

0   5

miles

High Wycombe

25 June: Colonel Hurry executes
a raid on West Wycombe, causing
alarm in London.

Kennet

Hungerford

Newbury

Reading

Windsor

LONDON

Brentford

Thames

31 July: Norton's attack on
Basing House is beaten off.

🏰 Basing House

Basingstoke

Farnham 🏰

Guildford

N

W   E

S

Test

Winchester

0   25

miles

MAP 39
Events Around Oxford
JUNE–AUGUST 1643

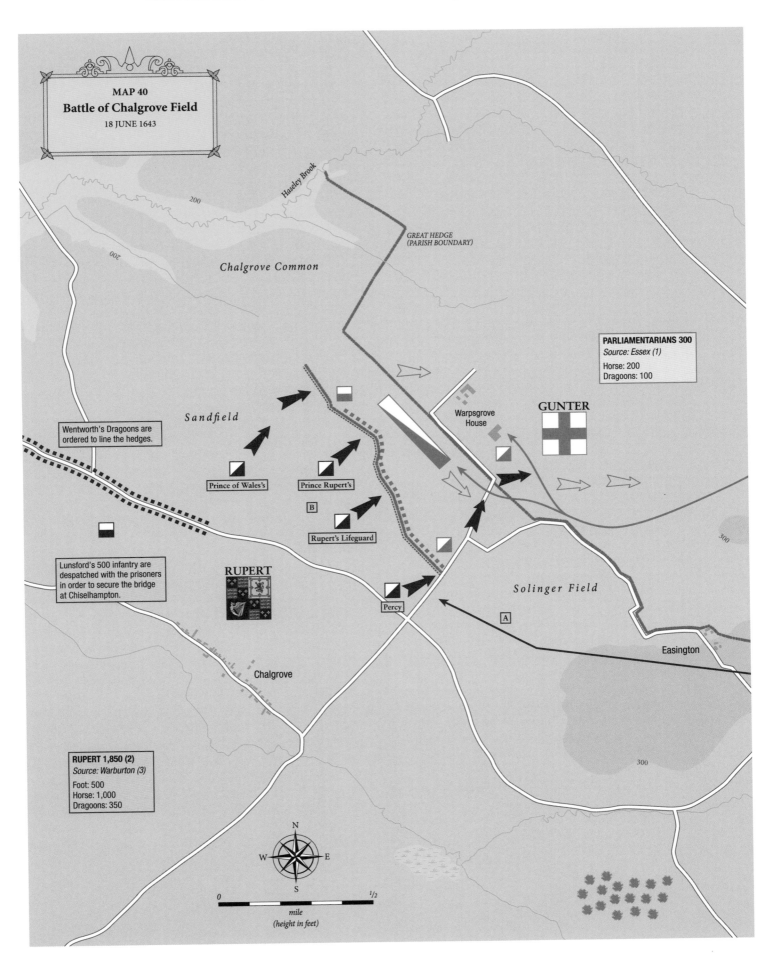

MAP 40
Battle of Chalgrove Field
18 JUNE 1643

Hasley Brook

GREAT HEDGE
(PARISH BOUNDARY)

Chalgrove Common

PARLIAMENTARIANS 300
Source: Essex (1)
Horse: 200
Dragoons: 100

Sandfield

Warpsgrove
House

GUNTER

Wentworth's Dragoons are
ordered to line the hedges.

Prince of Wales's

Prince Rupert's

B

Rupert's Lifeguard

Lunsford's 500 infantry are
despatched with the prisoners
in order to secure the bridge
at Chiselhampton.

RUPERT

Solinger Field

Percy

A

Easington

RUPERT 1,850 (2)
Source: Warburton (3)
Foot: 500
Horse: 1,000
Dragoons: 350

Chalgrove

N
W   E
S

0   1/2
mile
(height in feet)

The raid had not been completely successful, and the battle at Chalgrove was a small affair, but its consequences, like at Powick Bridge, were far reaching. Hampden was to die in agony from his wounds six days later; his loss, to the less radical element of the Parliamentarian cause, was to cut deep. Furthermore, the audacity of the Royalists did little to enhance Essex's standing, or his hold on command. He was not helped by another raid deep into the heart of his forces on 25 July, the day after Hampden's death. The turncoat Colonel Hurry received intelligence of a force of 500 foot and a troop of horse at West Wycombe.[26] He set off with 200 horse and 40 dragoons and arrived at the town in the mid-afternoon. The defenders had been warned and many were able to slip away before Hurry's men entered the town. Nevertheless, such a daring raid so close to the capital caused panic in London. Pym wrote to Essex in direct terms about his army's late performance, prompting Essex to offer his resignation. It was rejected, but it marked a watershed in Essex's wider command; he elected from that point onwards to concentrate on his own army in the Thames valley. It did, however, prompt Parliament to consider Essex's grievances. A subsequent committee, headed by Pym, agreed to settle arrears in pay and to raise new recruits and reinforce his cavalry.

After Adwalton Moor there was every expectation that Newcastle would capitalize on his victory and push south to contain the Midlands. However, on 20 July, his inertia and intentions were shaken when Lord Willoughby of Parham attacked and captured Gainsborough, thereby severing Royalist communication with the key town of Newark. Both sides reacted with some speed. Cavendish, who was still around Newark, was sent north immediately to recapture the town. At the same time orders were sent, by the Committee which managed the affairs of the Eastern Association, to Meldrum and Cromwell to move to the area with all speed in order to support Willoughby. The Parliamentarians came up against Cavendish's forlorn hope about a mile and a half from Gainsborough. The Lincolnshire troops led the Roundhead vanguard and pushed the Royalists back on to their main body atop a large hill to the south-east of the town. The Royalist force had about 30 troops of horse and dragoons, while the Parliamentarians had about 24 companies of horse and dragoons.[27] The Lincolnshire cavalry continued to advance but the going was steep and increasingly difficult. Cromwell recalled, 'when we recovered the top of the hill, we saw a great body of the enemy's horse facing us, at about a musket shot or less distance; and a good reserve of a full regiment of horse behind it'.[28]

The Roundheads charged the Royalist main body. Cromwell wrote, 'We came up horse to horse, where we disputed it with swords and pistils a pretty time.'[29] The Royalists began to fall back and the Lincolnshire cavalry sensed their opportunity and pressed home their attack. It was enough to break the Royalist resolve and they broke and were pursued for many miles by the jubilant horsemen from Nottingham and Lincoln. Cavendish, however, had held back his reserve and now moved to fall on the rear of the Roundhead cavalry but Cromwell had anticipated just such a move:

At last General Cavendish charged the Lincolners, and routed them. Immediately, I fell on his rear with my three troops; which did so astonish him, that he gave over the chase... I pressing on forced them

down the hill... and below the hill drove the General with some of his soldiers into a quagmire; where my Captain-lieutenant slew him with a thrust under his short ribs.[30]

Cromwell and his men wasted no time in relieving Willoughby and putting powder and provisions inside Gainsborough. While this was under way, intelligence reports of another Royalist force arriving from the north were received by Cromwell. Reinforced by some of Willoughby's foot soldiers, he set off north to intercept this new threat. After a short skirmish with a couple of Royalist troops, Cromwell suddenly found himself facing Newcastle's entire army, 'which, coming so unexpectedly, put us to new consultations'.[31] Cromwell realized the cavalry would have to stand to buy time for Willoughby's infantry to get back to Gainsborough. It was a hard-fought fighting withdrawal, which prompted Cromwell to claim that 'the honour of the retreat is due to God'.[32] Willoughby's men made it back to Gainsborough, where they barricaded themselves against the inevitable attack, and the cavalry continued their escape towards Lincoln.

On 30 July Willoughby surrendered Gainsborough and pulled back to Lincoln but, in the face of the large Royalist army, he was forced to abandon that town a few days later. Newcastle, somewhat characteristically, now lingered at his latest conquest before being prompted by Charles to move on to Hull. Lord Fairfax had been made the new governor there on 22 July and Thomas Fairfax had been busy in the interim, rebuilding the army following the defeat at Adwalton. He established a base at Beverley, just north of Hull, but was forced to abandon it at the end of August as Newcastle's force of 16,000 men, and a considerable siege train, approached. This inability of the Parliamentarian armies to hold their gains infuriated Cromwell. Furthermore, if Newcastle moved towards London, Cromwell was concerned about the ability of his forces to hold the Royalists. He wrote, in no uncertain terms, to the commissioners at Cambridge and to the Essex deputy lieutenants. He suggested that 'the whole association will be exposed [to] the fury and cruelty of the popish Armie' and 'it's no longer disputing, but out instantly all you can! Raise all your bands; send them to Huntingdon; – get up what volunteers you can; hasten your horses'.[33] Despite the threat and Cromwell's rhetoric, the response from the counties was poor. London, however, realized the gravity of the situation and resolved to increase the infantry of the associations to 10,000. Cromwell was delighted but he was less pleased to discover, on 10 August, that the Earl of Manchester was to be appointed as the commander of the Eastern Association. The earl was given clear orders to block the advance of Newcastle's forces towards the capital.

As it happened, Manchester's first alarm was not with Newcastle's army but with the troublesome Sir Hamon L'Estrange, at King's Lynn, who had finally declared for the King after refusing to pay taxes to Parliament. Manchester decided to blockade the town, which he referred to as 'a gangrene in the heart of the Association', rather than besiege it. He sent Captain William Poe with a small force, which arrived on the outskirts on 19 August. Poe was surprised by the strength of the defenders' equipment and stores, which included 40 pieces of ordnance, 1,200 muskets, 500 barrels of gunpowder, 'with bullet answerable', and three or four troops of horse.[34] In addition, he was soon to discover the determination of the

---

26 *Prince Rupert's Late Beating up* – there is an additional pamphlet detailing the raid – pp. 15–16.

27 Burne & Young, *Great Civil War*, p. 108.

28 Carlyle, *Cromwell's Letters*, vol. I., p. 134.

29 Ibid., p. 135.

30 Ibid.

31 Ibid., p. 136.

32 Ibid.

33 Ibid., p. 140; Holmes, *Eastern Association*, p. 92.

34 Ketton-Cremer, *Norfolk in the Civil War*, p. 208.

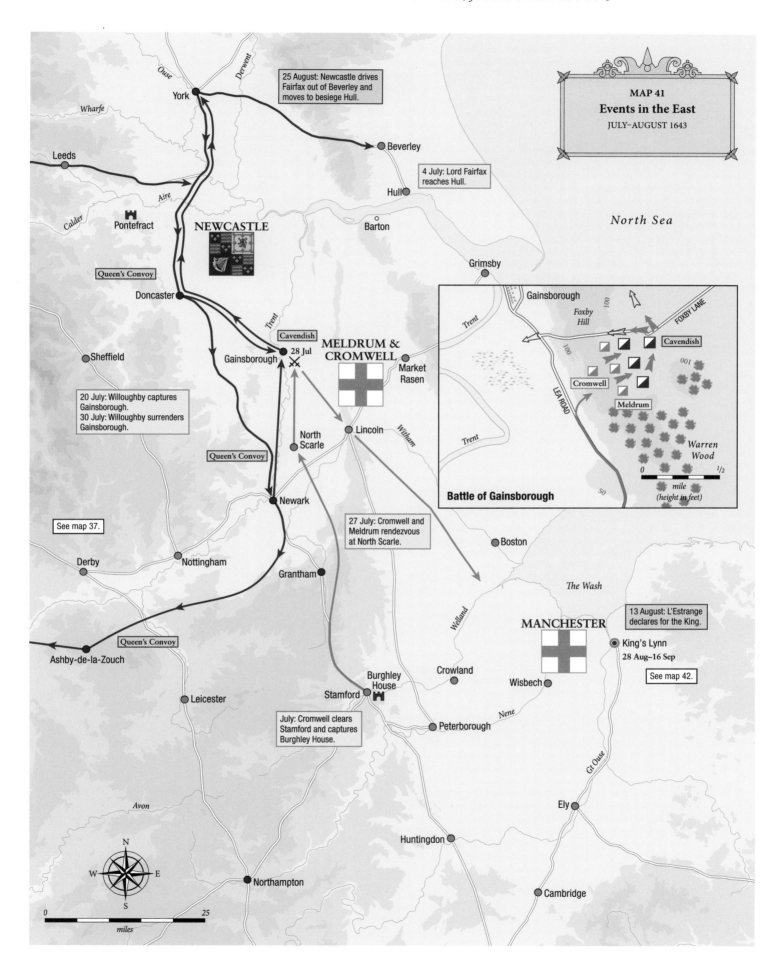

25 August: Newcastle drives Fairfax out of Beverley and moves to besiege Hull.

MAP 41
Events in the East
JULY–AUGUST 1643

4 July: Lord Fairfax reaches Hull.

North Sea

Leeds

Wharfe

York

Ouse

Derwent

Beverley

Hull

Barton

Calder

Pontefract

NEWCASTLE

Grimsby

Aire

Queen's Convoy

Doncaster

Sheffield

Trent

Gainsborough

Cavendish

28 Jul

MELDRUM & CROMWELL

Market Rasen

20 July: Willoughby captures Gainsborough.
30 July: Willoughby surrenders Gainsborough.

North Scarle

Lincoln

Witham

Queen's Convoy

See map 37.

Newark

27 July: Cromwell and Meldrum rendezvous at North Scarle.

Boston

Derby

Nottingham

Grantham

Welland

The Wash

MANCHESTER

13 August: L'Estrange declares for the King.

King's Lynn
28 Aug–16 Sep

See map 42.

Ashby-de-la-Zouch

Queen's Convoy

Leicester

Stamford

Burghley House

Crowland

Wisbech

July: Cromwell clears Stamford and captures Burghley House.

Peterborough

Nene

Avon

Gt. Ouse

Ely

N
W   E
S

Huntingdon

0   25
miles

Northampton

Cambridge

Battle of Gainsborough

Gainsborough

Trent

Foxby Hill

FOXBY LANE

100

Cavendish

100

Cromwell

001

Meldrum

LEA ROAD

Trent

Warren Wood

50

0   1/2
mile
(height in feet)

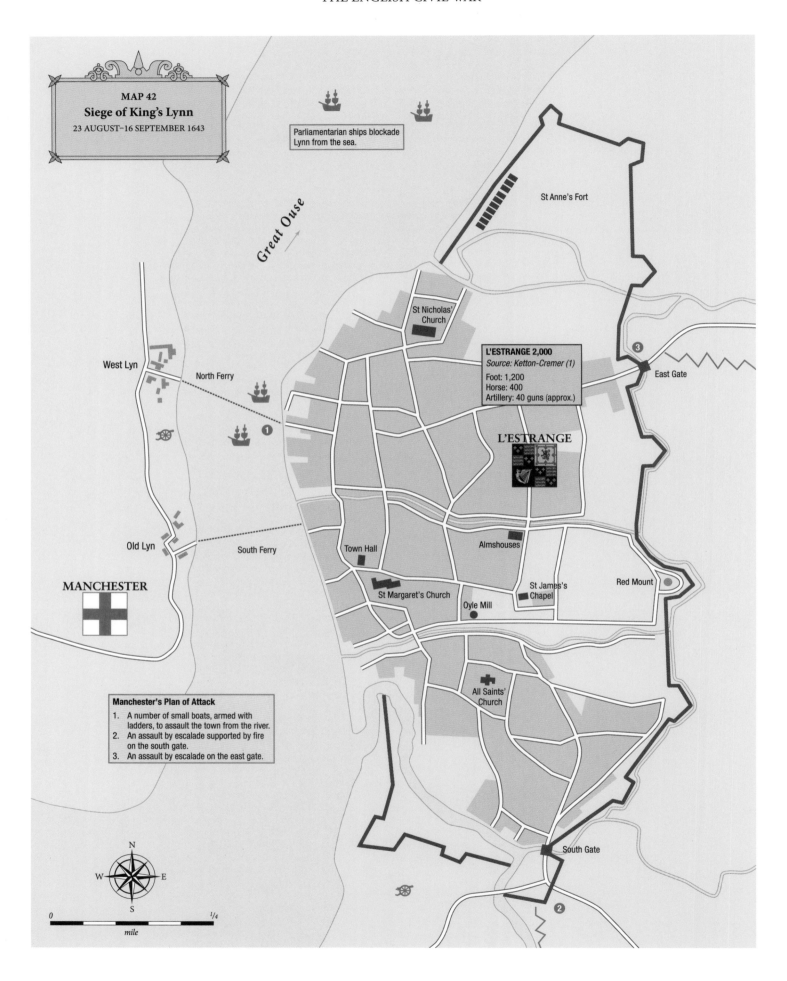

MAP 42
Siege of King's Lynn
23 AUGUST–16 SEPTEMBER 1643

Parliamentarian ships blockade
Lynn from the sea.

St Anne's Fort

Great Ouse

St Nicholas'
Church

West Lyn

North Ferry

L'ESTRANGE 2,000
Source: Ketton-Cremer (1)
Foot: 1,200
Horse: 400
Artillery: 40 guns (approx.)

East Gate

③

L'ESTRANGE

①

Old Lyn

South Ferry

MANCHESTER

Town Hall

Almshouses

Red Mount

St James's
Chapel

St Margaret's Church

Oyle Mill

All Saints'
Church

Manchester's Plan of Attack

1. A number of small boats, armed with ladders, to assault the town from the river.
2. An assault by escalade supported by fire on the south gate.
3. An assault by escalade on the east gate.

N
W   E
S

South Gate

②

0   1/4
mile

defenders when he, and his troop of horse, were attacked by L'Estrange's men, who sallied out from the town in some force. Poe wrote to the deputy lieutenants of the Eastern Association counties, impressing upon them the urgency of sending reinforcements with the utmost speed. Manchester arrived with the army a few days later and established his headquarters at Setch, about 4 miles south of Lynn.[35] The siege commenced on 28 August. West Lynn and Old Lynn were occupied and a battery set up on the west bank, which 'kept the Towne in continual Alarmes, and did so terrifie the people with their shot and Granadoes, that they durst hardly abide in their houses that were towards that side'.[36]

More and more reinforcements arrived in early September and, despite the questionable level of training and equipment of these men, Manchester elected to try to take the place by storm. A battery was established 'on a hill of firm ground' to the south but its progress was slow, 'they making up as fast as we should have beaten downe'.[37] The plan was to escalade the place simultaneously at the south and east gates and from boats assaulting from the river. Within the town, the Royalist defenders had been hopeful of assistance from Newcastle, who still had a considerable force at Gainsborough. However, the days passed and the likelihood diminished. Finally, on 16 September, Manchester made it known that an assault was imminent. He warned the Royalist hierarchy to move the women and children from the town or pay the consequences. It was enough to convince them to surrender and, after three weeks, the town was back under Parliamentarian control.

---

35 It is difficult to determine the size of Manchester's force. Many of the local trained
      bands failed to obey orders to muster – see Holmes, *Eastern Association*, p. 95.
36 Yaxley, *King's Lynn*; Anon, *Surrendering of King's Lyn*, p. 2.

37 Ibid.

CHAPTER 11

THE STRUGGLE FOR BRISTOL AND THE SOUTH-WEST, JUNE TO AUGUST 1643

With Bristol and Gloucester secure, but having failed to capture Worcester, Waller now concentrated his army around Bath. It was a precautionary measure; he had received reports of a Royalist advance east from Somerset. At Chard, the union of the armies of Prince Maurice and Hertford with those of Hopton and Grenville, had amassed a force of 6,300 men and 16 field guns.[1] However, two matters needed to be resolved before they could march towards Oxford in order to join the King for a drive on London. The first was to determine who was in overall command, and the second was to convince the Cornish soldiers to march beyond Somerset. As Hopton's leadership was pivotal in achieving the latter, it was most likely deemed logical that he should exercise overall command, leaving Maurice to command the horse. Having taken the surrender of the garrison at Dunster Castle, they marched east. At Wells they halted, and on 12 June the advance guard had a sharp skirmish with Waller's cavalry at Chewton Mendip, during which Maurice was injured and temporarily captured.[2] The two sides sized each other up and there was a pause for some weeks underpinned by a ceasefire. Hopton wrote to his old friend and comrade-in-arms Waller.[3] However, Waller turned down the offer to parley and instead both sides made good use of the hiatus. Hopton sought to establish a firm base for subsequent operations and Waller sought to augment his outnumbered force. The Parliamentarians were rewarded towards the end of the month with the arrival of Sir Arthur Haselrig and his regiment of cuirassiers.[4] This brought Waller's cavalry up to 2,500, but he was still heavily outnumbered in infantry, having only 1,500 musketeers and pikemen.

The offensive finally began on 2 July when the Royalists advanced and secured a crossing over the Avon at Bradford. Waller counter-moved his force to Claverton Down but was forced back by Hopton at Batheaston, and by Maurice at Claverton, the next day. He had little choice but to fall back on Bath but wasted no time in redeploying his army to cover the northern approaches to the city, on the slopes of Lansdown Hill. Early on 4 July Hopton, now united with Maurice, moved west to Charlcombe, from where he could see Waller's men on the high ground above. He wasted little time in dismissing the idea of executing an uphill assault and instead gave orders for the withdrawal of the force to Marshfield, from where he hoped to attack Waller's men at Lansdown from the north. Hopton recalled:

> … the next morning earlie Sr Wm. Waller drew out his whole Army over Lansdowne to that ende which lookes towards Marsfield, and there upon the verie point of the hill, over the high way suddenly raysed breast workes with faggotts and earth, and sent downe strong partyes of

horse into the field towards Marsfield, where they lighted upon a party of horse and beate them in.[5]

Hopton responded by giving the order for the entire Royalist army to march towards the Parliamentarians' main force, using Tog Hill and Freezing Hill as the axis of advance. Walter Slingsby, a colonel in the Royalist foot, recalled the moment he reached Tog Hill and secured a good view of the Parliamentarian position:

> In the brow of the hill, hee had raised brestworkes in which his cannon and greate store of small shott was placed; on either flanke hee was strengthned with a thicke wood which stood upon the declining of the hill, in which hee had putt store of muskeiteires; on his reare hee had a faire plaine where stood rang'd his reserves of horse and footte; some bodyes of horse with muskeiteires hee bestow'd upon some other places of the hill, where hee thought there was any accesse; thus fortyfied stood the foxe gazing at us…[6]

Hopton drove back the Parliamentarian cavalry pickets but, after two further hours of bickering fire, decided that Waller's position was, in point of fact, too strong and he gave the order to withdraw. Waller had always been conscious that the road to Oxford was now open for the Royalists and he felt compelled to take the fight to them. After a few minutes, two cavalry groups were despatched to charge into the Royalists flanks as they pulled back. Francis Dowet's troop of 200 horse was the first to deploy, followed shortly by William Carr's troop of a similar number. This checked the Royalist retreat and they turned, stood and deployed their artillery, which raked the Parliamentarian cavalry. Waller responded by sending the bulk of Robert Burghill's Regiment of Horse, supported by some dragoons, to maintain the offensive and to regain the initiative. A young Royalist cavalry captain watching on considered Waller's actions to be 'the boldest thing that I ever saw the enemy do; for a party of less than 1000 to charge an army of 6000 horse, foot and cannon, in their own ground, at least a mile and a half from their body'.[7] Fortune very nearly favoured the bold on this occasion and had it not been for the presence of groups of commanded musketeers deployed on either flank by Maurice, Burghill's troopers would have caused panic. The Royalist musketeers held their ground among the hedges and ditches until the Royalist cavalry were close before releasing a devastating volley at close range. The Parliamentarian cavalry reined up and then the Royalist cavalry, immediately followed and supported by the Cornish infantry,

---

1   Chadwyck-Healey, *Bellum Civile*, p. 47: 4,000 foot, 2,000 horse and 300 dragoons.

2   The date of this action varies in the sources from 9 to 14 June. I have taken the date from Gardiner, *Great Civil War*.

3   They had both served together during the Thirty Years' War in the Elector of Palatine's army.

4   They wore a complete suit of armour and were dubbed 'Lobsters' by the Royalists.

5   Chadwyck-Healey, op. cit., p. 53.

6   Slingsby, *Colonel Slingsby's relation of the battle of Lansdown and Roundway Down*, Clarendon MSS., Vol. 23, No. 1738 (2). This is reproduced in Chadwyck-Healey, op. cit., pp. 94–9. Slingsby is not to be confused with Sir Henry Slingsby.

7   Atkyns, *The vindication of Richard Atkyns*, p. 30.

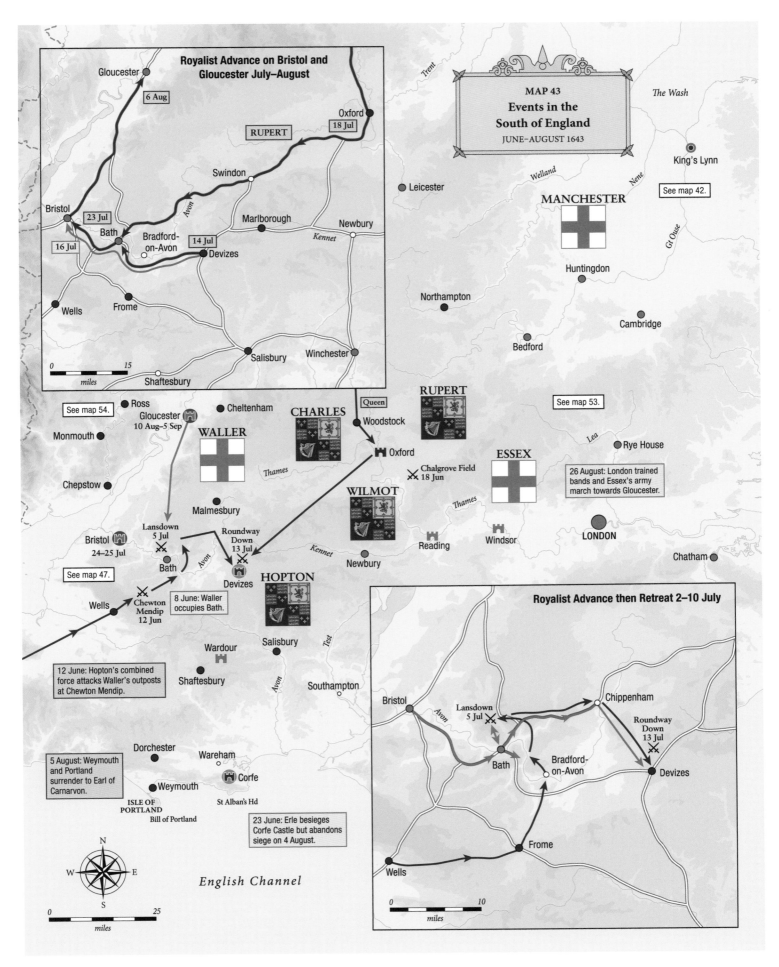

Royalist Advance on Bristol and Gloucester July–August

Gloucester

6 Aug

RUPERT

Oxford
18 Jul

Swindon

Bristol
23 Jul
Bath
16 Jul
Bradford-on-Avon
14 Jul
Devizes

Wells   Frome

Marlborough
Newbury
Kennet

Salisbury   Winchester

Shaftesbury

0   15
miles

MAP 43
Events in the South of England
JUNE–AUGUST 1643

Trent

The Wash

King's Lynn

Welland   Nene

See map 42.

Leicester

MANCHESTER

Huntingdon

Northampton

Bedford

Cambridge

See map 54.

Ross
Gloucester
10 Aug–5 Sep

Monmouth

Cheltenham

CHARLES

Queen

Woodstock

WALLER

Thames

RUPERT

See map 53.

Oxford

Chalgrove Field
18 Jun

ESSEX

Lea

Rye House

26 August: London trained bands and Essex's army march towards Gloucester.

Chepstow

Malmesbury

WILMOT

Bristol
24–25 Jul

Lansdown
5 Jul

Roundway Down
13 Jul

Kennet

Thames

Newbury

Reading   Windsor

LONDON

Chatham

See map 47.

Bath

Avon

Devizes

8 June: Waller occupies Bath.

HOPTON

Wells

Chewton Mendip
12 Jun

12 June: Hopton's combined force attacks Waller's outposts at Chewton Mendip.

Wardour

Shaftesbury

Salisbury

Test

Avon

Southampton

Dorchester   Wareham

5 August: Weymouth and Portland surrender to Earl of Carnarvon.

Weymouth   Corfe

ISLE OF PORTLAND
Bill of Portland

St Alban's Hd

23 June: Erle besieges Corfe Castle but abandons siege on 4 August.

N
W   E
S

English Channel

0   25
miles

Royalist Advance then Retreat 2–10 July

Chippenham

Lansdown
5 Jul

Roundway Down
13 Jul

Bristol

Avon

Bath   Bradford-on-Avon

Devizes

Frome

Wells

0   10
miles

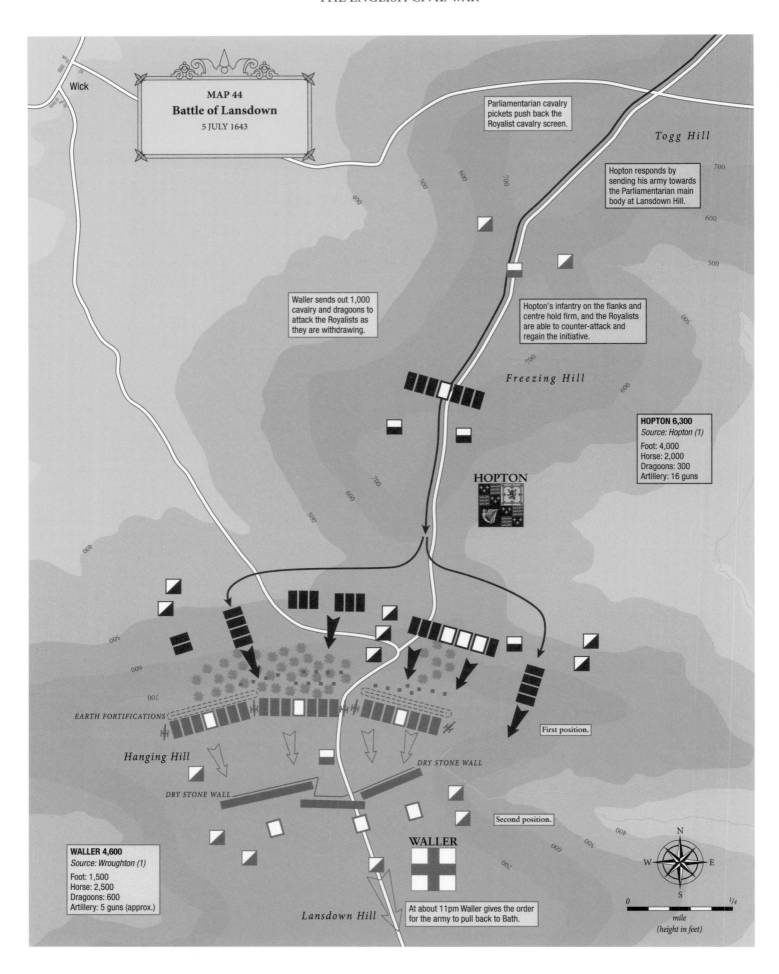

Wick

MAP 44
Battle of Lansdown
5 JULY 1643

Togg Hill

Parliamentarian cavalry pickets push back the Royalist cavalry screen.

Hopton responds by sending his army towards the Parliamentarian main body at Lansdown Hill.

Waller sends out 1,000 cavalry and dragoons to attack the Royalists as they are withdrawing.

Hopton's infantry on the flanks and centre hold firm, and the Royalists are able to counter-attack and regain the initiative.

Freezing Hill

HOPTON

HOPTON 6,300
Source: Hopton (1)
Foot: 4,000
Horse: 2,000
Dragoons: 300
Artillery: 16 guns

EARTH FORTIFICATIONS

First position.

Hanging Hill

DRY STONE WALL

DRY STONE WALL

Second position.

WALLER 4,600
Source: Wroughton (1)
Foot: 1,500
Horse: 2,500
Dragoons: 600
Artillery: 5 guns (approx.)

WALLER

At about 11pm Waller gives the order for the army to pull back to Bath.

Lansdown Hill

N
W E
S

0   1/4
mile
(height in feet)

drove back the cavalry and dragoons over Tog Hill to the top of Lansdown Hill, where they were left licking their wounds.

It was early afternoon and the day certainly held enough daylight for a major attack to be delivered on Lansdown Hill, but once again Hopton hesitated. He could see the strength of Waller's position, and close up it looked even more formidable than it had done from the top of Freezing Hill. Meanwhile, the Parliamentarian guns opened on the Royalists in the valley below and it was not long before they had their range. Taking large numbers of casualties, the Cornish infantry pleaded to be allowed to charge the hill and silence the guns. Slingsby recalled, 'Now did our footte believe noe men theire equals, and were soe apt to undertake anything... for they desir'd to fall on and cry'd lett us fetch those cannon'.[8] Hopton finally agreed, albeit reluctantly, to let the Cornishmen off the leash. 'Order was presently given to attempt the hill with horse and footte: greate partys of Muskeiteires was sent out of either of our wings to fall into those woodes'.[9] In the centre, the Royalist cavalry were the first up the hill but they were quickly driven back by the heavy weight of artillery fire from the well-sited guns, and from the Parliamentarian dragoons deployed in the woods on either side of the road.

Hopton renewed the attack, his intention being to send out 'strong partyes of musketiers on eache hand to seconde one another, to endeavour under the couvert of the inclosed groundes to gaine the flanck of the Enimy on the topp of the Hill, which they at last did'.[10] It took a Herculean effort to overwhelm Waller's men and the Royalists 'were five times charg'd and beaten back with disorder'. Captain Atkyns, a young cavalry commander in the thick of the fighting in the centre, recalled that 'when I came to the top of the hill, I saw Sir Bevill Grinvill's stand of pikes, which certainly preserved our army from a total rout, with the loss of his most precious life'.[11] Waller gave the order to his men to fall back to a drystone wall about 400 yards to their rear. The Royalists had taken the crest but they were exhausted and many of their cavalry had drifted away.[12] Slingsby recalled that the two armies took breath and eyed each other until dark. Both sides were spent. The Cornish infantry, which had behaved with such courage, were devastated at the loss of their leader Bevil Grenville and their morale plummeted accordingly.

As dusk fell, Hopton's position looked the most precarious, but it was to be Waller who blinked first. Withdrawing his army at this side of midnight, he once again pulled back to the safety of Bath. The Royalists awoke to see the Parliamentarian positions abandoned to their front and, soon after first light, they began their slow withdrawal back towards their camp at Marshfield. Losses are difficult to predict with any accuracy. The contemporary Parliamentarian newspaper *Mercurius Civicus* informs us that 'the certainty of the number on both sides is not knowne, but it is conceived there were not lesse than 2000, whereof the greatest part were Hoptonians'.[13] The Royalist newspaper *Mercurius Aulicus* noted that 'the rebels foote were absolutely routed, and all dispersed and cut off, his loss of officers and horse very great... we are confident we killed many hundreds of his men'.[14] The Parliamentarian post-battle report records the Royalist losses at 200 dead and 300 wounded, while Waller's losses were listed as 21 dead and

56 wounded.[15] Despite the Royalists claiming victory, the fact remained they had failed to take Bath. Furthermore, the performance of their cavalry and the loss of the talismanic Grenville had severely dented morale among the Cornish contingent.

Things were about to get a whole lot worse. Soon after they arrived back at Marshfield camp, an ammunition cart exploded in a ball of fire, badly injuring the Royalist leader and consuming the bulk of the army's powder. Captain Atkyns recalled that he 'found his lordship miserably burnt, his horse singed like parched leather'. His observation that 'the foot and cannon (by the loss of the ammunition) became wholly unserviceable to us' was, however, a greater and more immediate concern for the Royalist commanders.[16] The decision was made to move directly to Oxford and they spent the rest of the day burying their dead and making preparations. Meanwhile Waller, encouraged by the Royalists' misfortune, called up reinforcements from Bristol and, on 7 July, as soon as they arrived, he set off in immediate pursuit of Hopton's force in the hope of cutting it off before it was reinforced or before it reached the Royalist capital. They caught up with them at Chippenham on 9 July and forced them back to the relative safety of the castle and town of Devizes. The next day, Waller deployed his army on Roundway Hill to the north of the town, and offered battle. Hopton, badly burned, confined to a chair but conscious, realized that without powder and ammunition, his options were limited. A subsequent council of war elected to despatch Maurice and Hertford, with all the cavalry, to make a rush to Oxford in order to gather reinforcements and fresh powder. Meanwhile, Hopton, with the infantry and artillery, would hold the town until they returned. It was probably the only sensible option and the cavalry breakout was executed just in time, for early on the 11th the Parliamentarians surrounded the town and hauled a battery of heavier guns on to the hill to the east.

Waller was aware of the abscondment of the Royalist horse and sent urgent word to Essex to move west with all haste to intercept them, or any force that might endeavour to move from Oxford. However, his message was received too late to be effective.[17] Maurice reached Oxford on the night of the 11th to discover that two forces had already been despatched. The Earl of Crawford had departed on 9 July with a consignment of ammunition, escorted by 600 horse. The following day, Lord Wilmot had departed with his brigade of horse. Sir John Byron's brigade of cavalry was being readied and he and Maurice set off on the 12th to link up with Wilmot.[18] Waller had, in fact, intercepted Crawford, driven his cavalry away and captured the ammunition. He wasted little time in taunting Hopton with this news, while concurrently offering his friend the opportunity of surrender. Hopton was devastated but dragged out the negotiations. He needed to rest his men, preserve their ammunition and buy time for a response from Oxford. Realizing Hopton's intentions, Waller's forces attacked the town early on 12 July and 'beat them in from all their out posts and guards'. The next day a major assault was planned, but before this could be put into execution 'news came that the enemy from Oxford was within two miles, with two thousand horse'.[19]

Wilmot had concentrated his force (consisting of his own, Byron's and Crawford's cavalry) at Marlborough and marched, via the Bath to London

---

8   Slingsby, op. cit., p. 95.

9   Ibid.

10 Chadwyck-Healey, op. cit., p. 54.

11 Atkyns, op. cit., p. 32.

12 Burne & Young, *Great Civil War*, p. 82.

13 *Mercurius Civicus*, Number 7, dated Thursday July 6 to Thursday July 13, 1643. BL Thomason / 11:E.60[9].

14 *Mercurius Aulicus*, Week 27, 9 July 1643. BL Thomason / 11:E.60[18].

15 Anon, *A true relation of the great and glorious victory through Gods providence, obtained by Sir William Waller, Sir Arthur Haselrig and others of the Parliament forces*, p. 4.

16 Atkyns, op. cit., pp. 33–4.

17 Chadwyck-Healey, op. cit., p. 57.

18 Hertford stayed at Oxford.

19 Colonel in the Army, *A true relation*, p. 3; Scott, *Most Heavy Stroke*, p. 62, considers Waller's plans to have been optimistic given his numbers.

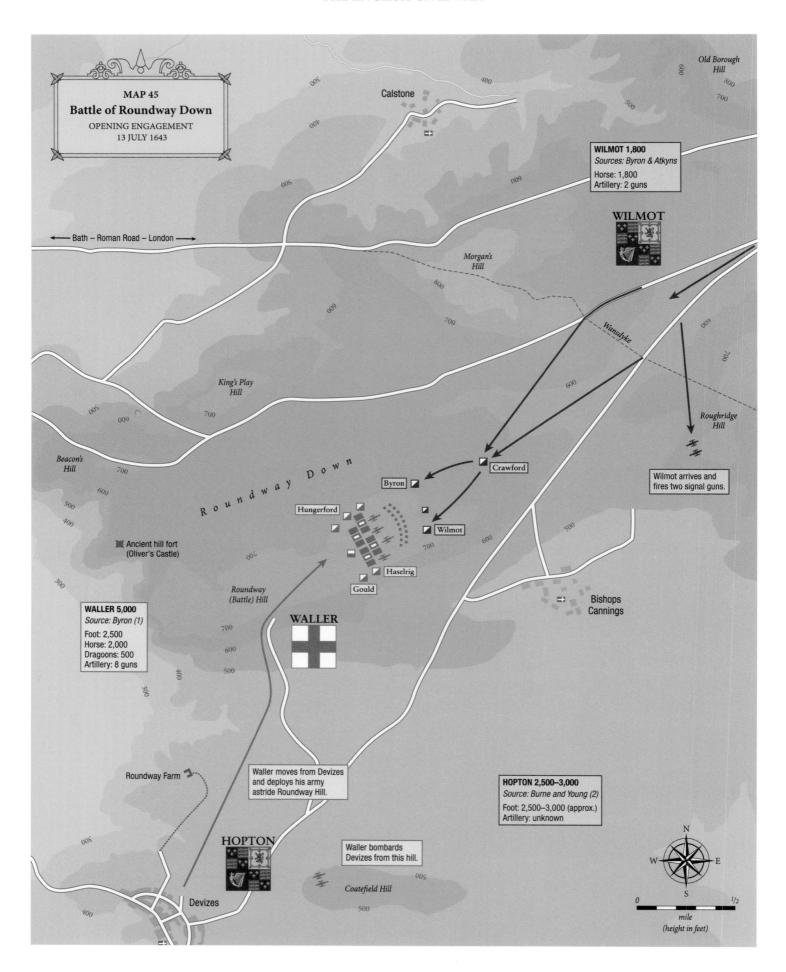

MAP 45

Battle of Roundway Down

OPENING ENGAGEMENT
13 JULY 1643

Old Borough
Hill

Calstone

WILMOT 1,800
Sources: Byron & Atkyns
Horse: 1,800
Artillery: 2 guns

WILMOT

← Bath – Roman Road – London →

Morgan's
Hill

Wansdyke

King's Play
Hill

Roughridge
Hill

Beacon's
Hill

Roundway Down

Crawford

Wilmot arrives and
fires two signal guns.

Byron

Hungerford

Wilmot

Ancient hill fort
(Oliver's Castle)

Haselrig

Bishops
Cannings

Gould

WALLER 5,000
Source: Byron (1)
Foot: 2,500
Horse: 2,000
Dragoons: 500
Artillery: 8 guns

Roundway
(Battle) Hill

WALLER

Roundway Farm

Waller moves from Devizes
and deploys his army
astride Roundway Hill.

HOPTON 2,500–3,000
Source: Burne and Young (2)
Foot: 2,500–3,000 (approx.)
Artillery: unknown

HOPTON

Waller bombards
Devizes from this hill.

Devizes

Coatefield Hill

N
W — E
S

0   1/2

mile
(height in feet)

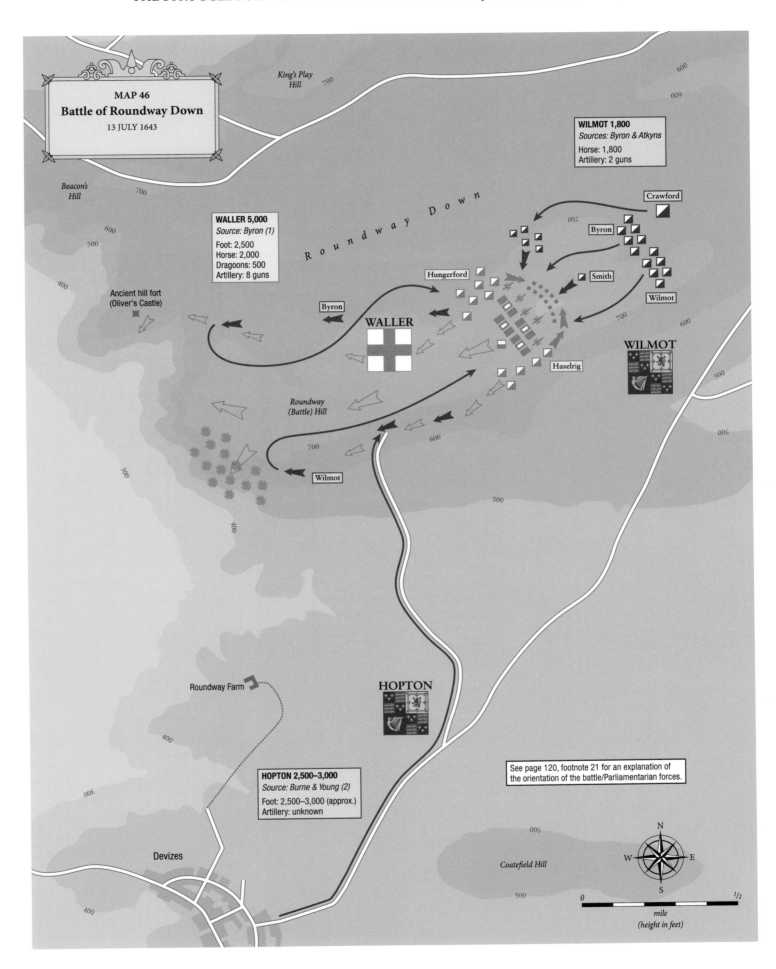

MAP 46

Battle of Roundway Down

13 JULY 1643

WILMOT 1,800
Sources: Byron & Atkyns
Horse: 1,800
Artillery: 2 guns

WALLER 5,000
Source: Byron (1)
Foot: 2,500
Horse: 2,000
Dragoons: 500
Artillery: 8 guns

King's Play Hill

Beacon's Hill

Roundway Down

Crawford

Byron

Smith

Wilmot

Hungerford

Byron

WALLER

WILMOT

Haselrig

Ancient hill fort (Oliver's Castle)

Roundway (Battle) Hill

Wilmot

Roundway Farm

HOPTON

See page 120, footnote 21 for an explanation of the orientation of the battle/Parliamentarian forces.

HOPTON 2,500–3,000
Source: Burne & Young (2)
Foot: 2,500–3,000 (approx.)
Artillery: unknown

Devizes

Coatefield Hill

N
W E
S

0   1/2

mile
(height in feet)

road, branching south on the fork a mile to the west of Beckhampton. Hopton, reported with some relief, that…

> Verie shortly after Prince Maurice and Lo[rd] Wilmot who were returned with a verie gallant party of the King's horse, appeared 3 miles off upon the hills, and haveing Ordnance with them gave two gunns for a warning to the Towne, which was answeared againe by the Earle of Marleborough from the old Castle where the Trayne was.[20]

Byron, who was with the Royalist horse on Roughridge Hill, recalled, 'we shot off our ordinance from an high hill that overlookes the Town, to let them know, that we were there for their assistance; at the same time Waller appeared with his whole army upon an opposite hill'.[21] Waller had moved his entire force to Roundway (Battle) Hill where he deployed 'the foot in the middle between the two wings of horse and the cannon before the foot'.[22] The terrain constricted the deployment and most of the horse on both wings were on sloping ground.

Wilmot, having only cavalry and two light guns, would have expected support from Hopton's infantry and sent word accordingly. However, Hopton, despite being able to see (at least some of) Wilmot's force, was concerned that Waller's movements were a ruse to get him to leave the security of the town barricades and walls. He delayed accordingly. Meanwhile, Byron recalled that 'it was resolved that we should immediately march towards them, and my Lord Wilmott very discretely ordered it, that only his brigade and mine should charge… and that the other troopes… should only stand as a reserve'.[23] The Royalist forlorn hope, consisting of 300 men under Sergeant Major Paul Smith, drove back Woodley's Dragoons sent down to counter their advance and then caused havoc in the Parliamentarian gun line.[24] This prompted Haselrig, who was placed on the far right, to charge Smith's men in order to enable the Parliamentarian forlorn hope to get away. Wilmot immediately responded by counter-charging Haselrig's 'Lobsters'. Captain Atkyns recalled, 'the charge was so suddain that I hardly had time to put on my Armes, we advanced at full trot, 3 deep, and kept in order'.[25] The two bodies of cavalry clashed in front of the right wing of Waller's guns and infantry. It was a furious engagement, during which time Atkyns found

himself face to face with Haselrig. He discharged his pistol, injuring the General of Horse. The heavy cuirassiers retreated but rallied and executed a second charge. This was met by Wilmot's and Byron's brigades, which had been seconded from the north of the hill. Byron remembered, 'they rallied themselves again and charged a second time, but with worst success; for then my brigade being drawn up to second my Lord Wilmot, they all ran away… and appeared no more in the battle'.[26]

The Royalist cavalry would have been deployed in the Swedish system, while those of Waller in the Dutch system – see the chapter 'Civil War Armies'. This resulted in the Parliamentarian horse having greater concentration of firepower, but they were quickly overlapped on both flanks, and this was their undoing.[27] The flight of Parliament's talismanic cavalry did little for morale, and Waller, with his right wing having collapsed, realized he would have to try to regain the initiative, and quickly. Waller's Horse on the left wing advanced towards Byron's and the latter commander ordered his men not to 'discharge a pistol till the enemy had spent all his shot'. This was studiously observed and when Byron charged and fell in with them his men were able to use their pistols and carbines, discharging them 'in their teeth'. Another brigade of Parliamentarian cavalry came up but they were hindered by Crawford's men, who had come around the left flank in a timely manner. The infantry was unable to fire for fear of hitting their own cavalry and so this rather extraordinary situation of close-quarter cavalry actions going on around the infantry persisted for some time. Byron recalled that the situation was only resolved when 'it pleased God to put new spirit into our tyr'd horse as well as into our men'.[28] The Parliamentarian cavalry broke on this flank and also fell back on the reserve horse and the whole fled with most of the Royalist cavalry in pursuit. They pursued them to the end of Roundway Hill (Oliver's Castle) and here they 'came to a precipice, where their fear made them so valiant that they galloped as if it had been plain ground, and many of them brake both their own and their horses' necks'.[29]

Behind them the Parliamentarian infantry remained on the field but they soon found themselves facing Hopton's infantry that had filed out of the town and moved north to the hill with some speed. As they advanced, they were joined by Wilmot's cavalry that had regrouped and made its way back to the field. Having lost their guns the Parliamentarian infantry put up a fight for a while, in the hope that Waller and some of the cavalry would return. Their hopes were dashed a short while later, when some of Byron's and Crawford's cavalry began to appear and a few troopers turned two of the captured guns upon their ranks. Realizing the game was up, they decided to try to move off in formation. Captain Slingsby recalled, 'But drawing over the downes, seeing severall bodyes of our horse pressing hard upon them on all sides, they began to fall in pieces.'[30]

It was, as *Mercurius Aulicus* recorded, 'a most absolute victory'.[31] The Royalists had killed 600 and captured 800, along with seven cannons, 26 colours of foot and eight colours of horse. The army of the Western Association had been badly cut up and Charles was quick to exploit the opportunity. Five days after the battle, he despatched Rupert with three infantry brigades (those of Grandison, Wentworth and Belasyse), two cavalry brigades (of Aston and Gerard) and nine troops of dragoons to join

20 Chadwyck-Healey, op. cit., p. 58.
21 Byron, *John Byron's Relation*, p. 3. This is at odds with Adair, *Roundhead General* and Burne, *Battlefields of England* who have Wilmot's force atop/astride Morgan's Hill. However, I agree with the English Heritage Battlefield Report that quotes Hopton's and Byron's eyewitness records. This places the Royalist signal guns on Roughridge Hill and not Morgan's Hill, because from the latter there is no line of sight to Devizes. I believe the Royalist cavalry were in the low ground to the north west of Roughridge Hill entering the bowl of Roundway Down and on the old road to Devizes. I base this on Atkyns' remark, 'there were four hills like the four corners of a dye… upon one of the hills we discharged our cannon…'. Furthermore, if the Royalists had arrived at Morgan's Hill, Waller would have arrayed his force facing north and that would have placed his back to the steep slopes down to Devizes, which seems unlikely. In addition, it does not explain why Waller, once beaten, withdrew to his left and not back and away from the attacking force. Scott, *Most Heavy Stroke*, agrees with this but believes the Royalists continued further down the road through Shepherds' Shore and then swung towards Roundway Hill from the north. That might be correct but it does not dovetail with the earlier eyewitness accounts that indicate that the Royalists in the town could see Wilmot's force. They would not have been able to do so if they had all passed at (old) Shepherds' Shore.
22 Atkyns, op. cit., p. 37.
23 Byron, op. cit., p. 4.
24 Scott, op. cit., p. 92.
25 Atkyns, op. cit., p. 37.
26 Byron, op. cit., p. 4.
27 Scott, op. cit., pp. 95–7, for an excellent explanation.
28 Byron, p. 5.
29 Ibid.
30 Slingsby, op. cit., p. 98.
31 *Mercurius Aulicus*, Issue 15, Jul 1643, BL Thomason / 11:E.62[3].

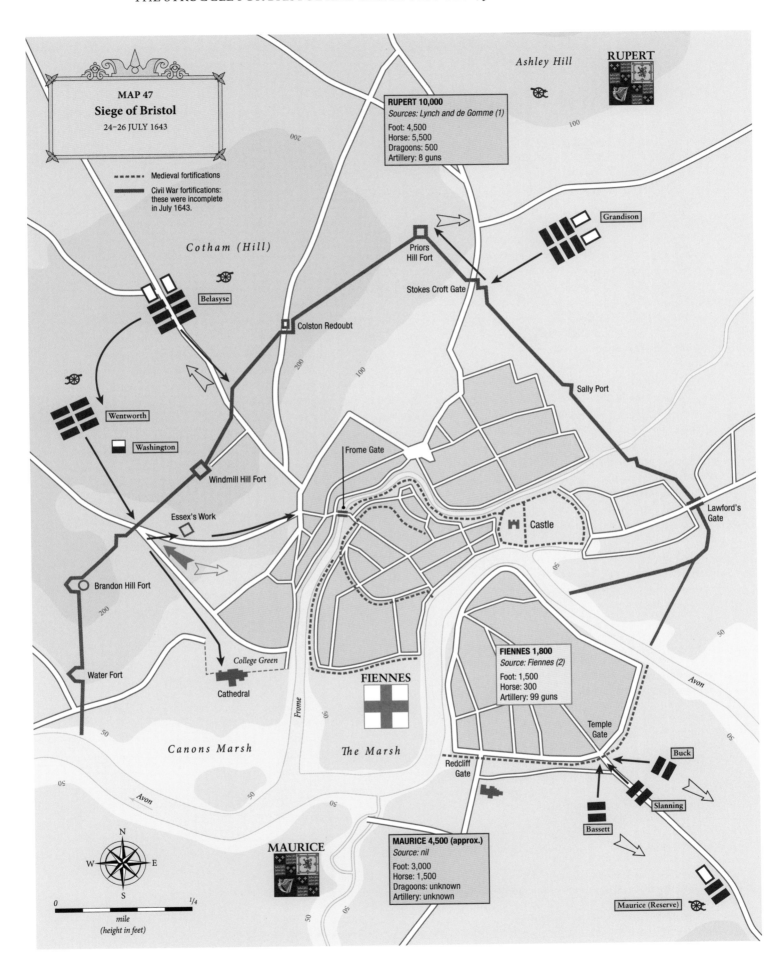

RUPERT

Ashley Hill

RUPERT 10,000
Sources: Lynch and de Gomme (1)
Foot: 4,500
Horse: 5,500
Dragoons: 500
Artillery: 8 guns

MAP 47
Siege of Bristol
24–26 JULY 1643

- - - - Medieval fortifications
▬▬▬ Civil War fortifications:
these were incomplete
in July 1643.

Cotham (Hill)

Grandison

Priors
Hill Fort

Stokes Croft Gate

Belasyse

Colston Redoubt

Sally Port

Wentworth

Frome Gate

Washington

Lawford's
Gate

Windmill Hill Fort

Castle

Essex's Work

Brandon Hill Fort

College Green

Water Fort

Cathedral

FIENNES 1,800
Source: Fiennes (2)
Foot: 1,500
Horse: 300
Artillery: 99 guns

Canons Marsh

FIENNES

The Marsh

Frome

Temple
Gate

Avon

Redcliff
Gate

Buck

Slanning

Bassett

N

W   E

S

0   1/4

mile
(height in feet)

MAURICE

MAURICE 4,500 (approx.)
Source: nil
Foot: 3,000
Horse: 1,500
Dragoons: unknown
Artillery: unknown

Maurice (Reserve)

Wilmot. Their mission was to seize Bristol and then move on Gloucester. The artillery train was small but quite cumbersome, consisting of only eight guns but a mass of stores and ammunition requiring nearly 60 carts and 400 horses.[32] The two Royalist armies moved towards Bristol and linked up on 23 July. Following his heavy defeat at Roundway on the 13th, Waller had pulled back to Bath, but soon left and set off, by a circuitous route, to London while the small garrison left there withdrew to Bristol.

The city of Bristol had been in Parliamentarian hands since November 1642 and Colonel Nathaniel Fiennes had arrived to assume command the following February. However, his garrison had been significantly reduced by the provision of 1,200 men and 60 barrels of powder to support Waller's army. Fiennes recalled, 'I held the security of Bristoll to be involved in the security of that Army, and that the destiny of the one, would be the fall of the other.'[33] In July 1643, therefore, his hastily reinforced garrison numbered just 1,800 men, but more worryingly he only had 50 barrels of powder.[34] To make matters worse, the planned fortifications for the city were far from complete.

Rupert summoned Fiennes to surrender on 24 July, which was duly rejected. His expert eye had noted the incompleteness of the city's defences and his intuition led him to conclude that the defenders' resolve was at a low ebb. At the Royalist council of war later that day, it was decided to dispense with a formal siege and take the place by storm and escalade. Rupert's three brigades (or 'tertias') would attack from the north, while Maurice would coordinate three attacks by the Cornish infantry from the south, led by Sir Nicholas Slanning, Colonel Buck and Lieutenant Bassett. On the 25th, a number of guns were moved into place to support these attacks. Once in position they opened fire on the defences in the afternoon and continued through the night in order to deny the garrison any sleep and damage morale still further. At daybreak on the 26th, the assault was to be delivered on the firing of a signal gun from Grandison's battery. However, at 3am the Cornish infantry attacked prematurely, precipitating events. Despite the attacks in this southern sector being against the old medieval walls, the ditch proved too deep for the ladders and fascines and, after about 30 minutes, the determined Cornishmen were driven back with considerable loss. Slanning and Buck were killed and Bassett was wounded.

To the north, Rupert signalled the advance despite the troops not being fully in place and the assault equipment, in some cases, still in transit. Grandison made a strong attack on the Stokes Croft gate. It lasted over an hour but the attackers failed to gain entry. Rupert then turned his attention and his force to Priors Hill Fort, which had been bombarded by the two

heavy 27-pounder guns most of the 25th. However, the fort's defences remained intact and Grandison's attack once again faltered. Grandison attempted to initiate a third assault but was mortally wounded in the process. The brigade fell back, the fire having left the bellies of the men. On the other side of Cotham Hill, Belasyse's attack by Windmill Hill Fort never really got going. The first troops to arrive at the ditch did not have ladders and under heavy fire they quickly fell back. To their right, Wentworth's Brigade, supported by Washington's dismounted dragoons, attacked the wall in between Windmill Hill Fort and Brandon Hill Fort. The low ground was masked by the convex nature of the adjacent hill on which the forts were constructed. With the dragoons keeping the heads of the defenders down, the infantry hurled granadoes and quickly gained access in considerable force. Many hundreds were inside the walls before any counter-attack could be launched.[35] It was about 4am when Fiennes led the counter, but it was easily driven back and in the melee the Royalists captured Essex Work, consolidating their hold in the area. Belasyse was ordered to support the breach and Wentworth's men pushed on to College Green and occupied the cathedral. Belasyse's men then pushed on towards the town, where a fearful firefight around Frome Gate lasted two hours. Rupert then summoned Grandison's men to join the fray, and was in the process of calling up the Cornish infantry when Fiennes indicated a desire to parley.

While the fighting was ongoing, Fiennes had summoned a council of war, at which, Fiennes wrote:

… it was unanimously resolved, that we should entertain a treaty with the enemy; and that… it were far better to save so many Commanders and Souldiers both of Horse and Foot, and so many honest men's persons and estates… than to expose them all to destruction by attempting in a furious and mad way to defend the towne and Castel for two or three dayes.[36]

In view of the hopelessness of the defenders' immediate situation and the fact that Essex's reinforcements would not have arrived in time, Fiennes decided to throw in the towel. It was a decision that the Parliamentarian high command subsequently viewed with anger and derision. Fiennes was attacked as a coward and a traitor. At his subsequent court martial he was condemned to death and only spared due to the influence of his father, Lord Saye and Sele. Nathaniel Fiennes was never to be offered field command again.

---

32 Roy, *Ordnance Papers*, pp. 226–59. The guns included 2 demi-cannon (27-pounder), 2 whole culverins (18-pounder), 2 quarter cannons (12-pounder), and 2x 6-pounders.

33 Fiennes, *A relation made in the House of Commons*, p. 10.

34 Ibid., p. 9. Some men had fallen back from Bath and another 200 under Captain Gore from Malmesbury.

35 Peachey, *Storming of Bristol*, p. 36.

36 Fiennes, *Concerning Bristol*, pp. 3–4.

CHAPTER 12
OPERATIONS IN THE NORTH, SEPTEMBER TO DECEMBER 1643

Tom Fairfax's small force (700 horse and 600 foot) was forced to pull back from his base at Beverley as Newcastle's numerically superior force moved south-east from York towards the fortified city and port of Hull. Fairfax wrote, 'They march on with their whole body, which was about 4000 Horse, and 12000 Foot. We stood till they were come very neare to us; I drew off thinking to make good ye Retreat with ye Horse.'[1] Fairfax reached Hull on 1 September, and Newcastle established a cordon around the place the following day. Tom's father, Lord Fairfax, had been made governor of Hull on 22 July and he had made good use of his time to strengthen the defences in and around the fortified port. Neither Fairfax was, however, to be content to wait for Newcastle to bring the fight to the Parliamentarian garrison; instead they opted for an active defence. Redoubts and batteries were constructed outside the walls and suspected Royalist sympathizers inside the city were rounded up and detained.

Newcastle established his artillery and baggage train at Cottingham (3 miles to the west) and began digging works for guns near the Derringham Dyke. That night the Royalists cut the fresh water supply to the city. The next morning the new work was clearly visible to the town's defenders and on Monday, 3 September, two guns were moved into the battery. A Parliamentarian participant recalled, 'all this while we were imployed in fitting our platfromes and fortiying the Walls with breast-works, and repairing the out-works…'.[2] Tuesday morning revealed work on a new and very large battery (Royal) opposite the north gate and that night a bridge of boats was built across the River Hull, giving the attackers access to the Holderness area. Two lighter guns were placed there in a hastily prepared battery. In response, Fairfax ordered the destruction of the old hospital at Charterhouse in order to construct a battery on the ruins to counter the large Royal battery to the north. Fairfax used a female labour force to conduct this dangerous work, prompting one observer to note 'that we have our Virgin Troopes, yet we can boast of our Troops of Virgins, who shewed so much diligence…'.[3]

On 8 September the Royal Battery was manned with a number of guns, including two massive demi-cannons nicknamed 'Gog' and 'Magog'.[4] The Royalist gunners prepared a large furnace to the rear of the battery, a dangerous prospect on any gun position, but their intentions soon became clear as they began to fire heated shot. One Parliamentarian recalled, 'They did heate their bullets, and shot them into the Towne, like their rage *red hot*.'[5] Fairfax added, 'But by ye Diligence and care of ye Governor (who caused every Inhabitant to watch his owne house, and where ever they saw these bullets to fall, to be ready to quench them, they prevented the

Danger.'[6] Fairfax placed some heavier culverins into the Charterhouse Battery to counter this new threat and ordered the construction of another work adjacent to it. Despite this, the Royalist guns were having a major impact on the battery in the ruins of Charterhouse and the old north gate and blockhouse. On 9 September, Fairfax decided to attempt a sally to destroy one of the Royalist batteries. It debouched from the Beverley Gate towards Anlaby, but it was driven back with considerable loss. Then, on 14 September Fairfax decided to open the sluice-gates and flood the area around the city. It was a masterstroke. The Royalists suddenly found their batteries and works under water and a sea of mud. They were forced to move the batteries to higher ground, which was essentially only to be found on the elevated roads and tracks and on the Derringham Dyke. The guns in the Royal Battery do not seem to have been too greatly affected by the flooding and they began firing some of the massive mortars with granadoes 'a foot in diameter' which, fortunately for the defenders, seem to have largely failed to hit any substantial targets within the city.

Newcastle was well aware that his cordon was only partially effective. The presence of Parliamentarian gun ships and naval craft moving freely along the River Humber frustrated Royalist efforts and provided succour to the besieged. He decided to deploy some troops on both the north and south banks, armed with light field guns, to engage the ships and drive them away. As they moved into place, they were bombarded by the warships *Lion* and *Unicorn*, and destroyed before it could be completed.[7] The cordon was so permeable that on 26 September Willoughby and Cromwell were able to cross the Humber from Barton (south bank) in a small boat into the city. They came to offer counsel, but their main aim was to remove Tom Fairfax and the 700 horse. They were badly needed for operations in Lincolnshire in conjunction with Manchester's army.[8] In exchange, 500 infantry were en route (under Meldrum) to assist the defenders of Hull. They arrived on 5 October.[9]

The Parliamentarians were enormously relieved during the month of September that Newcastle had not made a move on London. There is little doubt that Newcastle could have made better use of his large army, but it is perhaps an exaggeration to propose that Hull saved the Parliamentarian cause. William Widdrington was the senior Royalist in Lincolnshire, and both he and Henderson now received orders from Newcastle to gather a mounted force, from Newark, Lincoln and Gainsborough, and move to support the small Royalist garrison at Bolingbroke Castle. While they were moving east, Manchester moved his force up from Boston and drove in the Royalist pickets in Bolingbroke town and surrounded the castle. Later that

---

1 Fairfax, *Short memorials*, p. 217.
2 Anon, *Hulls managing*, p. 14.
3 Ibid., p. 15.
4 These guns purportedly fired 36-pound projectiles and were named (in the Book of Ezekiel) after the biblical enemies of God's people and allies of Satan.
5 Anon, *Hulls managing*, p. 15.

6 Fairfax, op. cit., p. 218.
7 Cooke, *Yorkshire Sieges*, p. 23; McNicol, *Kingston upon Hull*, p. 15.
8 The large numbers of horses were a heavy burden on the fast-dwindling supplies of drinking water. Manchester had concluded the siege at King's Lynn on 16 September – chapter 10.
9 Anon, *Hulls managing*, p. 18.

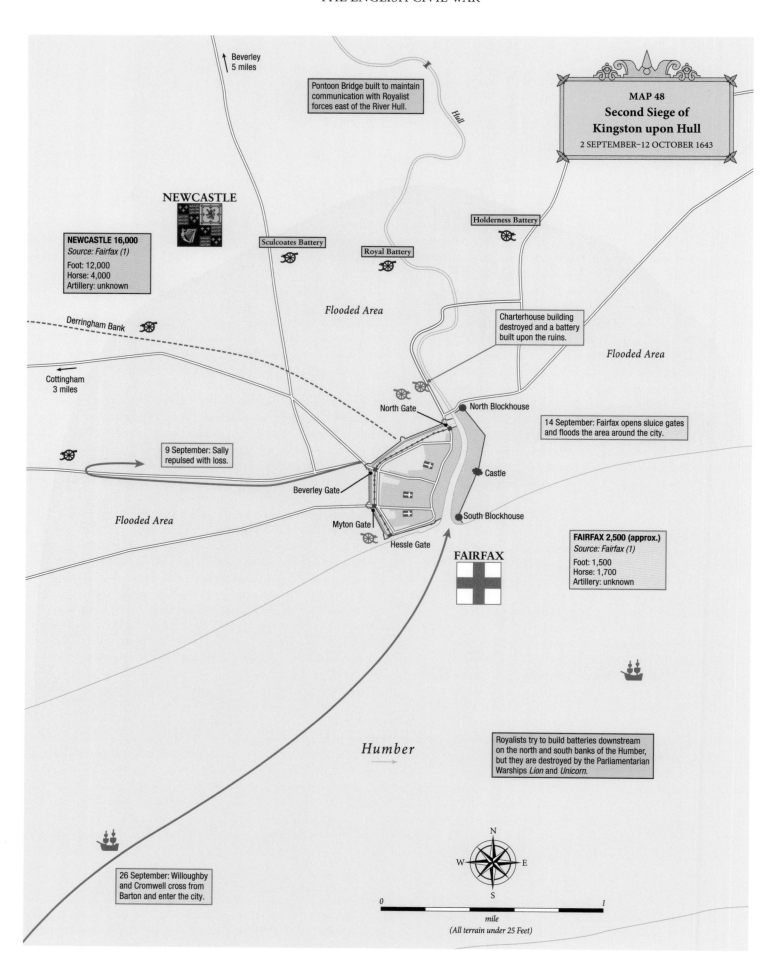

Beverley
5 miles

Pontoon Bridge built to maintain
communication with Royalist
forces east of the River Hull.

Hull

MAP 48
**Second Siege of
Kingston upon Hull**
2 SEPTEMBER–12 OCTOBER 1643

NEWCASTLE

Holderness Battery

NEWCASTLE 16,000
Source: Fairfax (1)
Foot: 12,000
Horse: 4,000
Artillery: unknown

Sculcoates Battery

Royal Battery

Flooded Area

Charterhouse building
destroyed and a battery
built upon the ruins.

Flooded Area

Derringham Bank

Cottingham
3 miles

North Gate

North Blockhouse

14 September: Fairfax opens sluice gates
and floods the area around the city.

9 September: Sally
repulsed with loss.

Castle

Beverley Gate

FAIRFAX 2,500 (approx.)
Source: Fairfax (1)
Foot: 1,500
Horse: 1,700
Artillery: unknown

Myton Gate

South Blockhouse

Hessle Gate

FAIRFAX

Flooded Area

Royalists try to build batteries downstream
on the north and south banks of the Humber,
but they are destroyed by the Parliamentarian
Warships *Lion* and *Unicorn*.

Humber

N
W   E
S

26 September: Willoughby
and Cromwell cross from
Barton and enter the city.

0   1
mile
(All terrain under 25 Feet)

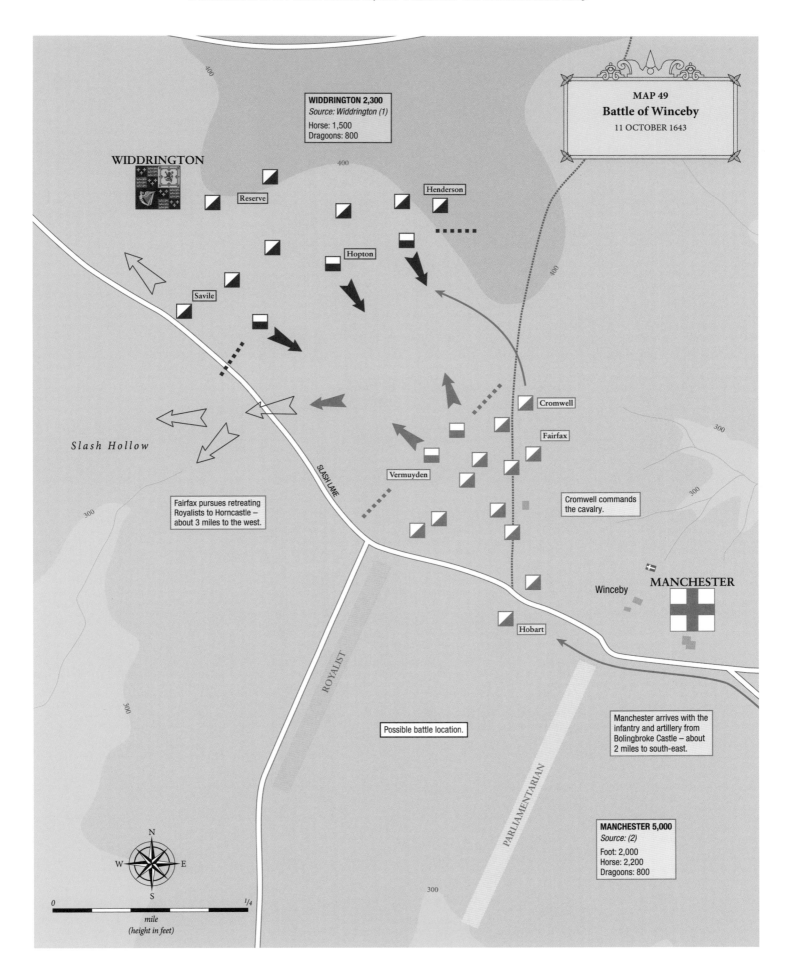

WIDDRINGTON 2,300
Source: Widdrington (1)
Horse: 1,500
Dragoons: 800

MAP 49
Battle of Winceby
11 OCTOBER 1643

WIDDRINGTON

Reserve

Henderson

Hopton

Savile

Cromwell

Fairfax

Slash Hollow

Vermuyden

Cromwell commands
the cavalry.

Fairfax pursues retreating
Royalists to Horncastle –
about 3 miles to the west.

SLASH LANE

Winceby

MANCHESTER

Hobart

ROYALIST

Manchester arrives with the
infantry and artillery from
Bolingbroke Castle – about
2 miles to south-east.

Possible battle location.

PARLIAMENTARIAN

N
W   E
S

MANCHESTER 5,000
Source: (2)
Foot: 2,000
Horse: 2,200
Dragoons: 800

0   1/4
mile
(height in feet)

day Manchester met up with Cromwell at Kirkby, while Fairfax's Horse was north of them at Hareby. During the day an alarm was raised on the sighting of a large mounted Royalist force and Fairfax sent Willoughby to investigate. They discovered the Royalists at Horncastle and returned to give their report. Manchester gave orders for the entire force to concentrate at Bolingbroke Hill at first light on 11 October.[10]

At the council of war, Manchester proposed taking the fight to the Royalists but Cromwell urged caution.[11] His mounts were exhausted, having been in constant action for the previous three days. Manchester was unconcerned and Fairfax recalled, 'we advanced again toward ye Enemy, and chusing a convenient ground to fight upon, we drew up ye Army there'.[12] Cromwell was given command of the horse and Manchester was to follow with the infantry. Cromwell divided the horse into six squadrons and placed Bartholomew Vermuyden's in front as the forlorn hope, while the Royalists had divided into four squadrons.[13] John Henderson was commanding that on the Royalist left, on the higher ground, while William Savile had command of the other two groups in the centre.[14] The Royalists were keen to get on with matters before the Parliamentarian infantry arrived from Bolingbroke. Some of their dragoons opened proceedings by advancing close to the Parliamentarian cavalry, dismounting and delivering a volley before pulling back to find cover for the inevitable response. What followed was a furious and bloody cavalry on cavalry engagement: 'Cromwell fell with resolution upon the enemy, immediately after their Dragooneers had given him the first volley, yet they were so nimble as with halfe pistol shot they gave him another, his horse was killed under him at the first charge and fell downe upon him.'[15]

Many in the Parliamentarian army thought that Cromwell had been killed. Indeed Ingram Hopton had knocked Cromwell to the ground for a second time, apparently intent on taking him prisoner, before being killed himself.[16] The heavy fire from the Royalist dragoons had taken most of the sting out of Cromwell's initial charge against Savile's two squadrons. Cromwell was somewhat shaken from his fall but was soon given another mount. Before he could rejoin his squadron, they had already executed a second charge, which drove the main body of Savile's horse back on their reserve. The discombobulated Royalists had no time to reorganize themselves before Fairfax's two squadrons were upon them. It was enough to break the Cavalier cohesion and put them to complete disorder. After about half an hour the fighting was effectively over. The Royalists fled back towards Horncastle and were pursued with unbridled vigour by Fairfax's squadrons.[17] At about the time the Royalist cavalry broke, the first elements of Manchester's infantry had arrived near Winceby and they quickly set about mopping up the small pockets of dragoons that had been left or whose mounts had deserted them in the heat of battle. Many were caught at the 'Winsby' Gate and surrendered.[18]

Losses are difficult to determine. Widdrington alluded to the complete loss of his dragoons and his horse was completely dispersed, allowing, by his own admission, the Parliamentarians to be 'at liberty to dispose of their forces what way they please'.[19] Winceby had been a short, sharp action but its consequences were far reaching. With Newcastle's main force still north of the Humber, the Parliamentarians in Lincolnshire began to tighten their grip. Lincoln surrendered on 20 October, Bolingbroke Castle on 14 November and Gainsborough on 20 December. At Hull, events had not been conclusive. Both sides had suffered misfortune – the defenders when the magazine in the north blockhouse was ignited through carelessness, and the attackers when a powder magazine had exploded at their artillery park. The arrival of Meldrum's infantry had energized the sallies from Hull and they had succeeded in destroying the batteries astride the Derringham Dyke and at Sculcoates and driving out an attack on the Charterhouse battery. But it was the major sally on the same day as the battle at Winceby that decided affairs. All the remaining Royalist batteries were overrun and many guns were captured. Lord Fairfax wrote in his report to Essex:

> … after two houres sharpe encounter, or thereabouts, they left the field: since that we have drawne into the Town their great Demi-Cannon, one Demi-Culverin, one Sacre [Saker], three Drakes and one case of small pieces, some armes and a carriage of great bullet, besides some powder, which was made use of against them.[20]

The next morning Newcastle's demoralized men were seen breaking camp. The Royalist commander had received the news of Winceby the same day and, if that were not bad enough, he was notified that his wife had passed away a few days earlier.

Newcastle decided not to march his army south to Lincolnshire in order to stem the tide, but instead, they were to march north and join the Royalist forces in and around Northumberland. On 25 September, the ratification of the Solemn League and Covenant forged a deal between the Parliamentarians and the Scottish Covenanters (see chapter 15). At the end of September some Covenanter forces had already occupied Berwick-upon-Tweed. The intervention in the north by many thousands of Scottish troops was bound to tip the scales back in Parliament's favour. Days later Charles responded by forming two new armies. Hopton was to establish the Western Army and advance with it east to London, while Byron was to form the new army in Cheshire and, in conjunction with Newcastle, block the Scots and re-establish control in Lancashire and Yorkshire. As a result of the Irish cessation, both these armies were to receive support from troops returning from Ireland.

In June Parliament had approved the appointment of Sir Thomas Myddleton as its commander of the six counties of north Wales. It was, at

10 Anon, *Earle of Manchester's forces and the Marquesse of Newcastle's forces*, pp. 3–5.

11 Ibid.

12 Fairfax, op. cit., p. 218. There is some dispute as to whether the Royalists were on the field first, thereby dictating the location of the Parliamentarian deployment or vice versa.

13 Dillingham, *The Parliament Scout*, 13–20 October 1643, p. 148; Rushworth, *Historical Collections*, part 3, vol. II, pp. 268–70.

14 The exact position of the battlefield remains the subject of debate. The map depicts the traditional location as marked on ordnance survey mapping and supported by English Heritage and Glenn Foard's assessment of aerial photography and hedge lines. A recent study, supported by some archaeology, by Stuart Weston (*Battlefield Survey of the Battle of Winceby*) indicates that the traditional area is not supported by the evidence thrown up by the survey. He proposes, but without archaeological evidence to support the claim, that the battlefield my well have been to the south of Slash Lane.

15 Anon, *Earle of Manchester's forces and the Marquesse of Newcastle's forces*, p. 6.

16 Burne & Young, *Great Civil War*, p. 114. They suggest this is the origin of the names 'Slash Lane' and 'Slash Hollow'; this is expanded upon in the English Heritage battlefield report.

17 Dillingham, *The Parliament Scout*, p. 148, suggests that they slew more than they should have done.

18 Brammer, *Winceby*, p. 89.

19 Rushworth, op. cit.

20 Fairfax, *Lord Fairfax, to His Excellency*, pp. 4–5.

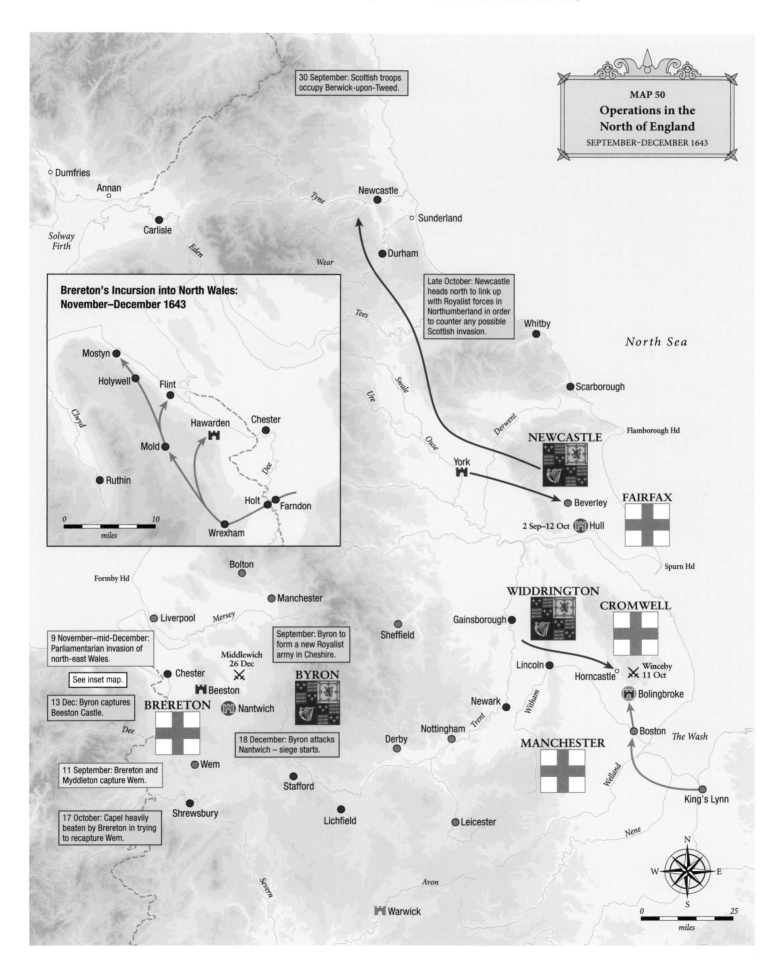

30 September: Scottish troops occupy Berwick-upon-Tweed.

MAP 50
Operations in the North of England
SEPTEMBER–DECEMBER 1643

Late October: Newcastle heads north to link up with Royalist forces in Northumberland in order to counter any possible Scottish invasion.

Brereton's Incursion into North Wales: November–December 1643

0   10
miles

North Sea

Dumfries

Annan

Solway Firth

Carlisle

Eden

Tyne

Newcastle

Sunderland

Wear

Durham

Tees

Whitby

Mostyn

Holywell

Flint

Clwyd

Chester

Hawarden

Mold

Dee

Ruthin

Holt

Farndon

Wrexham

Scarborough

Ure

Swale

Ouse

Derwent

Flamborough Hd

NEWCASTLE

York

Beverley

FAIRFAX

2 Sep–12 Oct   Hull

Spurn Hd

Bolton

Formby Hd

Manchester

Liverpool

Mersey

9 November–mid-December: Parliamentarian invasion of north-east Wales.

See inset map.

13 Dec: Byron captures Beeston Castle.

Middlewich 26 Dec

September: Byron to form a new Royalist army in Cheshire.

Chester

Beeston

BYRON

Nantwich

BRERETON

Dee

18 December: Byron attacks Nantwich – siege starts.

11 September: Brereton and Myddleton capture Wem.

Wem

17 October: Capel heavily beaten by Brereton in trying to recapture Wem.

Shrewsbury

Sheffield

Gainsborough

Lincoln

Newark

Derby

Nottingham

Trent

Stafford

Lichfield

Severn

Leicester

Avon

Warwick

WIDDRINGTON

CROMWELL

Horncastle

Winceby 11 Oct

Bolingbroke

Witham

Boston

The Wash

MANCHESTER

Welland

King's Lynn

Nene

N
W   E
S

0   25
miles

127

that time, more symbolic than representative as there were no troops and little sympathy in, what was effectively, Royalist Wales. However, on 11 September Myddleton and Brereton captured Wem and established a garrison there under Brereton's brother-in-law, Thomas Mytton. Lord Capel, the Royalist commander in Wales, made an abortive attempt to recapture the small town on 17 October but was beaten with considerable loss while trying to escape. On 9 November, Brereton's force crossed the River Dee at Holt, driving back the Royalist defenders and occupying Wrexham before nightfall. Some men stayed in the city, dismantled the church organ and melted down the lead pipes to make bullets.[21] The majority of the force pushed north and,

on 10 November, the garrison at Harwarden Castle surrendered. The towns of Mold and Holywell followed in quick succession, giving Brereton control of the western side of the Dee estuary.

However, Brereton's excursion into north Wales was about to come to an abrupt end. On 17 November the first of the reinforcements from Ireland arrived and landed at Mostyn. The small Roundhead garrison at Harwarden capitulated on 7 December and Byron captured Beeston a week later. On Christmas Day, Byron concentrated his force and cornered Brereton at Middlewich the next day. By mid-December the area was once again firmly back under Royalist control.

---

21 Gaunt, *Civil War in Wales*, p. 36.

CHAPTER 13
EVENTS IN DEVON, SEPTEMBER TO THE END OF 1643

Hopton's defeat of the Earl of Stamford at Stratton in May had secured Cornwall for the Royalists. Indeed, such was the scale of the victory that there was little prospect of the Parliamentarian army being able to mount a proactive defence of the adjacent Devon, outside the walls of their larger garrisons. Alas, Hopton's attempt to subjugate Devon was not to be. His Royalist Cornish army was ordered to link up with another Royalist army en route from Oxford. This combined force would then advance to challenge and destroy Waller. Hopton was, however, determined to keep the pressure on Stamford and he decided to leave John Berkeley and a regiment of horse in the county with orders to maintain the blockade of Exeter and to try to recruit more men for the King's cause.[1] Over the next three months, in the South-West, there were no major battles and little of significance was to occur. Most of the main towns remained under Parliament's control and the Parliamentarian navy not only circumvented the attempt at a land blockade of Exeter, but it also provided control of both banks of Exe estuary. Berkeley's grip, therefore, was tentative at best. However, that was all to change following the fall of Bristol in July. In early August, Maurice led the Western Army back to Devon and, following a failed attempt to capture the fishing village at Lyme Regis, he marched on Exeter.[2]

The defenders in Exeter had been busy shoring up defences and morale was high. They had conducted some isolated skirmishes against the besiegers and a 'hot fight' had taken place on the outskirts of the city on 31 July in the parish of St Thomas. Earlier in the month, Alexander Carew had made an attempt to break the blockade with a force despatched from Plymouth. It had been intercepted by Berkeley and driven back. Rumours that another force was being mustered in the towns of north Devon prompted Berkeley to despatch Colonel John Digby with a small force of 300 horse and dragoons to Torrington. He was soon supplemented by about 600 foot from Cornwall. The presence of these Royalists in north Devon spurred the towns into action. They collected a comparably sized force and, on 19 August, attacked Digby at Torrington. But the Royalist cavalry were in a different league entirely. The aggressive and decisive nature of their charges quickly demolished the cohesion of the Parliamentarian forces. Within days Bideford had fallen and Barnstaple and Appledore soon followed. Back at Exeter, the arrival of Maurice's large force to join the siege, coupled with news of the loss of these north Devon towns, caused an almost instantaneous collapse in morale within the city. Maurice, sensing the moment, offered generous terms and the city capitulated on 5 September, the Parliamentarian garrison marching out two days later.

Maurice now moved his force to besiege Dartmouth, while Digby advanced, with a reinforced group, to cordon Plymouth. Maurice had been led into a false sense of Royalist invincibility following the victory at Exeter, and he mistakenly believed that Dartmouth would be an easy target.

As a consequence, he wasted a full three weeks on the place, while the main objective at Plymouth was allowed precious time to prepare for the inevitable. Maurice's initial optimism had led him to conclude that the best plan would be to blockade Dartmouth and await its surrender. However, the defenders appeared to be made of sterner stuff, and when the weather turned, a large proportion of the Royalist force fell ill, including Maurice himself. Dartmouth was not an easy objective; sited on the west bank of the River Dart, it was surrounded by numerous outer fortifications some distance from the town. Maurice realized there was no easy solution and, having called up the heavy artillery, it was moved on arrival to the Warfleet valley in order to attack the castle and isolate the town. The plan worked and Dartmouth capitulated on 6 October, once again being offered generous terms.

Meanwhile, Derby had arrived on the outskirts of Plymouth on 15 September. Royalist optimism was high, but they could not have known that they were about to embark on one of the most destructive and enduring episodes of the entire war. The siege of Plymouth was to endure intermittently until January 1646 at enormous human cost and suffering. Plymouth had become a very important port in Tudor times as a key naval base for operations against France. In the early 17th century it had become a centre for Puritanism and the town wasted little time declaring for Parliament at the outbreak of hostilities in 1642. However, the numerous losses suffered by the Parliamentarian forces by autumn 1643 was having a significant effect on both the morale and long-term allegiance of the townsfolk. During the siege of Exeter, the governor at Plymouth, Alexander Carew, had offered up St Nicholas Island in exchange for a Royal pardon. His treachery was discovered and he was duly sent to London, tried and executed. Parliament was quick to respond to quell any further examples of treachery and failing nerve. On 30 September, Colonel James Wardlaw arrived by ship up Plymouth Sound with 500 reinforcements and a clear message for the authorities that 'no thought was to be given to surrender'.[3] Within weeks, amidst bickering, Wardlaw had replaced the mayor as military governor. He then energized the defenders, assumed absolute control, forced them to swear an oath to defend the town and, just to be sure, imprisoned any suspected Royalist sympathizers. He also took the offensive. In early October he attacked the Royalist outposts, taking a number of prisoners, along with two colours and some gunpowder. However, a second sally on 15 October overextended itself, and during the cavalry pursuit lost a number of men.[4]

Meanwhile, Maurice's arrival had been noted by the defenders, 'and now the enemy being settled in his quarters, at Plymton, Plymstoke, Causands, Buckland, Tamerton etc. With an army consisting of five Regiments of Horse, and nine Regiments of Foot'.[5] The cordon extended

---

1 Andriette, *Devon and Exeter*, p. 89.
2 Lyme Regis was saved by naval action.

3 Andriette, op. cit., p. 97.
4 Anon, *Late siege of Plymouth*, p. 2.
5 Ibid.

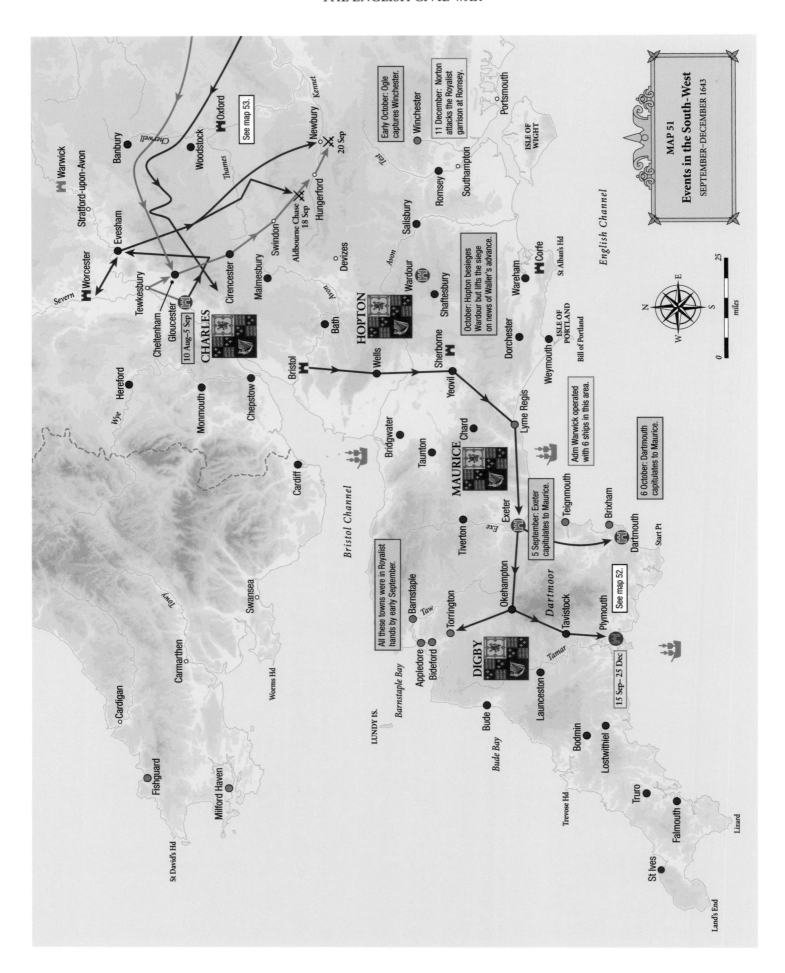

MAP 51
Events in the South-West
SEPTEMBER–DECEMBER 1643

Early October: Ogle captures Winchester.

11 December: Norton attacks the Royalist garrison at Romsey.

October: Hopton besieges Wardour but lifts the siege on news of Waller's advance.

Adm Warwick operated with 6 ships in this area.

5 September: Exeter capitulates to Maurice.

6 October: Dartmouth capitulates to Maurice.

All these towns were in Royalist hands by early September.

See map 52.

See map 53.

Newbury
20 Sep

Aldbourne Chase
18 Sep

Gloucester
10 Aug–5 Sep

CHARLES

HOPTON

MAURICE

DIGBY

15 Sep–25 Dec

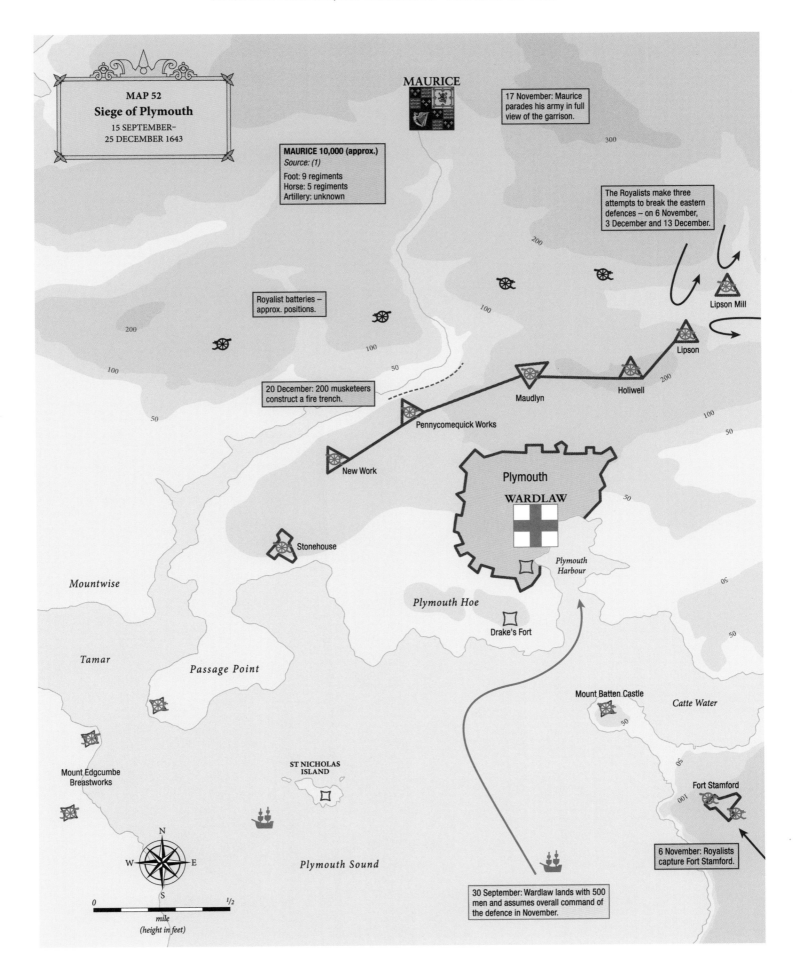

MAURICE

MAP 52
Siege of Plymouth
15 SEPTEMBER–
25 DECEMBER 1643

MAURICE 10,000 (approx.)
Source: (1)
Foot: 9 regiments
Horse: 5 regiments
Artillery: unknown

17 November: Maurice parades his army in full view of the garrison.

The Royalists make three attempts to break the eastern defences – on 6 November, 3 December and 13 December.

Royalist batteries – approx. positions.

300

200

100

100

50

200

100

50

50

Lipson Mill

Lipson

Holiwell

200

20 December: 200 musketeers construct a fire trench.

Maudlyn

Pennycomequick Works

100

50

New Work

Plymouth

WARDLAW

50

Stonehouse

Plymouth Harbour

Mountwise

Plymouth Hoe

Drake's Fort

50

Tamar

Passage Point

Mount Batten Castle

Catte Water

50

50

Mount Edgcumbe
Breastworks

ST NICHOLAS
ISLAND

50

Fort Stamford

100

N
W   E
S

Plymouth Sound

6 November: Royalists capture Fort Stamford.

0   1/2
mile
(height in feet)

30 September: Wardlaw lands with 500 men and assumes overall command of the defence in November.

131

6 miles, effectively cutting off the Plymouth peninsula from the River Tamar to the River Plym. Maurice was with the main force on the hills to the north, while Digby was sent over to the east with at least three regiments of foot, some horse and a few guns. His objective was the isolated Fort Stamford on the south bank of Catte Water. The fort was held by 300 men from William Herbert's and William Gould's regiments along with some men from Calmady's London Greycoats. They were supported by a small group of naval gunners.[6] The defenders dug in and despatched pleas for reinforcements and more ammunition. Their appeals went unheeded and on 6 November, with their ammunition expended, the defenders capitulated. It had been a fierce struggle, but with the structure in Digby's hands, the Royalists turned the fort's heavy guns against Wardlaw's ships and, more importantly, they began a bombardment of the main town. Later the same day, somewhat elated by the news, Maurice made an attempt to capture Lipson fort and mill, but his troops were repulsed.

On 17 November, Maurice decided to switch tactics and to parade his entire army, in full view of the garrison, on the hills to the north. The next day he sent in a summons for surrender. However, this psychological warfare was to backfire and merely served to strengthen Wardlaw's grip on the men and matters under his command. He immediately ordered the line of works to the north of the town to be strengthened. A few days later Wardlaw was apoplectic with rage on discovering a treasonous plot to blow up the Maudlin works, as one chronicler detailed: 'One Ellis Carkeet a malignant Mariner was accused and laid fast, for tampering with Roger Kneebone the chief gunner at Maudline Worke, to blow up the said worke, the powder roome being buryed in it, and he having the keyes.'[7] Two of Carkeet's accomplices, Henry Pike and Moses Collins, escaped to the Royalist lines but Carkeet was less fortunate. Pike and Collins, in an effort to ingratiate themselves, spilled evidence of certain weaknesses in the town's defences.

On 3 December, three hours before daylight, the two turncoats guided a small force of 400 musketeers to a crossing point. The Royalist plan was another attempt to capture Lipson fort from the east. The musketeers were supported by a second wave of five regiments of horse and four of foot. However, the Parliamentarians were alerted to the movements of the forlorn hope and attacked it in the flank as it moved into position. They succeeded in driving back the musketeers but they were now set upon by Maurice's main force and driven back within Lipson fort. An observer recalled, 'at which time some of the enemies Horse mixt themselves with ours, and came within pistol shot of the walls and were killed or taken'.[8] It was a dangerous moment for the defenders; if the critical end-fort had fallen, the Royalists would have been able to roll up the line, one fort after another. Acutely aware of this, the defenders fought with renewed zeal and managed to bring a small drake cannon into action. Its effect was immediate and after only discharging four cannister rounds they dispersed the Royalist horse. The fighting continued for some time yet, but after another couple of hours the Royalist line began to fall back. They were pursued by the Parliamentarian infantry, which had been sent up by Wardlaw from the town, and assisted by fire from the guns mounted on the works and a few naval guns from a ship east of the works in Catte Water. A number of Royalists were drowned as they attempted to cross the creek and others (including horses) were stuck fast in the thick mud and succumbed when the tide turned.

Ten days later, Maurice made another attempt on the eastern defences; this time against the Lipson Mill fort. Once again, the defenders held firm. Amidst an atmosphere of growing frustration, Maurice had another go at the (central) Maudlyn fort on 18 December. A preliminary artillery bombardment by heavy ordnance commenced proceedings and continued for two days. Then, during the night on the 20th, 200 musketeers stole forward and constructed a fire trench and earthwork within musket range between the Maudlyn and Pennycomequick forts. At dawn, when the Parliamentarians discovered the work, they attacked it but were beaten back. Two hours later, William Gould gathered a larger force and attacked a second time. The fight lasted several hours and eventually the Royalists once again were forced to pull back. Maurice was at his wits end, his force thoroughly demoralized and thinning daily through sickness. On Christmas Day he decided to lift the siege and pull back into Devon. It was to prove to be a costly failure for the Royalists. Plymouth remained a bastion of defiance and hope for the Parliamentarians in the West Country.

6   Barratt, *Sieges of the English Civil Wars*, p. 69.
7   Anon, *Late siege of Plymouth*, p. 8.
8   Ibid., p. 9.

CHAPTER 14
THE FIRST BATTLE OF NEWBURY, SEPTEMBER 1643

Six days after Bristol fell, Charles entered the city to popular acclaim. However, he had not come to wallow in the achievement; his mission was more delicate in nature – to govern and lay down the command status between the Marquis of Hertford and Prince Rupert. The former was Lord Lieutenant of the counties that encompassed Bristol and nominal commander of the King's western armies, and he therefore viewed Rupert as a mere auxiliary to that force. Rupert, however, saw things very differently. He had usurped Hertford by writing to the King and securing the governorship of Bristol. Charles's task was, therefore, to defuse this tempest and, having done so, to plan the next phase of Royalist operations. Rupert kept Bristol, a decision the Prince, and arguably the King, would later regret. Hertford was elevated to the King's inner council, a decision that took him to Oxford, and away from the area. Meanwhile, that council had to decide whether both armies of the centre (Oxford) and west should unite and, if so, what their role or roles should be.[1] In the end they agreed to leave them as separate forces.

The Western Army was to remain independent and was to be sent back to Devon (chapter 13). The command of this force was given to Maurice, while Hopton, ever anxious to avoid contention, agreed to become the Lieutenant Governor of Bristol (under Rupert) with a small force taken from Maurice's new force. Such blatant patronage in support of the King's two nephews caused indubitable friction and growing disgruntlement within the Royalist high command. The next mission for the Oxford army was more contentious. There were, in effect, two options on the table. Firstly, to move to besiege Gloucester, thereby opening up communications with Worcester and Shrewsbury and clearing the way for Welsh soldiers to deploy into England. Secondly, to move on London in concert with Newcastle's army from the north. Supporters of the second option saw Gloucester as a red herring. In the end, Rupert convinced the King to move on Gloucester. To be fair he assumed the affair would be over as quickly as Bristol, with the not inconsiderable benefits that the prosperous and geographically well-sited city provided, and that the second option could be put into effect once Gloucester was in Royalist hands. Many historians have since argued that this single decision was the ruination of the Royalist cause, in part because it appeared to be a tactical decision tackling a strategic problem; in part because the operation at Gloucester was anything but rapid; and, finally, in part because the Parliamentarian high command was, at this juncture in the war, in a state of disharmony.[2]

Many in London had, for some time, questioned Essex's capacity for command. On 25 July Waller had been given a hero's welcome in London. His defeat at Roundway Down was played down and blame shifted on to Essex's failure to move in support of the Western Association. Two days after

his return to the capital, Waller was recommended as the prime contender to command the new forces being raised in London. It was a decision, intended by the draftsman John Pym, to augment the ill-feeling between Essex and Waller. Essex responded by petitioning the House of Lords and requesting an independent inquiry into the loss of the west. Following a debate, the House agreed to Essex's petition and declared that a vindication as to Waller's conduct should be made public. At the same time, they agreed to a number of other subsidiary demands regarding pay and conditions for Essex's army – demands that Essex argued, quite rightly, had constrained the freedom of movement of his army in the first instance. To his credit, Pym set about making every effort to meet the needs of Essex's army, in the guise of money and men, but refused to be drawn on the subject of an inquiry. The Lords had held sway on this issue, but they chose to link the motion with proposals to re-open negotiations with the King, and in the end the Commons (narrowly) defeated the motion. The problems of Parliamentarian military high command had, for now, been kicked down the street.

The advance guard of the Royalist army reached the walls of Gloucester on 8 August. Charles arrived two days later, and ignoring Rupert's pleas to storm the walls, the King proceeded to summon the city. Two citizens with 'lean, pale, sharp, and bad visages' delivered the message that they were 'wholly bound to obey the commands of his majesty, signified by both houses of parliament: and are resolved, by God's help, to keep this city accordingly'.[3] By rejecting Rupert's option for a rapid storming and having his summons brusquely rejected, Charles had backed himself into a corner. He had to go ahead with the siege or lose face and, by so doing, he had denied himself the option of marching on London. Charles's hopes that all would be concluded in a matter of days were quickly dispelled. Within the week he returned to Oxford. He had to placate the flabbergasted Queen, who was furious and keen to discover how the King was going to win his kingdom back at the walls of Gloucester and not London.

A clergyman within the city recorded that 'The strength of Gloucester was no more than two regiments of foot, a hundred horse with the trained bands, and a few *reformadoes*; there were besides about a hundred horse and dragoons from Berkeley Castle, in the whole about fifteen hundred men, forty single barrels of gunpowder with slender artillery.'[4] As such, Gloucester had fewer men than Cirencester and Bristol, and furthermore, there were concerns over the new commander. The deputy-governor, Colonel Edward Massey, had taken control of the city the previous December. He was not a local man and his nomination, orchestrated through Waller's patronage, was not well received. In June, in an attempt to prove his worth, Massey led a raid deep into Royalist-held territory – it was a disaster. The siege,

---

1 Day, *Gloucester and Newbury*, p. 26 citing Hyde.
2 Part of the reason for the delay in taking Gloucester was Charles's risk/casualty aversion that significantly constrained Rupert.

3 Clarendon, vol. IV, p. 179.
4 Corbet, *Government of Gloucester*, p. 41.

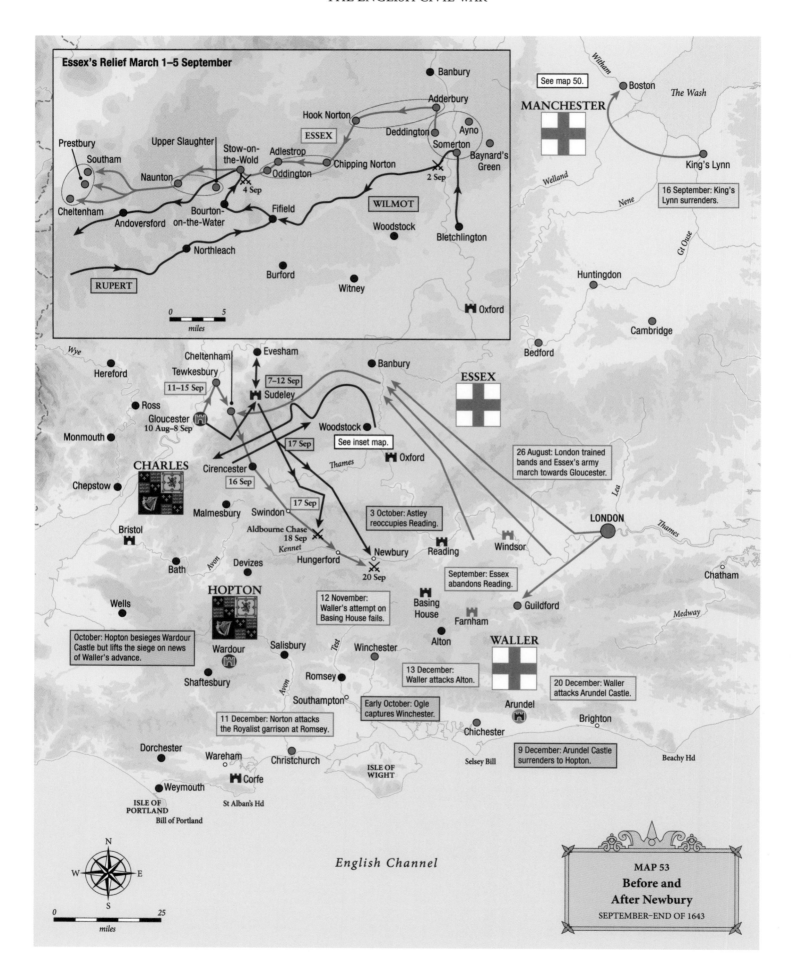

Essex's Relief March 1–5 September

Banbury

See map 50.

Boston

The Wash

Witham

MANCHESTER

King's Lynn

Welland

16 September: King's Lynn surrenders.

Nene

Adderbury

Hook Norton

Deddington

Ayno

ESSEX

Somerton

Baynard's Green

Prestbury

Southam

Upper Slaughter

Stow-on-the-Wold

Adlestrop

Naunton

Oddington

Chipping Norton

2 Sep

Cheltenham

Fifield

Bourton-on-the-Water

WILMOT

Woodstock

Andoversford

4 Sep

Bletchlington

Northleach

Burford

Witney

Oxford

RUPERT

0   5

miles

Huntingdon

Gt Ouse

Cambridge

Bedford

Wye

Cheltenham

Evesham

Banbury

Hereford

Tewkesbury

ESSEX

11–15 Sep

Sudeley

7–12 Sep

Ross

Gloucester
10 Aug–8 Sep

Woodstock

Monmouth

See inset map.

26 August: London trained bands and Essex's army march towards Gloucester.

Lea

17 Sep

Thames

Oxford

CHARLES

Cirencester

16 Sep

LONDON

Thames

Chepstow

17 Sep

Chatham

Malmesbury

Swindon

3 October: Astley reoccupies Reading.

Wells

Bath

Aldbourne Chase
18 Sep

Kennet

Newbury

Reading

Windsor

September: Essex abandons Reading.

Devizes

Hungerford

Guildford

Medway

Avon

20 Sep

12 November: Waller's attempt on Basing House fails.

Basing House

HOPTON

Farnham

October: Hopton besieges Wardour Castle but lifts the siege on news of Waller's advance.

Alton

WALLER

Salisbury

Test

Winchester

Wardour

13 December: Waller attacks Alton.

20 December: Waller attacks Arundel Castle.

Shaftesbury

Romsey

Avon

Southampton

Early October: Ogle captures Winchester.

Arundel

Brighton

11 December: Norton attacks the Royalist garrison at Romsey.

Chichester

Dorchester

Wareham

Christchurch

9 December: Arundel Castle surrenders to Hopton.

Selsey Bill

Beachy Hd

Corfe

ISLE OF WIGHT

Weymouth

St Alban's Hd

ISLE OF PORTLAND

Bill of Portland

English Channel

N
W   E
S

0   25

miles

MAP 53
**Before and
After Newbury**
SEPTEMBER–END OF 1643

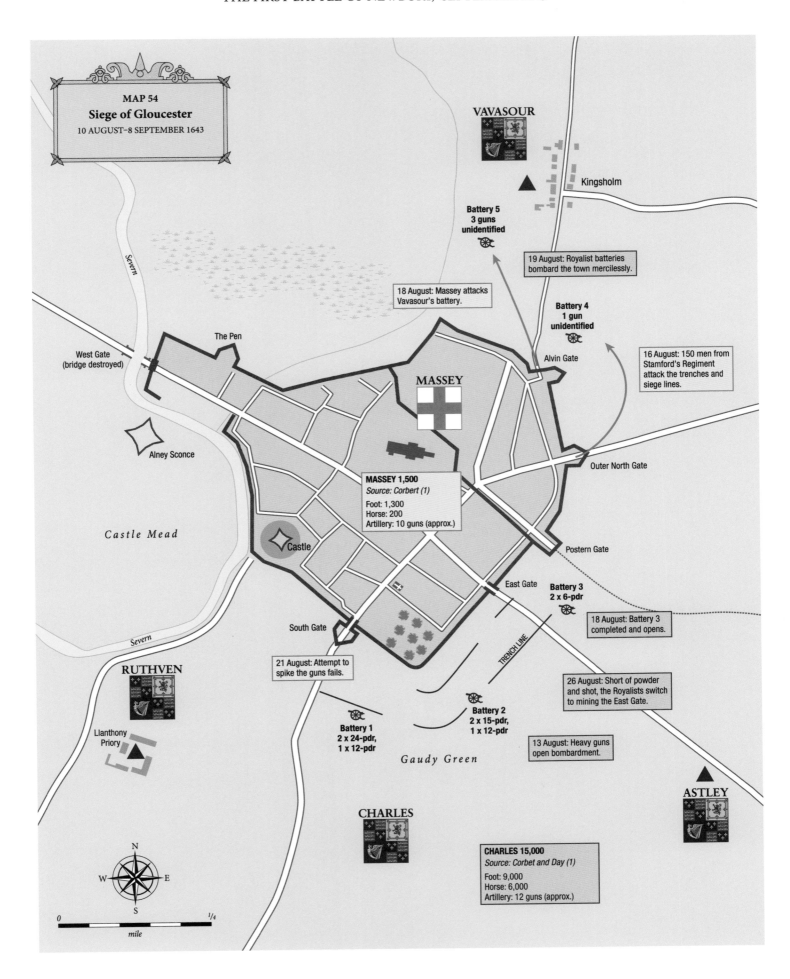

MAP 54
Siege of Gloucester
10 AUGUST–8 SEPTEMBER 1643

VAVASOUR

Kingsholm

Battery 5
3 guns
unidentified

19 August: Royalist batteries bombard the town mercilessly.

18 August: Massey attacks Vavasour's battery.

Battery 4
1 gun
unidentified

Alvin Gate

16 August: 150 men from Stamford's Regiment attack the trenches and siege lines.

The Pen

West Gate
(bridge destroyed)

MASSEY

Alney Sconce

Outer North Gate

MASSEY 1,500
Source: Corbert (1)

Foot: 1,300
Horse: 200
Artillery: 10 guns (approx.)

Castle Mead

Castle

Postern Gate

East Gate

Battery 3
2 x 6-pdr

18 August: Battery 3 completed and opens.

South Gate

TRENCH LINE

26 August: Short of powder and shot, the Royalists switch to mining the East Gate.

21 August: Attempt to spike the guns fails.

RUTHVEN

Battery 2
2 x 15-pdr,
1 x 12-pdr

Llanthony
Priory

Battery 1
2 x 24-pdr,
1 x 12-pdr

Gaudy Green

13 August: Heavy guns open bombardment.

ASTLEY

N
W   E
S

CHARLES

CHARLES 15,000
Source: Corbet and Day (1)

Foot: 9,000
Horse: 6,000
Artillery: 12 guns (approx.)

0   1/4
mile

Severn

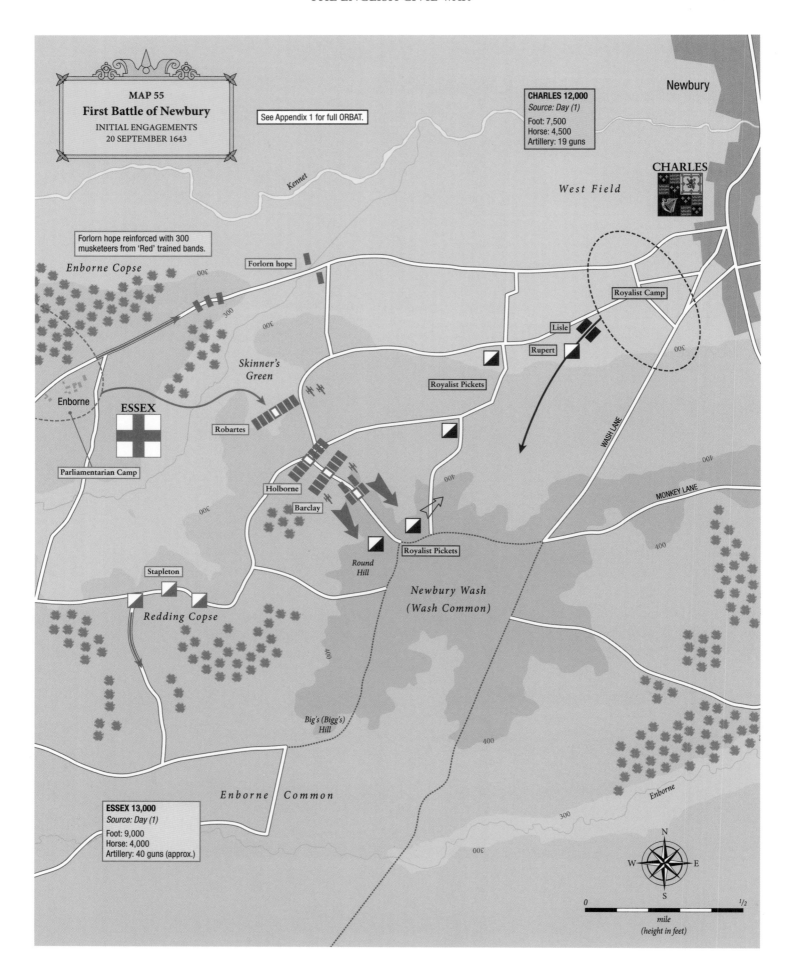

MAP 55

First Battle of Newbury

INITIAL ENGAGEMENTS
20 SEPTEMBER 1643

See Appendix 1 for full ORBAT.

CHARLES 12,000
Source: Day (1)
Foot: 7,500
Horse: 4,500
Artillery: 19 guns

Newbury

CHARLES

West Field

Kennet

Forlorn hope reinforced with 300
musketeers from 'Red' trained bands.

Enborne Copse

Royalist Camp

Forlorn hope

300

300

300

300

Lisle

Rupert

*Skinner's
Green*

Royalist Pickets

WASH LANE

Enborne

Robartes

ESSEX

400

400

MONKEY LANE

Parliamentarian Camp

Holborne

Barclay

300

400

Royalist Pickets

*Round
Hill*

Stapleton

*Newbury Wash
(Wash Common)*

400

Redding Copse

400

*Big's (Bigg's)
Hill*

Enborne   Common

300

300

ESSEX 13,000
Source: Day (1)
Foot: 9,000
Horse: 4,000
Artillery: 40 guns (approx.)

Enborne

N
W   E
S

0   1/2

mile
(height in feet)

therefore, was a chance for Massey to make amends.[5] Another advantage was the city's location. It remained relatively compact, bounded to the west by the River Severn with marshland to the north and north-east. This enabled the garrison to focus its defensive efforts to the east and south, where the outer suburbs were torched to clear fields of fire. Finally, Gloucester possessed a community determined to resist. In the words of John Corbet, Massey's chaplain, there were large swathes of the population 'who were held up by the deep sense of religion, or acknowledged a necessity to withstand a malicious or enraged enemy, whose implacable hatred urged them to offend by their own designs, and horrid threatenings [sic] to make the attempt more desperate'.[6]

The Royalist hopes that the city would capitulate quickly were undone. Furthermore, by making General Ruthven the siege commander in preference to Rupert, Charles had, to all intents and purposes, written the quick attack out of the script. Charles's Oxford army now had to be moved and concentrated for the siege. Corbet recalled that 'The King by this drew into the field before the towne, attended by Prince Charles, the Duke of York, Prince Rupert and General Ruthven, faced us with about six thousand horse and foote on that side [south at Tredworth], and two thousand horse on the other side' [northeast at Lower Walham].[7] The siege began in earnest on 10 August, with the engineers breaking ground to the south and east and destroying the pipes conveying water to the city. Massey's attempt to disrupt the works by fire had limited effect, as the Royalists deployed a number of musketeers to counter the fire from the ramparts. The Royalist batteries began to take shape and the massive army split into three camps to the south and north. Determined to delay Royalist operations as much as possible, he began a series of minor sallies against their works. However, their effect, like the counter-fire, was limited but it served to slow proceedings, the top priority of any garrison under siege. It should be added that the rather lacklustre performance by the Royalist siege gunners and the effect of the bad weather on mining operations also contributed to the delay.

On 19 August Essex finally received orders to march to the relief of the city. The day prior, all Parliamentarian soldiers in and around the Home Counties had been ordered to return to their colours on pain of death. Parliament also authorized the conscription of an additional 4,000 men to field two regiments of trained bands and three of auxiliaries. The groups met, on Friday 1 September near Brackley Heath, the 'general rendezvous' set by Essex. Sergeant Henry Foster recalled that 'it was goodly and glorious sight to see the whole Army of Horse and foot together; it is conceived by those that viewed our Army well, that wee did consist of 15,000 horse and foot, some speak of many more'.[8] Despite being short of provisions, Essex pushed on through the Cotswolds and brushed aside Wilmot's cavalry on 2 September. Another more concerted attack on 4 September, near Stow-on-the-Wold by Rupert and Wilmot, was also driven back as the Royalist cavalry was unable to respond to a preliminary bombardment by the Parliamentarian artillery, sharply followed by an infantry assault. The failure of 3,000 horse in open terrain to stop Essex's advance was a salutary

lesson to the Royalists. It was also a good example of the force multiplication advantages of combined operations against a single fighting component. When the vanguard of the Parliamentarian force reached the Prestbury hills on 5 September, Essex 'drew up his whole army in view of the City of Gloucester, and discharged 4 peeces of great Ordnance to give them notice of his approach'.[9]

Within Gloucester, Massey was down to the last three barrels of powder. The growing sense of hopelessness and isolation felt within the garrison in the preceding few days of the siege was instantly replaced by relief, jubilation and renewed determination. The Royalists, conversely, were crestfallen and angry. They torched their defence works and pulled back to the rendezvous at Birdlip Hill. Charles was determined to get something out of the failure and on 6 September he gave the order to march north to cut Essex's lines of communication (and retreat to London) and occupy Winchcombe and Sudeley Castle. Despite the size of the Parliamentarian army and their recent success, they were in no fit state to respond to Royalist manoeuvring. Essex's men were exhausted, half-starved and discipline evaporated as units went in search of food and shelter from the heavy rains. It was to be two more days before the army was once again collected near Gloucester. Essex left the city on 10 September and headed north, well aware that Charles had stolen a march. He moved to Tewkesbury, where he ordered a bridge to be built over the Severn. His intention was to deceive the Royalists into thinking he was going to attack Worcester. It worked, and as Royalist units headed north, he turned his army south, reaching Cirencester at nightfall on 15 September. The Roundhead objective was to clear Newbury and pass around the Royalists' right flank. Charles realized this and despatched Rupert's cavalry to delay them. Rupert, as ever, showed great determination and caught the Parliamentarian rearguard in a valley near Aldbourne.

The 20 September Royalist report (probably penned by Lord Digby) recorded the events as follows:

> Colonell Urrey with a party of a Thousand commanded men, was sent to follow them in the Reare from their quarters, whilst Prince Rupert with the body of the cavalry drew over the directest way to merrie him, and it was our good lucke to crosse his army just as our party had overtaken it upon the Downe, two miles on the Northwest side of Aubourne [Aldbourne].[10]

The Royalist cavalry drove the five regiments of Roundhead horse back on to their foot and artillery, and a Parliamentary report recalled that 'the enemy pursuing hotly both on Rere and Flank, our retreat was not without some confusion and losse'.[11] Rupert was keen to follow up his charge but was restrained, by other commanders, under the pretext that the main body of the Royalist force was still some way to the rear. The action was inconclusive but it had, from the Royalist perspective, achieved its aim. The delay inflicted on Essex's army had allowed the Royalists to close the gap and when his leading scouts arrived at Newbury to make preparations for the Roundhead army, they were driven out by a forlorn hope of Royalist cavalry. The race for Newbury had been won by the forces of the King.

Late on 19 September, the Parliamentarian forces, discovering that the Royalists held Newbury, and the only bridge across the River Kennet, established a camp 'about a mile and a halfe distant from Newbury

---

5   Gardiner (*Great Civil War*, vol. I, p. 198) suggests that Massey was in communication with the Royalists and was prepared to give up the city through an act of treachery. However, Day, op. cit., examines the evidence (pp. 43–4) and casts doubt on the timing of the letter.

6   Corbet, op. cit., p. 40.

7   Ibid., pp. 42–3.

8   Foster, *A true and exact relation*, p. 2. He was almost certainly with the Red trained bands based on his descriptions.

9   Anon, *Relief of Gloucester*, p. 8.

10 Digby, *Rebells neare Newbery*, p. 2.

11 Anon, *Relief of Gloucester*, p. 11.

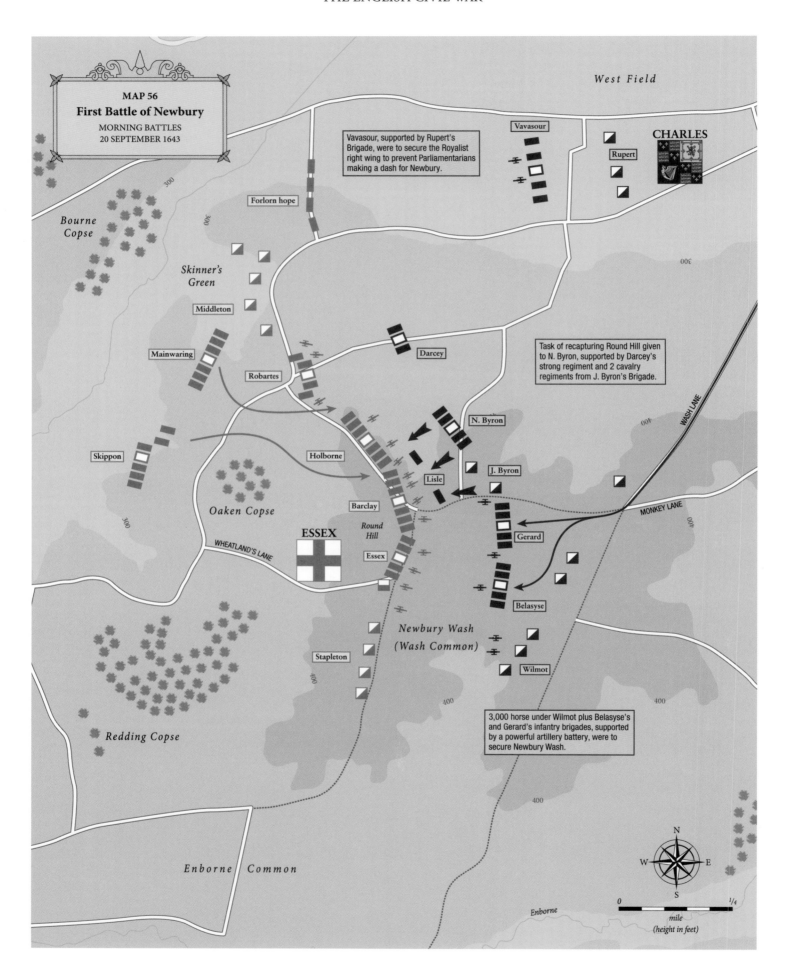

MAP 56

First Battle of Newbury

MORNING BATTLES
20 SEPTEMBER 1643

West Field

Vavasour, supported by Rupert's Brigade, were to secure the Royalist right wing to prevent Parliamentarians making a dash for Newbury.

Vavasour

Rupert

CHARLES

Bourne Copse

Forlorn hope

Skinner's Green

Middleton

300

Mainwaring

Darcey

Robartes

Task of recapturing Round Hill given to N. Byron, supported by Darcey's strong regiment and 2 cavalry regiments from J. Byron's Brigade.

N. Byron

WASH LANE

400

Skippon

Holborne

Lisle

J. Byron

MONKEY LANE

Oaken Copse

Barclay

Gerard

WHEATLAND'S LANE

Round Hill

ESSEX

Essex

300

Belasyse

Newbury Wash (Wash Common)

Wilmot

Stapleton

400

3,000 horse under Wilmot plus Belasyse's and Gerard's infantry brigades, supported by a powerful artillery battery, were to secure Newbury Wash.

400

400

Redding Copse

Enborne Common

N
W   E
S

Enborne

0   1/4

mile
(height in feet)

westward'.[12] On Charles's arrival in the town, he held a quick council and decided to pin the Parliamentarians by deploying his army south of the river into the area to the south-west of the town and by despatching some cavalry pickets to the high ground to the south.[13] As such, the Royalist plan was to deny ground and wait for Essex to make the first move. The Parliamentarian camp was established on Hampstead Park, some high ground west of Enborne village. Morale was not high, their hopes of finding shelter and food in Newbury quashed, and disappointment among the men was evident. Sergeant Foster remembered that 'this night our whole army quartered in an open field; we had no provisions but what little every one had in his Snapsack. We had now marched many dayes and nights with little food, or any sustenance, and little sleep.'[14] Essex was wily and experienced enough to realize that the best way to raise morale was to take the fight to the Royalists without delay. However, by advancing he was placing himself on the Wash plateau between two rivers and leaving his men the option of fighting or starving. On 20 September at about 3am silent reveille was called, orders issued and the army assembled. They moved before dawn, Essex personally leading the vanguard, consisting of seven regiments. Its objective was to secure the high ground to the east, a large round hill, referred to (rather misleadingly) in some accounts as Bigg's Hill.[15]

Essex's bold plan and audacious leadership seems to have worked, for Sergeant Foster referred to marching 'towards the enemy with the most cheerful and courageous spirits'. A far cry from the despondency of the previous evening. They advanced using the cover of darkness and the woods of Enborne Copse, shaking out into formation on Skinner's Green. Essex could see some Royalist troopers on top of Round Hill, 'but when his Excellency perceived that the enemies Forces had possest themselves of that hill, marching himself upon the head of his owne Reg[iment] and Col Barclays and Col Holborns Brigades, he charged so fiercely, that he beat them

from the hill, and kept it the whole day'.[16] As dawn broke Essex was in complete possession of Round Hill; it was to be the vital ground. The Royalist cavalry commander John Byron was quite clear that the loss was pivotal: 'Here another error was committed, and that a most gross and absurd one, in not viewing the ground, though we had day enough to have done it, and not possessing ourselves of those hills above the town by which the enemy was necessarily to march the next day to Reading.'[17] Essex was determined to hold the terrain and spread his 2,500 infantry across the top of the hill and ordered-up the two heavy demi-culverins, placing them in a commanding position overlooking the Newbury Wash and Kennet valley. Wash Common aside, almost all of the area fought over was covered by small enclosures, in which firepower was more important than pikes or cavalry; that mattered because Essex outnumbered the Royalists in both guns and muskets.

Some minutes later Rupert approached Round Hill to conduct a reconnaissance in force, with his cavalry Lifeguard of about 900 commanded musketeers to determine the strength of the Roundhead position. He quickly ascertained the seriousness of the situation and rode back to inform the King. Remaining in a blocking position was not an option, as Digby pointed out: 'by way of justification, I am to tell you that within the Enemies Domain a round hill not suspected nor observed by us the night before, from whence a battery would command all the plain before Newbury, where the King's army stood'.[18] The Council decided to split the army in three groups (see map 56). Sir William Vavasour would hold off any attempt to rush the town in the Kennet valley. Nicholas Byron, with a force of over 3,000 foot and 500 horse, would attack and recapture Round Hill from the southwest, while the balance of the army under Wilmot, over 2,000 infantry and a massive cavalry force 3,000 strong, would take possession of the high plateau of Newbury Wash. Once in possession of Round Hill and the Wash plateau, they would combine and drive the Parliamentarian army off to the west.

The Royalist optimism of the previous evening was quickly replaced by a mixture of antipathy and anticipation. The issuing of orders and the reorganization of the army were going to take some time. Meanwhile, Essex was also issuing orders for his cavalry to move in support of both wings: Stapleton to the right, deploying up Wheatland's Lane and then covering off the Newbury Wash, and Middleton to the left in Skinner's Green. The balance of three brigades of infantry was to move up from around Enborne village. Robartes' weak brigade was to deploy on the left of Holborne's Brigade to shore up that flank. Skippon's and Mainwaring's brigades were to remain to the rear in reserve.

While these plans were being implemented, Lisle's musketeers, having begun to probe forward, were embroiled in sporadic fire with both Barclay's and Holborne's infantry. Despite being outnumbered, they gave a good account of themselves as they waited for Nicholas Byron's infantry to march up from the valley floor. His nephew, John Byron, was at the front in support of this attack. He recalled the ferocity of the engagement:

> The commanded foot not being able to make good the place, my uncle Byron, who commanded the first tertia, instantly came up with part of the regiment of guards… but the service grew so hot, that in a very

---

12 Digby, *Rebells neare Newbery*, p. 4.

13 This decision was also taken due to the significant Parliamentarian sympathies displayed by the townsfolk.

14 Foster, *A true and exact relation*, p. 10.

15 The exact location of the Newbury battlefield remains contentious. The first detailed work by Money, published in 1881, has the battlefield spread from the Kennet to the Enborne rivers, with most of the action to the south nearer the latter waterway. In the 1880s Money convinced Gardiner of his conclusions and it is this version, therefore, that appeared in Gardiner's seminal work published in 1893. Burne and Young placed the battle further north in their 1959 *The Great Civil War*, only for Young in 1964 to return to Money's interpretation, but for different reasons. Money based his thesis on his deduction that Essex's army spent the night near Bigg's Hill (which he concluded to be well to the south of Round Hill and, for obvious reasons, to be near Bigg's cottage) and therefore deployed and fought further south, while Young concluded that the Parliamentarian forces would not fit in a frontage from the Kennet to Wash Common and that the battle area must have continued further south to the River Enborne. The crux of the matter, therefore, is whether the field extended 2 miles or 1.6 miles from north to south; the latter distance avoiding the deep gully south of Wash Common (or Newbury Wash) to the River Enborne. Scott, *The Battles of Newbury*, has adopted the Money/Young model but with clear caveats about actions in the south. While Day, *Gloucester and Newbury*, has the Parliamentary right and Royalist left at the southern extent of Wash Common and well north of the River Enborne. I have walked the ground and understand Young's concern, but my military appreciation tells me that Day is closer to the mark, but knowing the capability of the Royalist cavalry, Scott could also be correct. Under the circumstances, and in the absence of battlefield archaeology, the English Heritage Battlefield Report is a good compromise. I have therefore chosen to depict Day's detail but move it slightly further south in line with the English Heritage battlefield area.

16 Anon, *Relief of Gloucester*, pp. 12–13. There is contradiction in the eyewitness accounts as to whether there were Royalist troops on the hill. See Day, op. cit., pp. 165–6.

17 Byron, in a letter to Clarendon, published in Money, *Battles of Newbury*, p. 42.

18 Digby, *Rebells neare Newbery*, p. 5.

short time, of twelve ensigns that marched up with my Lord Gerard's regiment, eleven were brought off the field hurt… Upon this a confusion was heard among the foot, calling, horse! horse! whereupon I advanced with those two regiments I had and commanded them to halt while I went to view the ground, and to see what way there was to that place where the enemy's foot was drawn up, which I found to be enclosed with a high quick hedge and no passage into it, but by a narrow gap through which but one horse at a time could go and that not without difficulty.[19]

Skippon, Essex's sergeant major of foot, was with his commander watching the attacks, and it was agreed to call up his entire brigade and support it with Springate's Regiment and the Red Auxiliaries. At the same time Mainwaring's Regiment was sent to assist Robartes' troops who were being attacked in the lower ground.

On Newbury Wash, the mass of Royalist cavalry regiments was beginning to spread south along the eastern edge, followed by the foot regiments. Wilmot was in overall charge of the group, which consisted of his own brigade, the cavalry brigades of the Earl of Carnarvon and Charles Gerrard and two of John Byron's infantry regiments. Two-thirds of the Royalist horse were with him, but the gully to the south of the Wash constrained their deployable space. At much the same time, Stapleton had arrived opposite the Royalists at the western edge of the Wash and had begun to spread his horse south towards Enborne Common. The two massed cavalry formations now faced off for some time before the Royalists charged. Digby noted that 'this action was done merely by our horse, for (to say truth) our foot having found a hillocke in the Heath that sheltered them from the Enemies Cannon, would not be drawne a foot from thence'.[20] The young and impetuous Royalist cavalry officers had undervalued the ability and courage of their opponents and the attack failed with considerable loss. Stapleton's troopers did not move but waited until their counterparts were within pistol and carbine range before serving a massive volley upon them. As such, they had successfully executed the traditional system honed by the German Reiters.[21] A second charge quickly followed, so rapidly in fact that the Parliamentarian cavalry scarcely had time to reload. This time they were forced to counter-charge the Royalist horse. A quick third charge by the Royalists had some initial success but their follow up was devoid of infantry support and was heavily punished. A Parliamentarian supporter noted that 'Sir Philip Stapleton was here charged both in front and flanck, his whole regiment having spent both their pistols, and was so encompassed, that the enemy and ours, with both our whole bodies, were all mixed together, and in this confusion many were slaine.'[22]

While all this action was ongoing at the northern end of the field, a Parliamentarian soldier (or officer) known as 'T.V.' was observing down on the Kennet valley. He noted the 'King, Queen and Prince stood all the day upon a hill hard by, in sight of us, and beheld all'.[23] In fact, Henrietta Maria was not present at the Battle of Newbury and there is no evidence that the princes were either, but the King certainly was in action with his hand

firmly on the tiller. In the late morning, he ordered Vavasour's Brigade to advance against the reinforced Parliamentarian forlorn hope to their front. The two sides came very close but did not come to 'push of pike'. During one attack the Royalists captured one of Parliament's gun limbers and dragged it away. But for the most part, the attacks in this sector petered out and the two sides traded long-range musket fire.

In the centre, the fight was reaching a crescendo. Nicholas Byron had found a gap in the hedge, and had ordered it to be widened by the pioneers, when the Parliamentarian infantry opened fire. Byron's horse was shot in the throat and fell dying, while Lord Falkland was killed when he spurred his horse through the gap in the hedgerow. Nevertheless, the attack on Robartes' Brigade was prevailing and sustained. Mainwaring's Regiment was all but destroyed, carrying away part of Skippon's left. Byron recalled how he rallied his men:

… but not so soon but that the enemy had got away their field-pieces for fear of the worst, seeing us resolved not to give over, so I charged them a second time, Sir Thomas Aston being then come up with his [cavalry] regiment, we then beat them to the end of the close, where they faced us again, having the advantage of a hedge at their backs and poured in another volley of shott upon us.[24]

The situation for Essex's army at about midday was critical. If the Royalists penetrated the line and gained the road (running south-east from Skinner's Green to Newbury Wash), then they could engage the defending units in the flank and rear, and roll them up piecemeal. Digby described it as 'the hottest dispute that hath beene seene'.[25] The fate of the day hung precariously in the balance.

With Essex completely preoccupied at the front, both Barclay and Holborne, who had withdrawn to the rear, sensed the danger. 'Holborn perceiving with his Brigade gave the enemy a Round Salvo, and instantly his own and Colonell Barckley's Brigades and his Excell[ency's] Regiment again advancing beat back the enemy… and made good the place all the day after.'[26] Their intervention, by rallying their exhausted men, had stabilized the crisis but the danger was far from over. Essex moved some of Middleton's cavalry up behind Round Hill and gave orders for the nearly 3,000 musketeers in this composite group to deploy along the hedgerows. The battle continued in this sector, but the ferocity of the Royalist attacks waned. For Essex, the main effort now was to secure his right wing.

At Newbury Wash, Gerard's and Belasyse's brigades were under the command of Sir Jacob Astley. He and his officers were having a torrid time of trying to get the Royalist infantry to close with the Parliamentarians at the edge of the common.[27] Following Wilmot's failure to break Stapleton's cavalry, there had been a hiatus in this sector, during which time Essex reorganized his infantry and the Royalists called up more artillery. Sergeant Foster was with the trained bands; he remembered that 'when wee were come up into the field, our two regiments of the trained bands were placed in open campania upon the right wing of the whole army'.[28] It was not long before Foster and his comrades were being battered by the Royalist battery. Foster recalled:

19 Byron, in a letter to Clarendon, published in Money, *Battles of Newbery*, pp. 51–2.
20 Digby, *Rebells neare Newbery*, p. 5.
21 See the chapter on armies and tactics as well as Firth, *Cromwell's Army*, p. 128. This may have been due to the geographical constraints of Wash Common but it does place the quality of Essex's Horse in a different light.
22 Anon, *Relief of Gloucester*, p. 14.
23 T. V., *Battell neere Newbery*, p. 5.

24 Byron, in a letter to Clarendon, published in Money, *Battles of Newbery*, p. 52.
25 Digby, *Rebells neare Newbery*, p. 6.
26 Anon, *Relief of Gloucester*, p. 17.
27 Day makes the point that these were the same soldiers who had failed at Reading and Gloucester and been out of control after the fall of Bristol, p. 184.
28 Foster, *A true and exact relation*, p. 11.

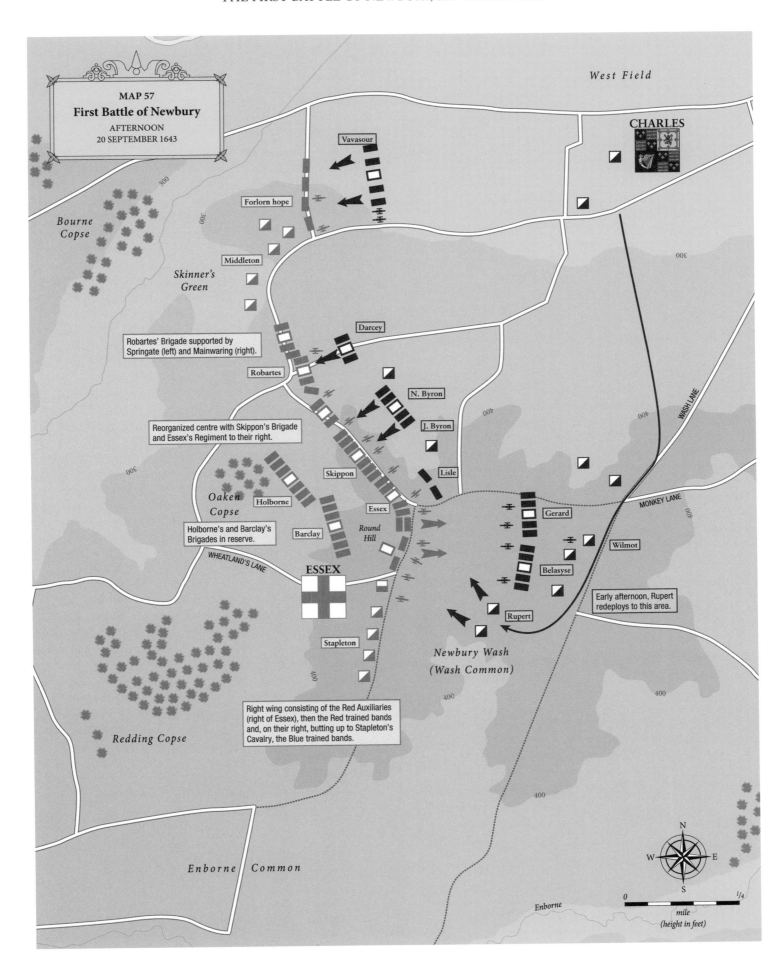

West Field

MAP 57

First Battle of Newbury

AFTERNOON
20 SEPTEMBER 1643

CHARLES

Vavasour

Bourne
Copse

Forlorn hope

Skinner's
Green

Middleton

Darcey

Robartes' Brigade supported by
Springate (left) and Mainwaring (right).

Robartes

N. Byron

J. Byron

Reorganized centre with Skippon's Brigade
and Essex's Regiment to their right.

Skippon

Lisle

Oaken
Copse

Holborne

Essex

Holborne's and Barclay's
Brigades in reserve.

Barclay

Round
Hill

Gerard

MONKEY LANE

Wilmot

Belasyse

WHEATLAND'S LANE

ESSEX

Early afternoon, Rupert
redeploys to this area.

Stapleton

Rupert

Newbury Wash
(Wash Common)

Redding Copse

Right wing consisting of the Red Auxiliaries
(right of Essex), then the Red trained bands
and, on their right, butting up to Stapleton's
Cavalry, the Blue trained bands.

Enborne Common

N
W   E
S

Enborne

0   1/4

mile
(height in feet)

WASH LANE

The enemy had there planted eight pieces of ordnance, and stood in a great body of horse and foot, wee being placed right opposite against them, and far lesse than twice musket shot distance from them. They began their battery against us with their great guns, above halfe an houre before we could get any of our guns up to us; our gunner dealt very ill with us, delaying to come up to us.[29]

Until the Parliamentarian cannon could be moved to counter the Royalist guns, Stapleton's reformed cavalry was asked to buy time. They charged twice against the Royalist infantry, and had considerable success against Gerard's units, which broke and sought refuge among Sir Charles Lucas's cavalry. The two heavy demi-culverins, brought up by the Parliamentarian vanguard on the first attack upon Round Hill, had played a pivotal role in engaging the floor of the Kennet valley, and in holding back the Royalist attacks in the centre, and now they were instrumental in destroying the cohesion of the Royalist foot on the right. As more and more Parliamentarian artillery arrived on the common, the two heavy guns began to neutralize the Royalist eight-gun battery (including the two 15-pound culverins) that had been firing continuously for over half an hour.

In the early afternoon, with news that the Royalists had failed to make a breakthrough on Round Hill or Newbury Wash, Rupert left the valley floor (one assumes with the King's permission and guidance) and moved with his Lifeguard to join Wilmot. Rupert had been everywhere that morning, but it is unclear as to exactly when he arrived on the common. On arrival, he found the Royalist infantry on the back foot, having been driven back by the combined Parliamentarian trained bands and auxiliaries. The latter had gained a firm lodgement on the common (forward of the road). Foster was with this group and noted the Royalists' failed attempt to win the hill:

… when our two regiments of the trained bands had thus plaid against the enemy for the space of three hours, or thereabout, our red regiment joyned to the blew which stood a little distance from us upon our left flank, where we gained the advantage of a little hill, which we maintained against the enemy halfe an hour: two regiments of the enemie's foot fought against us all this while to gain the hill, but could not.[30]

The Parliamentarian infantry had gained the ascendency, but their forward position had separated them from their guns and made them vulnerable to cavalry attack.

Rupert immediately saw this and seized the opportunity. About 500 horse, divided into two squadrons, charged. They surrounded the London infantry, who seem to have formed squares, and then thundered into the Parliamentarian gun line. Some of the guns were dragged away but the Roundhead foot stood firm, and their well-delivered musketry began to unseat large numbers of Rupert's troopers. Rupert charged a second time but the trained bands continued to hold their ground. Clarendon suggested that they 'behaved themselves to wonder, and were, in truth, the preservation of that army that day'.[31] In the immediate aftermath of the two cavalry charges they were then assailed by the Royalist infantry and suffered greatly. They eventually broke, seeking refuge among the hedges on the west of the common. Their flight could have been disastrous, for Essex had no reserves left but, as is so often the case when the critical moment arrives, the Royalists were exhausted and running desperately short of powder. The attack never materialized. Both sides were simply exhausted and in desperate need of water. As light began to fade, commanders were content to hold their ground and allow the infantry and gunners to engage in long-range musketry and artillery fire. The sun began setting soon after 6pm but sporadic firing continued for another four hours.

Charles was horrified and heartbroken at his losses, particularly among his noble officers. Exact numbers are difficult to tie down but they were probably over a thousand for each side.[32] Like Edgehill, the battle had been inconclusive. The Parliamentarians remained firm on the field of battle and the Royalists still held the road and, therefore, blocked the way for Essex's return to London. Nevertheless, Charles was disheartened and after a few hours he gave the order to pull back. Digby recalled what happened next:

It was thought fit to draw his Horse into Quarters on the other side of the River, and his foot into the Towne, principally to refresh them and to inable them for the next daies pursuit… too great a despaire of retreat might have made them opinionate a second fight in that disadvantagious place, where having not (to tell you the truth) Powder enough left for halfe such another day, having spent four score barrells in it, three score more than had served the turne at Edgehill, nor could we be assured that the supply from Oxford of 100 Barrelles more could come to us till the next day at noon.[33]

The next day, aware that the Royalists had pulled back, Essex's army marched cautiously east, by-passing the bridge at Newbury, and taking another route back to the capital. They were attacked in a rather half-hearted manner by Rupert's cavalry. It was, in a way, a rather desperate and frustrated attempt by the Royalists to dress up their failure at Newbury. London breathed a sigh a relief and celebrated on receipt of the wonderful news and again four days later when the victorious army marched proudly through the capital's streets. The opportunity for the Royalists to end the war before the year ran out had been squandered.

29 Ibid.
30 Ibid.
31 Clarendon, op. cit., p. 236.
32 Scott, *The Battles of Newbury*, p. 128.
33 Digby, *Rebells neare Newbery*, p. 7.

CHAPTER 15

IRISH CESSATION AND THE SCOTTISH COVENANT, 1643

With the formalization of the Confederate forces in Ireland in late 1642 (by the Confederation of Kilkenny; see chapter 3), there were now four separate armies involved in the Irish war: the Catholic Confederates, the Protestant forces consisting of Royalists (effectively the Irish army under James Butler, 1st Duke of Ormond), Parliamentarians (the so-called 'Lagan army' of British settlers living in Ulster) and the Scottish Covenanters under the command of Major General Robert Monro. The Protestants were bound by their anti-Catholicism and their determination to avoid the establishment of a nation with a church and government 'unavoidably hostile to her own religion and institutions, and unavoidably allied with the Continental powers who were her bitterest rivals'.[1] However, the outbreak of civil war in England in August 1642 had placed enormous pressure on this uncomfortable Protestant alliance and had, conversely, served to advance Catholic resolve.

In January 1643, Charles had instructed Ormond to open negotiations with the Confederates in order to air their complaints and gauge the best approach. His intention was not to resolve the enormous challenge of the Irish problem, but simply to pacify Irish Catholics, creating the conditions to release English soldiers from the Irish army to return to English soil and fight with their English brothers. The previous October, the Westminster Parliament had, in fact, despatched two representatives in an attempt to subvert the process with the Parliament and Privy Council in Dublin. They fled hot-foot in February, having failed to win over the Irish executive or the army, and just prior to the warrants issued by Charles for their arrest. Nevertheless, negotiations between the King and the Irish were inevitably going to take some time and, in the interim, the newly appointed Confederate generals were keen to use the hiatus to mobilize and further their cause and standing through the sword.

Owen Roe O'Neill, the Irish Confederate commander in Ulster, 'retired for a while into Longford and Leitrim, with the intention of nursing up an army in these rugged districts which would make him a match for his enemies'.[2] While John Burke, who was to command in Connaught, was actively engaged in enlisting the sympathies within his province. But it was in Leinster where Thomas Preston had been the most productive. By early January he 'was at the head of about 6,000 foot and 600 horse, and Lord Castlehevan, who acted as his lieutenant general, burned for an opportunity to distinguish himself'.[3] By 19 January, Preston's Leinster army had captured Bir Castle and the next day, without firing a shot, they occupied Banagher. However, his attempt in early February to block the Royalist force, under Viscount Ranelagh and Charles Coote, from their hasty retreat from Connacht back to Dublin ended in defeat at the Battle of Rathconnel. A month later, Preston was forced to retreat when Ormond advanced from

Dublin with the intention of capturing New Ross in order to disrupt communications between Kilkenny, the Confederate capital, and the ports of Waterford and Wexford. The siege was only in place a matter of days before Preston reappeared. Battle was offered and taken when Preston tried to block Ormond's withdrawal route to Dublin. On 18 March, the battle of Ross was another defeat for Preston's men, but they did succeed in driving the Royalists from their lands. Ormond's supply chain had been continually hampered throughout the operation by Confederate troops and sympathizers and, by the end of March, he limped back into Dublin with his half-starved army.

In spite of these military disagreements, Charles remained determined to continue negotiations with the Confederation. On 17 March discussions opened at Trim and a couple of weeks later the King dismissed Sir William Parsons, the Lord Chief Justice of Ireland, who had voiced his concern over the long-term Irish intentions towards the Protestants. On 23 April, with talks progressing slower than he would have hoped, Charles authorized Ormond to offer a cessation of hostilities to last for one year. So sensitive was this correspondence that the King encoded the last part of the message, which read, 'and as soon as that is done, Ormond Marquis must bring over the Irish army to Chester'.[4] The Irish Confederates were in no real hurry. While the assembly talked, the generals continued to wage war and strengthen their hand.

The Royalist garrison at Galway capitulated in June after hearing of Vavasour's defeat at Cloughlea earlier in the month. While on 10 June, O'Neill's Ulster army suffered a defeat at the hands of Stewart's Lagan army at Clones. O'Neill regrouped, reinforced by a number of men who defected from Preston's Leinster army, and defeated a government force under Lord Moore at Portlester in August. It was to be the last major action of the year. On 15 September, the cessation was finally signed, and on 23 October, the first English regiments began landing in Somerset. The following month more arrived at Mostyn in Flintshire (see map 50), bringing Brereton's excursion into north Wales to a rapid end. More regiments continued to arrive near Chester throughout December. Charles's Irish policy had, on paper at least, succeeded.

Monro's Scottish Covenanter army remained in Ireland, but by the end of 1642 their operations were limited in nature and tended to be conducted in concert with the British settlers. Meanwhile, back in Scotland, the outbreak of civil conflict in England had benefited the Covenanters by reducing any possibility of Charles seeking military revenge north of the border. As 1643 unfolded, however, the Covenanters had greater cause for concern. Royalist military successes in England did not bode well, but it was the exposure of a plan for a rising in Scotland backed by Irish Catholics that terrified them. Randal MacDonnell, Earl of Antrim, a Catholic landowner with estates in Scotland and Ireland, was captured at the end of

---

1   Gardiner, *Great Civil War*, vol. I, p. 120.
2   Meehan, *Confederation of Kilkenny*, p. 53.
3   Ibid., p. 56.

4   Gilbert, *Irish Confederation*, vol. II, p. 266.

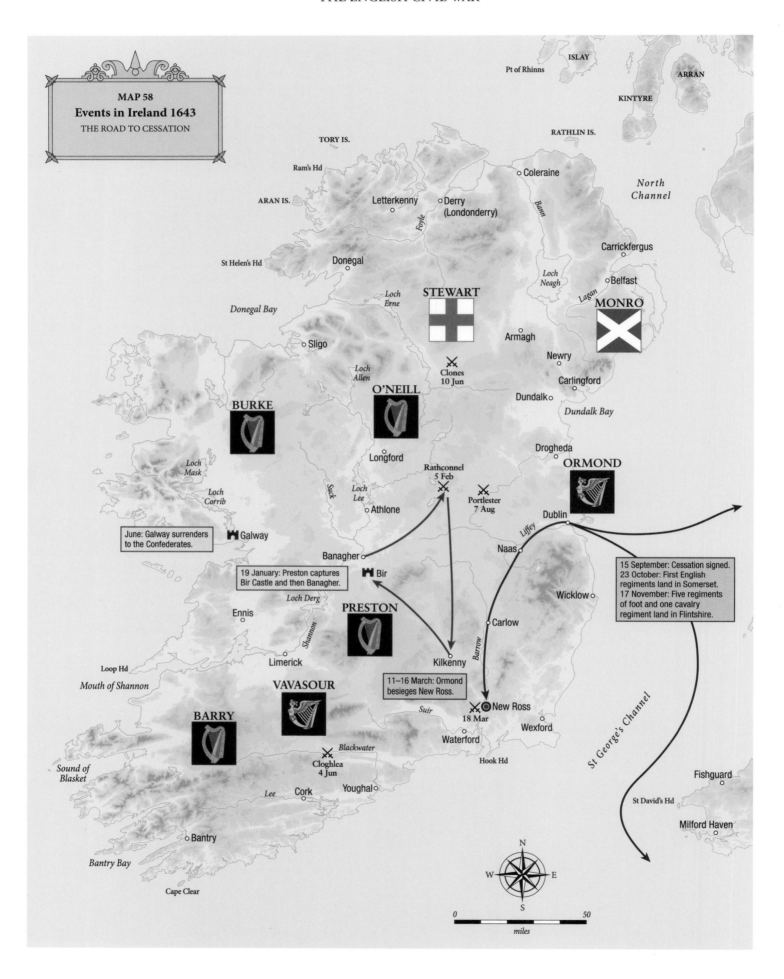

MAP 58

Events in Ireland 1643

THE ROAD TO CESSATION

ISLAY

Pt of Rhinns

ARRAN

KINTYRE

TORY IS.

RATHLIN IS.

Coleraine

North Channel

Ram's Hd

ARAN IS.

Letterkenny

Derry (Londonderry)

Foyle

Bann

Carrickfergus

St Helen's Hd

Donegal

Loch Neagh

Lagan

Belfast

Donegal Bay

Loch Erne

STEWART

MONRO

Sligo

Armagh

Loch Allen

Clones
10 Jun

Newry

BURKE

O'NEILL

Carlingford

Dundalk

Dundalk Bay

Loch Mask

Longford

Drogheda

Loch Corrib

Suck

Loch Lee

Rathconnel
5 Feb

ORMOND

June: Galway surrenders to the Confederates.

Galway

Athlone

Portlester
7 Aug

Dublin

Liffey

Banagher

Naas

19 January: Preston captures Bir Castle and then Banagher.

Bir

Loch Derg

Wicklow

15 September: Cessation signed.
23 October: First English regiments land in Somerset.
17 November: Five regiments of foot and one cavalry regiment land in Flintshire.

Ennis

PRESTON

Shannon

Carlow

Barrow

Limerick

Kilkenny

VAVASOUR

11–16 March: Ormond besieges New Ross.

Suir

New Ross
18 Mar

St George's Channel

Loop Hd

Mouth of Shannon

BARRY

Wexford

Waterford

Blackwater

Cloghlea
4 Jun

Hook Hd

Sound of Blasket

Lee

Cork

Youghal

Fishguard

St David's Hd

Bantry

Milford Haven

Bantry Bay

Cape Clear

N
W E
S

0   50
miles

MAP 59

A Nation Divided

THE SITUATION ON
9 DECEMBER 1643

Districts held by Parliament

Districts held by the King

Leven with the Covenanter
army of over 20,000 men.

October–December: Royalist
Troops returning from Ireland.

May 1643 by Monro's forces in Ulster. He was found to be carrying letters detailing a three-pronged uprising in Scotland (Hamilton in the centre, Montrose in the north and Robert Maxwell, Earl of Nithsdale, in the Western Borders) supported by an Irish invasion on the west coast. There was no evidence that Charles had been privy to the plan, but as he was, at that time, in communication with the Confederates at Kilkenny, there was every suspicion that he had been complicit.

These captured documents were sent to London, amidst tight security, at the end of June. Within days, news of Royalist victories at Adwalton Moor (30 June) and Roundway Down (13 July) had heightened tensions in London and Edinburgh further. A few days later delegates from the Westminster Parliament headed north. They arrived in Edinburgh on 7 August and within ten days the Solemn League and Covenant had been signed. This significant document laid, through divine sanction, the basis of an alliance between the Scottish General Assembly and the Parliamentarians to unite militarily against the King and to pledge to work for a civil and religious union. The Covenanters insisted on including a clause establishing Presbyterianism in England which sat uncomfortably with the Parliamentarians, who had simply wanted a civil and military union against the Royalists. But needs must and, by the time the document was ratified in London on 25 September, the military situation had changed and the clause regarding Presbyterianism was altered to one less prescriptive, swearing to preserve the Church of Scotland and reform the churches of England and Ireland.

On 29 November a second bill was passed, authorizing the Scots to raise an army at Parliament's expense. In fact, military preparations had been ongoing in Scotland since July and commanders had been nominated following the signing of the Solemn League and Covenant in August.

Scottish troops occupied Berwick at the end of September. The army, under Alexander Leslie, Earl of Leven, mustered in Berwickshire in the last few days of December. It was a considerable force, consisting of 18,000 foot, 3,000 horse (including 400 dragoons), and 60 pieces of ordnance.[5] As 1644 dawned they were poised to invade.

Charles was quick to denounce this alliance between Parliament and the Scots, and he summoned all the members of both Houses to attend a new Parliament to be convened at Oxford. He offered a 'free and general pardon' to those who accepted. It was not a hare-brained suggestion, for the numbers in the Commons had fallen to fewer than 200 out of the original 600 members, and the number of Lords was almost insignificant. Nevertheless, despite the arrival of a number of troops from Ireland, there was little room for optimism. The King's approach to the Catholics in Ireland and his connection with Irish Catholics with clannish ties to Scottish coreligionists heightened the perception of increasing links with Royalism and Catholicism. It betrayed the fact that many of the troops returning from Ireland were staunch Protestants and found little heart in the Royalist cause and even less of a desire to serve under so many Catholic commanders.

In response, Parliament had formed two new and large armies – one under the command of the Earl of Manchester in the east, and one under Waller in the west. The military crisis had settled. Essex had relieved Gloucester and held off the Royalist forces at Newbury. Things had stabilized in the south and the Royalists' position in the north had been weakened and was now decidedly precarious as the Covenanters massed on the Scottish border. As the year drew to a close, there was every reason for a rekindling of optimism within Parliament's ranks. On the other side, there was little doubt that 1643, from the Royalist perspective, was a year of several missed opportunities.

5 Kenyon & Ohlmeyer, *Military History*, p. 50.

CHAPTER 16
THE SCOTTISH INVASION, EARLY 1644

The Scottish invasion, when it came, was no surprise to the Royalists. In November 1643, Thomas Glemham had been relieved of his responsibilities as military governor at York and sent north with about 2,000 men. He detached a regiment of foot to monitor the border crossings. The Marquis of Newcastle, who had spent the last few weeks of 1643 in Derbyshire, felt compelled to move back to York in January 1644, although he was similarly compelled to leave sufficient men to secure his gains of the previous year across the Midlands. Savile, who had replaced Glemham at York, had died and his successor, Colonel John Belasyse, was en route from Oxford. Furthermore, the Yorkshire gentry had offered many thousands of new recruits and this matter, under the circumstances, was an offer that required his personal attention. As it happened, the recruits failed to materialize and Newcastle wrote to Rupert on 28 January outlining his concerns: 'I know they tell you, sir, that I have great force; truly I cannot march five thousand foot, and the horse not well armed.'[1]

On paper the Scottish army was four times that strength. The Scots had agreed, by the treaty with the English Parliament, to field 25,740 men.[2] In fact, by early 1644 far fewer had assembled north of the River Tweed. Many officers had failed to take command of their men, and provisions and materials, particularly ammunition, were in short supply. On 17 January the Committee of Estates and the force commander, General Alexander Leslie, Earl of Leven, decided that the invasion should go ahead, for it was fast consuming the inadequate rations and likely to disintegrate if left overly long in the barren wilderness of the Eastern Borders.[3] The Covenanter army crossed the Tweed two days later. It is difficult to be precise about the size of the force and most histories settle on 18,000 foot, 3,000 horse, 500 dragoons and a large amount of artillery.[4] However, more recent studies conclude that the force was considerably smaller, and this is supported by Newcastle's letter to Rupert at the end of January, by which time the intelligence should have been well honed on the matter, in which he writes that the enemy are 14,000 strong.[5] Whatever the numbers, the Covenanters significantly outnumbered the Royalist forces sent north or available to Newcastle to counter the invasion.

Glemham's screen force was ordered to pull back in the face of the Scottish advance. They destroyed key bridges and fell back on Newcastle to await the arrival of the Marquis with reinforcements. Time, therefore, was critical and it was Leven's intention to reach Newcastle by 27 January. As it transpired, however, a number of factors colluded, turning Leslie's lightning invasion into more of a forced march. The weather, not surprisingly, was none too kind. The Tweed had frozen, preventing Baillie's

column crossing at Kelso until the morning of the 23rd, snowdrifts blocked the roads, and when the snow melted, the rivers swelled and roads cut up. An eyewitness in the Scottish camp of General Leslie reported that 'Our army had a hard and difficult march in respect of the thaw, which so swelled the waters… that oftentimes it came to the middle, and sometimes the Arme pits of the Foot, insomuch that our Horse did not passe with little less difficulty'.[6] Movement of the heavier artillery was impossible and these guns were eventually loaded on to ships. On the night that Leven's advance guard crossed the Tweed, a letter had been drafted and sent to Glemham, explaining the rationale and intentions of the Covenanter army, in the hope that matters could be resolved peacefully. The need to wait for Glemham's response delayed matters further. Consequently, by 28 January, the Scots had just reached Morpeth (15 miles from their objective) but Leven was forced to wait again for his army to close up.

The following day, Newcastle departed York and headed north with 5,000 foot and 3,000 horse.[7] Newcastle had been delayed gathering his force but, once on the march, the Royalists made far better time than the northern invaders. By last light on 2 February the marquis entered Newcastle and joined forces with Glemham's men and the garrison. Since November, Glemham had turned his attention to improving the city's defences. He had cleared the ditch, plastered the outer walls, built a number of outworks and razed most of the outlying buildings outside the north walls.[8] Badly needed brass cannon, powder and muskets were landed from Danish ships.[9] At about noon on 3 February, the Marquis of Argyll arrived with the vanguard of the Covenanter army, approaching the city from the north. Unaware of Newcastle's arrival, they offered to parley.[10] Their overtures dismissed, Leven set about enforcing the point. An unfinished sconce to the northeast of the town near Shield-Field was quickly overrun but the attack on a sconce to the north of town was a far more demanding affair. The Scots attacked from the east and west but Colonel Charles Slingsby held them off for some considerable time supported by artillery fire from the north walls. After the loss of a number of men, Newcastle decided to withdraw the force and sent out eight troops of horse to assist the infantry in getting back safely. Leven responded by sending out five cavalry troops. Losses were light as the cavalry were unable to deploy and charge in the broken terrain, pitted by opencast mines. That night, in a clear statement of intent, the defenders torched the outlying suburbs to the east.

Until his heavy guns arrived Leven could do little but establish a cordon. North Shields was occupied, although Tynemouth Castle

---

1 Warburton, *Memoirs of Prince Rupert*, vol. II, p. 368.
2 Stevenson, *Scottish Revolution*, p. 295.
3 The Committee of Estates governed Scotland during the Wars of the Three Kingdoms when the Parliament of Scotland was not sitting.
4 Terry, *Leslie*, p. 176, citing Rushworth, *Historical Collections*.
5 Warburton, op. cit., p. 368. Other, more recent, works include Reid, *King's Armies*, p. 108 and Serdiville, *The Great Siege of Newcastle*, p. 56.
6 Bowles, *Scottish army*, p. 1.
7 Warburton, op. cit., pp. 370–1, in a letter from Sir Charles Lucas to Rupert.
8 Plastering of the medieval walls prevented the besiegers gaining footholds in the wall and climbing.
9 Reid, op. cit., p. 109.
10 A copy of Argyle's letter and the city's answer are included in Bowles, op. cit., pp. 9–13.

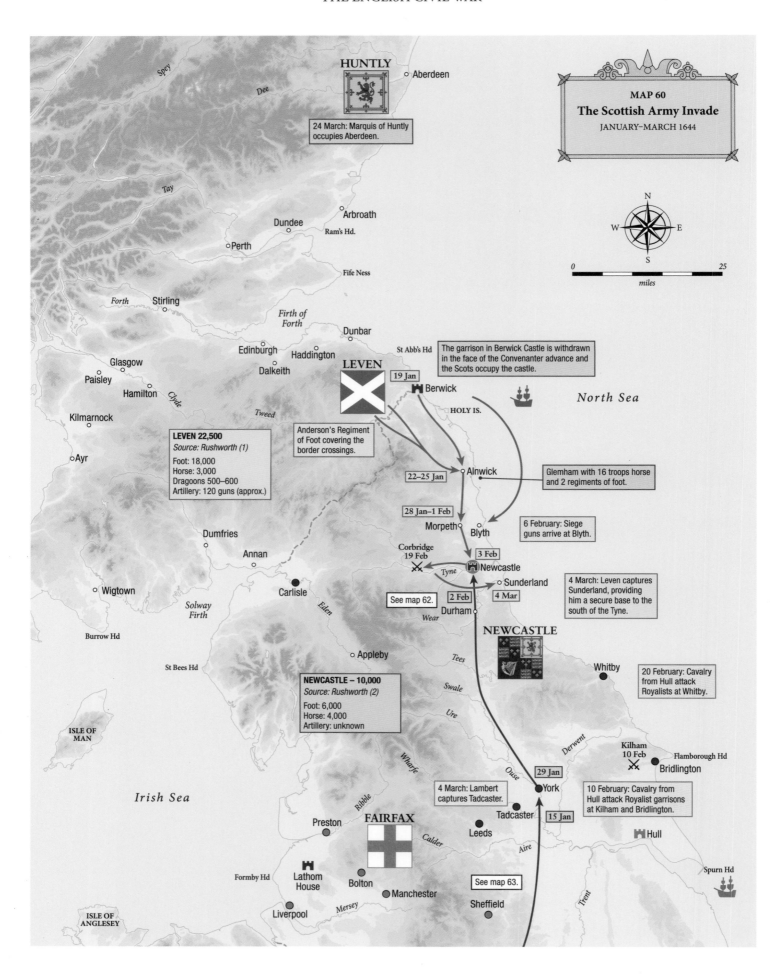

HUNTLY

24 March: Marquis of Huntly occupies Aberdeen.

MAP 60
The Scottish Army Invade
JANUARY–MARCH 1644

The garrison in Berwick Castle is withdrawn in the face of the Convenanter advance and the Scots occupy the castle.

LEVEN

19 Jan Berwick

North Sea

Anderson's Regiment of Foot covering the border crossings.

LEVEN 22,500
Source: Rushworth (1)
Foot: 18,000
Horse: 3,000
Dragoons 500–600
Artillery: 120 guns (approx.)

22–25 Jan Alnwick

Glemham with 16 troops horse and 2 regiments of foot.

28 Jan–1 Feb
Morpeth Blyth

6 February: Siege guns arrive at Blyth.

Corbridge
19 Feb
Tyne 3 Feb Newcastle

See map 62. 2 Feb Sunderland 4 Mar

4 March: Leven captures Sunderland, providing him a secure base to the south of the Tyne.

Durham
Wear

NEWCASTLE

20 February: Cavalry from Hull attack Royalists at Whitby.

NEWCASTLE – 10,000
Source: Rushworth (2)
Foot: 6,000
Horse: 4,000
Artillery: unknown

Whitby

Kilham
10 Feb Flamborough Hd
Bridlington

29 Jan York

10 February: Cavalry from Hull attack Royalist garrisons at Kilham and Bridlington.

4 March: Lambert captures Tadcaster.

Tadcaster 15 Jan

FAIRFAX

Leeds Hull

See map 63.

148

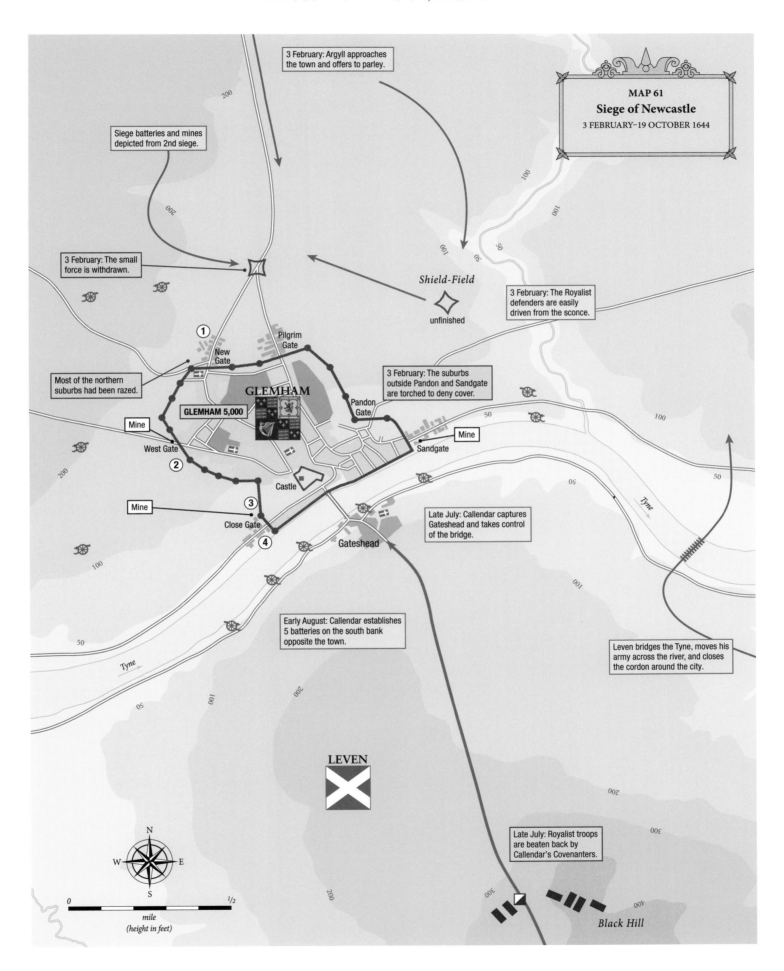

3 February: Argyll approaches the town and offers to parley.

MAP 61
Siege of Newcastle
3 FEBRUARY–19 OCTOBER 1644

Siege batteries and mines depicted from 2nd siege.

3 February: The small force is withdrawn.

3 February: The Royalist defenders are easily driven from the sconce.

Shield-Field

unfinished

① New Gate

Pilgrim Gate

Most of the northern suburbs had been razed.

GLEMHAM

GLEMHAM 5,000

Pandon Gate

3 February: The suburbs outside Pandon and Sandgate are torched to deny cover.

Mine

West Gate

②

Sandgate

Mine

Castle

③

Mine

Close Gate

④

Gateshead

Late July: Callendar captures Gateshead and takes control of the bridge.

Tyne

Early August: Callendar establishes 5 batteries on the south bank opposite the town.

Leven bridges the Tyne, moves his army across the river, and closes the cordon around the city.

Tyne

LEVEN

Late July: Royalist troops are beaten back by Callendar's Covenanters.

N
W E
S

0   1/2
mile
(height in feet)

Black Hill

remained in Royalist hands. The heavy guns arrived at Blyth port on 6 February and were outside the walls two days later. The same day Leven attempted to cross the River Tyne by building a pontoon bridge from captured vessels. However, the attempt failed due to a neap tide, which left many of the craft stuck fast in the mudbank, and a singular lack of fortitude by Colonel William Stuart who had been allocated the task. Newcastle, meanwhile, planned to get across the Tyne a few miles upstream and fall upon the Scottish horse quartered near Corbridge. The force of 25 troops of horse and 300 musketeers under Sir Marmaduke Langdale made good time, but they were shocked to find the Scots ready and waiting for them. The suspicion that one, or some, of the Scottish officers under the King's pay were haemorrhaging intelligence to their fellow countrymen was now confirmed.

The engagement at Corbridge was largely inconclusive in itself, but it did serve to galvanize Leven's subsequent operations in the region as well as to reinforce, in Newcastle's mind, that he did not have enough men to defend Newcastle and the full length of the Tyne. He noted, 'I found that there was so many fordable places betwixt Newburn and Hexham, about twelve miles distant one from the other, that it was impossible with my small number of foot to divide them so as to guard and make good every place.'[11] On 22 February, leaving a few thousand men north of Newcastle, Leven marched west with the balance of his army and crossed the River Tyne a few days later. The next day heavy snowstorms delayed operations, and it was to be some days before they could continue. An English entrepreneur, who signed his reports 'W. R.', was ensconced with the Scots and wrote to his superiors in London, 'On the 28 of Febr. With 15 Regiments of Foote, and 6 Regiments of Horse, we passed the River Tyne at severall Fordes near Bywell and Oringham, which if we had not done that day, the sudden alteration of the weather had made it some time impossible for us...'.[12] The Scots continued unopposed towards Sunderland and occupied the town on 4 March. Sunderland provided a secure base for Leven's army, which could be resupplied by sea. Furthermore, now south of the Tyne he could close the cordon around Newcastle and attack the Royalist lines of communication. Newcastle, determined to prevent this, marched south with speed to escape the cordon and bring the Covenanters to battle. His intention was to engage them in more open terrain, where his superior cavalry could be used decisively.

Reinforced by Lucas's Horse and 1,500 foot from Cumberland, Newcastle moved towards Sunderland on 6 March. He crossed the River Wear at New Bridge (under Lumley Castle) and despatched a cavalry force to clear the Scottish cavalry outpost from the high point to the east. The next day both armies were drawn up on elevated terrain facing each other. However, the ground was far from suitable for an open encounter, being enclosed with hedges and banks. Furthermore, the heavy snow, which had drifted to many feet in places, further impeded movement. Leven was quite clear of Newcastle's intentions and well aware of the strength of the Royalist cavalry. He refused to be drawn, maintaining his positions on the higher ground where his Scottish infantry would be at their most effective. A stand-off almost inevitably ensued. It continued into the morning of the third day, and with the prospect of another night in the open, Newcastle ordered a withdrawal to the Royalist base at Durham in order to rest and resupply his troops. Despite a show of force

to try to dissuade a Scottish pursuit, Leven nevertheless sent a large force to chase the retreating Royalists. Newcastle decided to turn and face the Scots. He recalled in his memoirs:

> ... being content to play with them at their own game, whilst we amused them by presenting some horse before them, our musketeers, which in the meantime stole down upon their flank towards their passage, gave them such a peal, that it made the passage which they retired over seem I believe a great deal straiter.[13]

Newcastle's force made it to the relative safety of Durham, but he had failed to draw the Scots into open battle and he was at a loss as to how to proceed.

Over the next few days some ships arrived at Sunderland in order to succour the Scottish force. Once resupplied and rested, Leven moved to capture the not inconsiderable fortress at South Shields. The first attempt on 16 March failed with some loss. The attackers came under heavy fire from the castle across the Tyne and a 'Dunkirk frigot' moored close to it. Leslie described the second attack which was made four days later:

> After we had considered of this repulse two or three dayes, and fasted on the nineteenth, the Fort was againe assaulted by another party; for the encouragement of which the Generall [Leven] went with them in person, and on the 20, being Wednesday in the morning, we tooke it with the losse of nine men, the hurt of more. In it wee found five Peeces of Iron Ordnance, seven Barrels of Powder, seventy Muskets; the men escaped in the dark to the water-side, where boats received them.[14]

Three days later Newcastle marched his army back from Durham in another attempt to gain a battle on favourable ground. He approached Sunderland along the flat ground to the north of the River Wear. Leven countermarched his army and, on 24 March, the two armies were once again facing each other. However, despite the flatter terrain, it was still interspersed with hedged enclosures and certainly not suitable for large-scale cavalry manoeuvres. In terms of numbers, both sides were evenly matched at about 6,000 men apiece. Following a general artillery bombardment, which was largely ineffectual due to the range, the Scots opened with an attack by Fraser's Dragoons. They dislodged a number of commanded musketeers that were lining the hedges along the main east–west road through Bolden. This triggered a wider attack and, at one stage, four Royalist regiments were engaged on the valley floor with six Scottish regiments.[15] The fight went on long after dark. It was, in the scheme of things, a bloody contest. Even *Mercurius Aulicus* admitted to 240 Royalist soldiers killed or captured.[16] Frustrated once again at not being able to capitalize on his cavalry, Newcastle gave orders for a withdrawal, which began at noon the next day. Leven took some time to realize the Royalist intentions, and when he did, he despatched the Covenanter horse, supported by some galloper guns,[17] to pursue them.

11 Firth, *Memoirs Duke of Newcastle*, pp. 350–1.
12 W. R., *Lord Generall of the Scottish Army*, p. 3.

13 Firth, op. cit., p. 353.
14 Terry, op. cit., p. 206, footnote.
15 Reid, op. cit., p. 115.
16 *Mercurius Aulicus*, dated March 30, 1644.
17 Galloper guns were lightweight guns used in the 17th and 18th centuries. The (relative) light weight enabled them to be moved during a battle to support mobile operations, particularly cavalry, hence the name. They were, in effect, the forerunner to horse artillery.

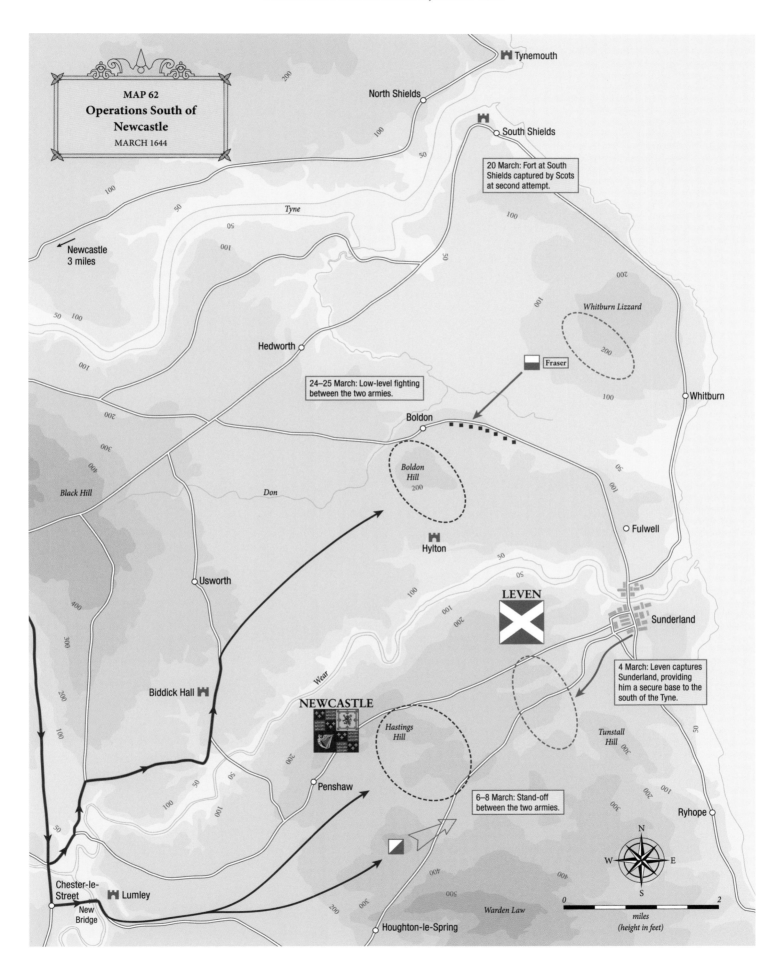

MAP 62

Operations South of Newcastle

MARCH 1644

Tynemouth

North Shields

South Shields

20 March: Fort at South Shields captured by Scots at second attempt.

Tyne

Newcastle 3 miles

Whitburn Lizzard

Hedworth

Fraser

24–25 March: Low-level fighting between the two armies.

Boldon

Whitburn

Boldon Hill 200

Black Hill

Don

Hylton

Fulwell

Usworth

LEVEN

Sunderland

4 March: Leven captures Sunderland, providing him a secure base to the south of the Tyne.

Wear

Biddick Hall

NEWCASTLE

Hastings Hill

Tunstall Hill

Penshaw

6–8 March: Stand-off between the two armies.

Ryhope

Chester-le-Street

Lumley

New Bridge

Warden Law

Houghton-le-Spring

N
W — E
S

0   miles   2
(height in feet)

Newcastle turned Charles Lucas's Brigade to charge the pursuing Scots. It was a minor victory in the scheme of things and the Royalists once again made it back to the relative safety of their base at Durham, but Newcastle remained unsure of just how to break the impasse.

Later that day, Newcastle wrote again to Rupert. He congratulated him on his actions in driving away the Parliamentarian besiegers from Newark and then took the opportunity to reiterate the importance of supporting him in the north:

I must assure your Highness, that the Scots are as big again in foot as I am, and their horse, I doubt, much better than ours are, so that if your Highness do not please to come hither, and that very soon too, the great game of your uncle's will be endangered, if not lost.[18]

With Tadcaster having been lost to Lambert's cavalry in early March, Newcastle's fears were well grounded. Then, on 31 March, Leven marched his army out of Sunderland and headed south. York was their next objective.

18 Warburton, op. cit., p. 397.

CHAPTER 17

NANTWICH AND NEWARK: THE BATTLES FOR CENTRAL ENGLAND, JANUARY TO MARCH 1644

The invasion of the Covenanter army in support of Parliament marked a turning point in the war. Charles was, however, seemingly unperturbed. The arrival of English soldiers from Ireland would, in his opinion, more than compensate for this treachery by his Scottish subjects. The King's intention was to build up another northern army under Lord Byron and base it in Cheshire. He combined the 3,200 soldiers from Ireland with about 1,000 horse from Oxford to create Byron's force. They soon got the better of Brereton's Parliamentarian forces in the Cheshire area and on Boxing Day drove them north following a forthright skirmish at Middleton. A week earlier, Byron had made an abortive attempt to capture Nantwich, the Parliamentarian headquarters in the county. Byron decided to establish a fairly loose cordon around the town and set about mopping up some of the Parliamentarian outposts in the county. However, by early January, Byron was growing impatient with Sir George Booth, the commander of the Nantwich garrison. On 10 January, Byron summoned the town but this was firmly rejected. With the Royalists running short of ammunition, and following a second verbal rebuff on 16 January, they made a second attempt to storm the place the next day. One regiment succeeded in breaking in the town's outer defences on the west side, but they were driven back by a determined counter-attack. Frustrated, Byron called off the attack. It was clear that the defenders could not last much longer and he could ill-afford more casualties. He pulled back and re-established the loose cordon.

However, unbeknown to Byron, a large Parliamentarian force was concentrating in and around Manchester in order to come to the aid of the townsfolk and lift the siege. Having recaptured Gainsborough, Fairfax was looking forward to moving into winter quarters, but Parliament had other ideas. Fairfax wrote:

> But in ye Coldest season of it, I was ordered by ye parliament to goe and raise ye seidge of Nantwich, which ye Ld Byron with ye Irish Army had reduced to great extremity, I was ye most unfit of all ye Forces, being ever ye worst paid, my men sickly, almost naked for want of clothes… But their Answer was a positive Direction to march, for it would admit of no Delay… upon my owne Credit got so much cloth as clothed 1500 Men, & all ready to march when these orders came to me.[1]

Fairfax's march, and the fact that the Royalist headquarters in Oxford were unaware of the concentration of forces at Manchester, is an early indication of another change in the dynamics of the war. The clear and unequivocal direction from London to Fairfax is a good example that the new Parliamentary Committee for War (known as the Committee of Both Kingdoms) was both able and willing to exert centralized control for strategic effect. The Royalist Council of War in Oxford had not developed the same level of sophistication and neither had it honed its intelligence gathering, analysis and dissemination with the same level of expertise.

Fairfax marched with 1,800 horse and 500 dragoons through Derbyshire and then north to Manchester. We know that Byron was aware of Fairfax's movement, and that he had asked Newcastle to do something to prevent it. But this did not happen, and we can only speculate that Newcastle's understandable preoccupation with the imminent Scottish invasion was the reason. Byron wrote:

> Some letters were intercepted from Sir Thomas Fairfax to Brereton; wherein he assured him to assist him with all that force, and to bring the foot of Staffordshire along with him to join with those of Lancashire. Whereupon I acquainted my Lord of Newcastle with the design, and desired him (this army then lying that way) to prevent Fairfax's march: which if he had done, the town had within a few days been delivered up to me.[2]

On arrival, Fairfax collected another 3,000 infantry from Brereton's depleted force and yet more from the counties of Lancashire and Cheshire. Despite concerns about the quality and cohesiveness of his new force, Fairfax set off south towards Nantwich on 21 January, as he recounted:

> With this Army we march to Nantwich, which was upon ye point of surrendering. When we were in 2 days march I had Intelligence yet ye Ld Byron had drawne off his Seidge, & intended to meet us in ye Field. I put my men in ye order I intended to fight, & so continued my march till we were within 3 miles of ye Towne.[3]

Byron, conversely, only got wind of Fairfax's approach after the Parliamentarian vanguard bumped a cavalry picket near Delamere in the early hours of 24 January. Byron's force had been somewhat depleted by the numerous minor exchanges in the seven weeks since he marched out from Chester. His foot was probably slightly fewer than 2,500 and his horse fewer than 1,000.[4] The ground surrounding Nantwich dictated that his army was split on the east and west banks of the River Weaver in order to prosecute the cordon and siege. With intelligence of an approaching Parliamentarian force on the Chester road, he gave orders for most of the army on the east bank to move to the west bank.

His intention was to engage the Parliamentarian force somewhere to the west of Nantwich, on the Chester road. However, that night, the temperature rose quickly and unexpectedly, causing a widespread thaw and

---

2 Letter, Byron to Ormond, dated 30 January 1644, from Carte, *Collection of Original Letters*, vol. II, p. 37.

3 Fairfax, op. cit., p. 219.

4 Dore & Lowe, *Battle of Nantwich*, pp. 99–100.

---

1 Fairfax, *Short memorials*, pp. 218–19.

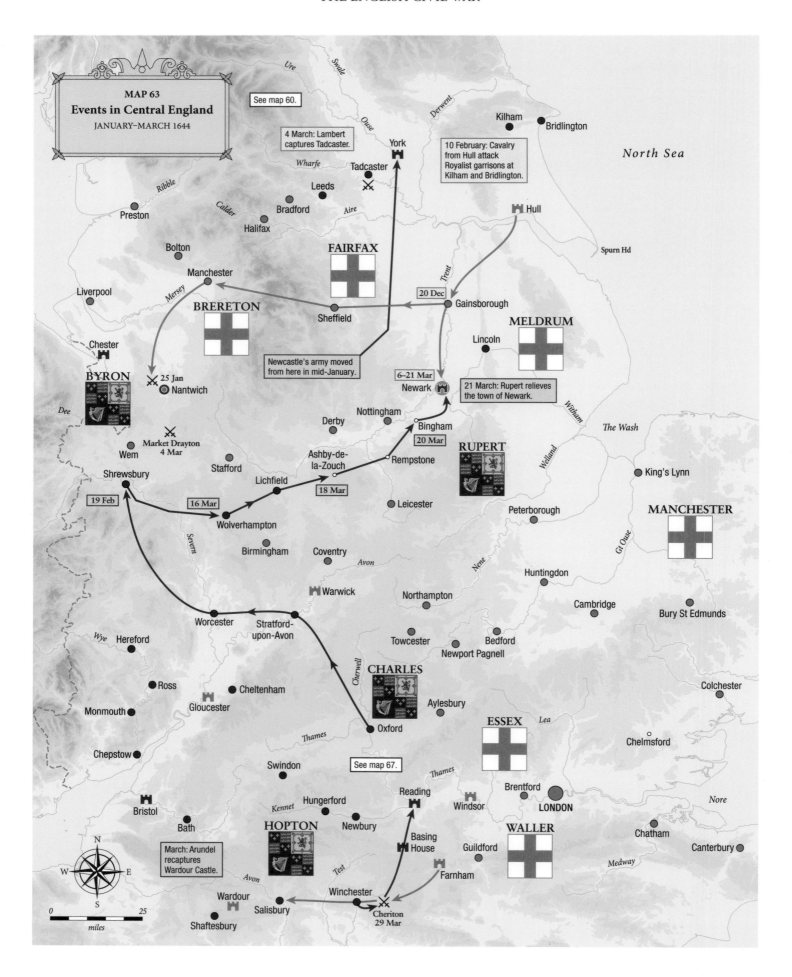

MAP 63
Events in Central England
JANUARY–MARCH 1644

See map 60.

Ure

Swale

4 March: Lambert captures Tadcaster.

York

10 February: Cavalry from Hull attack Royalist garrisons at Kilham and Bridlington.

Kilham
Bridlington

North Sea

Derwent

Tadcaster

Wharfe

Leeds

Calder

Bradford

Halifax

Aire

Preston

Ribble

Bolton

FAIRFAX

Hull

Spurn Hd

Liverpool

Manchester

Mersey

BRERETON

Sheffield

20 Dec

Gainsborough

Trent

Chester

Lincoln

MELDRUM

The Wash

BYRON

Dee

25 Jan
Nantwich

Newcastle's army moved from here in mid-January.

6–21 Mar
Newark

21 March: Rupert relieves the town of Newark.

Witham

Market Drayton
4 Mar

Wem

Derby

Nottingham

Bingham

20 Mar

Welland

King's Lynn

Ashby-de-la-Zouch

Rempstone

RUPERT

Shrewsbury

Stafford

Lichfield

18 Mar

Leicester

19 Feb

16 Mar

Wolverhampton

Severn

Birmingham

Coventry

Avon

Peterborough

Gt Ouse

MANCHESTER

Nene

Huntingdon

Cambridge

Bury St Edmunds

Warwick

Northampton

Worcester

Stratford-upon-Avon

Cherwell

CHARLES

Towcester

Bedford

Newport Pagnell

Colchester

Wye

Hereford

Ross

Cheltenham

Aylesbury

ESSEX

Lea

Chelmsford

Monmouth

Gloucester

Oxford

Thames

See map 67.

Thames

Brentford

LONDON

Nore

Chepstow

Swindon

Reading

Windsor

Chatham

March: Arundel recaptures Wardour Castle.

Bristol

Kennet

Hungerford

Newbury

Basing House

Guildford

WALLER

Canterbury

Medway

Bath

HOPTON

Farnham

Avon

Wardour

Salisbury

Winchester

Cheriton
29 Mar

N
W E
S

Shaftesbury

0   25
miles

a corresponding rise in the river. The swollen waters washed away the wooden pontoon bridge Byron had constructed north of Beambridge to maintain communication with both banks.[5] Consequently, the next morning, Byron was forced to make a rapid march south to use the bridge at Shrewbridge (1 mile to the south) in order to reunite his force. 'The night before we fought with them, a small river that ran betwixt our quarters, swelled so upon the falling of rain and melting of the snow, that one part of the army was forced to march six miles before it could join with the other', Byron wrote.[6] This may have upset his plans for a defensive position just north of Barbridge, forcing him instead to position his army around the village of Acton, an area that possessed few defensive qualities.

At first light on 25 January Fairfax moved towards Nantwich from his camp at Tilstone Heath. They arrived at Barbridge mid-morning and found their way barred by a small picket of 200 musketeers. He cleared this small force with a deliberate attack and approached Hurleston soon after midday. From the higher ground he could now see some of the Royalist forces to his front. Lacking full confidence in his rather ad hoc army, he decided to summon a council of war:

> We called a Councell, wherein it was debated whether we should attempt those in their workes (being divided from ye Rest of ye Army) or march into ye Towne, & relieve them, & by increase of more Force, be better able ye next day, to encounter them. The latter was resolved on.[7]

It is not clear whether all of Byron's forces had crossed the Weaver and were up in support.[8] Certainly Fairfax suggests they were not, so his plan was to move with speed across the ground north of Acton and enter the defences of Nantwich via the west gate. He was forced, therefore, to reorganize his foot into column. It was a risky manoeuvre, as he would leave his right flank exposed throughout, so the Parliamentarian foot were ordered to keep tight.

The deployment of the Royalist foot to counter this manoeuvre seems to have been made (according to Byron) by Colonel Gibson. The Royalist foot moved steadily north, trying to maintain formation over the numerous hedges and enclosures over the terrain to their front. Such was the slowness of their pace that the Parliamentarian forces had ample time to right face and advance into lines to receive the attack. At about half past three the attack began. Robert Byron's and Gibson's regiments seem to have been ahead of the two central regiments, giving the impression of a 'buffalo horn' attack. Whether this was by design or happenstance is unclear. The movement did give the impression that the Royalists, particularly on the Parliamentarian right, were coming around their flank and into the rear – an impression that was enhanced by the deployment of Byron's Horse, which moved around his younger brother's infantry. Their support was, however, severely hampered by the ground that was interspersed with hedges and enclosures. Fairfax adjusted his rear regiment, that of Booth and Holland, to counter this threat. Some while later, Gibson's men closed on the Parliamentarian vanguard to the east, thereby giving the impression of two separate attacks. 'Thus was ye battle divided, there being a Quarter of a mile betweene us', Fairfax wrote.[9] Both attacks appeared to be having

success, as Byron recalled: 'At the first encounter we had much the better of them, both our wings clearly beating both theirs, and were possessed of many of their colours.'[10] However, both attacks began to lose momentum and Byron attributes the failure to his regimental commanders in the centre, 'had not Col. Warren's men and Sir Mich. Erneleßs at the same time (notwithstanding all the endeavours of their officers) retreated, without almost fighting a stroke; so that the enemies battle fell into the flanks of both our wings'.[11] The Irish troops' resolve for the King's cause had been tested and failed alarmingly.

To make matters far worse, at about this time, the garrison debouched from Nantwich. A force of about 700 men quickly drove off Hunckes' token covering force and fell upon Gibson's rear and the right wing of Earnley's Regiment, before making their way to Acton and silencing the Royalist guns. It was the culminating point in the battle. The Royalist regiments collapsed like dominoes and, had there been two more hours of daylight, the consequences would have been even more catastrophic for the Royalists. As it was, some 200 were killed and over 1,000 taken prisoner. They lost all their guns and their field equipment. Fairfax had taken a fearful risk in crossing in front of Byron's force but fortune had favoured his boldness – helped in no small order by the slow reaction by Byron's force to exploit the opportunity and the timely sortie by the small garrison at Nantwich. Their intervention turned a success into a resounding victory. For the King the loss was a bitter blow, shattering his hopes that the intervention of the troops from Ireland would be decisive. The news that many of the Irish prisoners had taken the Covenant to fight for Parliament rubbed salt into the wound. Charles blamed Byron's leadership and reacted by ordering Rupert north to assume command. The Royalists had to reconquer Cheshire and Lancashire or risk being split into two separate geographic entities.

In mid-February Rupert moved north, with an excellent cavalry formation of 700 horse, and established his base at Shrewsbury, where he linked up with the remnants of Byron's force. Within days, two more Irish regiments, under Colonel Henry Tillier, joined him there. By 1 March he had begun a campaign to regain control of Shropshire and Cheshire. He started proceedings by beating up a Roundhead cavalry concentration at Market Drayton on 4 March. He then rode north to meet with John Byron who had moved back to Chester. The atmosphere between the two generals was a touch frosty at first, but the situation thawed within days when Rupert received the King's urgent instruction to move immediately to assist Newark, which was under siege.

At the tail end of 1643, Sir John Meldrum had supported Cromwell's cavalry in Lincolnshire, before taking over command of the operations around Gainsborough and assisting Fairfax at Hull. In mid-February 1644 the Committee of Both Kingdoms had ordered him to collect a strong force and advance on Newark. He arrived there on 29 February with a group of between 6,000 and 7,000 men, two mortars and 11 heavy guns, including a mighty 32-pounder dubbed 'Sweet Lips'.[12] He completed the investment of the town on 6 March, after a bitterly contested struggle for Muskham (draw) bridge and sconce. He then ordered a more substantial wooden bridge to be constructed and, once complete, he moved a pair of heavy guns

---

5 There is considerable confusion about the bridges at the time. See Dore & Lowe, op. cit., pp. 121–2.

6 Letter, Byron to Ormond, op. cit., p. 38.

7 Fairfax, loc. cit.

8 Barratt concludes, in *Battle of Nantwich*, p. 15, that Byron's horse was not up by the time Fairfax began this manoeuvre and I would concur.

9 Fairfax, loc. cit.

10 Letter, Byron to Ormond, op. cit., p. 38.

11 Ibid.

12 Matthews, *Sieges of Newark*, p. 28. The gun was named by the gunmaker in Hull after a local prostitute. As Matthews points out, quite what the Puritans made of this nickname is anybody's guess.

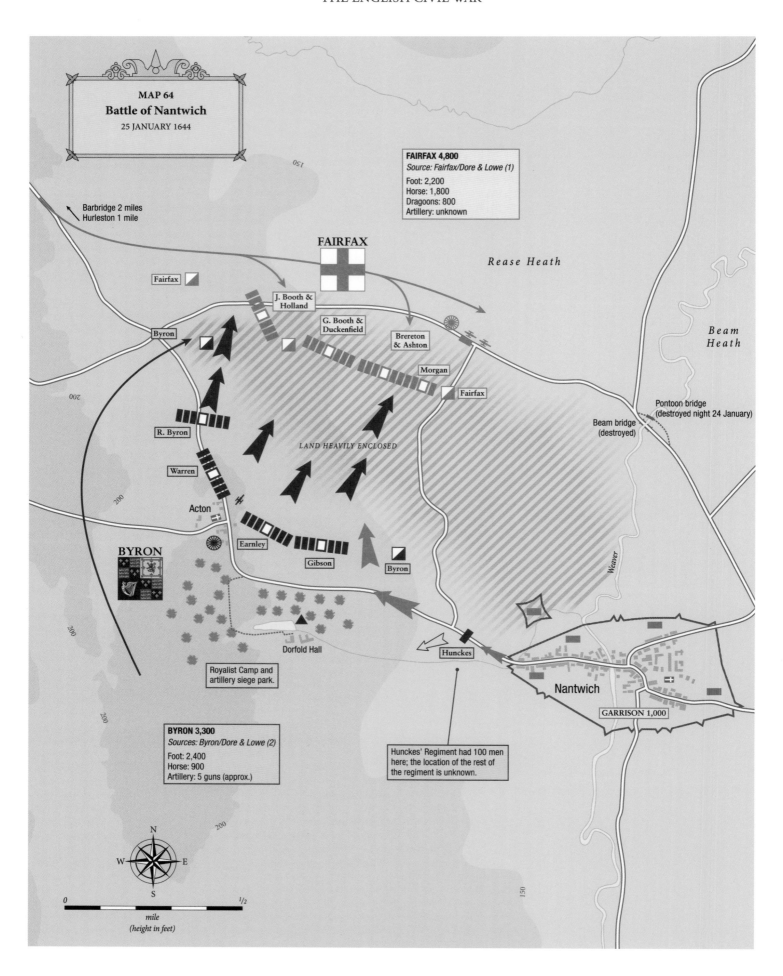

MAP 64

Battle of Nantwich

25 JANUARY 1644

FAIRFAX 4,800
Source: Fairfax/Dore & Lowe (1)
Foot: 2,200
Horse: 1,800
Dragoons: 800
Artillery: unknown

Barbridge 2 miles
Hurleston 1 mile

Rease Heath

FAIRFAX

Fairfax

J. Booth &
Holland

Byron

G. Booth &
Duckenfield

Brereton
& Ashton

*Beam
Heath*

R. Byron

Morgan

Fairfax

Warren

LAND HEAVILY ENCLOSED

Pontoon bridge
(destroyed night 24 January)

Beam bridge
(destroyed)

Acton

Earnley

BYRON

Gibson

Byron

Weaver

Dorfold Hall

Hunckes

Royalist Camp and
artillery siege park.

BYRON 3,300
Sources: Byron/Dore & Lowe (2)
Foot: 2,400
Horse: 900
Artillery: 5 guns (approx.)

Hunckes' Regiment had 100 men
here; the location of the rest of
the regiment is unknown.

Nantwich

GARRISON 1,000

N
W   E
S

0   1/2

mile
(height in feet)

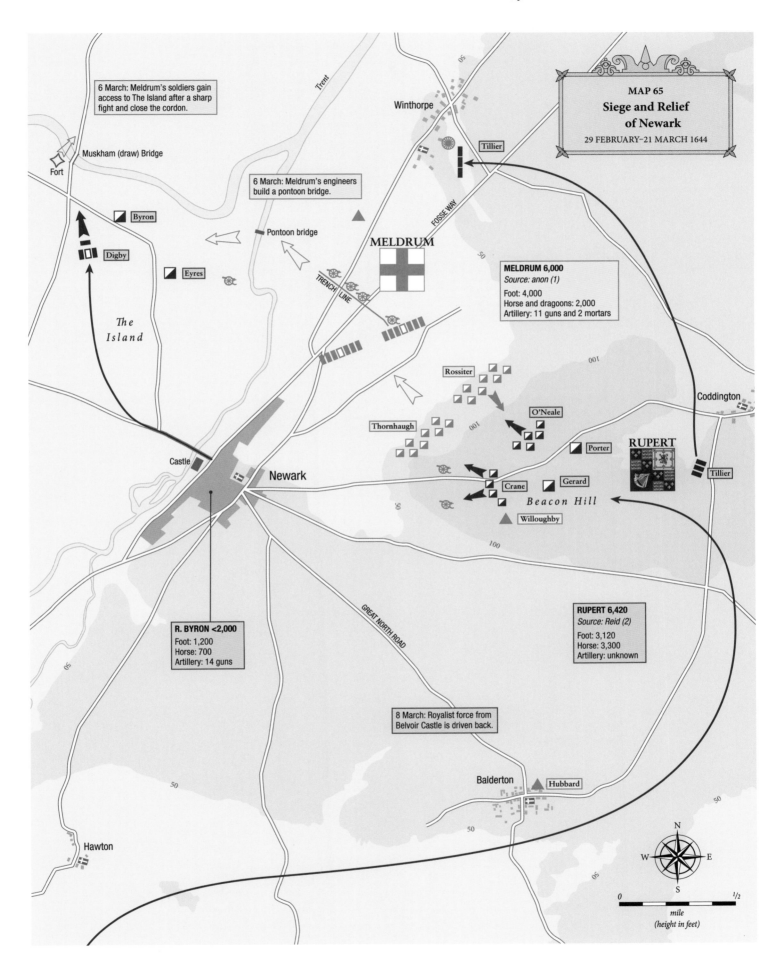

6 March: Meldrum's soldiers gain access to The Island after a sharp fight and close the cordon.

Muskham (draw) Bridge

Fort

6 March: Meldrum's engineers build a pontoon bridge.

Byron

Digby

Eyres

Pontoon bridge

The Island

Winthorpe

Tillier

Trent

FOSSE WAY

MELDRUM

TRENCH LINE

Castle

Newark

Rossiter

Thornhaugh

O'Neale

Porter

RUPERT

Tillier

Coddington

Crane

Gerard

Beacon Hill

Willoughby

R. BYRON <2,000
Foot: 1,200
Horse: 700
Artillery: 14 guns

GREAT NORTH ROAD

MELDRUM 6,000
Source: anon (1)
Foot: 4,000
Horse and dragoons: 2,000
Artillery: 11 guns and 2 mortars

MAP 65
Siege and Relief of Newark
29 FEBRUARY–21 MARCH 1644

RUPERT 6,420
Source: Reid (2)
Foot: 3,120
Horse: 3,300
Artillery: unknown

8 March: Royalist force from Belvoir Castle is driven back.

Balderton

Hubbard

Hawton

N
W   E
S

0   1/2

mile
(height in feet)

onto 'The Island' to bombard the northwest walls of the town and the castle. The Royalist garrison commander, Richard Byron, had over a thousand infantry and six troops of horse but this was inadequate to man the walls and commit to open battle by sally.[13] He had communicated his concerns in January to headquarters at Oxford but he began to feel increasingly isolated when Newcastle moved his army north (from the Midlands) in mid-January. An attempt to raise the siege on 8 March, by Gervase Lucas and the Newark Horse, was easily beaten off. Byron sent repeated requests for reinforcement and watched the Parliamentarian siege lines encroach towards the walls with growing apprehension.

Rupert moved across the Midlands, collecting reinforcements from every garrison along the route (see map 63). Meldrum had been kept abreast of Royalists movements and he sent out Edward Harrop, with a large body of cavalry, to try to disrupt Rupert's movement and the apparent ease with which he was able to recruit and expand the size of his force. It is not unreasonable to suggest that Harrop failed miserably in his task. On 20 March, Rupert was 10 miles short of his objective with a mixed force of over 6,000 men. Rupert gathered all the intelligence he could on the lie of the land and the Parliamentarian deployment and dispositions. He was only too well aware that his infantry was of dubious quality, largely comprised of garrison troops and not used to the particular challenges of standing in line of battle. He, therefore, elected for a short sharp action using his very capable cavalry and the more trustworthy of the foot soldiers. A little after midday, he broke camp with 1,000 horse and 500 infantry and made best speed north towards Newark. He did not approach, as suspected by Meldrum, from the west but had marched cross-country, leaving the Fosse Way, and approached from the south. As the first burst of dawn crested the sky on 21 March, Rupert was on Beacon Hill looking down on Meldrum's camp and siege lines. Meldrum, having been alerted to Rupert's presence, had withdrawn his forces and concentrated them around the siege lines (to

the north-east of the town). As Rupert had arrived, during the early morning hours, some of the last stragglers were still debouching from Beacon Hill.

Rupert decided not to wait for the rest of his force which was marching up the Great North Road. Sending Tillier's vanguard infantry to the north, in an attempt to attack and capture the pontoon bridge, he then charged the Parliamentarian cavalry to his front. Despite a successful counter-charge by Rossiter's man, Rupert succeeded in driving the Parliamentarians back down off the hill and behind their two lines of infantry. He would now have to wait for the balance of his infantry and his light artillery. Meanwhile, Tillier had failed to capture the bridge but he had closed the Lincoln road and this, as it turned out, was fortunate for the Royalists. For Meldrum rather lost his nerve and, still having the option of escaping over the bridge, ordered a retreat. Rupert ordered Tillier to hold his position and simultaneously ordered Byron to sally from the city and capture the Muskham Bridge.[14] As Byron's small force approached the defenders at the Muskham sconce they panicked, evacuated the fort and destroyed the drawbridge. Meldrum's entire force was now trapped. Realizing their predicament, some of his infantry mutinied and the next day Meldrum was forced into a humiliating surrender. One eyewitness recorded:

The rebels thus gone, we had the leasure to carry off their Arms and Ammunition, consisting of betwixt three and four thousand muskets, and a great quantity of Pikes and Pistolls, with the cannon they left behind... The number of slaine we know not; but we think they lost towards ninescore or two hundred, and we about half so many slaine and wounded. Thus, after just three weeks Siege, was Newark happily relieved.[15]

It was a remarkable feat, which did much to enhance Rupert's reputation while leaving that of Meldrum in tatters.

13 Richard was John Byron's eldest brother and succeeded to the title in 1652 on John Byron's death.

14 There is no record of just how he communicated with Byron.
15 Anon Eyewitness, *Rupert's raising of the siege*, p. 8.

CHAPTER 18
WALES: THE CONQUEST OF PEMBROKESHIRE, JANUARY TO MARCH 1644

When war had broken out in 1642, the direction Wales would take was not immediately apparent. Wales had been part of England since 1301, but it remained a separate entity with a different culture and language.[1] A fear of invasion by Catholics from Ireland or even Spain led to a general conservatism and a general loyalty towards the monarch. That loyalty was not, however, unquestioning. During the 1630s, Ship Tax had crippled Wales economically. By the end of the decade there were genuine concerns that it was driving ordinary Welshmen to poverty. The political crisis of 1641–42 at Westminster and the Irish rebellion across the water triggered panic in Wales, particularly in Pembrokeshire and Anglesey. Nevertheless, when Charles raised his Royal Standard in August 1642, it is not immediately apparent why virtually the whole of Wales came out in his support. Perhaps they were petrified by the alternatives. Wales did not have a strong commercial middling class and neither was it strongly in favour of Puritanism; it did, however, have an extensive and powerful Royalist elite and they were quick to overwhelm a fragmented opposition.[2] Within weeks all (bar one) of the Welsh counties had sent petitions of loyalty, obedience and support to the King and most counties had allowed control to be passed to pro-Royalist administrators and administrations. They quickly followed this show of allegiance by supplying large numbers of recruits and large amounts of materiel.

The situation in south-west Wales in 1643 was more complex. The rather lacklustre Earl of Carbery had wrestled Carmarthenshire and Cardiganshire from Parliamentary supporters, but he was less successful in Pembrokeshire. Parliament had invigorated the cause by sending naval ships to Milford Haven but, by the end of the year, the situation was in deadlock, with the Royalists holding most of the castles and large country houses, isolating many towns and villages with Parliamentarian sympathies. The Royalists attempted to break the deadlock by building a fort at Pill in order to command the Haven and thereby deny it as a safe naval anchorage. Parliament had stepped up its naval presence in the area at the back end of 1643 in an attempt to interdict the Royalist ships bringing back large numbers of troops from Ireland. Operating out of Milford Haven, Admiral Richard Swanley was reinforced by a strong fleet under Captain William Smith that set sail from Plymouth on 18 January. They arrived at Milford

five days later, having beaten around Land's End against inclement weather.[3] With this reinforcement in place, the Pembrokeshire Parliamentarian forces, under Colonel Rowland Laugharne, were stirred into action.

On 23 February, in a combined land and sea operation, Swanley and Laugharne attacked the unfinished fort at Pill. They bombarded the place from the sea and established a cordon on the land. (Naval) Captain William Smith, acting vice-admiral to Swanley, recorded that:

> About three of the clock in the morning they were landed, consisting of about 300 horse and foot [mainly seamen], with six field pieces of Ordnance; who preceding on their march, their Horse in the Front, they advanced before Pyll, about twelve of the clocke at no one. Or ships also were at anchor before the Fort…[4]

Two days later the small garrison and workforce surrendered and gave up a huge number of guns, powder and two ships, the *Globe of Bristol* and the *Providence*.[5] It marked a turning point, with many Royalist troops losing heart and evacuating the region. Simon Thelwall, a Welsh politician fighting for Parliament, recalled 'The news of the loss of this invincible fort quickly reached Haverford, where the great commanders, somewhat amazed, presently called a council, and therein, as appeared by the event, resolved nothing but a full purpose on our nearer approach to run away.'[6] Laugharne took command of the place the following morning before moving on to Roche Castle, which was summoned and delivered.

Swanley now ordered the navy to begin the bombardment of Tenby. Thelwall wrote that 'There was come to this place about by sea, the Vice-Admiral in the *Swallow*, and Captain Gettensby in the *Prosperous*, with the *Crescent* Frigate. We shot very thick upon the town before the land forces appeared.'[7] Tenby was a harder nut to crack and the Royalist garrison displayed considerably greater determination, but by 9 March the fort was also in the hands of Laugharne's forces. Carew Castle, the last Royalist stronghold, followed the next day, completing Parliament's conquest of Pembrokeshire. It remained a significant chink in the Royalists' Welsh armour.

---

1   Monmouthshire was, at this time, part of England although it was treated anomalously, with the result that its legal status as a Welsh county fell into some ambiguity and doubt until the 20th century, a situation that was not resolved until 1972.

2   Gaunt, *Civil War in Wales*, p. 16.

3   Smith, *Victorious successe of the ships*, p. 2.

4   Ibid., p. 5.

5   Ibid., p. 6.

6   Phillips, *Memoirs of the Civil War in Wales*, vol. II, p. 144.

7   Ibid., p. 145.

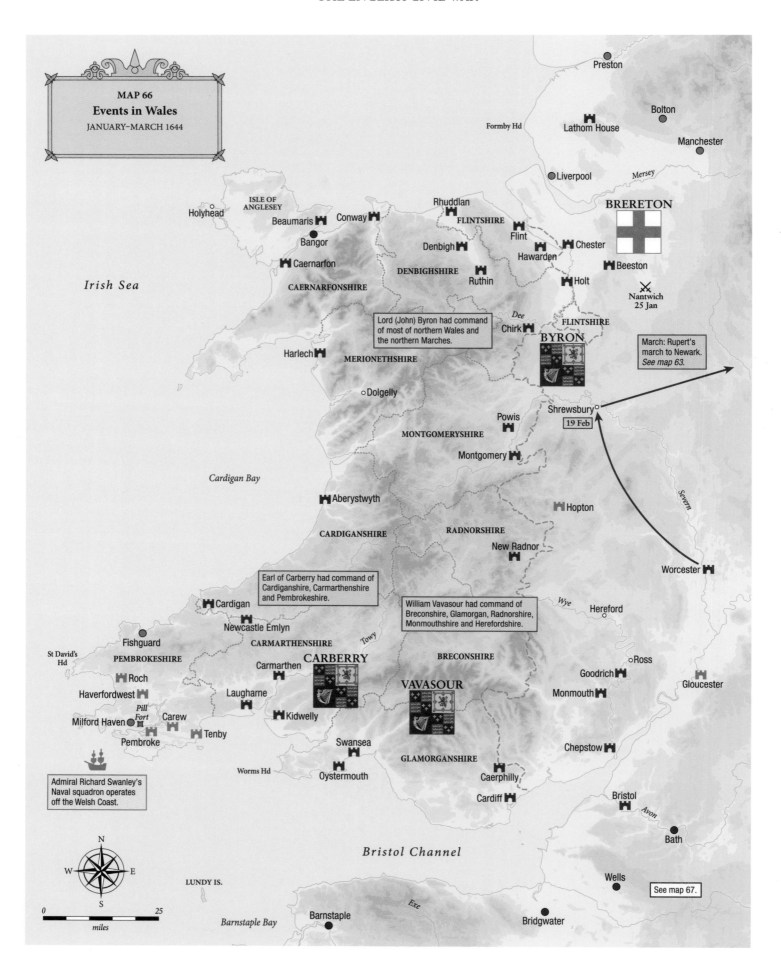

CHAPTER 19
WALLER'S OPERATIONS IN THE SOUTH, JANUARY TO APRIL 1644

Following the battle at Newbury, Hopton was summoned to a war council at Oriel College, Oxford, at which the King informed him of his new mission, 'that being reasonably well recovered of his hurts, he should draw into the field for the cleering of Dorsettshire, Wiltshire, and Hampshire, and so point forward as far as he could go towards London'.[1] In reality, Hopton had not fully recovered from his horrendous accident following the battle at Lansdown and, furthermore, Charles's ambitious plan for Hopton was not backed up by the provision of a suitable force or even the promise of reinforcements in due course. To make matters worse, even before his campaign got under way, he received news that a Roundhead force had attacked Winchester, and then, on 4 November, he received intelligence that Waller had moved towards the region from Windsor with a sizeable army. It may have been large, but it was untested, so Waller satisfied himself with conducting a series of sieges for the last few weeks of 1643 (see map 53). He aborted an attempt on Basing House but he defeated a Royalist outpost at Alton before moving towards Arundel Castle in late December. Hopton had only recently captured the castle and his apparent inability to counter Waller's advance led to renewed grumblings about his resolve in Oxford.

Waller captured Arundel Castle on 6 January, but before he could move west to confront Hopton heavy snow fell across the region and both sides went into winter quarters. This hiatus provided an opportunity for both sides to reorganize, replenish and reinforce their armies. For Waller's army, two new regiments of London trained bands were sent to replace the Westminster Regiment, which had behaved badly in front of Basing House, ultimately refusing to obey orders. In addition, a further 600 horse were (begrudgingly) sent from Essex's force to complete Waller's army, which now numbered about 10,000 men.[2] For the Royalists, Hopton did in fact receive a considerable reinforcement in early March, when Patrick Ruthven, the Earl of Forth, joined him with 1,200 foot, 800 horse and four cannon.[3] Forth was more senior than Hopton and his arrival was no coincidence (given the concerns in Oxford) and it could undoubtedly have led to awkwardness between the two men and consequent confusion in the army. However, Ruthven tactfully used his debilitative gout as a justification to leave Hopton in overall command.[4]

With an improvement in the weather, and with both forces reenergized, they now manoeuvred towards each other, commencing a taunting game of cat and mouse. In late March Hopton moved to Winchester and then, on receipt of intelligence that Waller had arranged a rendezvous at East Meon, he advanced towards the village. The two armies faced off for a day, but then

Hopton, thinking the stand-off might be a ruse to capture Winchester, doubled back towards New Alresford. Forth reached Alresford on 27 March with Waller's forces hot on their heels and slightly to the east. Hopton recalled that 'a mile and halfe before he came to Alsford, marching himselfe with Sir Edw. Stowell in the head of his brigade, did plainely discover Sir Wm. Belfore's troopes marching in the lane levell with them, and they were not a mile a sunder'.[5] The Royalists took possession of Alresford and their army encamped in Tichborne (or Sutton) Down, while Waller's army established themselves at 'Cheriton, to a place called by some, Lamborough-Field, where we quartered all night'.[6]

On the 28th both sides took stock of their situation and reconnoitred the lie of the land. For most of the day there were minor skirmishes in the area of East Down, the only open heathland in the vicinity, and for control of the southern hill that dominated the Parliamentarian camps.[7] By last light on the 28th it appears that the Royalists retained a foothold on that southern hill in a small copse. Hopton recalled:

> Wee disputed that ground that day with little partyes, and loose skirmishes, but towards the evening we gott the topp of the hill, and the view of the Enemye's quarters, where they encamped as is said before in a low field enclosed with a very thick hedge and ditch and theire ordnance planted upon the rysing of the hill behind them.[8]

Hopton placed there a strong picket under George Lisle, consisting of 1,000 musketeers and 500 horse.[9] Well aware of Waller's propensity for the unexpected, Hopton 'layed out the quarters for the whole army upon the same hill where they had stood in armes the night before, with command to

---

1 Hopton, *Bellum Civile*, p. 61.

2 *CSP-D* dated 4 March 1644 and H.T., *A glorious victorie*, p. 2.

3 Hopton, op. cit., p. 77. This raised his total strength to about 8,000. Walker, *Historical Discourses*, p. 7.

4 However, see Hopton, op. cit., p. 81, in which Hopton clearly states that Forth gave him orders at a critical moment.

5 Ibid., p. 79.

6 Archer, *Alsford*, p. 5. There remains doubt as to whether the battlefield is in the area of East Down (the traditional location) or in between the hill south of East Down, on the high ground overlooking Hinton Ampner. John Adair's detailed study (*Cheriton 1644*) concluded the latter; he is supported by another recent work by Laurence Spring, *The Battle of Cheriton*, and Malcolm Wanklyn, in his *Decisive Battles of the English Civil War*, suggests that Adair is 'probably correct'. Limited archaeological evidence is inconclusive but it does tend to support the traditional interpretation. However, detailed work over many years by Gary Chilcott and Adrien Webb has discovered that the only single area of over 200 acres of common and sheep pasture was at East Down. Therefore, in my opinion, East Down is the only candidate for the main cavalry action in accordance with the primary source accounts. It is also difficult to dispel Jones (*Letter from Captain Jones*, p. 6) in which he clearly states, 'the enemie lay in Sutton Down, we lay in Lumbourne field, we fought in East down between Cheriton and Alesford'.

7 H. T., op. cit., p. 4; Hopton, op. cit., p. 80.

8 Hopton, ibid.

9 The exact position of this copse/observation post is not clear but it was on the southern hill as it looked into the Parliamentary camps. The position annotated on map 68 is conjecture, although there is evidence of a copse on the ground.

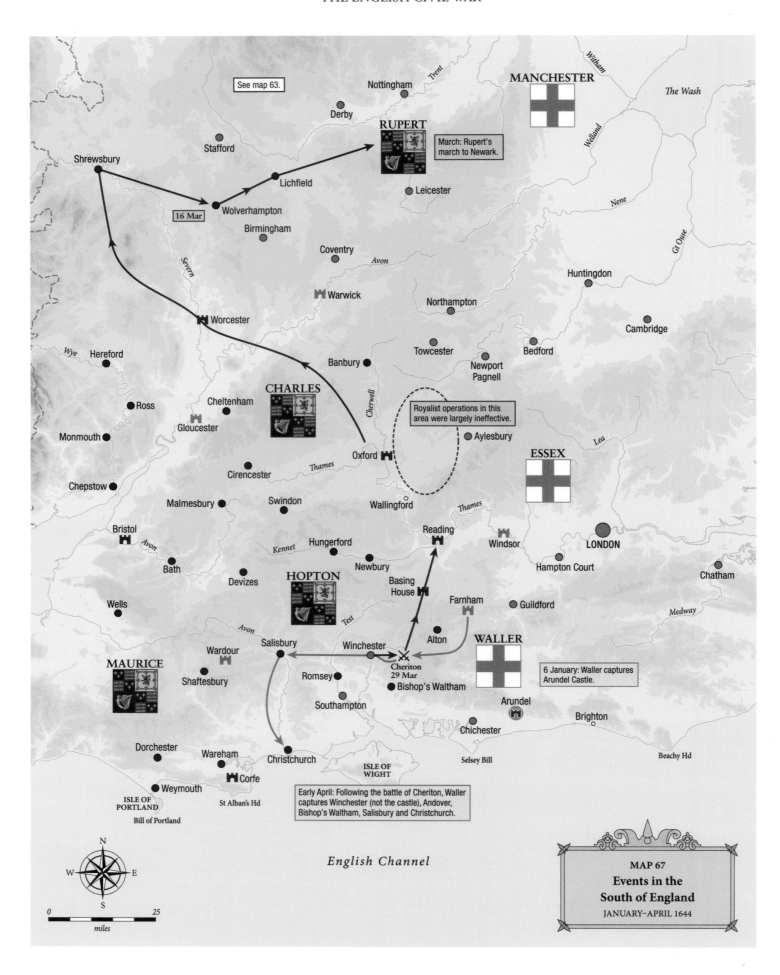

See map 63.

MANCHESTER

The Wash

Nottingham

Derby

RUPERT

March: Rupert's march to Newark.

Stafford

Shrewsbury

Lichfield

Leicester

16 Mar   Wolverhampton

Birmingham

Coventry   *Avon*

Warwick

Northampton

Huntingdon

Worcester

Wye   Hereford

Banbury

Towcester

Newport Pagnell

Bedford

Cambridge

Ross

CHARLES

Cheltenham

Gloucester

Royalist operations in this area were largely ineffective.

Aylesbury

ESSEX

Monmouth

Oxford

Cherwell

Chepstow

Cirencester

Thames

Malmesbury

Swindon

Wallingford

Thames   *Lea*

Reading

Windsor

LONDON

Bristol

Avon

Bath

Kennet

Hungerford

Newbury

Hampton Court

Chatham

Devizes

HOPTON

Basing House

Farnham

Guildford

Medway

Wells

Test

Avon

Salisbury

Winchester

Alton

WALLER

6 January: Waller captures Arundel Castle.

MAURICE

Wardour

Shaftesbury

Romsey

Cheriton 29 Mar

Bishop's Waltham

Southampton

Arundel

Brighton

Chichester

Dorchester

Wareham

Christchurch

ISLE OF WIGHT

Selsey Bill

Beachy Hd

Weymouth

Corfe

St Alban's Hd

Early April: Following the battle of Cheriton, Waller captures Winchester (not the castle), Andover, Bishop's Waltham, Salisbury and Christchurch.

ISLE OF PORTLAND

Bill of Portland

N   W   E   S

English Channel

0   25
miles

MAP 67

Events in the South of England

JANUARY–APRIL 1644

every horseman to rest by his horse, and every footeman by his armes, and every officer in his place'.[10] Not surprisingly, Lisle's men had a restless night. There were constant alarms, as sounds of movement and activity drifted across the night air. Before dawn, however, given the constant sounds of activity, Lisle concluded that Waller had broken camp and retreated.[11]

In fact Waller had other ideas. Before first light (at about 5am) he had sent a 1,000 musketeers, 300 horse and a couple of light guns to take Cheriton Wood and dominate the open land on East Down.[12] At the same time he dispatched a strong party of musketeers to line the hedges east of Cheriton near Lamborough Fields.[13] These movements were what Lisle's picket had heard. Without venturing out to confirm, they convinced themselves that the Parliamentarians were moving off under cover of darkness. Lisle sent word back to Hopton, who in turn informed Ruthven.[14] Ruthven then ordered the cavalry to be made ready to exploit the situation at dawn. However, Hopton was unsure and he decided to move to Lisle's observation post to see for himself. As dawn broke and the mist cleared, the two men could see the Roundhead troops concentrated on their left and right, those in Cheriton Wood completely dominating his position. They had not withdrawn at all and now held both flanks of the field with the Royalist picket between their jaws. Colonel Slingsby, a Royalist infantry commander, recorded that 'the Enemy had placed a thowsand musketeires and two peice of cannon in a thick wood which stood upon his right hand and helped him to aduance soe muche ground securely towardes the hill where wee intended to fight, which lay in the middle way or rather more towards his Camp'.[15]

Hopton raced back towards the Royalist lines and reported the reality to Ruthven, and he 'seeing the posture the Enemy was in, commanded the Lord Hopton to drawe the whole Army and cannon up to him to that ground, which he did accordingly'.[16] As the Royalist army advanced, they came under effective artillery and musket fire from Cheriton Wood. Hopton then 'commanded Coll. Appleyeard to draw out of the foote a commanded party of 1000 muskettiers, which he did, and devided them into 4 devisions, and in that order advanced towards the Enemy'.[17] Appleyard's men were initially driven back by accurate musket fire from the infantry along the edge of the wood and the attack quickly lost momentum. Hopton then intervened and ordered one of the divisions, under the command of his son Edward, to make a rush for the wood and to work around the flank of the Roundhead musketeers. 'Coll. Appleyeard with his party pursued them, and had the execution of a part of them through the wood, and possest himselfe of all theire ground of advantage, and tooke a horse Colours and some prisoners, but none of theire cannon, for they being light gunns were drawen off'.[18]

It is during this time that the Parliamentarian army had marched up the rear slope of southern hill. Lisle and his picket had extracted themselves by

this juncture. Captain Harley was in charge of a Parliamentarian company in the advance. He recalled:

> ... their was on the right hand of us – as we were now faced – a woode, which we did conceive might be of great advantage to us if it were maintained... on the left of us was hedges and a little village. We sent a very strong partee of muskettiers to line those hedges.[19]

Following the loss of Cheriton Wood, Harley recalled the disappointment of seeing the men fall back: 'Noe sooner they did see that the bullets would come otherwise then they would have them, but they made a foul retreat – I am confident I smelt them – with a fair paire of heeles, which do so discourage the rest.'[20]

About half a mile now separated the two armies and Ruthven advised Hopton to leave the next move to Waller:

> Having now possest all the ground of advantage on our side, his opinion was that wee should not hazard any farther attempt, for that he conceived the Enemy would now be forced, either to charge us upon their disadvantage, or to retire. The Lord Hopton remayn'd extremely satisfyed with that solid advice.[21]

It was probably about noon when Captain Harley recalled, 'the enemy being nowe possessed the woode, wee drewe downe *all* our horse into a heath, which stood betwixt the two hills'.[22] As Hopton was returning towards the centre of the Royalist position he realized that some of the infantry on the right wing had moved to clear the Parliamentarian dragoons that were lining the hedges near to Cheriton village. The attack was being executed by Henry Bard's Brigade. Hopton later claimed:

> ... he saw troopes of the right whing too farr advanced, and hotly engaged with the Enemy in the foote of the hill, and so hard prest, as when he came to the Lord Brainford, he found him much troubled with it, for, it seems the engagement was by the forwardnes of some particular officers, without order.[23]

But Slingsby records the event differently:

> This encourag'd us soe muche [i.e. the capture of Cheriton Wood] that wee made too muche hast to finishe the businesse... but wee were order'd to fall on from both wings, which was the only cause of theire standing to fight; for then the Enemy finds most of our strength drawne of the hill into a bottome, where hee had his desir'd advantage: and our first mischance hapned on our right wing, where Sir Henry Bard, leading on his Regiment further then hee had orders for.[24]

Whatever the cause, the tables were now about to be turned.

---

10 Hopton, op. cit. This is clearly the northern hill to the south of the Royalist bivouac areas on Sutton Common and near the road to Alresford.

11 There is evidence to suggest that news of the defeat at Newark had prompted suggestions that the Parliamentarians should retreat.

12 Portland MS, *Captain Robert Harley*, p. 108. This is almost certainly Cheriton Wood – as it is now called.

13 Jones, op. cit., pp. 2–3. Portland MS, *Harley*, loc. cit.

14 Hopton, op. cit., pp. 80–1.

15 Slingsby, *Bellum Civile*, p. 101. The question is, which hill is middle hill? As the Parliamentarians held Cheriton Wood, and the hedge line near Cheriton village, I believe this must be the hill of East Down. This fits with Captain Harley's account.

16 Hopton, op. cit., p. 80.

17 Ibid, p. 81.

18 Ibid.

19 Portland MS, *Harley*, loc. cit. This is a crucial account, as it is clear that the Parliamentarian position is atop the southern hill and not the hill above Hinton Ampner.

20 Portland MS, *Harley*, loc. cit.

21 Hopton, op. cit., p. 82.

22 Portland MS, *Harley*, loc. cit. The only area of open heathland large enough to accommodate so much cavalry was that from Cheriton Land to East Down.

23 Hopton, loc. cit.

24 Slingsby, loc. cit.

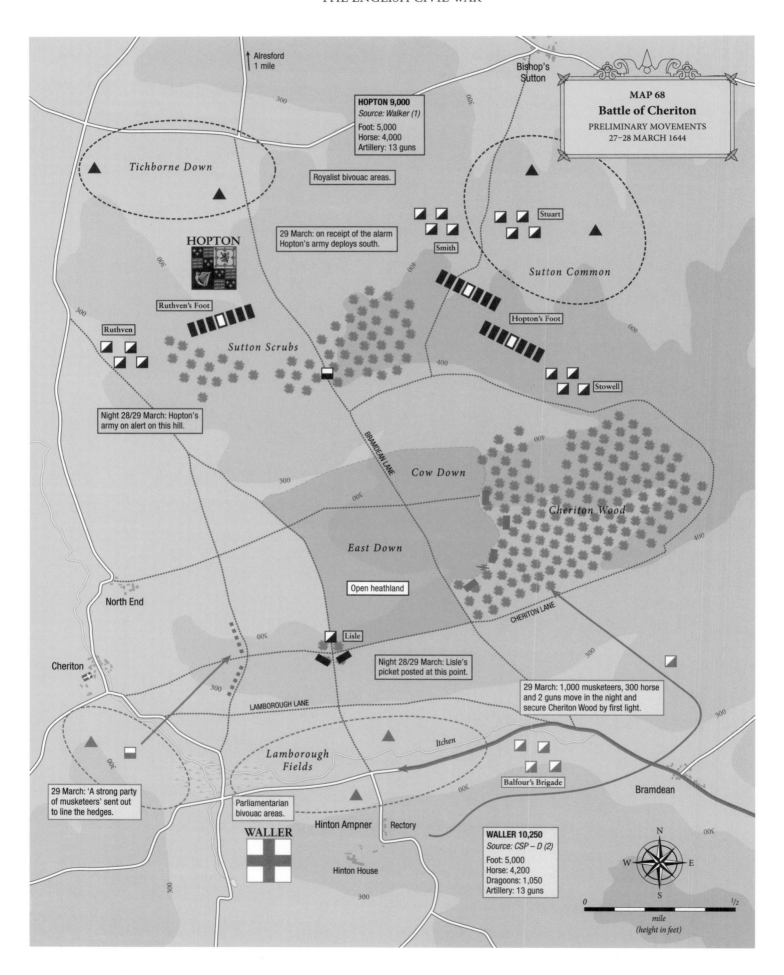

↑ Alresford
1 mile

Bishop's
Sutton

MAP 68
Battle of Cheriton
PRELIMINARY MOVEMENTS
27–28 MARCH 1644

Tichborne Down

HOPTON 9,000
Source: Walker (1)
Foot: 5,000
Horse: 4,000
Artillery: 13 guns

Royalist bivouac areas.

HOPTON

Stuart

29 March: on receipt of the alarm
Hopton's army deploys south.

Smith

Sutton Common

Ruthven's Foot

Hopton's Foot

Ruthven

Sutton Scrubs

Stowell

Night 28/29 March: Hopton's
army on alert on this hill.

Cow Down

Cheriton Wood

East Down

Open heathland

North End

BRAMDEAN LANE

Lisle

Night 28/29 March: Lisle's
picket posted at this point.

29 March: 1,000 musketeers, 300 horse
and 2 guns move in the night and
secure Cheriton Wood by first light.

CHERITON LANE

Cheriton

Itchen

*Lamborough
Fields*

Balfour's Brigade

LAMBOROUGH LANE

Bramdean

29 March: 'A strong party
of musketeers' sent out
to line the hedges.

Parliamentarian
bivouac areas.

Hinton Ampner

Rectory

WALLER

WALLER 10,250
Source: CSP – D (2)
Foot: 5,000
Horse: 4,200
Dragoons: 1,050
Artillery: 13 guns

Hinton House

N
W E
S

0   1/2
mile
(height in feet)

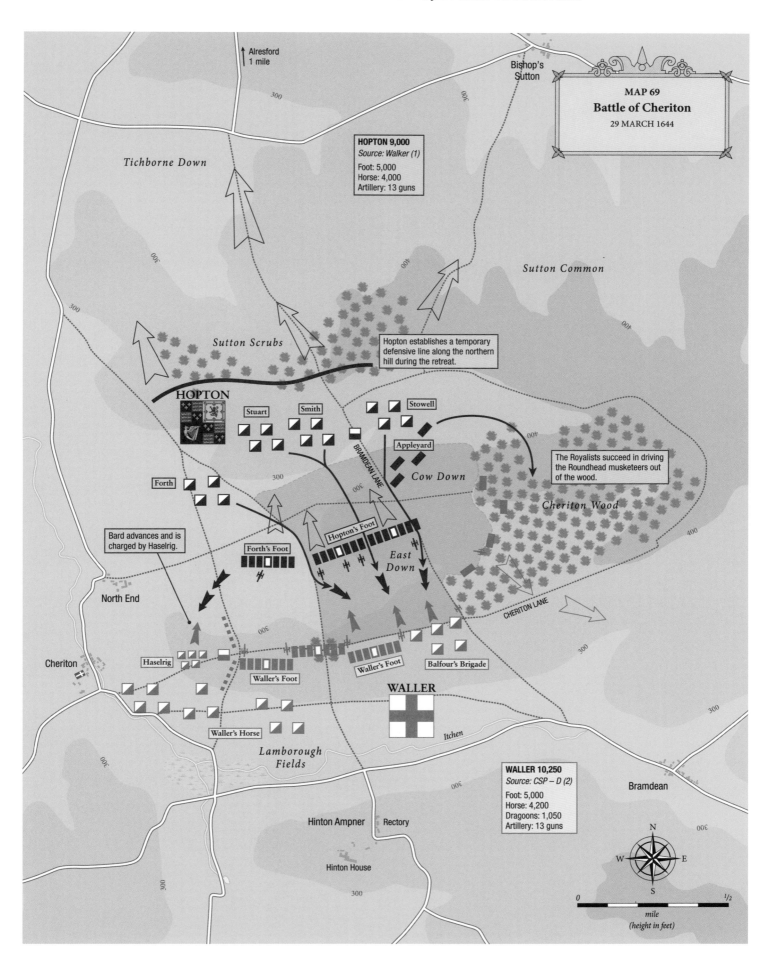

Alresford
1 mile

Bishop's
Sutton

MAP 69
Battle of Cheriton
29 MARCH 1644

Tichborne Down

300

300

Sutton Common

400

300

400

300

HOPTON 9,000
Source: Walker (1)
Foot: 5,000
Horse: 4,000
Artillery: 13 guns

Sutton Scrubs

Hopton establishes a temporary
defensive line along the northern
hill during the retreat.

HOPTON

Stuart   Smith   Stowell

Appleyard

Cow Down

The Royalists succeed in driving
the Roundhead musketeers out
of the wood.

400

Cheriton Wood

400

Forth

300

300

Hopton's Foot

Bard advances and is
charged by Haselrig.

*East
Down*

Forth's Foot

CHERITON LANE

North End

300

Cheriton

Haselrig

Waller's Foot

Waller's Foot

Balfour's Brigade

300

Waller's Horse

WALLER

Itchen

*Lamborough
Fields*

300

Bramdean

Hinton Ampner   Rectory

WALLER 10,250
Source: CSP – D (2)
Foot: 5,000
Horse: 4,200
Dragoons: 1,050
Artillery: 13 guns

Hinton House

300

N
W   E
S

300

0   1/2

mile
(height in feet)

The first regiment of Parliamentarian horse to arrive to counter the Royalist attack was the battle-hardened troopers of Sir Arthur Haselrig. Slingsby recalled that they made short work of Bard's Regiment. 'Out of his ground, who incontinently thrusts Sir Arthur Haselrig's regiment of horse, well arm'd, betwixt him and home, and theire in the view of our whole Army (much to our discouragement) kills and takes every man.'[25] This engagement drew the Royalist cavalry to the valley floor, which promoted a charge across the heath by all of Balfour's cavalry. Their first charge was repulsed but the second was more successful:

> They immediately try'd the second charge in which Captain Herbert of my Lord Hoptons Regiment was slaine, with a fresh body and were againe repulssed, and soe againe the third time, the foote keeping theire ground in a close body, not firing till within two pikes length, and then three rankes at a time, after turning up the butt end of theire musketts, charging theire pikes, and standing close, preserv'd themselues, and slew many of the enemy.[26]

This was a precursor to a series of a somewhat sporadic set of cavalry actions, interspersed with infantry engagements (largely) on the flanks. They continued for some three to four hours. Slingsby suggests that the cavalry could not get through the tight hedge-lined lanes and out on to the open heathland in sufficient numbers before being counter-charged.[27]

Towards the latter stages Waller's infantry began to advance. Gradually, the Royalist cavalry and infantry were beaten back to the top of the hill and, after making a brief stand, Hopton decided to retreat. He recalled:

> … making our reare as good as we could with some of the best of our horse and dragoons, we recovered our first ground upon the ridge of the hill by Alsford-towne, with all our Army, cannon and carriages; from whence we shewed so good a countenance towards the Enemy, that they gave us some respitt, unwilling (as it seem'd) to hazard theire whole army upon us.[28]

The Royalists had great difficulty maintaining discipline and in drawing off their cannon, but the Parliamentarians were tired and Waller was well aware that extending the attack beyond the northern hill and into Alresford was risky. However, some in the Parliamentarian high command disagreed, and while the matter was hotly debated, the Royalists took the opportunity to make good their escape.[29]

Hopton and Ruthven resolved to pull back to the north, rather than fall back on Winchester. In the early hours of 30 March, the exhausted Royalist troops reached Basing House, where they rested for a day before retreating further back towards Reading. Waller was not inclined to follow and instead moved west and captured Winchester (although the Royalist garrison held on to the castle), Bishop's Waltham, Andover, Salisbury, and finally, he cleared the Royalist garrison from the town of Christchurch. There can be little doubt that Cheriton was a significant, if not decisive, battle. It certainly repaired and enhanced Waller's reputation, although it is only fair to note that the leadership shown by both Ruthven and Hopton was somewhat questionable. More noteworthy perhaps, the engagement at Cheriton was to be the last offensive operation mounted by the Royalists for the rest of the First Civil War.[30]

25 Slingsby, Ibid, p. 102. They were armed as harquebusiers at this stage of the war.
26 Ibid.
27 Ibid.
28 Hopton, op. cit., p. 83.
29 Portland MS, *Harley*, op. cit., p. 109.
30 Adair, op. cit., pp. 148–9.

CHAPTER 20
THE GREAT SIEGE AND BATTLE IN YORKSHIRE, APRIL TO AUGUST 1644

Charles had signed Montrose's commission as Captain General of Scotland in February but gathering the clans had been problematic. The industrious Montrose had, therefore, spent much of March south of the border gathering a force in Cumberland, and in early April he crossed back into Scotland at Gretna Green at the head of a small contingent of 2,000 men. On 15 April the town of Dumfries threw open its gates and Montrose waited there for the promised reinforcement from the MacDonalds and Gordons. This intrusion, rather than invasion, had taken the Covenanters by surprise, but it was not long before a force had gathered at Selkirk to challenge Montrose's merry band. With no sign of any further reinforcements, and his force still woefully inadequate particularly in horse, Montrose was forced to pull back to Carlisle. Once there his English troops threatened to mutiny if Montrose moved back into Scotland.[1] Montrose's foray therefore failed completely. Meanwhile, the other Royalist laird, George Gordon the Marquis of Huntly, had made some small gains in Deeside. But when the Earl of Argyll, at the head of an army nearly 5,000 strong, recaptured Aberdeen in early May, Huntly fled and the gains were ceded. For now, the Royalist threat in Scotland had been smothered.

In the north of England, Leven's Scottish army and the Parliamentarian army of Lord Fairfax were beginning to tighten the noose around Newcastle's overstretched force. On 8 April Leven had cut the road south of Durham, forcing Newcastle to fight or pull back. While he pondered, considering his options, the Fairfaxes linked up and captured Selby on the 11th. Newcastle, conscious of the danger this posed to his rear, pulled back to York, which he entered on 18 April. Fairfax and Leven joined forces at Wetherby on 20 April, and three days later they had a loose cordon around York. Newcastle sent a desperate message to the King, escorted by the greater part of his cavalry. It was what he had predicted and feared. The great siege of York, the Royalist headquarters in the north, had begun.

Since 1642 a considerable amount of work had been undertaken to strengthen the defences of the city. At least five fortifications had been constructed outside the city walls.[2] The largest was a sconce on The Mount located outside the Micklegate Bar, on the Tadcaster road. Henry Slingsby, an infantry commander within the garrison, recalled:

> …the Scots rendezvous was upon Bramham Moor, where he & my Ld. Fairfax meets, & takes up their Quarters; The Scots at Bishopthorp & Middlethorp, my Ld Fairfax at Foulfourth & Hesslington, by making over Ouse a bridge of boats. Thus we were blockt up upon two sides of ye town, & ye rest we had open for about 3 weeks, until such times as my Ld Manchester came with his Norfolk men, whom it seem'd ye Scots did expect.[3]

The garrison had a plentiful supply of provisions but it was short of both money and powder.

Despite having a combined force of over 20,000 men, Fairfax and Leven appear to have done little in the first month of the siege. Fairfax noted that 'for this worke it was thought fit to have more men, the Towne being large in Compasse, and Strongly Manned'.[4] Nor do they appear to have closed the cordon between the rivers Ouse and Foss to the north of the city. The combined armies did, however, attack and destroy, or eliminate, a number of Royalist strongholds in castles and towns surrounding York. The most notable was at Stamford Bridge, where 80 Royalist infantry were captured, and Cawood Castle, which the Royalists tried unsuccessfully to recapture.[5] But Lord Fairfax and the Earl of Leven had concluded that more troops were required to prosecute the siege and 'therefore ye E. of Crawford, Lyndsey & myself [Tom Fairfax] were sent to ye E. of Manchester to desire him to Joyne with us in ye seidge, which he willingly consented to, bringing an addition of 6000 Foot, and 3000 Horse with him'.[6]

Manchester had surrounded and captured the city of Lincoln by 6 May (capturing 1,000 prisoners and eight guns) but he was not ready to move north for another three weeks.[7] Manchester's army, when it did finally arrive on 3 June, was allocated the northern section, closing the cordon. Another pontoon bridge was constructed over the River Ouse to the north and a fort built on the Scottish side to provide protection to the wooden connection. Two days later the besiegers made their first move. Manchester's and Leven's troops moved menacingly towards the city, to act as a distraction, while Fairfax moved onto Windmill Hill and established a heavy battery (battery 1) and then pushed on to Walmgate Bar where a three-gun battery (battery 2) was hastily placed.[8] On 6 June Manchester's men attacked the Bootham Bar, gaining a lodgement in the suburbs, where they began to dig a mine under St Mary's tower. The first major assault took place the next day when the Scots attacked the three Royalist forts to the south-west of the city. They captured all three, taking over 200 prisoners, although the Royalists did manage to recapture The Mount, the largest of the forts, after a swift counter-attack. Newcastle decided that the besiegers' task was being made too easy for them and, soon after this attack, he ordered the torching of the suburbs. Simeon Ashe, a chaplain in Manchester's army, recalled that 'upon Saturday the 8 day in the morning, a souldier of the Marquess of Newcastle was taken in the Earl of Manchester's leager: he was in a red suit, he had pitch, flax

---

1 Wedgwood, *Montrose*, p. 62.

2 Those depicted on map 71 are from Wenham, *The Great and Close Siege of York*. The exact locations are not known.

3 Parsons, *Henry Slingsby*, p. 107.

4 Fairfax, *Short memorials*, p. 220.

5 Wenham, op. cit., p. 18; Cook, *Yorkshire Sieges*, p. 34.

6 Fairfax, loc. cit.

7 Goode, *Successes of the Right Honorable the Earle of Manchester's army*, p. 6.

8 There were a number of dwellings outside the gates; these are not depicted, as the extent is unknown. However, it is clear that these had not been destroyed and, as such, they were a considerable advantage to the attackers.

and other materials upon him for fiering of the suburbs there, as yet free from the wasting flames'.[9]

Throughout early June Newcastle was aware that Prince Rupert, who was causing havoc in Lancashire, was most likely to be despatched to York with a relieving force.[10] He needed, therefore, to play for time and during the evening of 8 June sent a letter to Fairfax and Leven to do just that. The allied commanders were also well aware of Rupert's antics. In fact, they had been under pressure from the Committee of Both Kingdoms to despatch troops across the Pennines to counter the threat.[11] However, they had rejected the proposal of lifting the siege, but Newcastle's letter now opened the opportunity for a peaceful solution and the opportunity to move against Rupert. Newcastle prolonged communications and stalled at every opportunity, insisting that there should be a general ceasefire before any serious talks could resume. Having gained a week, a parley was scheduled for 3pm on 14 June and a tent was erected for the purpose to the south of the city. Newcastle stated the Royalist conditions for surrender, and the allied commissioners, having sought guidance, submitted counterproposals. The sticking point was the existence of Newcastle's army after capitulation. The next morning Newcastle gave his reply. Despite being a disappointment, it came as little surprise to the allied council. The ceasefire was at an end.

Following the raising of the siege at Newark, Rupert had returned to Oxford. It soon became apparent that a repeat performance of his operation to relieve Newark would be highly desirable at York. On 5 May Rupert headed north to Cheshire and then to the Marches in order to raise an army. By 23 May he had a force of 2,000 horse and 6,000 foot. He decided to cross the River Mersey at Stockport. He closed on the town two days later, causing panic among the town's large defence force. After a brief skirmish on the outskirts, the Parliamentarians pulled back into Stockport, but when Rupert advanced at the head of a large cavalry force it was enough to trigger a flight. The escaping troops (possibly as many as 2,000) made it to Manchester, although many were killed or captured during the flight. On 28 May, Rupert's force arrived on the outskirts of Bolton, hoping for a similar outcome. However, he was unaware that the 2,000-strong besieging force from Lathom House (under the command of Colonel Rigby) had withdrawn into the town the day prior. There were some 3,500 men and a number of pieces of ordnance within the Lancashire town. Rupert, once apprised, remained unperturbed. With the arrival of the Earl of Derby's troops, he now had between 10,000 and 12,000 men.[12] Rupert's summons was met by cannon fire and he immediately responded by ordering a general attack. It was repulsed with trifling loss. Rupert ordered a second attack, during which some Royalist horse gained access to the north-west of the town. They made their way through the streets causing mayhem, precipitating a complete collapse. What happened next has been subject to discriminatory accounts by both sides. Royalist reports record the killing of a number of soldiers in a great victory, while Parliamentarian accounts claim that a massacre took place following the collapse of the town's defences.

Two days later Rupert received another large reinforcement, when he linked up with Colonel Goring and the Northern Horse. His strength was now estimated at 6,000 foot and 7,000 horse and it was causing considerable

concern to the Committee of Both Kingdoms and no little panic among the Parliamentarian garrisons in Lancashire.[13] Rupert's next target was Liverpool. The city, and vital port, had been taken by Parliament in April 1643, and its loss had been felt acutely by the Royalists during the subsequent movement of troops from Ireland. The Parliamentarian garrison numbered a mere 600 men, but it was supplemented by sailors and could be supported by troops sent down the Mersey from Manchester. The Royalists arrived at the outskirts of the city on 7 June and began an immediate bombardment lasting two days. On 10 June, with the city's walls having collapsed in many places, the Royalist assault was delivered. It was beaten back, but the defenders decided to evacuate the place by sea and the next day Rupert had his prize. The force remained in the city for over a week during which time Rupert visited the Countess of Derby, Charlotte de la Tremoüille, at Lathom House, the brave defender who had defied the Parliamentarian siege force since February.

In the meantime, the Committee of Both Kingdoms was issuing orders to all the northern garrisons to move all their available troops to oppose Rupert's operations in Lancashire. Then, on 19 June, Rupert received a letter from the King. This letter, which became most contentious *ex post facto*, was taken by Rupert to be a direct order to march to the relief of York.[14] Rupert drew his force together and set off east across the Yorkshire Dales. By 26 June he was at the Royalist stronghold at Skipton, where he rested his force and sent word to Newcastle of his impending arrival. Meanwhile, inside York the Royalist defenders had withstood renewed attacks since 16 June when the ceasefire had ended. Early in the morning on the 16th, Manchester's artillery had battered a hole in the medieval walls next to St Mary's Tower. Slingsby remembered:

> … we fall to work & make it up with earth & sods; this happn'd in ye morning: at noon they spring ye mine under St. Mary's tower, & blows up one part of it, which falling outwards made ye access more easy; Then some at ye breach, some with Ladders, getts up & enters, near 500.[15]

General Lawrence Crawford led the attack at the head of a force of 500 or 600 men. They were quickly counter-attacked and driven back with the loss of 200 killed or taken prisoner. Meanwhile, at Walmgate Bar, Fairfax's artillery had reduced the structure to rubble and the defenders stole themselves for the inevitable assault. It never came. On 24 June, Newcastle ordered a sally from the Monk Bar, which was also largely ineffectual. The fact of the matter was that both sides were well aware that Rupert's large force was closing fast.

On 28 June the allied commanders lifted the siege, but they had every intention of maintaining the cordon. Meldrum's men in Manchester and Denbigh's men in Staffordshire were both ordered to move with haste to the area in order to provide sufficient forces to execute this plan. However, when they had failed to arrive by 1 July, the allied commanders were forced to abandon the siege lines, leaving many of the heavier guns and siege equipment in situ. Their priority now was to meet and defeat the Royalist force. They advanced a few miles to the south-west and deployed on a ridge

9   Ashe, *True intelligence from the English and Scottish forces*, Number 4, 8–17 June 1644, p. 1.

10 The garrison were able to receive signals from Pontefract Castle, which could be seen from the tower at York Minster. Cook, op. cit., p. 38.

11 Ibid., p. 36.

12 Ibid., p. 75.

13 Firth, *Marston Moor*, p. 20.

14 Rupert, *Memoirs*, vol. II, pp. 437–9. The letter remains controversial and Rupert is said to have carried it on his person for the rest of his life. Cook, ibid., pp. 172–4 gives a good analysis of the correspondence.

15 Parsons, op. cit., p. 109.

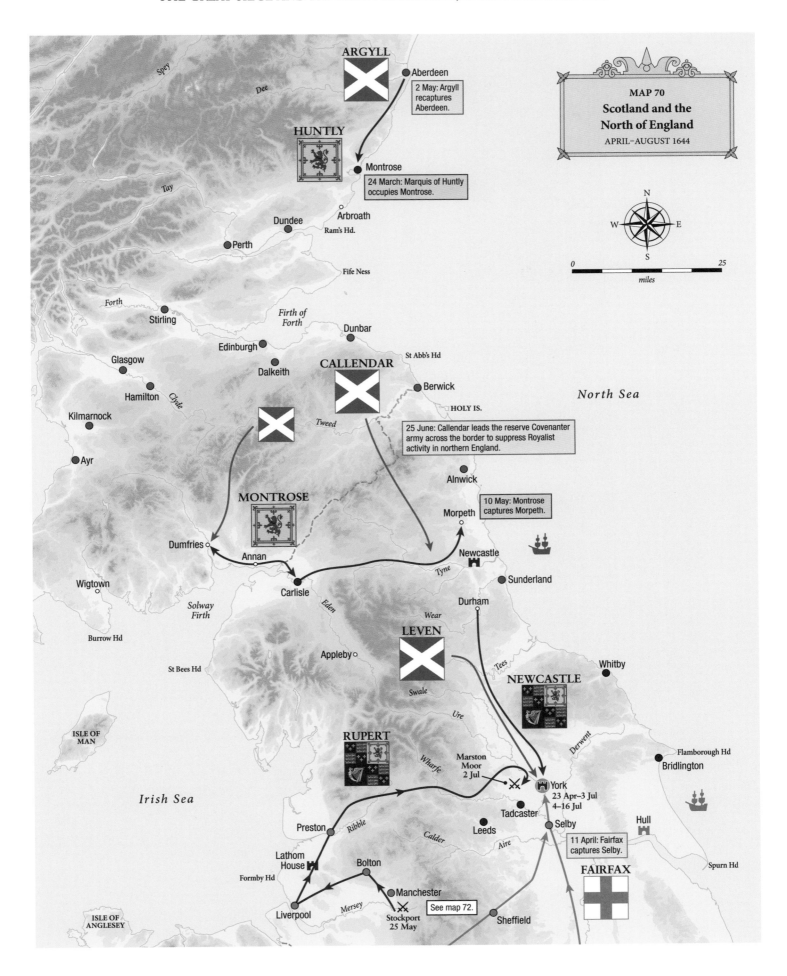

ARGYLL

Aberdeen

2 May: Argyll recaptures Aberdeen.

HUNTLY

Montrose

24 March: Marquis of Huntly occupies Montrose.

MAP 70
Scotland and the North of England
APRIL–AUGUST 1644

Spey

Dee

Dundee

Arbroath

Ram's Hd.

Perth

Tay

Fife Ness

N
W E
S

0   25
miles

Forth

Stirling

Edinburgh

Dunbar

CALLENDAR

St Abb's Hd

Glasgow

Dalkeith

Berwick

North Sea

Hamilton

Clyde

Firth of Forth

HOLY IS.

Tweed

Ayr

Kilmarnock

25 June: Callendar leads the reserve Covenanter army across the border to suppress Royalist activity in northern England.

Alnwick

MONTROSE

Morpeth

10 May: Montrose captures Morpeth.

Dumfries

Annan

Newcastle

Sunderland

Tyne

Carlisle

Eden

Durham

Solway Firth

Wigtown

Wear

LEVEN

Burrow Hd

Appleby

Whitby

St Bees Hd

Swale

Tees

NEWCASTLE

Ure

ISLE OF MAN

Derwent

RUPERT

Wharfe

Flamborough Hd

Bridlington

Marston Moor 2 Jul

Irish Sea

Preston

Ribble

Tadcaster

York
23 Apr–3 Jul
4–16 Jul

Hull

Leeds

Selby

Calder

Aire

11 April: Fairfax captures Selby.

Spurn Hd

Lathom House

Bolton

FAIRFAX

Formby Hd

Manchester

Mersey

See map 72.

ISLE OF ANGLESEY

Liverpool

Stockport 25 May

Sheffield

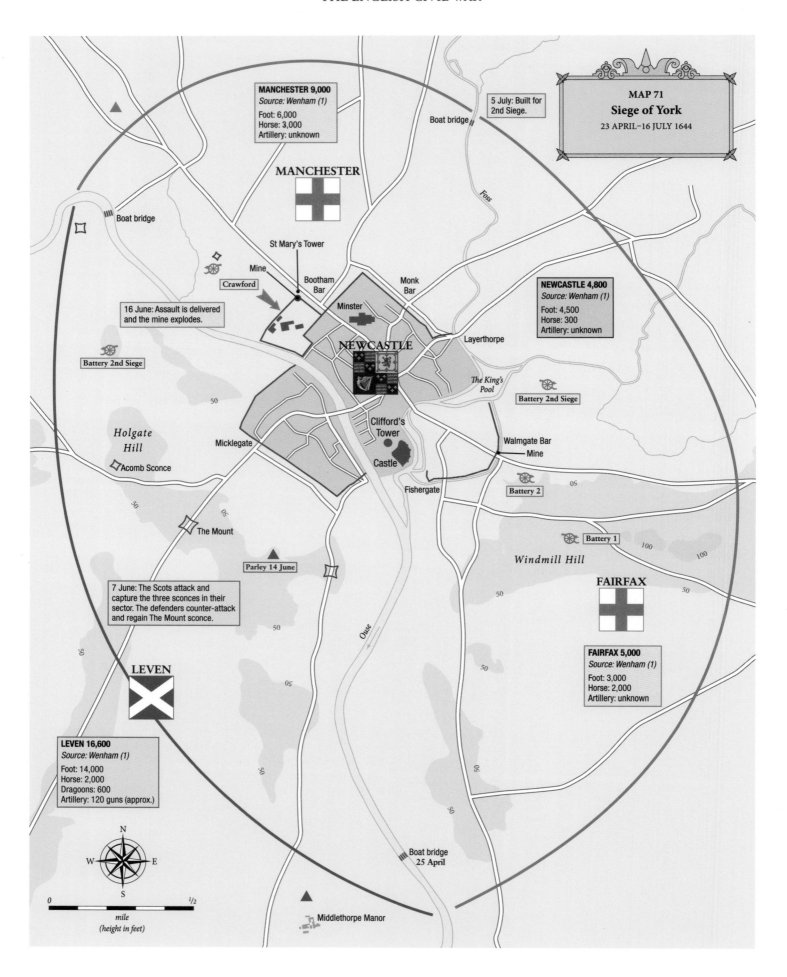

MANCHESTER 9,000
Source: Wenham (1)
Foot: 6,000
Horse: 3,000
Artillery: unknown

5 July: Built for 2nd Siege.

MAP 71
Siege of York
23 APRIL–16 JULY 1644

Boat bridge

MANCHESTER

Foss

Boat bridge

St Mary's Tower

Mine

Bootham Bar

Monk Bar

Crawford

16 June: Assault is delivered and the mine explodes.

Minster

NEWCASTLE 4,800
Source: Wenham (1)
Foot: 4,500
Horse: 300
Artillery: unknown

NEWCASTLE

Layerthorpe

Battery 2nd Siege

The King's Pool

Battery 2nd Siege

50

Clifford's Tower

Holgate Hill

Micklegate

Castle

Walmgate Bar
Mine

Acomb Sconce

Fishergate

Battery 2

50

The Mount

50

50

Battery 1

100

100

Windmill Hill

FAIRFAX

Parley 14 June

7 June: The Scots attack and capture the three sconces in their sector. The defenders counter-attack and regain The Mount sconce.

Ouse

50

FAIRFAX 5,000
Source: Wenham (1)
Foot: 3,000
Horse: 2,000
Artillery: unknown

50

50

LEVEN

50

LEVEN 16,600
Source: Wenham (1)
Foot: 14,000
Horse: 2,000
Dragoons: 600
Artillery: 120 guns (approx.)

N
W   E
S

0   1/2
mile
(height in feet)

Boat bridge
25 April

Middlethorpe Manor

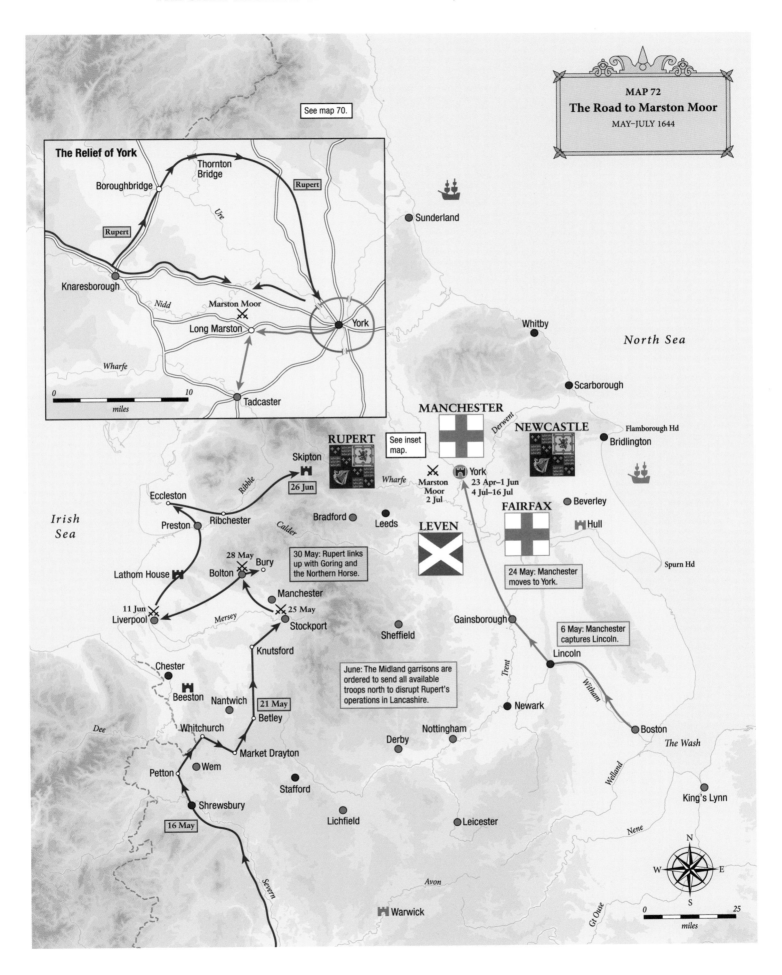

MAP 72
The Road to Marston Moor
MAY–JULY 1644

See map 70.

The Relief of York

Thornton
Bridge

Boroughbridge

Rupert

Knaresborough

Rupert

Ure

Nidd

Marston Moor

Long Marston

York

Wharfe

Tadcaster

0   10
miles

Sunderland

Whitby

North Sea

Scarborough

MANCHESTER

Derwent

NEWCASTLE

Flamborough Hd

Bridlington

RUPERT

See inset
map.

Skipton

Wharfe

Marston
Moor
2 Jul

York
23 Apr–1 Jun
4 Jul–16 Jul

26 Jun

Eccleston

Ribble

Bradford

Leeds

LEVEN

FAIRFAX

Beverley

Hull

Preston

Ribchester

Calder

*Irish
Sea*

24 May: Manchester
moves to York.

28 May
Bury

Lathom House

Bolton

30 May: Rupert links
up with Goring and
the Northern Horse.

Spurn Hd

11 Jun

Liverpool

Mersey

Manchester

25 May

Stockport

Sheffield

Gainsborough

6 May: Manchester
captures Lincoln.

Knutsford

Lincoln

Chester

Trent

Witham

Beeston

Nantwich

June: The Midland garrisons are
ordered to send all available
troops north to disrupt Rupert's
operations in Lancashire.

Newark

Dee

Whitchurch

21 May

Betley

Nottingham

Boston

The Wash

Derby

Petton

Wem

Market Drayton

Stafford

Lichfield

Leicester

King's Lynn

Nene

Shrewsbury

16 May

Severn

Avon

Warwick

Gt Ouse

N
W   E
S

0   25
miles

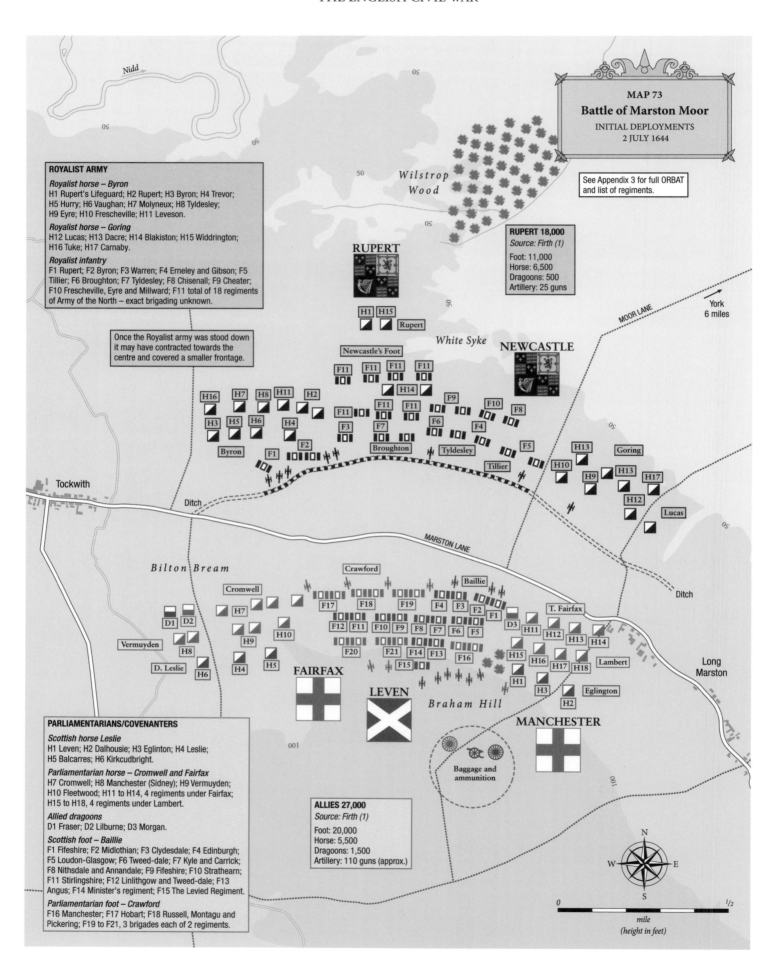

MAP 73

Battle of Marston Moor

INITIAL DEPLOYMENTS
2 JULY 1644

See Appendix 3 for full ORBAT and list of regiments.

RUPERT 18,000
Source: Firth (1)
Foot: 11,000
Horse: 6,500
Dragoons: 500
Artillery: 25 guns

ROYALIST ARMY

Royalist horse – Byron
H1 Rupert's Lifeguard; H2 Rupert; H3 Byron; H4 Trevor;
H5 Hurry; H6 Vaughan; H7 Molyneux; H8 Tyldesley;
H9 Eyre; H10 Frescheville; H11 Leveson.

Royalist horse – Goring
H12 Lucas; H13 Dacre; H14 Blakiston; H15 Widdrington;
H16 Tuke; H17 Carnaby.

Royalist infantry
F1 Rupert; F2 Byron; F3 Warren; F4 Erneley and Gibson; F5
Tillier; F6 Broughton; F7 Tyldesley; F8 Chisenall; F9 Cheater;
F10 Frescheville, Eyre and Millward; F11 total of 18 regiments
of Army of the North – exact brigading unknown.

Once the Royalist army was stood down
it may have contracted towards the
centre and covered a smaller frontage.

PARLIAMENTARIANS/COVENANTERS

Scottish horse Leslie
H1 Leven; H2 Dalhousie; H3 Eglinton; H4 Leslie;
H5 Balcarres; H6 Kirkcudbright.

Parliamentarian horse – Cromwell and Fairfax
H7 Cromwell; H8 Manchester (Sidney); H9 Vermuyden;
H10 Fleetwood; H11 to H14, 4 regiments under Fairfax;
H15 to H18, 4 regiments under Lambert.

Allied dragoons
D1 Fraser; D2 Lilburne; D3 Morgan.

Scottish foot – Baillie
F1 Fifeshire; F2 Midlothian; F3 Clydesdale; F4 Edinburgh;
F5 Loudon-Glasgow; F6 Tweed-dale; F7 Kyle and Carrick;
F8 Nithsdale and Annandale; F9 Fifeshire; F10 Strathearn;
F11 Stirlingshire; F12 Linlithgow and Tweed-dale; F13
Angus; F14 Minister's regiment; F15 The Levied Regiment.

Parliamentarian foot – Crawford
F16 Manchester; F17 Hobart; F18 Russell, Montagu and
Pickering; F19 to F21, 3 brigades each of 2 regiments.

ALLIES 27,000
Source: Firth (1)
Foot: 20,000
Horse: 5,500
Dragoons: 1,500
Artillery: 110 guns (approx.)

mile
(height in feet)

near the village of Long Marston. It was a relatively strong position. Rupert, at this juncture, was at the village of Knaresborough, but given the Parliamentarian dispositions an advance east towards York was most unwise. He was greatly outnumbered, and to have done so would have exposed his force to a flanking attack and placed the River Nidd on his left shoulder, severely hindering his line of retreat. Instead, on 1 July, Rupert sent a large cavalry force east down the Knaresborough road, while he marched with the balance of the army north. Crossing the River Ouse at Boroughbridge, and the River Swayle at Thornton, he then swung south and surprised the small Scottish force left to guard the northern pontoon bridge over the River Ouse near York. Meanwhile, the detached cavalry force on the Knaresborough road, which the Parliamentarians had thought was the Royalist vanguard, had completed the deception. Moments later a detachment of dragoons from Manchester's force, which had been left guarding the northern bridge of boats over the Ouse with the Scots, rode into the Parliamentarian position to report the ruse. The Royalist cavalry then rode east and joined Rupert, and the great city of York was relieved without a shot being fired.

Rupert remained with his army to the north of the city and sent word to Newcastle to prepare his troops for battle the following day. Newcastle was decidedly uncomfortable at the prospect of marching from the safety of York and offering battle to a numerically superior force. Furthermore, he was somewhat aghast that Rupert assumed he now enjoyed overall command. At some stage in the exchange, it appears that Newcastle agreed to deploy the garrison the following day only to be subsequently dissuaded by General King.[16] Nevertheless, Newcastle did move at the head of his force the next morning and met up with Rupert on the field at about 9am. He remained deeply sceptical about the wisdom of fighting, and 'after some conferences, he declared his mind to the Prince, desiring his Highness not to attempt anything as yet upon the enemy; for he had intelligence that there was some discontent between them, and that they were resolved to divide themselves, and so to raise the siege without fighting'.[17] Rupert was insistent, informing Newcastle that 'he had a letter from his Majesty (then at Oxford), with a positive and absolute command to fight the enemy; which in obedience, and according to his duty, he was bound to perform'.[18]

In fact, the previous day, the three allied commanders had long debated their future options. Fairfax recalled, 'we were divided in our opinions, what to doe. The English were for fighting them; the Scotts for Retreating, to gaine (as they alleged) both time & place of Advantage. This latter being resolved on, we marched away to Tadcaster; which made ye Enemy advance ye faster'.[19] In fact, the dissention between the commanders may have been deeper than Fairfax's memoirs suggest. The reinforcements from Denbigh and Meldrum were en route but they were not expected to arrive for many days.[20] Consequently, before dawn on 2 July, the allied forces began their march south towards Tadcaster. At much the same time Rupert's force began their move west towards Long Marston.[21] The allied rearguard on Braham Hill picked up the Royalist movement soon after dawn and watched the first elements begin to deploy on the lower ground to their front. By 9am, at much the same time that Rupert and Newcastle were having their tête-à-tête, the order was sent for an immediate return of the allied armies.[22] However, their reappearance was to take some time, as some of the Scottish foot had already reached Tadcaster, 6 miles to the south. The Royalist deployment was also taking considerable time. Newcastle's troops did not leave the confines of the city until past nine; they were held up crossing the single pontoon bridge and many could not resist the temptation to pillage the abandoned enemy siege lines as they marched.

Rupert, in his frustration, pondered attacking before Newcastle's Foot were on the field but decided that the opportunity had passed. Instead he decided to try to capture the west end of the ridge to the southeast of Tockwith in the area of Bilton Bream, where some of the allied rearguard were positioned. The Royalists were sharply beaten off and some of the allied horse was positioned there to anchor the left wing and prevent a recurrence.[23] As the hours passed, the two massive armies methodically took their places in the field. The Royalist forces numbered 11,000 foot and between 6,500 and 7,500 horse and 25 guns, while the allies numbered 20,000 foot, 7,000 horse and possibly as many as 75 guns.[24] The three allied commanders gathered atop Braham Hill, near a clump of trees (subsequently known as Cromwell's Plump), from where they enjoyed an unbroken view of the field. They were able to see the hedge-lined ditch filled with musketeers that marked the front of the Royalist position.[25] Leven, as the most experienced general and in charge of the lion's share of the allied force, assumed overall command.

The allied army was more or less in place by about 3pm. Much to Rupert's frustration, Newcastle's infantry had still not arrived. He sent word to Newcastle to hasten their arrival and busied himself with refining the deployment:

> … the right wing rested on some impassable hedges in order to protect his flank; in front was a deep ditch with a bank on this side, within which the greater part of the Royal artillery were placed in battery. A strong detachment of dragoons were scattered among the hedges, in order to protect these guns.[26]

16 Young, *Marston Moor*, p. 197, taken from an excerpt of Rupert's Diary. King (Lord Eythin) had served with Rupert in the Thirty Years' War and specifically at the battle at Vlotho in 1638, where Rupert's rashness had cost him his liberty. There was no love lost between these two soldiers.

17 Firth, *Memoirs Duke of Newcastle*, pp. 74–5.

18 Ibid.

19 Fairfax, loc. cit., p. 221.

20 Meldrum had a force of nearly 8,000 at Manchester and Denbigh another force of undisclosed size marching from Staffordshire.

21 All of Newcastle's garrison except for Bellasye's, Glemham's and Slingsby's regiments. Parsons, op. cit., p. 112.

22 Cook, *Road to Marston Moor*, p. 85.

23 During Civil War battles, armies were almost never anchored on key or distinctive terrain, or built-up areas.

24 Firth, *Marston Moor*, p. 23; Leslie, *Letter from Generall Leven, the Lord Fairfax, and the Earl of Manchester*, p. 11; Stewart, *Full relation of the late victory*, p. 10 (Royalist totals). Firth, *Marston Moor*, p. 23; Stewart, *Full relation of the late victory*, p. 1 (allied totals). There are no accurate numbers for the allied artillery and very little work has been done to resolve this. Stephen Bull, *The Furie of the Ordnance*, p. 155, suggests that the allies would have had at least 110 guns, but there is no tangible evidence to support this. Newman, *The Battle of Marston Moor 1644*, p. 62, based on cannon balls recovered from the field, suggests that most of these guns were the 3.5-pound Saker. The figures for infantry and cavalry dovetail with those of de Gomme, *Order of Majestie*, and the battle map. However, Reid, *All the King's Armies*, p. 140, suggests that the allied infantry total was nearer 15,000, making the armies more numerically balanced – he could be correct.

25 According to Leadman, *The Battle of Marston Moor*, p. 295, the hedge was on the south side of the ditch.

26 Rupert, op. cit., p. 450.

At around this time the allied artillery opened. Slingsby recalled that 'the enemy makes some shot at him as they were drawing up into Battalio… but this was only a shewing their teeth, for after 4 shots made them give over, and in Marston corn fields falls to singing psalms'.[27] Chaplain Simeon Ashe, was at the front of the allied centre, leading the singing of psalms with the soldiers of the Eastern Association. He recollected:

… before our foot could get back (which was about two or three a clock) the enemy was possessed of the Moore (a ground very advantageous) and had in many small bodies bespread themselves, that their Army did extend two miles (as its judged) in length: Yea, by the improving of this opportunite, they had by divers regiments of Muskettiers so lined the hedge and ditch betwixt themselves and us, that our Souldiers could not assault them, without very great apparent prejudice. We were compelled to draw upon our Army, and to place it in battalia in a large field of Rie, where the height of the corn, together with the showers of rain which then fell, prov'd no small inconvenience unto our Souldiers; yet being on an hill, we had the double advantage of the ground, and the wind.[28]

At about 4pm General King arrived with the 3,000 infantry and, as they took their place on the field, the three Royalist commanders had a confab.[29] It was an acrimonious affair, particularly between Rupert and King.[30] Newcastle reiterated his concern at action and 'asked his Highness what service he would be pleased to command him; who returned this answer, that he would begin no action upon the enemy, till early in the morning; desiring my Lord to repose himself till then'.[31] Why Rupert came to the conclusion that the allies, enjoying numerical advantage and better terrain, would remain inactive with three hours of daylight remaining is unclear. Nevertheless, the order was given and many of the Royalist formations were stood at ease in anticipation of their evening meal.[32] The Royalist stand-down was immediately detected by Leven and he decided to strike:

Our Army being thus Marshalled, towards six or seven of the clocke we advance about two hundred paces towards the Enemy, our Canon (which had plaid one or two houres before from the top of the Hill) was drawne forward for our best advantage, our signal was a white Paper, or handkerchiffe in our hats; our word was God with us. The Enemies signal was God and the King.[33]

The black clouds overhead broke, and peals of thunder accompanied the battle drums. The great battle had started and the Royalists were on the back foot.

'Wee came down the Hill in the bravest order, and with the greatest resolution that was ever seen', recalled Scoutmaster General Lionel Watson with Manchester's front brigades.[34] Such was the pace of the advance that they were in a 'running march' and had crossed the open ground between the two armies in a matter of a few minutes. The Royalists scrambled to their posts but the few musketeers in the ditch were quickly and easily overwhelmed; the heavy rain had extinguished many of their matches at the critical moment. Four small drake cannons placed there were quickly taken.[35] Some of the Eastern Association Foot began to move around the guns and the flank of Rupert's Bluecoats and Byron's Foot that had been sent there to protect the gun line. While in the centre one of Fairfax's brigades pushed on and drove back Broughton's Greencoats. However, the Scots on Fairfax's right, having penetrated the ditch, began to lose momentum. On both flanks, the allied horse had advanced and charged in concert with the foot. Captain Stewart was with the Scottish foot on the allied right flank, and recalled that the cavalry on this wing had several misfortunes, constrained by a narrow lane with steep banks topped with hedges lined with musketeers:[36]

Sir Thomas Fairfax charged gallantly, but the enemy keeping themselves in a body, and receiving them by threes and foures as they marched out of the Lane, and (by what mistake I know not) Sir Thomas Fairfax his new leavied regiment being in the Van, they wheeled about, and being hotly pursued by the enemy came back upon the L. Fairfax Foot, and the reserve of the Scottish Foot, broke them wholly, and trod the most part of them under foot.[37]

On the allied left Cromwell's cavalry movement was met by a corresponding advance by Byron's cavalry.[38] Watson, who was just to the right of this massed cavalry action, recalled that 'our front divisions of Horse charged their front, Lieutenant Generall Cromwels division of three hundred Horse, in which himselfe was in person, charged the first division of Prince Ruperts, in which himselfe was in person'.[39] In fact, at this juncture Rupert was still to the rear with the reserve cavalry. Cromwell's first charge was brought to a halt and Cromwell himself was injured. As Rupert arrived with the cavalry reserve they counter-charged the allies and a fierce and vicious cavalry engagement ensued: 'Cromwell's own division had a hard pull of it: for they were charged by Rupert's bravest men, both in Front and Flank: they stood at the swords point a pretty while, hacking one another.'[40] In fact, it was most likely the arrival of David Leslie's second-line cavalry that decided the struggle. Newcastle did his best to stem the flow of fleeing troopers from the right wing, 'which out of a panic fear had left the field, and run away with all the speed they could'.[41] Rupert was caught up in the rout and famously hid in a bean field to avoid capture.[42]

On the allied right, Tom Fairfax had cleared the lane and a host of other obstacles with his first wave of cavalry, but did not wait for the others to come up and reform. Being engaged with effective musket fire, he decided

27 Parsons, op. cit., p. 112.

28 Ashe, op. cit., p. 4.

29 Binns, *Cholmley*, p. 136. Not all of Newcastle's infantry may have been up by 4pm.

30 Binns, loc. cit., and see Barratt, *The Battle for York*, pp. 96–8, for a good account of this confrontation.

31 Firth, *Memoirs Duke of Newcastle*, p. 76.

32 Newman & Roberts, *Battle of the Five Armies*, p. 93. It is at this point that the Royalist lines 'condensed laterally' and presented a smaller frontage.

33 Ashe, op. cit., p. 5.

34 Watson, *Exact relation of the late battell neer York*, p. 5.

35 Ashe, loc. cit.

36 I assume this to be Moor Lane.

37 Stewart, op. cit., pp. 6–7.

38 Byron was criticized by Rupert for leaving the relative security of his rearwards position and in making this advance – Young, *Rupert's Diary*, p. 197. A good summary of this is in Tincey, *Marston Moor 1644*, p. 60 and Reid, op. cit., pp. 150–1. Newman, *Battle of the Five Armies*, pp. 70–1, suggests that the blame of Byron was designed to deflect blame on Rupert.

39 Watson, loc. cit.

40 Ibid.

41 Firth, *Memoirs Duke of Newcastle*, pp. 77–8.

42 Newman & Roberts, op. cit., p. 92, suggests that the whole story about a bean field and Rupert's hiding during the battle, to be Parliamentarian post-battle tittle tattle, with no supporting evidence.

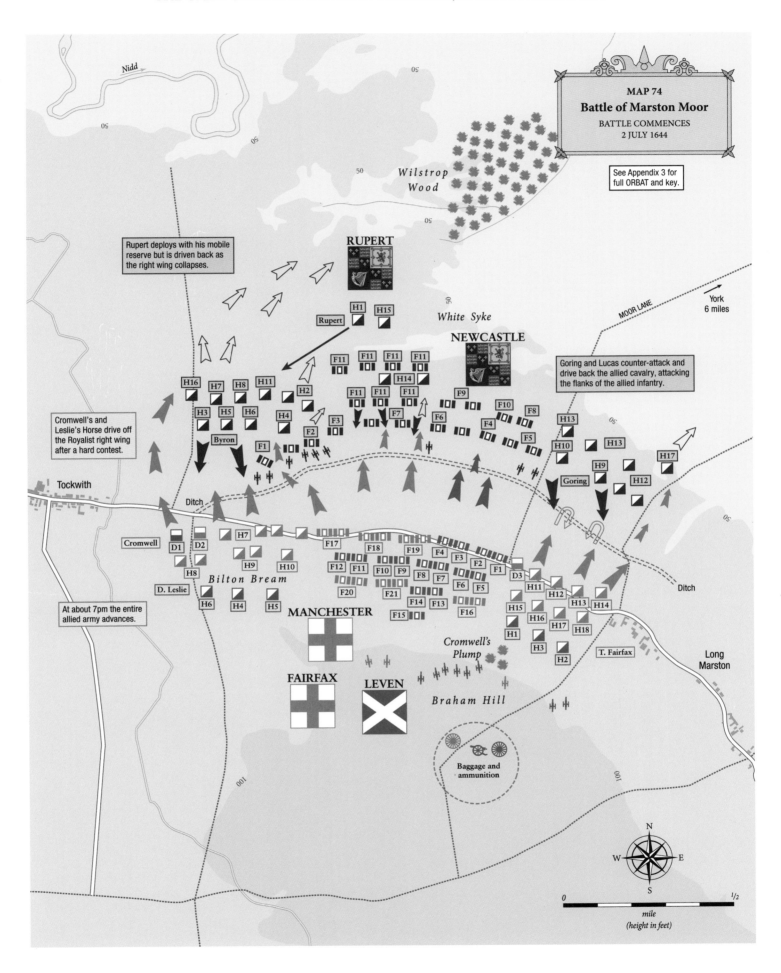

Nidd

Wilstrop Wood

MAP 74

Battle of Marston Moor

BATTLE COMMENCES
2 JULY 1644

See Appendix 3 for
full ORBAT and key.

RUPERT

Rupert deploys with his mobile
reserve but is driven back as
the right wing collapses.

H1   H15

Rupert

White Syke

York
6 miles

MOOR LANE

NEWCASTLE

F11 F11 F11 F11

H14

Goring and Lucas counter-attack and
drive back the allied cavalry, attacking
the flanks of the allied infantry.

F9

H16 H7 H8 H11

H2

F11 F11 F11

F10 F8

H13

H3 H5 H6

H4

F3   F7   F6

F4

H10   H13

Cromwell's and
Leslie's Horse drive off
the Royalist right wing
after a hard contest.

Byron

F2

F1

F5

H9

H17

Tockwith

Ditch

Goring

H12

At about 7pm the entire
allied army advances.

Cromwell

D1 D2

H7

F17   F18   F19   F4 F3 F2 F1

D3

Ditch

H9   H10

F12 F11 F10 F9 F8 F7 F6 F5

H11   H12   H13   H14

H8

Bilton Bream

F20

F21

F14 F13

H15 H16   H17 H18

D. Leslie

H6   H4   H5

F15   F16

H1

T. Fairfax

Long
Marston

MANCHESTER

H3

H2

Cromwell's
Plump

FAIRFAX

LEVEN

Braham Hill

Baggage and
ammunition

N
W   E
S

0   1/2

mile
(height in feet)

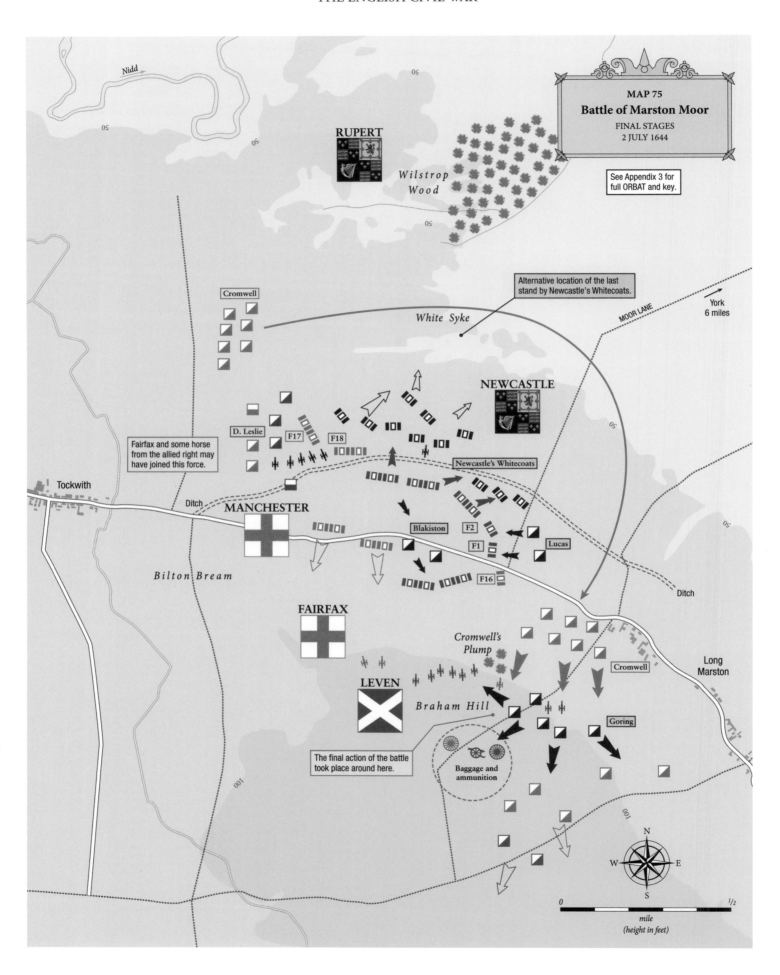

Nidd

50

50

50

RUPERT

Wilstrop Wood

50

MAP 75

Battle of Marston Moor

FINAL STAGES
2 JULY 1644

See Appendix 3 for
full ORBAT and key.

Cromwell

Alternative location of the last
stand by Newcastle's Whitecoats.

White Syke

MOOR LANE

York
6 miles

50

NEWCASTLE

D. Leslie

F17

F18

Fairfax and some horse
from the allied right may
have joined this force.

Newcastle's Whitecoats

50

Tockwith

Ditch

MANCHESTER

Blakiston

F2

F1

Lucas

Bilton Bream

F16

Ditch

FAIRFAX

*Cromwell's
Plump*

Cromwell

Long
Marston

LEVEN

Goring

Braham Hill

100

The final action of the battle
took place around here.

Baggage and
ammunition

100

100

N

W   E

S

0   1/2

mile

(height in feet)

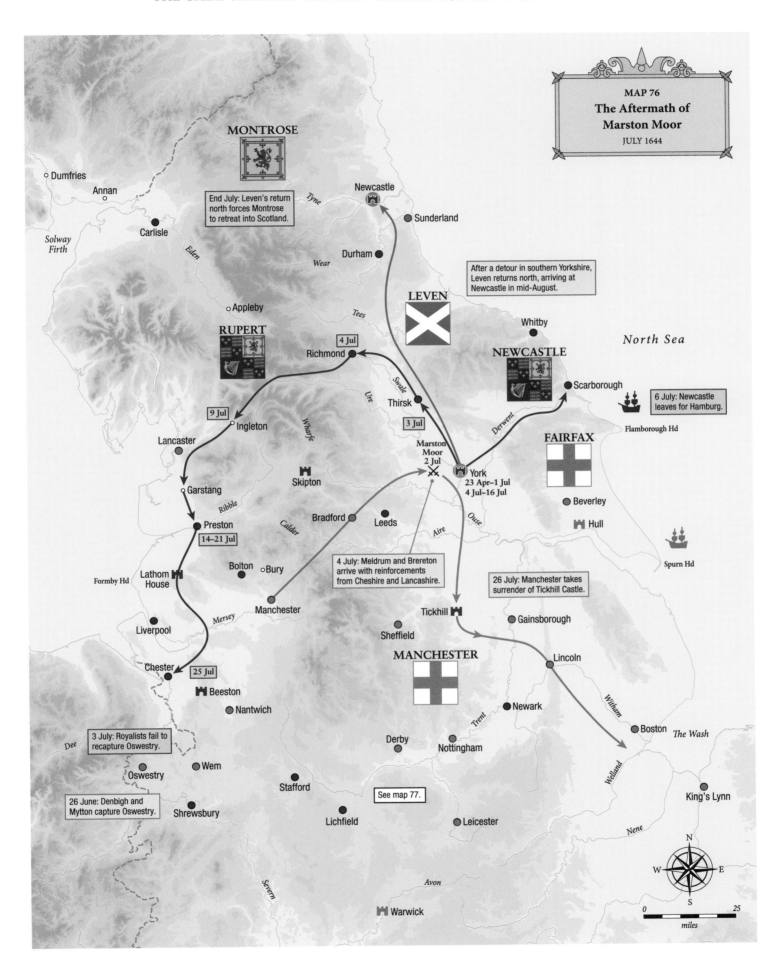

MAP 76

The Aftermath of Marston Moor

JULY 1644

MONTROSE

End July: Leven's return north forces Montrose to retreat into Scotland.

Dumfries

Annan

Solway Firth

Carlisle

Eden

Appleby

Wear

Tyne

Newcastle

Sunderland

Durham

LEVEN

After a detour in southern Yorkshire, Leven returns north, arriving at Newcastle in mid-August.

Tees

Whitby

North Sea

RUPERT

4 Jul

Richmond

Swale

Ure

Thirsk

NEWCASTLE

Scarborough

6 July: Newcastle leaves for Hamburg.

Flamborough Hd

9 Jul

Ingleton

Wharfe

3 Jul

Derwent

FAIRFAX

Lancaster

Skipton

Marston Moor 2 Jul

York 23 Apr–1 Jul 4 Jul–16 Jul

Garstang

Ribble

Calder

Bradford

Leeds

Beverley

Aire

Ouse

Hull

Preston

14–21 Jul

4 July: Meldrum and Brereton arrive with reinforcements from Cheshire and Lancashire.

26 July: Manchester takes surrender of Tickhill Castle.

Spurn Hd

Lathom House

Bolton

Bury

Formby Hd

Mersey

Manchester

Tickhill

Gainsborough

Liverpool

Sheffield

MANCHESTER

Lincoln

Witham

Chester

25 Jul

Beeston

Nantwich

Newark

Boston

The Wash

Dee

Trent

Derby

Nottingham

3 July: Royalists fail to recapture Oswestry.

Wem

Stafford

See map 77.

Leicester

Welland

King's Lynn

26 June: Denbigh and Mytton capture Oswestry.

Oswestry

Shrewsbury

Lichfield

Nene

N W E S

Severn

Avon

Warwick

0   25
miles

to charge Carnaby's Regiment on the far left of the Royalist line. Many of Fairfax's men then pursued the remnants of this broken force back on the road to York.[43] Lambert's second line of allied cavalry could not get up to Fairfax and had itself been counter-charged by Goring and Lucas. Meanwhile, in the centre, the infantry battle raged at an intensity never witnessed throughout the war.[44] The allied front-line troops cleared the ditch, driving back the Royalist foot on to their parent units. Despite this onslaught, the Royalist front line remained intact at this stage and King decided the time was ripe to launch the Northern Foot through the intervals of the front-line regiments. They fell on the allied infantry with considerable force. Ashe remembered that the attack fell heavily on Lord Fairfax's Brigade and that sometime 'afterwards by Marquesse New-castles Regiment of Foot, and by them furiously assaulted, did make a retreat in some disorder'.[45] Blakiston's Cavalry Regiment joined the attack and charged down on to Fairfax's men, but their overall effect appeared quite limited. Hamilton's Brigade, to the right of Fairfax's, also broke. The panic was infectious and it quickly spread to the second line. As they fell back in disorder, some of the Royalist cavalry under Lucas swung into their exposed flank of the Fifeshire and Midlothian Foot, where the Scottish pikemen were hard pressed to keep the rampant Royalist cavalry at bay. The balance of Goring's cavalry then pursued the broken allied right wing regiments back up Marston Hill and penetrated the allied position as far as the baggage train, which they sacked for good measure. Some of the allied infantry in the centre also broke (Fairfax's Foot and other regiments of the Northern Association) but enough remained to stem the flow and hold the line.

By this time, the allied right had broken, the allied centre was under severe pressure, but on the allied left they were now about to administer the *coup de grâce*. Cromwell and Leslie had destroyed the Royalist cavalry on this flank. Cholmley recorded that Cromwell kept his units close, 'still falling upon that quarter of the Prince's forces which seemed to make the most resistance'.[46] This resistance was being made by the Royalist foot. Many units had wheeled right to face the threat. Fraser's Dragoons were instrumental in driving back their Royalist counterparts, which were a significant threat to unsupported cavalry and, once accomplished, Leslie's cavalry and Manchester's infantry now began to fold up the Royalist infantry unit by unit. At the same time, Cromwell swung around the back of the field and caught Goring's men, who had formed a battle line, but they were too widely spread to put up an effective resistance. Both attacks were simultaneous and overwhelming. Royalist cohesion and morale collapsed as one. Newcastle's Whitecoats put up a stoic resistance to hold off the attack in the centre, which bought time for large numbers of the Royalist foot to quit the field, but the outcome had been decided.[47]

The battle was over by 9pm. Leven recalled the victory:

> … we put them wholly to the rout, killed many, and took their Officers and Colours, and by this time we had no enemy in the field. Wee took all their Ordnance, being in number 25, near 130 barrels of Powder… above a hundred Colours, & ten thousand Armes, besides two Waggons of Carbines and Pistols of spare Armes.[48]

Following the battle the locals were ordered to bury the dead. 'They reported that 4,550 dead bodies were buried at Marston Moor, of whom, they said, 3,000 had belonged to the Royalist army, and of these fully two-thirds were gentlemen.'[49] While the Royalists fled to York, the allied armies remained on the field. The next day they received the welcome reinforcements from Lancashire and Cheshire and returned to what was left of the siege lines around York.

The day prior both Rupert and Newcastle had departed from the city. Sir Hugh Cholmley, in his memories of the battle and aftermath, recalled that 'General King, considering the King's affairs absolutely destroyed by loss of this battle, persuaded the Marquis, against all the power of his other friends, to quit the kingdom.'[50] Newcastle rode with his family, escorted by two troops of cavalry, to Scarborough, where he departed for Hamburg. Rupert, meanwhile, marched with 'fifteene or sixteen hundred horse, and eight hundred foot'.[51] At Thirsk he linked up with Sir Robert Clavering, adding another nearly 2,000 men that he had raised in the north-east. A few days later he crossed the Pennines and by the end of the month he was back in Chester. Rupert's decision to fight near York had been a costly one; in addition to losing his beloved dog 'Boye', his reputation of invincibility was irrevocably damaged.[52] Once the siege had been resumed, Meldrum and Brereton returned to Lancashire to counter any attempt by Rupert to capitalize on their absence. Rupert had left Thomas Glemham in charge within the city. Slingsby summed up the mood: 'thus were we left at York, out of all hope of relief, ye town much distract'd, & every one ready to abandon her'.[53] The city was summoned, but Glemham refused to surrender. The allies erected new batteries (see map 71) and another smaller pontoon bridge over the Foss. By 11 July, Glemham requested a parley; four days later terms were agreed, and on 16 July the city was delivered to the Parliamentarian forces. A few days later Leven moved the Scottish army back north to join the Earl of Callendar's cordon at Newcastle and to recommence the siege, while Manchester led the Eastern Association army back south, leaving Fairfax to remain in and around York. The north had been conquered.

---

43 Fairfax himself appears to have stayed on the field. There are accounts that he linked up with Cromwell/Leslie when their cavalry completed the encirclement. Stewart, op. cit., p. 7.

44 Newman & Roberts, op. cit., p. 92.

45 Ashe, op. cit., p. 5.

46 Binns, op. cit., p. 137.

47 Reid, op. cit., p. 159, suggests that they were ordered by King to act as the sacrificial rearguard. There are contradictory accounts, however, as to exactly when in the battle and, indeed where, this encounter took place. However, the work by Newman & Roberts, op. cit., casts doubt on the White Syke position as this was largely a creation of 18th-century enclosures. Extensive battlefield detection by Paul Roberts confirms this theory as there were very few artefacts found in the area. He placed the last stand nearer the road, which is supported by finds and makes more sense as to the flow of the battle.

48 Leslie, *Letter from Generall Leven, the Lord Fairfax, and the Earl of Manchester*, p. 11. For a list of the Royalist colours see Stewart, op. cit, pp. 14–16.

49 Leadman, op. cit., p. 325.

50 Firth, *Memoirs Duke of Newcastle*, p. 82.

51 Stewart, op. cit., p. 12.

52 Boye was an iconic white hunting poodle given to Rupert while he had been imprisoned in Linz. Parliamentarian propaganda alleged that the dog was 'endowed' with magical powers.

53 Parsons, op. cit., p. 114.

CHAPTER 21
THE OXFORD CAMPAIGN, MAY TO AUGUST 1644

The defeat at Cheriton (chapter 19) put the Royalists on the back foot in the south and centre. If Oxford was to be protected, the Royalists needed to control Oxfordshire, Berkshire and Buckinghamshire.[1] Orders were given for the Royalist armies to concentrate near Marlborough and on 10 April Charles reviewed an army of 6,000 foot and 4,000 horse. At a subsequent council of war, the decision was taken to resume the offensive against Waller's army and destroy his force before they threatened Oxford. Charles was not confident of success, for on return to Oxford he packed off the Queen who was shortly expecting a child.[2] In fact, the orchestration of Parliamentarian arrangements for operations in the centre was far from tuneful. The Committee of Both Kingdoms ordered a rendezvous of all available Parliamentarian forces to take place at Aylesbury on 19 April. It never materialized for Manchester's force was under increasing pressure in Lincolnshire. Following his victory at Cheriton, Waller had pushed the Royalists back in Hampshire (see map 67) but he was then obliged to fall back to Farnham as the London Regiments had, once again, proved unreliable when separated too far from their homes.

The Committee of Both Kingdoms devised an alternative plan in early May. Waller's army, brought up to a strength of 10,000, was to recover Reading, while Essex, with a similar-sized force, was to capture Oxford. The coordinated offensive began on 14 May and the Royalist commanders decided to give up Reading (18 May) and then Abingdon (25 May) as the Parliamentarian armies advanced north. Charles was understandably concerned at the abandonment of one of the towns that had formed the ring of steel around Oxford and tried to countermand the order. The fact remained that the garrison there of no more than 500 men would not hold an open town without a castle. Essex sent his infantry to occupy the town that evening. Three days later, once all the Parliamentarian forces had closed up and been resupplied, Essex set off to skirt the city to the east and attack the city from the north, while Waller divided his force, half to remain to the south while the balance moved off to skirt the city to the west. Essex's force reached the village of Islip on 30 May and tried to cross the River Cherwell at Gosford (Kidlington). However, Lord Astley had covered the crossing with two well-placed 6-pounder guns, and drove back three attempts (on 30, 31 May and 1 June) by Essex's vanguard to cross. Essex moved north and made two more attempts, the first at Enslow Bridge (8 miles north of Oxford), and the second at Tackley Ford (9½ miles north). Once again, well-sited artillery and some determined musketry held the Parliamentarians back.[3] To the south, Waller had divided his army into two groups. One group, at the second attempt, crossed the Thames at Newbridge (8 miles west of Oxford), where they spent three nights repairing the bridge to enable the army to cross.[4] On 2 June, Waller's army crossed in force and moved towards Oxford only to receive orders from Essex to wait.

Charles now faced a significant dilemma. He was not yet surrounded, but time was certainly against him. With no hope of relief and enough supplies for two weeks at most, he decided to leave his second son Charles within the city (with an ad hoc group of advisors), and move between the two Parliamentarian armies and into the Cotswolds. The following morning (4 June) news that Charles and his army had slipped the noose set both Parliamentarian armies in pursuit, but morale was ebbing at an alarming rate, particularly within the ranks of Essex's force. Things were no more sanguine within the Royalist army and, on 5 June, Charles received the disturbing news that Tewkesbury had fallen to a *coup de main* operation the day before. He therefore altered his plans and marched directly for Worcester via Evesham, destroying the bridge at Pershore en route.[5] Meanwhile Essex and Waller had convened a meeting, which took place at Chipping Norton on 6 June.[6] The enmity between the two commanders resurfaced with vengeance, Waller no doubt incredulous that Essex had failed to cross a minor river on no fewer than five occasions and thereby allowed the King to escape. Essex, conversely, was in no mood to take lessons in tactical river crossings from Waller and he announced his intention of redirecting his army south to relieve Lyme Regis, which was at the time being besieged by Maurice. It was an extraordinary decision and one which, when it reached London, incurred the wrath and incredulity of the Committee of Both Kingdoms. New orders were sent to Essex with haste along with unequivocal instruction to stick to the script. But by the time the papers reached him, he was already in Devon.

Waller was delighted to be left to pursue the King and his army alone. His first objective, in conjunction with Massey and troops from Gloucester, was to capture and reduce Sudeley Castle, which he achieved on 9 June.[7] By now, the King was aware that Parliament's pursuit force was not stronger than his own, but he was unsure of just how best to proceed. On 12 June he decided to move away from Worcester in order to entice Waller away from the city and to link up with Rupert in and around Shrewsbury. Waller followed the King's army on the east bank of the River Severn, but then the Royalists doubled-back and began to move back towards the Cotswolds. Messages were sent to Oxford to prepare some field artillery to meet them at Witney. Waller was a day's march behind, but had the bridges over the Severn been intact, he would have caught the Royalist army and been able to bring it to battle. Instead he decided to break off the immediate pursuit and, having discounted an attack on Cirencester, he decided that Stow-on-the-Wold would be his next objective. The King, meanwhile, having evaded Waller, was now contemplating a rush on London. However, the idea was stymied by the Lords Commissioners at Oxford who

---

1 Toynbee & Young, *Cropredy Bridge, 1644*, p. 6.

2 The Queen gave birth to their ninth child (Princess Henrietta) at Exeter on 16 June 1644.

3 Toynbee & Young, op. cit., pp. 31–3.

4 Coe, *An exact diarie*, p. 3.

5 Peachey, *Richard Symonds*, p. 9.

6 There is some conjecture as to where this meeting took place, Toynbee & Young, op. cit., p. 49. However, Essex wrote from Chipping Norton that day, see *CSPD* dated 6 June 1644.

7 Coe, op. cit., p. 4, for details and list of prisoners.

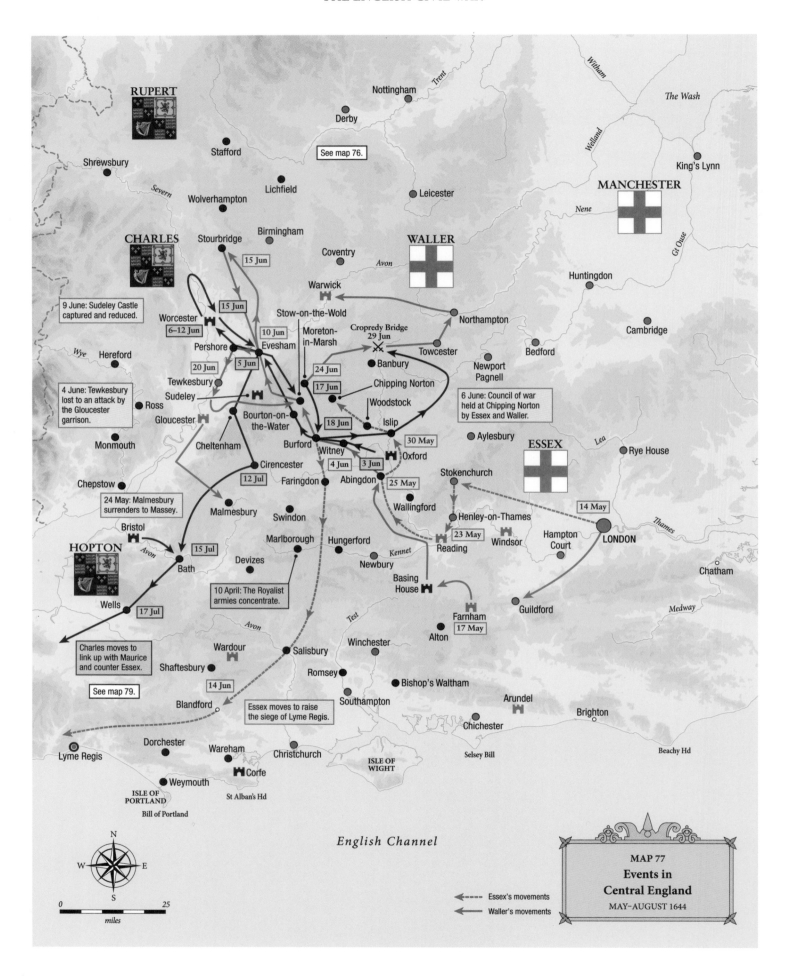

RUPERT

CHARLES

MANCHESTER

WALLER

Shrewsbury

Stafford

Derby

Nottingham

King's Lynn

Lichfield

Wolverhampton

See map 76.

Leicester

Stourbridge

Birmingham

Coventry

Huntingdon

15 Jun

15 Jun

Cambridge

9 June: Sudeley Castle
captured and reduced.

Worcester
6–12 Jun

Stow-on-the-
Wold

Warwick

Northampton

Pershore

10 Jun
Evesham

Moreton-
in-Marsh

Cropredy Bridge
29 Jun

Towcester

Bedford

Hereford

20 Jun

5 Jun

Banbury

Newport
Pagnell

Tewkesbury

24 Jun

4 June: Tewkesbury
lost to an attack by
the Gloucester
garrison.

Sudeley

17 Jun

Chipping Norton

6 June: Council of war
held at Chipping Norton
by Essex and Waller.

Ross

Woodstock

Bourton-on-
the-Water

Gloucester

Cheltenham

18 Jun

Islip

Aylesbury

ESSEX

Rye House

Monmouth

Burford

Witney

30 May

Oxford

Chepstow

Cirencester

4 Jun

3 Jun

25 May

Stokenchurch

14 May

12 Jul

Faringdon

Abingdon

Wallingford

24 May: Malmesbury
surrenders to Massey.

Malmesbury

Swindon

Henley-on-Thames

23 May

Hampton
Court

LONDON

Bristol

15 Jul

Marlborough

Hungerford

Reading

Windsor

Chatham

HOPTON

Bath

Devizes

Newbury

Kennet

Basing
House

Guildford

Medway

10 April: The Royalist
armies concentrate.

Farnham

17 May

Wells

17 Jul

Winchester

Alton

Charles moves to
link up with Maurice
and counter Essex.

Wardour

Salisbury

Romsey

Bishop's Waltham

Arundel

Brighton

See map 79.

14 Jun

Shaftesbury

Southampton

Chichester

Beachy Hd

Blandford

Essex moves to raise
the siege of Lyme Regis.

Dorchester

Wareham

Christchurch

**ISLE OF
WIGHT**

Selsey Bill

Lyme Regis

Weymouth

Corfe

St Alban's Hd

**ISLE OF
PORTLAND**

Bill of Portland

English Channel

N
W   E
S

0   25
miles

MAP 77
**Events in
Central England**
MAY–AUGUST 1644

— — → Essex's movements
———→ Waller's movements

180

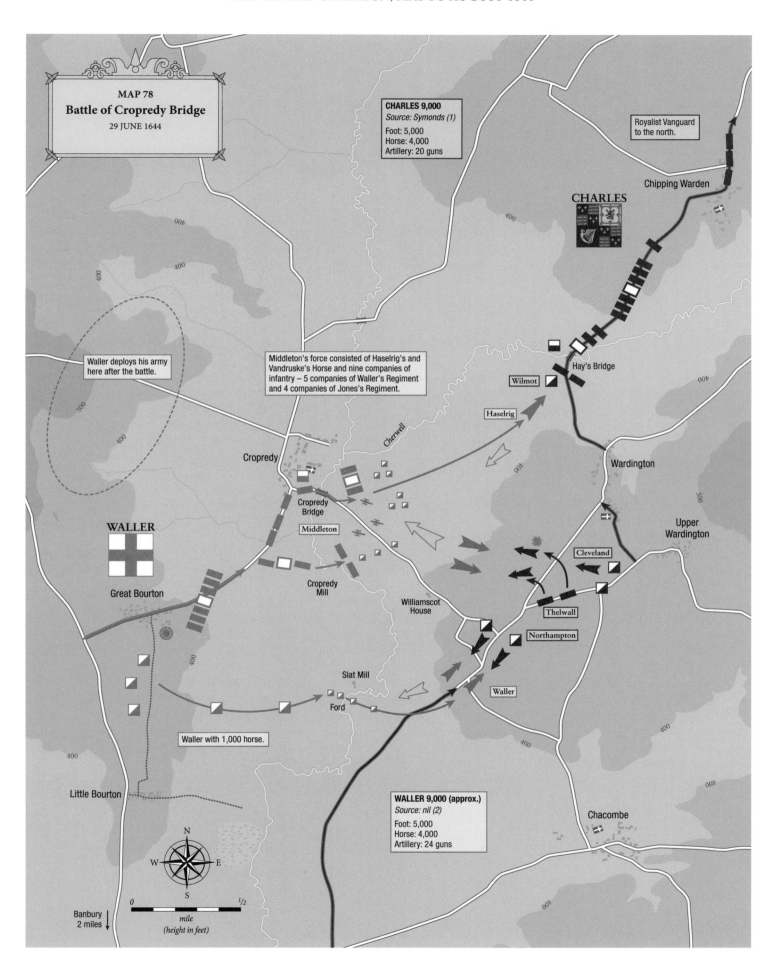

MAP 78

Battle of Cropredy Bridge

29 JUNE 1644

CHARLES 9,000
Source: Symonds (1)
Foot: 5,000
Horse: 4,000
Artillery: 20 guns

Royalist Vanguard to the north.

Chipping Warden

CHARLES

Waller deploys his army here after the battle.

Middleton's force consisted of Haselrig's and Vandruske's Horse and nine companies of infantry – 5 companies of Waller's Regiment and 4 companies of Jones's Regiment.

Wilmot

Hay's Bridge

Haselrig

Cherwell

Wardington

Cropredy

Upper Wardington

Cropredy Bridge

Middleton

WALLER

Cleveland

Cropredy Mill

Williamscot House

Thelwall

Great Bourton

Northampton

Slat Mill

Waller

Ford

Waller with 1,000 horse.

Little Bourton

WALLER 9,000 (approx.)
Source: nil (2)
Foot: 5,000
Horse: 4,000
Artillery: 24 guns

Chacombe

N
W   E
S

0   1/2
mile
(height in feet)

Banbury
2 miles ↓

had better memories of Edgehill and who feared that Waller's army would move to act as the hammer on the anvil of the London trained bands with the advancing Royalists caught between.

From 25 June it seems, therefore, that both commanders, if not intent on battle, were resigned to that outcome. Both armies were poised numerically at 9,000, but both commanders were anxious to secure favourable ground. The manoeuvrings of both forces over the period 25–28 June are a good example of some fairly sophisticated intelligence at work in both headquarters. By early morning on 29 June both armies were near Banbury. Waller had won the race for Crouch Hill (southwest of Banbury), and Charles mused over how to remove him from the feature without committing to battle. The two armies faced off for the rest of the day, as Richard Coe in the Tower Hamlet's Regiment recalled: 'Our horse and they faced one the other, the water being between them and us, we not willing to venture between them and the Castle, they not daring to come over to us, there we lay all night, but knew not their minds, as they it seems did ours.'[8] At about 8am the order was given for the Royalists to move north-east towards Daventry in order to 'observe Waller's motion and expect a fitter opportunity and place to give him battell'.[9] It had the desired effect, for 'we were no sooner on our March, but the Rebels drew off from their Ground, and coasted us on the other side of the River, but at such a distance that we did not at all believe they would have attempted us'.[10]

Waller, who had been monitoring the movement of the King's army from the west bank, had ordered his main body to advance off the high ground and move towards the River Cherwell and to prepare to strike in the flank of the Royalists, should the opportunity seem favourable. He paused at Great Bourton in order to survey the line of the King's army and to better gauge the terrain. He could see the three crossings over the Cherwell: the bridge at Cropredy, the ford to the south at Cropredy Mill and a ford further downstream near Slat Mill (see map 78). The Royalists had already moved a small party of dragoons under Colonel Thomas Hooper to cover the former. It is unclear whether Waller was committed at this stage to crossing the river and engaging the enemy in the flank, but it was certainly a development in the Royalists' dispositions that changed everything. Sir Edward Walker, the King's secretary-extraordinary to the Privy Council, who was with the monarch on the field, recalled:

Our Army marching in this order, certaine intelligence was brought that a boddy of three hundred Rebelles horse were within two Myles of our Van, intending to joyne with Waler, by which it was judged that they might be easily cut off by our quick advancing; whereupon, our formest horse, upon order, hastened their March...[11]

The vanguard, under the Earl of Brentford, hastened, while the rearguard under Cleveland, unaware of any increase in tempo, fell behind. A gap of over 1½ miles quickly opened between the centre (with the main body) and the rear.

As the Royalists became more strung out, Waller calculated that it was a risk worth taking and ordered an attack on the Royalist 'heel'. Middleton, with Haselrig's and Vandruske's cavalry, supported by 900 infantry and 11 guns (under Wemyss) made for Cropredy bridge and the ford to the south of it, while Waller, with 1,000 horse, crossed the ford at Slat Mill and swung north into Northampton's horse. The Royalist rearguard consisted of Northampton's and Cleveland's brigades of horse (500 each) and 100 commanded musketeers under Colonel Thelwall. Waller's group closed on Northampton's Brigade with speed and they, in turn, deployed to meet them. Both attacks were met by corresponding cavalry charges. The Royalist newssheet recorded the events:

Those Two most valiant Earles instantly faced about, and twice charged through the Rebels, and were so well seconded by their horse, and Sir Bernard Astley's Foot, that in a short time they Routed the Rebels, both horse and Foot, killed 150 in the place [and] tooke all their 14 pieces of Ordnance.[12]

To the north, Haselrig's Horse had headed off to try to capture Hay's Bridge and cut the Royalist army in two. Thomas Ellis, an officer in Waller's Parliamentarian army, remembered that 'Wee pursued them above a mile till we came to a bridge, where their foot made a stand, drew up and faced us... they overthrew a Carriage to barricado the bridge, and planted it with Muskettiers'.[13] Charles immediately drew up the main body north of Hay's bridge and sent a strong body of the King's Troop under Lord Wilmot back across the river to assist his rearguard. Both Parliamentarian groups were driven back on their artillery support but, despite a number of light guns having crossed the river and been deployed, they failed to stem the tide. Lieutenant Colonel John Birch, who was commanding Haselrig's Foot on the west bank near Cropredy, could see the problem quite clearly: 'But when there begun to bee need of shott, and that the Kings army began to drawe up, then it was found there was in these regiments, cullers, pikes, leather guns; but our shott was in the reare.'[14] James Wemyss, despite being a hugely experienced gunner, was unable to provide the level of artillery support at a critical moment in the battle. During the hurried retreat he not only lost most of his guns on the east bank but he lost his liberty too by being taken prisoner.[15] The Royalist reaction and follow up was swift and clinical. Waller's attack had failed completely. Still holding the bridge at Cropredy, he drew up his demoralized army on the high ground west of Cropredy village. The two sides faced each other for the remainder of the day. At dusk, when some heavier Royalist guns began to bombard the Parliamentarian forces, Waller gave the order to withdraw. It had been, not for the first time for Waller, a humiliating defeat.

8 Ibid., p. 5.
9 Walker, *Historical discourses*, p. 30.
10 Ibid., p. 31.
11 Ibid.

12 *Mercurius Aulicus*, Week 26, p. 1056.
13 Ellis, *Kings forces and Sir William Waller*, p. 4.
14 Webb, *Military Memoir of Colonel John Birch*, p. 13.
15 *CSPD* dated 30 June 1644 (Waller's report to the Committee).

CHAPTER 22
EVENTS IN THE SOUTH-WEST, APRIL TO AUGUST 1644

The meeting at Chipping Norton on 6 June (see chapter 21) between Essex and Waller reached a significant conclusion. The King, having slipped the cordon around Oxford, was heading off deep into the Cotswolds and beyond. Essex concluded, therefore, that he would leave Waller chasing the King, while he would better serve the cause by heading off south to raise the siege of Lyme Regis. The seeds of this plan had been sown by the Committee of Both Kingdoms themselves as early as 30 May in a letter to Essex:

> This Committee is clearly of opinion that it is necessary to send presently such a strength as may relieve Lyme, which will not only preserve that town which deserves so well, but be a means to prevent the levies of men and money now raising by a new Association in those parts, and to recover the whole West, whose affections are already very inclinable to the Parliament.[1]

However, it was never their intention that Essex should take his force to the area, and they expressed their dismay and no little anger on hearing that he had done just that a few days after that fateful meeting. Their instructions to halt his advance arrived as he entered Blandford on 14 June and prompted a stinging response from Essex.[2] He had absolutely no intention of turning back; it was a decision that he was to bitterly regret.

On 10 June, according to a Parliamentarian scout report, 'Maurice made an assault on the town [Lyme], made a breach and entered some part of it, but was repulsed with the loss of above 50 men.'[3] Five days later, with Essex's force fast approaching, Maurice lifted the siege. Essex then went on to capture Weymouth and Bridport before, like all military commanders devoid of a strategic plan and/or support, calling for a council of war.[4] He had achieved his initial aims in the area but, heavily influenced by some of his close advisors, namely Lord Robartes, he elected to remain and to regain full control of the West Country. The Committee of Both Kingdoms, somewhat exasperated but mildly placated, had reached the same decision and the same day a letter was despatched from London authorizing him to use his 'best endeavours for reducing the West'.[5] Before Essex's campaign could really get going, news arrived of Waller's reverse at Cropredy Bridge. Despite the seriousness of the failure, it must have solicited a wry smile from Essex. At the subsequent Royalist council after Cropredy, the King, fearful for the safety of the Queen, and amidst conflicting rumours as to the outcome of the events around York (chapter 20), elected to head south, link up with Hopton and Maurice, and pursue Essex.

By 15 July the King had reached Bath. He was relieved, but not surprised, to discover that Waller was not in pursuit.[6] However, this good news was tempered by the full and accurate report that reached his council outlining the extent of the Royalist defeat at Marston Moor.[7] He contemplated turning back and linking up with Rupert in the north. However, with Essex closing in on Exeter, his overriding concern was for the safety of his wife and this hardened his resolve. He was unaware that that very day the Queen, whose health was failing, had departed for France in a Flemish man-of-war.[8] Essex, meanwhile, had received intelligence that a Royalist force under the King was marching south-west. At Tiverton, on 5 July, he had another council and debated three options: to turn back and engage the King's army in Somerset; to lay siege to Exeter; or to continue west, relieve the siege of Plymouth, and reduce Royalist Cornwall. He elected for the latter option on the assumption that he had the full cooperation of Admiral Warwick and the Parliamentarian navy that was active off the coast, that he would receive local support in Cornwall, and finally, that Waller was hot on the King's heels. As it turned out, the first two assumptions were ungrounded and the latter, in the age of sail, was to be limited in scope.

On 23 July, with reports of Essex's continued westerly movement, Richard Grenville lifted the siege of Plymouth and moved swiftly with his force of about 4,000 north-east in order to avoid being surrounded.[9] Three days later Essex crossed the River Tamar and entered Cornwall. He appeared ostensibly oblivious that, by moving in to the geographically constrained area of the South-West peninsula, he was marching into a trap. Parliament, it seems, was more aware of Essex's predicament and ordered Waller to move as quickly as possible to the South-West in support. Furthermore, Waller was to despatch Middleton immediately with a strong force of 2,000 horse in advance of his army.[10] The same day, the Royalist armies concentrated at Okehampton, mustering about 16,000 men, and on 1 August this combined force crossed the Tamar and entered Cornwall. The Cornish, considering the King's army the lesser of two evils, gave them every support; Essex's men, conversely, despite Lord Robartes' assurances, had received nothing but hostility. Despite running short of supplies, Essex remained unperturbed; his faulty intelligence informed him the King had but 7,000 men and he remained convinced that Waller was hard on his tail. Furthermore, the terrain, consisting of small enclosures, narrow lanes, steep

---

1   *CSPD* dated 30 May 1644.
2   Ibid., dated 10am 14 June 1644.
3   Tibbutt, *Samuel Luke*, p. 666.
4   An attempt on Dorchester failed. Rushworth, *Historical Collections*, part 3, vol. II, p. 686.
5   Ibid., pp. 683–4.

6   Waller's army was still intact, but following the London regiments' poor performance at Cropredy and the subsequent desertion, his force was woefully short of infantry.
7   In fact, the Committee of Both Kingdoms had, at this stage, ordered Waller to stay in the Midlands and make good use of the fertile recruiting grounds.
8   Admiral Warwick had pursued the vessel and nearly intercepted it. Princess Henrietta was left within the confines of Exeter.
9   Richard Grenville was the brother of Bevil Grenville who, after serving in Ireland, had defected to the Royalists.
10 *CSPD* dated 24 July 1644. Middleton apparently tried to besiege Donnington Castle en route, which he failed to capture, merely serving to slow his westerly movement.

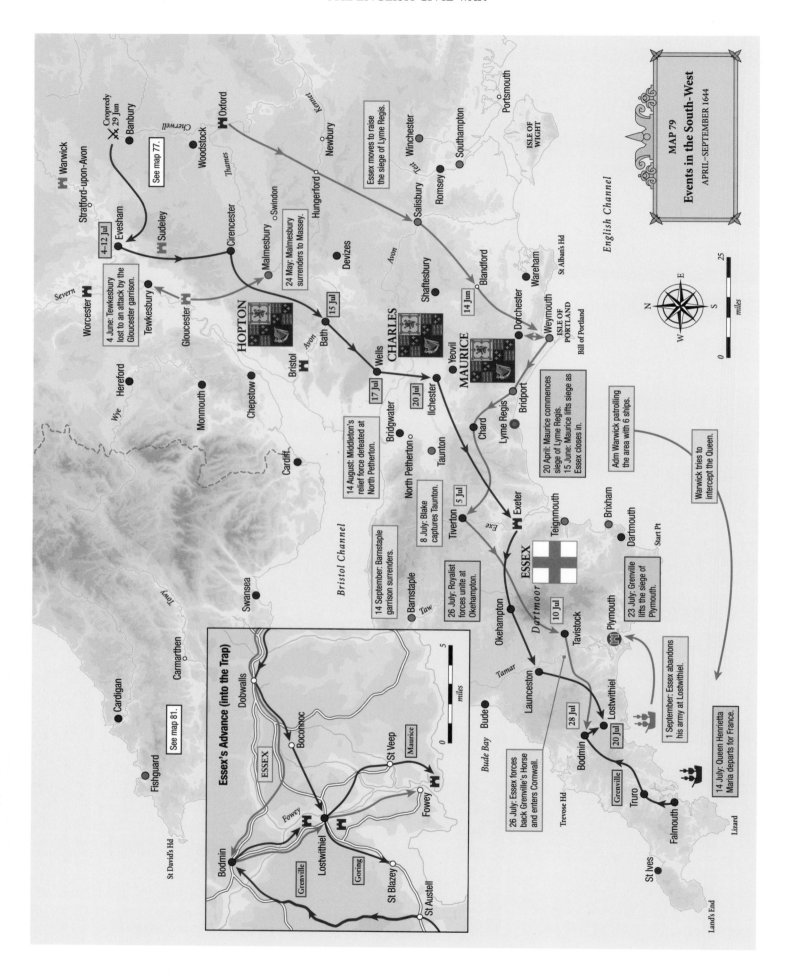

MAP 79
Events in the South-West
APRIL–SEPTEMBER 1644

Cropredy
29 Jun

Banbury

Warwick

Stratford-upon-Avon

Woodstock

See map 77.

Oxford

Newbury

Essex moves to raise the siege of Lyme Regis.

Winchester

Southampton

Portsmouth

ISLE OF WIGHT

Evesham

4–12 Jul

Sudeley

Cirencester

Malmesbury

Swindon

Hungerford

24 May: Malmesbury surrenders to Massey.

Devizes

Salisbury

Romsey

English Channel

N
W E
S

0   25   miles

Worcester

Severn

Tewkesbury

Gloucester

4 June: Tewkesbury lost to an attack by the Gloucester garrison.

HOPTON

15 Jul

Bath

Shaftesbury

Blandford

14 Jun

Dorchester

Wareham

St Alban's Hd

Weymouth

ISLE OF PORTLAND
Bill of Portland

Hereford

Wye

Monmouth

Chepstow

Bristol

Wells

CHARLES

17 Jul

Ilchester

Yeovil

MAURICE

20 Jul

Bridport

Lyme Regis

20 April: Maurice commences siege of Lyme Regis.
15 June: Maurice lifts siege as Essex closes in.

Cardiff

14 August: Middleton's relief force defeated at North Petherton.

Bridgwater

North Petherton

Taunton

Chard

Adm Warwick patrolling the area with 6 ships.

Bristol Channel

8 July: Blake captures Taunton.

Tiverton

5 Jul

Exeter

Exe

Teignmouth

Brixham

Dartmouth

Start Pt

Warwick tries to intercept the Queen.

Swansea

14 September: Barnstaple garrison surrenders.

Barnstaple

Taw

26 July: Royalist forces unite at Okehampton.

ESSEX

Carmarthen

Towy

Okehampton

10 Jul

Tavistock

Plymouth

23 July: Grenville lifts the siege of Plymouth.

Dartmoor

Cardigan

See map 81.

Fishguard

St David's Hd

Essex's Advance (into the Trap)

Dobwalls

Boconnoc

ESSEX

St Veep

Maurice

Fowey

Lostwithiel

Grenville   Goring

St Blazey

St Austell

Bodmin

0   5   miles

Launceston

Tamar

Bude

Bude Bay

26 July: Essex forces back Grenville's Horse and enters Cornwall.

28 Jul

Bodmin

20 Jul

Lostwithiel

1 September: Essex abandons his army at Lostwithiel.

Grenville

Truro

Falmouth

St Ives

Trevose Hd

14 July: Queen Henrietta Maria departs for France.

Land's End

Lizard

184

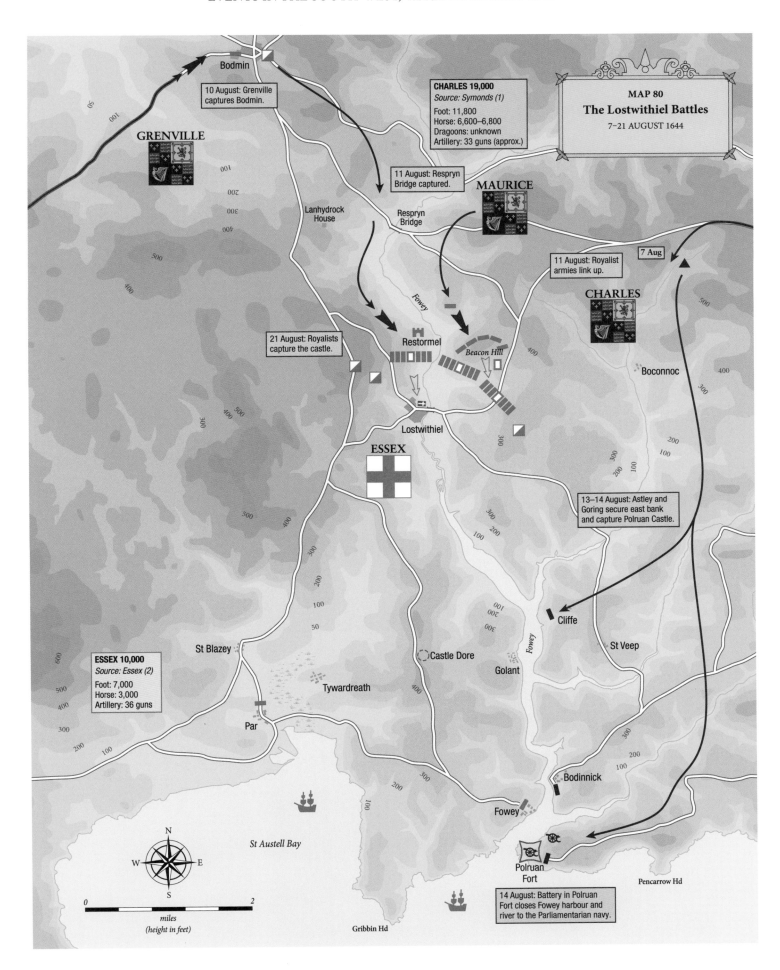

10 August: Grenville captures Bodmin.

Bodmin

GRENVILLE

CHARLES 19,000
Source: Symonds (1)
Foot: 11,800
Horse: 6,600–6,800
Dragoons: unknown
Artillery: 33 guns (approx.)

MAP 80
The Lostwithiel Battles
7–21 AUGUST 1644

11 August: Respryn Bridge captured.

Lanhydrock House

Respryn Bridge

MAURICE

11 August: Royalist armies link up.

7 Aug

21 August: Royalists capture the castle.

Fowey

Restormel

Beacon Hill

CHARLES

Boconnoc

Lostwithiel

ESSEX

13–14 August: Astley and Goring secure east bank and capture Polruan Castle.

ESSEX 10,000
Source: Essex (2)
Foot: 7,000
Horse: 3,000
Artillery: 36 guns

St Blazey

Castle Dore

Cliffe

St Veep

Golant

Tywardreath

Par

Bodinnick

Fowey

N
W E
S

St Austell Bay

Polruan Fort

Pencarrow Hd

14 August: Battery in Polruan Fort closes Fowey harbour and river to the Parliamentarian navy.

0   2
miles
(height in feet)

Gribbin Hd

185

hills and abundant creeks, favoured an army determined to remain on the defensive. Essex decided to create a defensive line from Bodmin to Lostwithiel and despatch Lord Robartes to secure the port at Fowey and establish communication with Warwick and the fleet. Robartes arrived there late on 3 August but there was no sign of Warwick. The same day the King's force advanced from the east and Grenville's from the west. On 4 August, a Royalist patrol 'met with a boy who told them of a many gay men in Lord Mohun's house' at Boconnoc. They raided the place, capturing a number of Parliamentarian officers and soliciting some key intelligence.[11] The noose had begun to tighten.

On 7 August the King's army marched towards Lostwithiel and camped in the vicinity of the battlefield of Braddock Down. The King wrote to Essex the same day, firmly of the belief that he would realize his predicament and settle for terms.[12] Essex's blunt reply arrived at the King's headquarters on 10 August. It stated that he had no authority to negotiate, but that he would send the letter to Parliament.[13] Amidst all the anticipation, evidence was forwarded to the King that Lord Wilmot had been corresponding with the enemy and he subsequently ordered his arrest.[14] It was a blow for the King; he despised turncoats and one so close to him cut deeper. By chance, Goring had arrived from Rupert's army in the north the day prior and seamlessly assumed the post as the King's Lieutenant General of Horse. The coincidence resulted in much speculation, and submissions emerged of loose talk by Wilmot portending the replacement of Charles with the Prince of Wales.[15]

Meanwhile, operations continued, with Grenville's force driving the Parliamentarians out of Bodmin on 10 August. They soon began closing the gap with the King's forces to the east. On 11 August, the Parliamentarian picket at Respryn abandoned the bridge to Grenville and the next day he established his headquarters in Lord Robartes' country residence at Lanhydrock. He was now able to close the link with the King's armies, completing the land cordon around Essex's army. With the loop closed, the precariousness of the situation suddenly appeared to dawn on Essex. The navy did not possess enough transports to evacuate the entire army from Fowey harbour. Furthermore, his hopes of relief from Waller's force were dealt a significant blow when he received notification from the Committee of Both Kingdoms, in a letter dated 9 August, that Waller was ensconced in Abingdon and would not be released until another force could be assembled there to hold the town.[16] It would have wiped the wry smile from Essex's face instantaneously. The boot was now on the other foot. In the meantime, Middleton's relief force of 1,500 horse and 500 dragoons had entered Somerset. They collected a large amount of provisions gathered by the county's commissioners, but considered the Royalist force at Chard too strong, and elected to bypass this force. They headed into the north of the county and into disaster. On 14 August, Middleton was defeated near Bridgwater by a similarly sized cavalry force under William Courtney and Francis Doddington. The Royalists captured 140 prisoners, and the balance of Middleton's dispirited cavalry galloped away towards Sherbourne.[17]

When Parliament received the combined reports detailing Essex's growing predicament and Middleton's apparently unpredicted setback, they reacted by ordering Waller to move to the area with all haste. Waller's movement was now Parliament's main effort, but their actions did not match their words. Waller made it clear that he was deficient in stores, munitions and animals but Parliament's quartermasters and suppliers spent the rest of the month vacillating and failed to provide him the wherewithal to complete his mission.[18] He never made it beyond Farnham.

On 13 and 14 August the Royalists captured most of the east bank of the Fowey River, including the lightly held castle at Polruan, in which they placed a battery of guns. This effectively denied both the river and the harbour at Fowey to Essex's army and Warwick's navy. Nevertheless, the Royalist high command remained undecided on how to bring Essex's force to battle in such undulating terrain. Based on reports of the state of affairs in the Parliamentarian camps, they contemplated starving them out. However, with Warwick's naval assistance, that was going to take an inordinately long time; furthermore, the Royalist supply lines were stretched to the limit and their provisions were fast diminishing. Charles realized that things needed to be brought to a head. On 21 August, under cover of an early morning mist, the three Royalist armies advanced and began to close in on Essex's defensive line. Grenville's and Maurice's troops moved towards their respective objectives – Restormel Castle and Beacon Hill. Part of Weare's Regiment, holding Restormel, panicked and ran, yielding the castle all too easily. On the Parliamentarian right, the forlorn hope was quickly driven back and within minutes the key terrain of Beacon Hill was also in Royalist hands. Quite how these two key positions were allowed to fall so easily remains a mystery, but it is clear that there was a great deal of misunderstanding among the defenders, whose orders were not as clear as they needed to be and whose reactions were slow and uncoordinated.[19] As Walker observed, 'the Rebels did very little by way of opposition, and were certainly surprised'.[20]

Despite attempts to recapture the castle and Beacon Hill, the Royalists continued to hold both positions into the night. However, according to Walker, losses were no more than 40 per army so the fortitude of these counter-attacks seems somewhat questionable. The following day, both sides contented themselves with long-range artillery duels, the Royalists, with no little irony, using some of Waller's (Wemyss's) guns captured from Cropredy.[21] They consolidated their hold on Beacon Hill by building a small redoubt. Although Essex retained Lostwithiel, the Royalist guns atop Beacon Hill could comfortably reach the town and the Parliamentarian troops and battery positioned there. On 24 August Symonds recalled that 'the forenoone was spent in great shott from them to our battery. No harme: we gott many of their bullets… in the afternoon about three of the clock the King went upon the hill, and divers came and told him that the enemy was gone towards Foye'.[22] When the Royalists advanced the next day, they were

11 Peachey, *Symonds*, p. 18.
12 Walker, *Historical discourses*, p. 53.
13 Ibid., p. 61.
14 He was imprisoned in Exeter Castle but permitted to leave two weeks later. He departed for exile in France.
15 Coate, *Cornwall in the Great Civil War*, p. 142. Meanwhile Hopton replaced Percy as the Master General of the Ordnance.
16 *CSPD* dated 9 August 1644 and reiterated in a letter dated 12 August 1644.
17 *Mercurius Aulicus*, dated 16 August 1644.

18 *CSPD* letters dated 17 August, 18 August and 2 September 1644.
19 Essex's version does not tally with other primary source accounts and this is all part of the post-Lostwithiel blame game; Essex, *Lord Generall his quarters*, p. 2. For Weare's account see *apologie of Colonell John Were*, p. 7, and *A true relation of the passages that were in his Ex[cellen]cies army after such time as Colonel Were came into it*, p. f.195v. At his court martial, he suggests that his men were given the order to pull out of the castle by Major William Boteler, who, Weare suggests, was acting on higher orders.
20 Walker, ibid., p. 66.
21 Ede-Borrett, *Lostwithiel 1644*, p. 33.
22 Peachey, op. cit., p. 22.

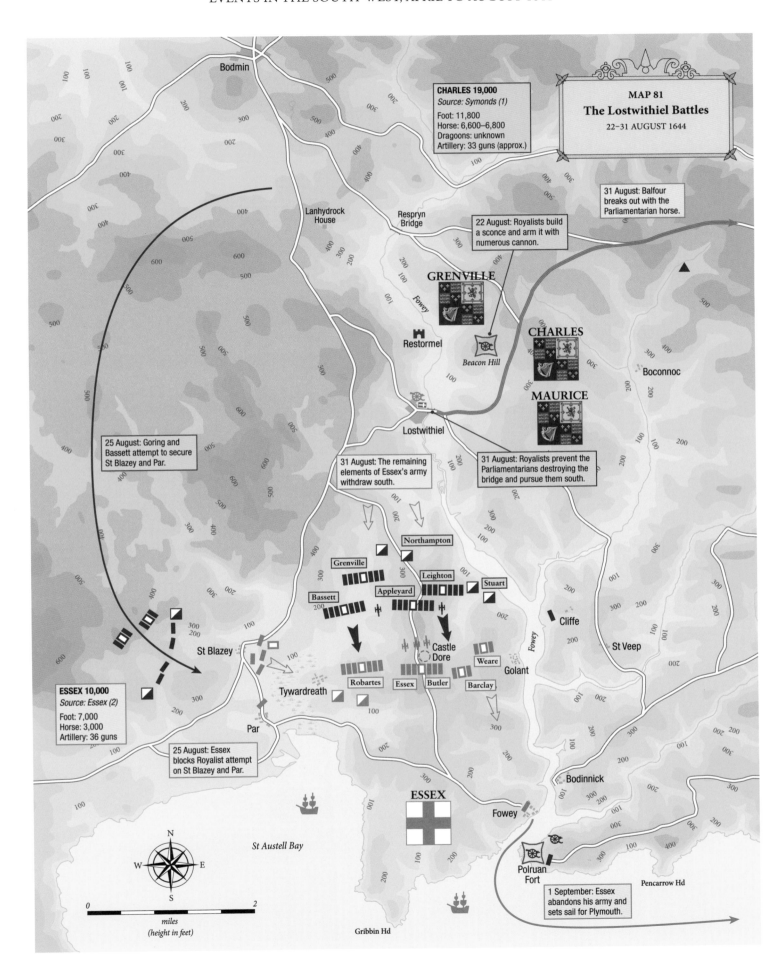

CHARLES 19,000
Source: Symonds (1)
Foot: 11,800
Horse: 6,600–6,800
Dragoons: unknown
Artillery: 33 guns (approx.)

MAP 81
The Lostwithiel Battles
22–31 AUGUST 1644

31 August: Balfour breaks out with the Parliamentarian horse.

22 August: Royalists build a sconce and arm it with numerous cannon.

GRENVILLE

Respryn Bridge

Restormel

CHARLES

Beacon Hill

Boconnoc

MAURICE

Lostwithiel

31 August: The remaining elements of Essex's army withdraw south.

31 August: Royalists prevent the Parliamentarians destroying the bridge and pursue them south.

25 August: Goring and Bassett attempt to secure St Blazey and Par.

Northampton

Grenville

Leighton

Stuart

Bassett

Appleyard

Cliffe

St Veep

St Blazey

Castle Dore

Weare

Golant

Robartes

Essex

Butler

Barclay

ESSEX 10,000
Source: Essex (2)
Foot: 7,000
Horse: 3,000
Artillery: 36 guns

Tywardreath

25 August: Essex blocks Royalist attempt on St Blazey and Par.

Par

Bodinnick

ESSEX

Fowey

St Austell Bay

Polruan Fort

Pencarrow Hd

1 September: Essex abandons his army and sets sail for Plymouth.

N
W   E
S

0   2
miles
(height in feet)

Gribbin Hd

Bodmin

Lanhydrock House

surprised to discover the Parliamentarian positions manned and reinforced. Essex's men had not pulled back, but had dug in and concealed themselves from the effective artillery fire. Maurice called off the attack, while an attempt to blow up a large amount of powder was thwarted, as Essex recalled: 'When 60 barrels of gunpowder, of the 100 you sent last, were to be brought from the bay an attempt was made by placing lighted matches in the waggons to explode the powder, but neither of them fired.'[23]

On 25 August the King decided to try to cut off the Parliamentarian lifeline to the sea by capturing St Blazey and Par. Goring, with 2,000 horse, and Bassett, with 1,500 foot, were sent to the area and Essex immediately responded by sending an all-arms force to protect his left flank.[24] Essex was now constrained to a small strip of land on the west bank of the Fowey, and although the Royalist forces outnumbered the Parliamentarians by two to one, the fact remained that the Royalist perimeter was far too extensive to be completely effective.[25] Furthermore, stocks of Royalist powder were running dangerously low. But Essex was not to know this and from his end of the telescope things were bleak indeed. On 27 August, he wrote to the Committee of Both Kingdoms outlining his concerns:

> Our duty here is so great that, if the enemy do not draw off or we receive succour speedily, we shall be put to great extremities, spending much ammunition and match, which we cannot afford, besides the fatigue of the soldiers, many of them not having been relieved for eight days.[26]

Having received no reply, a council of war three days later resolved that Balfour should break out with 2,000 horse and head for Plymouth. On 31 August at 3am, aided by the moonless night and some questionable work by the Royalist sentries, Balfour's Horse escaped.[27]

At the same time, Essex began to pull back the balance of his army towards Fowey in the hope that they could be evacuated by sea. He established a strong defensive line from Golant to Par through Castle Dore. The Royalist cavalry pursued them with vigour, determined not to let them escape, and the infantry was not far behind. A Parliamentarian officer recalled that 'the enemy having felt the Animosity of our Horse in breaking through their army, had little heart to pursue them; but presently with all

their force, fell on our Foot, on every side, supposing them to be all at their mercy, but resolved to show them no mercy at all'.[28] During the initial stages of the withdrawal discipline had begun to unravel, but the Royalist resolution not to give quarter hardened their resolve. With their backs to the sea, the Parliamentarians fought with a renewed fury, and at 4pm they executed a counter-attack to check the Royalist advance. The terrain hindered a combined attack by infantry and cavalry but they had checked the advance and the Royalist forces began to go firm. Towards evening, Essex ordered a second counter-attack to drive the Royalists back. It was successful to a point, but Northampton followed it up with a cavalry charge against some of Weare's isolated troops; they fled and carried many of Barclay's men with them. As light faded the Parliamentarians were driven further back. Night alone saved the force – for now.

That night Essex, Robartes and Merrick boarded a small craft and abandoned their army. They were transferred to a larger craft in the Channel and set sail for Plymouth. Philip Skippon was left in charge of the demoralized force and, at the council he called on 1 September, he proposed that they should select the honourable option and, like their cavalry, try to break out. However, after days of fighting, encumbered by large numbers of wounded comrades, enduring little sleep and meagre rations, the fire had been extinguished in their bellies. They convinced their officers of the futility of the situation and they, in turn, proposed that Skippon ask for terms. The next day the Parliamentarian soldiers marched away, leaving 45 guns, over 9,000 muskets and pikes. They were allowed to keep their colours and the officers their swords. Under terms, which many in the Royalist hierarchy considered far too lenient, Parliament's soldiers were to be given safe escort to the garrisons at Poole and Wareham. Their passage was, however, anything but safe; they were frequently attacked by Royalist soldiers and angry Cornish men and women en route.[29] Meanwhile, Essex was quick to try to deflect blame, suggesting that he had been hung out to dry by his political masters and through the petty jealousies of *other* generals. No names, no pack drill.[30] He was supported in that claim by two staunch advocates of the Parliamentarian cause, Denzil Lord Holles and Bulstrode Whitelocke, but the evidence suggests incompetence and lethargy rather than intrigue.[31] Either way, Parliament had suffered its worst defeat of the war, leaving many scratching their heads in London.

23 *CSPD* letters dated 27 August 1644.

24 Walker, op. cit., p. 68.

25 Wanklyn, *The Warrior Generals*, p. 118; Barratt, *South-West*, p. 96.

26 *CSPD*, loc. cit.

27 Walker, op. cit., pp. 70–1. It was all the more remarkable as two Parliamentary prisoners had warned the Royalists about the breakout earlier that day. Although Ede-Borrett, op. cit., p. 38 presents evidence that Balfour had to fight his way out.

28 R. B. & E. H., *Sad passages*, p. 4. Reid, *King's Armies*, p. 182, suggests that the Royalist attack was made in two columns.

29 Walker, op. cit., p. 80, suggests that only 1,000 made it to Poole safely, although Wanklyn, op. cit., p. 121, suggests the figure was nearer 3,000 – which seems more realistic. The figure of 800–900 in *CSPD* dated 14 September 1644 refers to the first elements only.

30 Rushworth, op. cit., pp. 701–3 for a copy of Essex's letter to Sir Philip Stapleton.

31 Holles, *Memoirs of Denzil Lord Holles*, p. 25; Whitelocke (ed.), *Memoirs*, p. 187.

CHAPTER 23

WAR IN THE CENTRE: THE SECOND BATTLE OF NEWBURY, AUGUST TO NOVEMBER 1644

During the weeks following the loss of Essex's army at Lostwithiel, both sides manoeuvred in an attempt to deliver the *coup de grâce*. Essex escaped blame for the disaster, and in order to divert any suggestion of tardiness on their part, the Committee of Both Kingdoms decided 'to write to Manchester, Waller, Behr, Skippon, Middleton, and Col. Cromwell to lay aside all disputes of their rights and privileges and to join heartily together in the present service'.[1] Alas, it was not to be. The campaign leading to the second battle at Newbury exposed escalating tensions between Essex, Manchester and Waller and a number of other officers, most notably Oliver Cromwell. On 14 October, after weeks of disagreement between Parliament's military commanders, the Committee were compelled to set a mechanism to ensure that they stuck to the political script and worked in unison to achieve the mission laid out within it.[2] Within days, in an attempt to deliver that decisive blow to Charles's army and end the war before winter, Parliament fielded an army of 11,000 foot and 8,000 horse.[3]

The King, at this time, had two large armies in the field – his own in the south-west and the rejuvenated army of Rupert that, post the battle at Marston Moor, had moved south during August and was now in Shropshire and Herefordshire.[4] The King's army marched slowly east and on 11 September it halted before the walls of Plymouth. Charles was hoping that recent events would have weakened their resolve. The garrison quickly disabused him, and leaving Grenville to blockade the town, he set off for Exeter. In early October he met with Rupert at Sherborne and they agreed a plan of action. Once reinforced with 4,000 cavalry and 2,000 infantry, Charles would take the offensive.[5] The King's proclamation, issued at Chard on 30 September, suggested that the Royalists' objective would be London; but Charles was under no illusion that the concentration of Parliament's armies in the south would make that improbable.[6] Instead, by way of preliminary operations, he was determined to raise the sieges of Banbury and Donnington castles and Basing House, before reinforcing Oxford and seeking winter quarters. However, the situation at Basing House was so desperate that the garrison would not have held out long enough to wait for the King. General Gage, who had recently joined the Royalist cause from an English regiment in Flanders, decided to take 250 horse and 400 infantry and march directly from Oxford. On 14 September he drove off the besieging force, relieved the garrison, replenished the stores and returned to

Oxford. Six days later he re-entered the Royalist capital with 100 prisoners and to huge acclaim.[7]

Alas, Gage's popular exploits had gained only a brief respite, for within a week the Parliamentarian forces had reoccupied Basingstoke and resumed the siege of Basing. A few days later, Horton was despatched to have another go at Donnington Castle. Charles grew increasingly anxious about news from Basing, and intelligence pertaining to Horton's planned mission against Donnington, and decided he could not wait for Rupert to return with the reinforcements. He decided to open proceedings by moving towards Waller's force at Andover. Despite the Royalist threat, the Parliamentarian armies remained dispersed. Manchester was at Reading and the remnants of Essex's army near Portsmouth. However, the King's sudden advance on 15 October spurred them into action and within five days they were all concentrated in and around Basingstoke. The matter of overall command had been addressed in a directive from the Committee of Both Kingdoms dated 14 October.[8] It is an extraordinary document, and its conclusions for the execution and unity of command were completely unsuited to military procedure and decision making. To all intents and purposes, the directive effectively placed the three armies under a sub-group, thereby conducting business by committee. To make matters worse, Essex was to fall ill and return to Reading, his absence being concealed from the men. Manchester was now the senior general on the newly formed committee and, since the battle of Marston Moor, his determination, rather than his commitment to the cause, was very much open to question.[9]

The decision to concentrate had, however, forced the Parliamentarians to lift the sieges of Banbury and Donnington. By the evening of 26 October, after some manoeuvring, both armies were within 3 miles of each other near Newbury. The Parliamentarians drew up in battalia beyond Thatcham and were determined to cut off the road to Oxford. They drove off a Royalist forward post on Clay Hill (to the east of the town) and established a number of guns on it from where they dominated the Oxford road and the Royalist strongpoint at Shaw House. The Royalist army was positioned in the wedge between the Kennet and Lambourn rivers. The three bridges north of the Lambourn were either destroyed or covered with fire and they had strengthened their positions along the riverbank with breastworks and entrenchments. They occupied several houses which extended beyond Newbury, including Shaw House on the north bank, which was fortified and supported by artillery.[10] In addition, the guns from Donnington Castle provided a considerable advantage as they could enfilade any attempt by the Parliamentarians to cross the Lambourn from the north.

1 *CSPD* dated 10 September 1644.

2 Wanklyn, *The Warrior Generals*, p. 129.

3 Money, *Battles of Newbury*, p. 142. These are Cromwell's figures from his evidence against the Earl of Manchester.

4 The King's army was about 10,000 strong and that of Rupert, which included Newcastle's forces, was about 14,000 strong, but widely spread.

5 These consisted of 2,000 horse from Newcastle's force under Marmaduke Langdale, 2,000 horse from Rupert's force under Gerard, and 2,000 infantry from the garrisons of Bristol and Bath.

6 Rushworth, *Historical Collections*, part 3, vol. II, pp. 715–6.

7 Money, op. cit., p. 139.

8 *CSPD* dated 14 October 1644.

9 See Wanklyn, op. cit., pp. 122–9 and Bruce, J., *The Quarrel between the Earl of Manchester and Oliver Cromwell, an episode of the Civil War* (Camden Society, 1875).

10 Money, op. cit., p. 152.

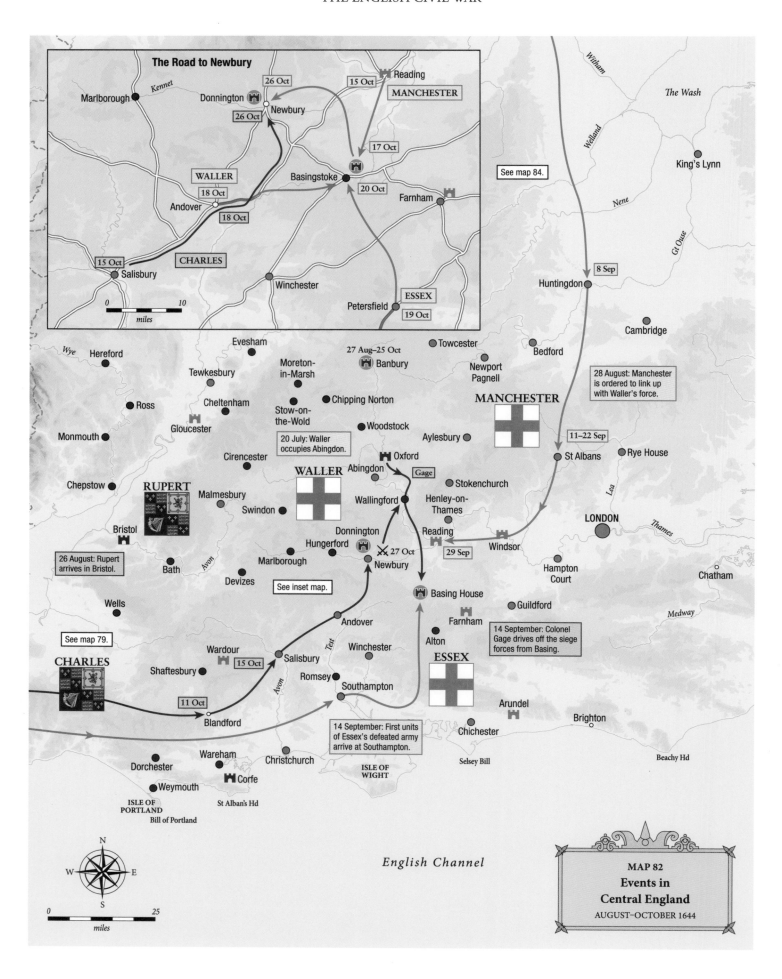

The Road to Newbury

Marlborough

Kennet

26 Oct
Donnington
26 Oct
Newbury

Reading
15 Oct
MANCHESTER

17 Oct

WALLER
18 Oct
Andover
18 Oct

Basingstoke
20 Oct

Farnham

See map 84.

CHARLES
15 Oct
Salisbury

Winchester

ESSEX
19 Oct
Petersfield

0   10
miles

The Wash

King's Lynn

Witham

Welland

Nene

Gt Ouse

8 Sep
Huntingdon

Cambridge

Evesham

27 Aug–25 Oct
Banbury

Towcester

Bedford

Hereford
Wye

Tewkesbury

Moreton-
in-Marsh

Newport
Pagnell

28 August: Manchester
is ordered to link up
with Waller's force.

Ross

Cheltenham

Stow-on-
the-Wold

Chipping Norton

11–22 Sep

Monmouth

Gloucester

Woodstock

Aylesbury

Rye House

MANCHESTER

Cirencester

20 July: Waller
occupies Abingdon.

Oxford

Gage

St Albans

Lea

Chepstow

RUPERT

Malmesbury

Swindon

WALLER

Abingdon

Wallingford

Henley-on-
Thames

Stokenchurch

LONDON

Thames

Bristol

Donnington

Hungerford

27 Oct

Reading

26 August: Rupert
arrives in Bristol.

Marlborough

Newbury

Windsor

29 Sep

Hampton
Court

Chatham

Bath

Devizes

See inset map.

Basing House

Guildford

Medway

Wells

Andover

Farnham

14 September: Colonel
Gage drives off the siege
forces from Basing.

See map 79.

Wardour

Salisbury

Winchester

Alton

CHARLES

15 Oct

Test

Shaftesbury

Romsey

Southampton

ESSEX

Arundel

11 Oct

Avon

Blandford

14 September: First units
of Essex's defeated army
arrive at Southampton.

Chichester

Brighton

Dorchester

Wareham

Christchurch

ISLE OF
WIGHT

Selsey Bill

Beachy Hd

Weymouth

Corfe

ISLE OF
PORTLAND

St Alban's Hd

Bill of Portland

N
W   E
S

0   25
miles

English Channel

MAP 82
Events in
Central England
AUGUST–OCTOBER 1644

Avon

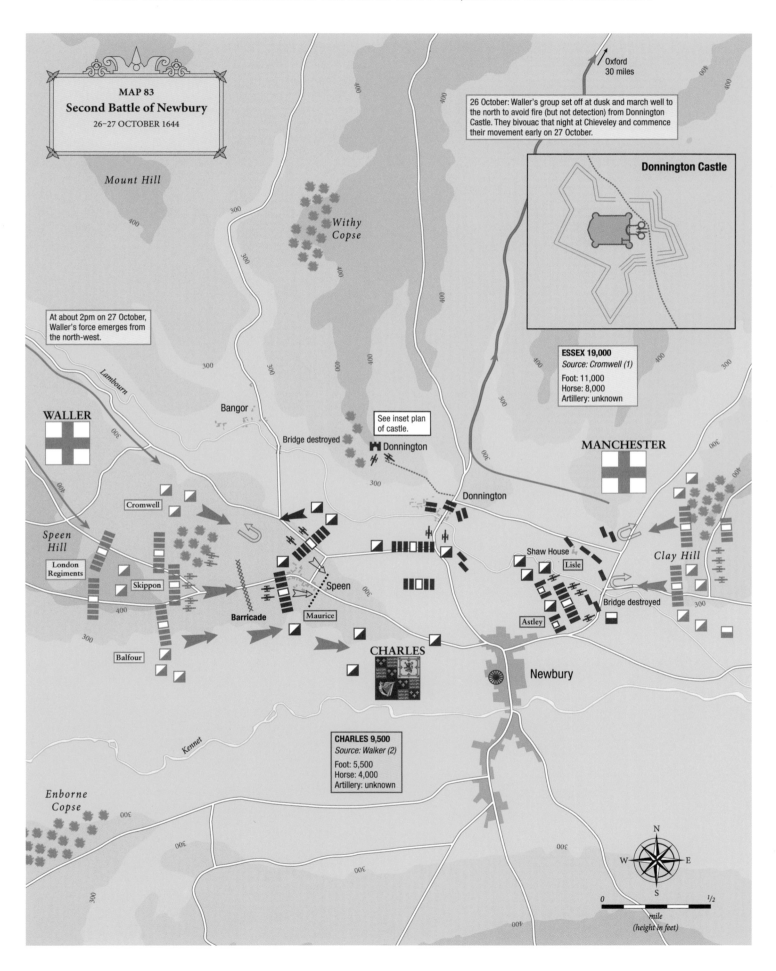

MAP 83

Second Battle of Newbury

26–27 OCTOBER 1644

Mount Hill

Withy Copse

Oxford
30 miles

26 October: Waller's group set off at dusk and march well to the north to avoid fire (but not detection) from Donnington Castle. They bivouac that night at Chieveley and commence their movement early on 27 October.

Donnington Castle

At about 2pm on 27 October, Waller's force emerges from the north-west.

ESSEX 19,000
Source: Cromwell (1)
Foot: 11,000
Horse: 8,000
Artillery: unknown

Lambourn

WALLER

Bangor

See inset plan of castle.

Bridge destroyed

Donnington

MANCHESTER

Donnington

Cromwell

Speen Hill

London Regiments

Skippon

Shaw House

Lisle

Clay Hill

Speen

Barricade

Maurice

Astley

Bridge destroyed

Balfour

CHARLES

Newbury

Kennet

CHARLES 9,500
Source: Walker (2)
Foot: 5,500
Horse: 4,000
Artillery: unknown

Enborne Copse

0   1/2
mile
(height in feet)

Waller and Manchester surveyed the Royalist defences from atop Clay Hill and decided that a frontal attack from the east would be too risky. Following a council of war, it was decided to 'divide their Forces; viz. That all the General's Horse and Foot, part of Manchester's Horse, and most of the Forces under the Command of Waller, should march to Speen-Hill; while the Earl of Manchester's Foot, and part of his Horse, to continue in the field near Shaw'.[11] The plan was for Waller's group to attack the Royalists from the west, while Manchester fell on them from the east. Waller's group set off at dusk and marched well to the north to avoid fire (but not detection) from Donnington Castle. They bivouacked that night at Chieveley and commenced their movement early on 27 October. At 7am, as per the plan, Manchester's force launched its diversionary attack from Clay Hill with the aim of keeping the defenders' eyes looking east and not north-west. They quickly drove back the Royalist infantry and, in their enthusiasm, crossed the line of the Lambourn. Having overextended themselves they were now vulnerable to a counter-attack, which was not long in coming. Despite lacking sufficient reserves, the infantry was able to withdraw under the cover of the Parliamentarian guns. By 9am the activity was all but over and both sides contented themselves with long-range cannonading. Meanwhile, Waller's group had forded the Lambourn at Boxford, where they drove off a weak Royalist picket, and came up on Wickham Heath and Speen Hill at about 2pm. They had to wait another hour for the guns to manoeuvre into position and for the ammunition and powder to be unloaded. The guns then opened fire; it was the signal for Waller's force to attack the Royalist barricades at Speen and for Manchester's force to re-commence their attack on Astley's men in and around Shaw House. For whatever reason, Manchester chose to ignore the signal.

To the west, Waller's forlorn hope drove back the Royalists, forcing the guns to pull back. Then Essex's Foot advanced towards the barricades. As they approached, word spread that the defences were manned by many of Maurice's Cornish infantry. With a score to settle and pride in need of restoration, Essex's men attacked with unbridled fury and tore down the barrier, capturing a number of guns and driving the Cornishmen back into the village. They established a second line of defence along the enclosures at the east end of the village. By this time light was fading fast and some of Balfour's Horse, supported by musketeers, made some progress in clearing the village before darkness. Walter Money, in his detailed history of the battle, suggests that there was great panic among the Cavaliers at this moment, that many ran away having thrown down their arms and that the King himself was in imminent danger.[12] Despite the danger, on Waller's left the advance by Cromwell's and Waller's Horse had been all too easily checked and driven back. Furthermore, to the east, Manchester's attack had not gone in on time, and when they did advance, they were easily picked off by the Royalist infantry who were well sited in ditches, along hedges and in the grounds and buildings of Shaw House. In the gloom some of the Parliamentarian foot in this part of the field fired on their own troops. The attack by Manchester's men quickly faltered, and a charge by some Royalist horse drove the infantry back up the hill, allowing the pursuing Royalist infantry to capture at least one light gun.

Despite the rather questionable series of attacks by the combined armies of Parliament, the Royalists were in the more precarious position. Trapped between two armies to the west and east and two rivers to the north and south, to have remained in position would have been most unwise. Charles had been in a similar dilemma at Oxford in June and, as he had done then, he decided to slip past both armies and head north. Just before midnight the Royalist army marched between the two Parliamentarian forces and made Wallingford before dawn. They made good speed, having deposited all their heavier artillery in Donnington Castle en route. It was a feat of escapology that had left the Parliamentarian commanders scratching their heads and scampering for scapegoats, for the second time in a matter of weeks. By 2 November Charles's army had been reinforced with Rupert's force from the west, and Northampton's Brigade from Banbury. In the meantime, Waller and Manchester, more by way of a sop, had resumed the siege of Donnington, but it was not long before the old divisions resurfaced. During one acrimonious exchange, Cromwell accused Manchester of undermining the war effort and treachery to the cause. It was enough to prompt a government enquiry. They were not to realize at the time that the enquiry was to create a new model, which would turn the tide of the war.

---

11 Rushworth, op. cit., p. 721.

12 Money, op. cit., pp. 167–8. Modern accounts do not see the situation in the same light.

CHAPTER 24

WALES, SCOTLAND AND THE NORTH OF ENGLAND, AUGUST TO THE END OF 1644

Following the Royalist defeat at Marston Moor, Montrose realized that he would be alone fighting the King's cause north of the border. The Earl of Antrim's promise of troops from Ireland had not come to pass, and by mid-August Montrose decided to head south in an attempt to rally support among his Lowland kinsmen.[1] His efforts to rally the temperate people of Fife and the Lothians were largely in vain. As he was losing faith, he received two encouraging pieces of news: firstly, that his cause might be considered sympathetically by some in the Highlands, and secondly, that troops had at last landed from Ireland. About 2,000 native Irish troops landed in Ardnamurchan in late July under the command of Alasdair MacColla MacDonald but their primary aim was not support to the King's cause but to bring vengeance upon a Highland foe. Binding clans for a wider political objective was a nigh on impossible task. In order to secure their line of withdrawal, MacColla's Irish troops seized and garrisoned Mingary Castle and then set off for Inverlochy through Campbell country, killing anyone and burning anything that got in their way.

Montrose, on being apprised of MacColla's arrival, summoned him to Blair Atholl. This combined army numbered a mere 3,000, all foot. Yet they were a force to be reckoned with, consisting of Highland warriors and seasoned Irish troops, the latter, in the main, led by officers who had served in the Spanish army of Flanders. They advanced south in the last days of August and, on 1 September, fell upon a considerable Covenanter army outside Perth. An 18th-century Scottish historian wrote that 'The general committee of estates at Edinburgh, hearing of the Irish progress, hastily raises out of the shires of Fife, Perth and Angus, an army of about 6,000 foot and 800 horse, with expert officers and commanders, ammunition, powder, ball, and four field pieces, to go upon the Irishes'.[2] Montrose lacked a balanced force, had a paucity of muskets and precious little powder, but his warriors broke Elcho's militia within minutes, executing the Highland charge which put the fear of God into the militia troops who fled the field.[3] Montrose then occupied Perth and reequipped and replenished his army before heading north.[4]

On 13 September they reached the outskirts of Aberdeen. MacColla's Irish troops were still with Montrose but many of his Highlanders had returned home to squirrel away their booty and they had been replaced by a few Highlanders under the Earl of Airlie.[5] The combined force numbered only 1,500 when they were confronted by the Covenanter force under Lord Burleigh, which enjoyed twice Montrose's numbers. Montrose summoned the city, and during the tense stand-off near Justice Mills, a young drummer boy was shot dead.[6] Montrose was incensed and ordered an immediate attack. His small cavalry group was placed on either wing, flanking his infantry. They repulsed a Covenanter cavalry charge on the right, before moving to assist the cavalry on the left as the infantry simultaneously advanced. The Irish gave a repeat performance of the Highland charge and this was enough to destroy Covenanter resolve for a second time. For a full three days, Aberdeen was at the mercy of the post-battle licentiousness that followed.

The Committee of Estates was by now mildly concerned and made the Marquis of Argyll commander of the new army that was to track down and eliminate Montrose and his merry band of followers. To create a force for Argyll, troops were withdrawn from Leven's army, which was by now back besieging Newcastle. However, the numbers were inadequate, and Argyll set off in October at the head of just 4,000 men. He headed north, lost the scent and then picked it up again, and in late October caught up with Montrose near Fyvie Castle. His numbers and the nature of the terrain prevented him achieving anything decisive. With winter approaching, Argyll headed south, while Montrose's men went off west to have another head-to-head with the Campbells. They were active in the area for many weeks, killing at least 900 Campbells of military age in the process.[7] One of MacColla's men recalled, 'we left neither house nor hold unburned, nor corn, nor cattle, that belonged to the whole name of Campbell'.[8] Montrose then headed north and sought refuge in the Great Glen, where he waited and planned for renewed offensives in the New Year.

In June 1644, the Earl of Callendar had been despatched with an army of 6,000 foot and 800 horse to deal with Montrose in Northumbria. He had pursued Montrose to Carlisle and besieged the city, but was ordered back towards Newcastle when Leven headed south for the allied concentration against York. Callendar, meanwhile, amused himself with capturing a number of Royalist outposts in July, including Stockport and Hartlepool. Then, sometime after Marston Moor, he received orders to move back towards Newcastle in anticipation of the return of Leven's main army and the resumption of the siege. He approached the city from the south and attacked some of the Royalist defenders on Black Hill south of Gateshead (see map 61). He drove them back the next day and, according to William Lithgow, 'chased them down the Gatesyde, and hushed them along the bridge, closed them within the towne'.[9] Lithgow described how Callendar erected five batteries on the south bank and 'was

---

1 Antrim was a Roman Catholic landed magnate in Scotland and Ireland, and the chief of Clan MacDonnell of Antrim. He had been ordered by the King to raise his Northern Irish MacDonalds and land them on the western coast of Scotland.

2 Spalding, *Memorable transactions in Scotland*, vol. II, p. 233.

3 The Highland charge consisted of two phases: firstly, the troops, armed with muskets, advanced to within a hundred yards and fired a volley, then they dropped the weapon and charged with their broadswords; Kenyon & Ohlmeyer, *Military History*, p. 55.

4 They made an attempt on Dundee but the city was too strongly held.

5 Gardiner, *Great Civil War*, vol. II, p. 143.

6 The Battle of Aberdeen is also known as the Battle or 'Fecht' of Justice Mills.

7 Kenyon & Ohlmeyer, op. cit., p. 58.

8 Wedgwood, *Montrose*, pp. 80–1.

9 Lithgow, *Siege of Newcastle*, p. 10.

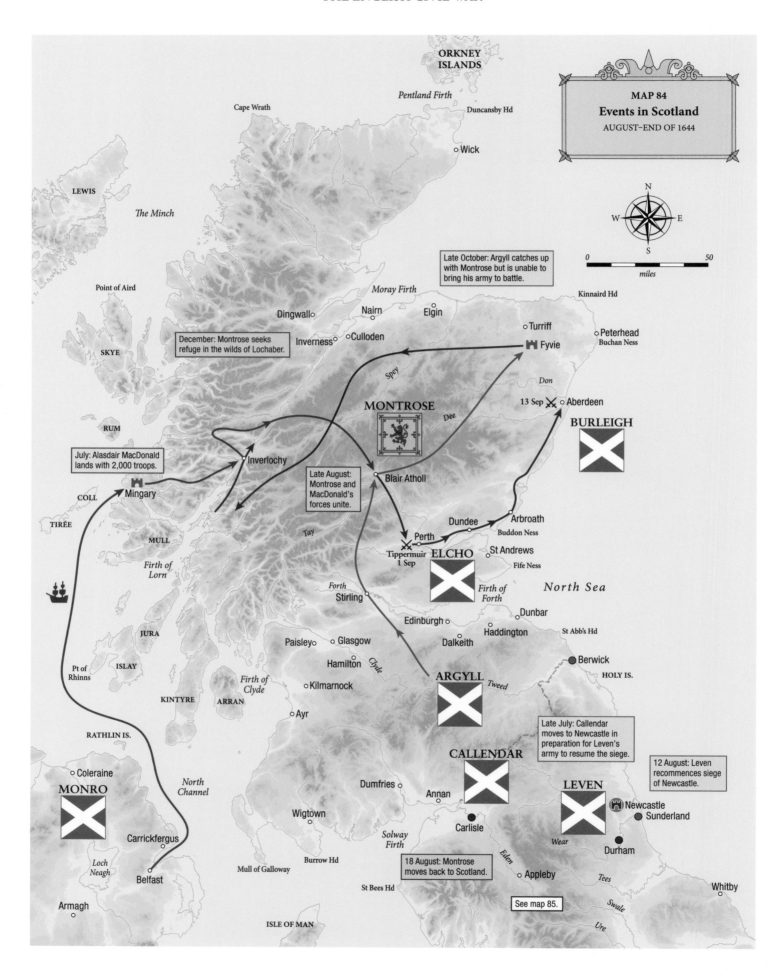

ORKNEY
ISLANDS

Pentland Firth

Cape Wrath

○ Wick
Duncansby Hd

MAP 84
Events in Scotland
AUGUST–END OF 1644

N
W   E
S

LEWIS

The Minch

0   50
miles

Point of Aird

SKYE

Moray Firth
Kinnaird Hd

Late October: Argyll catches up
with Montrose but is unable to
bring his army to battle.

Dingwall ○
Nairn ○   Elgin ○   ○ Turriff   ○ Peterhead
Inverness ○   ○ Culloden   Buchan Ness

December: Montrose seeks
refuge in the wilds of Lochaber.

Spey

⚑ Fyvie

RUM

Don

13 Sep ✗ ○ Aberdeen

MONTROSE

Dee

BURLEIGH

July: Alasdair MacDonald
lands with 2,000 troops.

Inverlochy ○

COLL
Mingary ⚑

Blair Atholl ○

Late August:
Montrose and
MacDonald's
forces unite.

TIRÉE

MULL

Tay

Dundee ○   ○ Arbroath
     Buddon Ness
Perth ○
✗   ELCHO
Tippermuir   ○ St Andrews
1 Sep   Fife Ness

Firth of
Lorn

North Sea

JURA

Firth of
Forth

Forth
Stirling ○

Dunbar ○
Edinburgh ○   ○ Haddington   St Abb's Hd
Dalkeith ○

Pt of
Rhinns
ISLAY

Paisley ○   ○ Glasgow
Hamilton ○
Clyde

ARGYLL

Tweed

● Berwick
HOLY IS.

KINTYRE
ARRAN

Firth of
Clyde

○ Kilmarnock

Ayr ○

RATHLIN IS.

Late July: Callendar
moves to Newcastle in
preparation for Leven's
army to resume the siege.

12 August: Leven
recommences siege
of Newcastle.

○ Coleraine

MONRO

North
Channel

CALLENDAR

LEVEN

Dumfries ○
Annan ○
Carlisle ○

⚑ ● Newcastle
● Sunderland

Carrickfergus ○

Wear

Durham ●

Loch
Neagh

Belfast ○

Wigtown ○

Burrow Hd

Mull of Galloway

Solway
Firth

18 August: Montrose
moves back to Scotland.

Eden

Appleby ○

Tees

Whitby ○

Armagh ○

St Bees Hd

See map 85.

Swale

Ure

ISLE OF MAN

194

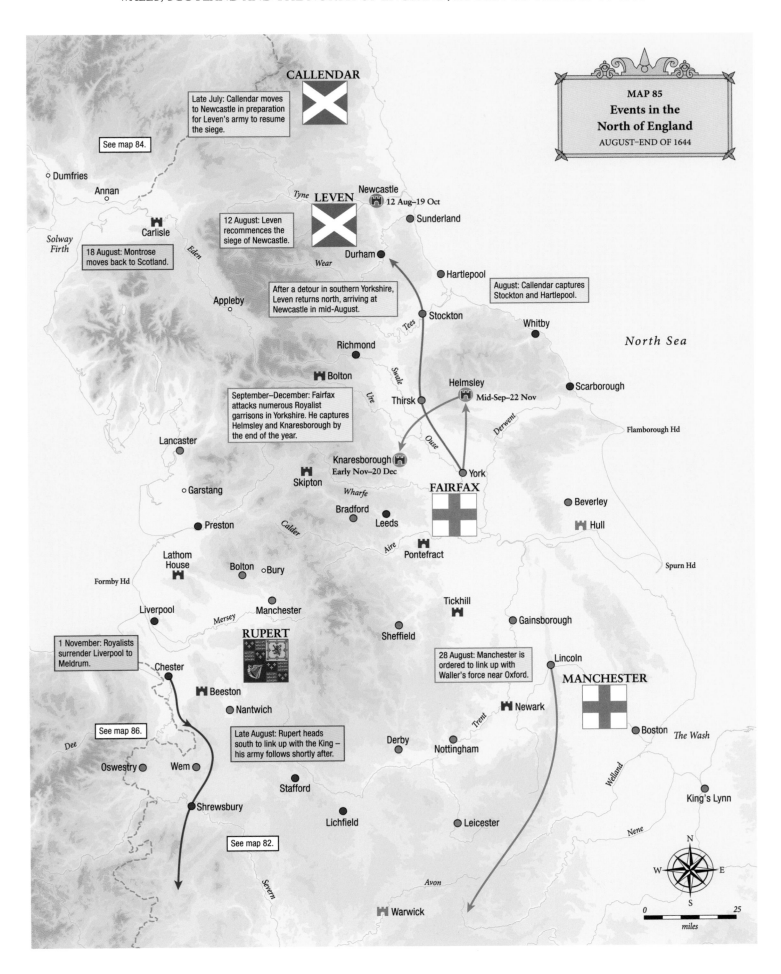

CALLENDAR

Late July: Callendar moves to Newcastle in preparation for Leven's army to resume the siege.

See map 84.

○ Dumfries

Annan

⌂ Carlisle

Solway Firth

18 August: Montrose moves back to Scotland.

Eden

Tyne LEVEN   Newcastle ⌂ 12 Aug–19 Oct

12 August: Leven recommences the siege of Newcastle.

● Sunderland

Durham ●

Wear

○ Appleby

After a detour in southern Yorkshire, Leven returns north, arriving at Newcastle in mid-August.

● Hartlepool

August: Callendar captures Stockton and Hartlepool.

Stockton ●

Tees

● Whitby

North Sea

Richmond ●

⌂ Bolton

Swale

Helmsley ⌂ Mid-Sep–22 Nov

● Scarborough

Thirsk ●

Ure

Derwent

Flamborough Hd

September–December: Fairfax attacks numerous Royalist garrisons in Yorkshire. He captures Helmsley and Knaresborough by the end of the year.

Lancaster ●

Knaresborough ⌂ Early Nov–20 Dec

Ouse

York ●

FAIRFAX

● Beverley

○ Garstang

⌂ Skipton

Wharfe

Bradford ●

● Leeds

⌂ Hull

● Preston

Calder

Aire

⌂ Pontefract

Spurn Hd

Lathom House ⌂

Bolton ● ○ Bury

Formby Hd

● Liverpool

● Manchester

Mersey

Tickhill ⌂

● Gainsborough

1 November: Royalists surrender Liverpool to Meldrum.

RUPERT

Sheffield ●

Lincoln ●

MANCHESTER

Chester ●

⌂ Beeston

● Nantwich

28 August: Manchester is ordered to link up with Waller's force near Oxford.

⌂ Newark

Trent

● Boston

The Wash

See map 86.

Dee

Late August: Rupert heads south to link up with the King – his army follows shortly after.

Oswestry ● Wem ●

Derby ●

Nottingham ●

● Stafford

Shrewsbury ●

● Lichfield

● Leicester

● King's Lynn

Welland

Nene

See map 82.

Severn

Avon

⌂ Warwick

N
W ✦ E
S

0 ___ miles ___ 25

MAP 85
Events in the
North of England
AUGUST–END OF 1644

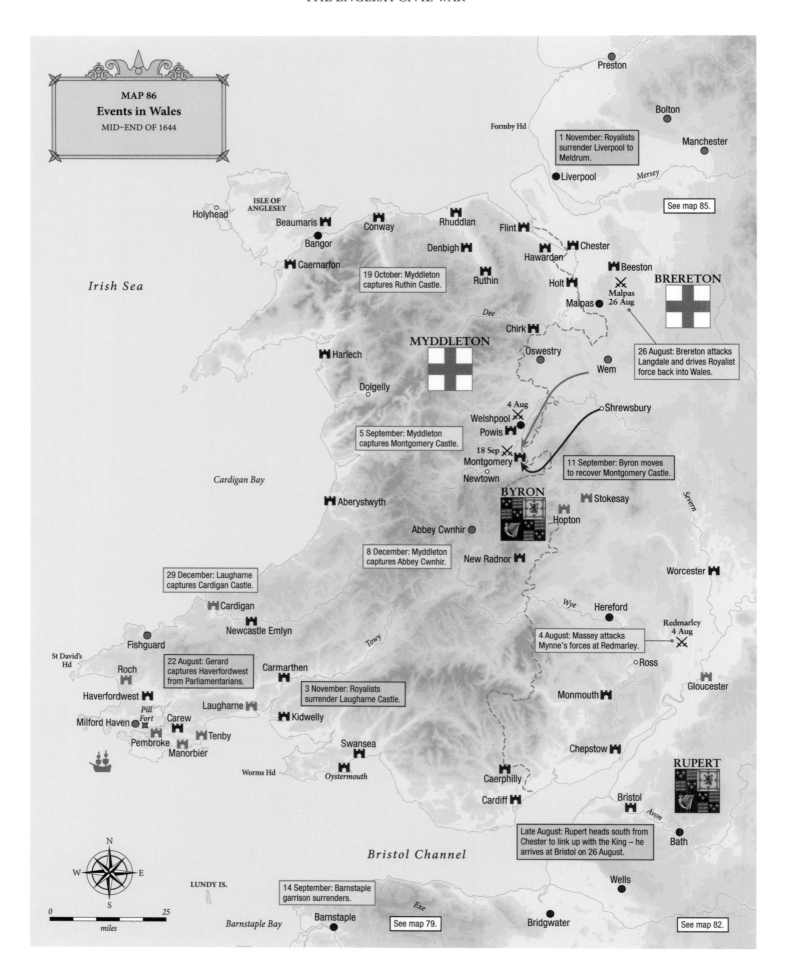

MAP 86

Events in Wales

MID–END OF 1644

Formby Hd

Preston

Bolton

Manchester

1 November: Royalists surrender Liverpool to Meldrum.

Liverpool

Mersey

See map 85.

Irish Sea

Holyhead

ISLE OF ANGLESEY

Beaumaris

Bangor

Caernarfon

Conway

Rhuddlan

Denbigh

Ruthin

Flint

Chester

Hawarden

Holt

Beeston

Malpas

Malpas 26 Aug

BRERETON

19 October: Myddleton captures Ruthin Castle.

Dee

Harlech

Chirk

MYDDLETON

Oswestry

Wem

26 August: Brereton attacks Langdale and drives Royalist force back into Wales.

Dolgelly

Shrewsbury

4 Aug

Welshpool

Powis

5 September: Myddleton captures Montgomery Castle.

18 Sep

Montgomery

Newtown

11 September: Byron moves to recover Montgomery Castle.

Severn

Cardigan Bay

Aberystwyth

BYRON

Stokesay

Hopton

Abbey Cwnhir

8 December: Myddleton captures Abbey Cwnhir.

New Radnor

Worcester

29 December: Laugharne captures Cardigan Castle.

Wye

Hereford

Redmarley 4 Aug

Cardigan

Newcastle Emlyn

4 August: Massey attacks Mynne's forces at Redmarley.

Ross

Fishguard

St David's Hd

Towy

22 August: Gerard captures Haverfordwest from Parliamentarians.

Roch

Carmarthen

3 November: Royalists surrender Laugharne Castle.

Monmouth

Gloucester

Haverfordwest

Pill Fort

Carew

Laugharne

Kidwelly

Milford Haven

Tenby

Pembroke

Manorbier

Swansea

Chepstow

Worms Hd

Oystermouth

Caerphilly

RUPERT

Cardiff

Bristol

Avon

Late August: Rupert heads south from Chester to link up with the King – he arrives at Bristol on 26 August.

Bath

Bristol Channel

N
W E
S

LUNDY IS.

Wells

14 September: Barnstaple garrison surrenders.

0   25

miles

Barnstaple Bay

Barnstaple

Exe

See map 79.

Bridgwater

See map 82.

ever personally directing' the guns, 'Pot-pieces [mortars], and other fireworkes of great importance'.[10] Leven arrived on 15 August and 'immediately built a bridge over the River of Keill boats, over which his Armie have safely and peaceably past'.[11] He then closed the cordon (although Sheffield Fort still remained in Royalist hands at this juncture) and built additional batteries on the north bank.

The walls of Newcastle were strong. Lithgow recorded that they were 'a great deal stronger than these of Yorke, and not unlike the walls of Avineon (Avignon), but especially of Jerusalem'.[12] Leven's engineers resorted to a combination of battering and mining to create the breaches. On 19 October, following a sustained bombardment by the breaching batteries, three mines were detonated, two to the west at the West Gate and Whitefriar Tower, and one to the east at Sandgate. Handpicked men from every regiment assaulted the four breaches (see points 1–4, map 61). They gained access at every breach, the post-siege despatch noting that 'they within the town made all the opposition they could, on the walls, and in the streets'.[13] The defenders fled to the castle but surrendered with little delay. Leven had lost 300 men killed and 800 injured but the prize was well worth it. The loss of Newcastle was the final nail in the coffin for the Royalist cause in the north. Leven captured Tynemouth Castle a few days later and then waited for new orders from the joint committee in London. They were to be a long time coming, as political intrigue and military infighting galvanized the Parliamentarian political and military hierarchy.

Following Marston Moor, Lord Fairfax had been left in the area and he decided to make his base within the walls of York. He turned his attention to reducing some of the remaining Royalist garrisons in Yorkshire. Thomas Fairfax arrived with a force at Helmsley Castle in September. His plan to starve the garrison does not appear to have worked and he was forced to call up heavy artillery to speed up the process. The castle fell on 22 November but not before Fairfax had been badly wounded during a sortie executed by Jordan Crossland's small garrison of 200 men. Knaresborough Castle was his next objective and he despatched Robert Lilburn to blockade the town and castle before the siege at Helmsley had been concluded.[14] On 12 November Lilburn attacked the town and drove the defenders into the castle. With the arrival of the heavier guns from Helmsley, Lilburn was able to prosecute the siege with renewed vigour. On 20 December the garrison surrendered. Fairfax now turned his attention to the castle at Pontefract, a strongpoint that had caused him considerable aggravation since Newcastle had captured and garrisoned the place two years earlier, following the Battle of Tadcaster. As the year came to an end the siege guns were being moved south from Knaresborough, but Pontefract was to remain a thorn in Fairfax's side for some time to come.

Since the defeat of Byron's army at Nantwich in January 1644, the Parliamentarians had slowly established a footprint within Shropshire and the Marches. Attempts by the Royalists to recapture Stokesay Castle in June and Oswestry in July were to fail. With Wem and Oswestry in Parliamentarian hands, this opened the possibility of a route into Wales along the Severn valley. In mid-1644, Thomas Myddleton, the Parliamentarian commander

in the Shropshire area, had executed a war of propaganda, distributing a manifesto in which he promised to deliver the northern Welsh from Royalist burden. It had been more of a publicity stunt than a realistic proposal but the movement of large numbers of Royalist forces to join Rupert in Yorkshire in June had now opened up the opportunity for military action. On 4 August Myddleton's forces raided Welshpool and captured a number of prisoners. He eyed Powis Castle but did not consider his force strong enough, for now, to move to attack.

Myddleton's attacks were being coordinated with Brereton's, in much the same way that the two men had done in late 1643, when they invaded northern Wales (see map 50). Accordingly, on 26 August, Brereton attacked Langdale's garrison force at Malpas and drove them back into northern Wales. Myddleton then received orders from London to move into north Wales and intercept a large powder convoy en route from Bristol to the Royalist defenders in Liverpool and Chester. He departed his base at Oswestry on 3 September and surprised the garrison at Newtown the next day, capturing 36 barrels of powder, 12 barrels of brimstone and huge quantities of match.[15] Emboldened by his success, Myddleton decided to try to capture the castle at Montgomery, which purportedly housed yet more valuable powder.[16] The castle was held by Lord (Black) Herbert of Chirbury, who had refused to install a Royalist garrison or play an active part in the war. Most of the walls around the castle and the town were in a bad state of repair and in some cases had been cleared away. In place of the medieval walls, ditches 'of two banks' had been dug. The castle essentially guarded one of a number of river corridor gateways into the heart of Wales that straddle the Welsh borderland and was situated on an important crossroads. It was an ideal objective for the Parliamentarians, providing a good foothold from which to launch sorties into Royalist territory and disrupt communication and supply lines.[17]

On 4 September Myddleton occupied the town and requested permission to occupy the castle. Herbert, unable to prevent Myddleton taking the place by force if he wished, agreed terms the following day.[18] It was not long before the Royalists moved to challenge the occupation. They were determined to attack Myddleton's force before it had time to improve the defences. On 6 September, Michael Earnley gathered a force of about 1,000 men from Shrewsbury and the surroundings garrisons, and marched towards Montgomery. Two days later Earnley surprised Myddleton's force in the open; he escaped with the cavalry (and dragoons), leaving Colonel Mytton with about 500 defenders within the castle. As Royalist reinforcements arrived, they put a strong cordon around the castle, but lacking any siege artillery their intention was to starve the garrison into submission. Mytton and his men had sufficient powder and musket ammunition but food supplies were limited. He was confident that Myddleton would return and was determined to hold out.

Myddleton wasted little time in securing support from both Brereton (at Chester) and Meldrum, who was at that time besieging Liverpool. Meldrum recalled that he 'resolved to contribute my best endeavours in that expedition, as well in regard of the importance of the service, as that

10 Ibid.

11 Ibid., p. 11. The exact location of this bridge is unknown – that shown on map 61 is diagrammatic only.

12 Ibid., p. 17.

13 Humbie, *Taking of the town of Newcastle by storm*, p. 5.

14 Cooke, *Yorkshire Sieges*, p. 77.

15 This is a good indicator of the high level of intelligence available to the Parliamentarian forces, and a correspondingly slick manner in intelligence transmission.

16 Worton, *Battle of Montgomery*, p. 34, suggests that Myddleton split his force and sent Lt Col Till and 250 hand-picked cavalry and dragoons to Newtown.

17 Walters & Hunnisett, *English Civil War Battlefield of Montgomery*, p. 1.

18 The terms were both civil and generous, Herbert being allowed to stay in the castle with his family and servants.

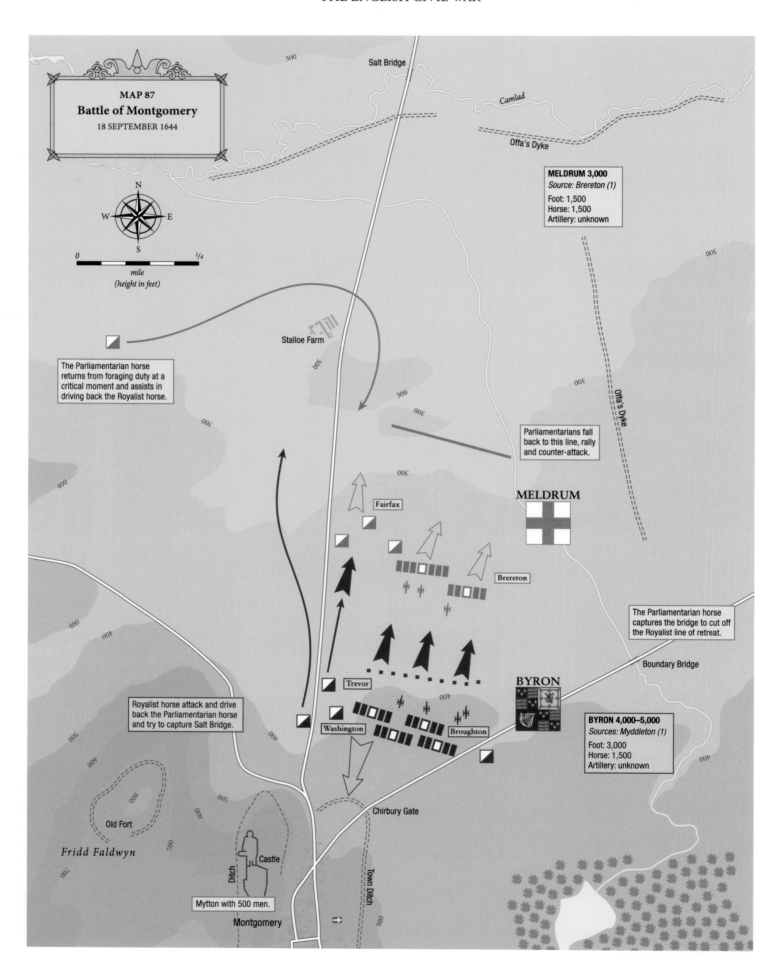

MAP 87
Battle of Montgomery
18 SEPTEMBER 1644

Salt Bridge

Camlad

Offa's Dyke

MELDRUM 3,000
Source: Brereton (1)
Foot: 1,500
Horse: 1,500
Artillery: unknown

N
W E
S

0 1/4
mile
(height in feet)

Stalloe Farm

The Parliamentarian horse returns from foraging duty at a critical moment and assists in driving back the Royalist horse.

Offa's Dyke

Parliamentarians fall back to this line, rally and counter-attack.

MELDRUM

Fairfax

Brereton

The Parliamentarian horse captures the bridge to cut off the Royalist line of retreat.

Boundary Bridge

Trevor

BYRON

Royalist horse attack and drive back the Parliamentarian horse and try to capture Salt Bridge.

Washington

Broughton

BYRON 4,000–5,000
Sources: Myddleton (1)
Foot: 3,000
Horse: 1,500
Artillery: unknown

Chirbury Gate

Old Fort

Fridd Faldwyn

Ditch

Castle

Town Ditch

Mytton with 500 men.

Montgomery

Liverpool was not to be attempted suddenly by such forces as I had'.[19] The combined forces, under Meldrum's overall command, totalled about 3,000 men and were split evenly between foot and horse. The Royalists, realizing that the Parliamentarians were likely to return in strength, were also sending reinforcements to the area. Lord Byron arrived on 17 September with a large force, bringing the total Royalist strength up to about 4,500 men.[20] Later that day Meldrum's force approached from the north and the Royalists yielded the ground to the north-east of the town and pulled back to the high ground around the castle, which encompassed their siege lines. Meldrum recalled:

> … we came thither on the 17th of this instant September, where we lay that night in the field that was most advantageous for us, which the enemy had possessed themselves of before, and deserted to our coming thither, placing themselves upon the mountain above the castle, a place of great advantage for them.[21]

Meldrum was able to determine that he was outnumbered; furthermore, any idea of attacking the Royalists on the dominating ground would have been quickly dismissed. Many Royalist commanders advocated a quick attack, but Byron, mindful of the garrison in the castle to his rear, was not so hasty. He elected to leave a strong force to contain the garrison and move steadily off the high ground and deploy on the gentle slope north of the town. The Parliamentarians, meanwhile, aware that the garrison required resupply, had decided to try to gather some local supplies from the surrounding countryside. Somewhat irresponsibly, given the circumstances, they had detached a third of their horse to undertake the task. Both armies were thus reduced in numbers, with the Royalists numbering about 3,700 and the Parliamentarians about 3,000.[22] The Royalists advanced and Myddleton recalled that they 'came up to our ground, and gave us battell'.[23]

The Royalist line was preceded by a line of skirmishers, which fell back as the main body of Royalist infantry advanced towards the Parliamentarian positions. On the Royalist left, the cavalry also advanced in tandem with the foot, and then charged. Arthur Trevor wrote, in a letter to the Marquis of Ormond after the battle, that 'the first charge was made by my brother upon all their horse, who killed Sir William Fayrefaix in the head of them

and put them all in disorder'.[24] In fact the fight was not quite as straightforward as Trevor's account suggests. Both cavalry groups were engaged for some time and Myddleton recalled that 'Sir William Fairfax, who had command of the horse, did most valiantly set upon their horse, and engaged himself so farre that he was taken prisoner, but presently fetched off by the valour of our men, but sore wounded'.[25] At the same time the Royalist foot advanced and the Parliamentarians waited and then fired their muskets in a single volley. It was a tactic that delivered a decisive amount of firepower and had been decisive in the past, but on this occasion, they fired too early and the advantage was lost.[26] The Royalists continued their advance and the two sides closed to 'push of pike'. Brereton recalled that it was a difficult moment, 'for they were much too hard for us, having many more pikes'. The Royalists could taste victory.

On the Royalist left, the initial success of Trevor's Horse had not been followed up. Whether it was because morale was low in some regiments, namely the Lancashire Horse, or whether at the critical moment the foraging parties of the Parliamentarian horse returned to tip the scales, is unclear. Trevor wrote that 'all the Lancashire horse ran without a blow struck; which disheartened the foot so infinitely, that being in disorder with the pursuit of the enemy they could not be persuaded to rally again'.[27] It was one of those extraordinary moments in combat, where for almost inexplicable reasons, a tide of optimism sweeps across one side while a cloud of despair engulfs the other. Brereton remembered a 'unanimous resolution, both in the horse and foot to fight it out to the last man'.[28] The Cheshire infantry behaved with particular distinction; their aggression and determination was infectious. After the battle, the Parliamentarian commander noted, with great delight, that the enemy 'were shamefully routed, by the pursuit of the victorie, which continued for a space of three miles: there are found dead upon this place five hundred… and twelve hundred prisoners'.[29]

The Parliamentarian horse pursued the broken Royalist forces and captured the bridge on the east of the battlefield, thereby cutting off the line of retreat towards Shrewsbury. A large number of the Royalist foot surrendered almost immediately, and many of the soldiers left in the siege lines were also swept up by the Parliamentarian cavalry and Mytton's garrison, which sallied out to join in the spoils. Montgomery was the largest battle that took place on Welsh soil. It was a decisive and important victory for Parliament. It came at an opportune time and it delivered a crippling blow to the Royalists in their heartlands, from which they never recovered. Myddleton went on to capture Powis Castle on 2 October and the abbey at Cwnhir in December, thereby establishing Parliamentarian ascendency in central Wales. The battle at Montgomery had made that possible; it had been a resounding success, blackened only by the loss of William Fairfax, who had died from his wounds. His widow was distraught at his death, but 'she grieved not that he died in this cause, but that he died so soon to do no more for it'.[30]

19 Brereton, Myddleton, & Meldrum, *Letters from Sir William Brereton, Sir Thomas Middleton, Sir John Meldrum*, p. 6.
20 Phillips, *Memoirs of the Civil War in Wales*, vol. I, p. 249.
21 Brereton, Myddleton, & Meldrum, op. cit., pp. 4–5.
22 Worton, op. cit., p. 85. There is little disagreement that the battlefield lies to the north of Montgomery, but doubt remains as to whether the key bridge was that at (or near) the current Salt Bridge or the bridge over to the east, annotated (on OS mapping) as County Boundary Bridge. Given the understandable preoccupation of the Parliamentarians with their lines of retreat, and the location of their base at Oswestry, I have little hesitation in concluding that Salt Bridge is the key bridge in question. The question of the orientation of the forces is less easy to square away. Worton's very detailed work disappointingly skips the issue, and Walters and Hunnisett's archaeological report has the two sides facing off (initially) at a 45-degree north-west to south-east line, while Abram, *Montgomery*, has the armies deployed on an east-west orientation, with the Royalist attack being made in a northerly direction. Based on my reading of the ground, and the primary source material, I have split the difference. I fully support Walters and Hunnisett's suggestion that action took place at both bridges, at different stages of the battle, thereby dovetailing with their archaeological evidence.
23 Brereton, Myddleton, & Meldrum, op. cit., p. 5.

24 Carte, *Collection of Original Letters*, Letter, Trevor to Ormond dated 23 Sep 1644, vol. I, pp. 64–6.
25 Brereton, Myddleton, & Meldrum, op. cit., p. 5.
26 Worton, op. cit., p. 87.
27 Carte, op. cit., pp. 64–6.
28 Brereton, Myddleton, & Meldrum, op. cit., p. 2.
29 Ibid., p. 7.
30 Firth, *Dictionary of National Biography*, 1885–1900, vol. 18., 'Fairfax, William (1609–1644)'. He was the nephew of Lord Fairfax and cousin of Tom.

CHAPTER 25
A TIME TO REFLECT: THE END OF 1644

Following the escape of Charles's army at Newbury, it was imperative that the Parliamentarians prevent the union of that force with Prince Rupert's force from Bristol. However, the commanders could only agree to disagree and decided instead to resume the siege of Donnington Castle and wait for the Royalists to return to collect their cannon. They did not have to wait long. A strong Royalist force departed Oxford on 6 November and moved south.[1] Their mission was threefold: to relieve Donnington, to recover the artillery, and to move to relieve the siege at Basing House. What followed was simply extraordinary. The King relieved Donnington on the morning of the 9th, without encountering any opposition, and then deployed his 11,000-strong force on Speenhamland facing east. Elements of the Parliamentarian army were there but the cavalry did not appear until nearly dark. That night the Royalists moved back and took up a strong position at Winterbourne. The Parliamentarian commanders Manchester, Waller and Balfour (Essex was still convalescing at Reading) seemed at a loss as to how to proceed. Morale was low, the weather was turning by the day and promises of pay and supplies failed to materialize. Among the generals, indecision turned to a war of words and the armies were ordered to remain in their bivouacs south of the Kennet. The Committee of Both Kingdoms was angry and perplexed at their decision and demanded answers. Meanwhile, on 22 November, the Royalist garrison at Basing House was relieved. The Royalists had achieved their aims and moved back to establish their winter quarters in and around Oxford, while the Parliamentarian commanders were summoned to London to explain themselves.

The campaign of 1644 was one of missed opportunities for both factions. A glance at map 88 reveals the extent of the Royalist failures in the north following Marston Moor, the loss of York and the 'coal city' of Newcastle. The lack of a Royalist national strategy, the failure to link up the Royalist armies and move on London, and the intervention of the Scottish Covenanters had effectively removed any possibility of the Royalists achieving an outright military victory. Charles had gambled and played the Irish card, a strategy which had both misfired and backfired. The significant triumph at Lostwithiel secured the South-West but provided little tangible geographical advantage to the King. The plethora of isolated Royalist garrisons were gallant and visible bastions to the King's cause, and a thorn in the side of the Parliamentarian commanders, but they were also a drain on Royalist resources and served to dilute rather than focus Royalist aims. By the end of 1644 Charles had dismissed the idea of a negotiated settlement. He had hardened his heart to achieving military victory, perhaps emboldened by his personal triumphs at Cropredy and Lostwithiel, and he demonstrated that determination by appointing Rupert as the lord general of the King's armies. Maurice took over Rupert's command in Wales and the Marches, while Goring took command of what was left of the western forces. That was the sum total of the Royalist winter hierarchical reorganization. Charles returned to Oxford in November 1644 in buoyant mood, but his optimism was severely misplaced.

The strengths and weaknesses of the Parliamentarian cause were the reverse of those of the King. The Royalists had a unified command and administrative system, while Parliament had individual army commands and a series of overlapping committees. Furthermore, their alliance with Scotland, and the duly formed Committee of Both Kingdoms, had developed cracks. Reliance on county militias complicated military planning. However, Parliament held two trump cards. The cities and counties under their regulation were far wealthier than those in the Royalist controlled areas. Furthermore, their control of the navy gave them an advantage in the prosecution of the war and, importantly, in limiting and interdicting foreign support to the Royalist cause. These advantages provided the Parliamentarians something that was denied to the King – namely, time. During the first two years of the war it was John Pym who made best use of that time, but he had died in December 1643. The reorganization of the Parliamentary administration in the wake of Pym's death and of the new alliance with Scotland resulted in the establishment of the Committee of Both Kingdoms, in which middle parties were more strongly represented. This angered the overall military commander, Essex, especially when vital resources were diverted from his army to those of Waller and Manchester. The resulting squabbles undermined the importance of the victory at Marston Moor and failed to deliver a corresponding blow against the Royalists in the south. Something had to give.

Waller and Cromwell addressed Parliament on 25 November and directly laid the blame on Manchester, Cromwell repeatedly referring to events at York and Marston Moor.[2] Manchester had no real defence to speak of. His comments following the debacle at Newbury now came back to haunt him: 'If we beat the King ninety-nine times, he would be King still, and his posterity, and we subjects still; but if *he* beat *us* but once, we should be hanged and our posterity undone.'[3] Essex, who had largely escaped blame from Cromwell (but not Waller), tried to shift the finger of blame on Cromwell for trying to drive a wedge between Parliament's Scottish allies. He had pre-empted Cromwell's accusations and in the wake of Newbury had convened a meeting with the Scottish Commissioners. Bulstrode Whitelocke had been present and recalled the words of the Lord Chancellor of Scotland that 'Ye ken vara weel that Lieutenant-General Cromwell is nae freend of oors; and since the advance of our army into England, he hath used all underhand and cunning means to take off from our honour and merit of this kingdom'.[4] It was a dangerous accusation and one that could be considered treasonable at a time when three other men were being tried under similar pretences.[5] But following Lostwithiel, Essex did not have a strong platform.

---

2 *CSPD Series of depositions illustrative of the charges brought by Lieut.-Gen. Cromwell against the Earl of Manchester, submitted to the examination of the Committee formerly appointed for the Lord General Essex's army*, dated 25 Nov 1644 to 6 Jan 1645.

3 Bruce, *Earl of Manchester and Oliver Cromwell*, p. LXX.

4 Whitelocke, *Memoirs*, p. 199.

5 Wanklyn, *Warrior Generals*, p. 140 – Alexander Carew and John Hotham senior and junior.

---

1 It comprised the forces that had been under Charles at Newbury, Rupert's force from the west, and a significant element of the Oxford garrison.

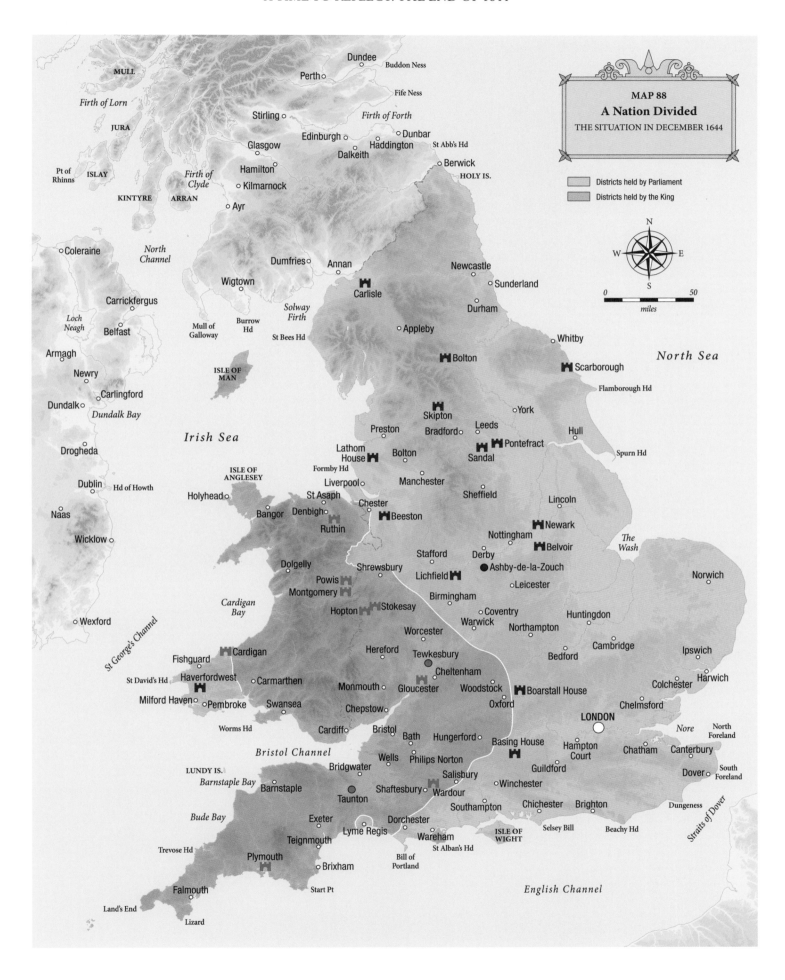

MULL

Firth of Lorn

JURA

Pt of
Rhinns   ISLAY

KINTYRE   ARRAN

Dundee
Perth   Buddon Ness

Fife Ness

Stirling   *Firth of Forth*

Glasgow   Edinburgh   Dunbar
              Dalkeith   Haddington   St Abb's Hd
Hamilton   Berwick
  Kilmarnock   HOLY IS.
  Ayr

*Firth of
Clyde*

Coleraine   *North
               Channel*

Dumfries   Annan   Newcastle
  Wigtown   Sunderland
                      Carlisle   Durham
Carrickfergus
         *Loch   Mull of   Burrow   *Solway
         Neagh*   Galloway   Hd   Firth*   Appleby
Belfast   St Bees Hd
Armagh

Newry
    Carlingford   ISLE OF
Dundalk   MAN   Whitby
         Dundalk Bay   Bolton
                                                          Scarborough
                                                 Flamborough Hd
Drogheda   Skipton   York
                              Irish Sea   Preston Bradford Leeds   Hull
Dublin   Lathom   Pontefract   Spurn Hd
    Hd of Howth   ISLE OF   House   Bolton   Sandal
                         ANGLESEY   Formby Hd
Naas   Liverpool Manchester
                   Holyhead   St Asaph   Sheffield   Lincoln
Wicklow   Bangor Denbigh Chester
                                      Ruthin   Beeston   Newark
                                                       Nottingham   Belvoir   *The
                                          Dolgelly   Derby   Wash*
Wexford   *Cardigan   Shrewsbury Stafford Lichfield Ashby-de-la-Zouch   Norwich
                 Bay*   Powis   Leicester
                        Montgomery   Birmingham
                                 Hopton Stokesay   Coventry   Huntingdon
                                                Warwick   Northampton
                               Worcester
St George's Channel   Hereford Tewkesbury   Cambridge   Ipswich
              Fishguard   Cardigan   Cheltenham   Bedford
St David's Hd Haverfordwest Carmarthen   Monmouth Gloucester Woodstock Boarstall House   Colchester Harwich
  Milford Haven Pembroke Swansea Chepstow   Oxford   Chelmsford
                                                        Basing House
         Worms Hd   Cardiff Bristol Bath Hungerford   LONDON   *Nore*   North
                                                                Hampton   Foreland
LUNDY IS.   *Bristol Channel*   Wells Philips Norton Court   Chatham Canterbury
Barnstaple Bay   Bridgwater   Salisbury Guildford   Dover   South
         Barnstaple   Shaftesbury Wardour Winchester   Foreland
              Taunton   Dorchester   Chichester Brighton   Dungeness
Bude Bay   Exeter   Lyme Regis   Wareham   ISLE OF   Selsey Bill Beachy Hd   *Straits of Dover*
         Teignmouth   St Alban's Hd WIGHT
Trevose Hd   Plymouth Brixham   Bill of
              Falmouth   Portland   *English Channel*
         Land's End   Start Pt
         Lizard

North Sea

W   N   E
     S
0   50
   miles

MAP 88
A Nation Divided
THE SITUATION IN DECEMBER 1644

☐ Districts held by Parliament
☐ Districts held by the King

Underpinning all of these differences was religion. Cromwell and others were determined to oppose rigid Scottish Presbyterianism, while many in Parliament feared the religious zeal and commitment to the cause of Cromwell's Eastern Association forces, in particular his cavalry. Conversely, the emergence of religious tolerance within the Assembly of Divines directly undermined both the philosophy and acceptance of Cromwell's religious separatism. All of this led to a bitter power struggle within the Parliamentarian ranks and heightened divisions between the three parties: the war-party, the peace-group and those vacillating between the two, known as the middle group. The former outflanked their opponents in December with the introduction of the Self-Denying Ordinance. This decree admitted fault on all sides and proposed a separation of political and military functions. It offered both an olive branch and an opportunity. It was quickly accepted by the Commons but the Lords were less enthusiastic. By removing all members of Parliament from the new army, many of the ennobled officers would be forced to hang up their swords. It was to prove to be a long and difficult fight to drive the bill into law.

On 31 December 1644, Parliament debated and agreed that the new army would 'be 16,000 foot, 8,000 horse, and 1,500 dragoons. That a foot regiment consist of 1,200 men. That a regiment of horse consist of 600 men. The pay to be according to the last establishment of the Lord General's army.'[6] Financing the force was the first challenge; finding sufficient numbers from the remnants of the armies of Essex, Manchester and Waller was the second. By the time the bill became law, the numbers for the infantry and cavalry had been revised down to 14,000 and 6,000 respectively.[7] Elevating the new army to a war footing was going to take time and it was resolved to raise another 8,500 in London and eastern and southern counties to meet the manpower requirements. The New Model Army did not, however, immediately replace the plethora of other forces fighting for Parliament in early 1645. These included the Scottish army under Leslie (21,000) the Northern Association under General Poyntz (10,000) and the Western association under Massey (approximately 8,000) plus a number of smaller bodies of troops. Charles Firth estimates that there were at least 60,000 or 70,000 soldiers, excluding the Scots, earning Parliament's 'shilling'.[8] Gradually, over the next two years, these forces were incorporated into the New Model Army.

On 13 January 1645 the Lords threw out the Self-Denying Ordinance, but this did not deter Parliament from continuing their work on the new army, and on 21 January they voted by 101 votes to 69 to make Thomas Fairfax the new commander-in-chief. Skippon was named as his major general, while the post of lieutenant general of horse was, pointedly, left vacant. Indeed, Cromwell understood that his political position, and his ongoing, very personal and highly public disagreement with Manchester effectively ruled out his nomination at this stage. Ironically, however, it was Cromwell's spat with Manchester that was to provide the lever with which to surge ahead with the establishment of Parliament's new army. For when the Lords threw out the Self-Denying Ordinance and the nomination of Fairfax as the commander, they did so because they wanted one of their own – namely Manchester – to have the post. Therefore, on 15 January, the two

committees charged with the investigation of the accusations laid at Manchester's feet suggested that the Lords' investigation of a member of the Commons – namely Cromwell – without the permission of the House of Commons had breached Parliamentary privilege. A categorical no-no in the Palace of Westminster in the 1640s. Furthermore, they were happy for both sides to state their positions and for Manchester to be able to conduct his defence. Backed into an unhappy corner, the Lords passed the bill for the New Model Army on 15 February. The passing of the Self-Denying Ordinance was a more protracted affair. With the news a week later that the King had rejected the latest set of propositions laid before him by the Parliamentary and Scottish commissioners, the Lords, devoid of other options, duly passed the bill into law on 3 April.

Although Fairfax was commanding but one, albeit the most significant, English army fighting for Parliament, most importantly he held complete authority of all the other forces. This was crucial to enable him to fight a national campaign, but as Malcolm Wanklyn points out, Fairfax's influence over strategic and operational-level decisions remained ultimately in Parliament's hands and (for now) with the Committee of Both Kingdoms. The irony was that the former army commanders and politicians, as *ipso facto* members of the committee, probably enjoyed greater influence over strategy and operations than they had as commanders in the field, or than Fairfax enjoyed, or was to enjoy, in his new appointment.[9] Nevertheless, one of the *raisons d'être* of the New Model Army was that it was a national force not constrained by county or local directives or needs. The lack of numbers, however, made impressment and county quotas a prerequisite and this led to a shortage of men (3,000 to 4,000 when the army deployed for the first time in May) but it also significantly reduced, in the short term, the mobility of the new army as many deserted and went back home.

The army was to have 12 regiments of infantry, 11 regiments of cavalry and a regiment of dragoons. Each infantry regiment had ten companies, the cavalry regiments six troops and the dragoon regiment ten troops. The amount of artillery was not specified and there was a simple explanation for this. Artillery, at this time and indeed up to 1855, was under the auspices of the Board of Ordnance and the direction of the Master of Ordnance.[10] However, Parliament would have directed the board to provide both guns and trained gunners to its armies and the New Model Army in particular. According to Lieutenant General Hammond's account, the artillery train consisted of four demi-culverins, four long sakers and 20 ordinary sakers. The accuracy of this is unclear as the train was supplied with two demi-culverin and eight sakers in April 1645, with another saker and three drakes being subsequently sent up to Windsor for the army.[11] Fairfax was required to produce his list of officers, from colonel to captain, whom he wanted to serve in the infantry and cavalry, and in what capacity. The House of Commons debated the names at great length and ultimately accepted the vast majority of proposals. The Lords, however, removed, relegated or reassigned as many as a third of Fairfax's suggestions. The approach of the new campaigning season and the Royalist opening salvos forced Parliament to cut short debate and allow the New Model Army to cut its teeth and get on with the job at hand.

---

6 *CSPD* dated 31 December 1644.
7 Ibid., dated 9 January 1645.
8 Firth, *Cromwell's Army*, p. 34.

9 Wanklyn, op. cit., pp. 143–4.
10 See the chapter 'Civil War Armies' on tactics and armies.
11 NA SP28/145 f.60r.

CHAPTER 26
NATIONWIDE DEVELOPMENTS, EARLY 1645

Following the Parliamentarian victory at Montgomery (chapter 24), Myddleton continued to expand and consolidate in central Wales, while Brereton moved back to Cheshire to begin preparations for the capture of Chester. Secured by the Royalists early in the war, Chester was a major base for them as well as a vital communications hub that connected the Royalist north with Wales, central England and, most importantly after 1644, Ireland. Chester had been in Brereton's sights since moving to the area in early 1643, but he considered the city too strong to tackle on his own. Pleas for help from other Parliamentarian commanders, or directly to the Committee of Both Kingdoms, had largely fallen on deaf ears. However, the loss of the north to the Royalists, the recent gains in central Wales and the rather unpredictable nature of Irish support to the King's cause, had given Brereton new purpose and optimism in his quest. He had his men construct a fort at Christleton, 2 miles to the south-east of the city on one of the main arterial routes. Byron tried to storm it on 19 January but Brereton had set an ambush and captured and killed many of Byron's troopers. A week later, emboldened by this minor victory, Brereton tried to storm Chester at night, but was easily repulsed. Aware that the city was short of provisions, Brereton sent troops across the River Dee and closed the land cordon, in the hope of starving them into capitulation. With the city open on the west side to the River Dee, Brereton was fully aware that the likelihood of success was small.

In December, Maurice had assumed Rupert's former command in Wales and the Marches. He left Oxford on 14 January and headed towards the area, but his first task was to raise an army. Willing volunteers had long since dried up and the Royalists were forced to press men to take the King's shilling. If he was to march to the relief of Chester, he had little choice but to take the Anglo-Irish regiments quartered around Shrewsbury, along with some of the garrison's gunners. Brereton had been aware of Maurice's mission soon after he left Oxford and, in mid-February, leaving sufficient troops to maintain the cordon, he established a defensive line to the south of Chester.[1] Maurice was also well aware of Brereton's intentions and he outwitted him by moving north, deep inside Wales. On 21 February he approached Chester from the west, driving off the few Parliamentarian troops in the cordon on the west bank of the Dee estuary, and entered the city. Any Royalist jubilation, however, was short lived for Brereton responded by despatching 600 troops, to link up with a corresponding number under Mytton's command in Shropshire, and they fell on the (by now) thinly guarded city of Shrewsbury.[2] The town was quickly overrun and the defenders in the castle surrendered at noon the following day. It was a devastating blow for the Royalists; they had not just lost their regional headquarters, but also a vital supply depot containing, *inter alia*, 2,000 weapons and 100 barrels of powder.[3] On the 27th Brereton entered the town, bringing reinforcements; the Parliamentarians, having captured the place, were determined to hold it. Maurice was severely

chastised for the loss of Shrewsbury, but to be fair to him he had few options: he was hamstrung by having to establish a new army in the area and hampered by the emergence of the Clubmen and, furthermore, by a shift in Welsh public opinion in favour of Parliament. Rather harshly, he never held independent field command again.

To the east the Royalists were also to suffer setbacks. On 22 February, after three weeks of trying, Meldrum finally captured the town of Scarborough, and with it, control of the port. Cholmley withdrew his force of 500 men back into the castle and settled down for a siege, hoping to hold out long enough for the long-overdue relief from Oxford to arrive. Meldrum tried to coerce Cholmley into capitulating, and when that failed, he sent for heavy guns. Cholmley remembered when the guns arrived, as he smugly recorded:

> … beeing to plant these ordnance neere to the sea cliff for more advantage to batter, Meldrum there in person giving directions about them, his hatt blows off his head, and he catching to save that, the winde being veerie great blowes his cloake over his face, and hee falls over the cliff amongst rockes and stones att least steeple height.[4]

It took Meldrum three days to recover from his fall. It was the least of his worries, for the removal of Cholmley and his troublesome band was to take many months and constitute a considerable drain on resources badly needed for other sieges in the region.

Help for Cholmley, however, was not forthcoming from Oxford, for the King was otherwise preoccupied. In short, the Royalists were on the back foot across the country. Hopes of support, in the guise of money and troops from abroad, had failed to materialize in sufficient quantity to be able to make a tangible difference. Peace negotiations with Parliament (the Treaty of Oxbridge) had not gone well and, on 10 January, just to rub a touch of salt into the King's wounds, Archbishop Laud was led to the scaffold at Tower Hill. Furthermore, hopes that the in-fighting between Parliament's generals would be fatal to their cause, were frustrated by intelligence that a compromise, of sorts, had been found through the Self-Denying Ordinance. At the same time, Rupert's attempt to drive the Parliamentarians out of Abingdon, who were too close for comfort, met with failure. A few days later Goring tried to capture Christchurch, in Dorset, but was also unsuccessful and then, at the end of February, news came through that Lewis Dyve had been driven out of Weymouth by a local Parliamentarian force.

Marmaduke Langdale provided the only cause for Royalist optimism. He opened the year with the rout of Ludlow's forces and the recapture of Salisbury. The following month he moved north with a force of about 1,700 men, mixed horse and foot (but only musketeers, no pikemen). His mission was to relieve the siege at Pontefract. He defeated Rossiter's cavalry force, about 2,000 strong, at Market Harborough on 25 February, before moving towards Newark.[5] His presence in the area was enough to disperse the small

---

1 This is another good example of the Parliamentarian intelligence system working well.
2 Worton, *Waging Civil War in Shropshire*, p. 123.
3 Wanklyn, *Warrior Generals*, p. 151.

4 Binns, *Cholmley*, p. 156.
5 Dudley to Rupert, *Mercurius Aulicus*, 2–9 March 1645, p. 1402.

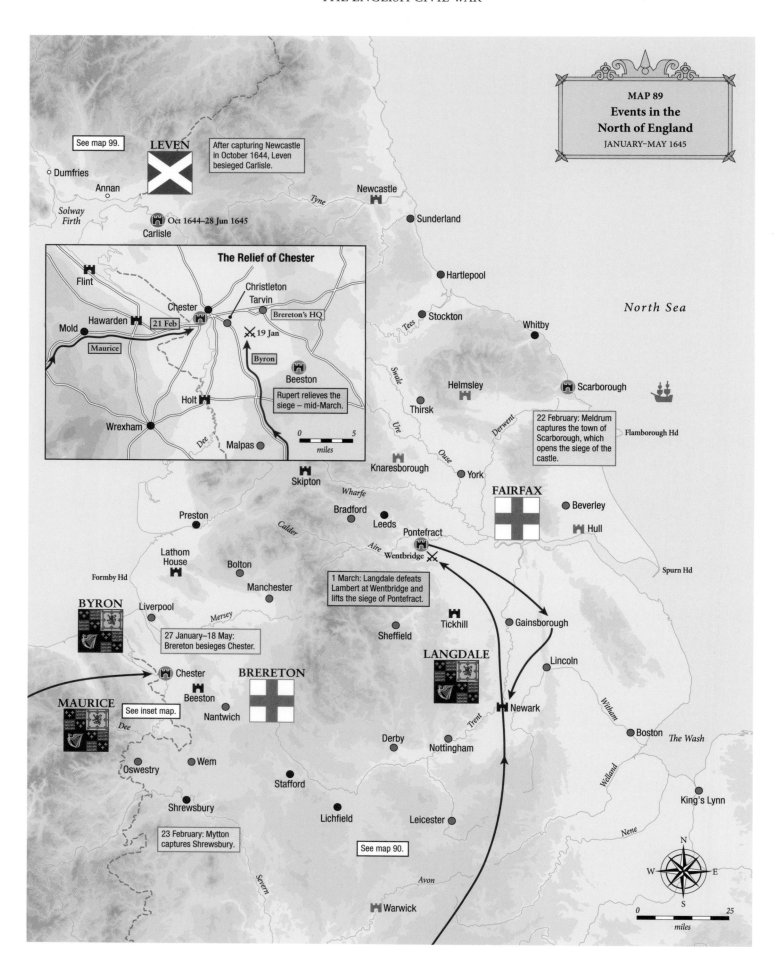

MAP 89
Events in the
North of England
JANUARY–MAY 1645

See map 99.

LEVEN

After capturing Newcastle in October 1644, Leven besieged Carlisle.

Dumfries

Annan

Solway Firth

Tyne

Newcastle

Oct 1644–28 Jun 1645

Carlisle

Sunderland

The Relief of Chester

Flint

Christleton

Tarvin

Chester

Brereton's HQ

Hawarden

21 Feb

Mold

Maurice

19 Jan

Byron

Beeston

Holt

Rupert relieves the siege – mid-March.

Wrexham

Dee

Malpas

0   5
miles

Hartlepool

North Sea

Tees

Stockton

Whitby

Swale

Helmsley

Scarborough

Thirsk

Ure

Derwent

22 February: Meldrum captures the town of Scarborough, which opens the siege of the castle.

Flamborough Hd

Knaresborough

Ouse

York

Skipton

Wharfe

FAIRFAX

Beverley

Bradford

Leeds

Hull

Preston

Calder

Pontefract

Aire

Wentbridge

Spurn Hd

Lathom House

Formby Hd

Bolton

Manchester

1 March: Langdale defeats Lambert at Wentbridge and lifts the siege of Pontefract.

BYRON

Liverpool

Mersey

Tickhill

Gainsborough

Sheffield

LANGDALE

Lincoln

27 January–18 May: Brereton besieges Chester.

Chester

BRERETON

Beeston

Nantwich

See inset map.

MAURICE

Dee

Newark

Trent

Boston

Witham

The Wash

Oswestry

Wem

Derby

Nottingham

Welland

Shrewsbury

Stafford

Lichfield

Leicester

King's Lynn

23 February: Mytton captures Shrewsbury.

See map 90.

Nene

Avon

N
W   E
S

Warwick

0   25
miles

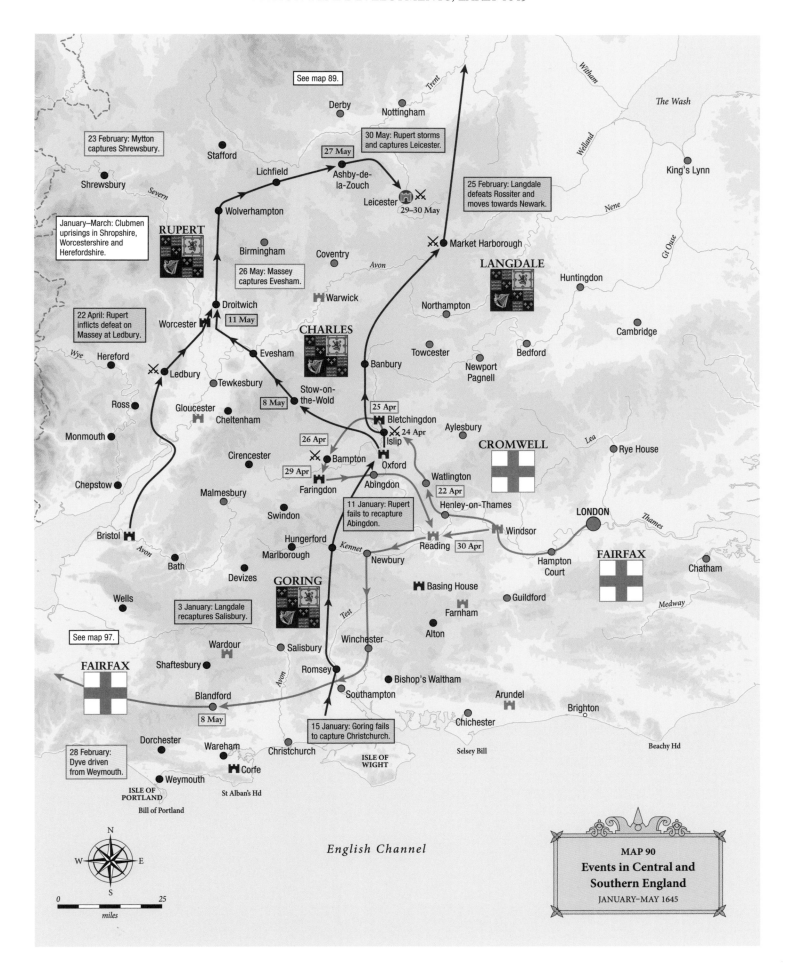

See map 89.

23 February: Mytton captures Shrewsbury.

30 May: Rupert storms and captures Leicester.

27 May

25 February: Langdale defeats Rossiter and moves towards Newark.

January–March: Clubmen uprisings in Shropshire, Worcestershire and Herefordshire.

RUPERT

26 May: Massey captures Evesham.

LANGDALE

22 April: Rupert inflicts defeat on Massey at Ledbury.

11 May

CHARLES

8 May

25 Apr

CROMWELL

26 Apr

29 Apr

11 January: Rupert fails to recapture Abingdon.

22 Apr

LONDON

30 Apr

FAIRFAX

3 January: Langdale recaptures Salisbury.

GORING

See map 97.

FAIRFAX

8 May

15 January: Goring fails to capture Christchurch.

28 February: Dyve driven from Weymouth.

English Channel

N
W   E
S

0   25
miles

MAP 90
Events in Central and
Southern England
JANUARY–MAY 1645

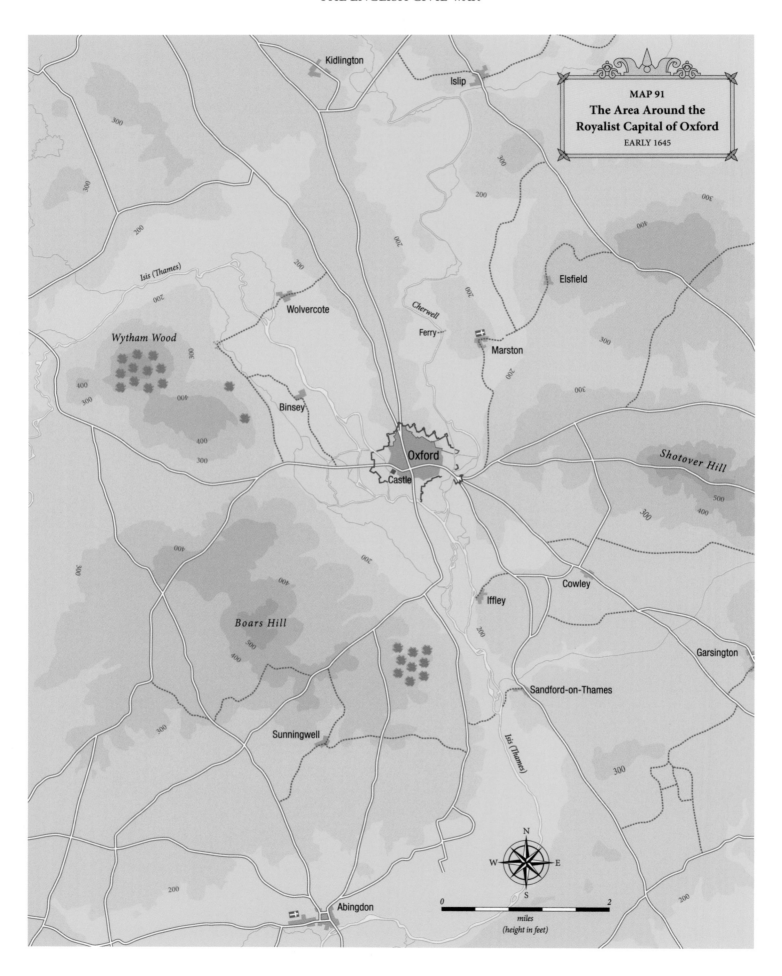

Kidlington

Islip

MAP 91
**The Area Around the
Royalist Capital of Oxford**
EARLY 1645

300

300

200

Isis (Thames)

200

200

400

Elsfield

300

Wolvercote

Cherwell

200

Wytham Wood

Ferry

300

Marston

200

300

Binsey

400

300

400

Oxford

Shotover Hill

300

Castle

500

400

400

300

Cowley

Iffley

200

Boars Hill

Garsington

500

Sandford-on-Thames

400

300

300

Sunningwell

Isis (Thames)

300

200

N

W   E

S

200

200

0   2

miles
(height in feet)

Abingdon

Parliamentarian force that was besieging Norwell House (just north of Newark). On 27 February, having been reinforced with 400 foot and 400 horse from Newark, he continued his northerly movement, crossing the River Don at Rossington. On 1 March, 3 miles south of Pontefract, Langdale deployed his force into battalia and moved towards the town and castle. Later that afternoon he clashed with Lambert's (similarly sized) forces at Wentbridge. The Royalists succeeded in driving the Parliamentarians back, and by keeping pace with their withdrawal, they prevented them from rallying. As the Roundheads approached Pontefract they were then attacked in their rear by a contingent of 200 musketeers from the garrison that had sallied from Pontefract Castle.[6] Parliamentarian losses were high, probably about 300 and 700–800 prisoners, plus a large amount of powder and ammunition was also captured, and quickly moved to the castle.[7] The siege was lifted, but it was a brief respite, for Lord Fairfax's men would return to the task once Langdale headed back south to Newark a few days later.

On 20 April, while the New Model Army was being assembled, the Committee of Both Kingdoms gave Cromwell orders to prevent the junction of the King's army (from Oxford) and that of Rupert (from Bristol):

Being informed that the enemy have mounted their ordnance at Oxford, and that Prince Maurice is come thither with 1,000 horse to convey his Majesty and those ordnance to join with the forces of the two Princes in Hereford and Worcester shires, and considering of what advantage it would be to the public to prevent this design of the enemy we have thought fit to employ in that service your two regiments, Col. Fiennes and the rest of that party which went with you into the west.[8]

Cromwell, and his supporters, had juggled the requirements of the Self-Denying Ordnance; his official role with the New Model Army was not endorsed until June. For now, he was doing God's work at the hands of his own command, but he was acutely aware that his success in executing the committee's orders to the letter would play a pivotal role in deciding his future role within the New Model.

Rupert ventured north in late April (at the same time that Cromwell received his orders) to deal with uprisings by Clubmen, who were refusing to comply with the demands of the Royalist commissionaires in Monmouthshire. On 22 April he cornered Colonel Massey at Ledbury and taught him, and his men, a sharp lesson in cavalry tactics. Cromwell, meanwhile, was draughting all the available mounts he could lay his hands on in the east and south-east, and he had already advanced towards Oxford to a prearranged rendezvous at Watlington. He despatched Major General Browne forward to Wheatley, to conduct a reconnaissance and to try to gather intelligence on the Royalist strengths, dispositions and intentions. That night he received reports that the King's convoy seemed ready to march from Oxford at any moment, and that the advance guard, the Earl of Northampton's Regiment, were quartered at Islip. Cromwell recorded that 'Wherefore in the evening I marched that way, hoping to have surprised them; but by mistake and falling on the forlorn-hope, they had an alarm there, and to their quarters, and so escaped me.'[9] Cromwell remained at Islip that night and the next day his force was attacked by Northampton, supported by Wilmot's and the Queen's regiments, that had come up from Oxford. He remembered the action:

The General's [Fairfax's – formerly Cromwell's own troop] Troop charged a whole squadron of the Enemy, and presently broke it. Our other Troops coming seasonable on, the rest of the Enemy were presently put into confusion; so that we had the chase of them three or four miles; wherein we killed many, and took near Two-hundred prisoners and about Four-hundred horse.[10]

It was an authoritative start to Cromwell's campaign. Many of the survivors escaped to Bletchingdon House, which Cromwell duly summoned the next morning. Perhaps wisely, Colonel Windebank, the garrison commander, decided to accept Cromwell's terms. Sending his newly acquired guns and the escorted prisoners back to Abingdon, Cromwell then crossed the River Cherwell and caught Lisle's infantry brigade at Burton (in-the-Bush) before pushing on to capture Faringdon Castle. Roger Burgess, the governor, received Cromwell's audacious note: 'I summon you to deliver into my hands the House, therein you are, and your Ammunition, with all things else there; together with your persons, to be disposed of as parliament shall appoint. Which if you refuse to do, you are to expect the utmost extremity of war.'[11] Burgess was not so easily intimidated, and with no sign of any infantry or siege artillery, his reply was derisive and to the point. Cromwell requested infantry from Abingdon but when none had come by 3am he decided to storm the place. He failed, lost 14 men and then withdrew east. However, he did not dwell near Oxford, for he had received intelligence that Goring was making his way with some speed from the south coast. Cromwell decided to pull back towards Reading, satisfied that, if nothing else, he had put the wind up the Oxford garrison.

In early April, Charles Gerard had been sent by the Royalists to regain control over the errant Pembrokeshire corner of south-west Wales (see chapter 30). At the same time, Berkeley and Grenville had decided to defeat the Parliamentarian garrison at Taunton, which had, since Blake captured the town the previous July, become a proverbial pea under the mattress. The town's plight was also to become a bugbear of Parliament, when stories of the defenders' and townsfolks' predicament filtered back to London. As it happened, marching to the relief of the place was to become the New Model Army's first mission. On 28 April, the Committee of Both Kingdoms ordered Fairfax to march to the south-west, taking no more than 6,000 foot and 2,500 horse and dragoons.[12] The remainder of the army were to continue to assist Cromwell in the Oxford area. Fairfax arrived at Blandford on 8 May and received news that the town had survived an assault that day. News of a more urgent nature also came into his headquarters. On 7 May Charles had departed Oxford and headed north. The King held a council of war at Stow-on-the-Wold that night, at which Goring and Digby pressed for the King to head south and engage the fledgling New Model Army. Rupert argued that the combined armies should move north, relieve Chester and then conduct a recruiting drive in the north, sweeping up the surviving infantry units from Newcastle's northern army and returning them to the colours. Charles concurred, but agreed to send Goring with 3,000 horse to assist the by now beleaguered garrison at Taunton. Westminster instructed Cromwell, with some of the New Model infantry and the forces in Abingdon, to keep in contact with the King's army in the Cotswolds. Fairfax was told to send a force to Taunton (under the command of Colonel Weldon) and wait for further instructions. The year 1645 was about to ignite.

---

6   Ibid., p. 1405.
7   Cook, *Yorkshire Sieges*, p. 97.
8   *CSPD* dated 20 April 1645.
9   Carlyle, vol. I, p. 181 (Letter XXV).

10 Ibid.
11 Ibid., p. 183 (Letter XXVI).
12 *CSPD* dated 28 April 1645.

CHAPTER 27

THE GREAT AND DECISIVE BATTLE AT NASEBY, 14 JUNE 1645

The two Royalist armies linked up at Droitwich on 11 May and then, with news that Brereton had lifted the siege at Chester (in the wake of the Royalist advance), the King headed east. General Browne, who commanded the Abingdon troops and the lion's share of Cromwell's pursuit force, grew increasingly concerned about the size of the Royalist army to his front and broke off the chase. Cromwell, technically lacking any official overall command capacity, was powerless to interfere. However, news of the relief of Taunton had changed things for the Parliamentarians. The committee ordered Fairfax to move to besiege Oxford and Cromwell and Browne were to return to assist him. They calculated that this would entice Charles to alter his plans and return south in defence of his capital. It was a more economical use of military resources, as it would mean the army would be less fatigued and better prepared to engage the King's forces on their return south. Furthermore, in the interim, leaving the army around Oxford might yield fruit of another kind. Meanwhile, a strong cavalry force under Bartholomew Vermuyden would continue north to link up with the Scots. The Committee of Both Kingdoms had ordered Leven to move south with his forces, link up with Lord Fairfax and await further instructions.[1] But Leven had other priorities. He was concerned that Charles would march up the west coast and link up with Montrose's forces and pose a threat to Scotland. Instead of marching south, he moved his army west and bivouacked around Appleby, where the balance of his force was positioned a few miles to the north, besieging Carlisle.

The consequence of all these moves was that there was no Parliamentarian force of any significance in the north Midlands – a point not lost on Rupert. Declining Byron's suggestion to attack Nantwich, Rupert elected to move towards Yorkshire, via Newark. This drive caused panic in Parliamentarian circles, as some thought that Rupert's intended objective was the Fens, the heartland of the Eastern Association. They reacted by ordering the immediate movement of troops from around Oxford. In fact, Rupert's objective was precisely calculated to distract Parliament's intentions around the Royalist capital. Sir Edward Walker, the King's Secretary of War noted that:

> Prince Rupert, whose Mastery and chiefest Delight is in Attempts of this kind, was easily induced to undertake it; to which end, Sir Marmaduke Langdale was sent to surround it with the Horse, and about the last of May 1645, a Recruit of 800 Horse under the Command of Sir Richard Willy, Governor of Newark being come up, the Army was drawn about the Town.[2]

The town was Leicester, which had an understrength garrison, insufficient artillery, a scarcity of equipment and, most crucially, inadequate defences. On 28 May Langdale, with the Northern Horse, had been sent to cut off the road between Coventry and Leicester. His troopers ended up chasing some of the garrison cavalry back to the walls and, the next day, the Royalist army arrived and invested the town. Major Innes was ordered to conduct a sally over St Sunday's Bridge and drive back the Royalists, 'which he accordingly did, and beat all the enemies parties close to their bodies, and hindered them from making any batteries that day'.[3] Innes then set fire to a number of houses in the suburb of St Leonard, so that they could not be used as cover by the attackers.

On 30 May Rupert sent in a summons offering generous terms but Colonel Grey (the garrison commander) and the town officials responded by detaining the Prince's trumpeter.[4] Rupert, visibly miffed, ordered the construction of a battery to the south of the town at Raw Dykes, where the old town walls had not been lined with earth. As the Royalists dug to the south, the townsfolk dug even more energetically opposite the batteries, in an attempt to backfill the walls. Rupert was, as ever, a man in a hurry and he did not wait for the gun platforms to be properly constructed before running out of patience. At 3pm he ordered some of the guns to open fire. Within three hours a 'practical' breach had been blasted and that evening the Royalists prepared to storm the town. A single gun fired at midnight; it was the signal for six separate and simultaneous attacks to commence. The main effort was at the breach. Lisle's men, who attacked there, were thrice driven back, but soon after midnight they gained a lodgement. At about the same time to the north, Astley's men had swarmed over the lesser and inadequately manned walls, and opened the gates for Northampton's Horse. They drove off a counter-attack by the Leicestershire cavalry and soon the town was engulfed in small-scale urban fights, as pockets of local forces refused to surrender. In response, the Royalists gave no quarter and this led to spiralling casualties and a number of atrocities. Fairfax's preacher, Joshua Sprigge, noted that 'The enemy put many to the sword at their first entrance, and dealt also extreme cruelly with the town, plundering all they had, and putting many to great ransoms, when they had taken away all their moneys and goods.'[5] The killing stopped by dawn, but the plundering went on for many days. Royalist losses were not light, at about 400 killed and many more injured. However, the losses endured by the townsfolk were so widespread that there was a collection on their behalf by Londoners who were keen to provide relief to the citizens of Leicester.[6]

Meanwhile, on 22 May Fairfax had arrived on the outskirts of Oxford. On 1 June, the Committee of Both Kingdoms sent an urgent communique to him:

---

1 *CSPD* dated 13 May 1645.
2 Walker, *Historical Discourses*, p. 127.

3 Pye, *Siege laid to the town of Leicester*, p. 4.
4 The trumpeter was also used as a messenger. They were trained to observe and report back on strengths, defences, morale etc.
5 Sprigge, *Anglia Rediviva*, p. 27.
6 Foard, *Naseby, The Decisive Campaign*, p. 120.

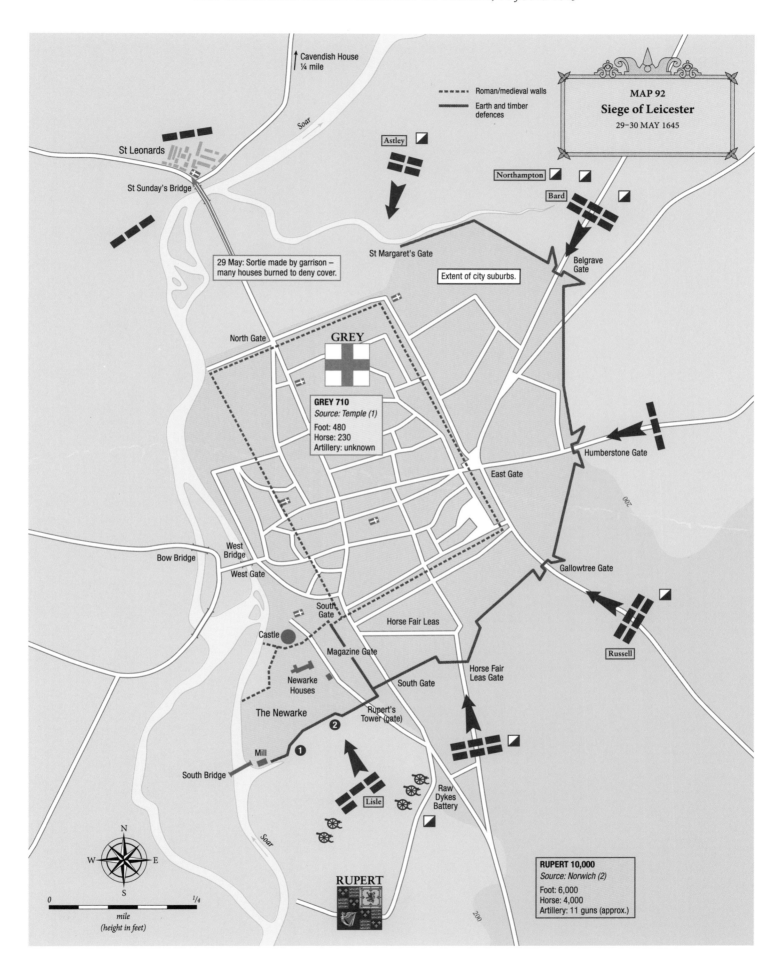

Cavendish House
¼ mile

St Leonards

St Sunday's Bridge

Soar

Astley

Northampton

Bard

29 May: Sortie made by garrison –
many houses burned to deny cover.

St Margaret's Gate

Belgrave
Gate

Extent of city suburbs.

North Gate

GREY

GREY 710
Source: Temple (1)
Foot: 480
Horse: 230
Artillery: unknown

Humberstone Gate

East Gate

Bow Bridge

West
Bridge

West Gate

Gallowtree Gate

South
Gate

Horse Fair Leas

Russell

Castle

Magazine Gate

South Gate

Horse Fair
Leas Gate

Newarke
Houses

The Newarke

Rupert's
Tower (gate)

Mill

1

2

Raw
Dykes
Battery

Lisle

South Bridge

Soar

N
W E
S

0   ¼
mile
(height in feet)

RUPERT

200

Roman/medieval walls

Earth and timber
defences

MAP 92
Siege of Leicester
29–30 MAY 1645

RUPERT 10,000
Source: Norwich (2)
Foot: 6,000
Horse: 4,000
Artillery: 11 guns (approx.)

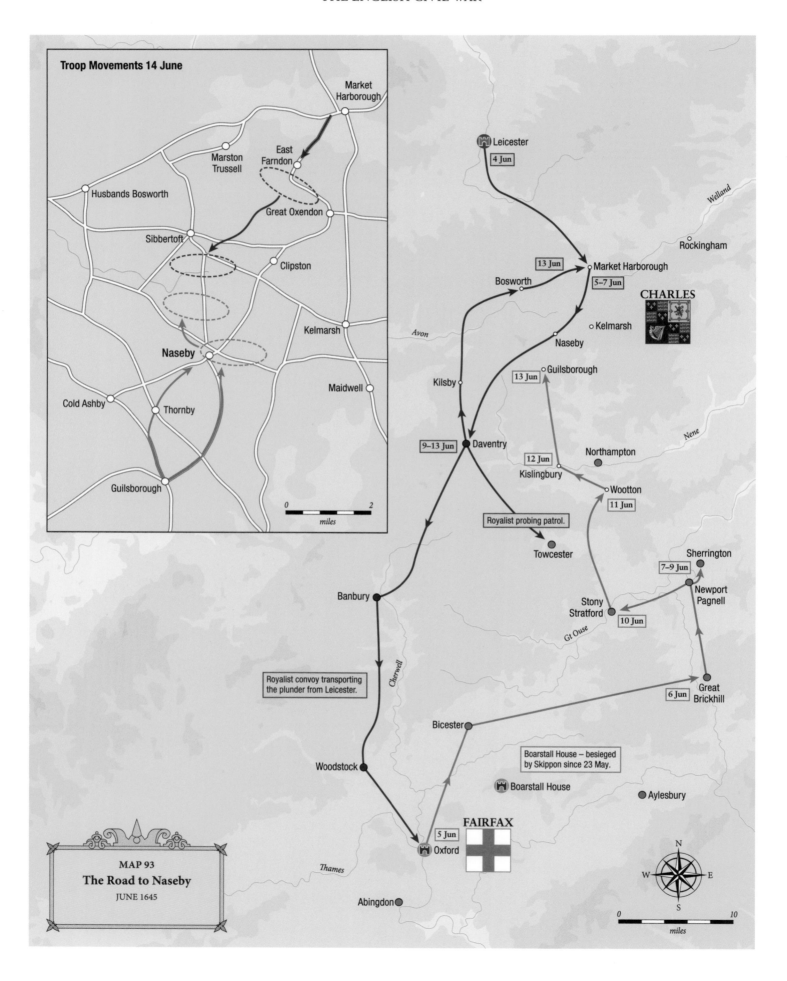

Troop Movements 14 June

Market Harborough

Marston Trussell

East Farndon

Husbands Bosworth

Great Oxendon

Sibbertoft

Clipston

Naseby

Kelmarsh

Cold Ashby

Thornby

Maidwell

Guilsborough

0   2
miles

Leicester
4 Jun

Welland

Rockingham

13 Jun   Market Harborough

Bosworth

5–7 Jun

CHARLES

Kelmarsh

Avon

Naseby

Kilsby

13 Jun   Guilsborough

Daventry

9–13 Jun

Northampton

Nene

12 Jun   Kislingbury

Wootton

11 Jun

Royalist probing patrol.

Towcester

Sherrington

7–9 Jun

Newport Pagnell

Stony Stratford

10 Jun

Gt Ouse

Banbury

Great Brickhill

6 Jun

Royalist convoy transporting the plunder from Leicester.

Cherwell

Bicester

Boarstall House – besieged by Skippon since 23 May.

Woodstock

Boarstall House

Aylesbury

5 Jun   Oxford

FAIRFAX

Thames

Abingdon

MAP 93
The Road to Naseby
JUNE 1645

N
W   E
S

0   10
miles

We have just received advertisement that the enemy has taken Leicester by storm, whereby those parts are much discouraged, besides there are no forces in the field to oppose them and protect the country. Upon consideration of the present state of affairs we conceive it very probable you will speedily receive orders to take the field.[7]

The original plans to sit tight around Oxford to bait Rupert's force were in tatters. Fairfax's redeployment orders followed almost immediately, yet he seemed slow to mobilize and react. Four days later he received a rebuke: 'since the writing of our former letter we have received yours of the 4th from Marston. We desire that you would not amuse yourself about Boarstall House but make all the speed you can to join Vermuyden's forces and those of the Association with Cromwell'.[8] The loss of Leicester, and the apparent tardiness demonstrated by Fairfax around Oxford, led to demands in some quarters in London for the reinstatement of a steering committee to accompany the New Model Army and thereby vest military control back firmly in political hands. However, there was even greater consensus in the Lower House for less political interference, and rather than shackle Fairfax with another political committee, they elected to cut the chains and give him free rein and full command. They did not, at this stage, place Cromwell as General of Horse, in the New Model Army, but the very same debate did reopen the issue and raised a new petition proposing Cromwell's appointment. On 8 June, Fairfax, exercising his full command, endorsed that petition and the pretence over Cromwell's military function was finally resolved.

Over the same period, the Parliamentarians received reports that the Royalist army, which had left Leicester on 4 June, was approaching Daventry. Northampton, which Fairfax had concluded was their objective, was therefore wide open. However, in order to use a better and faster road, Fairfax headed back south-west before crossing the River Great Ouse at Stony Stratford, and heading up Watling Street before turning off a few miles from Towcester. Unbeknown to him, the Royalists were probing south down Watling Street from Daventry. Samuel Luke, with the King's army, recalled that they entered Whittlewood forest, south of Towcester, where they halted and observed the Parliamentarian army.[9] The alarm got back to Daventry, where Symonds recalled that 'the King was hunting deare; when two mile off Daventry there came a strong alarm, so that the whole army was driven on Beacon [Borough] Hill, and lay there all night'.[10]

After spending the night near Wootton, Fairfax headed north towards Guilsborough. It was a potentially dangerous manoeuvre, exposing his left flank during the march. To counter this, he ordered a number of patrols, or commanded parties of horse, to move west. One of these patrols triggered an alarm by stumbling on a Royalist picket a few miles east of Daventry. Fairfax fully expected his army to be attacked that night and ordered every man to arms in situ, but in fact, the Royalists were waiting for a body of 1,200 horse to return from Oxford. The Royalist wait at Daventry had been necessary in order to despatch the mass of plunder from Leicester, and to transport requisitioned cattle, sheep and supplies from Leicestershire and Northamptonshire, back to the capital. Early in the morning of 13 June, Fairfax (now at Kislingbury) received reports that the King's army was once again on the move. They were not, however, heading east, but north.[11]

Soon after this report came in, Cromwell and the Eastern Association cavalry arrived, and Fairfax continued his northerly movement in a more tentative manner, the army reaching Guilsborough that evening. The Royalists had kept to their northerly route and then swung east through Bosworth to quarter that night near Market Harborough. During the night, as both sides sent out cavalry probing patrols and pickets, there were some low-level cavalry clashes near the small village of Naseby.

Throughout the campaign the intelligence picture in Fairfax's headquarters was far more sophisticated and precise than that of their counterparts. Consistently, they had a clearer picture of the strengths, dispositions and intentions of the King's army. This is perhaps not a surprise when taking into account the way intelligence was gathered at this time and the fact that the Royalists were operating in Parliamentarian territory.[12] However, there was another vital piece of intelligence that the Parliamentarian Scoutmaster General Watson's agents had intercepted. It was a communique from Goring, in which he stated that he would resolve matters in Taunton in three weeks (i.e. by the end of June) and, in the interim, he advised the King to 'stand on the defensive, and not engage till his forces were joyn'd'.[13] With this vital information it is not unreasonable to suppose that the King, on 13 June at his customary evening council, would have been uneasy about bringing on a battle without Goring's contingent. The question of whether Fairfax had this intelligence in advance of the battle is a contentious point, but Ellis, in his excellent work on intelligence during the civil wars, makes a good case that he was.[14]

Whatever the outcome of their respective councils on the evening of 13 June, both armies drew out of their quarters in the early hours of the following day. Sprigge, a Parliamentarian army chaplain, recalled, 'The general with the army advanced by three of the clock in the morning from Gilling [Guilsborough] towards Naseby, with an intention to follow close upon the enemy, and (if possible) retard their march with our horse till our foot could draw up to them.'[15] As they drew up on the high ground beyond the village of Naseby, orders were given for the army to deploy into battalia, while Fairfax and Cromwell surveyed the ground to their front. The Royalists moved south at about the same time, but formed up on a position around East Farndon (see inset map 93). Scoutmaster General Francis Ruce was sent forward to conduct a reconnaissance. His report that he could 'neither discover nor hear the Rebels' is puzzling and prompted Rupert to ride forward and take a look for himself.[16] Rupert not only fixed the New Model Army but realized that their position was a formidable one. He also noted that the army was still deploying.[17] As Rupert watched the Parliamentarian army move west to a new position on Closter Hill, he sent back the order for the Royalist army to move to a new position on the north side of Broad Moor, atop Dust Hill.[18] Symonds recalls, 'at seven of the clock, wee marched in Battalia back towards the enemy, who was then very neare; marching up the hills wee discovered

7 *CSPD* dated 1 June 1645.
8 *CSPD* dated 5 June 1645.
9 Tibbutt, *Samuel Luke* Letter 712, dated 11 June 1645.
10 Peachey, *Richard Symonds*, p. 55.
11 Foard, op. cit., pp. 184–6.
12 Ibid., p. 159.
13 Rushworth, *Historical Collections*, part 4, vol. I, p. 49.
14 Ellis, *Military Intelligence*, pp. 150–8.
15 Sprigge, op. cit., p. 37.
16 Walker, op. cit., p. 130. Walker accuses Ruce of lying, which is perhaps based on Slingsby's account, in which he states that they could see the enemy: Parsons, *Henry Slingsby*, p. 150.
17 The Parliamentarians may have initially deployed on Mill Hill, nearer the Clipston road. There is a suggestion that Cromwell considered the position too strong and, in order to entice the Royalists to battle, he convinced Fairfax of the need to redeploy. W.G., *A just apologie*, p. 5.
18 There is general agreement that the Royalist artillery did not make it to the battlefield, other than a few very light pieces.

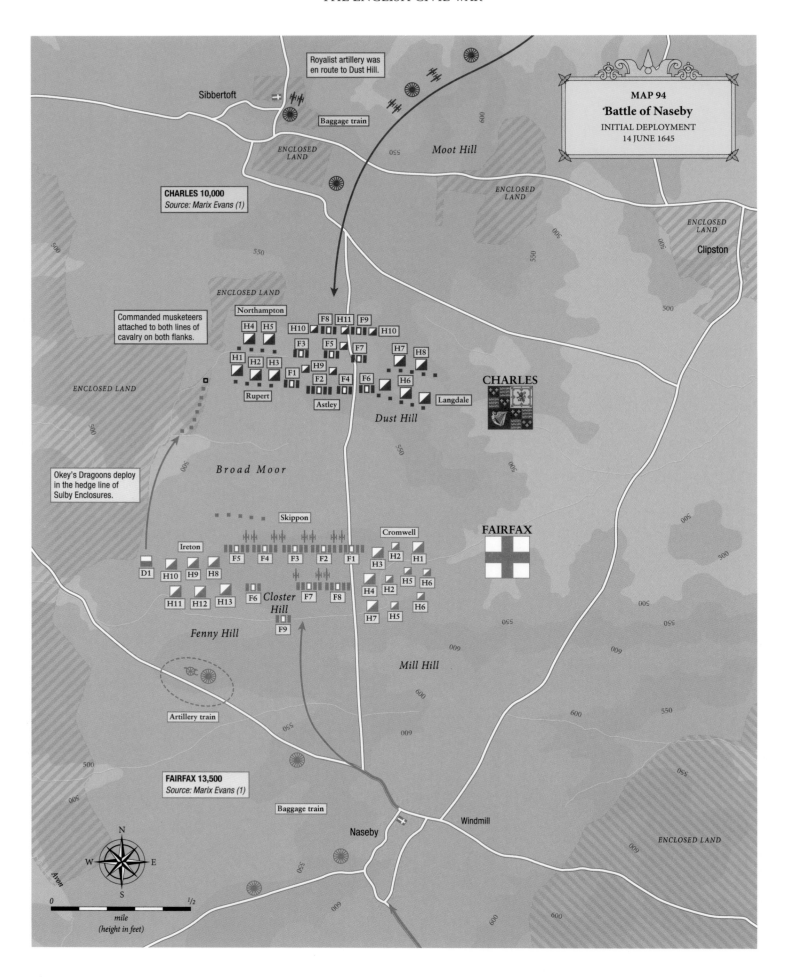

Royalist artillery was en route to Dust Hill.

Sibbertoft

Baggage train

ENCLOSED LAND

Moot Hill

600

550

ENCLOSED LAND

ENCLOSED LAND

Clipston

CHARLES 10,000
Source: Marix Evans (1)

550

500

550

500

Commanded musketeers attached to both lines of cavalry on both flanks.

ENCLOSED LAND

Northampton

H4 H5

H10 F8 H11 F9 H10

F3 F5 F7 H7 H8

H1 H2 H3

F1 H9 F2 F4 F6 H6

Rupert

Astley Langdale

Dust Hill

CHARLES

ENCLOSED LAND

500

550

Broad Moor

Okey's Dragoons deploy in the hedge line of Sulby Enclosures.

Skippon

FAIRFAX

Ireton Cromwell

F5 F4 F3 F2 F1 H2 H1

D1 H10 H9 H8 H3

H4 H2 H5 H6

H11 H12 H13 F6 F7 F8

Closter Hill H7 H5 H6

F9

Fenny Hill

Mill Hill

500

550

600

600

550

Artillery train

600

600

550

600

FAIRFAX 13,500
Source: Marix Evans (1)

500

550

Baggage train

Windmill

Naseby

550

ENCLOSED LAND

N
W   E
S

Avon

600

600

0   1/2

mile
(height in feet)

MAP 94
Battle of Naseby
INITIAL DEPLOYMENT
14 JUNE 1645

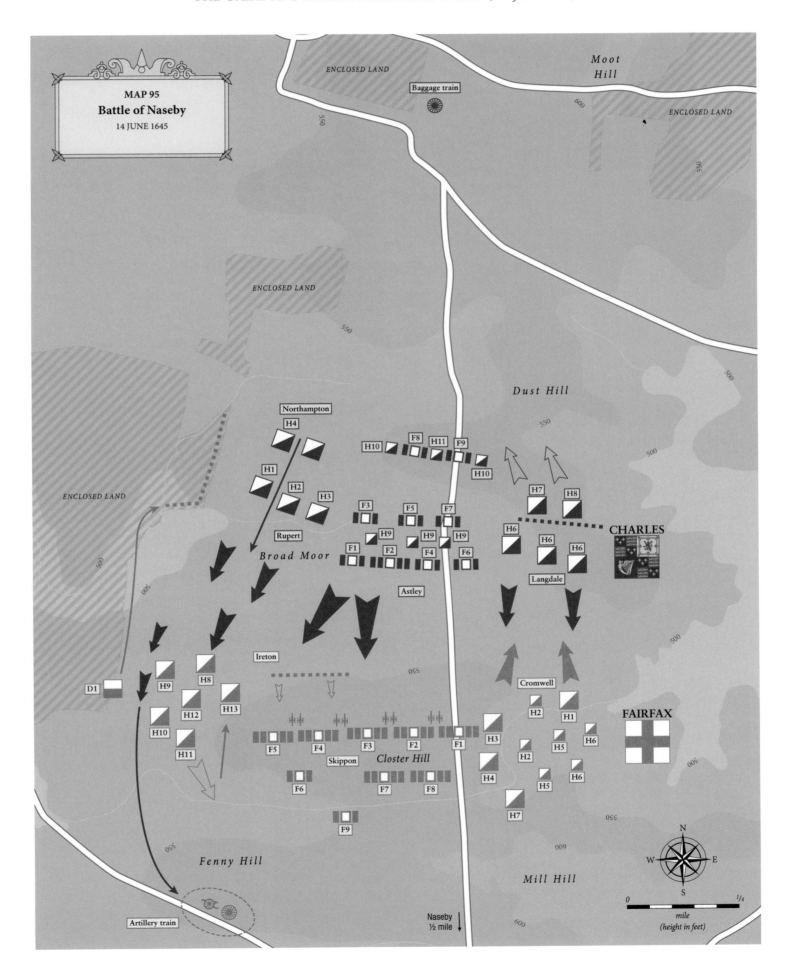

MAP 95
Battle of Naseby
14 JUNE 1645

Moot Hill

ENCLOSED LAND

Baggage train

ENCLOSED LAND

ENCLOSED LAND

ENCLOSED LAND

Dust Hill

Northampton

H4

H1

H2

H3

Rupert

Broad Moor

H10   F8   H11   F9

H10

H7   H8

F3   F5   F7

H9   H9   H9

F1   F2   F4   F6

H6   H6   H6

CHARLES

Langdale

Astley

Ireton

D1

H9   H8

H12   H13

H10

H11

Cromwell

H2   H1

H3   H6

FAIRFAX

F5   F4   F3   F2   F1

Skippon   Closter Hill

H2

H4   H5

F6

F7   F8

H5   H6

F9

H7

Fenny Hill

Artillery train

Naseby
½ mile

Mill Hill

N
W   E
S

0   1/4

mile
(height in feet)

some of the enemy's horse, in parties'.[19] Both armies took some time to deploy. The New Model Army numbered about 13,500 while that of the King about a third less, at about 10,000.[20]

Colonel John Okey, commanding the Parliamentarian dragoons, recalled that Fairfax, Cromwell and Skippon 'were so careful about the great work in hand; as that they soon drew us up into a body, in such a manner, as that we were presently ready to encounter with the Enemy, as the enemy was to fall upon us'.[21] Sprigge added that 'a Forlorn of Foot (musquetiers) consisting of about 300 [were deployed] down the steep of the hill towards the enemy, somewhere more than Carbine shot from the Main battail, who were ordered to retreat to the battail, whensoever they should be hard pressed upon by the Enemy'.[22] As the two sides deployed, Cromwell also realized the importance of the hedge line running up the west of the field, and ordered Okey, 'with all speed mount my men, and flank our left wing'.[23] It was a bold decision as Okey's men were desperately close to the Royalist right wing. But, as it transpired, this action was to have a considerable influence during the opening stages of the battle, and provided an undoubted advantage to the Parliamentarians. It was not, however, a precursor to a Parliamentarian attack. Fairfax was quite content to allow the Royalists to make that first move and Rupert was keen to oblige. Such was the Prince's determination to get on with things that he attacked as soon as the King's men reached Dust Hill. He wanted to take and keep the initiative, more especially as he could see that the Parliamentarians were still in the process of finalizing their movement across the slope of Closter Hill. On the Parliamentarian right, Cromwell was also in the process of redeploying the cavalry in three lines (instead of two) as he lacked sufficient space. The late arrival of the Lincolnshire Horse had exacerbated the problem.[24]

The battle opened sometime between 10 and 11am. It is unclear whether the fire from Okey's Dragoons pressed events or whether Rupert's confidence and impetuosity brought on the initial attack.[25] Whatever the reason, it is certain that the Royalists were not truly ready. Walker commented that 'the Heat of Prince Rupert, and his Opinion they durst not stand him, engaged us before we had either turned our Cannon or chosen fit Ground to fight on'.[26] Rupert's (right) cavalry wing outnumbered that of Ireton, but they suffered heavily during their advance from the flanking fire of Okey's Dragoons. Slingsby remembered that 'many of ye Regiment [were] wound'd by shot from ye hedge before we could joyne with theirs on y' wing'.[27] The subsequent cavalry on cavalry action was a protracted affair. Rupert halted his advance to shake out before charging and Ireton moved his cavalry slightly forward, off the gentle slope, to meet the charge. The two sides were motionless for a short time, the Royalists gaining composure and dressing before the charge. It is possible that they may have taken the opportunity during this hiatus to reload pistols, many having discharged them against

Okey's Dragoons as they had moved south. Ireton's divisions, for reasons of difficult terrain, did not meet the charge together. The right-hand divisions were further forward but they fared well in the initial clashes, driving back and routing their opponents, while one regiment (probably Ireton's own) even went on to attack Northampton's reserve.[28]

While this cavalry action was ongoing to the west, the Royalist left-wing cavalry to the east were also well advanced. In between them, the Royalist infantry had crossed Broad Moor, driven back the forlorn hope (500 deployed musketeers, largely deployed in front of Skippon's left wing) and started to climb Closter Hill. The Parliamentarian artillery appears to have only fired a few shots, as Symonds recalled: 'they kept their grownd on the top of the hill, and wee marched up to them through a bottom full of furse bushes; they shot two pieces of cannon'.[29] Walker supports this account of a lack of suppressing fire from the enemy artillery and records that the rounds that were fired were largely ineffectual: 'Presently our Forces advanced up the Hill, the Rebels only discharging five Pieces at them, but over shot them.'[30] Considering the Royalist advance from Dust Hill was over half a mile, this cannot have been through a lack of time but more likely that the gun platforms were too high to enable the barrels to be depressed to fire down into Broad Moor, and it supports the assertion that the rounds were fired high. The two blocks of infantry waited until they were within a few feet of each other before charging. It was a fairly even contest, ebbing and flowing, with both groups of pikemen and musketeers locked together in a deadly embrace. Howard's cavalry, which had been interposed between the two groups of Royalist foot, was helping to provide momentum to the attack.[31] The Parliamentarian lines began to fall back, as Walker describes:

> The Foot on either fide hardly saw each other until they were within Carbine Shot, and so only made one Volley; ours falling in with Sword and butt end of the Musquet did notable Execution; so much as I saw their Colours fall, and their Foot in great Disorder.[32]

To their right, Cromwell's cavalry advanced to meet that of the Royalist left wing under Langdale. Cromwell's front line suffered heavy casualties in the initial engagement with the Northern Horse, and Slingsby, who was with Langdale's wing, recalled that 'after they were close joyn'd, they stood a pritty while, & neither seem'd to yeild, till more came up to their flanks & put ym [them] to rout, & wheeling to our right took ym [them] in disorder, & so presently made our whole horse run'.[33] Cromwell's second and third lines undoubtedly had an impact, and the ferocity and discipline with which his elite Ironsides had fought took Langdale's troopers by complete surprise. George Bishop recalled the rout of the Royalist left wing. He wrote after the battle to the Scoutmaster General in London, detailing that Cromwell 'routed the King's left Wing; drove them clear away from that side, having not the least retreat, but was like a Torrent driving all before them'.[34]

Back on the Royalist right it would appear that Ireton's cavalry began to attack some of the Royalist infantry in the flank. According to Sprigge,

---

19 Peachey, op. cit., p. 55. Although Symonds recalls they had been on the move since 2am to get into position.

20 Exact numbers are contentious. See the notes for map 94 for an explanation of these numbers.

21 Okey, cited in Young, *Naseby 1645*, p. 338.

22 Sprigge, op. cit., p. 39.

23 Okey, op. cit., p. 338.

24 Sprigge, op. cit., p. 40.

25 The dragoons had pushed well north to the end of the enclosed land; there is considerable archaeological evidence of an extensive exchange of musketry in the area.

26 Walker, op. cit., p. 130.

27 Parsons, op. cit., pp. 151–2.

28 Foard, op. cit., p. 253.

29 Peachey, op. cit., p. 55.

30 Walker, op. cit., p. 130.

31 It is unclear how they achieved this, whether by pushing from the back or getting around the flanks.

32 Walker, op. cit., p. 130.

33 Sprigge, op. cit., p. 42.

34 Bishop, *Particular and exact relation of the victory*, pp. 1–2.

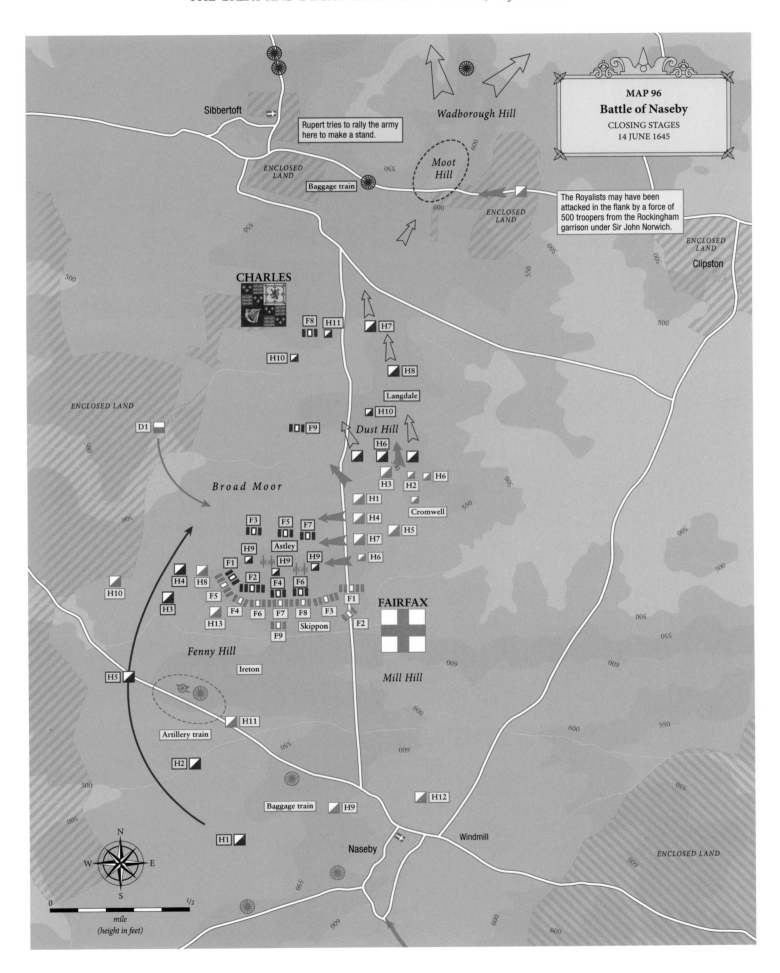

Sibbertoft

Rupert tries to rally the army
here to make a stand.

Wadborough Hill

MAP 96
Battle of Naseby
CLOSING STAGES
14 JUNE 1645

*ENCLOSED
LAND*

*Moot
Hill*

Baggage train

The Royalists may have been
attacked in the flank by a force of
500 troopers from the Rockingham
garrison under Sir John Norwich.

*ENCLOSED
LAND*

*ENCLOSED
LAND*

Clipston

CHARLES

F8 H11

H10

H7

H8

ENCLOSED LAND

Langdale

D1

H10

Dust Hill

F9

Broad Moor

H6

H3   H2   H6

H1

Cromwell

F3   F5   F7

H4

H5

H9 Astley

H7

F1   H9   H9

H6

H4 H8

F2

F4   F6

H10

F5

F1

FAIRFAX

H3

F4   F6   F7   F8   F3

H13

F2

Skippon

F9

Fenny Hill

Ireton

Mill Hill

H5

H11

Artillery train

H2

H12

Baggage train   H9

N

W   E

S

H1

Naseby

Windmill

ENCLOSED LAND

0   1/2

*mile
(height in feet)*

Ireton 'himself with great resolution fell in amongst the musketeers, where his horse being shot under him, and himself run through the thigh with a pike, and into the face with an halbert, was taken prisoner by the enemy'.[35] Ireton's loss seems to have had an effect upon his left-wing cavalry, with the two central regiments (probably Vermuden's and Fleetwood's) breaking and fleeing the field. Some of Rupert's troopers charged through the gap. Joshua Sprigge recorded that:

> The enemy having thus worsted our left wing pursued their advantage, and Prince Rupert himself having prosecuted his success upon the left wing almost to Naseby town, in his return summoned the train, offering them quarter, which being well defended with the firelocks, and a rearguard left for that purpose.[36]

But, as was so often the case, the Royalists failed to exploit their penetration. Wanklyn suggests this may have been due to the way Fairfax deployed his infantry and the force protection allocated to the artillery train.[37] Furthermore, many of Ireton's cavalry rallied and remained to provide support to the infantry on the left flank. Rupert needed infantry support of his own, but his commanded musketeers had been deployed to neutralize Okey's men and were some way off. It is probably about this point in the battle that Rupert returned to the King's entourage on Dust Hill only to realize that things were not going as well as he had hoped.

In the centre the infantry was still locked in a fearful struggle. Joshua Sprigge wrote that 'Fairfax's regiment on the right held firm, but almost all the rest of the main battle being overpressed, gave ground, and went off in some disorder, falling behind the reserves'.[38] The officers rallied their men and anchored the regiments on those behind. On the extreme left, Skippon's men continued to fight on with Ireton's cavalry, and during one of their counter-attacks, Ireton was recaptured and carried from the field. But the failure of the Royalist left and centre to make ground was now about to be dealt a terminal blow. A combination of discipline and the terrain had constrained large numbers of Cromwell's cavalry from pursuing Langdale's defeated Northern Horse. According to George Bishop, Fairfax was with Cromwell during his decisive charge, and having lost his helmet 'hee with Lieutenant General; Cromwell faced about to that wing, with some Divisions of Horse, [and] charged bareheaded'.[39] The Royalist foot on Closter Hill now found themselves surrounded. Rupert tried to gather as many of the Royalist horse and foot as he could muster, in order to counter-attack. Henry Slingsby, a Royalist observer at the battle, remembered the action with some frustration:

Ye prince on ye one hand, & Sr. Marmaduke Langdale on ye other, (ye King yet being upon ye place) having got together as many as they could, made an offer of a 2 [second] charge, but could not abide it; they being horse & foot in good order, & we but a few horse only, & those mightily discourag'd; y' so we were immediately made to run.[40]

The Royalist foot, 'seeing all their horse beaten out of the field, and surrounded by our horse and foot, they laid down their arms with condition not to be plundered'.[41] The decision was taken not to risk a charge by the Parliamentarian cavalry alone; the cavalry commanders decided to wait for their infantry. They did not take long to come up, but at that point the cavalry was reluctant to leave their recent spoils and give chase to the Royalist cavalry. Colonel Edward Wogan remembered that they were 'much discontented to leave all the plunder in the field to our foot... which was richly laden with plunder and could by no means be brought together for a long time'.[42] At first, the Royalist retreat was a controlled withdrawal; they tried to make a stand near their baggage train atop Moot Hill but were attacked and could not be rallied.[43] The retreat increasingly turned to a rout with every man for himself. Cromwell's post-battle letter to the speaker of the House of Commons summed up the extent of the victory:

> We after three Hours Fight very doubtful, at last Routed his Army, kill'd and took about five thousand, very many Officers, but of what Quality, we yet know not. We took also about two hundred Carriages, all he had, and all his Guns, being twelve in number, whereof two were Demi-Cannon, two Demi Culverins, and I think the rest Sacres [sakers]; we pursued the Enemy from three miles short of Harborough to nine beyond, even to the Sight of Leicester, whither the King fled.[44]

It was a catastrophic blow to the Royalist war effort, and to make matters considerably worse, the King's cabinet, containing all his personal correspondence, was taken among the spoils of the baggage train. It contained letters to and from his Queen in which they detailed plans to bring over foreigners and 'papists' from Ireland and from the Continent to fight for the Royalist cause. It was the evidence of treason that the King's enemies had long sought, and manna from heaven for the Parliamentarian propaganda machine. They wasted no time in publishing the correspondence, in a pamphlet entitled 'The King's Cabinet Opened'.[45] The disclosure of the King's duplicity did his cause no end of harm among his own supporters. While the King and the remnants of his broken army made off to the Welsh Marches, Fairfax moved to Leicester, and on 18 June, four days after the battle, the city was back in Parliament's hands.

35 Sprigge, op. cit., p. 42.
36 Ibid.
37 Wanklyn, *The Warrior Generals*, p. 164.
38 Sprigge, op. cit., p. 41.
39 Bishop, op. cit., p. 2.

40 Parsons, op. cit., p. 152.
41 Sprigge, op. cit., p. 353.
42 Wogan, E., *The Proceedings of the New-Moulded Army* in Young, op. cit., p. 367.
43 There is some contention as to which cavalry force attacked the Royalists at Moot Hill and Wadborough Hill. Mike Ingram, *Naseby: What happened after the battle?*, provides good evidence that it was in fact a Parliamentarian cavalry force from Rockingham Castle under the command of Sir John Norwich.
44 Fairfax, *Three letters*, p. 2.
45 Charles I, *The King's cabinet opened*.

CHAPTER 28

TAUNTON AND LANGPORT: EVENTS IN THE SOUTH-WEST, JANUARY TO JULY 1645

Following the Battle of Lostwithiel, Grenville was left to conduct operations against Plymouth, which remained the only Parliamentarian stronghold in Cornwall and Devon. However, Grenville's free rein was curtailed by Charles's reorganizations in the winter of 1644–45 and the establishment of a Council of the West under the nominal leadership of the teenage Prince of Wales.[1] Rupert warned the King that such an arrangement would be fraught with opportunities for intrigue. Goring had been left in charge of the South-West following Lostwithiel, but despite having a force of 1,500 horse and 3,000 foot, he was unable, or more accurately unwilling, to attempt the recapture of Weymouth.[2] Instead he returned to Exeter and demanded that both Grenville and Sir John Berkeley (the military governor), join him in undertaking a second siege of Taunton.[3] Grenville refused, citing his mission to capture Plymouth, and Berkeley similarly declined in forthright terms. However. the Council of the Prince of Wales decided otherwise, and some weeks later Grenville moved east only to discover that Goring had grown impatient, abandoned the plan and moved back into Dorset.

With Goring out of the way, Grenville, in an effort to strengthen his claim for overall command of the forces on the ground in the South-West, continued towards Taunton in order to besiege the place. He arrived on 2 April and, aware that Goring had been ordered back into the area, he was in a hurry. After a couple of days Grenville was injured in a preliminary operation to capture Wellington House (near Taunton) and had to be evacuated back to Exeter. Goring arrived back a few days later. But Grenville's Cornish soldiers refused to take orders from either Goring or Berkeley, and attempts by the Council of the Prince to resolve matters were unsuccessful. The impasse and internecine power struggle went on for many weeks. In consequence, the siege was never conducted with the necessary gusto. On 8 May an assault was easily repelled, and heavy fighting the next day still failed to dislodge the determined garrison.

Days turned to weeks, and by the end of June intelligence confirmed that a strong Parliamentarian force, a new army under Fairfax, was on its way to the area. The Royalists broke camp and the second siege was lifted. As it turned out, both Fairfax and Goring were soon to be ordered out of the South-West; the former to move towards Oxford on news that Charles had departed his capital, and the latter to link up with the King at Stow-on-the-Wold. Following the King's council at Stow-on-the-Wold, Goring was considered superfluous and sent back to Taunton with 3,000 men. He had only been there a matter of days when he received another urgent recall by the King, as events developed in the Midlands. However, Goring prevaricated and chose to ignore the several orders for his return. His heavy drinking certainly seemed to be affecting his judgement and he

wrote to the King (see chapter 27), placing his regional interests over the greater Royalist cause.

The victory at Naseby had dealt a fatal blow to the Royalist cause, although it is important to recognize that this was not wholly apparent at the time. Having recaptured Leicester, Fairfax had dismissed the idea of chasing the remnants of the King's army to the Welsh Marches. He elected instead to march back south, relieve Taunton and destroy Goring's force, arguably the last significant Royalist army. The third siege of the beleaguered town had begun at the end of May, but was beset with all of the earlier frictions affecting unity of effort and command. The garrison had been reinforced by 4,000 soldiers under the command of Colonel Weldon, who had been sent by Fairfax in May. Goring's force numbered nearly 11,000, but despite this, operations against the town were making little progress, aggravated by a growing alienation by the local population and armed action by the mounting faction of Clubmen. On 29 June, with news that the New Model Army was heading back south, Goring lifted the siege for the third and final time. His initial plan was to establish a Royalist rendezvous at Chard but this was countermanded by an order from Charles a day later. He ordered Goring to retain control of the West Country until the rest of the King's forces could join him. He realized the task of establishing a defensive line across Somerset was nigh on impossible; instead he concentrated on keeping open his lines of communication with the rest of the King's forces by holding north Somerset, the ports and the approaches to Bristol.

Goring planned to use the rivers Yeo and Parrett as obstacles and moved from Taunton to cover the key crossings from Bridport to Ilchester. Weldon's regiments broke out of Taunton, escaped and headed east. On 5 July they linked up with Fairfax at Crewkerne. The Parliamentarians now had about 16,000 men, having made a union with Massey's forces from Gloucestershire at Blandford on 2 July. Goring was heavily outnumbered. He decided to try to get Fairfax to split his force by conducting a feint towards Taunton. It succeeded, Fairfax splitting his force three ways.

> He had, at Long Sutton, under his immediate command nine regiments of infantry and seven regiments of horse intact, with one company of dragoons and the pikes of three infantry regiments, about 10,600 men in all, of which 2,800 were cavalry. Massie near Ilton, had 3,600 horse and dragoons; while between these two forces, and powerless to assist either Massie or Fairfax, was Montague, with about 1,700 horse and foot.[4]

At Isle Moor, on 8 July, Massey caught Goring's brother-in-law, George Porter, off-guard, taking 200 prisoners and nine colours.[5] Goring was

---

1   The King was worried that both he and the Prince of Wales could be captured together – Andriette, *Devon and Exeter*, p. 135.
2   Dyve had been driven from the town at the end of February.
3   The first siege had lasted from 23 September to 14 December 1644.

4   Browne, *From Leicester to Langport*, p. 262.
5   Fairfax, *The coppie of a letter*, p. 1. Porter's 1,500 troopers, quite inexplicably, had been given the day off and were bathing in the River Isle when Massey surprised them.

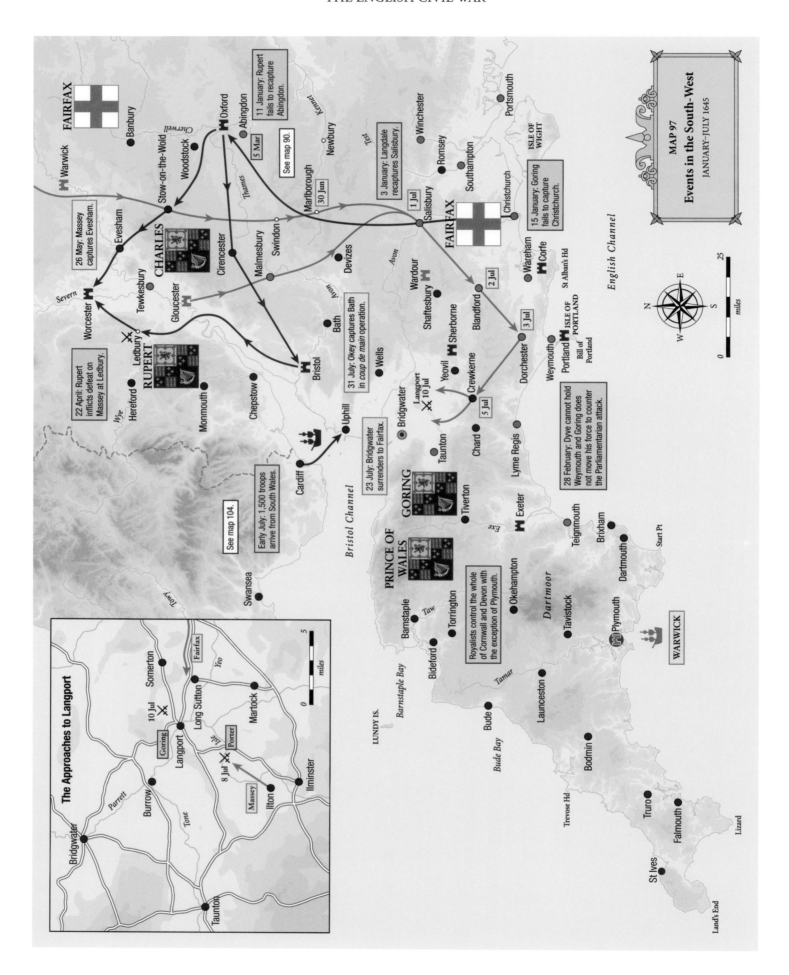

FAIRFAX

11 January: Rupert fails to recapture Abingdon.

5 Mar

See map 90.

3 January: Langdale recaptures Salisbury.

1 Jul

15 January: Goring fails to capture Christchurch.

FAIRFAX

Warwick

Banbury

Oxford

Abingdon

Woodstock

Stow-on-the-Wold

Evesham

26 May: Massey captures Evesham.

CHARLES

Marlborough

30 Jun

Swindon

Newbury

Winchester

Romsey

Southampton

Christchurch

Portsmouth

ISLE OF WIGHT

Cirencester

Malmesbury

Tewkesbury

Gloucester

Devizes

Wardour

Shaftesbury

Sherborne

Blandford

2 Jul

Wareham

Corfe

St Albans Hd

Severn

Worcester

Ledbury

RUPERT

Hereford

Bath

Wells

Bristol

31 July: Okey captures Bath in coup de main operation.

Yeovil

Crewkerne

Dorchester

3 Jul

Weymouth

Portland

ISLE OF PORTLAND

Bill of Portland

22 April: Rupert inflicts defeat on Massey at Ledbury.

Monmouth

Chepstow

Uphill

Langport 10 Jul

5 Jul

Bridgwater

Lyme Regis

28 February: Dyve cannot hold Weymouth and Goring does not move his force to counter the Parliamentarian attack.

See map 104.

Early July: 1,500 troops arrive from South Wales.

Cardiff

23 July: Bridgwater surrenders to Fairfax.

Taunton

Chard

GORING

Swansea

Bristol Channel

Tiverton

Exeter

PRINCE OF WALES

Exe

Royalists control the whole of Cornwall and Devon with the exception of Plymouth.

Barnstaple

Bideford

Torrington

Okehampton

Teignmouth

Brixham

Dartmouth

Start Pt

Taw

Dartmoor

Tavistock

Plymouth

WARWICK

LUNDY IS.

Barnstaple Bay

Bude

Launceston

Tamar

Bude Bay

Bodmin

English Channel

N
W E
S

0 miles 25

MAP 97
Events in the South-West
JANUARY–JULY 1645

Truro

St Ives

Falmouth

Lizard

Trevose Hd

Land's End

The Approaches to Langport

Somerton

Fairfax

Long Sutton

10 Jul

Yeo

Martock

Goring

Langport

Porter

8 Jul

Massey

Ilton

Ilminster

Burrow

Isle

Bridgwater

Parrett

Tone

Taunton

0 miles 5

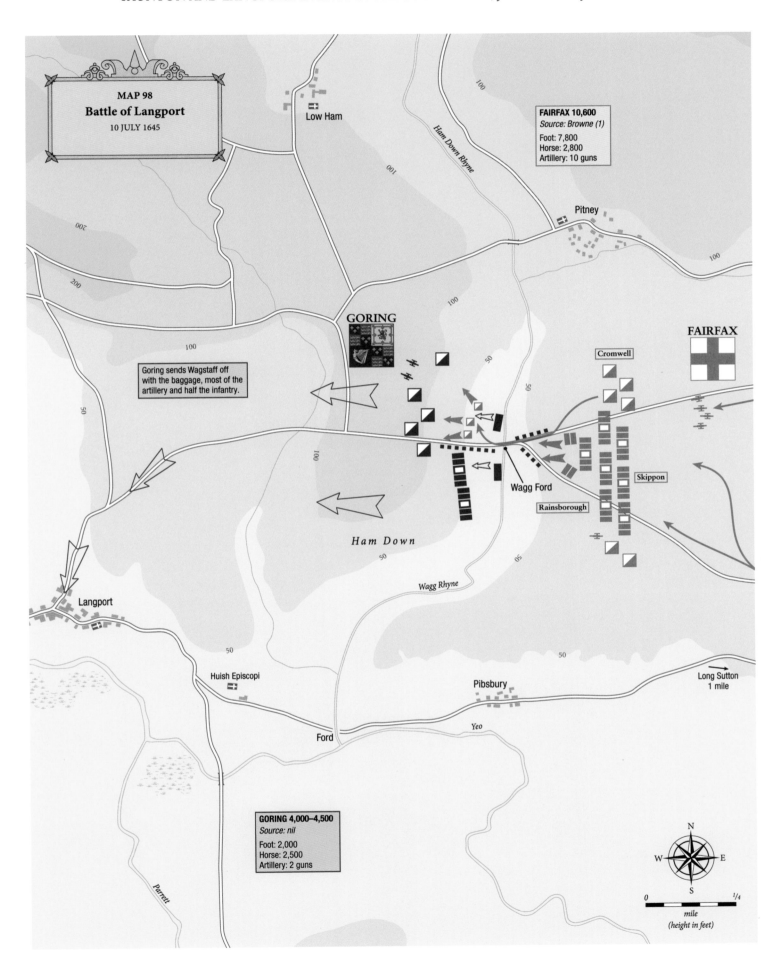

MAP 98

Battle of Langport

10 JULY 1645

Low Ham

Ham Down Rhyne

FAIRFAX 10,600
Source: Browne (1)
Foot: 7,800
Horse: 2,800
Artillery: 10 guns

100

100

200

200

Pitney

100

GORING

50

FAIRFAX

50

Goring sends Wagstaff off
with the baggage, most of the
artillery and half the infantry.

Cromwell

50

50

Wagg Ford

Skippon

Rainsborough

Ham Down

50

50

Langport

50

Wagg Rhyne

Long Sutton
1 mile

50

50

Huish Episcopi

Pibsbury

Yeo

Ford

GORING 4,000–4,500
Source: nil
Foot: 2,000
Horse: 2,500
Artillery: 2 guns

Parrett

N
W   E
S

0   1/4

mile
(height in feet)

furious with Porter, suggesting to his adjutant that 'he deserves to be pistoled for his Negligence or Cowardice'.[6] This unsettling development was followed by intelligence that Fairfax had crossed the River Yeo (at Yeovil) and was approaching from the east.[7] Goring pulled back to Langport, and sent off all the baggage and all but two guns to the strongly fortified garrison at Bridgwater. He hoped to hold the position until nightfall. Fairfax approached Langport very early on 10 July; he was short of supplies, his men were exhausted, and he realized that he could not wait for Massey's men to join him if he was going to cut off Goring before he withdrew north.[8] News then arrived that Goring was indeed withdrawing, and following a quick reconnaissance by Fairfax and his senior commanders, he elected to attack.

Goring had placed two regiments (Slaughter's and Wise's) directly at Wagg ford, and lined the hedges with 2,000 musketeers, mainly from the newly arrived troops from Wales. His cavalry was on the hillside and the infantry on the lower ground to their right. At about 10am Fairfax advanced from Long Sutton and moved his artillery to the high ground from where they opened a heavy and accurate fire before he moved about 1,500 commanded musketeers, under Colonel Rainsborough, forward as a forlorn hope to clear the Royalist musketeers from the hedges and to engage the regiments adjacent to the bridge. Captain Blackwell recorded:

> … the Royalists intended to draw off their Musquettiers, but before they could draw them off, we had engaged them by forlorne hopes of Musquettiers, drawn downe to the hedges, both on the right hand and the left of that passe, which they withstood a while stoutly; but having drawne up our great Guns, and given them about 50 or 60 great shot, their horse began to retreat, and their foote could not abide so much heat, as they found in our Musquettiers, of both forlorne hopes.[9]

As the Royalists fell back, Rainsborough's men pushed across the Wagg Rhyne and were followed almost immediately by a charge by three troops of horse led by Major Bethels. Lieutenant Colonel Lilburne described what happened next in his report to the House of Commons:

> It coming to Major Bethels turne to charge with his forlorne of horse… Bethell upon command given, led on his own troop through the water which was deepe and dirty and very narrow, the Enemy having a very large body at the top of the lane, many times over his number, charged them with as much gallantry as ever I saw men in my life, forceing them with the sword to give ground, which made way for Capt. Evinsons Troope to draw out of the lane, and front with him, driving the enemies great body and their reserve up the hill.[10]

In order to delay the follow-up, the fleeing Royalists set fire to houses in Langport. Cromwell's cavalry was leading the pursuit and they caught up with a couple of large groups of Royalist stragglers some 2 or 3 miles to the north. They took a number of prisoners but the main force escaped. Goring, most of the horse and the infantry that had departed earlier had made it to the safety of Bridgwater. Joshua Sprigge, our trusty chaplain, summed up the extent of the Parliamentarian victory:

> We pursued the enemy within two miles of Bridgewater… doing execution upon them all the way… took about fourteen hundred prisoners, about twelve hundred horse, and divers officers of quality… about thirty colours of horse and foot: and on the other hand, it was a victory as cheap to us as dear to them: we lost no officer, not twenty common soldiers; some fourteen or sixteen of major Bethel's troop were hurt, and himself shot in the right hand.[11]

Goring's optimism at having reached Bridgwater was short lived. Fairfax stormed the town on 21 July and it surrendered two days later. A surprise attack yielded Bath to Colonel Okey before the month was out, and Fairfax now eyed the vital city and port of Bristol. The defeat at Langport and the loss of Bridgwater effectively put an end to the King's plans in the South-West.

---

6 Bulstrode, *Memoirs and Reflections*, p. 137.

7 Goring assumed that Dyve (Sherborne Castle) was holding/denying the Yeovil crossing of the River Yeo; his failure to do so enabled Fairfax to get on to the north-east bank.

8 His forces were also suffering badly from large groups of Clubmen who threatened his lines of communication.

9 Blackwell, *Great defeat given to Goring's army*, p. 3.

10 Lilburne, *Full relation of the great battell*, p. 6.

11 Sprigge, *Anglia Rediviva*, p. 73.

CHAPTER 29
SCOTLAND IN 1645: MONTROSE'S ROYALIST CAMPAIGN

While Montrose laid up in the Great Glen, he allowed many of his Highlanders to go home for the winter. However, with news that Mackenzie of Seaforth was planning to attack down the valley with his considerable force of 5,000 men from the garrison at Inverness, Montrose elected to fight and recalled his men to the colours. While he gathered the clans, word was received that Argyll was approaching from the south with 3,000 men. He was in a trap, but he concluded that his men's hatred of the Campbells, coupled with Argyll's questionable military prowess, would not only prevail but serve to dishearten Seaforth's resolve to follow up. Montrose wasted no time in marching his 1,500 men south towards Argyll across the mountains in a terrible snowstorm.[1] On 31 January they crossed the Glen Roy and Glen Spean and the next day approached Inverlochy from the east. Having remained immobile during a moonlit night, they stole forward at first light and at the sound of the trumpet they charged. The Irish were on the flanks and the Highlanders in the centre. The Covenanters put up a good fight, for a short while, but once a few began to steal away, the flood unlocked. One of Montrose's many biographers wrote, 'Then ensued a terrible slaughter of the fugitives for nine miles without cessation. Of the enemy 1,500 were slain, among them many distinguished gentlemen and chieftains of the clan Campbell.'[2]

Inverlochy broke Argyll's power in the Highlands and added to Montrose's reputation of invincibility. His victory caused widespread alarm within the Committee of Estates in Edinburgh and led to a decision by Seaforth to disband his field army and retire back to Inverness.[3] Lieutenant General William Baillie hastened north to block any attempt by Montrose to move south. Montrose had no such intentions at this time, as his force was not strong enough, but he was also well aware that he could ill afford to rest on his laurels. Instead, he marched back north in the hope of rousing the support of the Gordons. He captured Elgin and established a temporary headquarters there and was soon rewarded with an important reinforcement, when Lord Gordon joined the Royalists with his clan cavalry. At the end of March, at the head of an army of 2,000 foot and 2,000 horse, Montrose headed south but he had great difficulty keeping his army in order and intact. To satisfy the Highlanders' desire for plunder, Montrose decided to storm Dundee on 4 April. A few miles to the west at Perth lay Baillie. He despatched a large part of his force to attack Montrose, but John Hurry, the Covenanter cavalry commander, failed to drive home this attack and, lacking any infantry support, the Royalists were able to melt back into the hills.[4] Baillie joined the pursuit as far as Brechin, before returning to Perth

but despatched, on orders of the Edinburgh committee, Colonel Hurry to continue north and pursue Montrose.

Hurry's small force, far from pursuing Montrose's army, was in fact being hunted by them. Hurry was forced to fight a series of rearguard actions as he evaded a general action, and on 7 May he finally reached the Covenanter garrison at Inverness. Reinforced by Seaforth's (and Sutherland's) men, Hurry then turned on Montrose who had camped a few miles to the east at Auldearn. The Covenanter numbers were now nearly 4,000, while those of Montrose barely mustered 2,000.[5] Montrose's men were spread across the glens. Exhaustion and inclement weather enticed the Royalists to seek shelter where they could. In the village itself were MacColla's Irish troops and Gordon of Moneymore's Regiment, while the balance of Montrose's infantry and cavalry were spread across the countryside in whatever lodging they could find.

The Covenanters marched from Inverness in the rain, and then 4 miles from the village of Auldearn they decided to clear their muskets 'which they were persuaded the rain had poysoned' and reload. It was a mistake, for 'the thundering report of this vollie, contrairie to ther expectatI by a suddain changeing of the wynd, carried throw the aire unto the eares of fyve or six scouts'.[6] The scouts raised the alarm and MacColla, realizing he needed to buy time for the Royalist troops to assemble, moved his troops out of the village and up onto Garlic Hill, while Moneymore's troops moved to a small hillock to the north-west of the village (known as Castle Hill). Both hills had some protection from ditches, enclosures and the former from marshy ground to the north-west. Hurry approached from the south-west, his troops constrained by the terrain and obstacles, but, in time, they came up against MacColla's men and a fearful fight ensued. Meanwhile Montrose was deploying the rest of his force. Patrick Gordon of Ruthven, one of the Gordon clansmen, recorded what happened next:

Whill Montros drawes up the foot to oppose the maine body of the enemies battell, Aboyne drawes a hundreth horse to charge the right winge, and my lord Gordon drawes forth so many to charge the left winge; whill M'Donell, who led the vane of the armie, is charged with a strong regiment of foot, and two troopes of horse.[7]

MacColla had with him the Royal Standard, giving Hurry the impression that this group constituted the Royalist main body. It most likely led him to approach with greater caution, all the while buying more time for Montrose.

With the cavalry on both sides constrained, the fight on Garlic Hill turned into an infantry firefight and Hurry's greater numbers were beginning

---

1   Montrose's force consisted of Alasdair MacColla MacDonald's Irish and the Stewarts, Macdonalds, MacLeans, and Camerons.

2   Murdoch and Morland-Simpson, *Marquis of Montrose 1639—1650*, p. 85. Argyll had removed himself from command that morning and left Duncan Campbell of Auchinbrek at the helm.

3   Kenyon & Ohlmeyer, *Military History*, p. 59.

4   This is the same John Hurry (or Urry) of Chalgrove Field 1643 – see chapter 10.

5   Reid, *Auldearn 1645*, considers Wishart's numbers to be inflated for the Covenanters and low in terms of the Royalist Horse, which he calculates to have been nearer 600.

6   Gordon, *Britane's distemper*, p. 123.

7   Ibid.

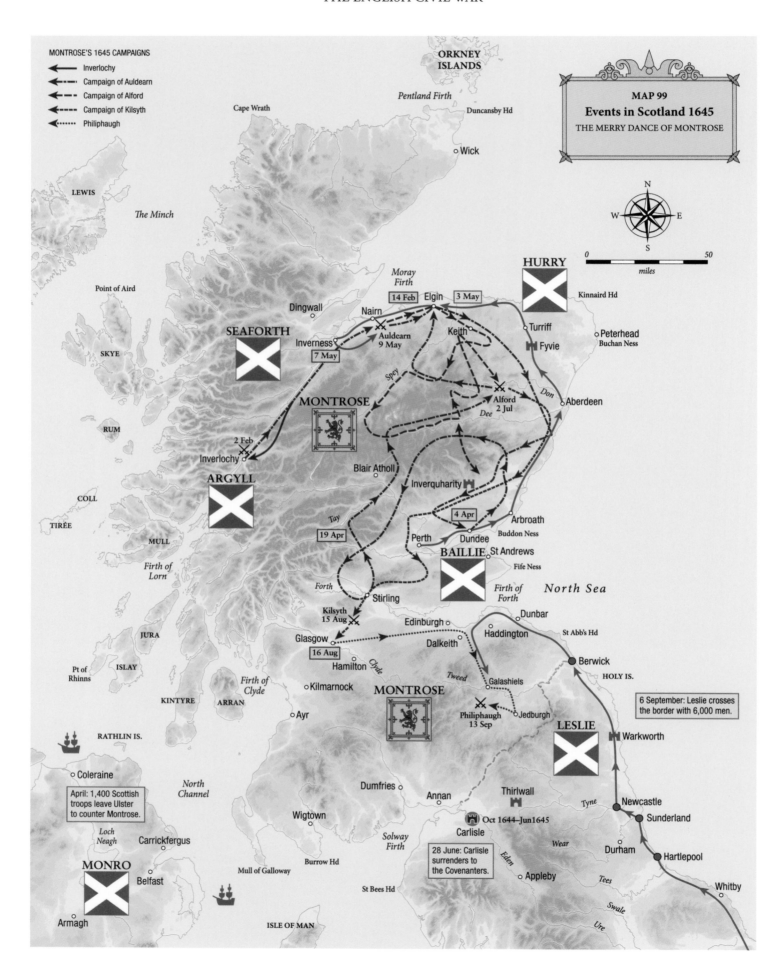

MONTROSE'S 1645 CAMPAIGNS

← Inverlochy
←·-·-· Campaign of Auldearn
←·- -·- Campaign of Alford
←- - - Campaign of Kilsyth
←······· Philiphaugh

ORKNEY
ISLANDS

Pentland Firth

Cape Wrath

Duncansby Hd

Wick

LEWIS

The Minch

Point of Aird

SKYE

Dingwall

SEAFORTH

Moray
Firth

14 Feb Elgin 3 May

HURRY

Kinnaird Hd

Nairn

Inverness

Auldearn
9 May

Keith

Turriff

Fyvie

Peterhead
Buchan Ness

MONTROSE

7 May

Spey

Alford
2 Jul

Dee

Don

Aberdeen

2 Feb

RUM

Inverlochy

ARGYLL

COLL

TIRÉE

Blair Atholl

Inverquharity

MULL

Firth of
Lorn

Tay

19 Apr

4 Apr

Arbroath
Buddon Ness

Perth

Dundee

St Andrews

JURA

BAILLIE

Fife Ness

North Sea

Forth

Stirling

Firth of
Forth

Pt of
Rhinns

ISLAY

Kilsyth
15 Aug

Edinburgh

Dunbar

ARRAN

KINTYRE

Firth of
Clyde

Glasgow

16 Aug

Hamilton

Clyde

Haddington

Dalkeith

St Abb's Hd

Berwick

HOLY IS.

Ayr

Kilmarnock

MONTROSE

Tweed

Galashiels

Philiphaugh
13 Sep

Jedburgh

LESLIE

Warkworth

RATHLIN IS.

Coleraine

April: 1,400 Scottish
troops leave Ulster
to counter Montrose.

North
Channel

Dumfries

Annan

Thirlwall

6 September: Leslie crosses
the border with 6,000 men.

Wigtown

Loch
Neagh

Carrickfergus

Burrow Hd

Solway
Firth

Carlisle

Oct 1644–Jun 1645

Eden

Appleby

Wear

Tyne

Newcastle

Sunderland

Durham

Hartlepool

MONRO

Belfast

Mull of Galloway

28 June: Carlisle
surrenders to
the Covenanters.

St Bees Hd

Tees

Swale

Whitby

Armagh

ISLE OF MAN

Ure

N

W   E

S

0   50
miles

MAP 99
Events in Scotland 1645
THE MERRY DANCE OF MONTROSE

to tell. MacColla 'with his men in both woods northward, made the first approach with his yallow banner and fired upon the enemy, and they gave him a repartee, so that his ensign was killed, the yallow banner fell 3 or 4 times, and he retires for recruits'.[8] Hurry's infantry drove the Irish back and they took up positions in the village itself. The Covenanters advanced, but they were quickly engulfed by enfilade fire from their left by Moneymore's troops on Castle Hill, and a hail of musketry from the Irish in the village. Behind Castle Hill, Gordon's Horse had collected on the Royalist right, while Montrose had the balance of the foot (the Strathbogie Regiment and some Irish levies) and Aboyne's Horse, to the rear left of the village. In the centre MacColla's men, having regained some composure, began to drive back Hurry's men but their counter-attack, due to the ground and enormity of the undertaking, soon lost momentum, as Patrick Gordon describes: 'The ground upon his left hand being all quagmire and bushes, was in this secund charge extreamly to his dissadvantage, wher his men could nether advance in order, nor fynd sure footing to stand, nor marche forward to helpe ther fellowes.'[9] MacColla's men were driven back a second time and when the Covenanters entered the village the fighting became intense, fought between small pockets of men in small spaces.

The cry went up in the Covenanter ranks that MacDonald [MacColla] and his men were routed. The battle hung in the balance and Montrose, realizing that the 'all or nothing' moment had arrived, ordered Aboyne's cavalry to charge into the Covenanter's right flank and the Strathbogie Foot to follow in support. The Covenanters' left flank protection was being provided by a troop of horse under Captain Drummond. At the critical moment Drummond appeared to panic, turning into his own infantry rather than towards the advancing Royalist cavalry. Patrick Gordon once again takes up the story. 'Hurry gives a word of command, whither wrong given or mistaken, Captain Drummond wheels his horse to the left for the right hand, and confuses the foot.'[10] The Covenanters fell back and at much the same time, Lord Gordon charged in on their left 'with a new form of fight, for he discharges all shooting of pistoles and carrabines, only with ther swords to charge quyt throwgh ther enemies'.[11] Assailed on both flanks and with MacColla's men attacking again in the centre and Strathbogie's infantry sweeping up in the wake of the cavalry, Hurry's men fell back to Garlic Hill where, once again, the fighting was brutal and hand to hand. Eventually, the Covenanters broke and poured down the back of the hill back towards the Inverness road. Hurry's losses were considerable, probably between 500 and 1,000 men (not quite the huge numbers in some secondary accounts).[12] Those of Montrose were almost certainly greater than generally reported at 200 killed and many more wounded.

In his memoirs, Gordon Ruthven writes that Montrose was keen to follow Hurry's men and 'resolves to take in Inverness, that their enemies should have no place of retreat', but on hearing that the action at Auldearn had stirred Baillie into action, changed his mind.[13] In reality Auldearn was a pyrrhic victory, and Montrose's losses were enough to enforce a period of inactivity for recruitment and recuperation. Hurry escaped to Inverness and

joined Baillie near Strathbogie. They moved back towards Montrose's force but in his weakened state a general action was most unwise. Montrose slipped the noose and headed south towards the Spey valley. Having escaped Baillie's immediate attentions, Montrose went on a recruiting drive as far south as Inverquharity Castle, while Baillie satisfied himself with besieging the Marquis of Huntly's castle. By late June, Montrose considered his force capable of challenging Baillie to battle. His anticipation was heightened on the news that Baillie had been ordered by the committee, who were dissatisfied with his handling of affairs to that point, to despatch a large part of his force to join the Marquis of Argyll. Argyll had been similarly ordered to advance on Montrose's men from the south. Baillie recalled that 'in exchange whereof, I was appointed to take unto me the Earle of Caffills's regiment of foot, some four hundred strong; whereby I was reduced to betwixt twelve and thirteen hundred foot, and about two hundred and sixty horsemen of the Lord Balcarras and Colonell Hackett's regiments'.[14]

Montrose caught up with Baillie near Keith and tried to entice him to battle, but the Royalists were in a strong position and Baillie ignored the bait. Montrose then pulled back south and Baillie had no choice (given his mission) but to follow. Montrose took the Suie road south, crossed the Dee at the boat bridge of Forbes, and then halted his force behind Gallow Hill. Bishop Wishart, the chaplain to Montrose's merry band, recorded what happened early on 2 July:

> Montrose ordered his men to get under arms ready for battle, and stationed them on a hill overlooking Alford. He was himself engaged with a troop of horse in observing the enemy's movements and bearing, and examining the fords of the Don, which runs by Alford, when he was informed that their horse and foot were hastening to a ford a mile distant from Alford, to cut off his retreat in the rear.[15]

Once Baillie's men had crossed the ford and advanced up the road they quickly realized they were in an ambush. Montrose's men slowly began to appear, in ever greater numbers, on Gallow Hill to their front. The sight would have been all the more remarkable as Montrose had ordered his men to strip down to their white linen shirts to cope with the oppressive heat.[16] Baillie had not intended to give battle but he knew he had no choice. With the river to his back, he noted that it 'was necessitate to buckle with the enemie, who were a little above our strength in horsemen, and twice as strong in foot'.[17]

Bishop Wishart waited for events to unfold. 'For a while both sides paused; the one side deeming it unsafe to storm the hill, the other unwilling to attack an enemy intrenched among deep ditches and marshes.'[18] The

8 Fraser, *Chronicles of the Frasers*, p. 295.
9 Gordon, op. cit., p. 123.
10 Fraser, op. cit., p. 295.
11 Gordon, op. cit., p. 126.
12 Reid suggests this number, based on musters of the Covenanter regiments some time later, while Wishart, *Memoirs of James Graham Marquis of Montrose*, p. 136, suggests 3,000 men were slain, and Spalding, *Memorable transactions in Scotland*, vol. II, p. 300, proposes that the number was 2,000.
13 Gordon, op. cit., p. 127.
14 Laing, *Letters and Journals of Robert Baillie, vol. II*, p. 419.
15 Wishart, *Montrose*, p. 108. I consider this primary source account to be crucial as to where Baillie crossed the River Don and how the battle unfolded. There are three schools of thought, although there are options for more (see Historic Scotland, *Inventory of Historic Battlefields – Battle of Alford*, pp. 9–12 and The Battlefields Trust – *Battle Report – Alford*, pp. 3–5). The first is that Baillie crossed at the main ford and engaged Montrose to the north of Gallow Hill; the second is that Baillie crossed the ford further east and engaged Montrose close to that ford; the final option is that Baillie crossed at the eastern ford and engaged Montrose up the gentler gradient towards Gallow Hill. On the balance of evidence, considering the missions/intentions of both leaders and the terrain, I believe the latter to be the most likely. This is the option put forward by Reid, *Auldearn 1645*, p. 71.
16 Wedgwood, *Montrose*, p. 105.
17 Laing, op. cit., p. 419.
18 Wishart, *Montrose*, p. 109.

battle opened on the Royalist right with a charge by Lord Gordon's Horse, which was met by a counter-charge by two (of three) squadrons of Balcarres' Regiment. Gordon Ruthven recorded that 'so headstrong and furious was the charge of the lord Gordoune, as his enemies ware not able to gainestand him, but ware all disordered and broken'.[19] In fact it was to be some time before Balcarres' men broke and then only because, as Baillie recalled, the third squadron did not attack Gordon's cavalry in the flank: 'The third, appointed for reserve, when I commanded them to second my Lord, and charge the enemie's horse in the flank, they went straight up in their ourses reare, and there flood untill they were all broken.'[20] The Royalist cavalry had been supported by commanded musketeers, under the command of Colonel Nathanial Gordon, and his quick thinking and aggression tipped the balance; he called out, 'Come, my men, down with those useless muskets and stab or hamstring the rebels' horses with your dirks.'[21] At the same time MacDonnell's Highlanders 'behaved bravely, running down the horse with their bowes and arrows'.[22] Once broken, Gordon led his men around the rear of the Covenanters and they crashed into the back of Halkett's Horse who were simultaneously charged in front by Aboyne's Horse.

In the centre, the Royalist foot advanced and closed on Baillie's infantry, who bravely stood their ground. Baillie reported:

> … our foot flood with myself and behaved themselves as became them, untill the enemie's horse charged in our reare, and in front we were overcharged with their foot; for they having six in fyle, did overwing us, who, to equall their front, had made the half ranks advance, and so received the charge at three deep.[23]

The writing was, however, on the wall. Once the Covenanter lines broke, it turned to a rout. The main battle had lasted no more than an hour but the pursuit of the beaten Covenanters continued until nightfall. It was a great victory for Montrose against a capable general and credible force. The Royalist losses were light but included the irreplaceable talisman Lord Gordon, who had been struck down by a musket ball in the closing stages of the battle. Baillie's army was no longer an effective force. Baillie blamed his failure and his predicament on constant political interference from Edinburgh and offered his immediate resignation.[24] It was refused. Instead he was ordered to assume command of Crawford-Lindsey's force, which was, to all intents and purposes, the last Covenanter army on Scottish soil.

The way was now open for Montrose to come down into the Lowlands. However, any aspirations he may have held of linking up with the King's army were undone by news of the utter disaster at Naseby.[25] At Fourdon Montrose was rejoined by MacColla and 1,600 reinforcements and, while he waited for Aboyne to appear (from Aberdeen) with replacement horses and more cavalry, he decided to make an attempt to capture Perth. It failed and Montrose's men were chased back into the hills by Baillie who had, by now, assumed command of Lindsey's force. A few days later Aboyne arrived at Dunkeld, bringing another 400 cavalry and 800 infantry. Montrose, at the head of the largest army to that point, now headed south into the Lowlands

– his objective was Glasgow. He by-passed Baillie's force and then camped en route at Kilsyth. Baillie was in pursuit, but with the clash at Alford fresh in his memory, he was keeping his distance. The temptation was too much for Montrose who decided to ambush them. He drew his army up adjacent to the road but Baillie got wind of the plan and, being well aware of the dangers of the terrain, decided to leave the road and 'marched with the regiments through the corns and over the braes, untill the unpaffible ground did hold us up'.[26] They could see the left flank of the Royalists about a mile to their front. That suited Baillie for he held a strong position, and the ground, with hills on his left and a river to his right, secured his flanks. He was happy to wait for Montrose to make the first move, but the committee representatives attached to Baillie's army had other ideas.

They urged that the high ground to the north would enable the troops to get around the Royalist flank. Baillie strongly expressed his concerns: 'I shew them I did not conceave that ground to be good, and that the rebells (if they would) might possess themselves of it before us.'[27] Baillie was overruled and, as the Covenanters began to redeploy, Montrose ordered his men to strip down to their white shirts, move to the higher ground and secure the key terrain. 'They obeyed with cheerful alacrity, and thus disencumbered, they stood ready for battle, determined to conquer or die.'[28] Montrose's men moved with speed over the heather while the Covenanters moved in formation. Baillie was monitoring the movement at one end of the field, but at the other he saw one of his battalion commanders (Major John Haldane) 'leading up an partie of musqueteers over the field, and toward a house near the glen, without any order from me'.[29] He sent word for Haldane to pull back, but by the time the order reached him the Highlanders were swarming around the crofters' dwellings, enclosures and dykes.[30] Soldiers on both sides now began to get sucked into the encounter, some with orders, others acting on impulse.

Baillie drew up his army in three bodies (see map 102); his right wing consisting of Balcarres' cavalry and 800 infantry (under General Holbourne) began to move first. All that stood in their way was a small troop of horse, which charged Balcarres' cavalry with great courage. Gordon of Ruthven recalled that the Covenanter infantry continued their advance: 'Those three regimentes, without brakeing of there ordour, lets them enter amongst them, and giveing fyre on all sydes, had well noire encompassed them.'[31] As the Royalist infantry closed, Aboyne took the initiative and charged. His troopers on their sturdy mounts were nevertheless hindered by the terrain and the stream and fired upon by the mass of Covenanter foot to their right. When they reached their fellow Highlanders, they were thinned in numbers and the horses spent. A counter-charge by Balcarres, who sensed the opportunity, easily drove them back. But they overextended their pursuit and they, in turn, were charged by the main cavalry under Nathanial Gordon and the Earl of Airlie. It was the decisive point in the battle. Balcarres' troopers were driven from the field. With no cavalry support the Covenanter infantry were now assailed in the front and flank with unbridled fury. MacColla's troops, in the centre, charged with such speed and ferocity that the Covenanter foot had no time to light their slow match. Baillie recalled that 'the rebells leapt over the dyke, and with downe heads fell on

19 Gordon, op. cit., p. 129.

20 Laing, op. cit., p. 419.

21 Wishart, *Montrose*, p. 110.

22 Fraser, op. cit., p. 299.

23 Laing, op. cit., p. 419.

24 Committee men were imbedded into Baillie's headquarters in much the same way they were in the headquarters of Parliament's armies in England.

25 They were also complicated by the loss of Carlisle on 28 June.

26 Laing, op. cit., p. 421.

27 Ibid.

28 Wishart, op. cit., p. 123.

29 Laing, op. cit., p. 421.

30 Maclean of Treshnish held the post with a hundred men; Wishart, op. cit., p. 123.

31 Gordon, op. cit., p. 140.

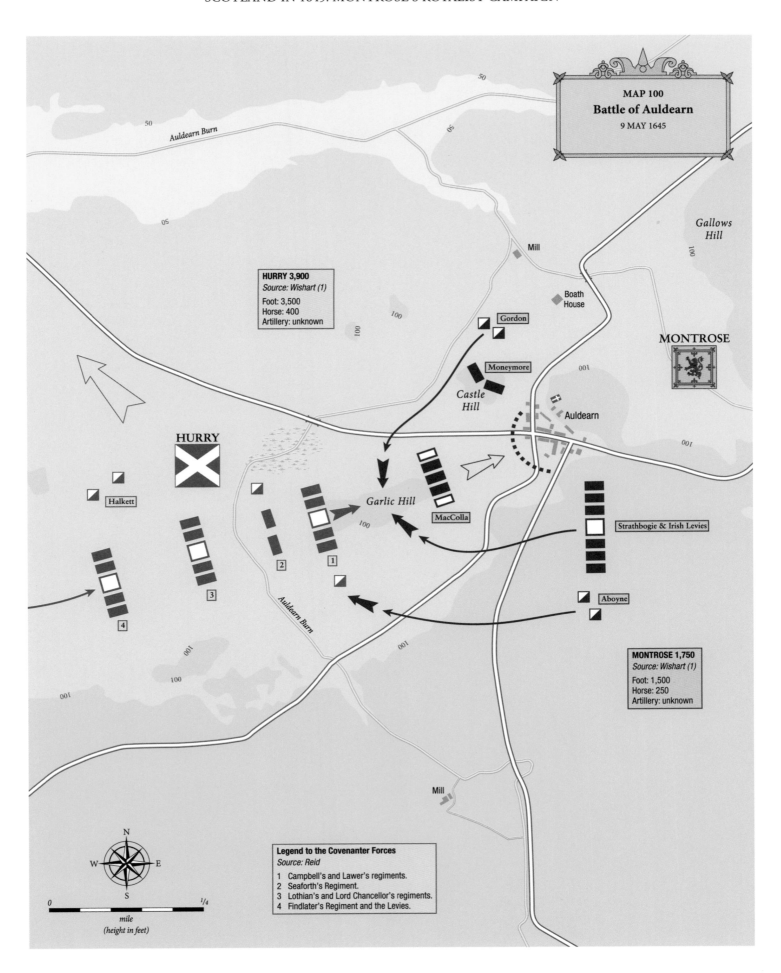

MAP 100

Battle of Auldearn

9 MAY 1645

Auldearn Burn

50

50

05

50

OS

Gallows
Hill

100

Mill

Boath
House

MONTROSE

HURRY 3,900
Source: Wishart (1)
Foot: 3,500
Horse: 400
Artillery: unknown

Gordon

100

100

Moneymore

Castle
Hill

100

Auldearn

001

100

HURRY

Garlic Hill

MacColla

Halkett

100

Strathbogie & Irish Levies

2

1

001

3

Aboyne

Auldearn Burn

4

001

001

100

100

Mill

MONTROSE 1,750
Source: Wishart (1)
Foot: 1,500
Horse: 250
Artillery: unknown

N
W E
S

0   1/4
mile
(height in feet)

Legend to the Covenanter Forces
Source: Reid

1 Campbell's and Lawer's regiments.
2 Seaforth's Regiment.
3 Lothian's and Lord Chancellor's regiments.
4 Findlater's Regiment and the Levies.

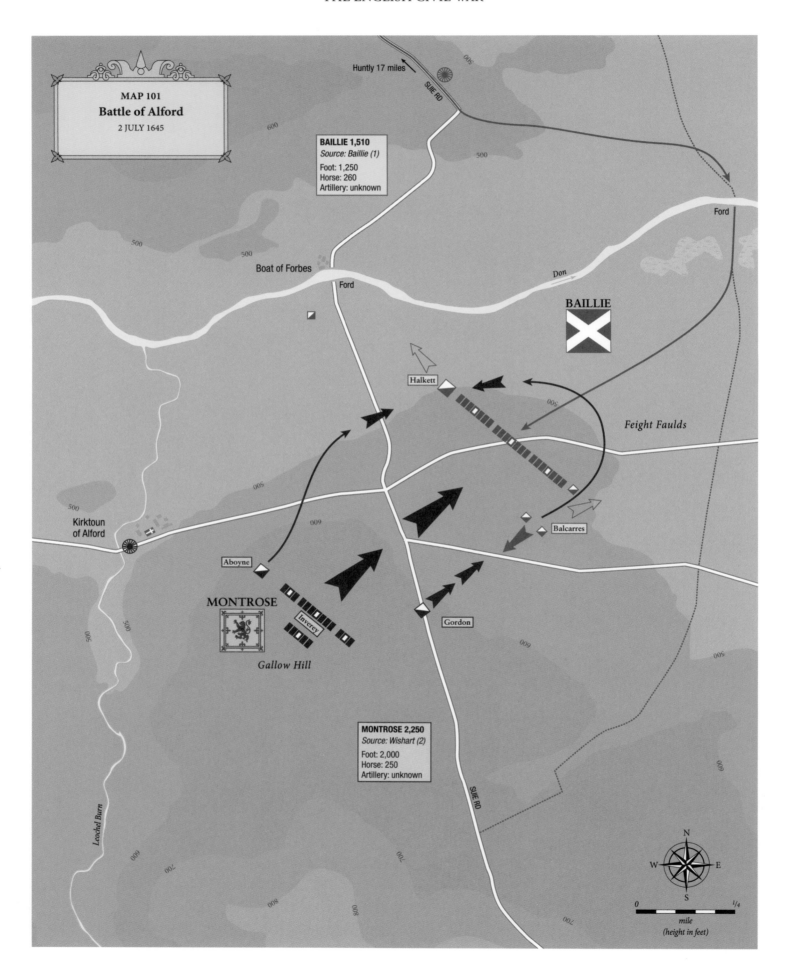

MAP 101
Battle of Alford
2 JULY 1645

Huntly 17 miles

SUIE RD

600

500

500

BAILLIE 1,510
Source: Baillie (1)
Foot: 1,250
Horse: 260
Artillery: unknown

500

500

Boat of Forbes

Ford

Ford

Don

BAILLIE

Halkett

Feight Faulds

500

500

Kirktoun
of Alford

500

009

Balcarres

Aboyne

500

MONTROSE

Inverey

Gordon

Gallow Hill

009

500

500

MONTROSE 2,250
Source: Wishart (2)
Foot: 2,000
Horse: 250
Artillery: unknown

SUIE RD

600

Leochel Burn

600

700

700

800

800

700

N
W   E
S

0   1/4

mile
(height in feet)

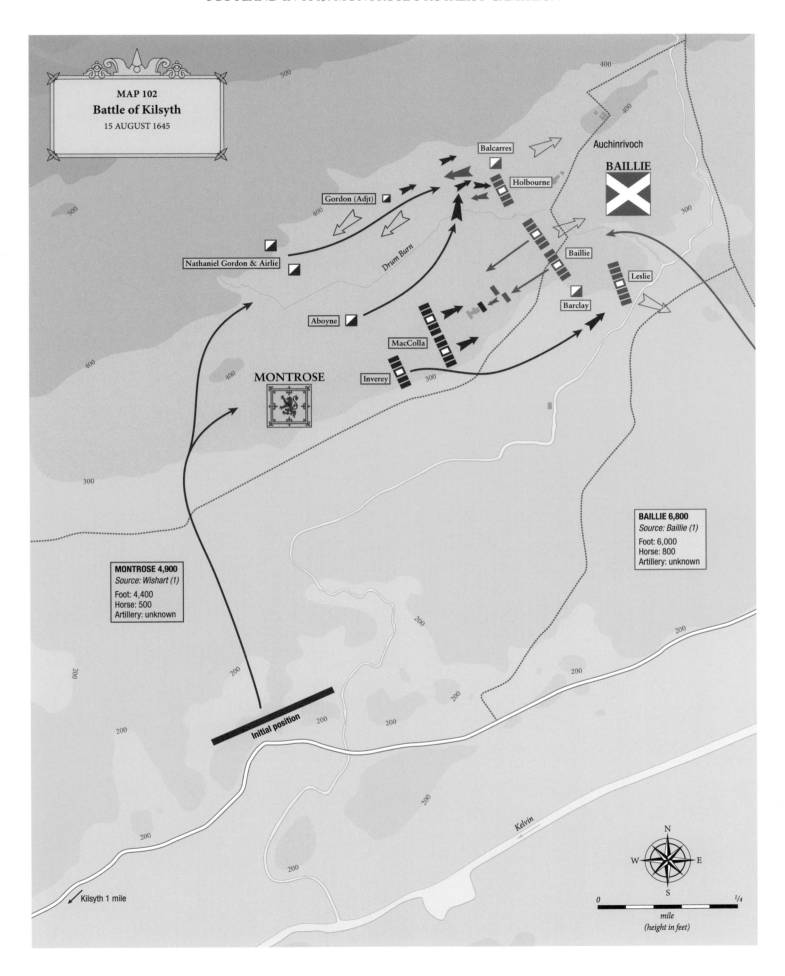

MAP 102
Battle of Kilsyth
15 AUGUST 1645

Auchinrivoch

Balcarres

BAILLIE

Holbourne

Gordon (Adjt)

Nathaniel Gordon & Airlie

Drum Burn

Baillie

Aboyne

Leslie

MacColla

Barclay

Inverey

MONTROSE

BAILLIE 6,800
Source: Baillie (1)
Foot: 6,000
Horse: 800
Artillery: unknown

MONTROSE 4,900
Source: Wishart (1)
Foot: 4,400
Horse: 500
Artillery: unknown

Initial position

Kelvin

Kilsyth 1 mile

0   1/4
mile
(height in feet)

N
W   E
S

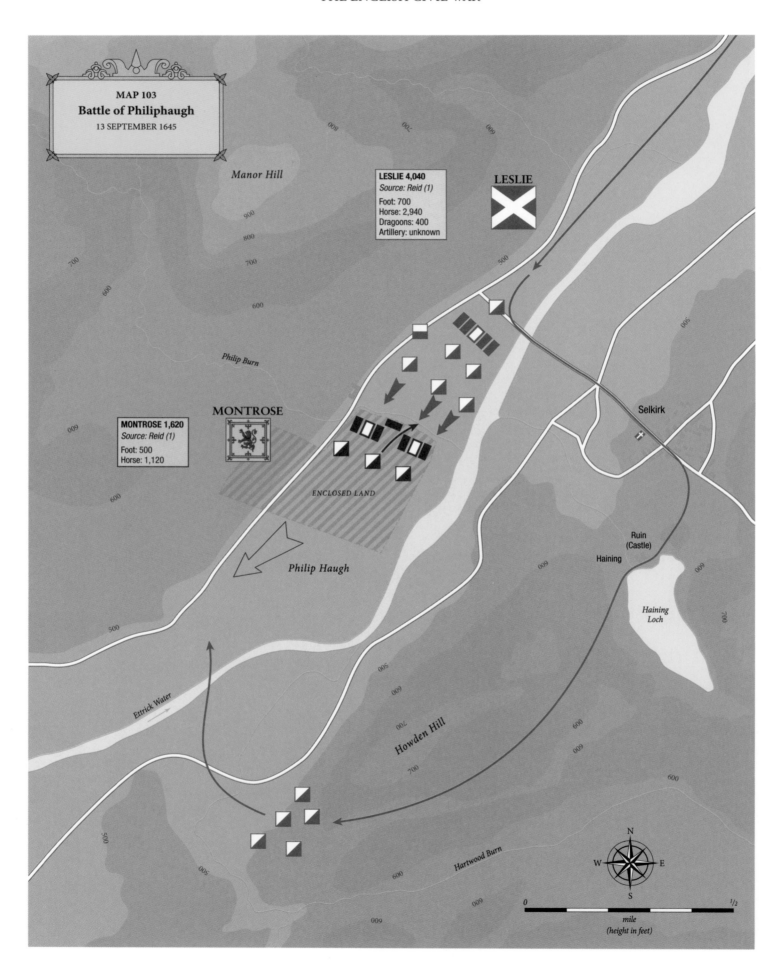

MAP 103
Battle of Philiphaugh
13 SEPTEMBER 1645

Manor Hill

LESLIE 4,040
Source: Reid (1)
Foot: 700
Horse: 2,940
Dragoons: 400
Artillery: unknown

LESLIE

Philip Burn

MONTROSE

MONTROSE 1,620
Source: Reid (1)
Foot: 500
Horse: 1,120

Selkirk

ENCLOSED LAND

Ruin
(Castle)

Haining

Philip Haugh

Haining
Loch

Ettrick Water

Howden Hill

Hartwood Burn

N
W   E
S

0   mile   1/2
(height in feet)

and broke these regiments'.[32] Almost instantaneously the cohesion of the Covenanter army collapsed and attempts to rally the men were futile. Most of the cavalry escaped but the infantry that ran were ruthlessly pursued for many miles through the hills.

Montrose's army stayed on the field for two days dealing with the wounded and burying the dead before resuming their march towards Glasgow.[33] The city was taken without opposition on 16 August, but Montrose's refusal to allow the Highlanders and Irish to pillage the place led to widespread desertion. In early September MacColla decided his job was done and set off to re-establish MacDonald hegemony in the Western Isles. Despite the loss of MacColla's warriors, Montrose decided to march on Edinburgh. Then, at this critical moment, Aboyne decided to take the Gordons back off north, leaving Montrose with a mere 500 infantry and fewer than 100 horse. He changed his plan and decided to head south and link with the King's armies. With reports of plague in Edinburgh, he gave the city a wide berth and headed into the borders.[34] On 6 September David Leslie, who had been sent north by Leven (see chapters 30 and 31), crossed the border at Berwick at the head of 5,000 to 6,000 men.[35] His initial intention was to march towards Edinburgh and secure the capital, but on receiving news that Montrose was in the borders, he swung south and set off in pursuit. Montrose, conversely, had received intelligence of Leslie's arrival and headed west to evade him. On 11 September, Leslie was reinforced by two cavalry regiments at Gladsmuir, and leaving most of his infantry to follow on, he departed with speed into the borders with a force that was entirely horsed. It comprised cavalry, dragoons and some mounted infantry and numbered about 4,000.[36]

Montrose was camped in and around Selkirk. His officers (and most of the cavalry) were in dwellings in the town itself, while the men were bivouacked across the river at Philiphaugh.[37] On the night of 12 September Leslie's men attacked one of the Royalist outposts at a small settlement called Sunderland, about 3 miles to the north. Reports from some of the survivors who escaped were foolishly dismissed and, in the early morning mist, the Covenanters advanced with both cover and surprise on their side. 'They were already within half a mile, and marching up in order, when Montrose's scouts came flying in with the tidings.'[38] The Covenanter force attacked down the valley and the Royalists scrambled from their bivouacs into firing positions among the many enclosures. Leslie's cavalry charged at Montrose's right wing, but constrained by the burn and by the good firing positions of the Irish infantry, they were unable to penetrate their line. The Royalist cavalry counter-charged, but they were quickly overwhelmed and a body of Irish musketeers had to deploy forward from the enclosed area to assist in their extraction. Leslie then switched to attack the Royalist left, for he had split his force, sending about half across the river, which then attacked Montrose's men in the flank and rear and threatened to cut off their retreat. It had the desired effect. Suddenly, as if on the flick of a switch, it was every man for himself. Montrose's gallant fighters realized that the game was finally up. Bishop Wishart witnessed what happened next: 'For the foot there was little hope in flight; they stood firm and fought resolutely, till offered quarter, when they threw down their arms and yielded. But, notwithstanding the promise of quarter, these defenceless men were every one butchered in cold blood by Leslie's own orders.'[39] Montrose's extraordinary year was over.

---

32 Laing, op. cit., p. 422.
33 This delay is perhaps indicative of the ferocity of the fighting.
34 Gordon, op. cit., p. 146.
35 Ibid.
36 Reid, *Auldearn 1645*, p. 85.

37 Wishart, op. cit., p. 142 states that the infantry were as far away as Harehead Wood.
38 Ibid. , p. 143.
39 Ibid., p. 144.

CHAPTER 30

POST-NASEBY, PART 1: WALES AND THE SOUTH, TO THE END OF 1645

Following the heavy defeat at Naseby, the King had been trying to raise an army in south Wales in order to reignite his cause. It was an uphill struggle. In Herefordshire, the newly raised levies deserted as quickly as they were mustered, and the Welsh Commissioners of Array were generally and quite understandably unenthusiastic. Despite Charles Gerard's early victories in 1645 at Newcastle Emlyn, and the capture and recapture of Picton and Carew castles respectively, the fact remained that Gerard's policies did little to enamour the Welsh people to the Royalist cause. The new garrisons created by Gerard were commanded by Englishmen, or non-locals, and his policy of removing cattle and burning corn to deny supplies to the Parliamentarians was both provocative and counterproductive. Renewed Royalist attempts to gain new reinforcements from Ireland had come to nothing, but the news that Charles was trying to reach agreement to bring Irish Catholics to Wales solicited fierce condemnation from many Welsh Royalists. Complaints and petitions led to defections and, subsequently, open resistance.

In Glamorgan and Monmouthshire, the men raised for the King's cause were restyled as the 'Peaceable Army'. They were placed under the command and control of the local gentry, who declared continued allegiance to the crown, but on certain conditions. Charles, not a man of arbitration but desperate for recruits, felt compelled to meet the leaders in Cardiff in early August. He was shocked at their tone and tenacity. They demanded the removal of Gerard, along with the English garrison (and commander) from Cardiff. They sought a promise that there would be no increases to existing taxes or creation of new duties. Finally, they sought a personal declaration of allegiance to the Protestant church. Visibly shaken, Charles granted their requests and by so doing lost Wales. The King departed soon after and headed off north, while Gerard was relieved of command and replaced by Jacob Astley. South Wales no longer offered a place of refuge for the King, and with his departure, the Royalist cause quickly collapsed. In Pembrokeshire, Laugharne wasted little time in capitalizing on developments and took the offensive. He defeated a small force at Colby Moor on 1 August, before storming the castle at Haverfordwest. Carew and Picton castles were swept up a few weeks later and in October he occupied Carmarthen. By the end of 1645, Pembrokeshire was entirely in Parliamentarian hands. More significantly, the 'Peaceable Army' secured control of Glamorgan and looked to Parliament for their delivery from 'papists, heavy taxes, acquisitive garrisons and other burdens'.[1]

Charles had effectively wasted three weeks of precious time in July with his Welsh initiatives, before eventually deciding to move with the forces he had at his disposal, cross the River Severn and join forces with Goring in the south-west. It was a plan not without some risk, for the Parliamentarian navy at Milford Haven, under Admiral Moulton, had increased their patrols and had already intercepted some Royalist transport ships in the Bristol

Channel.[2] Before Charles had even set off, he received news of Goring's defeat at Langport but, nevertheless, remained determined to link up with the remnants of his army at Bridgwater.[3] On 24 July, while about to cross the Severn from the ferry port at Black Rock, the King received the devastating news that Bridgwater had capitulated. To make matters worse, Leven's Scottish army were in the area, having captured Canon Frome on 23 July, and were now closing in on Hereford.

Three independent but interrelated schemes developed in the wake of these events. Firstly, a growing rift between the English Parliament and the Scottish army led to the latter opening communication with the King in order to seek mutually acceptable terms. While the King entertained the idea, he simultaneously resurrected his earlier plan to move his force north and link up with Montrose. On 28 July, Rupert, who had wind of the King's proposal, wrote to Richmond in an attempt to dissuade the King from marching north. Rupert anticipated, quite correctly, that Richmond would share the correspondence with the King and went on to suggest that 'His Majesty hath now no way left to preserve his posterity, kingdom, and nobility, but by a treaty'.[4] Charles rejected the idea out of hand and, by so doing, he rejected the idea of compromise; as Gardiner wrote, 'he saw his own resolution in the light of Divine will strengthening and comprehending it'.[5] With news of Royalist losses in Pembrokeshire and Yorkshire, and the closing in of Fairfax's army towards Bristol, it is hard to understand what hope Charles still congregated for his cause.

On 5 August the King set off from Cardiff, through the Welsh mountains, reaching Welbeck on the 15th and Doncaster three days later. He had with him 2,200 horse and 400 foot and he remained ever-optimistic for further recruits from Yorkshire and subsequent union with Montrose.[6] While at Doncaster he received intelligence of two military groups, apparently closing towards his location. The first was a large force of 4,000 Scots under David Leslie (despatched by Leven who was still conducting the siege of Hereford) and the second was a large force, from the Northern Association army under General Poyntz, that had been ordered south 'so as to join with the forces under the command of Lieut.-Genl.[7] David Leslie, and for the more speedy and unanimous prosecution of this service against the enemy'.[8] Charles wasted no time in issuing orders to head back south towards Newark, fearful that Leslie would catch him in the flank. Wasting little time at Newark, he then headed to Huntingdon, which he reached on

---

2 Lynch, *King & Parliament*, pp. 140–1.

3 In fact, Goring had retreated west with about 2,000 horse and left Hugh Wyndham in charge of the garrison at Bridgwater.

4 Warburton, *Memoirs of Prince Rupert*, vol. III, p. 149.

5 Gardiner, *Great Civil War*, vol. II, p. 283.

6 Peachey, *Richard Symonds*, p. 64.

7 The Scottish force consisted of eight regiments of horse, one of dragoons and 500 mounted musketeers. Terry, *Leslie*, p. 375.

8 *CSPD* dated 15 August 1645.

---

1 Gaunt, *Civil War in Wales*, p. 56

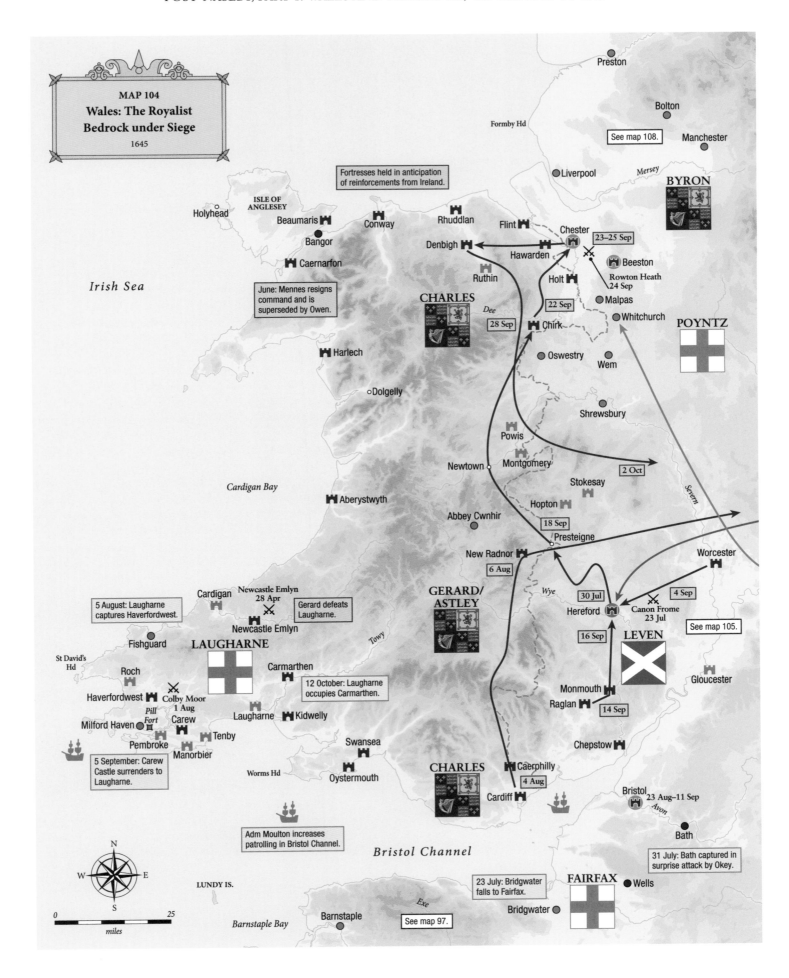

MAP 104

Wales: The Royalist Bedrock under Siege

1645

Fortresses held in anticipation of reinforcements from Ireland.

See map 108.

BYRON

Formby Hd

Mersey

Preston

Bolton

Manchester

Liverpool

Holyhead

ISLE OF ANGLESEY

Irish Sea

Beaumaris

Bangor

Conway

Rhuddlan

Flint

Chester

23–25 Sep

Beeston

Rowton Heath 24 Sep

Caernarfon

Denbigh

Hawarden

Ruthin

Holt

Malpas

Whitchurch

POYNTZ

June: Mennes resigns command and is superseded by Owen.

CHARLES

Dee

22 Sep

Chirk

28 Sep

Oswestry

Wem

Harlech

Dolgelly

Shrewsbury

Powis

Cardigan Bay

Newtown

Montgomery

Stokesay

2 Oct

Aberystwyth

Hopton

Abbey Cwnhir

18 Sep

Presteigne

Severn

New Radnor

6 Aug

Worcester

Cardigan

Newcastle Emlyn 28 Apr

Gerard defeats Laugharne.

GERARD/ ASTLEY

Wye

30 Jul

4 Sep

5 August: Laugharne captures Haverfordwest.

Newcastle Emlyn

Hereford

Canon Frome 23 Jul

See map 105.

Fishguard

LAUGHARNE

Carmarthen

16 Sep

LEVEN

St David's Hd

Roch

12 October: Laugharne occupies Carmarthen.

Gloucester

Haverfordwest

Colby Moor 1 Aug

Towy

Monmouth

Pill Fort

Carew

Laugharne

Kidwelly

Raglan

14 Sep

Milford Haven

Tenby

Pembroke

Manorbier

Swansea

Chepstow

5 September: Carew Castle surrenders to Laugharne.

Worms Hd

Oystermouth

CHARLES

Caerphilly

4 Aug

Bristol

23 Aug–11 Sep

Adm Moulton increases patrolling in Bristol Channel.

Cardiff

Avon

Bristol Channel

Bath

31 July: Bath captured in surprise attack by Okey.

N W E S

LUNDY IS.

23 July: Bridgwater falls to Fairfax.

FAIRFAX

Wells

0 ———— 25

miles

Barnstaple

Barnstaple Bay

Exe

Bridgwater

See map 97.

25 August. The day prior he had received news of Montrose's great victory at Kilsyth. It did little to lift his spirits. He was unaware, at that time, that this news from Scotland had diverted Leslie from his original mission, and probably saved a potentially decisive encounter.

Leslie had received the news at Nottingham and had been ordered back to Scotland by the Edinburgh Committee. Meanwhile, Leven's position in front of Hereford had grown increasingly precarious. Symonds recorded that General Crawford 'was slayne at a salley before the towne; they weare gott near the towne, and had made two breaches but were repulsed'.[9] For a number of days, the Scots had been desperately short of provisions and Leven had grown progressively concerned at being geographically static in between Royalist Worcester and Astley's new endeavours to reenergize the Royalist cause in Wales.[10] With news of Charles's small force returning to the area (they entered Worcester on 31 August) and having lost the not inconsiderable force under David Leslie, he decided to raise the siege. His force left the area in some haste on 1 September. Crossing the River Severn at Upton, he moved through Warwickshire, reaching Nuneaton ten days later.[11] By late September, Leven's army was once again back in North Yorkshire and news of Leven's precipitous withdrawal was greeted with contempt in London. It served to confirm many of the more recent suspicions about the resolve of the Scottish forces to the cause of the Committee of Both Kingdoms.

Following the capture of Bridgwater, Fairfax turned back eastwards in order to capture the Royalist castle at Sherborne. It was well garrisoned under the command of Lewis Dyves who had fled his seat in Parliamentarian-controlled Bedfordshire early in the war.[12] The Parliamentarians established a cordon on 2 August and 'a storm was intended, but upon second thoughts diverted; the army seeing recruits come so far below expectation, both in time and number, it behoved them to take more than ordinary care of their men'.[13] Fairfax decided to wait for the siege train. It arrived on 11 August, and by the 14th the heavy ordnance had blasted two significant breaches. The next morning at dawn, with offers of capitulation rejected, a mine was fired and the castle successfully stormed. With Sherborne in Parliament's possession, Fairfax's lines of communication to the west were shortened. Some of his close advisors proposed a campaign to completely reduce the South-West, but others saw Bristol as a much more significant prize. Bristol was not without risk, for there were reports that Rupert had a force of 3,000 foot and horse that was prepared to sally from within. Furthermore, the King was now back in the area with a similar number, more recruits could potentially arrive from Wales at any moment, Goring could fall on their rear from the south-west, and finally, just for good measure, plague was raging through the city.[14] Despite this, in the end Fairfax decided that the city was the next obvious objective:

> … seeing our judgments lead us to make Bristol our next design, as the greatest service we can do for the public; as for the sickness, let us trust God with the army, who will be as ready to protect us in the siege from infection, as in the field from the bullet…[15]

Fairfax closed in on Bristol on 22 August, having captured Nunney Castle en route. The advance guard established a position 'within musket-shot' to the south at Pile Hill.[16] Fairfax arrived the next day and established his headquarters at Hanham to the south-east. In desperation, Rupert had begun destroying some of the outlying villages and suburbs. Cromwell recalled that 'upon our advance, the enemy fired Bedminster, Clifton, and some other villages lying near to the City; and would have fired more, if our unexpected coming had not hindered'.[17] Henry Ireton had been despatched with a large force of horse and dragoons, supported by 500 foot, to protect the villages and secure the north bank. Over the next couple of days, the Parliamentarian troops established a cordon around the city. Siege batteries were opened on Pile Hill, and on 28 August the fort at Portishead was captured, thereby closing the River Avon to Royalist shipping and cutting sea communications. However, it was not long before bad weather set in, stultifying the tempo of events and the fortitude of the besiegers. Thomas Rainsborough recalled that 'the weather was so extreme wet, that both man and Horse with hard duty grew weak, and died in the Field… the Army was unfit for Assault'.[18] Cromwell noted that 'our Horse were forced to be upon exceeding great duty; to stand by the Foot, lest the Foot, being so weak in all their posts, might receive an affront'.[19]

The Royalists, meanwhile, capitalized on the Parliamentarians' misfortune and lethargy and made a number of sorties. *Mercurius Aulicus* claimed they had been hugely successful, killing scores of Parliamentarian foot. Cromwell, however, was more dismissive of the effectiveness of these sallies, claiming that they lost no more than 30 men as a result. That may be so, but Rupert's men were also tasked to gain intelligence on the besieging force, and this they were certainly able to do. Their reports were not encouraging, and they were inexorably instrumental in shaping Rupert's response to the first summons Fairfax sent in to the city on 4 September. Fairfax had resolved to storm the city should it be necessary. Rupert was aware that an assault was imminent, and with no word from the King (who by this stage was a few miles to the north at Hereford) he sought to buy time. The Royalists arranged to send Fairfax their own proposals, which reached him as late as 7 September. The demands were entirely unsatisfactory and, after two more days of fruitless negotiation, and with patience running out, Fairfax ordered the assault.

At 2am on 10 September a large bonfire was lit at Fairfax's (new) headquarters atop Ashley Hill. On the forward slopes four heavy guns began to fire at Priors Hill Fort. It was the signal for the series of assaults to commence. The Royalists were waiting for them but the sheer weight and number of attacks soon began to tell. Those on the west and north walls were opportunist in nature; those to the south, executed by Colonel Weldon's Brigade, were thwarted by their ladders being too short, while the attack up the river was undone by adverse tides. But the attacks on the east walls by Colonel Montagu's and Colonel Rainsborough's brigades were completely successful. Rupert recalled in his report:

> … they entered the line where the townsmen and new Welsh were, as at Stokescroft gate, where the Officer-in-Chief, who was Major of the town, was slain in the place, and at Lawford's gate, where many of the officers and soldiers were taken and killed, and at the same time they stormed Prior-hill fort, and took it, which was the loss of the whole line.[20]

9 Peachey, *Richard Symonds*, p. 68.
10 Terry, *Leslie*, p. 376.
11 Hamper, *William Dugdale*, p. 81.
12 There were more than 400 men, 18 guns and a mortar.
13 Sprigge, *Anglia Rediviva*, p. 91.
14 In fact, Rupert had far fewer, as he outlined in *A declaration of His Highness Prince Rupert*, p. 6. Written after the fall of the city and in order to gain some justification, the actual garrison may have been nearer 1,000 cavalry and 3,000 infantry, regular and auxiliary.
15 Ibid., p. 98.
16 Modern name is 'Windmill Hill'.
17 Carlyle, *Cromwell's Letters*, p. 200.
18 Rainsborough, *Storming Bristoll*, p. 16.
19 Carlyle, op. cit.
20 Warburton, op. cit., p. 175.

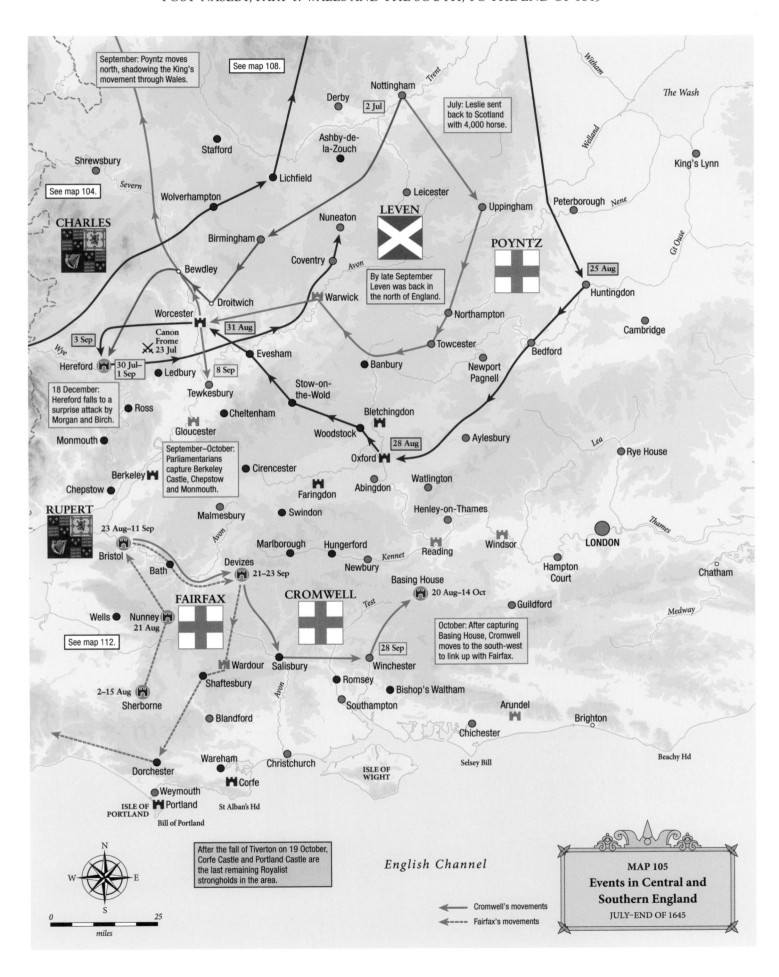

September: Poyntz moves north, shadowing the King's movement through Wales.

See map 108.

July: Leslie sent back to Scotland with 4,000 horse.

By late September Leven was back in the north of England.

See map 104.

Canon Frome 23 Jul

18 December: Hereford falls to a surprise attack by Morgan and Birch.

September–October: Parliamentarians capture Berkeley Castle, Chepstow and Monmouth.

October: After capturing Basing House, Cromwell moves to the south-west to link up with Fairfax.

See map 112.

After the fall of Tiverton on 19 October, Corfe Castle and Portland Castle are the last remaining Royalist strongholds in the area.

English Channel

N
W E
S

0   25
miles

Cromwell's movements
Fairfax's movements

MAP 105
Events in Central and Southern England
JULY–END OF 1645

Place names and labels: Shrewsbury, Stafford, Derby, Nottingham, Ashby-de-la-Zouch, The Wash, King's Lynn, Lichfield, Wolverhampton, Birmingham, Bewdley, Leicester, Uppingham, Peterborough, CHARLES, Nuneaton, LEVEN, POYNTZ, Huntingdon, Coventry, Droitwich, Worcester, Warwick, Northampton, Bedford, Cambridge, Hereford, Ledbury, Evesham, Banbury, Towcester, Newport Pagnell, Tewkesbury, Ross, Cheltenham, Stow-on-the-Wold, Bletchingdon, Aylesbury, Rye House, Gloucester, Woodstock, Monmouth, Berkeley, Cirencester, Oxford, Abingdon, Watlington, Chepstow, Faringdon, Henley-on-Thames, Malmesbury, Swindon, RUPERT, Windsor, LONDON, Bristol, Bath, Devizes, Marlborough, Hungerford, Reading, Hampton Court, Chatham, Newbury, Basing House, Guildford, Medway, FAIRFAX, CROMWELL, Wells, Nunney, Winchester, Wardour, Salisbury, Romsey, Shaftesbury, Bishop's Waltham, Southampton, Arundel, Brighton, Sherborne, Blandford, Chichester, Dorchester, Wareham, Christchurch, ISLE OF WIGHT, Selsey Bill, Beachy Hd, Corfe, Weymouth, Portland, St Alban's Hd, ISLE OF PORTLAND, Bill of Portland

Dates: 2 Jul, 25 Aug, 3 Sep, 31 Aug, 30 Jul–1 Sep, 8 Sep, 28 Aug, 23 Aug–11 Sep, 21–23 Sep, 20 Aug–14 Oct, 21 Aug, 28 Sep, 2–15 Aug

Rivers: Trent, Witham, Welland, Nene, Gt Ouse, Severn, Avon, Wye, Lea, Thames, Kennet, Test, Avon

233

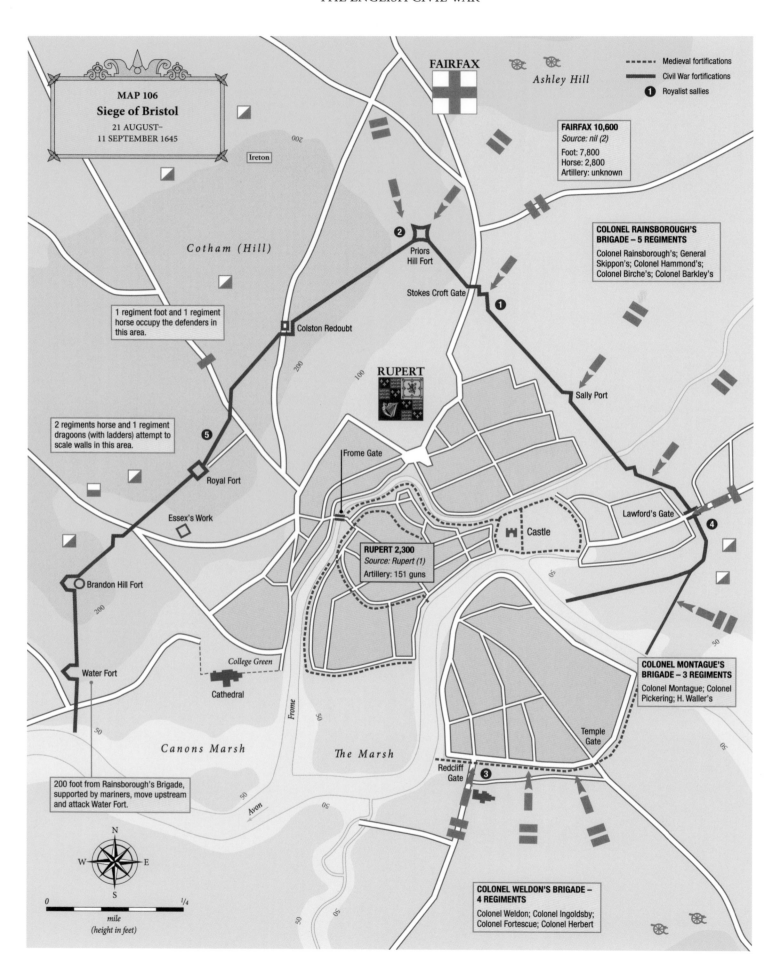

FAIRFAX

Ashley Hill

- - - - Medieval fortifications
———— Civil War fortifications
① Royalist sallies

MAP 106
Siege of Bristol
21 AUGUST–
11 SEPTEMBER 1645

Ireton

FAIRFAX 10,600
Source: nil (2)
Foot: 7,800
Horse: 2,800
Artillery: unknown

Cotham (Hill)

②
Priors
Hill Fort

Stokes Croft Gate

①

COLONEL RAINSBOROUGH'S BRIGADE – 5 REGIMENTS

Colonel Rainsborough's; General Skippon's; Colonel Hammond's; Colonel Birche's; Colonel Barkley's

1 regiment foot and 1 regiment horse occupy the defenders in this area.

Colston Redoubt

RUPERT

Sally Port

2 regiments horse and 1 regiment dragoons (with ladders) attempt to scale walls in this area.

⑤

Frome Gate

Royal Fort

Essex's Work

Lawford's Gate

④

Castle

RUPERT 2,300
Source: Rupert (1)
Artillery: 151 guns

Brandon Hill Fort

College Green

Cathedral

Water Fort

COLONEL MONTAGUE'S BRIGADE – 3 REGIMENTS

Colonel Montague; Colonel Pickering; H. Waller's

Temple Gate

Canons Marsh

Frome

The Marsh

Redcliff Gate

③

200 foot from Rainsborough's Brigade, supported by mariners, move upstream and attack Water Fort.

Avon

N
W E
S

0   1/4

mile
(height in feet)

COLONEL WELDON'S BRIGADE – 4 REGIMENTS

Colonel Weldon; Colonel Ingoldsby; Colonel Fortescue; Colonel Herbert

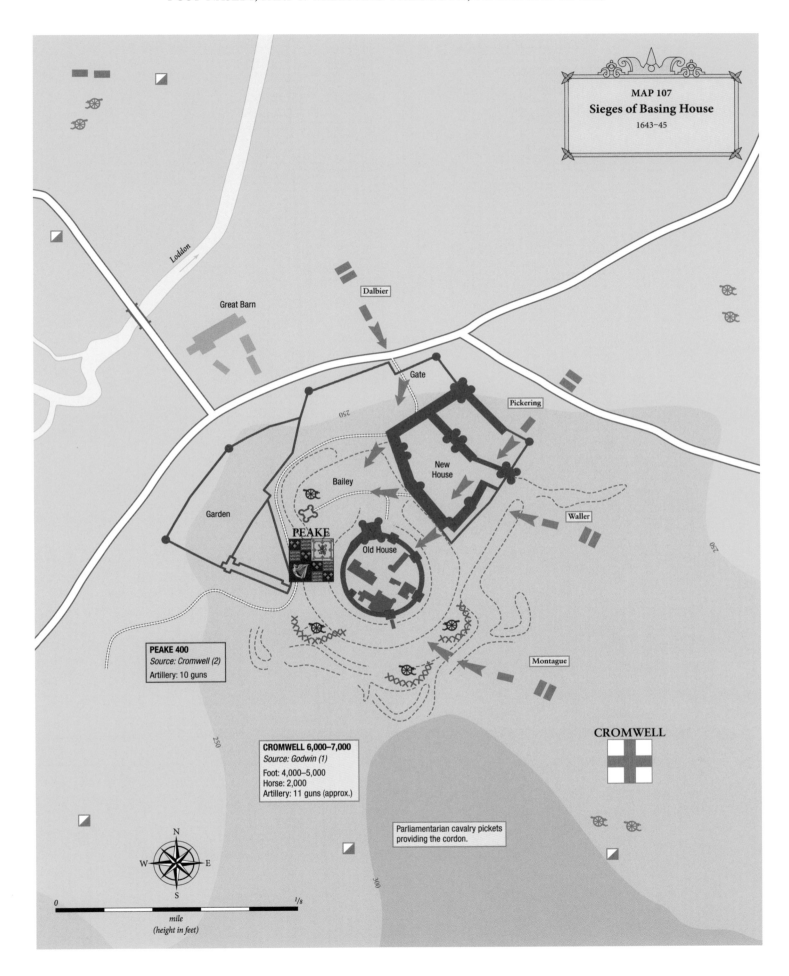

MAP 107
Sieges of Basing House
1643–45

Loddon

Great Barn

Dalbier

Gate

Pickering

New
House

Bailey

Garden

PEAKE

Old House

Waller

Montague

PEAKE 400
Source: Cromwell (2)
Artillery: 10 guns

CROMWELL 6,000–7,000
Source: Godwin (1)
Foot: 4,000–5,000
Horse: 2,000
Artillery: 11 guns (approx.)

CROMWELL

Parliamentarian cavalry pickets
providing the cordon.

250

250

250

300

N
W   E
S

0   1/8

mile
(height in feet)

The cavalry were quick to exploit the lodgement at Lawford's gate, as Sprigge noted: 'Colonel Montague and colonel Pickering with their regiments at Lawford's-gate entered speedily, and recovered twenty-two great guns, and took many prisoners in the works, major Desborough advancing with the horse after them'.[21] The Royalists were still in possession of Priors Hill Fort and the balance retreated to Royal Fort and Colston Redoubt. However, further resistance was clearly futile, and while Fairfax was considering the next course of action, 'the Prince sent out a trumpet to the General to desire a treaty for the surrender of the Town'.[22]

On 11 September the Royalist force marched out of the city and returned to Oxford. Waiting for Rupert on his arrival in the city was a letter from the King in which he expressed his extreme displeasure at the loss of Bristol, stripped him of his rank, cashiered his regiments of horse and foot, dismissed him from further service and closed with 'my conclusion is, to desire you to seek your subsistence until it shall please God to determine of my condition, somewhere beyond seas'.[23] The Governor of Oxford, Colonel Will Legge, was considered complicit to Rupert's apparent feebleness, removed and placed under arrest. The loss of Bristol was followed by news that Montrose's run of fortune had come to an end at Philiphaugh, but Charles remained defiant and determined. He decided to move towards Newark and thereby draw the Parliamentarian forces away from Chester (see chapter 31). By so doing he was effectively abandoning the west and this enabled Fairfax to turn his attention towards mopping up a number of garrisons and outposts which 'like vipers in the bowels, infested the midland parts'.[24] Berkeley Castle fell to Thomas Rainsborough in September, and in October, after Fairfax had departed with the army back into Somerset, Morgan captured Chepstow and Monmouth.

A second force under Cromwell, consisting of three regiments of foot and three of horse, was sent to clear the garrisons to the east.[25] On 21 September he began a siege of Devizes which put up a token resistance, while Pickering took the surrender of Lacock House a few miles to the north. The next day Cromwell moved to Winchester, where he had a more challenging task of convincing the bishop, who had taken refuge in the castle, to surrender. After two refused summonses, the gunners went to work 'and made a breach in the wall near the Black Tower; which, after about 200 shot, we thought stormable; and purposed on Monday [6 October] morning to attempt it'.[26] However, at 10pm the garrison commander had seen enough to convince him that capitulation was his best course of action. From Winchester, Cromwell marched to Basing House, the proverbial 'viper', which had been under its third siege since 20 August, when the Dutchman, Colonel John Dalbier, had arrived with instructions to take the place once and for all.[27] While he had enough guns, he lacked manpower, with only 1,000 men and four troops of horse to conduct the assaults.[28] Cromwell arrived on 8 October, bringing with him more guns and, crucially, a number of infantry. The *Moderate Intelligencer* (a Parliamentarian notebook) recorded that 'they that write from Bazing [and] say that Lieut-General Cromwell makes the number now before it between six and seven thousand horse and foot; he brought with him five great guns, two of them demi-cannons (32-pounders), one whole cannon (63-pounder)'.[29] Orders were sent to the garrison at Windsor Castle to send '100 whole cannon shot of 63 lbs., 300 demi-cannon shot (English) of 32 lbs., 300 whole culverin shot of 18 lbs., 200 granado shells of 13 inches, 200 demiculverin shot of 9 lbs., 50 granado shells of 10 inches, and one great mortar piece'.[30]

Work began on the gun positions on 8 October and was completed four days later. Cromwell sent in a summons with a clear warning that rejection would result in no mercy from his gunners and subsequently his infantry. He was in no mood for games. The largely Catholic defenders had heard such rhetoric before and rolled the dice. They erred, for they had not heard such rhetoric from a man like Cromwell. The guns opened and made short work of the drawbridge leading to the Old House and the walls of the New House. The assault was planned for 14 October. At 2am the men moved to their four assault concentration areas and, as the sun rose, the assaults went in. Cromwell recalled the events with some satisfaction:

> … we stormed this morning after six of the clock; the signal for falling on was the firing four of our cannon, which being done, our men fell on with great resolution and cheerfulness; we took the two Houses without any considerable loss to ourselves. Colonel Pickering stormed the New House, passed through, and got the gate of the Old House, whereupon they summoned a parley, which our men would not hear.[31]

There was no formal surrender. The rich pickings probably saved some of the Catholic defenders, but after about three hours, nearly 100 lay dead in the smoking ruins. Cromwell had lost about half that number. The house burned for another day and Cromwell recommended its destruction on the grounds that it would require many men to garrison. Cromwell's job in the area completed, he turned his men around and marched west towards Exeter, where he linked up with Fairfax at Crediton on 24 October.

21 Sprigge, op. cit., p. 116.
22 Carlyle, op. cit., p. 204.
23 Warburton, op. cit., p. 185. Letter from King Charles to Rupert dated 14 September 1645.
24 Sprigge, op. cit., p. 138.
25 Godwin, *Civil War in Hampshire*, p. 324.
26 Carlyle, op. cit., p. 207.

27 Godwin, op. cit., p. 320.
28 Barratt, *Sieges of the English Civil Wars*, p. 150.
29 Godwin, op. cit., p. 346.
30 Ibid., p. 345.
31 Carlyle, op. cit., p. 209.

CHAPTER 31
POST-NASEBY, PART 2: THE NORTH, TO THE END OF 1645

In accordance with the Self-Denying Ordinance, Lord Fairfax resigned his command in April 1645. He was replaced in May as commander of the Northern Association army by Sydenham Poyntz, who had returned from service on the Continent at an opportune moment. Although devoid of any large Royalist armies, the north still had a number of well-fortified and garrisoned fortresses and strongholds flying flags in support of the King. Poyntz's first success was to bring to an end the (five-month) long and protracted siege of Pontefract Castle. However, it was only brought about by offering generous terms that allowed the not inconsiderable garrison to march out with full honours and take themselves off to reinforce Newark.[1] The siege of Scarborough Castle had been no less troublesome for the Parliamentarians. In May, Meldrum had been killed in the trenches and replaced by Matthew Boynton. On 25 July, when the garrison ran low on powder and rations, Boynton finally agreed terms with Cholmley.[2] The illness that raked the garrison meant that a mere 50 men (one-third of the force) were strong enough to march out and make their way to Newark.[3]

At the beginning of August, Poyntz had been ordered south to link up with David Leslie's force, which had been detached by Leven to deal with the King's army marching north in the hope of linking up with Montrose (see chapter 30). The King, desperate to avoid both forces, headed swiftly back south to the security of Newark. He was not pursued, for Leslie had received news of Montrose's victory at Kilsyth and was, consequently, ordered to send part of his force back to Scotland to deal with him. His men, however, were not amenable to their force being split up and determined to return en masse, and they set off instantly. By the time London was made aware that Leslie's force had gone completely, almost two weeks had elapsed.[4] A few days later Poyntz received the following order: 'We are now advertised that the forces of the King are about [Chipping] Campden, whether he intends for Bristol or Hereford we know not, but desire you to follow him wherever he shall go, according to the intelligence you get of his movements.'[5] The King eluded Poyntz at Worcester before moving to Hereford, where the siege by Leven's force had been recently abandoned. However, Poyntz was constrained by having to wait near Tewkesbury for reinforcements to his horse and, after a number of days, his intelligence officers lost the scent. A few days later he was alerted to the King's second northerly movement and he headed off in order to try to prevent the Royalist force crossing the River Severn at Bridgnorth. Charles had moved north through the Welsh hills, by-passing Poyntz, and had reached Chirk Castle by 22 September. His force numbered about 4,000, mostly horse, and it was here that he received reports about the dire state of affairs in Chester.

The city of Chester had been besieged on and off since July 1643. Strategically positioned at the gateway to north Wales (and the Royalist recruiting grounds), the city was to play a key role during the war. The loyalty of most of the powerful merchant families, such as that headed by Sir Francis Gamull who dominated the city (and became colonel of the city guard), supported the King and so, early in the conflict, it had been secured for the Royalists. William Brereton, the commander of Parliament's forces in Cheshire, Shropshire, Lancashire and Staffordshire, conducted a relentless military campaign against the Royalists in the Welsh border counties and against the city of Chester. At the end of 1643, with the imminent arrival of troops from Ireland, the north Midlands assumed greater significance in the struggle and the King decided to send Lord Byron to assume command of the region for the Royalists. Throughout 1644 both Byron's and Brereton's fortunes had waxed and waned but Royalist failures in other parts of the country had stripped Byron of many of his better troops, and from October 1644 the city of Chester was in a virtually permanent stage of siege. The defeat of Byron's force at Nantwich in January 1644 (chapter 17), and his failure at Montgomery in September the same year (chapter 24), led to an abandonment of fighting the Parliamentarians in open battle and to a withdrawal within the walls of the city. Brereton, however, was facing difficulties of his own, and did not press his advantage, electing instead to implement a loose blockade and to establish a ring of garrisons around the city (see inset map – map 108), known as the Leaguer of Chester.

The Dee River protected Chester (from assault but not artillery) to the south and west. The fortified defences to the north and east had been built up as the war had progressed, but those to the north and north-east had been abandoned due to lack of resources and a sufficient number of defenders (see map 109).[6] Byron had long expected an assault on the city, and when it came, he was returning from visiting some of his outposts in north Wales:

The rebels accomplished their design that night, being the 20th of September 1645 betwixt two and three o'clock in the morning, and entered the works at the same place I had formerly given warning of… Boughton Turnpike, where upon the alarm, one Aldersley, a Lieutenant who commanded there, met them very gallantly with his guard… upon the death of that officer, the soldiers quitted their guard and the Enemy's party of foot, being then all entered, opened the Turnpike and let in their horse.[7]

Byron sent word to his outlying garrisons and ordered them to send troops to the city, while he returned there with all haste. The defenders torched the eastern suburbs and withdrew back inside the medieval walls, while the

---

1 Holmes (ed.), *The Sieges of Pontefract Castle 1644–1648*, p. 144.
2 The fact that the Royalists could not resupply this garrison from the sea is a good indicator of the naval dominance of the Parliamentarian fleet at this stage of the war.
3 Cooke, *Yorkshire Sieges*, p. 180.
4 *CSPD* dated 30 August 1645.
5 Ibid., dated 1 September 1645.
6 *County of Chester*, vol. V, Part 1, The City of Chester, p. 3.
7 Byron, *Account of the Siege of Chester*, p. 56.

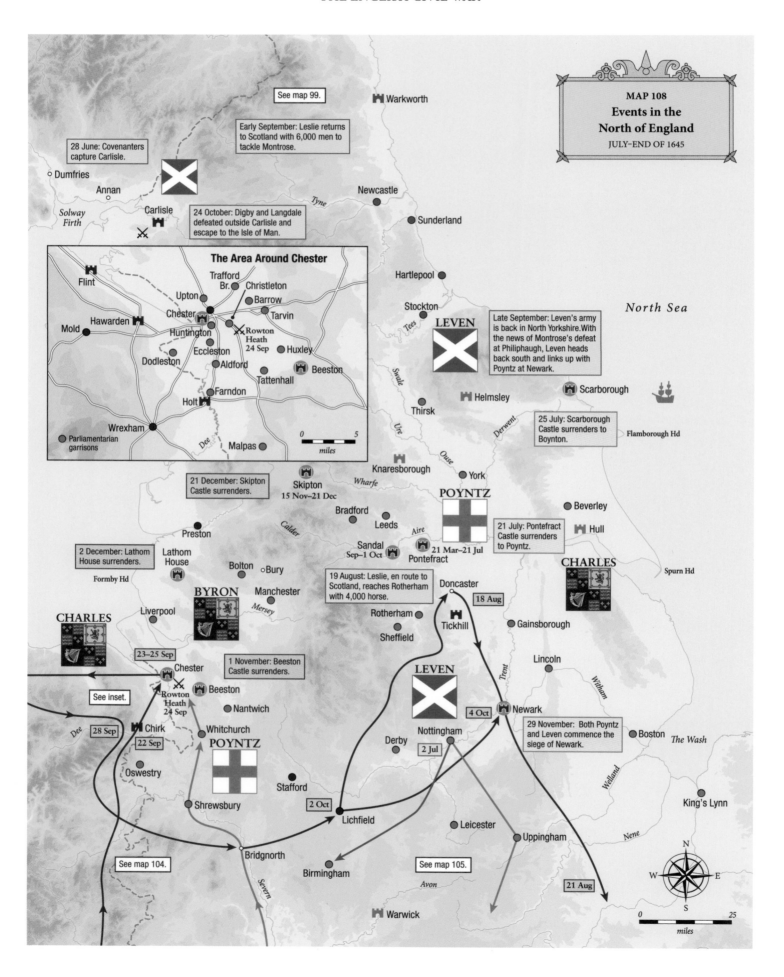

See map 99.

⌂ Warkworth

28 June: Covenanters capture Carlisle.

Early September: Leslie returns to Scotland with 6,000 men to tackle Montrose.

MAP 108
Events in the
North of England
JULY–END OF 1645

○ Dumfries

Annan

Tyne

● Newcastle

Solway Firth

Carlisle ⌂

24 October: Digby and Langdale defeated outside Carlisle and escape to the Isle of Man.

● Sunderland

North Sea

The Area Around Chester

⌂ Flint

Trafford Br.

Christleton

Upton ●

● Barrow

Chester ⌂

● Tarvin

Hawarden ⌂

Huntington

Rowton Heath 24 Sep

Mold ●

● Huxley

Dodleston ●

Eccleston ●

Aldford ●

Tattenhall ●

⌂ Beeston

Farndon ●

Holt ⌂

Wrexham ●

● Hartlepool

● Stockton

Tees

LEVEN

Late September: Leven's army is back in North Yorkshire. With the news of Montrose's defeat at Philiphaugh, Leven heads back south and links up with Poyntz at Newark.

⌂ Helmsley

⌂ Scarborough

● Thirsk

Swale

25 July: Scarborough Castle surrenders to Boynton.

Flamborough Hd

● Parliamentarian garrisons

● Malpas

0   5
miles

Dee

Ure

Derwent

Knaresborough ⌂

● York

Ouse

21 December: Skipton Castle surrenders.

⌂ Skipton
15 Nov–21 Dec

Wharfe

POYNTZ

● Beverley

21 July: Pontefract Castle surrenders to Poyntz.

⌂ Hull

Bradford ●

● Leeds

Aire

2 December: Lathom House surrenders.

● Preston

Calder

Sandal
Sep–1 Oct

⌂ Pontefract
21 Mar–21 Jul

CHARLES

Lathom House ⌂

Bolton ●

○ Bury

Spurn Hd

Formby Hd

BYRON

● Manchester

Mersey

19 August: Leslie, en route to Scotland, reaches Rotherham with 4,000 horse.

○ Doncaster

18 Aug

CHARLES

Liverpool ●

Rotherham ●

⌂ Tickhill

● Gainsborough

● Sheffield

23–25 Sep

Chester ⌂

1 November: Beeston Castle surrenders.

● Lincoln

Trent

See inset.

Rowton Heath 24 Sep

⌂ Beeston

LEVEN

Witham

● Nantwich

4 Oct

⌂ Newark

28 Sep

Dee

⌂ Chirk

● Whitchurch

Nottingham ●

29 November: Both Poyntz and Leven commence the siege of Newark.

● Boston

The Wash

22 Sep

POYNTZ

Derby ●

2 Jul

● Oswestry

● Stafford

Welland

● King's Lynn

● Shrewsbury

2 Oct

Lichfield ●

● Leicester

Uppingham ●

Nene

See map 104.

Bridgnorth ○

N

Birmingham ●

See map 105.

Avon

21 Aug

W   E

Severn

⌂ Warwick

S

0   25
miles

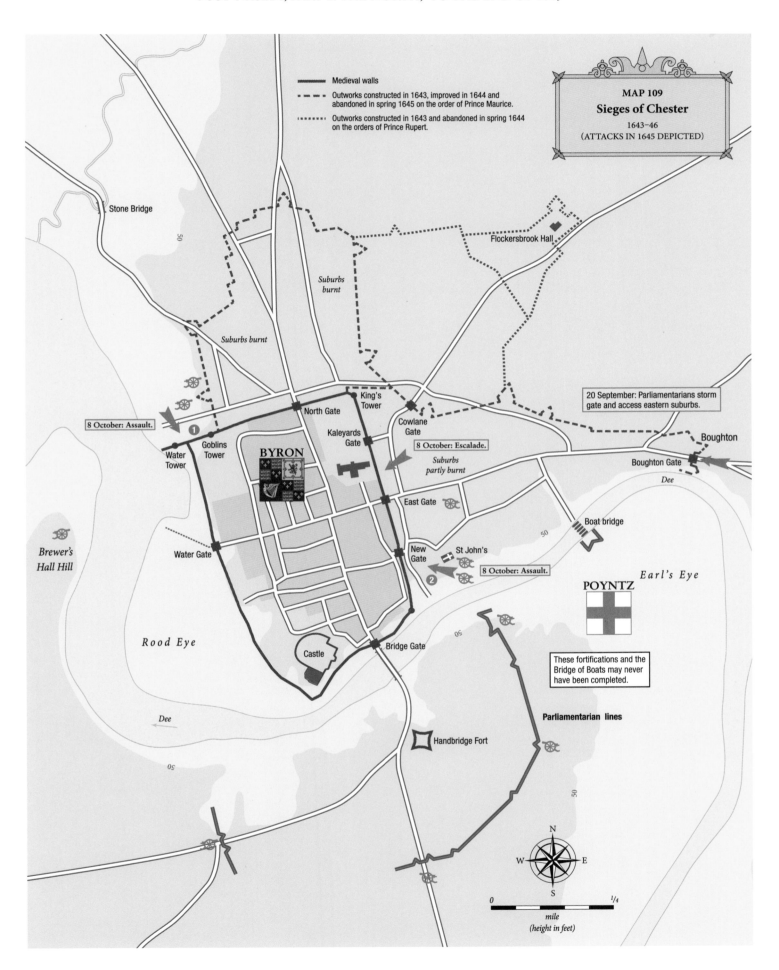

Medieval walls

Outworks constructed in 1643, improved in 1644 and abandoned in spring 1645 on the order of Prince Maurice.

Outworks constructed in 1643 and abandoned in spring 1644 on the orders of Prince Rupert.

MAP 109

Sieges of Chester

1643–46
(ATTACKS IN 1645 DEPICTED)

Stone Bridge

Flockersbrook Hall

Suburbs burnt

Suburbs burnt

20 September: Parliamentarians storm gate and access eastern suburbs.

King's Tower

8 October: Assault.

North Gate

Cowlane Gate

Boughton

Goblins Tower

Kaleyards Gate

8 October: Escalade.

Boughton Gate

Water Tower

BYRON

Suburbs partly burnt

Dee

Brewer's Hall Hill

Boat bridge

East Gate

Water Gate

New Gate

St John's

Earl's Eye

8 October: Assault.

POYNTZ

Rood Eye

These fortifications and the Bridge of Boats may never have been completed.

Castle

Bridge Gate

Parliamentarian lines

Dee

Handbridge Fort

N
W E
S

0   1/4

mile
(*height in feet*)

attackers brought up artillery. On 22 September the heavy guns blasted a wide breach in the area of New Gate. That night they stormed the opening and walls in three or four places, but they failed to gain an effective lodgement. With intelligence that the King was approaching the city with a sizeable force, the siege was again put on hold and the besiegers withdrew.[8]

Late on 23 September the King entered the city, with about 1,000 troops, after a tiring march. Meanwhile Langdale, with a 3,000-strong cavalry force, had been sent south in order to cross the River Dee at Holt, with the mission of attacking the Chester besieging force from the rear. As he advanced up the Whitchurch road towards the city, Langdale received a report of a large Parliamentarian force to the south.[9] This was Poyntz's force, which had failed to catch the King at Worcester, and had been shadowing his northerly movement. At Millers Heath, Langdale turned to face his pursuers, and at about 9am on 24 September, as Poyntz's troopers appeared in the early morning light, Langdale's Dragoons opened fire from the hedge lines. Poyntz's full force was not up but he had hoped to surprise Langdale; instead the boot was on the other foot. The hedge on either side of the lane prevented him deploying his vanguard and driving off the dismounted cavalrymen. After about a few minutes of frenzied close-quarter fighting, Poyntz gave the order to pull back. Both forces remained on the field – Langdale at Rowton Heath and Poyntz at Hatton Heath. Realizing their forces were evenly balanced, both commanders sent messengers requesting reinforcements and, specifically, some infantry.

Poyntz recalled, in his report to the Speaker of the House of Commons, that 'whereupon I sent to Chester for some foot, which was very seasonably sent me'.[10] Approximately 350 horse and 500 foot arrived after some hours under the command of Colonel Jones, who had led the assault on the city four days earlier. Langdale was less fortunate. The Royalist garrison did not react with quite the same urgency, and by the time they realized Langdale's predicament, it was too late.[11] Nathaniel Lancaster (a Parliamentarian chaplain) recalled that 'the enemy in Chester perceiving that [forces had been despatched], sent about one thousand horse and foot upon the rear of Collonel Jones, yet by two hundred horse and as many foot, sent out of the suburbs by Adjt. Louthaine, those were repelled and driven another way'.[12] The Royalist messenger who finally got through to Langdale could do little more than transmit an order for him to 'retreat towards the city'.[13] It was an unhappy suggestion, the execution of which would have trapped him between the two Parliamentarian forces. Langdale decided his best option was to deploy for battle on Rowton Heath, drive back Poyntz's force and seek an alternative route to the city. 'The Enemy formed themselves into a body upon Routon Heath, two miles from Chester and stood in Batalia', a Parliamentarian report later noted.[14] Colonel Parsons, commanding Poyntz's reserve, recalled that at some time after 4pm, 'the enemy advanced with their whole body, and the General…

tooke care of, and led up the van divisions, with which after a round volley of shot from the foot, he joyned battell, charging the enemy in Front and Flank'.[15]

The Parliamentarian report summarized the fierce (largely) cavalry on cavalry engagement that followed:

> They had the Wind and Sun; we had God with us, which was our Word, counterpoising all disadvantages, and countermanding all strength; a little before five a clock, we joyned in a terrible storm, firing in the faces of one another, hacking and slashing with swords neither party gain'd or lost a foot of ground, as if everyone was resolved there to breathe their last: Whilst the dispute was so hot and doubtfull, our Musquetiers so galled their horse, that their Rear fled, perceiving their losse by them, upon whom they made no Execution.[16]

The collapse of Langdale's rear left him no option but to pull back towards Chester, trapping his men between Poyntz and the Parliamentarian siege lines. Some of his troopers panicked and fled for the safety of Wales, crossing the Dee at Fardon, but Langdale managed to keep the majority formed up and they moved back, albeit in haste, towards Chester. It was not long before they were attacked by a strong force which debouched from the suburbs.

The Royalist forces within Chester could now plainly see Langdale's plight and a number of sallies were made from the eastern suburbs. What followed was a series of chaotic small fights involving horse and foot, which, 'satiated with slaughter, prisoners and booty', went on for some time before Langdale's men managed to extricate themselves. Some fled west towards Farndon bridge while others galloped north from where they moved, sometime later, to the relative safety of the city. Charles had witnessed the rather bloody and decidedly depressing affair from the Cathedral tower: 'as he was talking with a Captaine, a bullet from St. John's [suburb] gave him a salute, narrowly missing the King, hit the said Captaine in the head and killed him on the spot'.[17] Charles decided to escape from the city while he still could.[18] Later that day, Parliamentarian scouts reported that 'the King with a party of about five or six hundred was seen going into Wales'.[19]

Byron's report on the battle at Rowton Heath is rather dismissive of the intensity of Langdale's struggle to reach the city. He wrote that 'the night drawing on, he made his retreat without great loss'. But the preliminary Parliamentarian report suggests a very different outcome: 'It is generally conjectured 800 slaine, 1500 men and 2000 horse taken.' The list of Royalist officers captured during the battle and skirmishes runs to three pages, making a mockery of Byron's rather trivializing submission.[20] Although Rowton Heath was a relatively minor affair, it had far-reaching consequences. It prevented the King from proceeding to Scotland (for what that was worth at this stage); it significantly reduced the strength of horse within the King's army and badly dented the overall morale of the Royalist force; but, most notably, it sealed the fate of Chester, and with it, any hope of further reinforcements from Ireland.[21]

---

8 Nathanial Lancaster's account in Barratt, *The Siege of Chester and the Battle of Rowton Heath*, p. 45.

9 Morris & Lawson, *The Siege of Chester*, pp. 118–9. Poyntz tried to inform the besiegers that his force was making best speed towards them. His messenger was caught and the cat's head was out of the bag.

10 Poyntz to Lenthall, in Morris & Lawson, op. cit., p. 117.

11 For an account of why this (most likely) came about, see the English Heritage Battlefield Report: Rowton Heath (S) 1645, p. 9.

12 Nathanial Lancaster's account in Barratt, op. cit., p. 47. Byron states this was about 4pm.

13 Anon, *An account of the siege of Chester*, p. 36.

14 Anon, *The Kings forces totally routed by the Parliaments army*, p. 7.

15 Morris & Lawson, op. cit., p. 119.

16 Anon, *The Kings forces totally routed by the Parliaments army*, p. 8.

17 Poyntz to Lenthall, in Morris & Lawson, op. cit., p. 121.

18 Byron, *Account of the Siege of Chester*, p. 58.

19 Morris & Lawson, op. cit., p. 120.

20 Anon, *The Kings forces totally routed by the Parliaments army*, pp. 13–15. See also Brereton, *Letter Books*, vol. II, pp. 70–8 for a full list of prisoners.

21 Particularly as Bristol had also fallen in September.

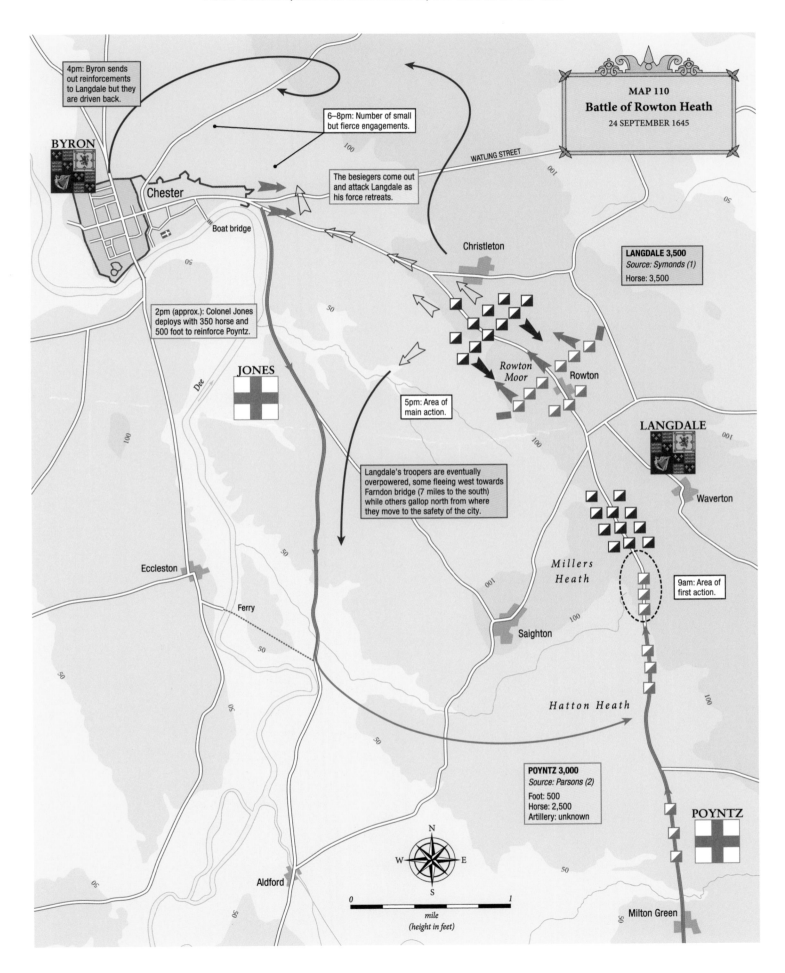

4pm: Byron sends out reinforcements to Langdale but they are driven back.

6–8pm: Number of small but fierce engagements.

The besiegers come out and attack Langdale as his force retreats.

MAP 110
Battle of Rowton Heath
24 SEPTEMBER 1645

WATLING STREET

BYRON

Chester

Boat bridge

Christleton

LANGDALE 3,500
Source: Symonds (1)
Horse: 3,500

2pm (approx.): Colonel Jones deploys with 350 horse and 500 foot to reinforce Poyntz.

JONES

Dee

Rowton Moor

Rowton

5pm: Area of main action.

LANGDALE

Langdale's troopers are eventually overpowered, some fleeing west towards Farndon bridge (7 miles to the south) while others gallop north from where they move to the safety of the city.

Waverton

Millers Heath

Eccleston

Ferry

9am: Area of first action.

Saighton

Hatton Heath

POYNTZ 3,000
Source: Parsons (2)
Foot: 500
Horse: 2,500
Artillery: unknown

Aldford

N
W E
S

POYNTZ

0   1
mile
(height in feet)

Milton Green

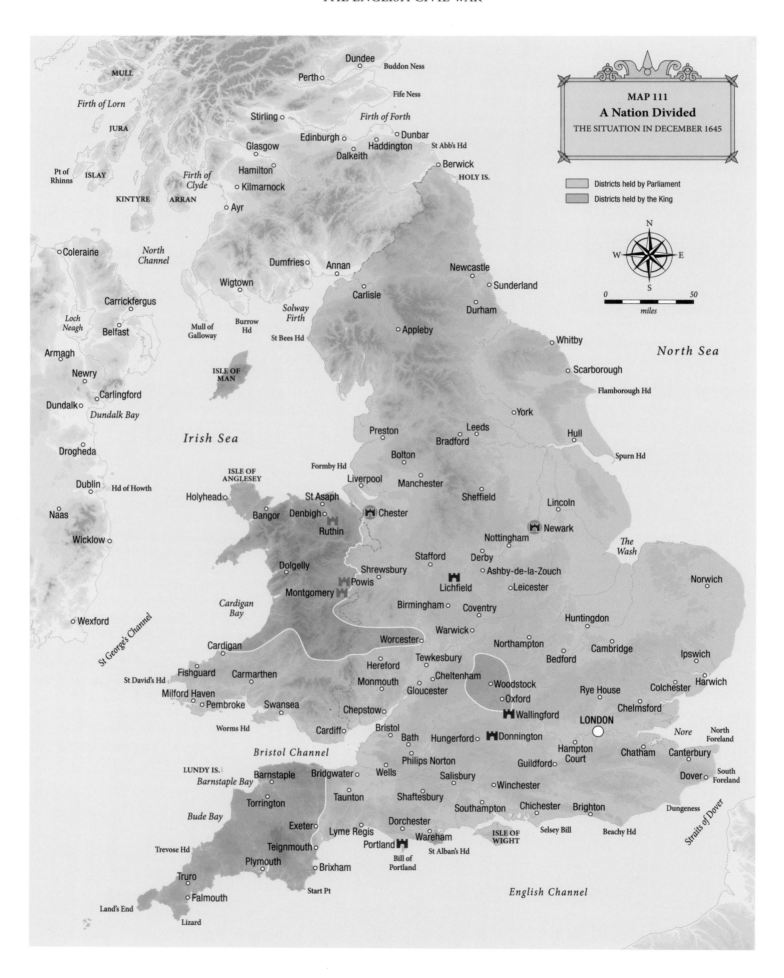

MULL

Firth of Lorn

JURA

Pt of
Rhinns   ISLAY

*Firth of
Clyde*

KINTYRE   ARRAN

Coleraine

*North
Channel*

Carrickfergus

*Loch
Neagh*   Belfast

Armagh

Newry

Carlingford

Dundalk

Dundalk Bay

Irish Sea

Drogheda

Dublin   Hd of Howth

Naas

Wicklow

ISLE OF
MAN

Wexford

St George's Channel

*Cardigan
Bay*

St David's Hd

Fishguard   Carmarthen

Milford Haven

Pembroke   Swansea

Worms Hd

LUNDY IS.

Barnstaple Bay

Bude Bay

Trevose Hd

Truro

Land's End

Lizard

Dundee   Buddon Ness

Perth

Fife Ness

Stirling

Glasgow   Edinburgh   Dunbar
Haddington   St Abb's Hd
Dalkeith   Berwick
Hamilton   HOLY IS.
Kilmarnock

Ayr

Dumfries   Annan   Newcastle
Wigtown   Carlisle   Sunderland
Durham

Mull of
Galloway   Burrow
Hd   Appleby   Whitby

St Bees Hd   Scarborough

North Sea

Flamborough Hd

York

Preston   Leeds   Hull
Bradford   Spurn Hd
Bolton

Formby Hd   Liverpool   Manchester   Lincoln
Sheffield

ISLE OF
ANGLESEY

Holyhead   St Asaph   Chester   Newark
Bangor   Denbigh   Nottingham   *The
Ruthin   Wash*

Dolgelly   Shrewsbury   Stafford   Derby   Norwich
Powis   Ashby-de-la-Zouch
Montgomery   Lichfield   Leicester
Birmingham   Coventry
Warwick   Huntingdon
Cardigan   Worcester   Northampton   Cambridge
Tewkesbury   Bedford   Ipswich
Cheltenham   Harwich
Hereford   Woodstock   Rye House   Colchester
Monmouth   Gloucester   Oxford   Chelmsford
Chepstow   Wallingford
Cardiff   Bristol   LONDON   *Nore*   *North
Bath   Hungerford   Donnington   Foreland*
Philips Norton   Hampton   Chatham   Canterbury
Wells   Court
Bridgwater   Salisbury   Guildford   Dover
Barnstaple   Winchester   South
Taunton   Chichester   Foreland
Torrington   Shaftesbury   Southampton   Brighton
Dorchester   Selsey Bill   Beachy Hd
Exeter   Lyme Regis   Wareham   ISLE OF
Teignmouth   Portland   WIGHT   *Straits of Dover*
Plymouth   Bill of   St Alban's Hd   Dungeness
Brixham   Portland
Start Pt   *English Channel*

Falmouth

MAP 111

A Nation Divided

THE SITUATION IN DECEMBER 1645

Districts held by Parliament

Districts held by the King

N

W   E

S

0   50

miles

The King reached Denbigh Castle on 26 September where he received news of Montrose's defeat at Philiphaugh. Lord Digby, the King's advisor, wrote to Byron that day in upbeat terms, extolling the determination of the Chester garrison and residents, and promising to send provisions and reinforcements.[22] The latter consisted of a few troops of horse under the command of William Blakestone and their primary task was to keep open the line of communication, and retreat, into Wales. However, Byron did not see things through the same pair of rose-tinted spectacles, well aware of the true nature of Blakestone's mission. He wrote to Ormond, begging for powder and men. The next day Byron reported to Digby that Poyntz's men were already on the Welsh side of the Dee, and suggested that the only sensible course of action was for the King to gather all available men from Wales and return to Chester. He was well aware that it was wishful thinking – Byron was on his own.

The day after the King's departure, Poyntz (who had assumed command of the operation) offered Byron the option of surrender, which he duly rejected.[23] Poyntz responded by occupying the northern suburbs, which had largely been abandoned by the Royalists a couple of months earlier, and reinforcing the batteries in the eastern suburbs. He also ordered the construction of a number of new batteries surrounding the city. At Handbridge, to the south, they built a line of entrenchments with gun emplacements and established a battery atop a small hillock known as Brewer's and maintained communication by the construction of a bridge of boats from Dee Lane to Earle's Eye.[24] On 8 October Poyntz sent in another summons. Byron asked for '14 days to give his Majesty an account of your demands and receive his further pleasure'.[25] Poyntz was in no mood for games, and responded by ordering all the batteries to open and provide an energetic bombardment upon the town. The eastern breach (by New Gate) was enlarged and a new breach was made in the north walls (see points 1 and 2, map 109). Later the same day, a few hours before dusk, a three-pronged attack was launched. The full-scale assault was beaten off, among furious fighting that saw columns of troops assault the two breaches, while fresh waves of troops attempted an escalade on the northern section of the east wall. At the first breach, it soon became apparent that the slope was too steep, and the Royalist barricades too effective, for it to be taken easily. At the second breach in the north walls, desperate fighting raged for much of the evening and night, but by dawn the unsuccessful attacks had been called off. Byron's men had fought with enormous bravery and no further (immediate) attempts were made to storm the city. Brereton returned in mid-October and reassumed control of the siege operations and elected to try to starve the garrison into submission. Chester, for now, still beat with a Royalist heart.[26] Beeston Castle, the Royalist outpost a few miles to the south-east of the city was, however, less fortunate and was forced to surrender on 6 November.

Charles's despondency at the news of Montrose was tempered by the arrival, on 28 September, of Prince Maurice and nearly 1,000 horse.

He wasted no time contriving a new plan and, somewhat optimistically, ordered Goring to join him at Newark. Charles reached Newark on 4 October, but the prospect of Goring joining him there was remote. Not, however, for the same reasons that had prevented Goring joining the King prior to Naseby. Fairfax had been delayed in moving back into the South-West to engage Goring due to a lack of money to pay his already disgruntled soldiers. Funds arrived on 14 October, and once paid the soldiers had an instantaneous change of heart and Fairfax set off almost immediately, while Cromwell, who had captured Basing House the same day, was following up. By 19 October Fairfax had captured Tiverton Castle; there was now no Royalist garrison between Exeter and London. With winter setting in, and with his army exhausted from almost constant campaigning, a council of war elected to go into winter quarters, in and around Exeter, from where they would plan the siege with expectant prospect of success. They remained poised, however, to strike at Goring if he made any attempt to move east. Consequently, with no news from Goring, Charles now seized on another rather extraordinary plan, this one put forward by Richard Willis, the governor of Newark. He planned to destroy the last remaining Royalist garrisons and strongholds in the Midlands – Newark, Ashby, Tutbury, Lichfield, Belvoir, Weston, Bridgnorth and Denbigh – thereby creating an army that would then march into the South-West to join Goring. That such an astonishing plan gained traction is indicative of the rather desperate state of the King's mind, and the dismal state of the King's council at this stage of the war.

Not surprisingly, it did not come to pass, but a plan to despatch Digby, with Langdale's Horse, north to link up with Montrose did pass muster. They dislodged and surprised an unsuspecting force of Parliamentarian infantry at Sherburn-in-Elmet on 15 October, but were chased off with loss by a strong cavalry group under Colonel Copley later in the day. Digby and Langdale finally made it to Carlisle on 21 October, only to be defeated by a Covenanter force under John Brown, which debouched from the city. Three days later both Digby and Langdale escaped to the Isle of Man to join the Earl of Derby, who had fled there in 1643.

In the Midlands, Parliamentarian forces had begun to sweep up a number of Royalist outposts and to close in on the Royalist stronghold at Newark. The Royalist outpost at Shelford Manor was taken on 3 November and that at Wilverton Hall followed the next day. By the end of November, Leven had come back south and joined Poyntz (who had moved west in the interim) and the two armies began the third siege of Newark. Charles had escaped the city at the beginning of the month and returned to Oxford, where, on his arrival, he was bombarded with advice to seek terms and end the war. Charles would entertain no such suggestions and became increasingly insular. On 18 December he received the news that Hereford had fallen to a surprise attack, with growing distress. As the penultimate year of the first English Civil War came to a close, and a deep winter chill froze the Thames and Severn rivers, Charles had run out of options.

---

22 Morris & Lawson, op. cit., p. 123.

23 Poyntz had assumed command from Colonel Jones – William Brereton was in London and did not return until October.

24 There is no primary source evidence to conclude that these defences were ever completed.

25 Brereton, op. cit., vol. II, p. 87.

26 An attempt by Vaughan to march to the relief of Chester on 1 November was defeated by Colonel Jones.

CHAPTER 32
SWEEPING UP THE SOUTH-WEST, JANUARY TO APRIL 1646

Fairfax had turned his attention back to the South-West in early October, and once Cromwell had captured Basing House, he moved to join him. In the interim, Fairfax captured Tiverton Castle when, as luck would have it, a round shot broke the chain holding up the drawbridge, 'whereupon the bridge fell down, and our men immediately, without staying for orders, possessed themselves of the bridge, and entered the works'.[1] Fairfax's and Cromwell's armies were united at Crediton on 24 October. They had Exeter firmly in their sights, having gathered intelligence that all was not well with the western Royalists. The disheartening news of Royalist failures from other parts of the country, and the likely departure of the Prince of Wales to France, led some to advise negotiation with Parliament.[2] Goring and Grenville were still at each other's throats, the latter objecting to the former claim for overall command, and the former blaming the latter for the desertion of the Cornish levies. Goring had a point: Grenville's rough-hand tactics in rounding up the trained bands, and punishing deserters, drove many into the arms of the Parliamentarians. Goring's relationship with the newly appointed Governor of Exeter, Sir John Berkeley, was no better, and on 22 October, he departed the city with his cavalry (to Okehampton), leaving the garrison to face the advancing Parliamentarians alone. A few weeks later Goring quit the Royalist cause altogether, pleading ill health (not entirely untrue for he was a heavy drinker) and set sail for France, never to return.

Meanwhile Grenville, without consulting the Prince of Wales, withdrew his force west of the Tamar. When summoned to Truro to explain himself, he suggested that Cornwall was the only loyal county in the region and that he could and would defend it if a deep trench were cut from Barnstaple to the English Channel.[3] Amidst this internecine squabbling, the Royalists were fortunate that the Parliamentarians had not made better use of the time and opportunity. However, in truth Fairfax's army was utterly exhausted and sickness raked the ranks. At the Parliamentarian council of war at the end of October, Fairfax had elected to move to secure the eastern approaches to Exeter and several garrisons were ordered to be established on the eastern bank of the River Clyst.[4] These fortifications were complete by mid-November and Fairfax elected to try to capture, by *coup de main*, Powderham Castle on the west bank. The attempt on 14 December failed, but it shook up Berkeley, who had sallied out of Exeter to assist the defenders and sent urgent word to the Prince of Wales for reinforcement. Fairfax contented himself with the capture of the village of Exminster, and with snow lying thickly on the ground and the soldiers on both sides in dire need of suitable winter clothing and lodgings, it brought hostilities to an end until the New Year.

On 27 December the Prince of Wales, perhaps in response to Berkeley's pleading, moved his headquarters to Tavistock with a view to taking the fight to the Parliamentarians. His intention was to combine the Devon trained bands and the raising of men in Devon, through *posse comitatus*, to link up with a brigade under General Guy and the rump of Goring's men (now under Wentworth's command), providing a force of about 5,000 horse and 6,000 foot.[5] However, Fairfax's intelligence service was aware of the plan in the embryonic stages and he decided to strike first. On 9 January, Cromwell fell on Wentworth's quarters at Bovey Tracey, capturing some 400 horses and many prisoners. The haul of men could have been greater, as Sprigge noted:

> It was almost supper time with them when our men entered the town, most of them at that instant were playing at cards, but our soldiers took up the stakes for many of their principal officers, who, being together in one room, threw their stakes of money out at the window, which whilst our soldiers were scrambling for they escaped out at a back door.[6]

The Parliamentarians also attacked the Royalist quarters at Ashburton and Totnes, before moving to storm the port of Dartmouth. The key port was a great prize and Fairfax proudly reported the feat in a letter to the House of Lords in which he reported the capture of '103 pieces of ordnance, and about 600 prisoners, and 100 horse, with good proportion of arms and ammunition'.[7]

The loss of Dartmouth necessitated lifting the Royalist siege of Plymouth, but it did throw up the besieging forces under Digby for use within the general army. However, when Digby refused to take orders from Grenville, the Prince of Wales gave supreme command to Hopton, in the hope that this would put an end to this internal squabbling. It did not, and by mid-January Grenville was under arrest for refusing to serve under the newly appointed Royalist commander.[8] More bad news was to follow. On 26 January, the defenders at Powderham decided to surrender the structure to Colonel Hammond, completing the encirclement of Exeter. Hopton felt compelled to take the offensive, moving from Stratton to Torrington, with the aim of driving off Fairfax's men and relieving Exeter. It was a bold move with an army that, by his own description, consisted of the foot that were 'full of necessities, complaints, and all sorts of distempers'; the horse that were 'never able to surprize or attempt upon the enemy, but ever liable to be surprized by them'; and of the artillery of which 'I had none, nor as much as carriages to carry our small proportion of ammunition, materials and provisions'.[9]

---

1 Sprigge, *Anglia Rediviva*, p. 155.
2 Charles had written to the Prince of Wales on 5 August instructing him to convey himself to France if he was in danger of falling into rebel hands – Clarendon, *History of the Rebellion*, vol. IV, p. 78.
3 Coate, *Cornwall*, p. 197.
4 Stoyle, *Deliverance to Destruction*, p. 111.
5 Barratt, *South West*, p. 129.
6 Sprigge, op. cit., p. 177.
7 Ibid., p. 184.
8 On 21 January he was sent to prison on St Michael's Mount.
9 Carte, *Collection of Original Letters*, pp. 109–10.

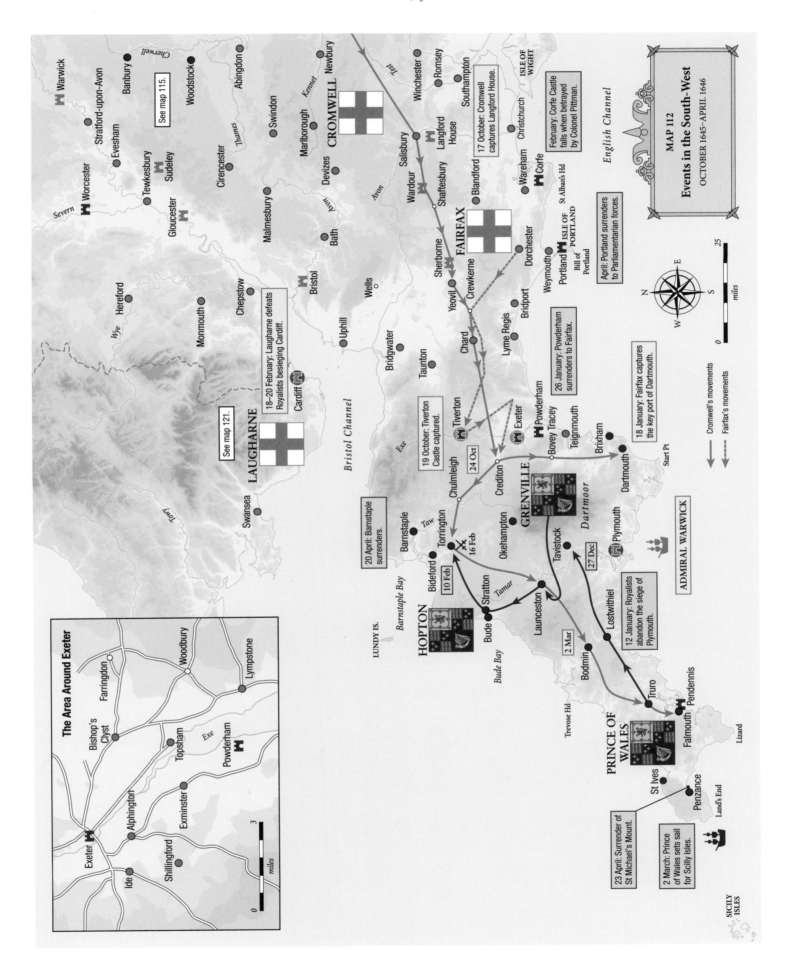

The Area Around Exeter

Woodbury
Farringdon
Lympstone
Bishop's Clyst
Topsham
Powderham
Exeter
Alphington
Exminster
Ide
Shillingford

miles
0   3

MAP 112
Events in the South-West
OCTOBER 1645–APRIL 1646

17 October: Cromwell captures Langford House.

February: Corfe Castle falls when betrayed by Colonel Pittman.

April: Portland surrenders to Parliamentarian forces.

26 January: Powderham surrenders to Fairfax.

18 January: Fairfax captures the key port of Dartmouth.

18–20 February: Laugharne defeats Royalists besieging Cardiff.

See map 121.

See map 115.

19 October: Tiverton Castle captured.

20 April: Barnstaple surrenders.

12 January: Royalists abandon the siege of Plymouth.

23 April: Surrender of St Michael's Mount.

2 March: Prince of Wales sets sail for Scilly Isles.

CROMWELL

FAIRFAX

LAUGHARNE

GRENVILLE

HOPTON

PRINCE OF WALES

ADMIRAL WARWICK

Cromwell's movements
Fairfax's movements

English Channel

Bristol Channel

N   E   S   W

miles
0   25

10 Feb
16 Feb
24 Oct
2 Mar
27 Dec

Fairfax received low-level intelligence of provisions being moved west out of Launceston, and this intelligence was almost immediately backed-up by further reports that Hopton was on the move towards Torrington. Leaving Hardress Waller to maintain the cordon around Exeter, Fairfax ordered a concentration of Parliamentarian forces at Crediton. On 14 February, with slightly fewer troops than he had hoped, he set off north to engage Hopton's force. The Parliamentarian army numbered 6,000 men, and while Hopton's army was of a similar size, he was decidedly short in infantry. Fairfax's advance was hampered by some appalling weather and he arrived at Chulmleigh (about 12 miles to the east of Torrington) late on 14 February. He received reports that the River Taw was in full flood (following the thaw) and that all the bridges were down. Sending pioneers forward to effect repairs, his army encamped in and around Chulmleigh for the night. Hopton was aware of Fairfax's movements but resolved to stand and fight for, as he wrote, 'to draw that body of horse and foot into Cornwall ('twas easily foreseen) was utterly ruinous, the country not being able to maintain them'; furthermore, the position at Torrington offered 'cover for my foot, and opportunity to make good use of my horse'.[10]

Fairfax had reservations about pressing an attack, for the bad weather seemed set to stay. Rain and drizzle would affect his firearms and negate his advantage in infantry. Furthermore, and mindful of the fate of Essex's army in the confines of the South-West, his lack of provisions, Hopton's advantage in cavalry, and the proximity of a strong Royalist garrison at Barnstaple on his right flank, all served to urge caution. Following significant discussions, during which staying put or withdrawing offered little by way of solutions, Fairfax 'resolved to go on to try what God would do for us, and trust him for weather, subsistence, and all things'.[11] On 16 February Fairfax ordered the army to rendezvous about 6 miles east of the town at Rings Ash. Simultaneously, the forlorn hope was sent forward towards Great Torrington. As the army advanced the weather improved; God was keeping his side of the bargain. The forlorn hope surprised a party of Royalist dragoons in Stevenstone House (a mile to the east of the map) and then pursued them westwards, compelling Fairfax to order the balance of the army to move up in support. The Royalists established themselves in a strong position, behind the barricades within the town, but it was a dangerous place to fight a defensive action. Hopton recalled:

> I sent out Major General Webb with 200 horse to our guards to give me a more perfect account of the motion and countenance of the enemy, and when he should feel it necessary to draw off the guards with him, which he performed very gallantly, entertaining continual skirmishes with the enemy till he came within a mile of Torrington, where with the assistance of 300 musketeers that I sent out to him, he held the enemy up till night.[12]

From the hills to the east of Great Torrington Fairfax was able to observe the town and the Royalist defences. Hopton had made that fatal error of placing a river to his back and line of retreat. Fairfax had seen what he needed to see and, as night was falling, he retired to prepare his orders. He gave immediate word that there would not be a general action until the following day.

In the process of setting guards, the Parliamentarian officers perceived noises from the town, which indicated that the Royalists appeared to be retreating. A small party of dragoons was sent forward to investigate, and for the second time that day they got embroiled in a firefight, necessitating additional troops to be sent forward to facilitate their extraction. The forlorn hope went towards the barricades and were soon followed by the reserve; within minutes there was an extensive firefight, 'and being thus far engaged, the general being on the field, and seeing the general resolution of the soldiery, held fit that the whole regiments in order after them should fall on, and so both sides were accordingly engaged in the dark, for some two hours'.[13] Eventually the Parliamentarian soldiers drove the Royalists from their barricades, and after a 'push of pike and but-end of musket', entered the town. The Royalists fled as the Parliamentarian horse came galloping through the streets past their infantry. The defenders poured out of the west and south of the town, over the two bridges; the barricades near these bridges held up the pursuing cavalry long enough to enable most of the Royalist cavalry and a sizeable force of infantry to make good their escape under cover of darkness and confusion. A group of about 200 prisoners were herded into the village church when the structure suddenly exploded, killing them all along with many of the Parliamentarian soldiers guarding them. Sprigge recorded that this was the work of 'a desperate villain, one [Robert] Watts, whom the enemy had hired with thirty pounds for that purpose, as he himself confessed the next day, when he was pulled out from under the rubbish and timber'.[14] The immensity of the blast (estimated to have been 80 barrels of powder) caused consternation, which worsened as many of the thatched roofs caught alight.

By dawn order was restored and while Fairfax's officers took stock of the situation, the men tended to the wounded. Torrington was in Parliament's hands. It had not been a decisive victory, but the effect on Royalist morale in the region was both significant and instantaneous. It certainly marked the beginning of the end for the King's cause in the South-West. Hopton pulled back to Stratton, where he was ordered to make a stand. He was not put to the test, for Fairfax elected to march towards Launceston, and thence to Bodmin. He reached the small Cornish town on 2 March, and that night the Prince of Wales, accompanied by Hyde and Culpeper, set sail in the *Phoenix* to the Isles of Scilly. Meanwhile, Hopton's force was slowly disintegrating as it was being pressed back towards Truro. On 8 March he sent nearly a thousand men into Pendennis Castle in a last-ditch attempt to keep the Royalist flag flying in Cornwall. Four days later he surrendered and agreed to disband the Royalist western army and take himself abroad. Frustratingly for Fairfax, his attempts to get John Arundell, the governor in Pendennis, to surrender proved futile and he was compelled to leave a portion of his force to conduct a siege of the place.

On 25 March Fairfax was received like a hero in Plymouth, where '300 pieces of ordnance discharged to welcome him thither'.[15] While at Exeter, Hardress Waller had maintained a close cordon on the city and when the heavy guns had arrived from Lyme, they were put to immediate use against the walls. Fairfax arrived back at Crediton on 29 March, and two days later he marched his entire (available) force to the hills to the north of the city. With every man in view of the north wall and castle, Fairfax summoned Berkeley to surrender. It was enough to convince Berkeley that further resistance was futile. By 9 April the negotiations ended, and the surrender took place four days later. The terms were surprisingly favourable, highlighting perhaps a tacit understanding that the civil struggle was

---

10 Ibid., p. 112.
11 Fairfax, *Sir Thomas Fairfax letter*, p. 3.
12 Carte, op. cit., p. 112.

13 Sprigge, op. cit., pp. 195–6.
14 Ibid., p. 196.
15 Ibid., p. 240.

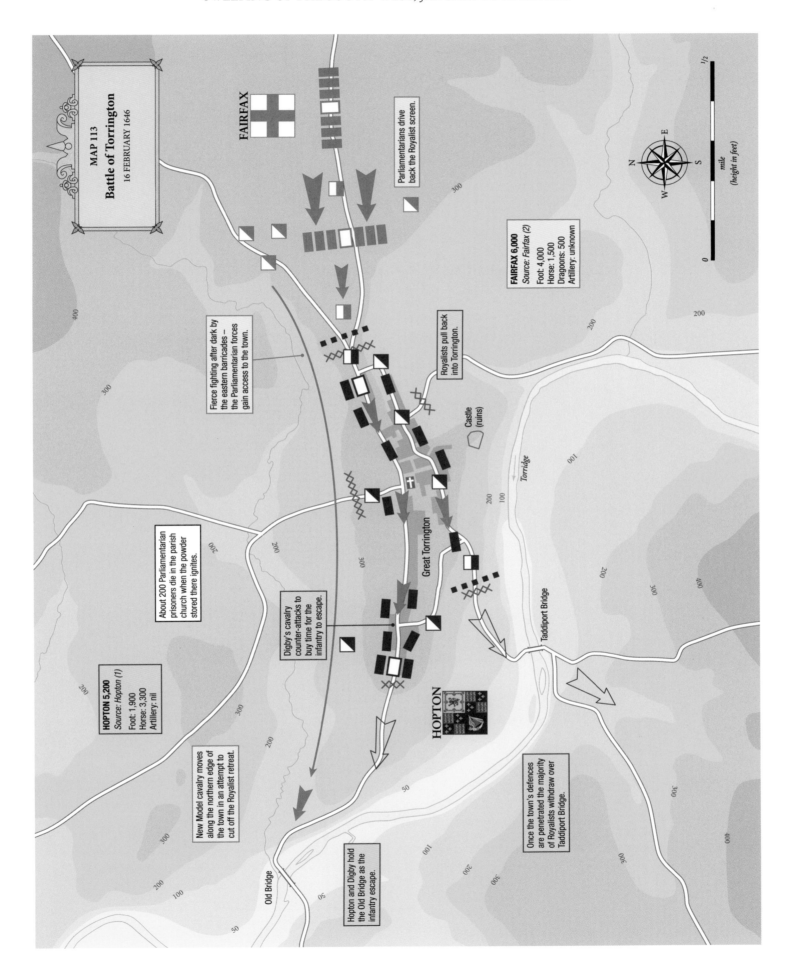

FAIRFAX

MAP 113
Battle of Torrington
16 FEBRUARY 1646

Parliamentarians drive back the Royalist screen.

FAIRFAX 6,000
Source: Fairfax (2)
Foot: 4,000
Horse: 1,500
Dragoons: 500
Artillery: unknown

Fierce fighting after dark by the eastern barricades – the Parliamentarian forces gain access to the town.

Royalists pull back into Torrington.

Castle (ruins)

Great Torrington

Torridge

Taddiport Bridge

About 200 Parliamentarian prisoners die in the parish church when the powder stored there ignites.

Digby's cavalry counter-attacks to buy time for the infantry to escape.

New Model cavalry moves along the northern edge of the town in an attempt to cut off the Royalist retreat.

HOPTON 5,200
Source: Hopton (1)
Foot: 1,900
Horse: 3,300
Artillery: nil

HOPTON

Once the town's defences are penetrated the majority of Royalists withdraw over Taddiport Bridge.

Old Bridge

Hopton and Digby hold the Old Bridge as the infantry escape.

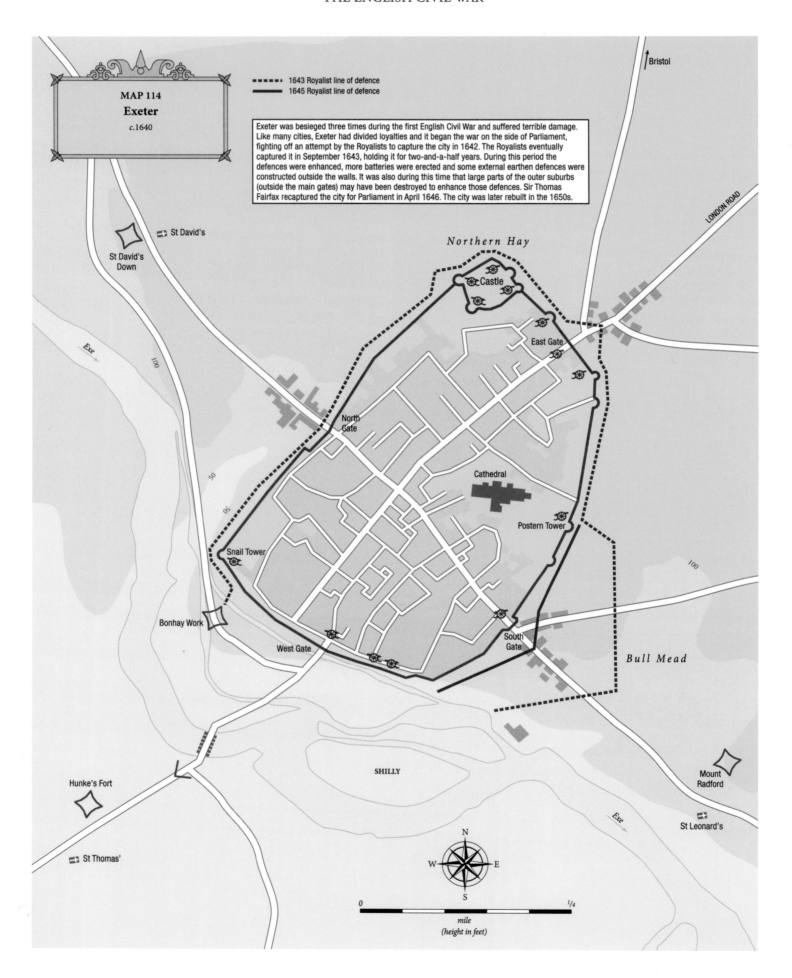

- - - - 1643 Royalist line of defence
——— 1645 Royalist line of defence

MAP 114
Exeter
c.1640

Exeter was besieged three times during the first English Civil War and suffered terrible damage. Like many cities, Exeter had divided loyalties and it began the war on the side of Parliament, fighting off an attempt by the Royalists to capture the city in 1642. The Royalists eventually captured it in September 1643, holding it for two-and-a-half years. During this period the defences were enhanced, more batteries were erected and some external earthen defences were constructed outside the walls. It was also during this time that large parts of the outer suburbs (outside the main gates) may have been destroyed to enhance those defences. Sir Thomas Fairfax recaptured the city for Parliament in April 1646. The city was later rebuilt in the 1650s.

Bristol

LONDON ROAD

Northern Hay

Castle

St David's

St David's Down

Exe

100

East Gate

50

North Gate

50

Cathedral

Postern Tower

100

Snail Tower

Bonhay Work

West Gate

South Gate

Bull Mead

SHILLY

Hunke's Fort

Mount Radford

Exe

St Thomas'

St Leonard's

N
W E
S

0   1/4
mile
(height in feet)

coming to an end. There was more to lose than be gained by harsh terms or treatment at this juncture. On 13 April the garrison marched out with their arms and full honours, and assurances were given for the protection of civilians and property (including churches). Princess Henrietta and her household were also given full liberty to pass.[16] Fairfax was not there to witness the ceremony; he had departed with a large force to summon Barnstaple, which capitulated on 20 April. The next day Fairfax was on the move again, back towards the Royalist capital, in order to orchestrate the siege of Oxford. With the exception of the fortress at Pendennis, the South-West was in Parliament's hands.

16 Anon, *The Articles of Exeter*.

CHAPTER 33

THE END OF THE FIRST CIVIL WAR, 1646

By early 1646 the war in England was almost at an end. The first Royalist bastion to fall was the great city of Chester. Byron had delayed repeated summonses by Brereton throughout January, but as any hope of relief faded, he negotiated surrender. On 3 February the garrison marched out and retreated through north Wales to Caernarfon.[1] Brereton appointed Colonel Michael Jones as the governor and left a garrison of 1,500 foot and 200 horse within the city.[2] Leaving a number of troops to blockade the many Royalist castles in north Wales, he then marched with his army towards Stafford and Lichfield where Royalist resistance continued. Brereton wrote:

> We have sent a strong party consisting of three Chesh. foot coys under Col. Massey and one of Col. Mytton's under Lt. Col. Twisteton, who have blocked up Hawarden Cas. And secured those passages, and they are likewise seconded by the regts of Chesh. And the Derbysh. horse. We have sent another party this day [14 January] to block up Holt…[3]

Any hopes that these Welsh strongholds would yield quickly were soon dashed. Harwarden held out until mid-March, while Holt hung on until January the following year.

Brereton met with no serious armed resistance at Stafford and quickly moved on to Lichfield, where Sir Thomas Tyldesley had prepared the garrison for a far more serious defence. Brereton captured the city on 9 March and began a siege of The Close which lasted four months.[4] He established his headquarters on the high ground to the north and erected a number of earthworks. A more recent history of the County of Stafford noted that:

> The central spire of the cathedral was used by the royalists as a vantage point, and when they also flaunted regimental colours and officers' sashes from it on May Day, it became a symbol of resistance in the eyes of the parliamentarians. Brereton also believed that it not only contained the powder magazine but also housed 'their ladies and grandees'. He subjected it to five days' bombardment, and on 12 May it collapsed.[5]

However, Lichfield Close was to hold out for another two months, the garrison of 84 officers and 700 soldiers finally surrendering on 10 July.

Jacob Astley had replaced the decidedly unpopular Charles Gerard as commander of Royalist forces in Wales. Astley was not to disappoint the King, for he not only sorted out the many Royalist garrisons, but he also raised a force of 3,000 horse and foot from Wales and Worcestershire. It was to be the last Royalist field army of the First Civil War. In March, Astley departed at the head of this force, destined for Oxford, where he was to link up with the King's forces there. The Committee of Both Kingdoms wrote to Colonel Birch at Hereford on 2 March:

> We are informed that Sir Jacob Astley continues upon the borders of Herefordshire daily plundering and raising contribution upon the country, whereby he supports himself and hinders the supply that otherwise would come to your garrison. We have designed several forces under the command of Col. Morgan to endeavour the breaking of those [Royalist] forces, and desire you to send to his rendezvous by the 16th inst. 500 or 600 horse and foot, or more if you can spare them, to receive his orders for this service.[6]

Roundhead intelligence had been monitoring Astley for some time, but realizing the size of the Royalist force they sent word to Brereton for the assistance of his horse and despatched colonels Fleetwood and Waller into west Oxfordshire with about a thousand horse.

Birch joined Morgan at Gloucester on 15 March. Their combined forces numbered about 1,700 and this force was further supplemented by 600 men from the Evesham garrison.[7] Astley was aware that a Roundhead force was manoeuvring to intercept him, and he spent a few days trying to evade it. Morgan decided to pull back to Chipping Campden on 19 March, leaving spies to watch the river crossings. It was a risky strategy, for Morgan was not entirely sure that Astley's intentions were for Lichfield or Oxford.[8] However, Astley took the bait and early the next day Morgan received timely intelligence that Astley was crossing at Bidford-on-Avon. He sent word to Fleetwood and Brereton, requesting urgent support from the latter. Morgan and Birch monitored the stronger Royalist force crossing the vale and advancing south, but declined battle when they began their ascent on Broadway Hill. Instead a number of skirmishers were sent out to delay the Royalist vanguard to buy time. Morgan recalled, 'the Lord Astley still continuing his march, and Sir W. Brereton not come up, was forced to hold him in action for the space of four Hours, Skirmishing with parties, and keeping my body drawn up in the most advantageous place for pursuit in case he should pass me'.[9] By 9am Astley's force was at the top of Broadway Hill, but keen not to lose large numbers of men in a general engagement, he remained a respectable distance and gave orders for his force to move around the right flank of Morgan's men.

Morgan appears to have let them go and then, at about 3pm, he followed with a view to attacking them in the rear. Morgan wrote in his post-battle despatch:

> I resolved to pursue, thinking it more advantageous to follow upon his rear, then at that time to draw out to meet him in the field; and in my

---

1 Byron was forced into exile in June 1646 after an attempt on his life. He died in 1652, childless, in Paris.

2 *County of Chester*, vol. V, Part 1, p. 5.

3 Dore, *Letter Books of William Brereton*, vol. II., letter 1246, p. 522.

4 'The Close' is a historic set of medieval buildings surrounding Lichfield Cathedral.

5 *County of Stafford*, vol. 14, p. 19.

6 *CSPD* 2 March 1946.

7 Webb, *Military memoire Colonel John Birch*, p. 34.

8 R. S., *Battell fought at Stow in the Would*, p. A2.

9 Morgan, *Morgan Governor of Glocester's letter*, p. 4.

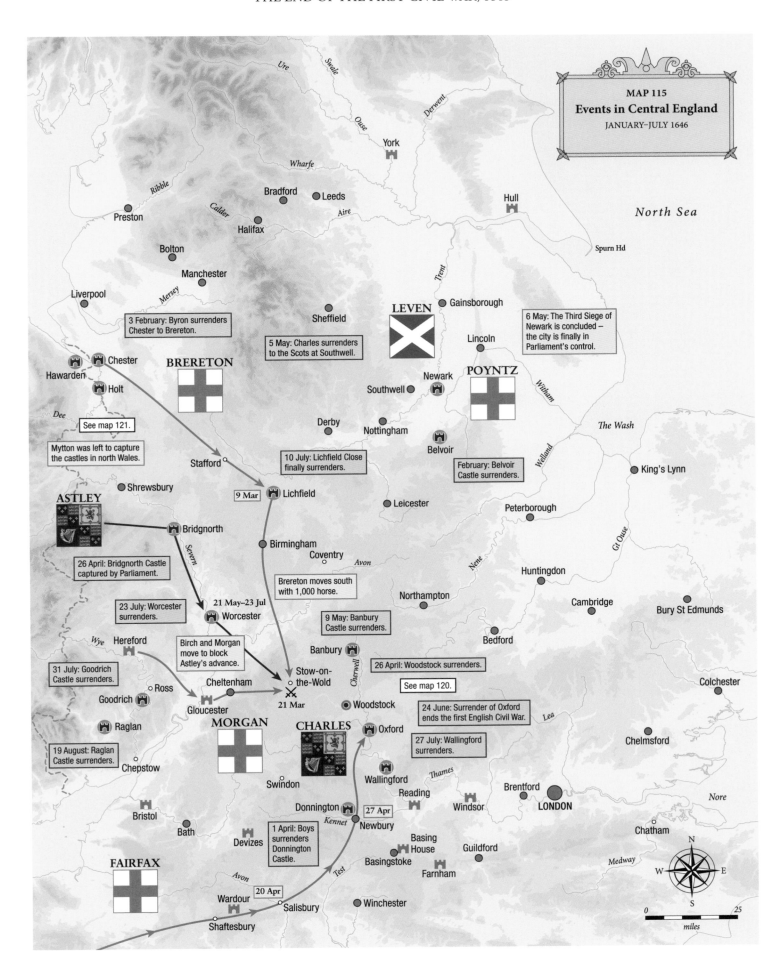

MAP 115
Events in Central England
JANUARY–JULY 1646

North Sea

Spurn Hd

York

Hull

Ure

Swale

Ouse

Derwent

Wharfe

Bradford

Leeds

Aire

Preston

Ribble

Calder

Halifax

Bolton

Manchester

Liverpool

Mersey

Sheffield

Gainsborough

LEVEN

Lincoln

6 May: The Third Siege of
Newark is concluded –
the city is finally in
Parliament's control.

5 May: Charles surrenders
to the Scots at Southwell.

3 February: Byron surrenders
Chester to Brereton.

Chester

BRERETON

Newark

POYNTZ

Southwell

Trent

Witham

Hawarden

Holt

Dee

Derby

Nottingham

Belvoir

February: Belvoir
Castle surrenders.

The Wash

See map 121.

Mytton was left to capture
the castles in north Wales.

Stafford

Shrewsbury

ASTLEY

9 Mar Lichfield

10 July: Lichfield Close
finally surrenders.

Leicester

King's Lynn

Welland

Peterborough

Gt Ouse

Bridgnorth

Severn

26 April: Bridgnorth Castle
captured by Parliament.

Birmingham

Coventry

Avon

Brereton moves south
with 1,000 horse.

Northampton

Nene

Huntingdon

Cambridge

Bury St Edmunds

Bedford

23 July: Worcester
surrenders.

21 May–23 Jul
Worcester

9 May: Banbury
Castle surrenders.

Wye

Hereford

Birch and Morgan
move to block
Astley's advance.

Cheltenham

Banbury

26 April: Woodstock surrenders.

Colchester

31 July: Goodrich
Castle surrenders.

Ross

Goodrich

Stow-on-
the-Wold

Cherwell

See map 120.

Gloucester

21 Mar

Woodstock

24 June: Surrender of Oxford
ends the first English Civil War.

Lea

Chelmsford

Raglan

MORGAN

CHARLES

Oxford

27 July: Wallingford
surrenders.

19 August: Raglan
Castle surrenders.

Chepstow

Swindon

Wallingford

Thames

Reading

Brentford

LONDON

Nore

Donnington

27 Apr

Newbury

Windsor

Bristol

Kennet

1 April: Boys
surrenders
Donnington
Castle.

Basing
House

Guildford

Chatham

Bath

Devizes

Basingstoke

Farnham

Medway

FAIRFAX

Avon

Test

Winchester

N

W   E

S

Wardour

20 Apr

Salisbury

Shaftesbury

0   25

miles

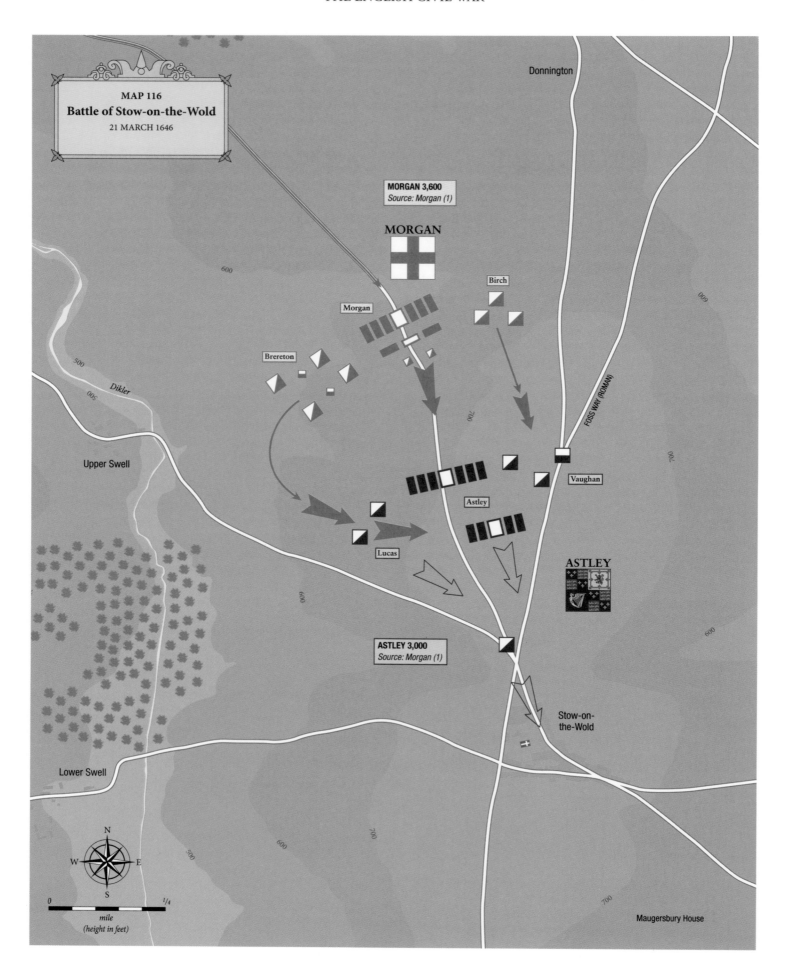

MAP 116
Battle of Stow-on-the-Wold
21 MARCH 1646

Donnington

MORGAN 3,600
Source: Morgan (1)

MORGAN

Morgan

Birch

Brereton

FOSS WAY (ROMAN)

Vaughan

Astley

Upper Swell

Lucas

ASTLEY

ASTLEY 3,000
Source: Morgan (1)

Dikler

600

500

500

700

600

700

700

600

Stow-on-the-Wold

Lower Swell

600

700

500

N
W   E
S

0   1/4

mile
(height in feet)

Maugersbury House

pursuit Sir William Brereton came up with 800 horse (of whom I desired to receive orders, but he referred the whole command of the field to me) then being equal in number to the Lord Astley's force.[10]

The Parliamentarians marched for the rest of the day and through the night. Morgan had received intelligence that some Royalist horse from Oxford were about 7 miles from Stow-on-the-Wold, and he hastened to make an attack on their rearguard.[11] As they advanced south, they discovered Astley deployed for battle facing his pursuers on a piece of open land north of Stow. The Parliamentarians deployed facing them. Morgan led the vanguard in the centre, consisting of 400 horse and 200 foot, with the balance of foot to his rear, while Brereton with his 800 horse and dragoons were on the right and the balance of the Gloucester and Hereford Horse on the left under Birch.[12] The two sides then stood off (for about an hour) waiting for first light.

Morgan appears to have spearheaded the attack with his vanguard, followed by a two-pronged cavalry advance, and then charged, on both the left and right. Birch, who had his horse shot from beneath him, recalled that 'hott it was for a while; their reformadoes standing stoutly to it' and the report in the *Moderate Intelligencer* confirmed that 'the dispute was hot, and the Parliament's forces were worsted twice, yet so as some maintained the fight, while others rallied'.[13] It went on to note that 'at last a party, not very numerous, took courage, charged home and routed the enemy'. It appears that Morgan broke the Royalists in the centre after a fierce struggle, and then 'Brereton with our right wing of Horse charged their left of Horse and Foot, and totally routed them, pursuing them into Stow'.[14] Over 1,500 men were killed or captured and there is some evidence that 200 were slain as they surrendered in the town.[15] One of the captured was Astley, of whom John Vicars, a schoolmaster, poetaster, and polemic, wrote: 'Astley being taken captive and wearied in this fight… the soldiers brought him a drum to sit and rest himself upon', which once he had sat he addressed the soldiers, '"Gentlemen, yee may now sit downe and play, for you have done your worke, if you fall not out among your selves".'[16] Prophetic words indeed.[17]

The last battle of the First Civil War had been fought. Charles received the news with growing dejection. The next day he wrote to his Queen:

> Ill success, mean spirits and Montreuil's juggling, have so vexed me that I cannot give thee so clear or good account as I hoped… now I come to that which I believe will trouble thee, for I am sure it doth me most, which is the message I am now sending to London… that I am forced to hazard this upon mere necessity, having neither force to resist, nor sufficient to escape to any secure place, and yet I have not, nor (by the grace of God) will ever depart from my main grounds.[18]

As the days passed the news grew even gloomier. Sir John Boys had surrendered Donnington Castle in early April and then came the news of the fall of Exeter, Barnstaple and St Michael's Mount to Fairfax's New Model Army. The South-West had fallen, and the noose was tightening around Oxford and the surrounding garrisons of Wallingford, Woodstock, Banbury, Faringdon and Boarstall House (see map 120). On 26 April, the first garrison at Woodstock surrendered. With intelligence that Fairfax was marching on Oxford, Charles decided to escape from the city disguised as a servant. For over a week a charged atmosphere pervaded in London – 'the King had escaped, the King was not in the City'. Then came news that on 5 May the monarch had ridden into the Scottish headquarters at Southwell, and given himself up.

The Scots had established a camp in the area in late November the previous year. Leven had marched south towards Newark with a large force, in order to establish a cordon around the Royalists' second major city. While waiting for other Parliamentarian forces that were en route, the Scots attacked the bridge at Muskham and captured it a few days later. They quickly dislodged the Royalists in the sconce covering the bridge, and forced them back, ceding the 'Island', upon which the Scots quickly established themselves. In early December, Poyntz and Rossiter had also moved to the area, having left a not inconsiderable force to maintain the cordon at Belvoir Castle. The Parliamentarians moved to the south and east of Newark, but the cordon was far from watertight. Furthermore, since the last siege (March 1644), the Royalists had constructed two large sconces on the east bank of the River Trent (the Queen's Sconce to the south and the King's Sconce to the north) as well as a whole host of other earthworks, 'so that the whole town seemed almost invincible (as it was defensible) because it was so well defended with men, arms, ammunition, and artillery'.[19] Inside the city, the recently installed governor, Henry Lord Belasyse, had a force of nearly a thousand horse (for foraging purposes), 3,000 infantry and about another 1,000 townsfolk, all armed and eager.[20]

The Royalists were not shy in taking the fight to the Parliamentarians and Scots. In December they fell on Rossiter's quarters to the south, but were beaten off. In January, it was Poyntz's turn, when a Royalist party sallied out to Farndon and took a hundred prisoners. Poyntz was forced to defend himself at the point of the sword, before the attackers were driven back. Then in February, Belasyse tried to recapture the bridge at Muskham from the Scots, but the attackers were repulsed after a fierce fight that lasted many hours. More Scottish troops arrived from Yorkshire in January, and additional Parliamentarian troops continued to trickle in from the Eastern Association over the same period. However, the capture of Belvoir Castle, in early February, freed another 1,000 men and a heavy mortar, which had been called up from Reading. The arrival of additional forces enabled Poyntz to close the cordon and build a line of defences on the east bank. The first line was started in early February and completed in the third week of March. At the same time the Scots fortified the Island, constructing a huge camp which they called 'Edinburgh'. A second, more concerted attack by the Royalists towards the Scottish positions around Muskham bridge in early March highlighted the need for better communication with the Island, and an additional bridge of boats was built at Crankley Point. It was further strengthened by the construction of a large sconce, and a pinnace armed with two small guns and 40 musketeers was brought up the river.[21]

10 Ibid., pp. 4–5.
11 Morgan, *A true relation by Colonell Morgan*, p. 5.
12 I have this information from Simon Marsh who has studied the battle in depth.
13 Birch, ibid., p. 35. *Moderate Intelligencer* report 23 March 1646, p. 359.
14 R.S., op. cit., p. A4.
15 Birch, op. cit. and *Moderate Intelligencer*, op. cit.
16 Vicars, *The burning-bush*, p. 399.
17 Hyett, *The Last battle*, pp. 37–42.
18 Bruce, *Charles I in 1646*, pp. 27–8. Jean de Montreuil was a young diplomat who had been sent by Charles to deal with the Scots Commissioners in London and Edinburgh.

19 Franck, *Northern Memoirs*, pp. 269–70.
20 Wood, *Nottinghamshire*, p. 107. The former governor, Sir Richard Willys, had resigned his position in support of Prince Rupert in October 1645.
21 Ibid., p. 110.

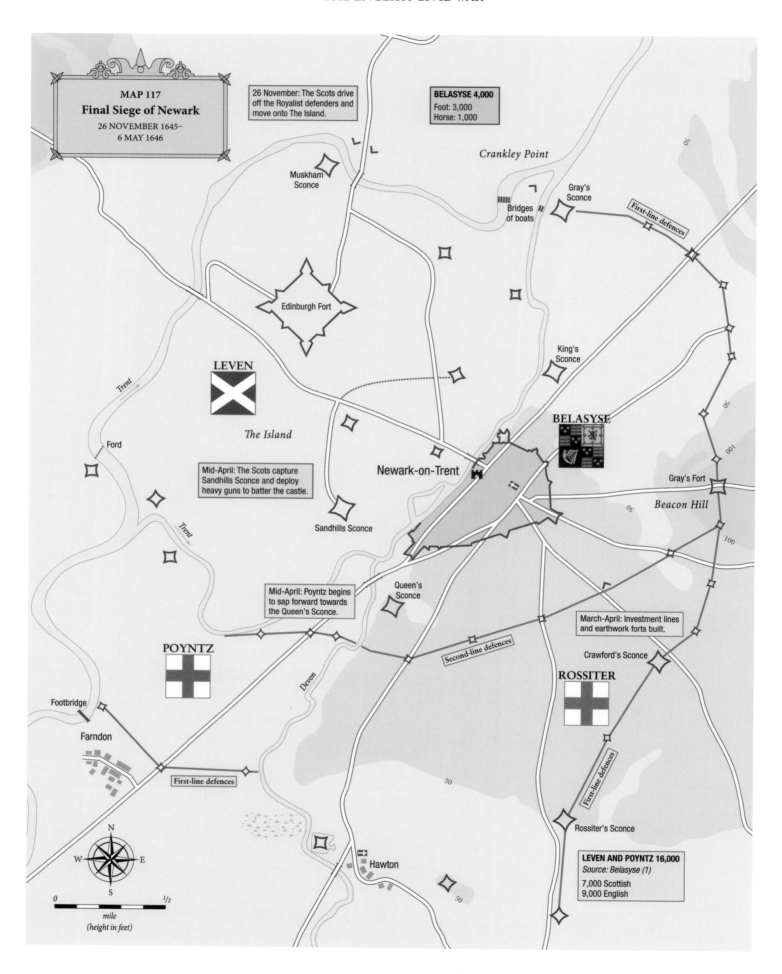

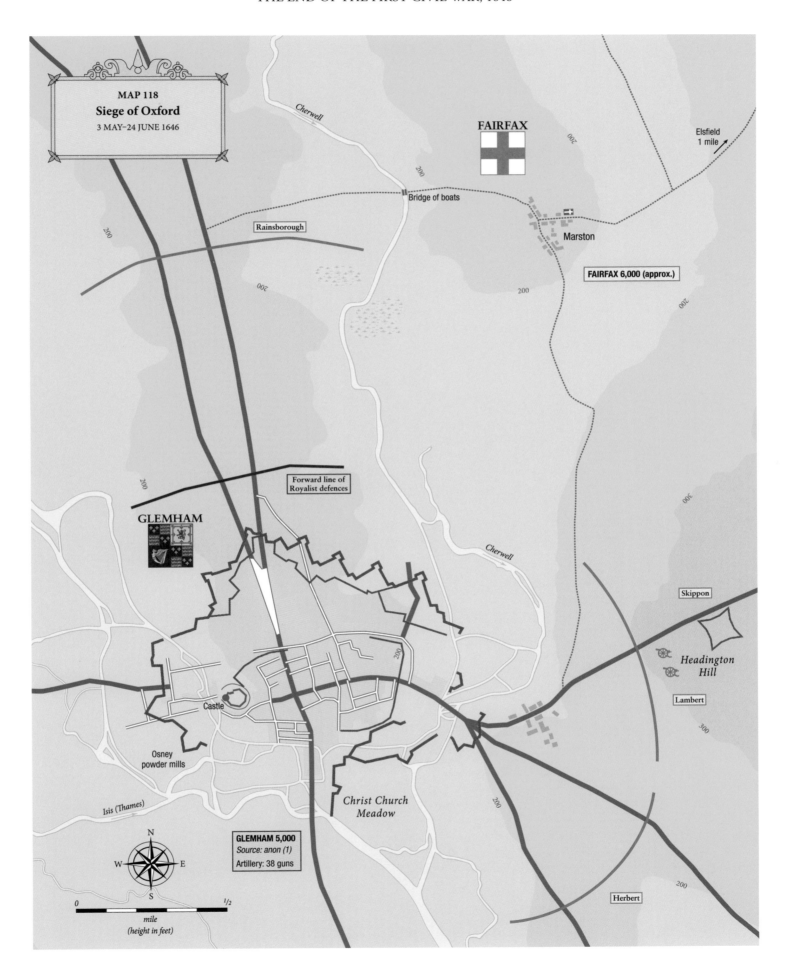

MAP 118
Siege of Oxford
3 MAY–24 JUNE 1646

FAIRFAX

Elsfield
1 mile

Cherwell

Bridge of boats

Rainsborough

Marston

FAIRFAX 6,000 (approx.)

Forward line of
Royalist defences

GLEMHAM

Cherwell

Skippon

Headington
Hill

Lambert

Castle

Osney
powder mills

Isis (Thames)

Christ Church
Meadow

Herbert

GLEMHAM 5,000
Source: anon (1)
Artillery: 38 guns

N
W   E
S

0   1/2

mile
(height in feet)

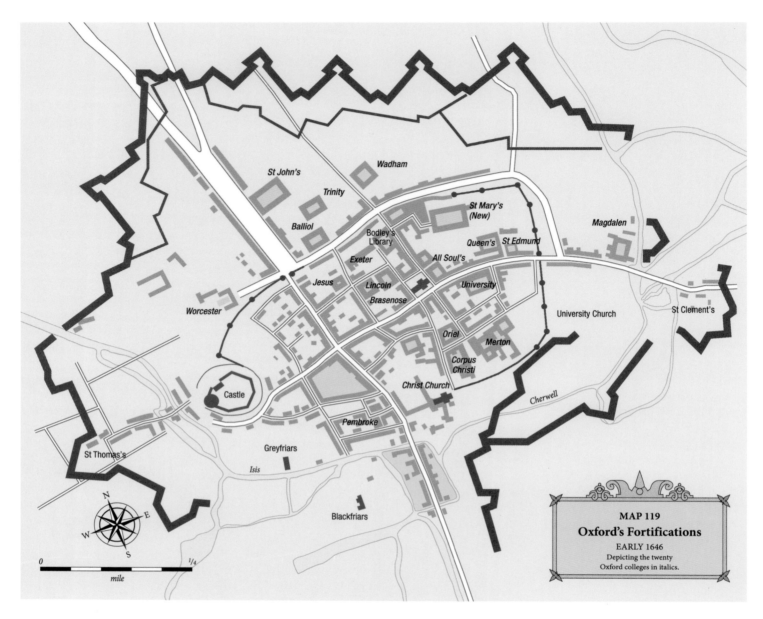

St John's

Wadham

Trinity

St Mary's
(New)

Balliol

Magdalen

Bodley's
Library

Queen's   St Edmund

Exeter

All Soul's

Jesus

Lincoln

University

Worcester

Brasenose

University Church

St Clement's

Oriel

Merton

Corpus
Christi

Castle

Christ Church

Cherwell

Pembroke

Greyfriars

St Thomas's

Isis

Blackfriars

MAP 119
Oxford's Fortifications
EARLY 1646
Depicting the twenty
Oxford colleges in italics.

0   1/4

mile

By the end of March, Newark was tightly invested, and the siege ordnance began to arrive in considerable quantities. It was placed in the earthwork forts and batteries positioned every few hundred yards from the town's perimeter. On 28 March, Poyntz summoned Belasyse to surrender. He responded by asking for a 'pass' for some of his officers to go to the King, so that 'I may know His Majesties pleasure whether according to his letter, he will wind up the business in general, or leave me to steer my own course'.[22] He was refused and the Parliamentarians stepped up their siege works and began their bombardment. By mid-April the course of the River Trent had been diverted and Parliament's engineers had constructed a battery south of the Queen's Sconce, from where they began sapping forward towards the massive defensive earthwork.[23] Meanwhile, the Scots had captured the Sandhills Sconce and placed heavy guns into it and began to batter the west face of the castle. Belasyse was aware that separate negotiations were ongoing between the King and Edinburgh on the one

hand, and the King and Westminster on the other.[24] At some stage in early April he received word from Charles allowing him to negotiate for the surrender of Newark, if the King had not appeared before the Scots' camp before 4 or 5 May.[25] While he waited for events elsewhere to play out he continued to conduct the defence amidst a backdrop of malnutrition, fever and plague. By the end of April, the English and Scots were within musket range of the walls and Poyntz sent in a second summons. Belasyse agreed to parley, planning to drag out proceedings in order to meet the King's timeline. The King arrived at Southwell on 5 May as he had projected, but his negotiations with the Scots did not go well. In order to ingratiate himself with his captors, Charles agreed to give up the town of Newark as a gesture of good faith. Terms were agreed at midnight on 6 May, and the Royalist garrison marched out two days later. Only Oxford and Worcester remained for the King.

On 4 April Fairfax had despatched Ireton's regiments from the New Model Army to march directly to Oxford and join the forces assembling

22 Belasyse, *Reducing of Newark* p. 8.

23 Poyntz tried to divert the course of the river by damming it; he hoped to stop the mills in the town producing corn and gunpowder and to force the townsfolk to rely on wells for their drinking water.

24 Wood, op. cit., p. 113.

25 Ibid., p. 115.

there for the siege of the city. Fairfax arrived before Oxford on 1 May, having learned of the King's escape while en route, and immediately commenced preparations for a siege. In the preceding days, Royalist troops from all over the country had been trickling into the city, including the garrison from Woodstock and 700 men under John Berkeley, who had marched from Exeter. Oxford was not an easy objective; the rivers Isis and Cherwell made the approaches on three sides most troublesome. Furthermore, while Woodstock may have been captured, there remained the Royalist ring of garrisons at Radcot, Faringdon, Wallingford and Boarstall House – see map 120. Whereupon Fairfax, having satisfied himself that the outer garrisons were isolated, concluded that Oxford was 'no place to be taken at a running pull, but likely rather to prove a business of time, hazard, and industry'.[26] Fairfax may have deliberately exaggerated the complexity of the task, for the war was all but over, and he was reluctant to lose further lives and the fabric of the celebrated city.[27]

The New Model Army moved towards the city on 2 May, and the following day Fairfax conducted a council of war. It was decided that a large fortification would be erected atop Headington Hill, sufficient to quarter 3,000 men; another quarter was to be established to the north of Oxford; and a bridge was to be built over the River Cherwell near Marston in order to maintain communication with the forces astride the river. The artillery train was placed at Elsfield, a mile or so from Marston village, where Fairfax established himself, not for the first time, in the house of Unton Croke.[28] An enormous amount of siege equipment was provided to Fairfax's men, including 500 barrels of gunpowder, 1,000 granadoes, 600 mortar shells, 30 tons of shot, 40 tons of match, 200 ladders and nearly 2,000 entrenching tools.[29] Construction of the siege lines was exhaustive drudgery, and to complicate matters, many Parliamentarian soldiers had been detached to contain the numerous Royalist garrisons surrounding Oxford. Sprigge noted:

> … several forces were taken forth and designed for the blocking up of other garrisons, viz. some for Farringdon, under the command of colonel sir Robert Pye; others for Radcot, under the command of colonel Cook; and others for Wallingford, under the command of colonel Paine and colonel Barkestend on Berkshire side, and colonel Temple on Oxfordshire side; others for Borstal-house.[30]

Inside the city, the garrison commander Sir Thomas Glemham had about 5,000 regular troops as well as the regiments raised from the many colleges and townsfolk (Town and Gown) providing, perhaps, another 2,500 men and women. In terms of artillery, 'the defenders had thirty-eight pieces of ordnance, whereof twenty-six were of brass, seventy barrels of powder in his magazine, and two powder mills at Osney, which brought in a daily supply of powder. Furthermore, the city was provisioned for six months'.[31] Fairfax was undoubtedly correct in urging caution, and despite his other commitments around Oxfordshire, the construction of the siege works continued under cannon shot from the city and from the Royalist batteries at Magdalen Bridge and St Clements. By 11 May the lines were complete

on the east side of the city, and Fairfax sent in a summons to Glemham. The Oxford commander asked for more time and explicitly for two messengers to be allowed to leave and seek the King's guidance on the matter. On 12 May the Parliamentarian trumpeter, who had been sent in to the town, returned with the message that there were 'besides the duke of York and the two princes, many other persons of eminency, lords, knights, and parliament (members of the Junto) men, and other gentry and clergy, besides the inhabitants, all concerned in the business' so that he could not possibly bring the negotiation to a rapid conclusion.[32] Fairfax had been alerted to the presence of Prince Rupert within the city the day prior, when he made a sortie out of the north gate and ended up embroiled in a firefight with Rainsborough's infantry. Dugdale recalled that Prince Rupert was 'pickering in ye fields on N. of Oxford, was shot in ye upper parte of ye arme, being the first wound he ever yet received'.[33]

Fairfax realized he would have to turn up the heat and, on 13 May, proceedings opened when the first shot was fired from the cannon in the large fort on Headington Hill. It landed with little ceremony in Christ Church meadow, but the next rounds began to creep towards the college and town buildings. It was enough. Two days later Glemham sent word to Fairfax offering to negotiate. For Glemham, agreeing to parley was the easy bit, for he was not acting as merely the military governor of a city but representing the interests of the King's Privy Council. Within the walls over the preceding days, tempers had flared, and while the military were against any form of capitulation, Glemham required the endorsement of the Privy Council as justification to either continue discussions, or to continue their defence. Unable to circle the square, Glemham decided to negotiate and maintain the defence. On 18 May, the two Royalist and Parliamentarian delegations met at Unton Croke's house (in Marston, where Fairfax was lodging) to discuss terms. Initial attempts broke down and were adjourned until 22 May. These also broke down, the Royalists claiming that Fairfax's demands were unreasonable. Over the next two weeks, negotiations were interspersed with exchanges of cannon shot and some low-level sallies. A round shot from Magdalen bridge battery killed Colonel Cotsworth on Headington Hill. Meanwhile, Fairfax's engineers considered ways to divert some of the many water channels surrounding the city to force the defenders to capitulate without bloodshed.

It is clear from correspondence from Fairfax to his father (at Bath) that the city accepted the inevitable and it was just a matter of time. He wrote on 13 June, 'Our treaty doth still continue… We think Monday will conclude all the rest. I think they do really desire to conclude with us.'[34] Discontent within the city, between the civil and military administrations, seems to have abated when the contents of a letter, sent by the King from Newcastle in mid-May, was printed and distributed. It contained orders instructing the Oxford commanders to make reasonable terms and stop the effusion of blood of 'our' subjects.[35] On 20 June the articles had been signed, agreeing to hand over the city at 10am on 24 June. The Duke of York was to be escorted to join the other members of the royal family in London. Princes Rupert and Maurice were given passes to remain in the country (but not London) for six months before they would receive their passes to depart. Glemham and his garrison were able to leave with full honours and, at a point 15 miles from the city, lay down their arms and disperse. Most significantly, the Great Seal and other

26 Sprigge, *Anglia Rediviva*, p. 257.

27 Barratt, *Cavalier Capital*, p. 197.

28 This house still stands (I can see it from my study window as I pen this text) and is known as 'Cromwell's House'. In fact, Cromwell had his quarters at Wheatley.

29 Barratt, op. cit., p. 199.

30 Sprigge, op. cit., p. 258.

31 Rigaud, *Lines formed round Oxford*, pp. 374–5.

32 Sprigge, op. cit., p. 263.

33 Varley, *The Siege of Oxford*, p. 136.

34 Bell, *Correspondence of the Fairfax family*, p. 294.

35 Hamper (ed.), *William Dugdale*, pp. 89–90.

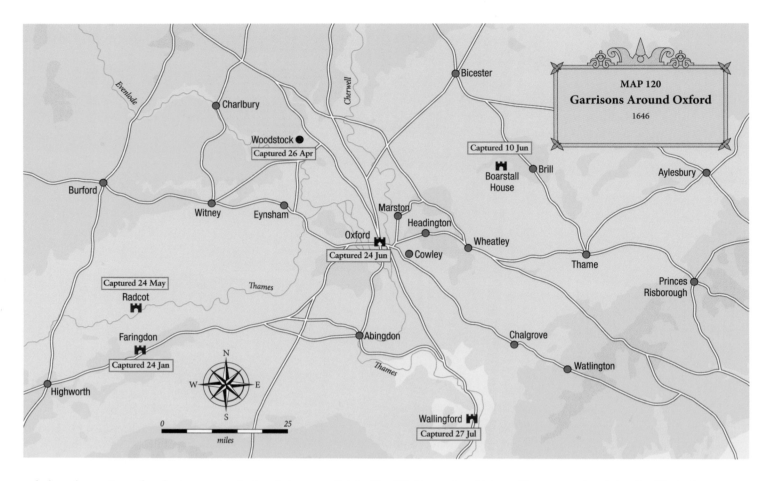

symbols and trappings of authority were to be handed over to Fairfax.[36] It was all hugely significant.

Following his victory over Astley at Stow-on-the-Wold, Morgan moved towards Worcester, 'The Faithful City', and summoned the governor, Colonel Henry Washington, to surrender. Washington rejected the summons, confident that Parliament's priority was Oxford, and that the finite siege resources were destined for the Royalist capital. He was also all too aware that such a respite was temporary, and he used the time to resupply the city's stores, collect timber and firewood from Shrawley Wood and clear the ground outside the walls, pulling down St Oswald's hospital.[37] On 16 May Fairfax wrote to Washington once again, requesting him to see common sense, avoid bloodshed and surrender. Washington, acutely conscious of his reputation as a professional soldier, once again refused. The siege began three days later amidst considerable concern among the civil population. Of the 6,000 inhabitants, many considered that

Washington's ambition paid scant regard to their safety. The Parliamentarians established a camp to the north-east of the city and on the west bank of the River Severn near the suburb of St John's (see map 154). In June they completed their encirclement to the north by building a bridge of boats, but any hope that news of the surrender of Oxford was going to bring a swift end to the siege at Worcester were quickly dashed. The siege dragged on into July, with conditions growing steadily worse within the walls. Finally, with powder running dangerously low, terms were finally agreed on 23 July. Following a moving service in the cathedral, the garrison marched out. Four days later the last of the outlying Oxford garrisons at Wallingford Castle surrendered to Fairfax, and on the last day of July the garrison at Goodrich Castle marched out to the tune of 'Sir Henry Lingen's Fancy'.[38] In England, only Pendennis Castle in Cornwall and Raglan Castle in Monmouthshire remained defiant for the Royalist cause. They were both to fall within weeks.

36 Anon, *Surrender of Oxford & Farringdon*, pp. 3–16.
37 Willis Bund, *Worcestershire*, p. 178.
38 Barratt, *Sieges of the English Civil Wars*, p. 117.

CHAPTER 34

WALES, SCOTLAND AND IRELAND IN 1646

The steady progress of Royalist collapse in England was mirrored in Wales, not through military action but by widespread disillusionment and desertion of the Royalist cause. Those who remained loyal were forced to retreat into the many castles. Those castles on the north Wales coast were particularly important, as they might yet serve as landing places for reinforcements from Ireland. But Charles's intentions towards Catholic Irish troops, and his dalliance with the Scots, was causing widespread discontent and anger among the Royalist core in Wales. Anger turned to action, and in 1645 county after county turned and petitioned the King. The replacement of the unpopular Charles Gerard, with the more understanding Jacob Astley, had done little to curb dissatisfaction with the King's strategies. In the south-west of Wales, Cardiganshire and Carmarthenshire followed Pembrokeshire in September 1645, in breaking away from the Royalist yoke; although the garrison at Aberystwyth Castle was to hold out until April the following year.

In central and north-eastern Wales, many of the castles and fortified houses changed hands many times. Even Montgomery Castle had briefly changed sides in 1645 when its governor, Sir John Price, had once again decided to support the King. He was to change his mind in July, a few weeks after the pivotal battle at Naseby. However, the loss of Chester was the beginning of the end for the Royalist cause in northern Wales. Many Welsh troops had fallen at the battle of Rowton Moor, and those that remained were stripped out by Charles during his final visit (following that battle) in late September 1645 (see chapter 31). Nevertheless, Parliament's task in north Wales was far from easy. Many of the fortresses dated from the English medieval conquest and were formidable structures. At the start of 1646, there were a considerable number still garrisoned by Royalist forces, including, Caernarfon,[1] Chirk, Conway, Rhuddlan, Flint, Holt, Harwarden, Ruthin, Denbigh and Harlech.

In 1643 Chirk Castle, which belonged to the Myddleton family, had been seized by forces loyal to the King. In mid-1646 Thomas Myddelton had successfully bribed the Royalist garrison to return control to him. Harwarden surrendered in March following the fall of Chester. However, the task facing Thomas Mytton, in reducing the remaining castles, was far from straightforward. Some of his commanders wrote to him in May outlining their difficulties:

> We have closely besieged Holt Castle, Denbigh, Carnarvon, and Flint, all places of exceeding great strength. Our forces are so many that all the countries under our command can hardly afford us provision. We are put to use our utmost skill to get maintenance this way; then you may judge how hard it is with us for want of pay, without which our soldiers will not continue patiently to go on in their hard and difficult duty that hitherto they have undergone.[2]

Mytton captured Caernarfon in early June, and two weeks later the Royalist defenders on Anglesey submitted to the Parliamentary commissioners sent there to discuss terms.

With Conway blockaded, Mytton was able to turn his attention to capturing the smaller fortresses. Rhuddlan Castle capitulated in July and Flint Castle was surrendered by Roger Mostyn on 24 August, but Denbigh Castle was a harder nut to crack. Mytton had summoned the governor, Colonel William Salusbury, a few days after the capture of Ruthin in April. His response left Mytton no choice but to commence the prosecution of a regular siege, and with a paucity of guns and equipment it was to be no easy task. As other castles fell, Mytton hoped that Salusbury would acknowledge the hopelessness of the Royalist situation and spare the town's inhabitants from further hardship. Salusbury sought guidance from his sovereign, and managed to get a messenger out through the cordon in late August. The man returned with a letter from the King (who was at this stage a prisoner of the Scots at Newcastle upon Tyne): 'I heartily thank you for your loyall constancie, and assure you that whensoever it shall please God to enable me to show my thankfullness to my friends. I will particularly remember you.'[3] Accompanying the letter was a Royal Warrant authorizing Salusbury to surrender the castle. Terms were agreed on 14 October and the garrison marched out 12 days later.

Mytton had stormed the town of Conway on 8 August, as one chronicler recorded:

> [He] surprised the main-guard, killed a corporal and a gentleman there, wounded many, took a major, one Capt. Wynne, an old cow-driver, four lieutenants, four ensigns, twenty-two soldiers of fortune, and fifty townsmen in arms. Many [Irish] were commanded to be tied back-to-back to be cast over-board, and sent by water to their own country![4]

Mytton summoned John Owen in the castle but was, once again, to be disappointed by his reply: 'as for your summons, I shall hold this castle as long as it pleaseth God, for his Majesty'.[5] Owen and his small garrison held out until 18 November but they were not the last castle in the north of Wales to finally succumb. Holt bridge (over the River Dee) had been secured for Parliament in December 1645, but the castle overlooking the crossing held out for the whole of 1646. Sir Richard Lloyd eventually accepted terms in January 1647. John Owen's younger brother William had the dubious honour of commanding the last of the Royalist castles in north Wales. Harlech was remote and access was difficult for heavier siege guns, but articles for surrender were finally agreed on 15 March 1647. Parliament finally had full control of Wales; it had been no easy task.

---

1 The Welsh spelling now used is Caernarfon.
2 Phillips, *Civil War in Wales*, vol. II, p. 306.

3 Ibid., p. 331.
4 Ibid., pp. 325–6.
5 Ibid., p. 327.

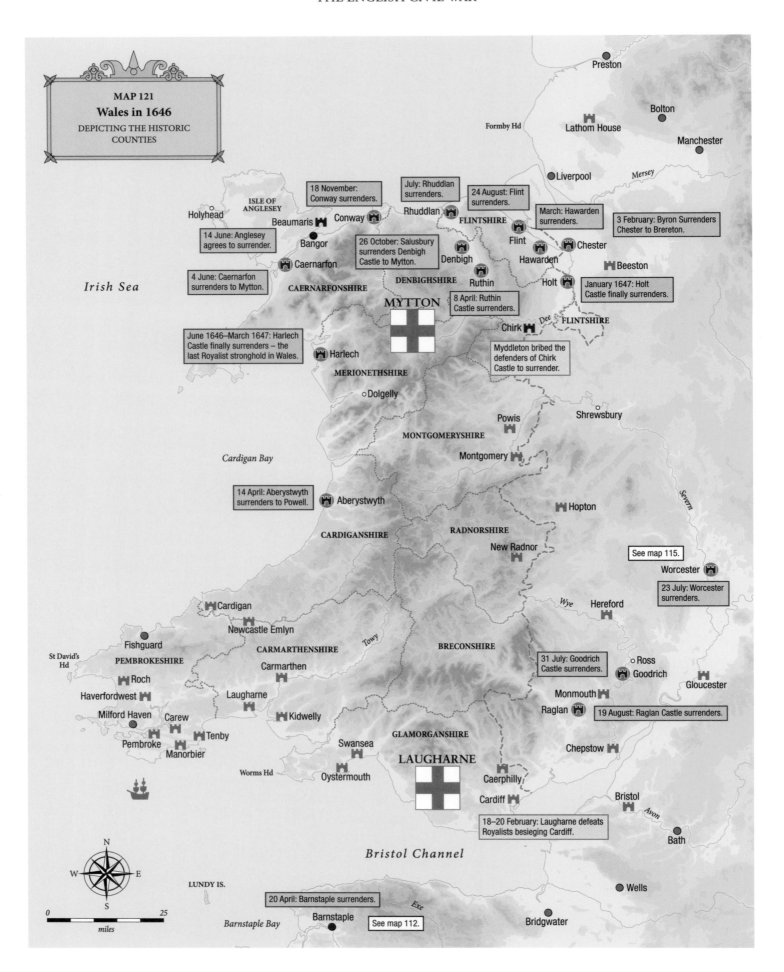

MAP 121
Wales in 1646
DEPICTING THE HISTORIC
COUNTIES

Preston

Bolton

Lathom House

Formby Hd

Manchester

ISLE OF
ANGLESEY

Liverpool

Mersey

Holyhead

18 November:
Conway surrenders.

July: Rhuddlan
surrenders.

24 August: Flint
surrenders.

March: Hawarden
surrenders.

3 February: Byron Surrenders
Chester to Brereton.

Beaumaris

Conway

Rhuddlan

FLINTSHIRE

Irish Sea

14 June: Anglesey
agrees to surrender.

Bangor

26 October: Salusbury
surrenders Denbigh
Castle to Mytton.

Denbigh

Flint

Hawarden

Chester

Caernarfon

CAERNARFONSHIRE

DENBIGHSHIRE

Ruthin

Holt

Beeston

January 1647: Holt
Castle finally surrenders.

4 June: Caernarfon
surrenders to Mytton.

MYTTON

8 April: Ruthin
Castle surrenders.

Chirk

Dee

FLINTSHIRE

June 1646–March 1647: Harlech
Castle finally surrenders – the
last Royalist stronghold in Wales.

Harlech

Myddleton bribed the
defenders of Chirk
Castle to surrender.

MERIONETHSHIRE

Dolgelly

Shrewsbury

Powis

Cardigan Bay

MONTGOMERYSHIRE

Montgomery

Severn

14 April: Aberystwyth
surrenders to Powell.

Aberystwyth

Hopton

CARDIGANSHIRE

RADNORSHIRE

New Radnor

See map 115.

Worcester

Wye

Hereford

23 July: Worcester
surrenders.

Cardigan

Newcastle Emlyn

St David's
Hd

Fishguard

Towy

BRECONSHIRE

31 July: Goodrich
Castle surrenders.

Ross

Goodrich

PEMBROKESHIRE

CARMARTHENSHIRE

Carmarthen

Gloucester

Roch

Haverfordwest

Laugharne

Kidwelly

Monmouth

Raglan

19 August: Raglan Castle surrenders.

Milford Haven

Carew

Tenby

GLAMORGANSHIRE

Chepstow

Pembroke

Manorbier

Swansea

LAUGHARNE

Caerphilly

Bristol

Worms Hd

Oystermouth

Cardiff

Avon

18–20 February: Laugharne defeats
Royalists besieging Cardiff.

Bath

Bristol Channel

N

W   E

S

LUNDY IS.

20 April: Barnstaple surrenders.

Wells

0   25

miles

Barnstaple Bay

Barnstaple

See map 112.

Exe

Bridgwater

In Scotland, Montrose's extraordinary year had come to an end at Philiphaugh in September 1645. With only a thousand men left, his options were limited. He spent the last few months of the year trying to tie Huntly down in an attempt to join forces (specifically his Gordon cavalry), and set about the recapture of Inverness. However, Huntly proved elusive, electing instead to use his force of 2,000 foot and 600 horse in the prosecution of private vendettas. There was some good news: MacColla had defeated the Campbells at Callander in February and there was news of the young Lord Napier's defence of Kincardine Castle the following month.[6] But for the most part this was a difficult time for Montrose and the Royalists north of the border. The Covenanters had amassed a strong force under Middleton in Aberdeenshire. By early 1646 it was nearly 2,500 strong (mainly horse) and it quickly reoccupied Aberdeen. Huntly's failure to cooperate with Montrose had effectively allowed elements of Middleton's force to cross the Spey and fall on Montrose as he attempted to besiege Inverness.

From the start of the wars, clan loyalty had proved a potent mix. For the most part the clans remained motivated by the same three issues that had led them to take sides in 1638: namely, loyalties to the King, the church and clan heritage. Montrose had secured the support of most of the west Highland clans, and following his success in 1645 the MacNabs, MacDougalls and Lamonts had thrown in their lot with the Scottish Royalists.[7] But it remained a fickle arrangement, and from 1644 to 1646 much had hung on Montrose's leadership and success. In June 1646, the return of the Earl of Antrim from Ireland changed that balance of clan loyalties. Antrim had returned with the understanding that the King was making his way to Scotland with a view to reigniting the struggle. Curiously, Antrim's arrival coincided with the King's instructions to Montrose to disband his forces and seek exile in France. Montrose sought guarantees for his men before complying, and the King wrote again in June and July:

> The most sensible part of my misfortunes is to see my friends in d'Stress and not to be able to help them, and of this you are the chief. Wherefore, according to that real freedom and friendship which is between us, as I cannot absolutely command you to accept of unhandsome conditions, so I must tell you that I believe your refusal will put you in a far worse state than your compliance will… For if this opportunity be let slip, you must not expect any more treaties. In which case you must either conquer all Scotland or be inevitably ruined.[8]

At the end of July, following a meeting with Middleton, Montrose accepted the terms and, assembling his army at Rattray near Blairgowrie, bade his men farewell. He set sail for exile in Norway on 3 September. The other Scottish Royalists, however, refused to disperse. Huntly, seemingly reenergized with Montrose's departure, seized the burgh of Banff, while MacColla, having linked up with Antrim, tried to raise an army of over 20,000 men from the enemies of the Campbell clans. Their plans represented a real threat to peace, not just in Scotland but (potentially) in England too.

Charles soon grasped that his gamble to surrender to the Scots had been a mistake. The Covenanters had attempted to compel the King to repudiate Montrose, order the Marquis of Ormond (in Ireland) to break off negotiations with the Irish Confederates, accept the Covenant and, finally, to give his assent to the making of the 'religious settlement' that both Covenanter Scotland and Parliamentarian England sought. Unfortunately for Charles, the recognition of his error came after he had ordered Newark to surrender and Montrose to disband. Charles was quickly whisked away by the Scots, north to Newcastle, for fear that the Parliamentarians would attempt to recover him by force. His close personal council, however, were advised to escape before they were handed over as prisoners to the 'English'. Alone, he wrote to his wife on 28 May and handed the letter to Jean de Montreuil for despatch:

> … I am confident that he will have that credit to make clearly appear the false juggling of the Scots, and the base usage that I have had since I came to this army, which 'tis not to be expected that anybody else can have, and I desire thee to avow that the Queen of England concurs with me in this advice.[9]

But the Queen had long since despaired of his tiresome conscience: 'surely', she wrote, 'it would be better to be a Presbyterian king than no sort of king at all'.

Charles had been deluding himself in thinking that he could persuade the Covenanters to join Montrose and the Irish, and that the whole would march against the Parliamentarians. Charles had, in fact, written to Ormond and outlined his plan. It was another error in judgement. Ormond had, in turn, shared the information with Monro, the commander of the Scottish Covenanters in Ulster, and he, furious and bewildered at any suggestion of linking hands with the Irish 'rebels', had sent the letter post-haste to Parliament. It was read out in the House on 6 June. Five days later, Charles, entirely unaware that his duplicity had been exposed, wrote to Parliament in an attempt to open negotiations, and as a gesture of appeasement ordered the garrison at Oxford to seek terms. Despite Monro's revelation, the House of Lords and the City were favourable, but the Commons remained immoveable. While all this was playing out and Monro waited for clarification from either London or Edinburgh, he was defeated in open battle by Owen O'Neill, changing the situation in and with Ireland dramatically.

Following the Cessation of Arms signed by Ormond and the Confederates in September 1643 the situation in Ireland had, to all intents and purposes, been put on hold (chapter 15). Of the four separate armies the Irish Confederates were now allied with the Protestant Royalists under Ormond, while their Protestant opponents remained the 'Lagan army' of British settlers living in Ulster and the (Scottish) Covenanters under the command of Robert Monro.[10] During 1644, 10,000 Royalist troops had left Ireland and another 2,000 departed under MacColla to join Montrose (chapter 24). In December 1644, Ormond was able to renew the Cessation of Arms but their offensive against Monro's men was both uncoordinated and ineffective. Following the Royalist losses at Naseby, the King commissioned the Earl of Glamorgan to negotiate a secret treaty with the Confederates. He was entirely successful; having agreed to significant religious concessions and substantial Catholic tolerance, the Confederates agreed to supply an army of 10,000 men. Charles was, however, forced to repudiate the treaty once the details became public in London. In December 1645, Glamorgan was arrested and Irish politics were thrown into disarray. O'Neill and Preston decided the time was right to re-invigorate the struggle; the Irish peace was over.

---

6   Buchan, *Marquis of Montrose*, p. 204. Napier was able to escape into exile.

7   Robertson, *Royalists at War in Scotland and Ireland*, p. 143.

8   Buchan, op. cit., p. 207.

9   Bruce, *Charles I in 1646*, p. 41.

10 It should be stated that Lord Inchiquin had abandoned the Royalist cause by this juncture and declared for Parliament in July 1644. He was appointed Lord President of Munster, by Parliament, in January 1645.

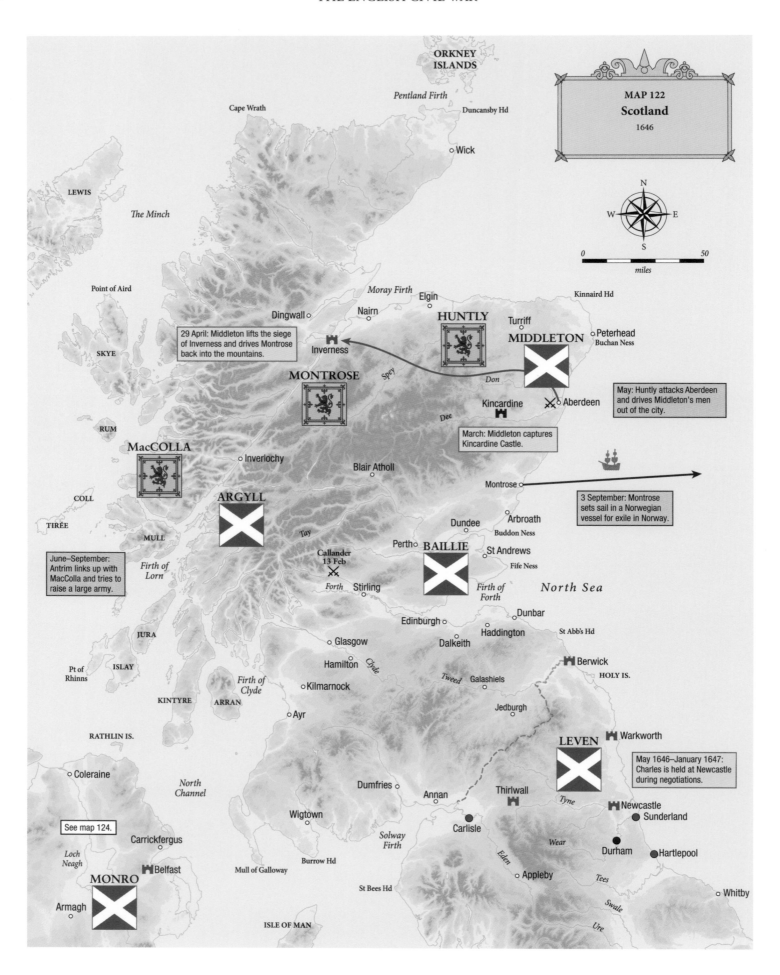

ORKNEY
ISLANDS

Pentland Firth

Cape Wrath

Duncansby Hd

Wick

LEWIS

The Minch

Point of Aird

SKYE

Dingwall

Nairn

Moray Firth

Elgin

Turriff

Kinnaird Hd

Peterhead
Buchan Ness

HUNTLY

MIDDLETON

29 April: Middleton lifts the siege of Inverness and drives Montrose back into the mountains.

Inverness

Spey

MONTROSE

Don

May: Huntly attacks Aberdeen and drives Middleton's men out of the city.

Kincardine

Aberdeen

RUM

Dee

March: Middleton captures Kincardine Castle.

MacCOLLA

Inverlochy

Blair Atholl

COLL

Montrose

3 September: Montrose sets sail in a Norwegian vessel for exile in Norway.

TIRÉE

ARGYLL

Tay

Dundee

Arbroath
Buddon Ness

MULL

Perth

BAILLIE

St Andrews

Fife Ness

North Sea

*Firth of
Lorn*

Callander
13 Feb

*Firth of
Forth*

June–September: Antrim links up with MacColla and tries to raise a large army.

Forth

Stirling

JURA

Edinburgh

Dunbar

Pt of
Rhinns

ISLAY

*Firth of
Clyde*

Glasgow

Haddington

St Abb's Hd

Dalkeith

KINTYRE

ARRAN

Hamilton

Clyde

Kilmarnock

Galashiels

Berwick

HOLY IS.

Ayr

Tweed

Jedburgh

RATHLIN IS.

Warkworth

LEVEN

Coleraine

*North
Channel*

Dumfries

Annan

Thirlwall

May 1646–January 1647: Charles is held at Newcastle during negotiations.

Tyne

See map 124.

Wigtown

Carlisle

Newcastle

Sunderland

Carrickfergus

*Loch
Neagh*

Belfast

Mull of Galloway

Burrow Hd

*Solway
Firth*

Wear

Durham

Hartlepool

MONRO

St Bees Hd

Appleby

Eden

Tees

Whitby

Armagh

ISLE OF MAN

Swale

Ure

MAP 122
Scotland
1646

N
W   E
S

0   50
miles

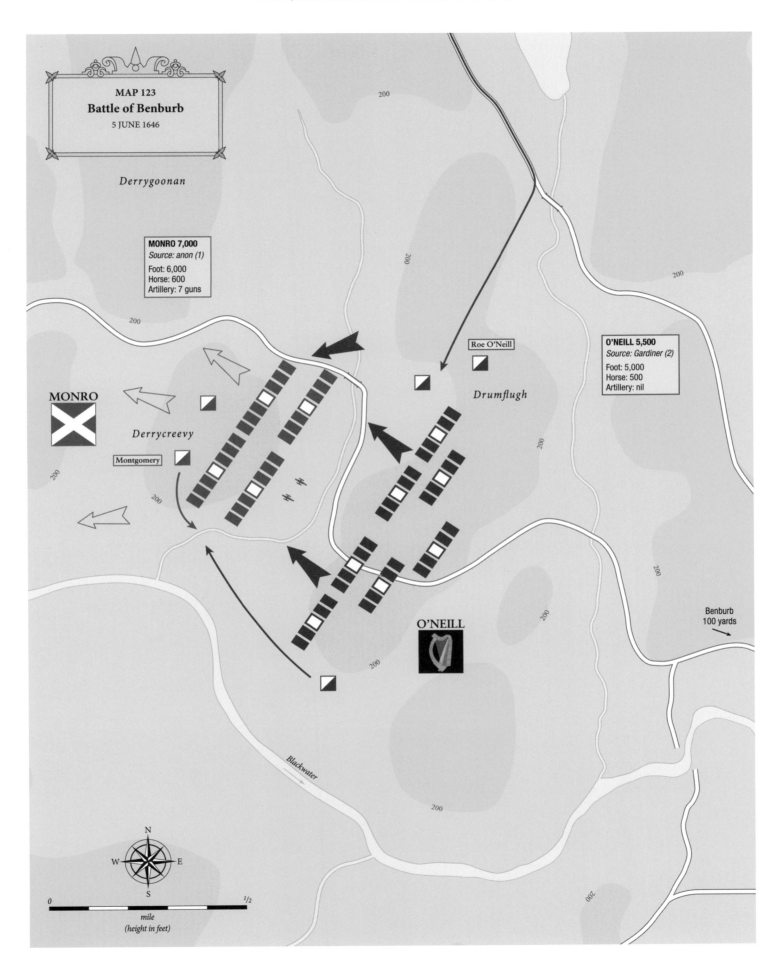

MAP 123

Battle of Benburb

5 JUNE 1646

Derrygoonan

MONRO 7,000
Source: anon (1)
Foot: 6,000
Horse: 600
Artillery: 7 guns

O'NEILL 5,500
Source: Gardiner (2)
Foot: 5,000
Horse: 500
Artillery: nil

Roe O'Neill

Drumflugh

MONRO

Derrycreevy

Montgomery

O'NEILL

Benburb
100 yards

Blackwater

0   1/2

mile
(height in feet)

N
W   E
S

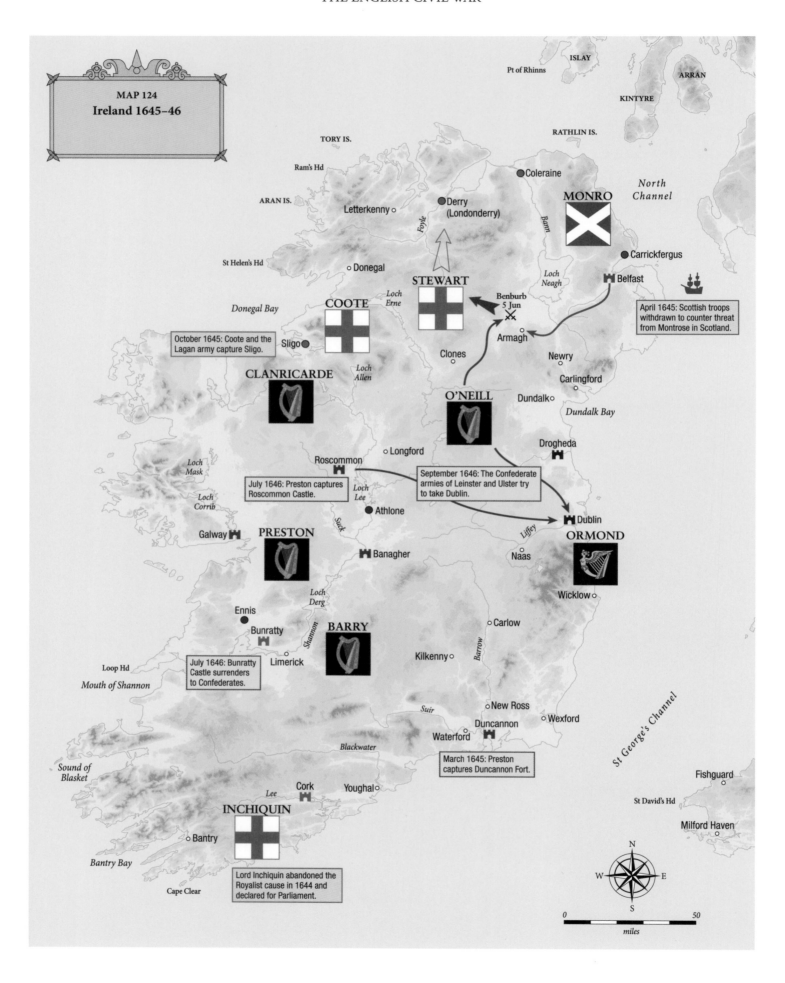

MAP 124
Ireland 1645–46

ISLAY

Pt of Rhinns

ARRAN

KINTYRE

RATHLIN IS.

TORY IS.

Ram's Hd

● Coleraine

North Channel

ARAN IS.

Letterkenny ○

● Derry (Londonderry)

Foyle

MONRO

● Carrickfergus

St Helen's Hd

○ Donegal

Bann

Loch Neagh

🏰 Belfast

STEWART

Benburb 5 Jun

Donegal Bay

COOTE

Loch Erne

October 1645: Coote and the Lagan army capture Sligo.

Sligo ●

Armagh ○

April 1645: Scottish troops withdrawn to counter threat from Montrose in Scotland.

Loch Allen

Clones ○

Newry ●

CLANRICARDE

Carlingford ●

O'NEILL

Dundalk ●

Dundalk Bay

○ Longford

Drogheda 🏰

Roscommon 🏰

July 1646: Preston captures Roscommon Castle.

September 1646: The Confederate armies of Leinster and Ulster try to take Dublin.

Loch Mask

Loch Lee

Loch Corrib

● Athlone

Suck

🏰 Dublin

Liffey

Galway 🏰

PRESTON

ORMOND

🏰 Banagher

Naas ●

Wicklow ●

Loch Derg

Ennis ●

● Bunratty

Shannon

BARRY

Carlow ●

July 1646: Bunratty Castle surrenders to Confederates.

○ Limerick

Kilkenny ●

Barrow

Loop Hd

Mouth of Shannon

Suir

● New Ross

Blackwater

Duncannon 🏰

○ Wexford

Waterford ●

March 1645: Preston captures Duncannon Fort.

St George's Channel

Sound of Blasket

Cork 🏰

Youghal ○

Fishguard ●

Lee

St David's Hd

INCHIQUIN

Milford Haven ●

Bantry ○

Bantry Bay

Lord Inchiquin abandoned the Royalist cause in 1644 and declared for Parliament.

Cape Clear

N
W E
S

0 ————— 50

miles

The arrival, at the end of 1645, of the papal nuncio, Giovanni Battista Rinuccini, had thrown the Glamorgan Treaty under the bus, but had also provided both funding and a large consignment of weapons from the Vatican. News that O'Neill had advanced north towards Charlemont (an Irish Confederate stronghold between Armagh and Loch Ney) was enough to draw Monro from the counties of Antrim and Down and the environs of Belfast. Monro had about 6,000 foot (mainly Scottish but including some English regiments), about 600 horse (including many lancers) and seven field guns (two of which were probably robinets).[11] His aim was to link up with elements of the Lagan army and a small force of about 250 infantry and 100 cavalry under the command of his son-in-law, Colonel George Monro, that was marching south from Coleraine. On 4 June at Poyntz Pass, Monro received news of the size and proximity of O'Neill's force and he ordered a general rendezvous at Armagh. O'Neill had anticipated Monro's intentions and reacted by moving across the River Blackwater to a strong position west of Benburb. He detached the majority of his cavalry, and a proportion of infantry to move north under the command of Brien Roe O'Neill, in order to intercept the Covenanter force from Coleraine.

With the river crossing at Benburb in O'Neill's hands, and that at Charlemont strongly defended by Confederate militia, Monro was forced to march well to the west and cross the River Blackwater at Caledon. By the time he had crossed, and his force had marched north and then east towards Benburb, it was early evening on 5 June, and his exhausted troops finally came up against the Irish. Monro, rather arrogantly, expected O'Neill to withdraw back towards Charlemont as his force came into view. Instead he found a strong Irish skirmish line which wasted no time in disrupting Monro's men as they jockeyed for position on the opposite hill. O'Neill had given his troops a lengthy 'Caesar-like' oration to fire them up. It went on for several minutes, interspersed with prayers and hymns, and closed with the words: 'If to shune death you fly and leave your fellowe souldiers in action, you will be no better esteemed in the world than bloudie Cain, who morthered [murdered] his own innocent brother Abell. Stricke, therefore, drum and sound trumpet for battle: advance, fight, live and raigne.'[12]

Monro was taken aback by the Irish resolve. It was clear that O'Neill had selected his ground wisely and his army was plainly drawn up for battle. Furthermore, his position restricted Monro to a lesser, narrower and lower hill opposite the Irish force. Monro moved his infantry into two lines, placing his artillery on the front of the slope and his cavalry to the rear. The British artillery opened proceedings and then Montgomery's cavalry attempted to secure a crossing over the brook dividing the forces. They were immediately counter-charged and driven back by the Irish cavalry, Montgomery being taken prisoner in the process.[13] No sooner was this action concluded when Brien Roe O'Neill's force returned, having surprised and routed the column from Coleraine near Dungannon (about 6 miles north of Benburb). Suitably reinforced, O'Neill gave the signal for a general advance across the frontage; it was about 8pm. Monro's cavalry charged the

advancing infantry, but a combination of the exhaustion of the horses (from their long march) and the difficult terrain rendered the charge largely ineffectual. The tide of Irish infantry drove over the artillery and came to push of pike with Monro's first line. A second attempt by Monro's cavalry also failed and merely served to expose their left flank, which was quickly attacked by O'Neill's men. It turned out to be the catalyst of the British collapse. As darkness fell the entire British line fell back in complete disorder, the cavalry having long since departed the field. In the rout that followed there was no quarter. As many as 4,000 of Monro's men were killed or taken; they lost all their artillery and nearly all their weapons and baggage.

Benburb was the largest set-piece battle of the struggle in Ireland. Celebrations rang out across the Catholic community, and a few days later, O'Neill followed up by advancing towards Stewart's forces, driving them back into Derry and Tyrone. It was a huge embarrassment for Monro's forces and Parliament's cause. It was also a wake-up call for the latter, who had to accept that, whatever their differences with the Covenanters, they could not do without them while the Irish rebellion continued. Plans were quickly put in place to start recruiting officers and men for an army to quell the uprising, and re-establish Anglo-Scottish ascendancy and Protestantism.[14]

The King's recent communication and the Irish victory at Benburb had left Ormond facing a real dilemma. Was he to continue negotiation with the Parliamentary and Covenanter commissioners or with the Irish council? A communication from the King in early July clarified things. In this, he confirmed that Ormond was to seek out the Irish peace as soon as possible. At the end of July, Ormond and the Supreme Council (at Kilkenny) announced the peace, but it was never going to be that simple. A few days after the announcement, Rinuccini, the papal nuncio, pronounced that all Catholics who took the oath of confederation offered under the terms of the peace treaty would commit perjury.[15] The following month, with emotions running high, O'Neill and Preston, following victories at Roscommon and Bunratty castles in July, advanced on Dublin and attempted to seize the city. However, unbeknown to O'Neill, Preston had opened secret negotiations with Ormond and the advance towards the capital floundered. In fact, by this stage O'Neill's army numbered between 8,500 and 11,500 and outnumbered Ormond by four to one, but he lacked the heavy artillery to make an attempt on Dublin a realistic prospect.[16] A stand-off ensued, but the Confederates had missed a golden opportunity to capture the capital and prevent it falling into the hands of the Parliamentarians.

In November, Parliament sent a number of commissioners to the city to open negotiations with Ormond. But the King's representative was unwilling to agree to their terms or relinquish the city. He refused to move on the issue of Dublin or Ireland without positive direction from the King. This arrived in early 1647. Charles directed Ormond to restore the breach with the Irish, providing he could do this with honour and good conscience. By the end of 1646, it was clear that Charles's Irish policy had been a complete failure.

---

11 Anon, *A bloody fight at Black-Water in Ireland*.

12 Gilbert, *History of affairs in Ireland*, vol. I, Part 1, pp. 111–12. The authenticity of the words in this speech is somewhat dubious.

13 Ibid., p. 114.

14 Wedgwood, *King's War*, p. 563.

15 Gardiner, *Great Civil War*, vol. III, p. 156.

16 Lenihan, *Confederate Catholics*, p. 97.

CHAPTER 35

IRELAND 1647: BEYOND REDEMPTION

By early 1647 the fractures between the Irish landed and landless factions, the Irish Supreme Council and the King's representative Ormond, were beyond redemption. The only thing that unified them all was a clear understanding that the future of Ireland depended upon the restoration of the King. A victory by the Scottish Covenanters or the English Parliamentarians (or a combination) would be utterly devastating to the Catholic cause within Ireland. Help from the Vatican had merely served to create an illusion that the Irish could win victory through force. The Vatican's misunderstanding of the Irish clans, their differing loyalties and internecine struggles was eclipsed, only just, by a similar ignorance portrayed by their own sovereign. Charles's instructions to Ormond to reopen negotiations with the Irish was both hopeful and naïve. By mid-January, the citizens of Dublin had refused to find the 1,500 troops to furnish the last remaining fighting group under his command. Ormond was in the unenviable position of having to surrender to either the papal nuncio or the English Parliamentarians. Deciding that the latter was the lesser of the two evils, in early February he offered to surrender his position as Lord Lieutenant of Ireland to Westminster without conditions. Ormond's decision was received with a mixture of indignation and dread by the Confederates. The burden of responsibility for Ireland now fell on Parliament's shoulders.

Ormond's successor, Colonel Michael Jones, was appointed on 9 April but he was not to arrive in Dublin until June. Parliament remained locked in a crisis over the establishment and fielding of the New Model Army (see chapter 36). Until this was solved Ireland was firmly on the back burner. Colonel Michael Jones arrived at the head of 2,000 of Parliament's troops and two weeks later Ormond completed the formalities of handover and returned to England in July. In the meantime, the Confederates reignited the struggle against the Parliamentarians, with General Preston taking Carlow Castle in April and the castles at Naas (St David's) and Maynooth in July. Preston's next move was to besiege Trim and, by so doing, he would place greater pressure on Jones's position in Dublin. Jones decided that sitting tight in the capital was no longer an option. On 1 August he departed Dublin at the head of his force, and four days later joined up with soldiers under Henry Tichborne from Drogheda, those under Colonel Moore from Dundalk and finally a contingent of horse under Colonel Conway. Suitably reinforced, Jones then moved towards Trim, prompting Preston to lift the siege of the castle there and pull back south across the River Boyne. Jones followed the Confederate force and on 8 August, at about 10am, they 'came to a place called Linchesknocke, within one mile whereof the enemy was drawne up on Dungan Hill'.[1]

Preston had over 7,000 men, having been reinforced by a significant number of Highlanders under Alastair MacColla, who had fled to Ireland in May having been defeated on the coast in Kintyre by a combined force led by Argyll and Leslie. Preston deployed his large force on the higher ground of Dungan's Hill with MacColla's 1,500 'Redshanks' on the left in lower ground among some trees, with a bog to their left flank. The intentions of the Confederate commander are unclear, but his subsequent reactions suggest that he might have been caught unprepared by Jones's rapid advance. Jones's advance guard debouched from the wood line to the north and, when in range of the Irish guns, they came under fire. However, it is clear that the fire had little effect. One Irish historian suggested that Preston's impetuosity got the better of him, and instead of holding his higher ground and waiting for the Parliamentarians to attack, 'he charged down the hill to break the columns of the parliamentarians, but was encountered with a firmness which threw his men into confusion. His artillery were so placed as to be useless, and his cavalry were drawn up in marshy ground, where they were at the mercy of the enemy.'[2]

Jones's battle report stated that 'about 12 of the clock the Armies joined Battell, continuing for about two hours: our two Wings of Horse with some foot having broken both the Wings of the Enemy, our main Body advanced, and broke theirs'.[3] The advance of the Parliamentarians seems to have been masked, to a degree, by tall crops, which concealed their numbers and perhaps their intentions. A cavalry charge by the Irish cavalry on the right never seems to have got going, and once they were counter-charged by the Parliamentarian horse it appears that the Irish quit the field, leaving Preston's infantry to hold the main attack. The strong skirmish line held out for a time, and MacColla's Highlanders displayed their customary courage by attacking into the flank of the Parliamentarian force as many as three times, but what happened next is unclear. It appears that the 'Redshanks' broke cover and retreated west, finding themselves in the large area of bog. According to the Parliamentarians, a similar number of the Irish infantry appear to have headed off in the same direction: 'Whereupon, about 3,000 of the Rebels betaking themselves to the Bog, they there drew up in a Body.'[4]

Jones ordered the bog to be surrounded by both horse and foot and then he sent in the infantry where 'they put to the sword all not admitted to quarter; such of the Rebels as left the Bog fell into the power of our Horse'.[5] It is difficult to be precise about the numbers killed in Preston's army. Figures vary from 2,500 to Jones's estimate of 5,470. However, as he accounts for only 20 fatalities on the Parliamentarian side, such estimates must be taken with a pinch of salt. Nevertheless, it is clear that a bloody slaughter took place following the collapse of Preston's army. Perhaps this was a demonstration of the 1644 act of 'Ordinance of no quarter to the Irish', but it was more likely revenge for Benburb, and an opportunity for Jones to stamp his mark.[6]

The defeat at Dungan's Hill was a heavy one for the Confederates to bear. The next day Jones marched his army to Maynooth, forcing the Confederates to surrender the castle. Within days the Irish had destroyed and abandoned their garrisons at Naas, Sigginstown (Wexford), Harristown (Wexford), Collinstown

---

1 Jones, *Victory obtained against the rebels at Dungons-Hill*, p. 8; Culme, *A diary and relation of passages*, p. 3. These two Parliamentary accounts are the only primary sources and are virtually identical. It is difficult to provide a balanced account of events without a Confederate source.

2 Haverty, *History of Ireland*, p. 563.

3 Jones, op. cit., p. 10.

4 Ibid.

5 Ibid.

6 The *Ordinance of no quarter to the Irish* was a decree of the English Parliament, passed on 24 October 1644, in response to the Irish Confederation of Kilkenny's threat to send troops from Ireland to support the King.

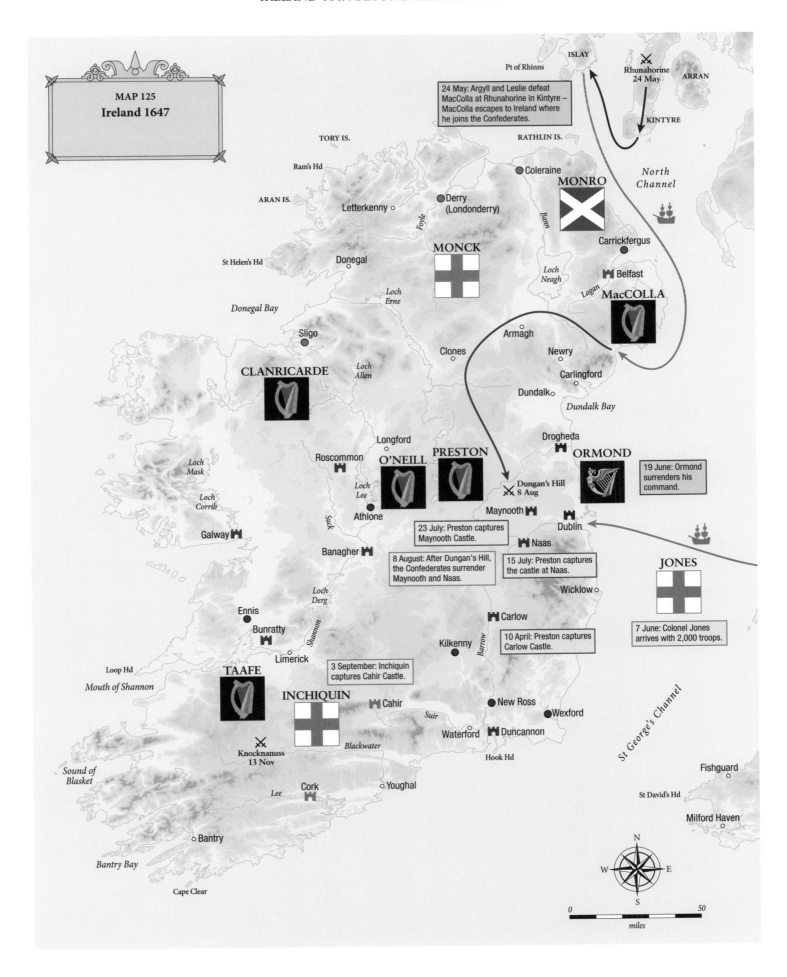

MAP 125
Ireland 1647

24 May: Argyll and Leslie defeat MacColla at Rhunahorine in Kintyre – MacColla escapes to Ireland where he joins the Confederates.

ISLAY

Pt of Rhinns

Rhunahorine
24 May

ARRAN

KINTYRE

North Channel

TORY IS.

RATHLIN IS.

Ram's Hd

Coleraine

MONRO

ARAN IS.

Letterkenny

Derry (Londonderry)

Carrickfergus

MONCK

Belfast

St Helen's Hd

Donegal

Loch Neagh

Bann

Foyle

MacCOLLA

Loch Erne

Lagan

Donegal Bay

Sligo

Armagh

Newry

CLANRICARDE

Clones

Carlingford

Loch Allen

Dundalk

Dundalk Bay

Drogheda

Loch Mask

Longford

O'NEILL

PRESTON

ORMOND

19 June: Ormond surrenders his command.

Roscommon

Loch Lee

Dungan's Hill 8 Aug

Loch Corrib

Athlone

Maynooth

Dublin

Galway

23 July: Preston captures Maynooth Castle.

Naas

Suck

Banagher

8 August: After Dungan's Hill, the Confederates surrender Maynooth and Naas.

15 July: Preston captures the castle at Naas.

JONES

Loch Derg

Carlow

Wicklow

7 June: Colonel Jones arrives with 2,000 troops.

Ennis

Bunratty

Kilkenny

10 April: Preston captures Carlow Castle.

Shannon

Limerick

Barrow

Loop Hd

3 September: Inchiquin captures Cahir Castle.

St George's Channel

TAAFE

Mouth of Shannon

INCHIQUIN

Cahir

New Ross

Fishguard

Suir

Wexford

Knocknanuss 13 Nov

Waterford

Duncannon

St David's Hd

Blackwater

Hook Hd

Sound of Blasket

Milford Haven

Lee

Cork

Youghal

Bantry

Bantry Bay

Cape Clear

N
W — E
S

0   50
miles

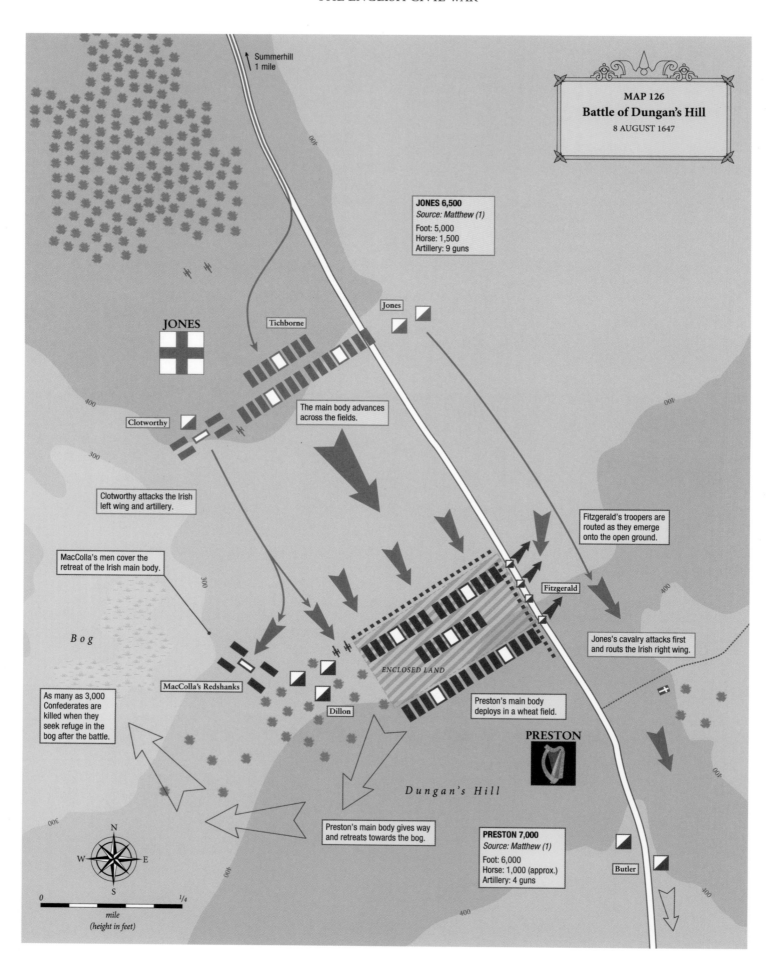

Summerhill
1 mile

MAP 126
Battle of Dungan's Hill
8 AUGUST 1647

JONES 6,500
Source: Matthew (1)
Foot: 5,000
Horse: 1,500
Artillery: 9 guns

Jones

JONES

Tichborne

The main body advances
across the fields.

Clotworthy

Clotworthy attacks the Irish
left wing and artillery.

Fitzgerald's troopers are
routed as they emerge
onto the open ground.

MacColla's men cover the
retreat of the Irish main body.

Fitzgerald

Bog

Jones's cavalry attacks first
and routs the Irish right wing.

ENCLOSED LAND

As many as 3,000
Confederates are
killed when they
seek refuge in the
bog after the battle.

MacColla's Redshanks

Dillon

Preston's main body
deploys in a wheat field.

PRESTON

Dungan's Hill

Preston's main body gives way
and retreats towards the bog.

PRESTON 7,000
Source: Matthew (1)
Foot: 6,000
Horse: 1,000 (approx.)
Artillery: 4 guns

Butler

N
W E
S

0   1/4
mile
(height in feet)

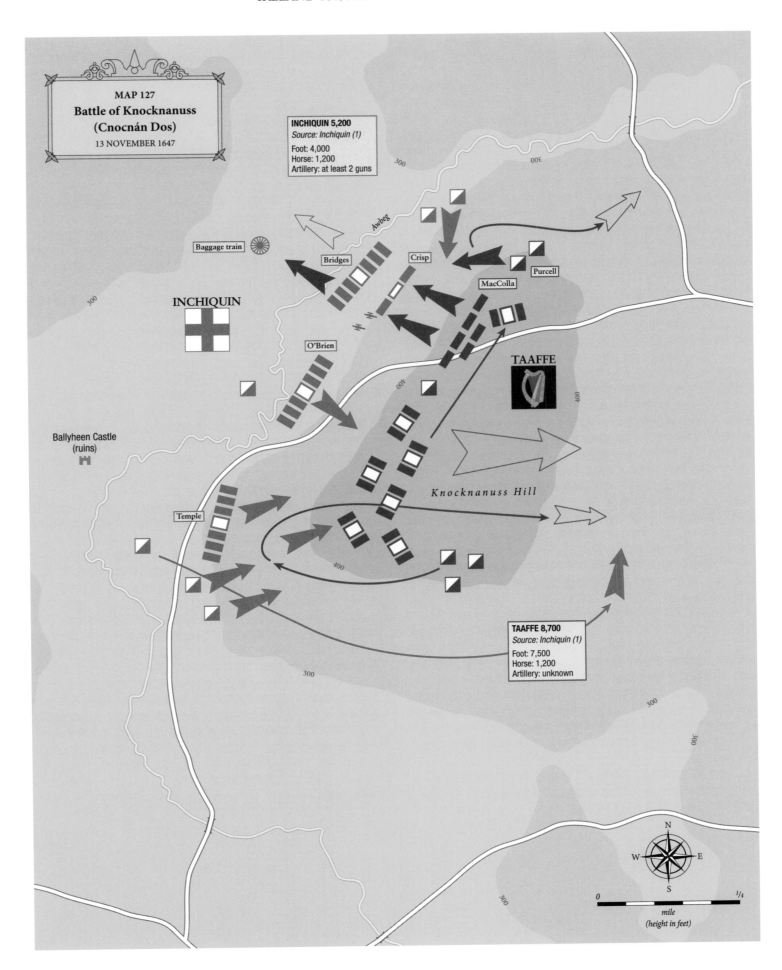

MAP 127
**Battle of Knocknanuss
(Cnocnán Dos)**
13 NOVEMBER 1647

INCHIQUIN 5,200
Source: Inchiquin (1)
Foot: 4,000
Horse: 1,200
Artillery: at least 2 guns

Baggage train

Awbeg

Bridges

Crisp

Purcell

MacColla

INCHIQUIN

O'Brien

TAAFFE

Ballyheen Castle
(ruins)

Knocknanuss Hill

Temple

TAAFFE 8,700
Source: Inchiquin (1)
Foot: 7,500
Horse: 1,200
Artillery: unknown

N
W E
S

0   1/4
mile
(height in feet)

(Westmeath) and Castlewarden (Kildare).[7] The Supreme Council called on O'Neill to move back into Leinster to counter the advances by Jones's seemingly invincible army. O'Neill had a large army, possibly as many as 12,000 men, and Irish accounts recount that he responded to the call and 'so harassed Jones by his rapid movements and by those inscrutable tactics which have obtained for him the title of the *Irish Fabius*, that the Parliamentary general was scared from the open country, and sought shelter behind the walls of Dublin'.[8] However, the reality was somewhat different. Sustaining a large *invading* army in central Ireland was an impossible task, and by 10 August, Jones was on his way back to Dublin.

Meanwhile, in Munster Lord Inchiquin was conducting a vicious campaign that resulted in the capture of the significant castle at Cahir in early September. The follow-up operation and the sack of the Rock of Cashel (a medieval complex on a hilltop overlooking the town) the following day, where numerous unarmed civilians were murdered and the cathedral desecrated, was yet another reminder of the brutality and callousness of the Irish conflict. Inchiquin's 'successes' and the apparent freedom of manoeuvre he was able to exercise (he marched to the very walls of Kilkenny) encouraged Jones to resume the offensive. Leaving Dublin on 2 October, he marched north to join forces with General Monck, who had arrived back in Ireland in September to take command of Parliament's forces in Ulster. Their united army consisted of 6,000 foot and 1,600 horse.[9] But the old adage that small armies were defeated while large armies starved was entirely apposite. During the month of October, Jones and Monck cleared northern Leinster of Confederate garrisons, including Athboy and Portlester. O'Neill's resistance was constrained by the fact that he had detached troops (including MacColla's Redshanks) to Taaffe. Furthermore, he remained in southern Leinster ready to intervene if Jones's force should move south and try to link up with Inchiquin. The Supreme Council decided to act to prevent such an outcome by ordering Taaffe to attack Inchiquin pre-emptively.

In addition to MacColla's 1,500 foot, Taaffe had been reinforced by three regiments from Connaught, raising his numbers to 7,500 foot and 1,200 horse.[10] Inchiquin's force at this juncture numbered 4,000 foot and 1,200 horse.[11] By 12 November, Taaffe had established his army on the high ground of Knocknanuss; the same day Inchiquin marched westwards through Ballyclough and camped within 3 miles of the Irish position. The next morning Inchiquin tried to entice Taaffe to give up the high ground and 'fight upon a fair plain'. Taaffe ignored the inducement and Inchiquin was compelled to deploy his force to the west, facing east, with the River Awbeg to his back (although it was not a large obstacle). It was Inchiquin's intention to make a main attack against the Irish right, which included MacColla's Redshanks and, accordingly, he placed his artillery there to provide supporting fire. At about 2am, Inchiquin noted that, 'after two shot was made (one whereof slew a Trumpeter of theirs) they perceiving that the Ordnance would force them from that ground, presently came on down the hill to meet our men'.[12] In fact, MacColla was worried that the Parliamentarians would outflank his position to his right and decided to strike first. Purcell was the first to attack, his troopers charging into Colonel Crisp's forlorn hope. Crisp was taken prisoner, along with Major Brown, who was slain along with 40 men. Colonel William Bridges' men were able to seek some respite from the Irish horse

by clambering back towards the ditch along the river. However, it was not long before Purcell's Irish horse were counter-charged and driven back by the Parliamentarian cavalry. The sight of the felling cavalry enticed Bridges' men to run uphill after them. It was a big mistake. MacColla's infantry, who had followed in the wake of Purcell's Horse, fell on the disorganized Parliamentarian foot. Having fired and then discarded their muskets, they charged and completed their grisly business with claymore and *targe*.[13] They also captured the two guns and turned one against the fleeing Parliamentarians. Having driven many across the river, MacColla's men were then distracted by the large baggage train that now lay at their mercy.

At the same time that the Irish attacked on their right, Taaffe had ordered the Irish horse on the left to charge downhill. He also had the presence of mind to redeploy the Munster Foot over to the right, to protect that flank which had been vacated by the advance of MacColla's men. Inchiquin responded by ordering Temple's men to march to their right, in order to give the impression that they were going to undertake a right flanking manoeuvre.[14] A Parliamentarian officer recorded:

> To prevent this, the Rebels resolved immediately to fall on: to this end they advanced with their Horse before their foot, to charge; but that error being soon espied by our, our shot [foot] were commanded presently to advance under the shelter of a ditch that parted them and us.[15]

The Parliamentarian cavalry counter-charged the Irish horse and immediately broke their resolve, forcing them back; they then collided with their infantry. Inchiquin had sent Temple's infantry immediately behind his horse. Now in disarray with their formation undone, the Irish infantry did not wait for the Parliamentarian foot to gain the summit before breaking and running in the same direction as their cavalry.

Inchiquin, satisfied that the Irish right wing was irrecoverably broken, turned his attention back to his left wing where he was 'presented with the rufull [rueful] spectacle of his men's slaughters and the Rebels overturning all before them even to our wagons'.[16] He immediately deployed his reserves, along with some of O'Brien's tercia, to move to the north. They engaged MacColla's men in the flank as they were returning to the field, having ransacked the baggage train. In the scramble that followed many of the Highlanders were slain and MacColla was killed, purportedly having requested quarter. Inchiquin's cavalry continued the pursuit and the killing across the hills went on well into the night. Inchiquin estimated that 3,000 men were slain and over 6,000 arms captured. It was an unmitigated disaster for the Confederates, leaving the detestable Inchiquin in control of most of Munster.

The Supreme Council were at a loss as to how best to proceed. There was talk of offering the Protectorate of Ireland to a foreign prince or in inviting the Prince of Wales from France, but the influence of Rinuccini pervaded. He insisted that, from the religious perspective, nothing should happen without the sanction of the Pope. As it turned out, events in England and Scotland were (once again) to dictate the outcome and determine the arrangements in Ireland.

---

7   Jones, op. cit., p. 12.

8   Haverty, op. cit., p. 564.

9   Gardiner, *Great Civil War*, vol. III, p. 108.

10 These are the figures in Inchiquin, *Lord Inchiquine in Munster in Ireland*, and an officer of the Parliaments army, *Battell of Knocknones*. In reality, the Confederate numbers may have been slightly lower – perhaps nearer 6,000 foot.

11 Ibid.

12 Inchiquin, op. cit., p. 3.

13 Ó Súilleabháin, *Battle of Knocknanuss*, p. 62.

14 Ibid., p. 63, suggests that Inchiquin's troops got around the back of the hill and then surprised the Irish but I can find no evidence to support this assertion. He may have got this from Haverty, op. cit., p. 566, but as neither Inchiquin nor the Parliamentary report mention this feat, it appears to be conjecture.

15 Officer of the Parliaments army, *Battell of Knocknones*, p. 7.

16 Ibid., p. 8.

CHAPTER 36
THE KING'S INTRANSIGENCE, 1647

On 2 January Charles wrote to his Queen in desperation: 'I must tell thee that now I am declared what I have really beene ever since I came to this army, which is a prisoner... the difference being only this, that heerefore my escape was easy anufe [enough], but now it is most difficult, if not impossible.'[1] The Scots, realizing that there was nothing to be gained from prolonging negotiations with the King, changed tack and entered into negotiations with the English Parliament. They agreed to hand over the sovereign in exchange for money owed to them for their services during the war. Parliament's commissioners arrived at the end of the month and Charles was moved to Holmby (Holdenby) House in Northamptonshire. Ten days later the last of the Scottish troops departed English soil. Leslie and the Covenanters, amidst cries of being 'traitor Scots who sold their king', marched against the last of the Royalist bastions in Scotland.[2] By mid-March the last Royalist stronghold had also fallen in Wales. On the surface it appeared as though Parliament had achieved complete victory. Despite this, there existed a real danger of anarchy across England and Wales, unless they could fill the void and quickly.

It was one thing to defeat the King but quite another to know what to do with him. The Presbyterian peers accepted a number of concessions during their negotiations with the King. Charles agreed to concede to Presbyterianism for three years, the existence of a militia for ten years and, furthermore, he would no longer have to sign the Covenant. While the peers saw this as a natural process of Parliamentary statesmanship, Charles saw it as an opportunity to renege on matters downstream. Despite Charles's apparent compliance and geniality, there were many that suspected his motives and were concerned that the sacrifices of the previous years were in danger of being thrown on the rocks. Reinstating the King may fill the void but it would not solve the underlying problem.

The other major issue facing the Parliamentarians was money. The nation's coffers were empty and the levels of taxation unacceptably high. However, there could be no diminution of dues without the complete or partial disbandment of the army. This was an explosive topic. The process of that disbandment became entwined with the ongoing struggle within Parliament. In the spring of 1647, Denzil Holles and Philip Stapleton held sway in Westminster and they were determined to disband the New Model Army. A number of regiments, whose commanders were sympathetic to the Presbyterian cause, were earmarked for service (out of the way) in Ireland, while the rest were to be disbanded and dispersed.[3] The army, not surprisingly, reacted with hostility. They felt they had earned a right to a say in the settlement of the kingdom and they wanted assurances from Parliament on the settlement of arrears of pay and indemnity from prosecution for past acts.[4] The pot was beginning to simmer.

Fairfax ordered the New Model to stay well clear of London, but he was well aware that he lacked the necessary political credentials and clout, and quickly yielded political direction and control of the army to Cromwell. The latter officer moved with speed and decisiveness, well aware that Holles had commenced the creation of a counter army from soldiers in the outlying garrisons and loyal Presbyterians in the New Model. By the end of May 1647, matters were running out of control. Rainsborough's Regiment, while waiting to be embarked at Portsmouth, mutinied and set off to Oxford to secure the army's artillery amidst rumours that Parliament was attempting to seize it (for use by the other force). A few days later even Fairfax's own regiment mutinied. On 31 May Cromwell ordered Cornet George Joyce (a junior officer in Fairfax's Horse) to ride to Oxford in order to safeguard the artillery, and from there to take a body of 500 horse and to secure the King at Holmby House. Cromwell had undoubtedly crossed a red line, but he was more than aware that the Presbyterians were openly preparing the London militia and, more alarmingly, had opened negotiations with the French ambassadors and Scottish commissioners to 'bring another army into England'.[5]

Fairfax called for a General Council of the Army, which, once met, drew up the 'Solemn Engagement', stating that the army would not disband until satisfactory arrangements had been made. A general rendezvous, for the wider army officer corps, was organized to take place at Newmarket. On 4–5 June, they gave their wholehearted assent to the Solemn Engagement. Five days later, in order to reinforce the point, the New Model Army marched south towards London, stopping at Royston. With no optimistic signs emanating from Parliament, two days later they continued towards London, prompting panic in the city. The Militia Committee ordered the trained bands to mobilize on pain of death (only the Westminster Regiment appeared in any strength) and shops were ordered closed. The New Model Army stopped short once again and Parliament requested a statement outlining all the army's demands. It resulted in the Declaration of the Army, which was the first attempt by the army to set out their political objectives. It was in the hands of Parliament's commissioners by 15 June and made worrying reading. In short, the declaration warned that erring members of Parliament should be brought to book, as well as erring kings. Its authorship was unmistakably Ireton's and it was promptly followed by a charge, made in the name of the army, against 11 members of the House, including Holles and Stapleton. The House was powerless and, in a bid to buy time, they agreed to look into both the declaration and the charges against some of its members. By July Holles, and the key protagonists among the Presbyterians, were losing their grip on matters. On 16 July a number of Presbyterian members asked for leave of

---

1 Bruce, *Charles I in 1646*, p. 99.

2 Wedgwood, *King's War*, p. 611.

3 About 8,400 foot were destined for Ireland (along with 1,200 dragoons and 3,000 horse), leaving about 6,000 foot to be disbanded.

4 They also wanted volunteers exempted from future service; widows and orphans of soldiers killed in action/service to receive a pension; and soldiers to be compensated for their material and/or financial losses and enough money set aside for the short-term quartering of soldiers on disbandment.

5 Rushworth, *Historical Collections*, part 4, vol. II, p. 517.

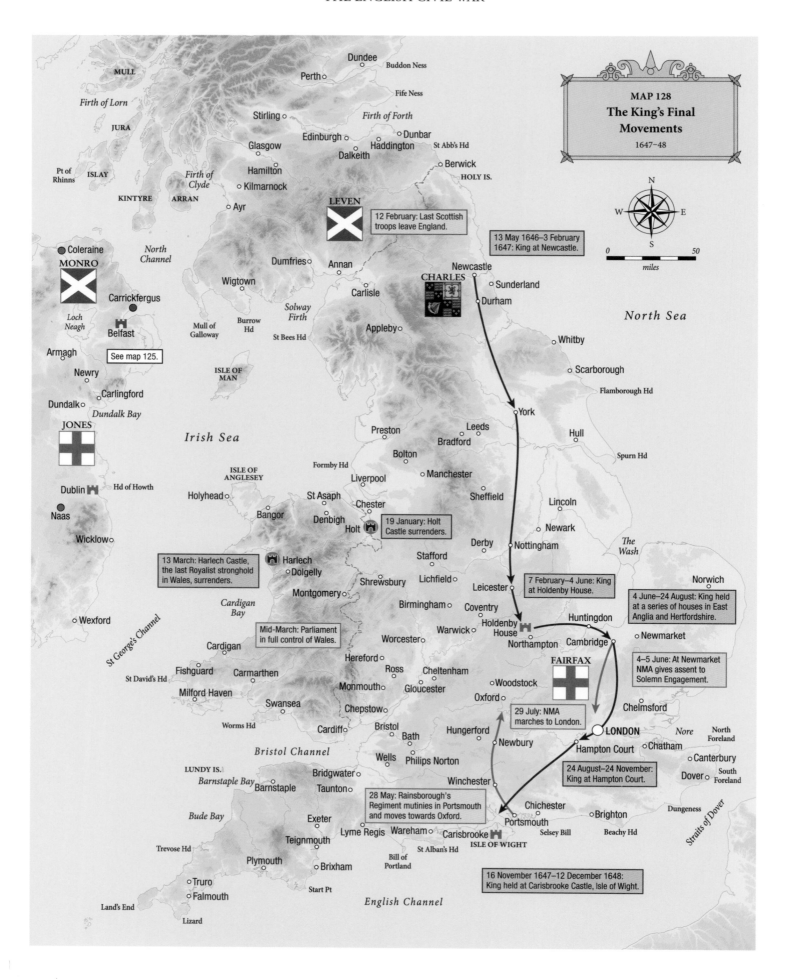

MAP 128
The King's Final
Movements
1647–48

MULL

Firth of Lorn

JURA

Dundee

Buddon Ness

Perth

Fife Ness

Pt of
Rhinns

ISLAY

KINTYRE

ARRAN

Stirling

Glasgow

Edinburgh

Dunbar

Firth of Forth

Haddington

St Abb's Hd

Dalkeith

Hamilton

Berwick

HOLY IS.

Kilmarnock

Ayr

LEVEN

12 February: Last Scottish
troops leave England.

13 May 1646–3 February
1647: King at Newcastle.

0   50
miles

Coleraine

MONRO

*North
Channel*

Dumfries

Annan

Carlisle

Newcastle

CHARLES

Sunderland

Durham

North Sea

Carrickfergus

*Loch
Neagh*

Belfast

*Solway
Firth*

Appleby

Whitby

Armagh

Mull of
Galloway

Burrow
Hd

St Bees Hd

Scarborough

See map 125.

Newry

ISLE OF
MAN

Flamborough Hd

Carlingford

Dundalk

Dundalk Bay

JONES

Irish Sea

York

Leeds

Hull

Preston

Bradford

Spurn Hd

Dublin

Hd of Howth

Bolton

Manchester

Sheffield

Lincoln

*The
Wash*

Naas

Wicklow

ISLE OF
ANGLESEY

Formby Hd

Liverpool

Holyhead

St Asaph

Chester

Bangor

Denbigh

Holt

19 January: Holt
Castle surrenders.

Derby

Newark

Nottingham

Norwich

13 March: Harlech Castle,
the last Royalist stronghold
in Wales, surrenders.

Harlech

Dolgelly

Shrewsbury

Stafford

Lichfield

Leicester

7 February–4 June: King
at Holdenby House.

4 June–24 August: King held
at a series of houses in East
Anglia and Hertfordshire.

Montgomery

*Cardigan
Bay*

Birmingham

Coventry

Holdenby
House

Huntingdon

Wexford

Warwick

Northampton

Cambridge

Newmarket

Mid-March: Parliament
in full control of Wales.

Cardigan

Worcester

FAIRFAX

4–5 June: At Newmarket
NMA gives assent to
Solemn Engagement.

St George's Channel

Fishguard

Hereford

Ross

Cheltenham

Woodstock

Chelmsford

St David's Hd

Carmarthen

Monmouth

Gloucester

Oxford

Milford Haven

Swansea

Chepstow

29 July: NMA
marches to London.

LONDON

Nore

*North
Foreland*

Worms Hd

Cardiff

Bristol

Bath

Hungerford

Hampton Court

Chatham

Bristol Channel

Wells

Newbury

24 August–24 November:
King at Hampton Court.

Canterbury

Philips Norton

Dover

South
Foreland

LUNDY IS.

Bridgwater

Winchester

Barnstaple Bay

Barnstaple

Taunton

28 May: Rainsborough's
Regiment mutinies in Portsmouth
and moves towards Oxford.

Chichester

Brighton

Dungeness

Bude Bay

Exeter

Portsmouth

Selsey Bill

Beachy Hd

Teignmouth

Lyme Regis

Wareham

Carisbrooke

Straits of Dover

Trevose Hd

St Alban's Hd

ISLE OF WIGHT

Plymouth

Brixham

Bill of
Portland

Truro

Start Pt

16 November 1647–12 December 1648:
King held at Carisbrooke Castle, Isle of Wight.

Falmouth

Land's End

English Channel

Lizard

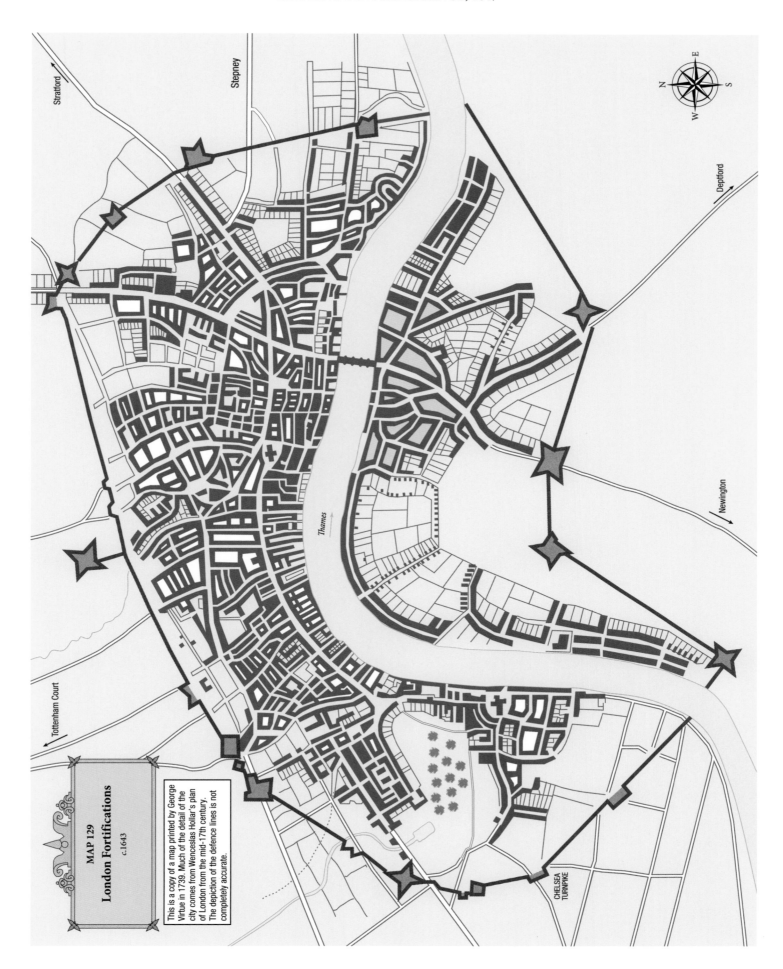

Stepney

Deptford

Newington

Thames

Tottenham Court

MAP 129
London Fortifications
c.1643

This is a copy of a map printed by George Virtue in 1739. Much of the detail of the city comes from Wenceslas Hollar's plan of London from the mid-17th century. The depiction of the defence lines is not completely accurate.

CHELSEA TURNPIKE

absence and effectively abandoned the struggle. Three days later Fairfax was given overall command of all the forces in England and Wales.[6] On 29 July the New Model Army marched to London, entering the city on 6 August, having received confirmation from the city's authorities that the gates would be opened. The Lord Mayor and Alderman welcomed Fairfax at Hyde Park and the army passed through and on to their new quarters at Croydon. In theory, at least, Parliament and the army were again one voice.

If the army's dealings with Parliament had outlined their political ambitions and intentions, their interaction with the King manifested the extent of those ambitions. On 9 September the Army Council discussed terms for the King's restoration, and in October they opened new negotiations. There can be little doubt that the terms offered to Charles provided the best chance of a principled conclusion and an honourable restoration. Yet he spurned the opportunity and the Royal Council was dismissed. It is a decision for which he has received almost universal historical criticism, but he, in fact, even at this hour, remained optimistic that his three-kingdom military alliance could still become a reality. In Scotland, the hard-line Covenanters had been replaced by men who had opposed intervention in 1644 and they now controlled the executive. In Ireland, Parliament's heavy handedness was opening up options for Irish support and the possible return of Ormond. Finally, in England and Wales, there was little doubt that the unpopularity of the army, and the taxation to support it, played directly into the King's hands. On 11 November Charles escaped from Hampton Court and turned up two days later at Carisbrooke Castle on the Isle of Wight. He had hoped that his freedom would enhance his position in brokering a deal to realize the alliance. As it turned out, the military governor on the Isle of Wight, Robert Hammond, an erstwhile friend of Cromwell's, whom the King had hoped to coerce, incarcerated him again.

The army understandably saw itself as the champion of the people. It was a perception that had developed in mid-1647 when the army's grievances were echoed by a group of civilian writers and activists collectively known as the Levellers. The most influential Leveller was John Lilburne, a former Parliamentarian soldier, who had resigned his commission in 1645 after refusing to sign the Solemn League and Covenant. His central theme was that an entirely new form of government, answerable to the people, should be constituted from the turmoil of the civil war. The legitimate authority of Parliament's members was 'inferior' to 'theirs who chose them'.[7] It struck a chord with many of the officers in the army, and on 28 October the Council of the Army met at Putney to discuss 'The Case of the Armie and the Agreement of the People'. The problem, from Cromwell's perspective, was that the Putney Debates, as they became known, threatened not just Parliament but also the unity of the New Model Army itself. In November a mutiny by two regiments in Hertfordshire was ruthlessly suppressed. Private Richard Arnold was shot as an example. The Council of Officers then decided to abandon all negotiations with the King and, furthermore, given his continued duplicity, to bring him to trial as the enemy of the people – sentiments that gained further traction when a letter was intercepted on 24 November, in which the King tells his Queen to plan on negotiations with the Scottish Presbyterians rather than the army.[8] On Boxing Day, Charles signed an 'Engagement' with the Scots by which, in return for intervention by a Scottish army to restore him to power, he would agree to restore Presbyterianism in England for three years, to supress the opinions and practices of Independents and to appoint an English Privy Council with a considerable number of Scotsmen. In so doing, he had sown the seeds of a second civil conflict.

---

6   Gardiner, *Great Civil War*, vol. III, p. 327.

7   Worden, *English Civil Wars*, p. 94.
8   Gardiner, op. cit., vol. IV, pp. 27–9. There is much controversy about this letter, known as the 'saddle-letter' as it was discovered in the courier's saddle.

CHAPTER 37

WAR REIGNITES IN WALES, 1648

The Second Civil War was of little significance militarily. Nevertheless, military coercion played a significant role in events in 1648 and in the eventual regicide. The passing by the House of Commons, on 3 January 1648, of the 'Vote of No Addresses' closed any further negotiation with the monarch. This, in turn, reignited the struggle by three main groups. The first were the Scots, with whom Charles had signed a treaty on Boxing Day. However, their immediate involvement in affairs had been slowed by internecine quarrels (chapter 39). The other two groups included former Royalists and a number of ex-Parliamentarians, who were united in their determination for a return to some form of normality. The Vote of No Addresses, in their opinion, stymied advancement in this direction. Violence at the local level had been rising throughout 1647, and clashes between rival groups of civilians and soldiers were commonplace. Committee men were imprisoned, holding them to ransom for arrears in local funding, Clubmen activity increased exponentially, and to make matters worse, the plague had a hold in numerous counties.[1] The nation was a stone's throw away from a complete breakdown in law and order.

Royalist intentions were straightforward enough, but the goals of the ex-Parliamentarians were largely driven by a return to order. In the main, they had no desire to see the restoration of the monarch, and were more interested in influencing the actions and decisions of Parliament and bringing about meaningful settlement. As such their uprisings were small, localized and largely ineffectual and quickly dealt with. Also ineffectual were the (purely) Royalist uprisings in Cornwall and Yorkshire, as insufficient numbers re-rallied to their cause. It was only in Wales and Essex, where the Royalists were able to capitalize on the open discontent of ex-Parliamentarians, that the insurrection gained traction.[2] Pembroke had been loyal to Parliament throughout the war but in early 1648 its governor, Colonel John Poyer, refused to cooperate with Colonel Fleming, Parliament's envoy sent to oversee the disbandment of local troops. Poyer, like many other Parliamentarian commanders in the shire, was furious that so many former Royalists (who were late in changing sides) were given control of numerous county governments.[3] Matters came to a head on 23 March, when Poyer declared for the King, effectively tossing a cat among the pigeons. Fleming and his small band of men beat a hasty retreat.

Colonel Reade was summarily despatched from Bristol, by sea, to restore order. His men landed at Pwllcrochan on 28 March, but were swiftly dealt with by Poyer's ever-growing band of followers. Poyer then marched towards Carmarthen and linked up with Rice Powell, taking control of Tenby en route, their combined force numbering about 3,500 men. By now word reached the King of Poyer's exploits and, if Thomas Burdett (one of his jailers at Carisbrooke) is to be believed, the King 'seemes to dislike the proceedings of Poyer and his adherents and it is

hoped will not in the least countenance their design'.[4] It is much more likely that the King was hugely encouraged by the defection of a key Parliamentarian, and by news of their troublesome exploits in southern Wales. Parliament was certainly concerned and ordered Colonel Horton to move west from his bases in Brecon in order to thwart the insurrection and nip the growing discontent in the bud. Having linked up with Fleming, Horton intended to block Poyer's advance by destroying a number of bridges over the River Towy, while Fleming was sent north to seize a pass. The latter commander was, however, lured into an ambush and was later found dead in the church at Llandeilo. On 1 May, when news of Fleming's demise reached the Army Council of War at Windsor, Fairfax ordered Cromwell to the area with two regiments of horse. The same day Waller was despatched to Cornwall, in order to keep the lid on another simmering pot.

Back in Wales, before Cromwell had arrived, Laugharne decided to throw in his lot with Poyer. The combined force proceeded to capture both Swansea and Neath, before pressing eastwards with Cardiff in their sights. Their force numbered about 6,500 foot and horse and was growing daily.[5] Horton had moved to block them, arriving at St Fagans on 4 May. He deployed elements of his 3,000-strong force forward, to cover the key crossings over the rivers Taff and Ely facing west. The same day, Laugharne's force closed to within 3 miles of Horton's men and there was some minor skirmishing on the 5th and 6th. While Laugharne deliberated his next move, he wrote to the commissioners outlining his grievances. On news of Cromwell's approaching cavalry he realized his options would be limited if he waited overly long. Instead, on 7 May, he decided to march back east towards Cardiff and give battle. Hopton recalled that 'the enemy advanced with their Body towards us, and we having some notice of it, drew forth, and took the best ground the place could afford'.[6]

The battle was fought early on the 8th. The two armies faced off across the Nant Dowlais stream, deploying on the higher ground to the west and east. The lower ground was wet and muddy and the whole area was heavily enclosed with both hedges and fences.[7] Laugharne had a limited amount of cavalry, but he appears to have sent the majority of it under Butler's command around the Parliamentarian left flank. They entered the town of St Fagans unopposed, but then, rather strangely, do not appear to have taken any further part in proceedings. About 60 horse under Laugharne advanced towards the Parliamentarian right but were easily beaten back. With these somewhat farcical cavalry actions completed, the main bodies of formed infantry in the centre now advanced towards each other. Horton recalled that 'we had a sharp dispute with them for about two hours: in our

---

1 Morrill, *Revolt of the Provinces*, p. 125.

2 Anderson, *Civil Wars*, p. 128.

3 Gaunt, *Civil War in Wales*, p. 66.

4 Anon, *Declaration from the Isle of Wight*, p. 2.

5 Anon, *Colonell Poyer's forces in Wales*, p. 2; Laugharne, *A declaration by Major General Laughorn*, p. 13.

6 Laugharne, ibid.

7 Gaunt, op. cit., p. 68. There are only scant accounts of the battle by the Parliamentarians with which to build a picture of what happened – this version (and the map) has been taken from Gaunt's work.

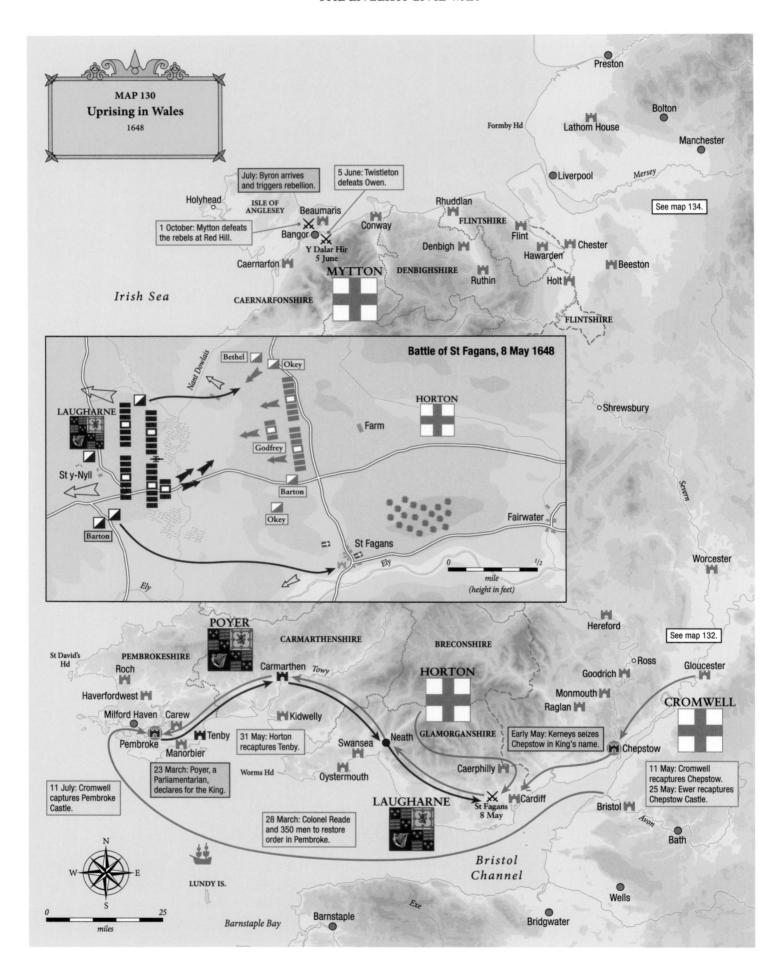

MAP 130
Uprising in Wales
1648

July: Byron arrives and triggers rebellion.

5 June: Twistleton defeats Owen.

1 October: Mytton defeats the rebels at Red Hill.

Preston

Bolton

Formby Hd

Lathom House

Manchester

Liverpool

Mersey

Holyhead

ISLE OF ANGLESEY

Beaumaris

Rhuddlan

FLINTSHIRE

See map 134.

Bangor

Conway

Denbigh

Flint

Hawarden

Chester

Y Dalar Hir
5 June

MYTTON

DENBIGHSHIRE

Ruthin

Holt

Beeston

Caernarfon

Irish Sea

CAERNARFONSHIRE

FLINTSHIRE

Battle of St Fagans, 8 May 1648

Nant Dowlais

Bethel

Okey

LAUGHARNE

HORTON

Shrewsbury

Farm

St y-Nyll

Godfrey

Barton

Okey

Barton

St Fagans

Ely

Fairwater

Ely

0   1/2
mile
(height in feet)

Severn

Worcester

POYER

CARMARTHENSHIRE

BRECONSHIRE

See map 132.

St David's Hd

PEMBROKESHIRE

Roch

Carmarthen   *Towy*

Hereford

Ross

Goodrich

Gloucester

HORTON

Haverfordwest

Kidwelly

Monmouth

CROMWELL

Milford Haven   Carew

Raglan

Pembroke   Tenby

31 May: Horton recaptures Tenby.

Swansea   Neath

GLAMORGANSHIRE

Early May: Kerneys seizes Chepstow in King's name.

Chepstow

Manorbier

Caerphilly

11 July: Cromwell captures Pembroke Castle.

23 March: Poyer, a Parliamentarian, declares for the King.

Worms Hd

Oystermouth

LAUGHARNE

St Fagans
8 May

Cardiff

Bristol

11 May: Cromwell recaptures Chepstow.
25 May: Ewer recaptures Chepstow Castle.

28 March: Colonel Reade and 350 men to restore order in Pembroke.

Avon

N
W   E
S

LUNDY IS.

Bath

Bristol Channel

Wells

0   25
miles

Barnstaple Bay

Barnstaple

Exe

Bridgwater

276

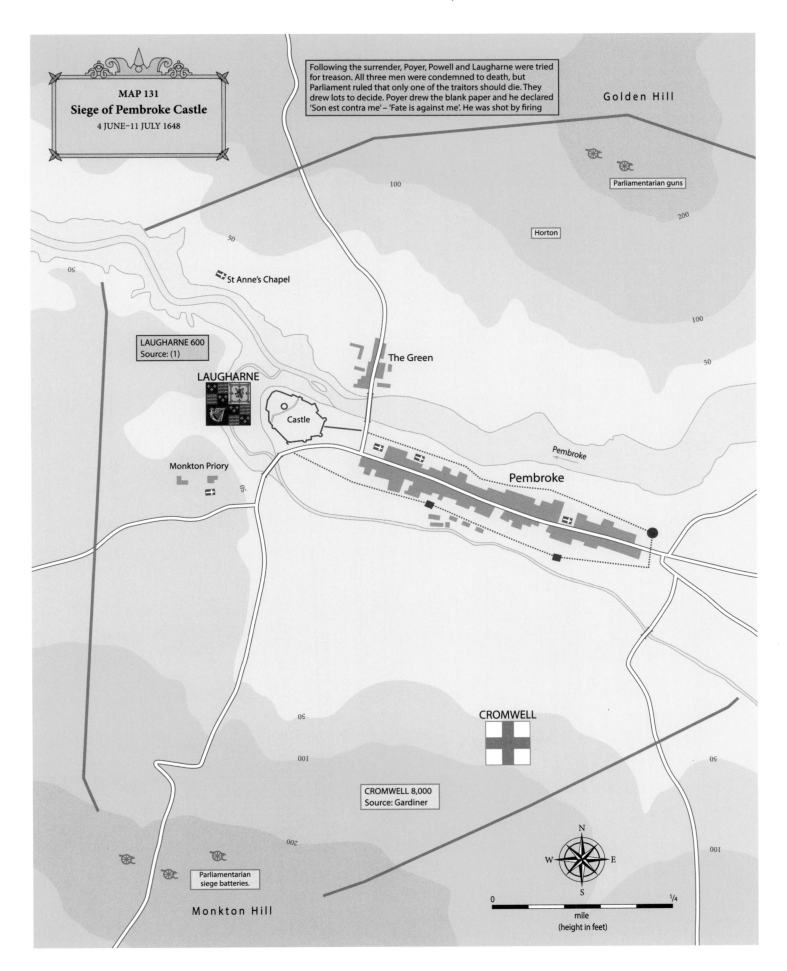

MAP 131
Siege of Pembroke Castle
4 JUNE–11 JULY 1648

Following the surrender, Poyer, Powell and Laugharne were tried for treason. All three men were condemned to death, but Parliament ruled that only one of the traitors should die. They drew lots to decide. Poyer drew the blank paper and he declared 'Son est contra me' – 'Fate is against me'. He was shot by firing

Golden Hill

100

200

Parliamentarian guns

Horton

50

50

St Anne's Chapel

100

LAUGHARNE 600
Source: (1)

The Green

50

LAUGHARNE

Pembroke

Castle

Pembroke

Monkton Priory

50

CROMWELL

50

100

50

CROMWELL 8,000
Source: Gardiner

200

100

50

N

W   E

S

200

Parliamentarian
siege batteries.

Monkton Hill

0   ¼
mile
(height in feet)

disadvantages, the Lord of Horse wonderfully encouraged both our Officers and Soldiers, that unanimously (as the Hedges and Bogs would permit) they charged the Enemy, who were wholly Routed and pursued about seven miles'.[8] Laugharne's losses were considerable: 3,000 men were killed, injured or captured and 4,000 weapons were lost, along with over a thousand horse.[9] Horton's losses were light, except in horse, which had to stand the enemy's shot to second the foot.

Laugharne's depleted and demoralized force limped back towards Pembrokeshire, pursued by Horton's small group, secure in the knowledge that Cromwell was not far behind. In fact, Cromwell had had to settle matters at Chepstow first – the town that had been seized in the King's name, by Nicholas Kerneys, in early May. The town was back in Parliament's hands by 11 May and, leaving Colonel Ewer to capture the castle where the defenders had ensconced themselves, Cromwell continued west.[10] He arrived in Pembrokeshire on 24 May, by which time only Tenby and Pembroke remained under Royalist control. Horton had surrounded the former (which capitulated at the end of May), leaving Cromwell to move directly to the latter.

'The condition here with us is very good, wee lye now before Pembroke castle, and have taken a village which doth command the Towne, and part of the Castle, in which wee have placed Batteries, that play into the Towne daily.'[11] However Cromwell's early assessment was overoptimistic, for the castle, built on a great mass of limestone rock, was almost totally surrounded by the Pembroke River and was considered one of the strongest fortresses in Britain. Initially Cromwell only had light guns to settle the matter. These were placed on Golden Hill to the north, and Monkton Hill to the south, but such inferior ordnance was not going to breach the 20-foot-thick walls. Heavier guns were being transported by sea, and until they arrived Cromwell hoped that Laugharne and Poyer would see sense

– they didn't. Cromwell then made an attempt to escalade the walls on 4 June, but the 'ladders were too short, and the breach so as men could not get over'.[12] Then, towards the end of June, came news that the vessel carrying the siege train had sunk in a storm at the mouth of the Severn.[13] Following another failed escalade on 24 June, Cromwell was growing increasingly angry and not a little anxious at news that the Scots were preparing to cross the border (chapter 39). The guns were, however, quickly recovered from the mud of the Severn, and arrived on 4 July. They were moved with haste to the battery on Monkton Hill and their effect was immediate, with the walls being breached in several places. On 11 July, with supplies running low and with fissures in the southern curtain, the town surrendered. Cromwell was finally free to move north to deal with the new emergency.

However, Wales was not yet free of Royalist rebellion. In May, Mytton had been besieged by a force raised by John Owen, who led an insurrection throughout Caernarfonshire. Finding himself virtually besieged, Mytton summoned support from Twistleton at Denbigh. As Twistleton moved west with 200 men he found his way blocked by Owen and 250 rebels on the coast road near Y Dalar Hir. The more disciplined troops drove back Owen's force and captured 60, leaving the remainder to take to the hills. The next month Byron arrived on the Isle of Anglesey, bearing news of a Scottish invasion. It was enough to incite another rising in north Wales, but Parliament's intelligence had been forewarned of Byron's movements, and they were prepared. A force of 1,500 men under Mytton and Middleton crossed the Menai Straight in a fleet of small ships assembled at Conway. The Royalists came out to meet them and the two sides clashed at Red Hill on 1 October. Again, the rebels were no match for professional soldiers, and they were quickly beaten and fled. By the end of the year Wales was, more or less, back under Parliament's control.

---

8 Laugharne, op. cit.

9 Laugharne, op. cit., p. 14; Anon, *Colonell Poyers forces in Wales* – last page.

10 The castle fell on 25 May, following a heavy bombardment and escalade, during which Kerneys fell along with many of his rebels.

11 Anon, *Sir Marmaduke Langdale*, p. 1.

12 Carlyle, *Cromwell's Letters*, vol. I, part IV, p. 4.

13 Gardiner, *Great Civil War*, vol. IV, p. 154.

CHAPTER 38
WAR REIGNITES IN ENGLAND, 1648

The eastern counties had been some of Parliament's strongest supporters at the start of civil conflict in 1642, but they now proved equally determined against the military rule under which they found themselves subjected. Unrest in London had spread to Kent and Essex and, on 24 April, a riot broke out in Norwich. A petition containing 30,000 signatures from (the county of) Essex arrived in London expressing support for the King and demanding an end to military administration. These disturbances on their own were a mere distraction, but when combined with insurrection in Wales and news of Langdale's occupation of Berwick for the King, they constituted a serious challenge to Fairfax and the Council of the Army. Cromwell was sent west to deal with Wales (chapter 37) and, on 10 May, Fairfax received orders to march north. With the army effectively out of the way, civil disturbance in the south and east came to the boil. On 12 May there was a two-day riot at Bury St Edmunds, and then a group marched to London from Surrey, proclaiming they did so 'For God and King Charles'. Following an attempt by the Canterbury authorities to supress another petition calling for the disbandment of the New Model Army, the storm finally broke on 21 May.

Two days earlier a young man had stepped ashore near Sandwich claiming to be the Prince of Wales. Despite his appearance, his claim was widely accepted and was enough to trigger a general uprising across the surrounding countryside. Rochester, Sittingbourne, Faversham and Sandwich were seized in the King's name. The following day, at a meeting at Rochester, it was agreed that the Kentish Royalists would gather, armed, at Blackheath on 30 May and march towards London in support of the petition. On 26 May matters escalated when Dartford and Deptford were seized by the insurgents, and a naval revolt broke out the next day, when six ships of the Parliamentarian fleet declared for the King. The guns of these warships proceeded to deliver the castles of Deal, Sandown and Walmer, while the castle at Dover found itself under siege. More worryingly, for the Parliamentarian authorities, the Kentish rebels were about to link hands with their brothers from Essex, after a bridge of boats was thrown across the Thames to facilitate communication.

Fairfax's earlier order to march north was rescinded and he was tasked to restore peace. For now, the security of London was a far more pressing issue than dealing with the Scots. Fairfax moved directly to Blackheath, sent Major Gibbons to relieve Dover, and positioned a strong force at Croydon to ward off any attempt on his rear by the rebels in Surrey. He then pushed on to Gravesend and deployed a strong reconnaissance force towards Rochester, where the main body of insurgents had congregated. Numbers were reported to be in the region of 7,000 men, 'all well accoutred, being most of them very sufficient men of ability, and not wanting of honourable resolutions'.[1] Reconnaissance reports confirmed that the road to Rochester was blocked, so Fairfax swung south, through the North Downs, having decided to cross the River Medway at Maidstone. When news of Fairfax's movements materialized, the Earl of Norwich, a Sussex gentleman who had

assumed command of the Kentish Royalists, detached 1,000 men to Aylesford and a similar number towards Maidstone, while the balance remained in and around Rochester.[2]

In Maidstone were positioned Brockman's Regiment of Foot and Manie's Regiment of Horse, with overall command appearing to have been vested with Gamaliel Dudley, the military governor of the town.[3] Most of the forces remained inside the town, although some had been deployed covering the bridge at East Farleigh. The Royalists' eight guns were positioned at the top of Gabriel's Hill, facing west and covering the bridge, while earthworks were thrown up covering the southern approaches.[4] During the afternoon, Fairfax's light cavalry arrived at Barming Heath; their report convinced the army commander to manoeuvre rather than try to take the main bridge head-on. Moving south to East Farleigh, Fairfax's men had to clear the lightly defended bridge, before crossing the Medway and swinging east.[5] As the heavier cavalry then advanced along the road towards Maidstone, they were counter-charged by some of Manie's heavy cavalry and driven back towards their main body of infantry who were following. Any Royalist elation was short lived, for Fairfax counter-charged and drove the Royalists back to the bridge at Tovil, which was defended by Royalist foot. At about 7pm Fairfax ordered his dragoons to clear and capture the bridge, before advancing up to Stone Street and north over the River Len and to the outskirts of Maidstone. He arrived there, with the forlorn hope, some two hours later.[6]

The streets were heavily barricaded and many of the Royalist guns on Gabriel's Hill had been repositioned to cover the threat from the south. When Fairfax came up, light was fading and with his artillery train some 3 miles to the rear, he decided to delay an all-out assault until the following morning. However, his vanguard had already closed with the defenders and, as was often the case, their bickering fire soon became a general engagement. John Rushworth, a 17th-century historian, wrote in his extensive history of the wars:

> … the fight begun about Seven of the clock at night, about a mile from Maidstone, and before we could beat them from hedge to hedge, and get in at the Barracado's, it was past Nine, and after we had entered the Town, we disputed every street and turning; they having Eight pieces of Canon, which they discharged above Twenty times upon our men in the streets, and by God's mighty help and assistance we overcame them between twelve and one o'clock at night.[7]

---

1 Carter, *Unfortunate expedition of Kent, Essex, and Colchester*, p. 80.

2 George Goring, First Earl of Norwich, was the father of George Goring who had fought extensively in the first English Civil War. Carter, op. cit., p. 82.

3 Carter, op. cit., p. 88. Dudley's original force was probably nearer 800 men but he was reinforced by troops from Aylesford during the early evening.

4 Marsh, *Battalia – Maidstone*, p. 49.

5 Carter, op. cit., p. 88, suggests Fairfax almost got over without a fight, but Gardiner, *Great Civil War*, vol. IV, p. 141, suggests otherwise.

6 Fairfax, *Fairfax to the House of Peers*, p. 1.

7 Rushworth, *Lord Fairfax's forces at Maidstone*, pp. 3–4.

The fighting was fierce and resolute; both sides 'disputed the Loss of every foot... from street to street, porch to porch, often falling on the enemy's horse with only their swords, in such a gallant manner'.[8]

Once the town was taken, Fairfax moved a strong force immediately to the north of the town in order to counter any attempt by Norwich's forces moving south from Rochester. In his subsequent report to the House of Lords, Fairfax noted that 'there were neare 300 slaine, and about 1,300 prisoners, many of them being taken the next morning early in the woods, hop-yards and fields whither they fled'.[9] With the loss of Maidstone and with Fairfax's men in control of the pass at Aylesford, some of the disheartened Kentish men dispersed. About 3,000 fled towards Blackheath and over the Thames at Greenwich and Woolwich and into Essex. However, with the insurgents in disarray, Fairfax somewhat bungled the pursuit. Instead of using his force as the hammer to drive the insurgents against the anvil of Skipton's men in the city, he chose to despatch a small force under Colonel Whalley and, by so doing, enabled many of Norwich's men to escape. Meanwhile, Colonel Rich was sent to assist Gibbons in the relief of Dover Castle.[10] Dover surrendered on 5 June, and three days later Canterbury capitulated to Ireton. Despite Deal, Sandown and Walmer castles remaining in Royalist hands, Fairfax now moved his army to Essex, where another Royalist uprising was gaining traction.

Fairfax left Colonel Rich in Kent with the task of capturing the castles. His mission was made all the more challenging as the Prince of Wales had sent support to the Channel forts by sea from France and the Netherlands. The first in early July succeeded in providing support at Deal and Sandown, but the fleet was later beaten back by a Parliamentarian naval force, when it tried to succour Walmer.[11] By 12 July Walmer was back in Parliament's hands, but the other two forts continued to hold out. Then, on 22 July, the Prince of Wales's full fleet arrived off Yarmouth and was only prevented from landing by a small body of men assembled by the local magistrates. The fleet then moved to the Kent coast and, on 14 August, they tried to relieve the siege of Deal, but were driven back by Rich's infantry. Deal then surrendered on 25 August and Sandown followed on 5 September. The crisis on land had passed but the naval dimension had alarmed the Parliamentarian and New Model commanders alike. They had been used, during the long years of war, to their own naval supremacy. On 27 May, six ships had mutinied and declared for the King; they were joined by three ships from the North Sea fleet a few days later.[12] Admiral Warwick hastened to Portsmouth to secure the loyalty of the squadron stationed there, before that was also turned. He arrived in the nick of time. Then, with news of the disaster at Maidstone, some of the mutinous ships reverted back to Parliament, as the leaders of the naval uprising descended into an internecine struggle about what to do next.

The crisis now entered a new phase and the (real) Prince of Wales decided to go on the offensive. On 30 August he sailed up the Thames estuary and confronted Warwick. For several hours the two fleets manoeuvred, each trying to get into a favourable position, but the heavy squalls eventually forced both fleets to drop anchor. That night the Prince of Wales, conscious of the dangers of losing his fleet on the sands, drew off and headed back to the Netherlands. For now, the crisis had passed.

Then, in September, the Prince's fleet was blockaded by Warwick at Helvoetsluys, but the Dutch States General took great and justifiable indignation at the two navies bringing their civil conflict into Dutch waters. Following intense diplomatic pressure, Warwick was forced to lift the blockade and return to the Kent coast in November.

Back on land, on 4 June Norwich had left his army under the command of William Compton on the south bank and crossed by ferry boat near Greenwich before moving to Stratford where many of the Essex men had purportedly gathered. However, when Norwich failed to return after a few days, Compton, realizing the danger, ordered his force to disperse.[13] When Norwich did finally return, he found no troops at Stratford and decided to move to Chelmsford, where Charles Lucas and Colonel Farre had enticed many of the Essex trained bands to rally for the King. Some of the Kentish men had crossed the Thames and joined them. The Royalist force numbered approximately 6,000 horse and foot, but they lacked arms and ammunition.[14] On 10 June they marched towards Braintree but, at Lucas's persuasion, they then moved to Colchester in order to gain more recruits and more military hardware from the city. They reached Colchester on 12 June and found many of the inhabitants far from amenable to their cause, but after a short delay, the gates were thrown open.

Command was nominally in the hands of Norwich but in practice it was Lucas to whom most looked for leadership. Lucas was a professional and capable soldier with battle experience from the Low Countries during the Thirty Years' War. With intelligence that Fairfax was a mere day's march away, Lucas needed to act fast. He deployed his force astride the London (Roman) road. The hedges protected his infantry but his cavalry on both flanks was more exposed. Fairfax, when he came up, wasted no time in ordering an attack, for he was keen to retake control of the city as soon as possible. He was, however, surprised at the skill and determination of the Royalist infantry and eventually had to employ his superior cavalry to settle the issue. Outflanked, the Royalist defences quickly disintegrated and, having lost 500 men, they pulled back to the safety of the city's walls. Fairfax's soldiers, their tails up, followed, but they were lured into a carefully prepared trap at Head Gate and severely mauled before beating a hasty retreat. Fairfax continued through the night to try to capture the city by escalade, but to no avail. By dawn, following a council of war, he reluctantly accepted the need for a siege. He ordered a cordon to be established with haste, to prevent the Royalist horse making good their escape, and sent parties up and downstream to cut off the Colne in order to thwart both escape and resupply.

Inside and outside the city both sides prepared their defences. On 24 June 1,000 men joined Fairfax from Suffolk, bringing his army up to nearly 7,000.[15] They were positioned on the north bank, where they erected Fort Suffolk, and were given the task of watching the north and east gates, along with Colonel Ewer's cavalry. The circumvallation was complete on 2 July but the siege works took another two weeks to complete. These works were not only extensive, but also fashioned a tight and effective cordon. However, a paucity in ammunition frustrated the Parliamentarian gunners and their attempts to batter the walls. From the period 16 July to mid-August, Fairfax seemed content to starve the defenders into submission. Towards the end of the month the water pipe supplying the city

---

8   Carter, op. cit., p. 91.

9   Fairfax, op. cit., p. 3.

10 Ibid., p. 4.

11 D. R., *Great fight at Walmer Castle*.

12 Kenyon & Ohlmeyer, *Military History*, chapter 5; Capp, *Naval Operations*, p. 182.

13 Carter, op. cit., p. 104.

14 Charles II, *A great fight at Colchester*, p. 2.

15 Townsend, *The Siege of Colchester*, p. 25. This was a bitter blow to the Royalists as they hoped these troops would arrive as allies rather than antagonists.

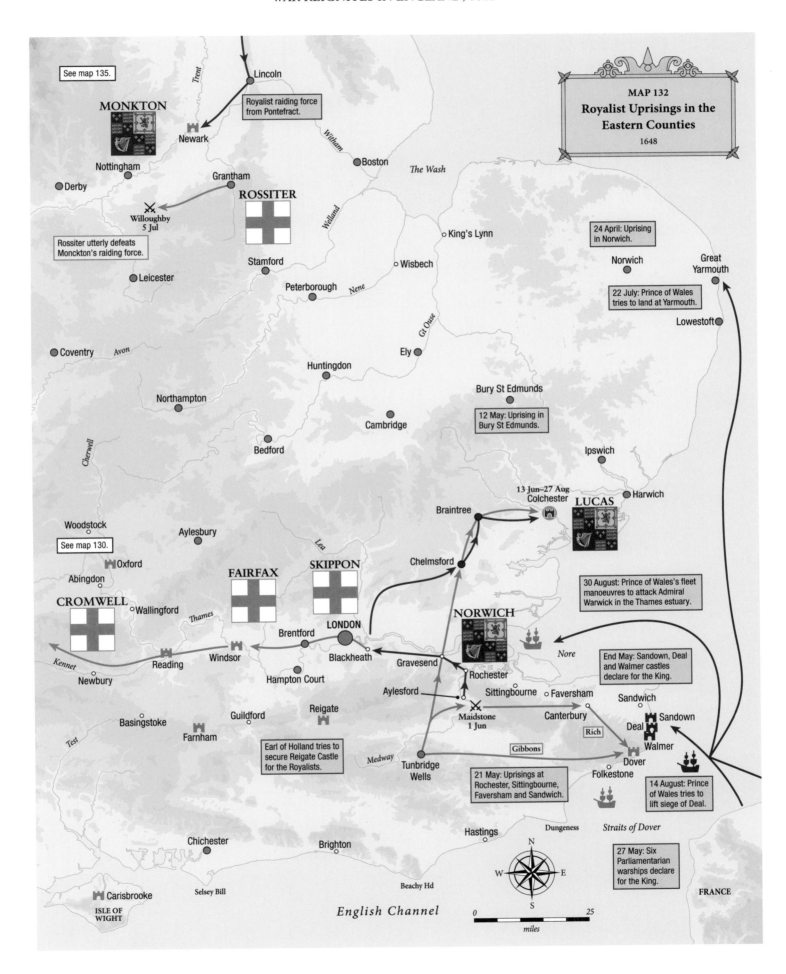

See map 135.

MONKTON

Trent

Lincoln

Royalist raiding force
from Pontefract.

Newark

Nottingham

Derby

Grantham

Witham

Boston

The Wash

ROSSITER

Willoughby
5 Jul

Rossiter utterly defeats
Monckton's raiding force.

Stamford

Leicester

Welland

King's Lynn

Wisbech

Peterborough

Nene

24 April: Uprising
in Norwich.

Norwich

Great
Yarmouth

22 July: Prince of Wales
tries to land at Yarmouth.

Lowestoft

Coventry

Avon

Cherwell

Northampton

Huntingdon

Gt Ouse

Ely

Bury St Edmunds

12 May: Uprising in
Bury St Edmunds.

Ipswich

Woodstock

Aylesbury

Cambridge

Bedford

Harwich

See map 130.

Oxford

Abingdon

FAIRFAX

SKIPPON

Lea

13 Jun–27 Aug
Colchester

LUCAS

Braintree

CROMWELL

Wallingford

Thames

Brentford

LONDON

Chelmsford

30 August: Prince of Wales's
fleet manoeuvres to attack Admiral
Warwick in the Thames estuary.

NORWICH

Kennet

Reading

Windsor

Blackheath

Newbury

Hampton Court

Gravesend

Rochester

Nore

End May: Sandown, Deal
and Walmer castles
declare for the King.

Aylesford

Sittingbourne

Faversham

Sandwich

Basingstoke

Guildford

Reigate

Earl of Holland tries to
secure Reigate Castle
for the Royalists.

Medway

Maidstone
1 Jun

Rich

Canterbury

Sandown

Deal

Walmer

Farnham

Test

Tunbridge
Wells

Gibbons

Dover

Folkestone

21 May: Uprisings at
Rochester, Sittingbourne,
Faversham and Sandwich.

14 August: Prince
of Wales tries to
lift siege of Deal.

Chichester

Brighton

Hastings

Dungeness

Straits of Dover

27 May: Six
Parliamentarian
warships declare
for the King.

Carisbrooke

Selsey Bill

Beachy Hd

N

FRANCE

ISLE OF
WIGHT

English Channel

0   25

W   E

S

miles

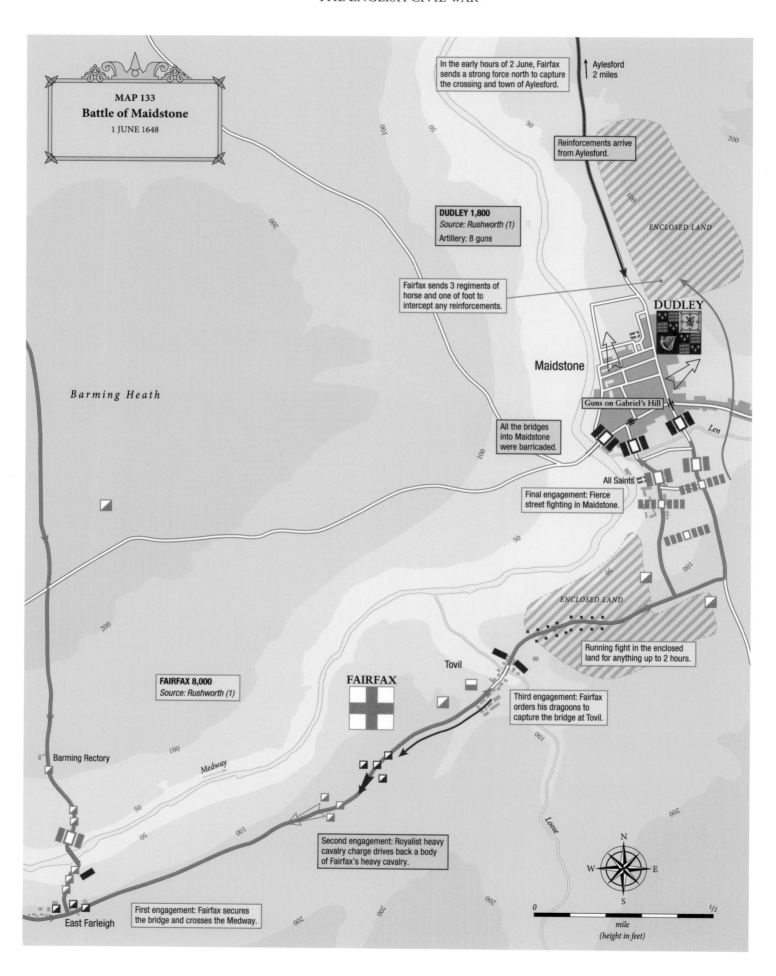

MAP 133
Battle of Maidstone
1 JUNE 1648

In the early hours of 2 June, Fairfax sends a strong force north to capture the crossing and town of Aylesford.

↑ Aylesford
2 miles

Reinforcements arrive from Aylesford.

ENCLOSED LAND

DUDLEY 1,800
Source: Rushworth (1)
Artillery: 8 guns

Fairfax sends 3 regiments of horse and one of foot to intercept any reinforcements.

DUDLEY

Maidstone

Guns on Gabriel's Hill

Barming Heath

All the bridges into Maidstone were barricaded.

Len

All Saints

Final engagement: Fierce street fighting in Maidstone.

ENCLOSED LAND

Running fight in the enclosed land for anything up to 2 hours.

Tovil

FAIRFAX 8,000
Source: Rushworth (1)

FAIRFAX

Third engagement: Fairfax orders his dragoons to capture the bridge at Tovil.

Barming Rectory

Medway

Second engagement: Royalist heavy cavalry charge drives back a body of Fairfax's heavy cavalry.

First engagement: Fairfax secures the bridge and crosses the Medway.

East Farleigh

Loose

N
W — E
S

0   1/2
mile
(height in feet)

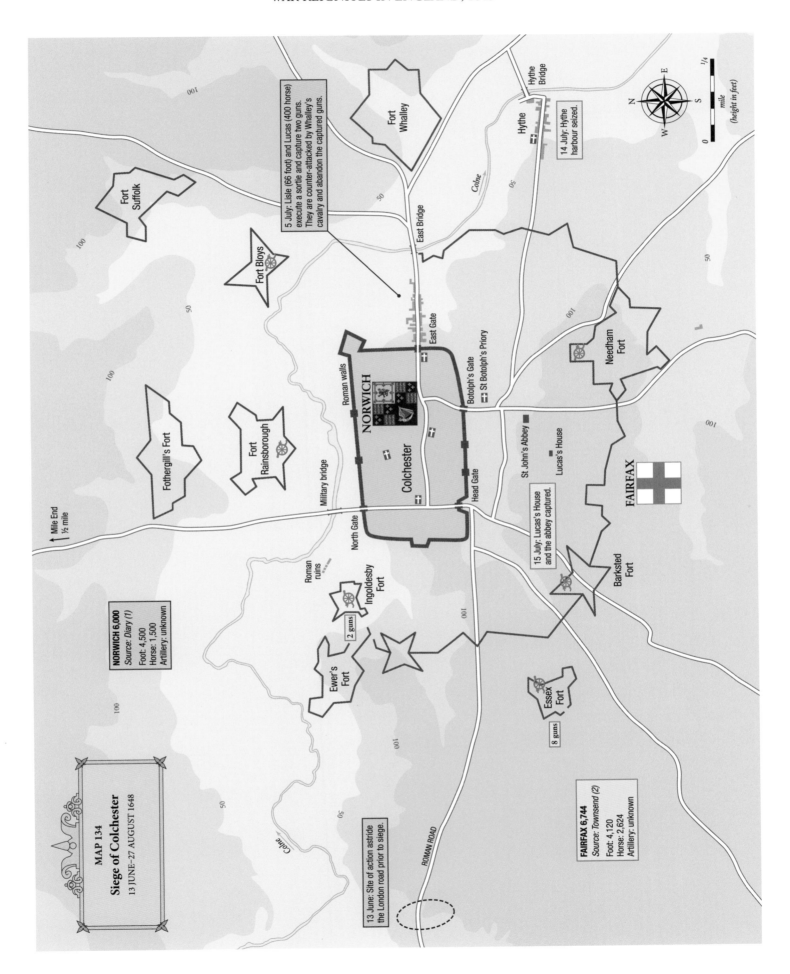

MAP 134
Siege of Colchester
13 JUNE–27 AUGUST 1648

NORWICH 6,000
Source: Diary (1)
Foot: 4,500
Horse: 1,500
Artillery: unknown

FAIRFAX 6,744
Source: Townsend (2)
Foot: 4,120
Horse: 2,624
Artillery: unknown

5 July: Lisle (66 foot) and Lucas (400 horse) execute a sortie and capture two guns. They are counter-attacked by Whalley's cavalry and abandon the captured guns.

14 July: Hythe harbour seized.

15 July: Lucas's House and the abbey captured.

13 June: Site of action astride the London road prior to siege.

Fort Whalley

Fort Suffolk

Fort Bloys

Fothergill's Fort

Fort Rainsborough

Ingoldesby Fort

Ewer's Fort

Essex Fort

Needham Fort

Barksted Fort

NORWICH

Colchester

Roman walls

North Gate

Head Gate

East Gate

East Bridge

Botolph's Gate

St Botolph's Priory

St John's Abbey

Lucas's House

Hythe

Hythe Bridge

Military bridge

Roman ruins

Mile End ½ mile

Colne

ROMAN ROAD

FAIRFAX

2 guns

8 guns

had been cut.[16] As conditions deteriorated inside the walls, and hunger took a hold, the civilians turned on the military defenders. This resulted in a constant stream of deserters, and on 16 August, Norwich wrote to Fairfax asking for mercy and free passage for the civilians. Fairfax realized what was going on and it was denied. Three days later Norwich wrote again, this time asking for terms. Finally, on 27 August Norwich agreed terms and surrendered the city the following day. But Fairfax was not done; he was determined to make an example. He had Lisle and Lucas executed for breaking their parole. Meanwhile, Norwich was transferred to a prison, to await the judgement of Parliament.

---

16 Cooper & Elrington (ed.), *A History of the County of Essex*, vol. 9.

CHAPTER 39
THE BATTLE OF PRESTON: THE DEATH BLOW TO ROYALISM, 1648

Charles's Boxing Day 'Engagement' (chapter 36) with the Scots provided the Duke of Hamilton the opportunity to create a wider coalition of conservative Covenanters in Scotland, as well as Royalists and Presbyterians from Scotland, Ireland and England.[1] On 3 April Lord Inchiquin had declared for the King and now supported an alliance with the Irish Confederates and the Scots. Alas, however, internecine divisions within the Irish ranks, stirred up by Archbishop Rinuccini, had, by late May, precluded any hope of Irish involvement. Furthermore, the path to collaboration with the English Royalists was far from straightforward. The Covenanters no longer trusted the Parliamentarians to deliver on the ideals of the 1641 Scottish revolution, but they were equally wary of the King's duplicitous propensity. By April the Engagers, a faction of the Scottish Covenanters, who made 'The Engagement' with King Charles I in December 1647, had taken control of the Scottish Parliament and had begun to raise an Engager Army (to be led by Hamilton); in addition, they had opened communication with (the northern Royalists) Marmaduke Langdale and Philip Musgrave. The former had seized Berwick Castle and the latter Carlisle Castle, in anticipation of the invasion.

When Hamilton finally crossed the border on 8 July, he had an army of about 14,000 men[2] – far fewer than he would have hoped, but his numbers were bolstered by about 3,000 men from the Royalists at Carlisle and those of Langdale, which arrived a few days later. Nevertheless, this Scottish force could not be compared with the army that had marched south under the Earl of Leven in January 1644. Hamilton's army consisted of many raw recruits. Insubordination prevailed between many of his senior commanders, he lacked money, and he had a paucity of good artillery. If that were not enough, his staff seemed incapable of sound military planning, and insufficient logistical preparation all contrived to erode force cohesion and flexibility. George Monro, who commanded the forces sent over from Ulster, refused to subordinate himself under Hamilton's key lieutenants, Baillie and Callendar, and therefore elected to detach himself to the rear of the main body.[3] Hamilton was unsure as to how to resolve these differences, but he was clear that he needed to act swiftly in order to capitalize on the fact that Fairfax was embroiled in Essex, and Cromwell in south Wales. But his hope of a speedy advance was soon thwarted as he was forced to wait over a week for his army to get their act together before moving south to engage Lambert's force around Penrith. The day before they finally crossed the start line, Cromwell had concluded business in Pembrokeshire and was already heading north with speed.

On 14 July Lambert was waiting for the Scottish vanguard as it approached his sentinels at Warwick Bridge. His force numbered about 4,000. The Parliamentarians gave a good account of themselves and fell back, as planned, to Appleby.[4] Two days later, once the Scottish infantry had closed up, Hamilton resumed the advance, and early on 17 July, they came up against Lambert's forces at Appleby. Once again, the Scottish horse had to wait for the infantry to close up in order to dislodge the Parliamentarian foot and dragoons from around the bridge, 'which was strongly manned with musketeers, and could not possibly with our horse be forced'.[5] They finally arrived as the sun was setting, but their attack, in the pouring rain, failed. Lambert considered he had done all he could to delay matters and, under cover of darkness, he pulled back to Bowes and thence to Barnard Castle, having left a small force to keep hold of Appleby Castle.[6] Hamilton followed up but was then, once again, forced to halt his army, this time for a full two weeks at Kirkby Thore (just north of Appleby). An anonymous military observer, embedded in Hamilton's headquarters, wrote in a letter to his friend in England sometime after the event, 'Yet it was necessary and requisite, in respect we still wanted the main materials and sinews of the Army... there being in store with us no more than ten barrels of powder, other ammunition proportionable, no artillery at all [and] no meal.'[7] While there, Hamilton received a number of reinforcements, bringing his army up to 14,000 – 10,000 foot and 4,000 horse.

Lambert had also received some reinforcements, troops from Yorkshire and six troops of horse sent north in advance by Cromwell.[8] The scouts of both forces remained in touch despite the two armies being 25 miles apart. Cromwell had reached Leicester on 1 August and Nottingham four days later. However, when he arrived at Doncaster on 8 August, he was forced to wait four days for the arrival of a siege train from Hull. He took the opportunity to antagonize the Royalists at Pontefract – their report makes the first recorded reference to the term 'Ironsides'.[9] Meanwhile, Lambert moved south and he and Cromwell joined forces at Wetherby on 13 August. The arrival of Cromwell's army could not have come soon enough for the Parliamentarians in the north. It coincided with both Scarborough and Tynemouth castles declaring for the King.

Hamilton recommenced his move south on 9 August. His intention was to link up with Lord Byron, who was in the process of stirring the Royalists in north Wales. Meanwhile, Langdale, with his 3,000 foot and 600 horse, had been detached and had ridden to the south-east, in the hope of persuading the governor at Skipton Castle to declare for the King. During the move towards Skipton, he was at Settle on 13 August when he received

---

1 Kenyon & Ohlmeyer, *Military History*, p. 63.
2 The exact number is difficult to determine. See Bull & Seed, *Bloody Preston*, p. 37.
3 Monro's force was about 3,000 strong.
4 Hamilton, *Bloody newes from the Scottish Army*.
5 Anon, *A letter from Holland*, p. 2. For a good account of this struggle see Hill & Watkinson, *Lambert's Campaigns in the North*, pp. 75–86.
6 The troops left in Appleby Castle (200 foot and 60 horse) surrendered to the Scots on 31 July and were, therefore, wasted.
7 Anon, *A letter from Holland*, p. 3.
8 Hill & Watkinson, op. cit., pp. 91–2. The total of these reinforcements was about 2,600 men – 1,000 foot and 1,600 horse.
9 Anon, *Resolution of the Kings Majesties subjects*, p. 3.

some disturbing intelligence on the size and proximity of a large Parliamentarian force coming in his direction: 'When hearing the Parliament's forces were gathered together and marching towards me, I went to acquaint Duke of Hamilton therewith to Horneby.'[10] Despite this vital intelligence, Hamilton decided to push on towards Preston, 'where his army being numerous in Foot, he might have the greater advantage upon his enemy in those enclosed countries'.[11] Hamilton's cavalry vanguard reached Preston on 16 August, but then crossed the River Ribble and moved further south towards Wigan in search of badly needed provisions. Meanwhile Cromwell's force continued to close from the east, and at Clitheroe he held a council of war and decided to interpose his army between the Scots and the Royalists in order to cut their line of retreat. He crossed to the north bank of the River Ribble and, after staying the night at Stonyhurst, pushed on towards Preston.[12]

At dawn on 17 August, Hamilton's cavalry under Middleton were still some way south of Preston, his infantry under Baillie was about to cross the River Ribble to join them, and Landale's army was entering Preston on the Longridge road. Meanwhile, Monro's men were more than a day's march to the north, near Kirkby Lonsdale. Cromwell had a good idea of the whereabouts of Monro's force and knew that he was pushing Langdale's Royalists to his front, but he would have been unaware that Hamilton's force was split either side of the Ribble. Hamilton was under the impression that Cromwell's force had divided, and that a body had already moved to relieve Manchester. He was not, therefore, overly concerned at reports of Parliamentarians to the east. He was to pay dearly for his lack of caution.

Before the sun was up, a strong forlorn hope, consisting of Northern Association troops under Major Smithson (who were familiar with the terrain) closed up on Langdale's rearguard.[13] The Royalists made a stand about 2 miles from Preston, while Langdale rode into the town to confer with Hamilton. The Scottish commander decided to ignore (more up to date) reports that the Parliamentarians were complete, and gave orders to Langdale to hold them off, while he crossed the Ribble with the infantry to join up with the cavalry near Wigan. Langdale recalled that 'the enemy coming the same way I had marched, fell upon my Quarter, where we continued skirmishing in all six houres, in all which time the Scots sent me no relief'.[14] Cromwell's main body had been some way to the rear of his forlorn hope and it was not until 4pm that they came up and began driving the Royalists back towards Preston. In fact, some of Hamilton's rearguard cavalry was sent to assist Langdale, but they were quickly driven back by Twistleton's Regiment of Horse operating on Cromwell's right flank. Captain Hodgson noted:

> ... at last comes a party of Scots lancers, and charged Major Smithson in the lane, passing by us, and put him to retreat; but they were routed immediately, and one of their commanders was running away, and I being aware of him, stepped into the lane, and dismounted him, and clapped into the saddle, and our horse came up in pursuit.[15]

As Cromwell's men advanced, from hedge to hedge, towards Preston, Hamilton finally accepted the scale of the attack and realized the precariousness of his position. His army was spread out along a 40-mile front and was about to be attacked in the centre by a force four times stronger than he had anticipated. While he fell back, Lambert ordered the Lancashire Foot (who were in the second line) to move around the Royalist right flank and down a narrow defile through the woods known as Watery Lane.[16] Cromwell wrote sometime later:

> ... at the last the Enemy was put into disorder; many men slain, many prisoners taken: the Duke, with most of the Scots horse and foot, retreated over the Bridge; where, after a very hot dispute, betwixt the Lancashire regiments, part of my Lord General's, and them, being often at push of pike, they were beaten from the Bridge; and our horse and foot, following them, killed many and took divers prisoners; and we possessed the Bridge.[17]

After so many hours without support Langdale's defence finally began to collapse and, at that point, Cromwell's and Harrison's regiments of horse burst through the centre, killing many of the fleeing Royalists, and subsequently, the Scottish infantry seeking refuge within the town.[18] Hamilton and Langdale, having left the men to their fate, escaped by wading across the river at the ford to Penwortham.

Meanwhile Baillie organized the immediately available Scottish infantry on the south bank of the River Ribble, around the small village of Walton-le-Dale, while Callendar brought up the balance of the infantry and positioned them on Walton Hill. After some time, Hamilton rejoined his reorganized but demoralized force on Walton Hill and immediately sent orders to Middleton (16 miles away at Wigan) to return with all haste. Neither side had any artillery, but the Lancashire infantry made better use of their heavy weight of musketry fire from the north bank. Langdale, who had remained with Hamilton, recalled that 'the Parliament's forces beat the Scots from the bridge presently, and so came over into all the lanes that we could not joyne with the foote';[19] Hodgson remembered that 'there was a long dispute before the bridge was gained'.[20] Cromwell now had a toehold south of the Ribble but light was fading fast and fighting soon petered out. Cromwell recorded that 'they lost four or five thousand arms. The number of slain we, judge to be about a thousand; the prisoners we took about four thousand'.[21]

Hamilton had been dealt a serious blow, but his army was still a force to be reckoned with. He convened a council of war in the driving wind and rain, and fell prey to the prolific negativity of his commanders. Callendar convinced him to withdraw under cover of darkness and link up with Middleton, who, Hamilton assumed and hoped, was already making his way back north. They abandoned their baggage, which included most of their spare powder, a decision they were to bitterly regret. Unfortunately for Hamilton, Middleton took a different route north to the one they were taking south and bumped into the advancing Parliamentarian vanguard before extracting himself. In the confusion, he managed to locate Hamilton's main body and then swung west in order to act as a rearguard to Hamilton's

10 Langdale, *Late fight at Preston*, p. 2. Many histories have concluded that Hamilton had no idea of Cromwell's whereabouts until the morning of 17 August; that was clearly not the case.

11 Ibid.

12 Stonyhurst was the house of Mr Sherburn and is now a grand Catholic school. The table on which Cromwell slept in his full armour is still there.

13 Bull & Seed, op. cit., p. 63; Hill & Watkinson, *Sanderson's War*, p. 120.

14 Langdale, op. cit., pp. 2–3.

15 Slingsby & Hodgson, *Original Memoirs, written during the Great Civil war*, p. 117.

16 There were joined a short while later by Cromwell's Regiment of Foot.

17 Carlyle, *Cromwell's Letters*, vol. I, part IV, p. 28.

18 Two brigades of Scottish infantry had not made it across the river.

19 Langdale, op. cit., p. 3.

20 Slingsby & Hodgson, op. cit., p. 120.

21 Carlyle, op. cit., p. 28.

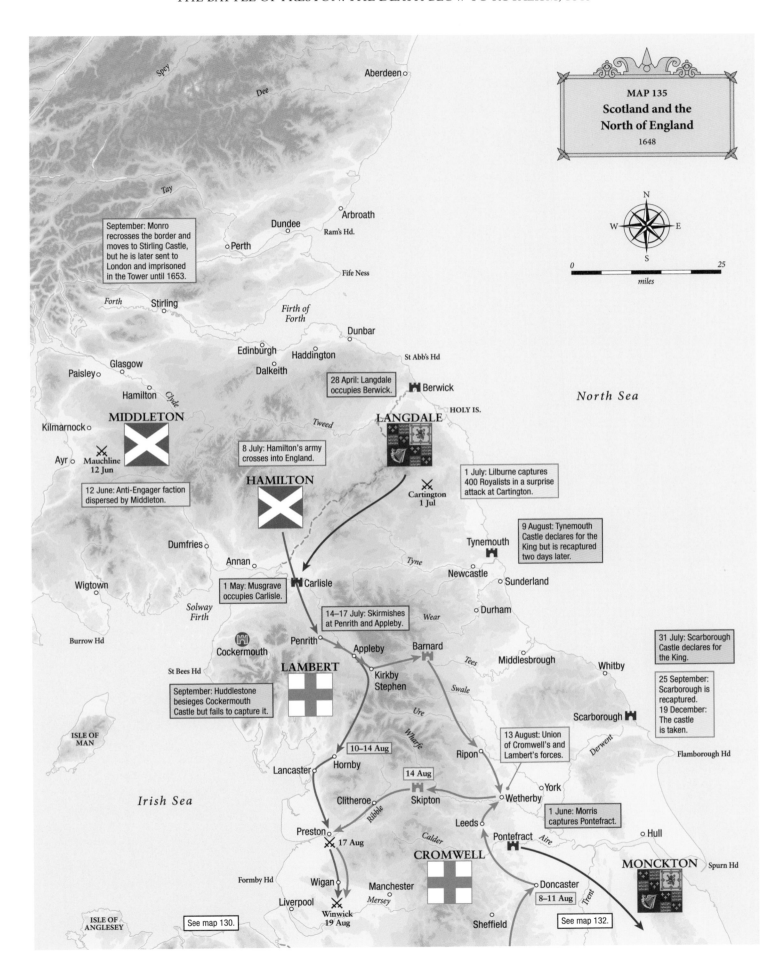

MAP 135
Scotland and the
North of England
1648

September: Monro recrosses the border and moves to Stirling Castle, but he is later sent to London and imprisoned in the Tower until 1653.

28 April: Langdale occupies Berwick.

8 July: Hamilton's army crosses into England.

12 June: Anti-Engager faction dispersed by Middleton.

1 July: Lilburne captures 400 Royalists in a surprise attack at Cartington.

9 August: Tynemouth Castle declares for the King but is recaptured two days later.

1 May: Musgrave occupies Carlisle.

14–17 July: Skirmishes at Penrith and Appleby.

31 July: Scarborough Castle declares for the King.

25 September: Scarborough is recaptured.
19 December: The castle is taken.

September: Huddlestone besieges Cockermouth Castle but fails to capture it.

13 August: Union of Cromwell's and Lambert's forces.

10–14 Aug

14 Aug

1 June: Morris captures Pontefract.

17 Aug

8–11 Aug

See map 130.

See map 132.

Winwick 19 Aug

North Sea

Irish Sea

Solway Firth

MIDDLETON

HAMILTON

LANGDALE

LAMBERT

CROMWELL

MONCKTON

Aberdeen
Spey
Dee
Tay
Dundee
Arbroath
Ram's Hd.
Perth
Fife Ness
Firth of Forth
Forth
Stirling
Dunbar
Edinburgh
Haddington
St Abb's Hd
Glasgow
Dalkeith
Berwick
Paisley
HOLY IS.
Hamilton
Clyde
Tweed
Kilmarnock
Ayr
Mauchline 12 Jun
Cartington 1 Jul
Dumfries
Tyne
Tynemouth
Annan
Newcastle
Sunderland
Wigtown
Carlisle
Wear
Durham
Burrow Hd
Cockermouth
Penrith
Appleby
Barnard
Tees
Middlesbrough
Whitby
St Bees Hd
Kirkby Stephen
Swale
Scarborough
Ure
Flamborough Hd
ISLE OF MAN
Wharfe
Ripon
Lancaster
Hornby
York
Clitheroe
Skipton
Wetherby
Ribble
Leeds
Hull
Preston
Calder
Pontefract
Aire
Spurn Hd
Formby Hd
Wigan
Manchester
Doncaster
Trent
Liverpool
Mersey
ISLE OF ANGLESEY
Sheffield

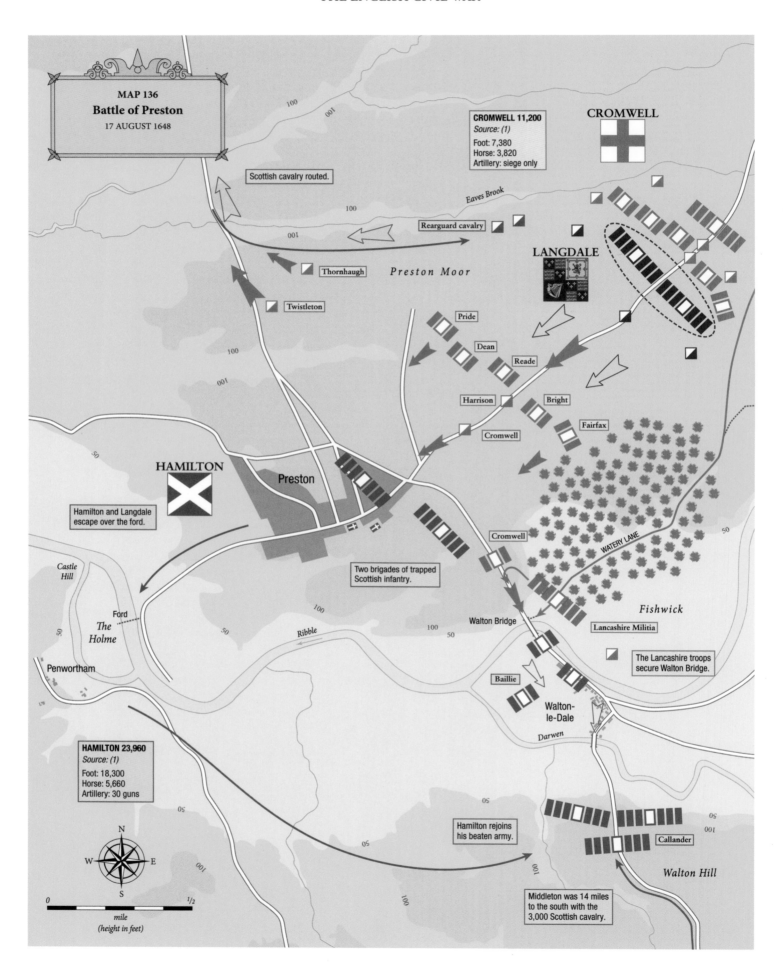

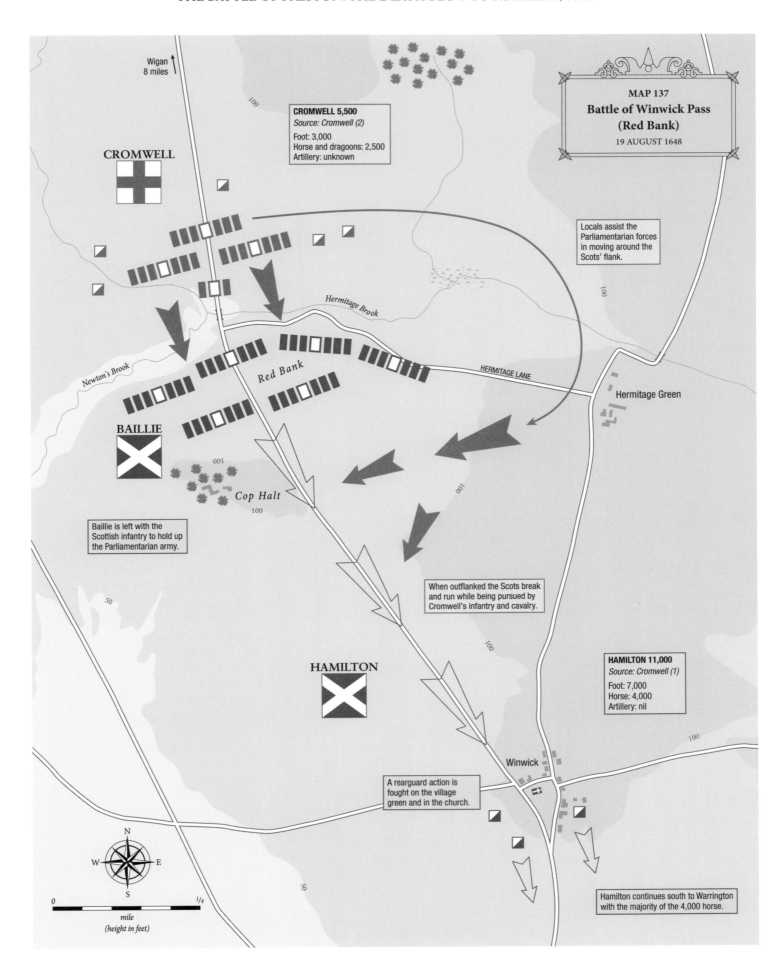

MAP 137
**Battle of Winwick Pass
(Red Bank)**
19 AUGUST 1648

Wigan
8 miles

CROMWELL 5,500
Source: Cromwell (2)
Foot: 3,000
Horse and dragoons: 2,500
Artillery: unknown

CROMWELL

Locals assist the
Parliamentarian forces
in moving around the
Scots' flank.

Hermitage Brook

HERMITAGE LANE

Hermitage Green

Newton's Brook

Red Bank

BAILLIE

Cop Halt

Baillie is left with the
Scottish infantry to hold up
the Parliamentarian army.

When outflanked the Scots break
and run while being pursued by
Cromwell's infantry and cavalry.

HAMILTON 11,000
Source: Cromwell (1)
Foot: 7,000
Horse: 4,000
Artillery: nil

HAMILTON

Winwick

A rearguard action is
fought on the village
green and in the church.

Hamilton continues south to Warrington
with the majority of the 4,000 horse.

N
W   E
S

0   1/4
mile
(height in feet)

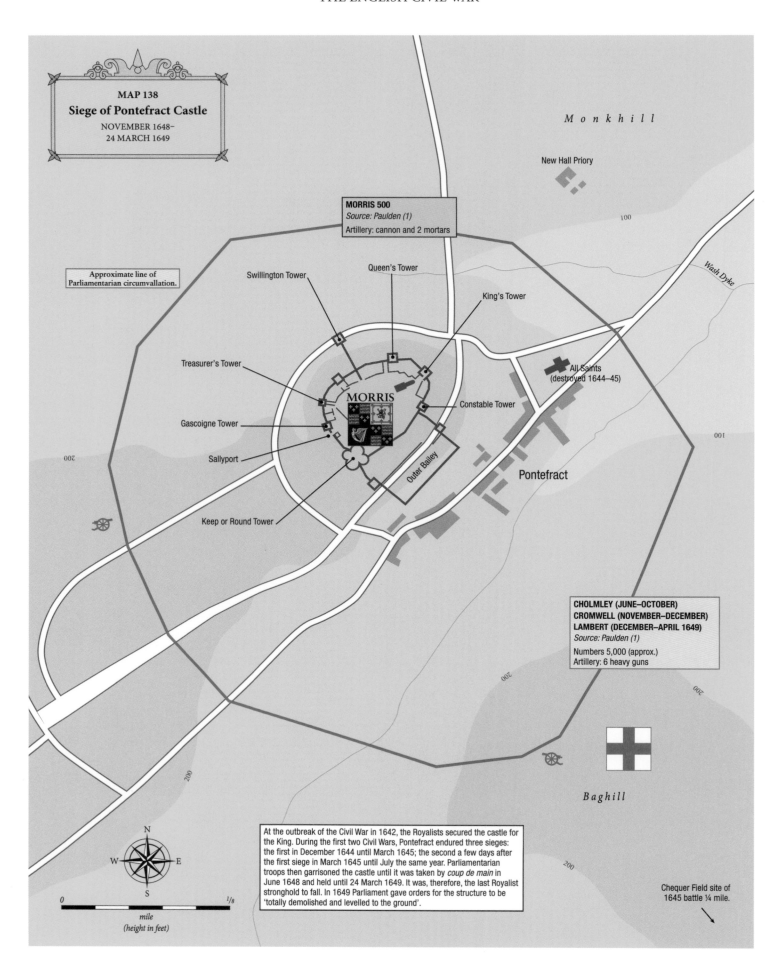

MAP 138
Siege of Pontefract Castle
NOVEMBER 1648–
24 MARCH 1649

M o n k h i l l

New Hall Priory

MORRIS 500
Source: Paulden (1)
Artillery: cannon and 2 mortars

Wash Dyke

Approximate line of
Parliamentarian circumvallation.

Swillington Tower

Queen's Tower

King's Tower

Treasurer's Tower

All Saints
(destroyed 1644–45)

MORRIS

Gascoigne Tower

Constable Tower

Sallyport

Outer Bailey

Pontefract

Keep or Round Tower

CHOLMLEY (JUNE–OCTOBER)
CROMWELL (NOVEMBER–DECEMBER)
LAMBERT (DECEMBER–APRIL 1649)
Source: Paulden (1)
Numbers 5,000 (approx.)
Artillery: 6 heavy guns

Baghill

At the outbreak of the Civil War in 1642, the Royalists secured the castle for
the King. During the first two Civil Wars, Pontefract endured three sieges:
the first in December 1644 until March 1645; the second a few days after
the first siege in March 1645 until July the same year. Parliamentarian
troops then garrisoned the castle until it was taken by *coup de main* in
June 1648 and held until 24 March 1649. It was, therefore, the last Royalist
stronghold to fall. In 1649 Parliament gave orders for the structure to be
'totally demolished and levelled to the ground'.

N
W   E
S

0   1/8
mile
(height in feet)

Chequer Field site of
1645 battle ¼ mile.

force and screen their retreat. Cromwell despatched Colonel Thornhaugh in pursuit and the two cavalry formations fought a series of actions as the Scots retreated south. Thornhaugh, leading from the front, and choosing not to wear any armour, was killed by Scottish lancers at Chorley. The Scots entered Wigan as light was fading on 18 August, and Cromwell halted the chase. He recalled that 'we lay that night in the field close by the Enemy; being very dirty and weary, and having marched twelve miles of such ground as I never rode in all my life, the day being very wet'.[22]

The next morning the Scots continued their southerly movement and, 3 miles outside Warrington, they came to a halt and established a strong defensive line among the many hedges, where, 'in a narrow lane, they made a stand with a Body of Pikes, and lined the hedges with muskets, who so rudely entertained the pursuing enemy, that they were compelled to stop'.[23] Captain Hodgson concurred that 'the foot drawn up in a most advantageous place, and snaffled our forlorn, and put them to retreat'.[24] The Parliamentarian main body was some way behind, and it took several hours for them to arrive. When they did, Cromwell threw them straight into the fight and they did not disappoint. The Scots held their ground, but what did for them were the locals, who were only too happy to guide the Roundhead infantry through fields and woods in order to outflank the Scots' position at Red Bank.[25] Hamilton's men began to fall back towards the small village of Winwick, but during their withdrawal, they were overtaken. With their powder spent, they ran for their lives, many seeking refuge in the village church, while others ran on 'crying, Mercy, Mercy... until they came to Warrington Bridge where Baily [Baillie] made Conditions for Quarter, and rendered himself and 4000 of them Prisoners'.[26]

The scale of the defeat was hard for the Scots to grasp. It is estimated that 2,000 Scots and Royalists were killed. The 3,000 or so cavalry had largely escaped intact and made off towards Chester. Cromwell gave chase, and a large number were captured when trapped by the Cheshire Parliamentarians, as they tried to cross the River Dee. The remainder was swept up through sheer exhaustion, as they headed east in an attempt to get to Pontefract. Cromwell then headed back north, to execute the other task in his orders from Derby House – the recapture of Carlisle and Berwick.[27] On 21 September, his army advanced into Scotland and was welcomed in Edinburgh by the Earl of Leven and the new ruling party. At the subsequent peace treaty, Berwick and Carlisle castles were surrendered. Furthermore, Monro was taken prisoner to London and his forces were shipped back to Ulster.

The battle at Preston had, to all intents and purposes, brought an end to the second English Civil War. However, there remained the Royalist occupation of Pontefract and Scarborough castles to be resolved. Royalist officers Colonel John Morris and Captain Thomas Paulden had captured the stronghold at Pontefract on 1 June and, just over a week later, about 800 Parliamentarians were deployed from Leeds to establish a cordon. Lacking the right equipment, they were unable to prosecute a formal siege and their numbers were inadequate to establish an effective blockade. The garrison were thus very active in conducting long-range sallies from their base. They successfully attacked Ferrybridge and Lincoln in late June and early July, before being thwarted in their attempt at Gainsborough, and were finally routed at Willoughby Field on 5 July.[28] The defenders then hatched a scheme in mid-October to capture Colonel Thomas Rainsborough, who had been sent by Fairfax to replace Henry Cholmley in command. The Royalists' plan was to exchange Rainsborough for Langdale, who had been captured at Nottingham some weeks after the battle at Preston. On 27 October, Paulden and 22 handpicked men arrived at Doncaster and surprised Rainsborough in his quarters. Refusing to be taken prisoner, he was run through in the ensuing melee.[29] Cholmley's lax cordon was blamed for the debacle but Cromwell's men were bent on revenge for the murder of Rainsborough.

Cromwell arrived at Pontefract on 30 October and wrote a full summary to Derby House in mid-November:

> The place is very well known to be one of the strongest inland garrisons in the Kingdom; well-watered; situated upon a rock in every part of it, and therefore difficult to mine. The walls very thick and high, with strong towers; and if battered, very difficult to access, by reason of the depth and steepness of the graft.[30]

He requested 500 barrels of powder and six good siege guns, to be speedily sent down from Hull. Having summoned Morris on 9 November, and received the anticipated response, Cromwell ordered the completion of earthen banks connecting a series of forts set in circumvallation around the castle. The defenders abandoned New Hall Priory and set it on fire, but the Parliamentarians arrived quickly on the scene, put out the fire and occupied it themselves. They also gained a valuable foothold in All Saint's Church, just below the eastern walls of the castle.[31]

Lambert arrived from Newcastle on 28 November to allow Cromwell to return to London (see chapter 40). He departed some nine days later. By the first week in December, three sides of the circumvallation around the castle had been completed, and battery positions had been constructed on Baghill and to the west. However, much to Lambert's frustration, the siege guns had not yet arrived from Hull, a situation that was made all the more exasperating by news from Scarborough that the siege was nearing its end, leaving Pontefract the sole Royalist bastion in the country. The heavy guns and ammunition finally arrived in mid-January and their fire rapidly succeeded in forcing the garrison to remove their artillery from the tops of the towers but seems to have done little damage to the structure itself. News of the King's execution, when it reached the Royalist defenders, only served to re-energize the defenders' struggle. A Royalist paper announced that 'the *King-Choppers* are as active in mischief as such Thieves and murderers need to be...'.[32] The Parliamentarians responded by throwing letters, wrapped around stones, into the castle offering terms and on 25 March the garrison finally surrendered. Work began almost immediately to level the structure. The emergency in the north was finally over.

---

22 Ibid., p. 29.

23 Heath, *Chronicle of The Late Intestine War*, p. 178. The site has been identified as Hermitage Green Lane.

24 Slingsby & Hodgson, op. cit., p. 122.

25 Bull & Seed, op. cit., p. 80.

26 Heath, op. cit., p. 178. Altogether 20 regiments surrendered and 70 colours were captured.

27 Derby House was the name given to the Committee of Both Houses that had assumed responsibility for conducting the war from the Committee of Both Kingdoms. It was so called because it met at Derby House, London.

28 See Beardsley, *Willoughby Field*.

29 Paulden, *Pontefract Castle*, p. 15.

30 Carlyle, op. cit., pp. 72–3.

31 Hill & Watkinson, op. cit., p. 122.

32 Ibid., p. 132.

CHAPTER 40
THE 'ENDGAME': REGICIDE, 1649

The latest intervention by the Scots and significant civil unrest from both sides of the divide had effectively been dealt with, but the fallout from both was to have political consequences. On the one hand, the case for peace had been strengthened, and Parliament, aghast that violence had reignited across England and Wales, were desperate for some form of negotiated settlement. On the other, the army, emboldened by Parliament's need to call on them to tackle both emergencies, hardened their resolve against any form of peace compromise. They were not prepared to hazard their lives further, because a misguided Parliament was incapable of dealing with an untrustworthy monarch. The full impact of the army's politicization (since 1647) was now about to be realized. No sooner had the army done their work to ensure Parliament's position and safety than Parliament rescinded its 'Vote of No Addresses' (chapter 37) and despatched commissioners to Carisbrooke Castle to reopen negotiations with the King. The army were, however, quite clear that the King had crossed a red line through his secret negotiation with the Scots and his willingness to subject his English subjects to foreign invasion. They had decided that the King was not to be trusted; furthermore, they were adamant that they had a voice in any political settlement. The King, conversely, saw Parliament's desire to talk as a weakness and had completely failed to grasp the army's consequence or influence in the matter.

Religion continued to play a key role, even at this stage of events. Fundamentalism continued to cloud judgement. For Charles his divinity was as clear as it ever had been, while for the puritanical element of the army, God's Providence drove everything. They had risked and dedicated their lives to God; all they needed was a sign of what God wanted them to do in continuance of His crusade. Charles's behaviour was that sign; it was also a forfeiture of his right to be regarded as God's anointed. Thus, the scene was set for the dialogue of the deaf. The initial negotiations with the King at Newport started well enough but soon stalled on the matter of religion, when the commissioners reiterated their demand for the abolition of the prayer-book and episcopacy, and for the introduction of Presbyterianism in their place. Charles eventually conceded that he would accept the latter for a period of three years. It was rejected on the grounds that the King's intention to revoke the concession after the three years was unequivocal. The King did, however, agree to surrender control of the militia, to subject the selection of his personal ministers to Parliament for approval and to concede the right to governance of Ireland.

As these negotiations continued, unrest in radical elements within the army grew. Lacking the support of Fairfax and with Cromwell (perhaps deliberately) still in the north, but nevertheless convinced of God's direction, Henry Ireton decided to act. He produced a new set of propositions enshrined in a document called 'The Remonstrance of the Army'. This revolutionary document called for the monarch to be brought to justice, but stopped short of proposing the abolition of the monarchy. Fairfax and the Council of Officers initially rejected Ireton's proposals and, instead, sent their own terms to the King, outlining the conditions he would have to accept in order for the army to maintain his position and security. Charles, demonstrating a fundamental misreading of the situation, rejected them

out of hand. Meanwhile, the commissioners had returned to Parliament with the King's answer to their four bills. Although he had rejected the religious proposals, there was enough progress for the conservatives, acutely conscious of the army's manoeuvrings, to expedite a vote agreeing that there was now sufficient basis for further negotiation. The army, realizing that they were about to be side-lined, acted quickly.

On 18 November the army council decided to adopt Ireton's 'Remonstrance'. A week later, Colonel Ewer was sent to replace Colonel Hammond of his charge at Carisbrooke Castle and, on 1 December, Fairfax ordered that the King be moved to Hurst Castle. The next day the army marched back into London and Fairfax installed his military headquarters in Whitehall. The military coup was bloodless and complete, but it was about to cross another red line. On 6 December Colonel Thomas Pride, acting on Ireton's orders but with Fairfax's knowledge, marched his soldiers to Parliament's lobby. His task was simple: to deny entrance to any member who had voted for continued negotiation with the King. A total of 186 members were excluded, of whom 45 were arrested and imprisoned; 86 chose to abstain and stayed away, leaving a rump Parliament of 154 members. This latter group were split between the conformists (those who accepted events and bent with the wind) and the revolutionaries (those who actively supported putting the King on trial).[1] The need to remove Charles had taken a large step forward; how to do this and how to replace him was less clear.

In the evening of the day of 'Pride's Purge', Cromwell finally returned from the north and, on arrival, declared his support for the Remonstrance and the purge. The Parliamentarian Edmund Ludlow noted that 'He declared that he had not been acquainted with this design; yet since it was done, he was glad of it, and would endeavour to maintain it.'[2] Cromwell's absence and rather tardy extraction from Pontefract has solicited criticism and accusation, but in fairness Cromwell had remained hesitant, at least initially. It was only once his attempts at parley with the King had been rebuffed that his mind was made up. Perhaps it was the sign from God that he had been awaiting. Even then his attention turned to the trial and not the sentence.[3] Cromwell, well aware of the significance of the army's actions was, nevertheless, like his colleagues, absolved of any wrongdoing in his mind through the manifestation of God's guidance. He was clear on the need for an open trial, with legal charges brought, drawn up and vindicated – vindication, that is, for their 'bringing' not their 'addressing'. Fairfax, uncomfortable and somewhat out of his depth, increasingly distanced himself from these discussions and Cromwell seamlessly replaced him. In the meantime, Charles had been moved from the rather austere surroundings of Hurst Castle to Windsor. Conditions were much more to his liking, but the irony that the seeds of his destruction had been sown within the same walls was not to become apparent for a while yet.

---

1 Anderson, *Civil Wars*, p. 132.
2 Firth, *Memoirs of Edmund Ludlow*, vol. I, pp. 211–12.
3 Fraser, *Cromwell*, p. 271; Anderson, op. cit., p. 134.

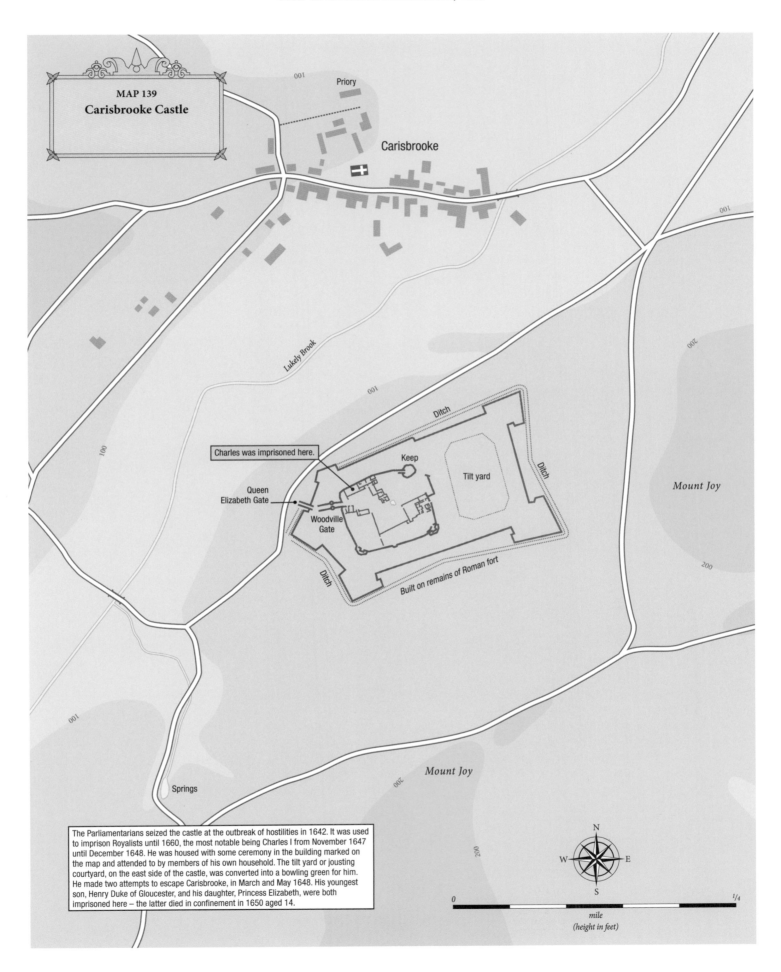

MAP 139

Carisbrooke Castle

Priory

Carisbrooke

Lukely Brook

Ditch

Charles was imprisoned here.

Keep

Tilt yard

Queen Elizabeth Gate

Woodville Gate

Ditch

Built on remains of Roman fort

Mount Joy

Mount Joy

Springs

The Parliamentarians seized the castle at the outbreak of hostilities in 1642. It was used to imprison Royalists until 1660, the most notable being Charles I from November 1647 until December 1648. He was housed with some ceremony in the building marked on the map and attended to by members of his own household. The tilt yard or jousting courtyard, on the east side of the castle, was converted into a bowling green for him. He made two attempts to escape Carisbrooke, in March and May 1648. His youngest son, Henry Duke of Gloucester, and his daughter, Princess Elizabeth, were both imprisoned here – the latter died in confinement in 1650 aged 14.

0   1/4

mile
(height in feet)

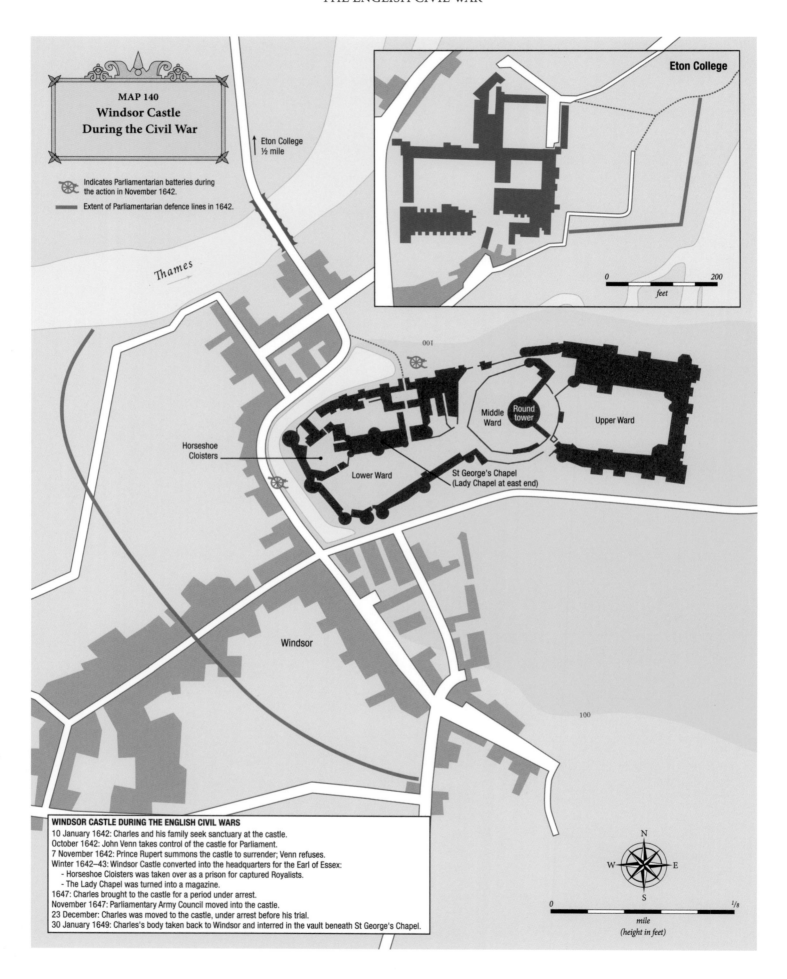

MAP 140
**Windsor Castle
During the Civil War**

Eton College
½ mile

Indicates Parliamentarian batteries during the action in November 1642.

Extent of Parliamentarian defence lines in 1642.

Eton College

0   200
feet

Thames

100

Middle Ward

Round tower

Upper Ward

Horseshoe Cloisters

Lower Ward

St George's Chapel
(Lady Chapel at east end)

100

Windsor

WINDSOR CASTLE DURING THE ENGLISH CIVIL WARS
10 January 1642: Charles and his family seek sanctuary at the castle.
October 1642: John Venn takes control of the castle for Parliament.
7 November 1642: Prince Rupert summons the castle to surrender; Venn refuses.
Winter 1642–43: Windsor Castle converted into the headquarters for the Earl of Essex:
    - Horseshoe Cloisters was taken over as a prison for captured Royalists.
    - The Lady Chapel was turned into a magazine.
1647: Charles brought to the castle for a period under arrest.
November 1647: Parliamentary Army Council moved into the castle.
23 December: Charles was moved to the castle, under arrest before his trial.
30 January 1649: Charles's body taken back to Windsor and interred in the vault beneath St George's Chapel.

N
W   E
S

0   1/8
mile
(height in feet)

On 28 December the 'Rump' outlined the plans for a special court for the trial of the King. They went to the Lords in early January and were forcibly rejected. Furthermore, the High Court judges refused to have anything to do with these proposals for a 'kangaroo court'. The Commons simply side-lined the Lords, by declaring themselves the supreme representative of the people, and then, equally adroitly, sidestepped the High Court by bringing in John Bradshaw, a relatively unknown Cheshire lawyer, to act as president. The trial opened on 20 January and, after the preliminaries, the charges were read out and Bradshaw asked the King to answer. With great conviction he retorted:

> England was never an elective Kingdom, but a hereditary Kingdom for near these thousands years; therefore let me know by what Authority I am called thither; I do stand more for the liberty of my people than any here that come to be my pretend judges; and therefore let me know by what lawful Authority I am seated here, and I will answer it. Otherwise I will not.[4]

Following a series of both public and private sittings, Charles was found guilty of treason against the people and sentenced to death. When the sentence was pronounced, he was denied the right of reply. He was executed on 30 January, going to his death unrepentant, firm in the belief that he had always tried to do the best for his people.

In death, Charles better served the cause of the monarchy than he had done during his life. The publication of *Eikon Basilike*, a few days later, purportedly the dead King's memoirs, fuelled the myth of martyrdom.[5] On 31 January the acting powers had to fill the vacuum, and quickly. Ireland was incorporated into the new state while Scotland, a separate nation, was allowed to make its own decisions with regard to a monarchy. They wasted little time in exercising that independence and declared the Prince of Wales as their new King on 5 February. Two days later, almost in defiance, the Rump Parliament elected to abolish both the English monarchy and the House of Lords.[6] A week later the English Council of State was established. Over the next few weeks and months, the Council consolidated the changes that the revolution had initiated. However, no matter how justified they felt in the eyes of God, the fact remained they had undoubtedly acted outside the law of the land. It was to be both their Achilles heel and their poisoned chalice. Even before the executioner's axe had fallen, the simmering Irish pot was coming back to the boil.

---

4 Robertson, *Tyrannicide Brief*, pp. 156–7.

5 It is unclear if the book is the work of Charles; after the Restoration, John Gauden, Bishop of Worcester, claimed to have written it

6 The acts were passed into law on 17 and 19 March, respectively.

CHAPTER 41
CROMWELL AND PARLIAMENT'S ARMY IN IRELAND, 1649–52

Ormond's attempt, in early 1648, to unite Irish Royalists and Confederates resulted in the Inchiquin Truce, and a tentative alliance between the Engagers, the Irish Royalists and the Supreme Council (at Kilkenny). The truce had been vehemently opposed by Rinuccini (read Rome) and, consequently, split the country: the Royalists, led by Inchiquin and a number of moderate Confederates, on the one side; the clerical party and the more extreme Confederates, who relied on military support from O'Neill and the Army of Ulster, on the other. Much of 1649 was, therefore, taken up with the internecine struggle between O'Neill and the Supreme Council, enabling the Protestants to seize Carrickfergus, Belfast and Coleraine in September.[1] At much the same time, the defeat of the Royalists and Scots in England (chapter 39) served to reinforce the importance of Ireland to the King's cause. In late September, Ormond landed at Cork with the express mission of uniting the factions in Ireland under the King's banner.[2] Rinuccini had alienated large swathes of Catholics with threats of excommunication, and had been called back to Rome to have his knuckles rapped. This eased matters for Ormond and, on 17 January 1649, the second Ormond Peace Treaty was signed amidst assurances of religious tolerance and the promise to repeal the abhorrent penal laws.

Following the second treaty, four factional armies existed in Ireland, two supporting the King and two Parliament. The former included Ormond's Royalists (with Inchiquin's Munster Protestants and the old English Catholic Loyalists) and the Ulster Gaelic Catholics under O'Neill. The latter included the English Parliamentarian troops under Major General Michael Jones and Sir Charles Coote, as well as the remnants of Monro's Scots in Ulster.[3] Ormond's treaty had come days before the King's trial in Westminster, undoubtedly raising fears in London of yet another Royalist uprising. Their concerns would have been heightened by the news – on the very day that court proceedings opened against the King – that Prince Rupert (and his brother Maurice) had set sail from the Netherlands with a squadron of 11 ships, destined for Ireland.[4] Parliament's attempt to intercept the fleet in the channel failed. On arrival off the Irish coast at the end of the month, Rupert fortified Kinsale harbour and made contact with Ormond. Parliament responded by ramping up their naval presence in the Irish Sea and St George's Channel by sending 30 warships and 40 armed merchantmen. Parliament was to receive another setback in mid-February,

when the Scottish Presbytery of Belfast denounced the execution of the King, and encouraged all Ulster Scots to refuse to cooperate with Monck and Coote. This served to further confuse the ethnic and religious make-up of the divide. The Scots were now split into the 'Resolutioners', supporters of Charles II, and the 'Remonstrants', supporters of Parliament.[5]

Back in London, with the trial concluded, the Council of State turned its attention to tackling its first national emergency. On 15 March they agreed to mobilize an army for operations in Ireland under the command of Cromwell. For the Parliamentarians the moment was opportune; they could finally subdue the Royalist rebels and wreak their vengeance on an ungodly people. Cromwell's army was to consist of 12,000 veterans, a massive war-chest of £100,000 and a huge siege train of 56 large guns and 600 barrels of powder plus the requisite shot.[6] Along with the supplies to feed, clothe and equip his army, and the wherewithal to move the entire siege and baggage train, the logistic plans took time to implement. In the meantime, the Council of State satisfied themselves with news that their navy had regained control of the seas and, by 22 May, had blockaded Rupert's fleet in Kinsale harbour.

Ormond was keen to take the fight to the Parliamentarians and, in mid-May, the Confederate Catholics and Protestant Royalists were clearing a way for their advance on Dublin, while the Lagan army of Western Ulster (about 7,000 men) besieged Coote in Londonderry. Coote conducted a skilful defence, helped by the fact that the Irish had no siege guns. However, the tide began to turn in May, when Robert Stewart (the former Lagan commander) escaped from prison in London and returned to Ulster to take command of the siege. In early July, Monro, with 2,000 Ulster Scots, arrived to help Stewart. He also had 12 light field guns. They were not much use against the walls but they were capable of sinking any supply ship that tried to break through the blockade by sailing up the River Foyle.

Ormond remained frustrated in his efforts to join forces with O'Neill's powerful Ulster Gaelic Catholic army. Those efforts were then dealt a blow in early May, when O'Neill, in an extraordinary show of duplicity, perhaps driven through an almost inbred suspicion, agreed a three-month cessation of hostilities with Monck. Unperturbed, Ormond mustered 14,000 men near Carlow and then marched north to remove the Parliamentarian garrisons in north Leinster, before advancing on the capital. By the end of July his forces had captured Drogheda, Dundalk, Newry, Carlingford and Trim.[7] But when Ormond moved his force to isolate O'Neill's army from providing support to Monck at Dundalk, the Ulster Catholics moved north towards Londonderry. Once there, thanks to his truce with the Parliamentarians, O'Neill agreed to supply Coote's men with ammunition

---

1 They were lost again to the Ulster Scots in early 1649.

2 He was able to land at Cork as Inchiquin had declared for the King in April 1648. He arrived with arms, paid for by the French, to equip 4,000 infantry and 1,000 cavalry.

3 Reilly, *Cromwell, An Honourable Enemy*, p. 28. The latter were to change sides once news of the regicide reached the Belfast Presbyterians.

4 Morrah, *Rupert of the Rhine*, pp. 237–8. Rupert was on the 52-gun *Constant Reformation*, his brother on the 46-gun *Convertine* and Rear Admiral Mennes in the 40-gun *Swallow*, while the fleet included five smaller vessels and three Dutch East Indiamen.

5 McKeiver, *A New History of Cromwell's Irish Campaign*, p. 56.

6 Kenyon & Ohlmeyer, *Military History*, p. 98.

7 Drogheda ran out of ammunition and surrendered on 11 July. Nearly all the garrison signed up to serve with the victors.

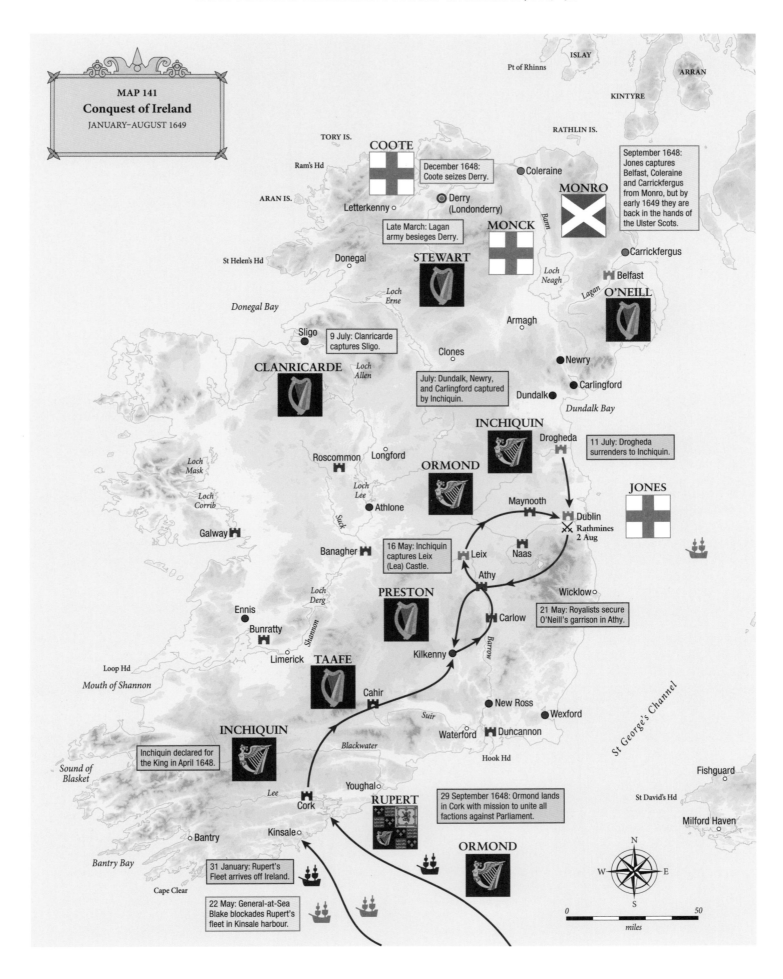

MAP 141

Conquest of Ireland

JANUARY–AUGUST 1649

ISLAY

Pt of Rhinns

ARRAN

KINTYRE

RATHLIN IS.

TORY IS.

COOTE

December 1648:
Coote seizes Derry.

Coleraine

MONRO

Ram's Hd

ARAN IS.

Letterkenny

Derry
(Londonderry)

Late March: Lagan
army besieges Derry.

MONCK

Bann

Carrickfergus

September 1648:
Jones captures
Belfast, Coleraine
and Carrickfergus
from Monro, but by
early 1649 they are
back in the hands of
the Ulster Scots.

St Helen's Hd

Donegal

STEWART

Loch
Neagh

Belfast

Loch
Erne

Lagan

O'NEILL

Donegal Bay

Armagh

Sligo

9 July: Clanricarde
captures Sligo.

Clones

Newry

Carlingford

CLANRICARDE

Loch
Allen

July: Dundalk, Newry,
and Carlingford captured
by Inchiquin.

Dundalk

Dundalk Bay

INCHIQUIN

Drogheda

11 July: Drogheda
surrenders to Inchiquin.

Loch
Mask

Roscommon

Longford

ORMOND

JONES

Loch
Lee

Maynooth

Dublin

Loch
Corrib

Suck

Athlone

Rathmines
2 Aug

Galway

Banagher

16 May: Inchiquin
captures Leix
(Lea) Castle.

Leix

Naas

Athy

Wicklow

PRESTON

Carlow

21 May: Royalists secure
O'Neill's garrison in Athy.

Loch
Derg

Ennis

Barrow

Bunratty

Shannon

Limerick

TAAFE

Kilkenny

Loop Hd

Mouth of Shannon

Cahir

New Ross

Suir

Wexford

Waterford

Duncannon

INCHIQUIN

Blackwater

Hook Hd

Fishguard

Sound of
Blasket

Inchiquin declared for
the King in April 1648.

Lee

Youghal

St David's Hd

Cork

RUPERT

29 September 1648: Ormond lands
in Cork with mission to unite all
factions against Parliament.

Milford Haven

Kinsale

Bantry

ORMOND

St George's Channel

Bantry Bay

31 January: Rupert's
Fleet arrives off Ireland.

N

Cape Clear

22 May: General-at-Sea
Blake blockades Rupert's
fleet in Kinsale harbour.

W   E

S

0   50

miles

and gunpowder. Frustratingly for the besiegers, they were not strong enough to challenge O'Neill in battle and were forced to lift the siege and withdraw – Stewart towards Connacht and Monro's forces to Coleraine and Belfast. Yet Parliament was deeply ill at ease over Monck's and Coote's 'arrangements' with O'Neill. Indeed, Monck was summoned back to London to explain himself. Once there, he stated his case, and by a margin they accepted his actions were 'necessary for the preservation of the Parliament of England's interest'.[8]

Ormond, meanwhile, now moved forces for the ultimate prize – Dublin. 'The possession of the capital, he supposed, would not only secure the King's interest in Ireland, but also cause an extensive rising in his favour throughout England.'[9] He was more than aware that Cromwell's arrival was imminent, but he was not unduly concerned, writing on 18 July that 'we shall more dread his money than his face'.[10] On 25 July, Ormond left Lord Dillon with 2,000 foot and 500 horse to cover the northern approaches towards the city and then crossed the River Liffey, with the balance of his force (5,000 foot and 2,000 horse), to close off the city from the south and deny the Parliamentarians access to grazing lands. However, Ormond lacked sufficient infantry, artillery and engineer stores to enable him to conduct a formal siege against a city the size of Dublin. Furthermore, he had received conflicting reports of Cromwell's intended landing site. On 27 July Ormond decided to send Inchiquin, with three regiments of horse, south into Munster to organize the province's defences and to prevent the defection of any coastal town that might facilitate the landing of Cromwell's large army.[11]

On 28 July Ormond's forces stormed and captured the outlying Parliamentarian garrison of Rathfarnham Castle, 3 miles south of Dublin. Despite their success Ormond was uneasy and, having lost Inchiquin and much of his cavalry, he considered raising the siege and retiring to Drogheda. The Irish officers would hear nothing of it, and proposed that they move closer to the city and capture Baggotrath Castle, from where they could establish a foothold and prosecute subsequent operations. Ormond agreed to conduct a reconnaissance, and recalled that 'it was ordered that my Lord of Castlehaven, General Preston, and Major-General Purcell, should view the place; and if they found it capable of strengthening in one night's work, then to cause men with materials to be sent as soon as it was dark'.[12] On 1 August Purcell was sent forward with 1,500 infantry to capture Baggotrath Castle, but the operation misfired when guides lost their bearings.[13] They did not reach the castle until an hour before daybreak on 2 August. Consequently, when Ormond arrived with the main body of the army at dawn, the structure had not been strengthened or prepared. Realizing the precariousness of the situation, Ormond gave orders for the army's deployment and then retired to sleep off the night's exertions. At 9am sounds of firing disturbed his slumbers. Jones had sallied out of the city in force and had attacked across the frontage.

According to a letter written by a colonel within the garrison, the Parliamentarians had 7,000 foot and 500 horse.[14] To this figure has to be added the reinforcements (1,600 foot and 600–700 horse) that arrived between 22 and 23 July. Jones was quite clear of his intentions: 'Drew I out twelve hundred horse and four thousand foot, not then intending further than the beating up of the enemy's quarters.'[15] The attack was quick, excellently delivered and very successful, as Ormond recalled:

> Before I got an hundred yards from my tent, all those I left working were beaten out, and the enemy had routed and killed Sir W. Vaughan… this was the right wing of our army; and it was not long before I saw it wholly defeated, and many of them running away towards the hills of Wicklow… Hereupon I went to the battalia… where I left them till I should either come or send them orders. How they were forced thence, or upon what occasion they charged, I know not; but I soon after perceived the enemy's horse had gotten round and was going through a lane… at this and at the running away of Reilly's regiment, our foot were so discouraged that they fought no more.[16]

With Ormond's men on the run, Jones let go of the leash, and his men pursued Ormond's men for many miles, and captured a large number who took refuge in the castles at Rathmines and Rathcar. Jones estimated his tally to be 4,000 killed and 2,500 prisoners; as well they 'took on the place three demi-cannons, one large square gun, carrying a ball of twelve pounds, one saker drake, and one mortar piece; all these brass'.[17] Ormond, in his post-battle letter to the King, painted a very different picture, claiming losses at 600 and making no mention of those taken prisoner, or the loss of his baggage, arms, ammunition, artillery and a money chest containing £4,000. Whatever the losses, the significance of the victory at Rathmines is unequivocal: it was the turning point of the war in Ireland and it paved the way for what was to follow. Jones decided to capitalize on his victory, and made a dash for Drogheda in order to try to convince the governor of the futility of continued defiance. Ormond, meanwhile, withdrew to Kilkenny, but on hearing of Jones's plans for Drogheda, moved north to Tecroghan (near Trim) and despatched Arthur Aston to assume command of the garrison.[18] Reinforcing the garrison to over 2,000 foot and 300 effective horse, Ormond withdrew back towards Trim, and Jones did likewise back to Dublin to await Cromwell's arrival.[19] Ormond's position was now very precarious, but he was to receive some positive news on 12 August. O'Neill, at the end of his three-month cessation, had finally agreed to join the Royalists. By then the opportunity had passed.

On 13 August Cromwell set sail from Milford Haven 'with the van of his army in thirty-two ships. Commissary-General Ireton, his son-in-law, followed two days after, with the main body of the army in forty-two vessels. His chaplain, Hugh Peters, with twenty sail brought up the rear. Three regiments were left behind for want of shipping.'[20] Cromwell had heard about Jones's resounding victory, which he described as 'an astonishing mercie', as he was about to set sail.[21] He wasted no time in changing their

---

8 Murphy, *Cromwell in Ireland*, p. 18.
9 Ibid., p. 23.
10 Gardiner, *Commonwealth and Protectorate*, vol. I, p. 99.
11 Murphy, op. cit., p. 27, estimates the number to have been about 1,100.
12 Ibid., p. 29.
13 The guide(s) may have done this on purpose – see Murphy, op. cit., p. 29, footnote 2.
14 R. C., *The present condition of Dublin*, p. 2. This almost certainly includes the reinforcements that arrived on 22 and 23 July from England – Murphy, op. cit., p. 26.

15 Cary, *Memorials of the Great Civil War*, vol. II, p. 161
16 Murphy, op. cit., pp. 30–1.
17 Cary, op. cit., p. 161.
18 He could only muster about 3,000 men.
19 The defenders of Drogheda were a mixture of Irish and English Protestants and Catholics. See McKeiver, op. cit., chapter 3.
20 Murphy, op. cit., pp. 73–4. It would appear that Ireton was destined for Munster but moved to Dublin because of bad weather – *Moderate Intelligencer* dated August 30.
21 Carlyle, *Cromwell's Letters*, vol. I, p. 134.

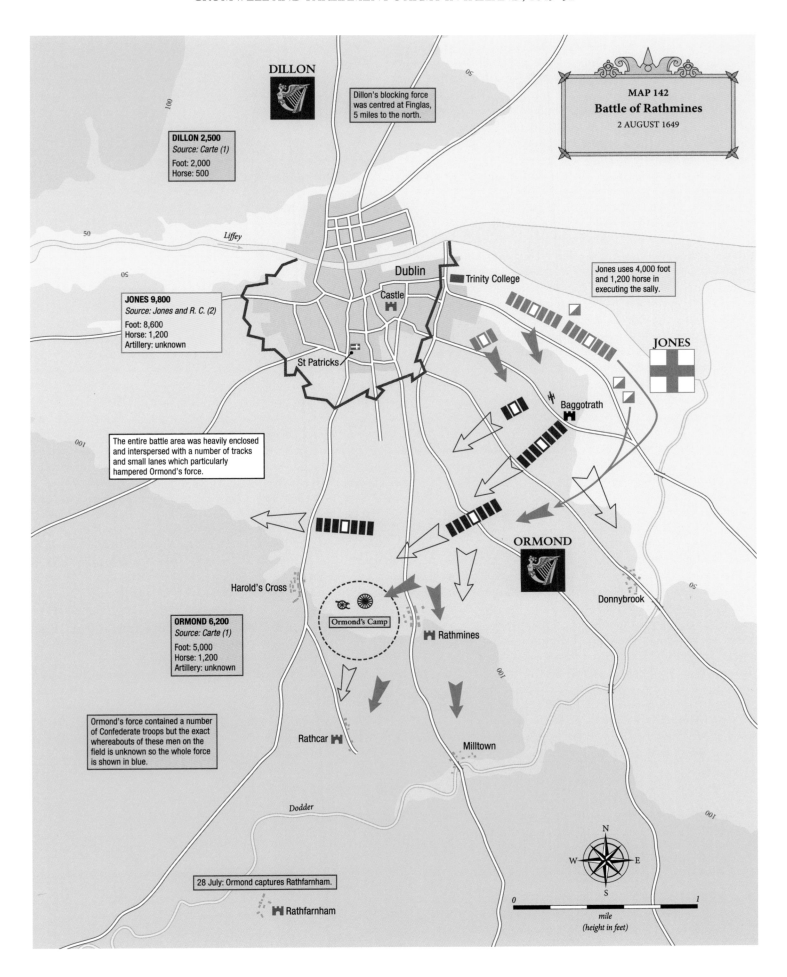

DILLON

Dillon's blocking force was centred at Finglas, 5 miles to the north.

MAP 142
Battle of Rathmines
2 AUGUST 1649

DILLON 2,500
Source: Carte (1)
Foot: 2,000
Horse: 500

Jones uses 4,000 foot and 1,200 horse in executing the sally.

Dublin

Trinity College

Castle

JONES

JONES 9,800
Source: Jones and R. C. (2)
Foot: 8,600
Horse: 1,200
Artillery: unknown

St Patricks

Baggotrath

The entire battle area was heavily enclosed and interspersed with a number of tracks and small lanes which particularly hampered Ormond's force.

ORMOND

Donnybrook

Harold's Cross

Ormond's Camp

ORMOND 6,200
Source: Carte (1)
Foot: 5,000
Horse: 1,200
Artillery: unknown

Rathmines

Rathcar

Milltown

Ormond's force contained a number of Confederate troops but the exact whereabouts of these men on the field is unknown so the whole force is shown in blue.

Dodder

N
W   E
S

0   1
mile
(height in feet)

28 July: Ormond captures Rathfarnham.

Rathfarnham

Liffey

destination to Dublin. Cromwell arrived in the city on 15 August, and Ireton a few days later. His army numbered 17,000 men, many of whom were battle-hardened veterans of the wars in England and Wales, many of whom were happy to die for God and their talismanic leader and many of whom were happy to get to grips with Catholics or their allies.[22] Worryingly, they were fired up to treat the Irish people as the Israelites in Joshua's time were bidden to treat the Canaanites. Ethnic cleansing was clearly on the menu. It was enough to solicit two declarations from Cromwell while he was in Dublin; the second, issued on 24 August, spelt out his determination to avoid unnecessary civilian casualties:

> … I do hereby warn and require all officers, soldiers, and others under my command, henceforth to forbear all such evil practices as aforesaid, and not to do any wrong or violence towards country people or persons whatsoever, unless they be actually in arms or office with the enemy, and not to meddle with the goods of such without special order.[23]

Cromwell saw no reason to delay matters and, in the final days of August, he 'rendezvoused with eight regiments of foot, six of horse and some troops of dragoons, three miles on the north side of Dublin'.[24] Having selected 12 of those regiments, amounting to about 10,000 men, he despatched the newly promoted Lieutenant General Jones to take the vanguard and march directly to Drogheda. Cromwell followed with the main body the next day, while George Ayscue transported the siege artillery, ammunition and engineer stores by sea. Bad weather delayed the arrival of the guns and it was not until 5 September that they were unloaded and moved to their two prepared battery positions to the south-east of the town. They were ready to open on 9 September and Cromwell duly sent Aston a summons, to which he received no satisfactory answer, and the great guns exploded into life. Drogheda was a formidable fortress, Aston a professional soldier of considerable repute and his garrison some of the best Royalist troops in the whole of Ireland. Nevertheless, Aston was relying on Ormond appearing over the horizon, at the head of a large force, to offer battle and to drive off the besieging army. In reality Ormond was having all sorts of problems concentrating forces. O'Neill pontificated about the many thousands he could muster, but remained rooted in and around Derry, while Ulick Fion Burke, the Marquess of Clanricarde,[25] and Inchiquin seemed equally unaware of the urgency and had not moved from Connaught and Munster respectively. Ormond himself only sported a few infantrymen and about a thousand horse; for now, he was relying on the formidable nature of Drogheda's walls and defences to delay Cromwell.

The Parliamentarian plan to crack Drogheda was straightforward enough, as Cromwell noted:

> … the place pitched upon was that part of the Town-wall next a Church called St. Mary's; which was the rather chosen because we did hope that if we did enter and possess that Church, we should be the better able to keep it against their horse and foot until we could make way for the entrance of our horse; and we did not conceive that any part of the Town would afford the like advantage for that purpose with this.[26]

This had the advantage that both assault columns would be able to provide each other mutual support. As such, it was not a textbook siege; there was to be no cordon and no planned diversionary attacks; Cromwell was clearly hoping the defenders would simply surrender. Aston conducted a sally on 7 September that killed and wounded a few of the besiegers but was otherwise ineffectual. Instead, he concentrated on retrenching behind the areas where Cromwell's batteries were breaching. After two days the huge guns had done their work and, on 10 September at about 5pm, they 'began the Storm: and after some hot dispute we entered, about seven or eight hundred men; the Enemy disputing it very stiffly with us'.[27]

Both attacks were driven back and Hewson's men were driven across the ravine and had to be supported by the regiments of Venables and Phayre. They, in turn, drove the Royalist defenders back through the breach and across their own retrenchments. To the south, Colonel Castle was shot in the head and this seemed the cause of the attack beginning to waver. Cromwell intervened personally to maintain the attacking momentum. After a while, both attacks gained lodgements and the defenders quickly began to lose heart. The Parliamentarian soldiers then poured through the breaches, and Aston and 300 men fell back to the security of Mill Mount. Cromwell recorded that 'our men getting up to them, were ordered by me to put them all to the sword'.[28] Cromwell, in the heat of the moment, also ordered every man bearing arms within the walls to be put to the sword. About 2,000 were slain (Cromwell's estimate) and others fled over the bridge to the north, where the slaughter continued for the rest of the night and into the following day.[29] Many defenders escaped through St Sunday's Gate, while others took refuge in two towers attached to the great walls. Cromwell noted:

> … from one of the said Towers, notwithstanding their condition, they killed and wounded some of our men. When they submitted, their officers were knocked on the head; and every tenth man of the soldiers killed; and the rest shipped for the Barbadoes. The soldiers in the other Tower were all spared, as to their lives only; and shipped likewise for the Barbadoes.[30]

The bloody siege of Drogheda was over in a matter of hours but the repercussions live long in memories to this day. Colonel Hewson recalled that 'in this slaughter there was by my observation, at least 3,000 dead bodies lay in the fort and the streets, whereof there could not be 150 of them of our own army, for I lost more than any other regiment and there was not sixty killed outright of my men'.[31] There is no evidence that the massacre included civilians, but given the size of Aston's garrison and the fact that some men were saved (and exported), some civilians must have

---

22 This included about 5,000 men who were attached to his field force from the garrison at Dublin.
23 Murphy, op. cit., pp. 77–9.
24 Carlyle, op. cit., p. 150. Cromwell does not indicate which regiments he took. There is considerable confusion over dates. I have used Cromwell's dates from his letters/reports.
25 Clanricarde is an interesting character and complex player in Irish affairs of the time. During the Irish Confederate Wars, he supported the Royalist James Butler in defending Ireland for Charles I against the Parliamentarians by uniting Catholic and Protestant nobles (himself being Catholic). He did not initially join the Catholic Confederate Ireland, but instead helped to broker a military alliance between the Confederates and English Royalists. After Ormond fled the country, Clanricarde became the Lord Lieutenant and the leading Royalist in Ireland.
26 Ibid.
27 Carlisle, loc. cit., p. 151.
28 Ibid., p. 152.
29 McKeiver, op. cit. disputes this – see pp. 95–6.
30 Ibid.
31 Ibbitson, *Perfect occurrences*, Issue 144, 28 September–4 October 1649, p. 1276.

(inevitably) been caught up in the atrocities.[32] Tom Reilly, in his excellent work on Drogheda, sums up the situation from the side of the combatants: 'Cromwell may well have had no moral right to take the lives of the defending garrison of Drogheda, but he certainly had the law on his side.' There are plenty of other examples in history where the garrison, having refused the summons, were put to the sword. Indeed, massacres had been an integral part of the struggle in Ireland, in this period (and others); furthermore, the vast majority of the victims of Drogheda were, in fact, English.[33] It is therefore curious that Cromwell (and Drogheda) has been singled out for unwavering notoriety of brutality to the Irish.

> The speedy capture of Drogheda and the merciless massacre of its inhabitants had the effect which they desired. It spread abroad the terror of his name; it cut off the best body of the Irish troops, and disheartened the rest to such a degree, that it was a greater loss in itself and more fatal in its consequences than the rout at Rathmines.[34]

Ormond's 19th-century biographer perfectly captures Cromwell's intentions at Drogheda and the importance of what passed at Drogheda to Cromwell's strategic plans for the conquest of the country. The dominoes now started to fall. As Ormond recalled in his letter to the King, 'immediately upon this I ordered the burning and quitting of Trim and Dundalk: but fear so possessed those in both places, that neither was so done, but that the Rebels have possessed them with garrisons, and are now marching with all their power towards Wexford'.[35] Cromwell sent three regiments north, under Colonel Robert Venables, to join forces with Sir Charles Coote in Ulster, while he returned to Dublin with the main body of his army and prepared to advance into the Confederate heartlands of southern Ireland. On 15 September Venables garrisoned Dundalk, which had been abandoned, while Coote liberated Coleraine, where the Irish Royalist garrison were massacred without mercy.[36] Then, on 21 September Venables captured Carlingford, assisted by a naval squadron which bombarded the town as he attacked. The next day he secured Newry. The resolve of the Ulster Scots was clearly on the wane and, on 30 September, the garrison at Belfast surrendered without a fight. Coote and Venables then joined forces and spent the rest of the year mopping up the Royalist forces under Montgomery, and the Ulster Scots under Monro. On 13 December they captured Carrickfergus, giving the Parliamentarians absolute control over Ulster with the exceptions of Charlemont and Enniskillen.

Cromwell left Dublin on 23 September and marched south; his objective was Wexford, a notorious base for privateers conducting raids on English shipping. His army was about 11,000 strong, and to ease his logistical burden and expedite movement, he hugged the coast and was shadowed by a supporting fleet. He arrived before Wexford on 1 October, having swept up the Royalist garrisons at Arklow, Ferns and Enniscorthy. Meanwhile, Ormond moved his headquarters to New Ross and despatched a further 1,000 troops under Colonel David Sinnott to reinforce Wexford.

The county town of Wexford was strategically sited with a harbour sheltered by two capes, the southern point being guarded by Rosslare fort. This was Cromwell's first objective and he outwitted his opponents by crossing the Slaney River, well north, and then swinging south and attacking Wexford from a southerly direction. Jones led the attack on the Rosslare fort and the garrison fled in panic as he approached with an advance guard of mounted dragoons. With this fort in his hands, the fleet carrying the heavy guns and supplies was able to enter the harbour. They unloaded the siege train to the south of the castle, and Cromwell's gunners quickly established a battery at the south-eastern corner of the town and castle. His army, by this stage having garrisoned the many forts he had captured en route, was about 9,000 strong.

On 3 October, while his infantry and gunners prepared their defences and battery positions, Cromwell issued a summons for surrender. Sinnott, as instructed by Ormond, played for time and, as the days passed, he received additional reinforcements from the north. Ormond decided to make a show of force with 1,800 horse on the north bank, but turned tail sharply when Cromwell responded by despatching Jones with a similar force to challenge him. By 10 September Cromwell's patience had run out. He later wrote:

> … upon Thursday, the 11th instant (our batteries being finished the night before), we began to play betimes in the morning; and having spent near a hundred shot, the Governor's stomach came down; and he sent to me to give leave for four persons, intrusted by him, to come unto me, and offer terms of surrender.[37]

While this was ongoing the captain of the castle (Captain Stafford) decided to allow the Parliamentarian soldiers to enter. When the town's defenders noticed their presence, they panicked, some running to the town's marketplace, others surrendering in situ, while the rest made for the shore and a number of small boats. Cromwell reported that 'our men perceiving, ran violently upon the Town with their ladders, and stormed it. And when they were come into the market-place, the Enemy making a stiff resistance, our forces brake them; and then put all to the sword that came in their way'.[38]

Cromwell and his officers appear to have done little to restrain their men and, as such, given the nature of ongoing negotiations, the actions at Wexford are difficult to excuse, being entirely devoid of both legality and morality. However, it is important to highlight that, unlike at Drogheda, Cromwell did not give a direct order. Much of the post-Wexford atrocities are, like Drogheda, the subject of Royalist propaganda and folklore.[39] The loss of Wexford and 2,000 men was another major blow to the Royalist–Confederate coalition, reducing Ormond's field army to fewer than 3,000. For Cromwell it offered up a marvellous, well-placed naval base, numerous ships from the Irish privateering fleet, over 100 (land and sea) guns of various calibres, as well as 'great quantities of iron, hides, tallow, salt, pipe and barrel staves'.

Cromwell was now ready to move on Munster, but he first had to remove the garrison at New Ross. Sir Lucas Taaffe, the governor there, persuaded the Marquis of Ormond to allow him to surrender the town on terms, and it was in Cromwell's hands by 19 October. The same day the Council of State

32 Unfortunately, there is no space in this work to debate what happened at Drogheda; the best studies on this are undoubtedly those by Tom Reilly and Philip McKeiver.

33 McKeiver, op. cit., p. 107, citing Hamilton, *Irish Rebellion*

34 Carte, *James, Duke of Ormond*, vol. III, p. 477.

35 Carte, *Collection of Original Letters*, vol. II, p. 412.

36 As there was no formal summons *per se* the Protestant inhabitants opened the gates. Therefore, the massacre at Coleraine is a far clearer war crime than events at Drogheda.

37 Carlyle, op. cit., p. 165.

38 Ibid., p. 169.

39 McKeiver, op. cit., chapter 4.

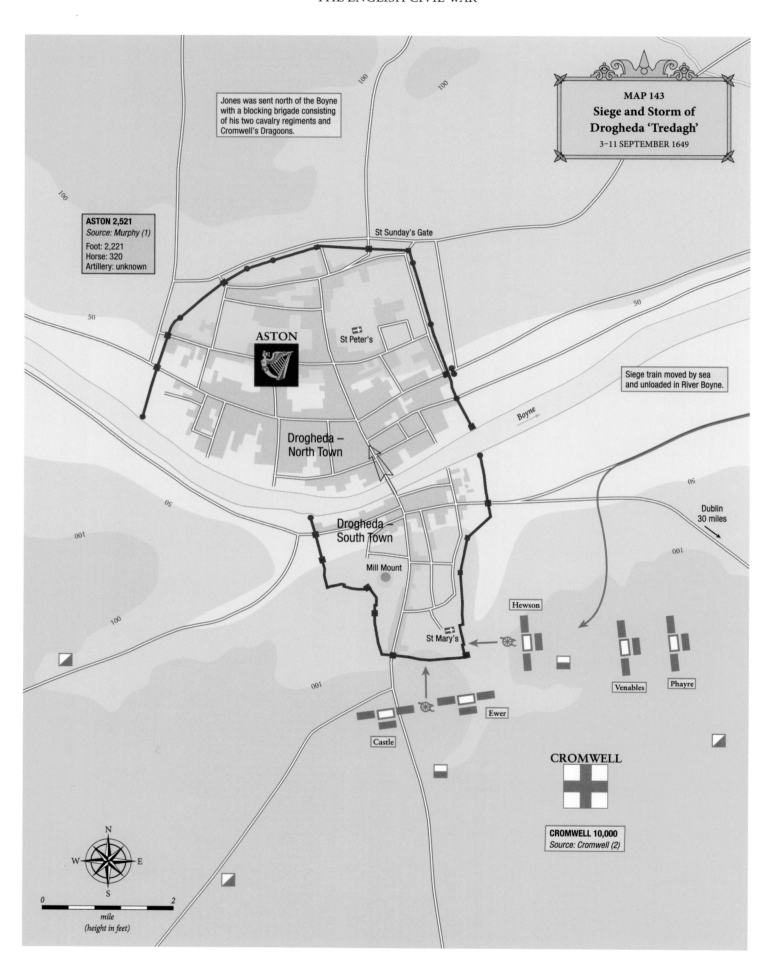

Jones was sent north of the Boyne with a blocking brigade consisting of his two cavalry regiments and Cromwell's Dragoons.

MAP 143
Siege and Storm of Drogheda 'Tredagh'
3–11 SEPTEMBER 1649

St Sunday's Gate

ASTON 2,521
Source: Murphy (1)
Foot: 2,221
Horse: 320
Artillery: unknown

ASTON

St Peter's

Siege train moved by sea and unloaded in River Boyne.

Boyne

Drogheda – North Town

50

Dublin 30 miles

Drogheda – South Town

Mill Mount

Hewson

Venables

Phayre

St Mary's

Ewer

Castle

CROMWELL

CROMWELL 10,000
Source: Cromwell (2)

N
W E
S

0   2
mile
(height in feet)

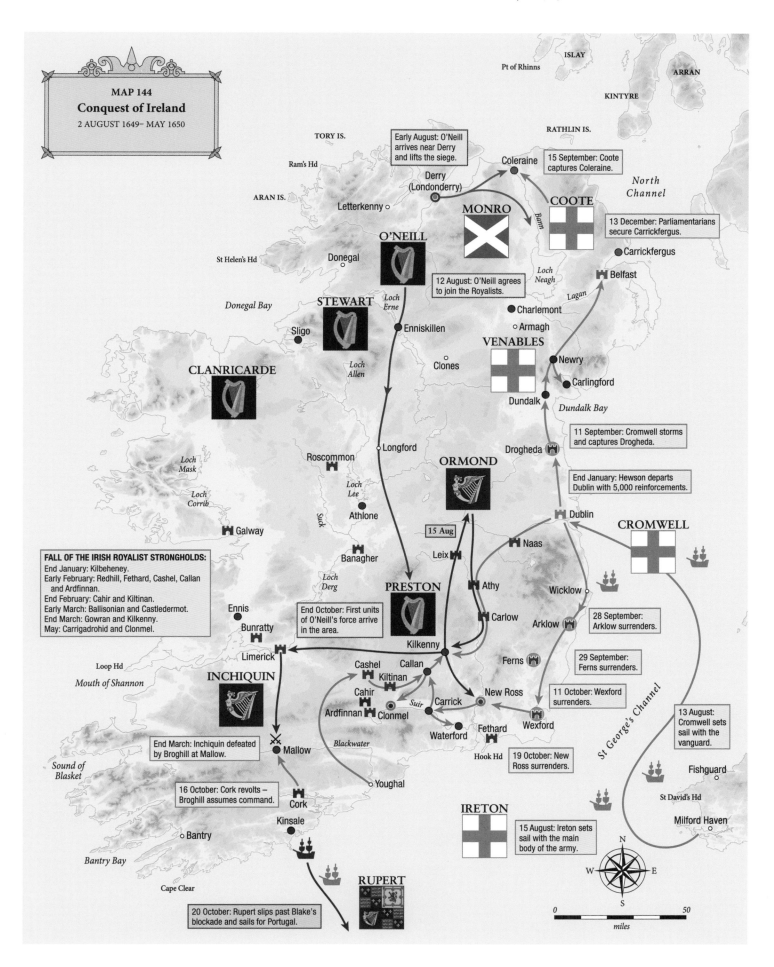

MAP 144
Conquest of Ireland
2 AUGUST 1649– MAY 1650

TORY IS.

ISLAY

Pt of Rhinns

ARRAN

KINTYRE

Ram's Hd

RATHLIN IS.

Early August: O'Neill arrives near Derry and lifts the siege.

Coleraine

15 September: Coote captures Coleraine.

Derry (Londonderry)

North Channel

ARAN IS.

Letterkenny

MONRO

COOTE

St Helen's Hd

O'NEILL

Bann

13 December: Parliamentarians secure Carrickfergus.

Donegal

Carrickfergus

Donegal Bay

STEWART

Loch Erne

12 August: O'Neill agrees to join the Royalists.

Loch Neagh

Belfast

Sligo

Enniskillen

Charlemont

Lagan

Armagh

VENABLES

Newry

Loch Allen

Clones

Carlingford

CLANRICARDE

Dundalk

Dundalk Bay

Loch Mask

Longford

11 September: Cromwell storms and captures Drogheda.

Loch Corrib

Roscommon

Drogheda

End January: Hewson departs Dublin with 5,000 reinforcements.

ORMOND

Loch Lee

Athlone

Dublin

CROMWELL

Suck

Galway

Naas

15 Aug

Leix

Loch Derg

Banagher

Athy

Wicklow

PRESTON

FALL OF THE IRISH ROYALIST STRONGHOLDS:
End January: Kilbeheney.
Early February: Redhill, Fethard, Cashel, Callan and Ardfinnan.
End February: Cahir and Kiltinan.
Early March: Ballisonian and Castledermot.
End March: Gowran and Kilkenny.
May: Carrigadrohid and Clonmel.

Carlow

Ennis

28 September: Arklow surrenders.

Arklow

Bunratty

End October: First units of O'Neill's force arrive in the area.

Ferns

29 September: Ferns surrenders.

Kilkenny

Limerick

Loop Hd

Mouth of Shannon

Cashel

Callan

11 October: Wexford surrenders.

Kiltinan

INCHIQUIN

Cahir

Suir

Carrick

New Ross

Ardfinnan

Clonmel

13 August: Cromwell sets sail with the vanguard.

St George's Channel

Waterford

Fethard

Wexford

End March: Inchiquin defeated by Broghill at Mallow.

Blackwater

Mallow

Hook Hd

19 October: New Ross surrenders.

Sound of Blasket

Fishguard

16 October: Cork revolts – Broghill assumes command.

Youghal

St David's Hd

Cork

Milford Haven

Bantry

Kinsale

IRETON

15 August: Ireton sets sail with the main body of the army.

N

Bantry Bay

W   E

Cape Clear

RUPERT

S

0   50

20 October: Rupert slips past Blake's blockade and sails for Portugal.

miles

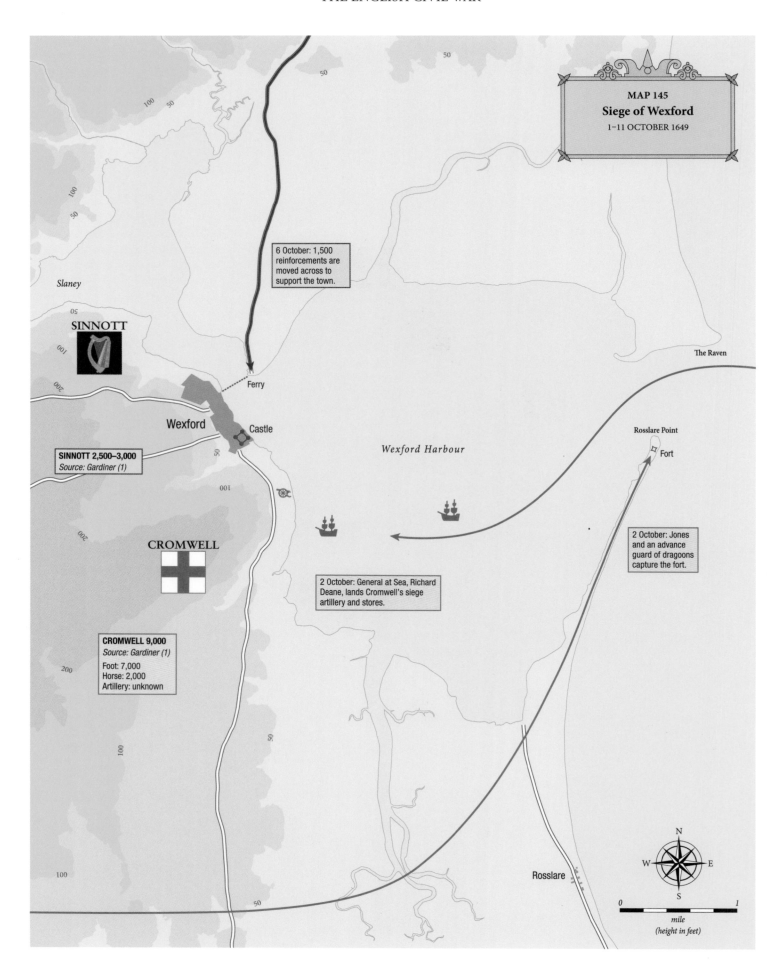

50

50

100

50

100

50

Slaney

05

100

SINNOTT

200

Wexford

50

SINNOTT 2,500–3,000
Source: Gardiner (1)

100

200

CROMWELL

CROMWELL 9,000
Source: Gardiner (1)
Foot: 7,000
Horse: 2,000
Artillery: unknown

200

100

100

50

50

6 October: 1,500
reinforcements are
moved across to
support the town.

Ferry

Castle

Wexford Harbour

The Raven

Rosslare Point

Fort

2 October: Jones
and an advance
guard of dragoons
capture the fort.

2 October: General at Sea, Richard
Deane, lands Cromwell's siege
artillery and stores.

Rosslare

MAP 145
Siege of Wexford
1–11 OCTOBER 1649

N
W   E
S

0   1

mile
(height in feet)

informed Cromwell that a reinforcement of 5,000 troops was fully prepared to depart for Ireland. The following day, Rupert slipped past Blake's blockading fleet and made for the Tagus estuary, having agreed terms with the Portuguese King Joao IV. Meanwhile, at New Ross, Cromwell ordered his pioneers to build a bridge of boats across the fast-flowing River Barrow to facilitate his advance into Munster. Despite all this, Ormond remained optimistic. He had finally concluded matters with an ageing and ill O'Neill, and some of the units of the Lagan army began to appear by the end of October. With plague rife in Cromwell's army, and he himself afflicted, Jones was despatched north with all able-bodied men in an attempt to capture Kilkenny. The venture was thwarted at Thomastown, where the Royalists blew the bridge. Cromwell then despatched Reynolds to capture Carrick, which was in Parliament's hands by 19 November. Cromwell then advanced to Waterford, arriving before the gates on 24 November, only to learn that Ormond had moved and was in the process of trying to recapture Carrick. In the end, both Ormond's attempt at Carrick and Cromwell's at Waterford were to fail, and both sides agreed to withdraw into winter quarters.

From Parliament's perspective, the initial stages of Cromwell's Irish campaign had been a resounding success. As 1650 dawned, Cromwell's overriding concerns were not for the enemy he faced, but for the illness and dysentery that raked his ranks. He was to lose over 1,000 men that winter, including Jones, who succumbed to the fever at Dungarvan on 10 December. His death was much lamented by Cromwell and his contribution to Parliament's victory in Ireland has undoubtedly not received the approbation it deserves.[40] For the Royalists, it was time to face up to the reality of the situation and, on 15 December, Ormond wrote to the King:

> This I hold it my duty to give your Majesty timely notice of, to the end that during this winter provision may be made, or that, if you find that impossible, you should not be deceived by relying on the bare name of a kingdom and armies being at your command, when without those necessaries that can be of no consideration nor continuance.[41]

Cromwell's offensive to capture the Confederate capital at Kilkenny, and the Royalist stronghold at Clonmel, started on 29 January 1650. The speed of their advance took the Royalists by surprise and, one by one, the castles and strongholds and key towns in Kilkenny, Waterford and southern Tipperary fell to the Parliamentarian onslaught. By the end of February, with Cromwell's forces closing in on three sides, Ormond and the Confederate Commissioners fled to Limerick. A month later, Kilkenny was surrounded, the great guns opened on 25 March, and two days later the town fell. Earlier in the month Inchiquin had advanced with three cavalry regiments towards Mallow, but had been intercepted and routed by Lord Broghill. Inchiquin retreated into Connaught with the last of the Munster Protestants. However, it was enough to bring them to the table. The following month, on 26 April, a treaty was drawn up and signed by the Protestant Royalists, the Ulster Scots and the Lagan army, agreeing to lay down their arms.

Back in London, the Council of State, acutely aware of the growing threat of a Royalist invasion from Scotland, wanted Cromwell to return to England, but he was equally determined to finish the job in Ireland, by taking the last two Royalist strongholds at Clonmel and Limerick. Cromwell's army arrived on the north side of Clonmel on 27 April and,

after delivering a summons, which was rejected by Hugh O'Neill the governor, the gunners began to prepare battery positions on Gallows Hill, the high ground to the north. The guns arrived about two weeks later, and the heavy ordnance soon battered a sizeable breach in the north wall. O'Neill then ordered the area behind the breach to be turned into a large-scale killing zone. He blocked off the lane, into which the breach fed, and sited two cannon at the south end, at the same time barricading the lower floors and manning the upper storeys with soldiers.[42] Unaware of this activity, Cromwell ordered the storm at 8am on 16 May.[43] Colonel Clume led Parliament's soldiers of the New Model Army into the breach, unaware that they were about to receive the greatest check in their short but bloody history. O'Neill waited for about a thousand men to have entered the retrenched area before releasing the maelstrom. The effect was devastating and Cromwell, unaccustomed to defeat, ordered those who pulled back, to get back into the town. By last light he had lost 1,500 men, but crucially, he had not broken Irish resistance.

That night O'Neill and his garrison slipped out over the River Suir on the road to Waterford. The town's authorities then offered terms, which Cromwell, unaware that the garrison had escaped, accepted. They entered the town the next morning and, discovering the duplicity, he sent a flying column to attack O'Neill's men. They caught up with them and killed 200 stragglers, but for Cromwell it was scant recompense, his army having just suffered its sharpest check to date. Cromwell could not delay his departure any longer and perhaps the events at Clonmel influenced his decision. The following day he departed Ireland, leaving Ireton in command. For the next three months, the new commander was fully occupied reducing the remaining Irish strongholds in Leinster and Munster.

Further north Reynolds and Hewson were embroiled in the siege of Tecroghan Castle. Robert Talbot was holding out with a garrison of 1,500, inspired by the presence of Lady Fitzgerald, who resided in the castle. Talbot's confidence was boosted by news of a Confederate relief column, under Castlehaven and Clanricarde, numbering nearly 4,000, approaching from the east. Their advance was blocked, but the Irish under Colonel Burke broke the English line on the right; much to his chagrin, the troops in the centre did not hold. Castlehaven and most of his men fled. A few hundred under Colonel Burke succeeded in fighting their way through to Tecroghan, destroying part of the English siege works and capturing a cannon in the process. Their appearance and supplies rejuvenated the defence but Clanricarde and Castlehaven could not agree on how to proceed, and Talbot felt compelled to take Reynolds's lenient terms two days later. Meanwhile Coote had fallen on the Irish Ulster army, now under the command of Heber MacMahon, Bishop of Clogher, at Scarrifholis. MacMahon had assembled his force (4,000 foot and 600 horse) in south Armagh, with the aim of marching through the centre of Ulster, thereby cutting Coote's garrison at Derry from Venables' command at Carrickfergus. MacMahon marched his men north then west, and was encamped on the Doonglebe/Tullygay hill, overlooking the ford at Scarrifholis, 2 miles west of Letterkenny. Although he outnumbered Coote's force, which came out to meet it, MacMahon had no military experience and disregarded the advice of those in his camp who did. The result was more of the same as the Irish force was decimated, with nearly 3,000 of the Ulster army killed on the field and during the subsequent pursuit.

---

40 Day, *Jones and the Defeat of Royalist Ireland*, p. 1.
41 Carte, *Collection of Original Letters*, vol. II, pp. 417–21.
42 Gentles, *New Model Army*, p. 374; Reilly, op. cit., p. 238.
43 I have used the date and reasoning from Gentles, ibid.

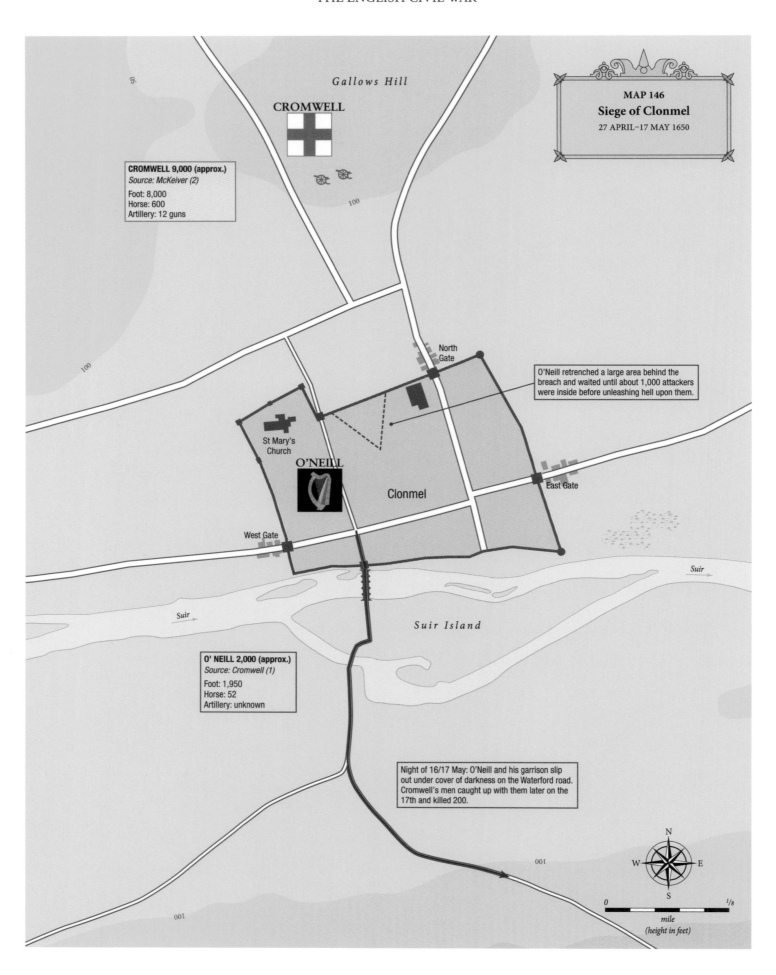

Gallows Hill

CROMWELL

CROMWELL 9,000 (approx.)
Source: McKeiver (2)
Foot: 8,000
Horse: 600
Artillery: 12 guns

MAP 146
Siege of Clonmel
27 APRIL–17 MAY 1650

North
Gate

O'Neill retrenched a large area behind the breach and waited until about 1,000 attackers were inside before unleashing hell upon them.

St Mary's
Church

O'NEILL

Clonmel

East Gate

West Gate

Suir

Suir Island

O' NEILL 2,000 (approx.)
Source: Cromwell (1)
Foot: 1,950
Horse: 52
Artillery: unknown

Suir

Night of 16/17 May: O'Neill and his garrison slip out under cover of darkness on the Waterford road. Cromwell's men caught up with them later on the 17th and killed 200.

N
W E
S

0   1/8
mile
(height in feet)

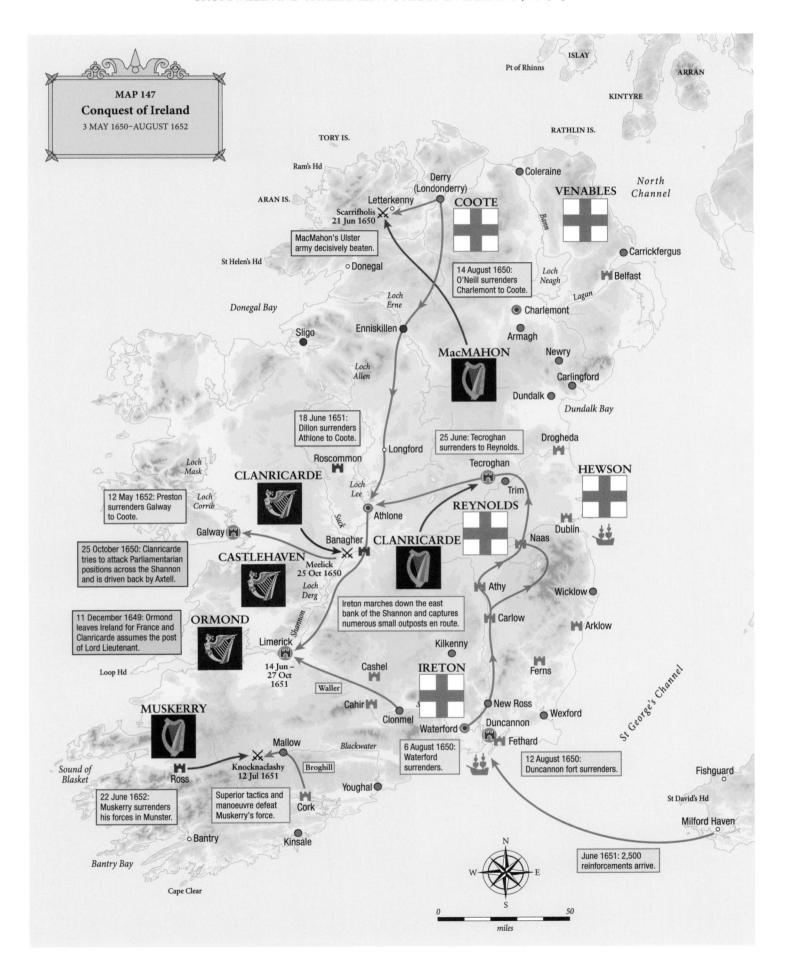

MAP 147
Conquest of Ireland
3 MAY 1650–AUGUST 1652

ISLAY

Pt of Rhinns

ARRAN

KINTYRE

TORY IS.

RATHLIN IS.

Ram's Hd

Coleraine

North Channel

VENABLES

Derry (Londonderry)

ARAN IS.

Letterkenny

COOTE

Scarrifholis 21 Jun 1650

Carrickfergus

MacMahon's Ulster army decisively beaten.

St Helen's Hd

Donegal

Loch Neagh

Belfast

Lagan

14 August 1650: O'Neill surrenders Charlemont to Coote.

Loch Erne

Charlemont

Donegal Bay

Sligo

Enniskillen

Armagh

Newry

MacMAHON

Loch Allen

Carlingford

Dundalk

Dundalk Bay

18 June 1651: Dillon surrenders Athlone to Coote.

Longford

25 June: Tecroghan surrenders to Reynolds.

Drogheda

Loch Mask

Roscommon

Tecroghan

HEWSON

CLANRICARDE

Loch Lee

Trim

Loch Corrib

Athlone

12 May 1652: Preston surrenders Galway to Coote.

REYNOLDS

Galway

Stuck

Banagher

CLANRICARDE

Naas

Dublin

25 October 1650: Clanricarde tries to attack Parliamentarian positions across the Shannon and is driven back by Axtell.

CASTLEHAVEN

Meelick 25 Oct 1650

Athy

Wicklow

Loch Derg

Ireton marches down the east bank of the Shannon and captures numerous small outposts en route.

Carlow

Arklow

11 December 1649: Ormond leaves Ireland for France and Clanricarde assumes the post of Lord Lieutenant.

ORMOND

Shannon

Limerick

Kilkenny

14 Jun – 27 Oct 1651

Ferns

Loop Hd

Cashel

IRETON

Waller

Cahir

New Ross

Wexford

St George's Channel

MUSKERRY

Clonmel

Waterford

Duncannon

Mallow

6 August 1650: Waterford surrenders.

Fethard

12 August 1650: Duncannon fort surrenders.

Fishguard

Sound of Blasket

Knocknaclashy 12 Jul 1651

Broghill

Ross

Blackwater

Youghal

St David's Hd

22 June 1652: Muskerry surrenders his forces in Munster.

Superior tactics and manoeuvre defeat Muskerry's force.

Cork

Milford Haven

Bantry

Kinsale

June 1651: 2,500 reinforcements arrive.

Bantry Bay

Cape Clear

N
W E
S

0   miles   50

To the south, the town of Waterford, and the nearby fortress of Duncannon, were the only major Irish strongholds left in southern Munster. In late July Ireton decided to capture them both before moving west to tackle Ormond in Limerick. He moved to isolate Waterford from land and used a naval squadron to blockade the harbour, before advancing his infantry and heavy artillery to tighten the noose. Thomas Preston refused Ireton's offer to surrender despite being perilously short of powder. As the townsfolk watched the Parliamentarian gunners prepare their massive guns, resolve crumbled and the mayor and aldermen persuaded Preston to give up what was clearly a hopeless struggle. They surrendered on 6 August and the fort at Duncannon capitulated less than a week later. Ormond had tried to rally the Irish forces to move against Ireton at Waterford but he was wholly ignored. The numerous defeats had destroyed the last vestiges of loyalty of the Catholics towards the King's lieutenant and many suggested that, for his own safety, he leave Ireland.[44]

With most of Ulster and Leinster, and a large proportion of Munster, under Parliamentarian control, Ireton was now poised to cross the River Shannon and root out the remaining vestiges of Irish resistance in the more remote province of Connacht. His first objective was the formidable fortress at Limerick, and his plan to take it was elaborate. He sent Hardress Waller directly towards the town, while moving with his main force north to link up with Coote at Athlone, where Dillon had agreed to surrender the key crossing over the Shannon. However, when Ireton approached Athlone, he was irritated to discover that Dillon had no such intentions. After trying to force the crossing, Ireton set off down the east bank of the Shannon, leaving Coote to deal with the duplicitous Dillon. Clanricarde, who was poised to assume responsibility as lord lieutenant from Ormond, had decided to gather a force of about 3,000 and move to support Dillon and, at the same time, cut Ireton's lines of communication. Coote anticipated the move and sent Colonel Daniel Axtell to intercept Clanricarde. He surprised the Irish in a ferocious night attack on Meelick Island, which all but destroyed the Irish force.[45]

Ireton arrived in front of Limerick on 6 October and, after summoning the governor to surrender, received the anticipated rebuff. Having conducted a full reconnaissance of the place, he then withdrew into winter cantonments as the weather worsened. In January 1651, Edmund Ludlow arrived in Ireland to assume the post of lieutenant general to Ireton. He was accompanied by three Parliamentary commissioners, whose task was to organize civil government in Ireland after the 'troubles'. Having received a number of reinforcements during the winter, Ireton had reorganized his forces, and with more reinforcements in the pipeline, his army was to grow to a staggering 30,000 men by the summer. The Irish armies that remained had neither the manpower nor the resources to match those of Ireton. Dillon had remained at Athlone (Coote having failed to dislodge him) with 500 men, O'Neill was at Limerick with 2,000, Preston had a similar number in Galway, and there existed three armies of a few thousand men each in central Connaught (Clanricarde), County Kerry (Muskerry) and as a mobile reserve in Connaught (Castlehaven). Ireton's first objective in 1651 was to conclude matters at Limerick. However, he realized that he needed

to conduct the siege from both sides of the Shannon and, for that to work, he needed to get the Irish armies to divide their forces.

While Ireton marched towards Limerick from Cashel, having placed Broghill on his right to provide flank protection from a possible attack by Viscount Muskerry, Coote and Hewson attacked Dillon's small, but well-placed, force at Athlone. They succeeded in driving Dillon back and secured the key crossing point over the Shannon, opening up the invasion of Connacht and giving them access to the west bank. Ireton, meanwhile, was able to move, apparently undetected, to O'Briensbridge, about 8 miles north of Limerick on the east bank of the Shannon. Once there, his engineers built a military road to the riverbank. They crossed in strength on 1 June, and drove back a counter-attack by Castlehaven, and then consolidated the crossing point with an earthwork *tête-de-pont*. Ireton then marched south and closed on Limerick from the north and south-east and, by 14 June, he had surrounded the town. He detached a force of 1,500 men under Reynolds, to link up with Coote and begin the process by attacking Portumna, the seat of Clanricarde. The garrison there surrendered in late June. Coote then marched his combined force towards Galway.

Meanwhile, at Limerick, Ireton made an attempt to storm Thomond Bridge and gain access to the town. It failed when the Irish blew the bridge, but in the process of executing the attack, Ireton secured the fort on the west bank and his artillery (that had been moved by ship down the Shannon) was quickly moved into batteries within the structure. On 23 June an amphibious assault also failed, as one participant recalled:

> The attempt was to be made by boates and part of the float bridge for carrying over horse and men; 2 of the boates passeing over hastily before they could be seconded and landing about 80 men the enemie fell on them in multitudes putting all to the sword but one, which so discouraged those who were to follow that the designe was wholy laid by.[46]

Following these failures Ireton set about closing the cordon, constructing an extensive circumvention and starving out the garrison. Although he was not overly concerned about a relieving force he was, however, keen to bring the town to heel as soon as possible.

To the south Muskerry advanced, as Ireton anticipated, from his base at Ross Castle. Lord Broghill moved to intercept him and the two sides met at Knocknaclashy on 12 July. The Irish outnumbered the Parliamentarian force, but Broghill made good use of the ground and his cavalry to outmanoeuvre the Irish who stood firm, but they were, as so often was the case with the Irish battles, eventually overwhelmed by superior tactics. It was to be the last pitched battle of the Irish Confederate Wars, and the removal of Muskerry sounded the death knell for Limerick. Ireton was determined to starve out the garrison before the winter and O'Neill was equally determined to wait for the cold weather to drive away the besiegers. 'You labour to beat us out with bombshells, but we will beat you out with snowballs', was the brag by one of the Irish sentries.[47] To avoid that eventuality, Ireton then decided that a more proactive approach was required and resorted to a new plan, which he later attributed to God's guidance. He moved a number of pieces of heavy artillery and a few mortars into Fort Cromwell; from here they began to batter a large breach. Once the guns were in place they opened on 22 October and three days later terms

---

44 Ormond left Ireland for France on 11 December. He was replaced by Clanricarde as lord lieutenant. Ormond joined Charles II during his long exile and became one of the King's most trusted advisors. He allied himself with Sir Edward Hyde and Sir Edward Nicholas in trying to steer the King away from wild schemes to regain the throne.

45 Axtell was later court-martialled by Ireton for killing prisoners taken at Meelick, after promise of quarter.

46 Gilbert, *Diaries of the proceedings of the forces in Ireland*, entry dated 23 June 1651.

47 Gardiner, op. cit., vol. II, pp. 121–2.

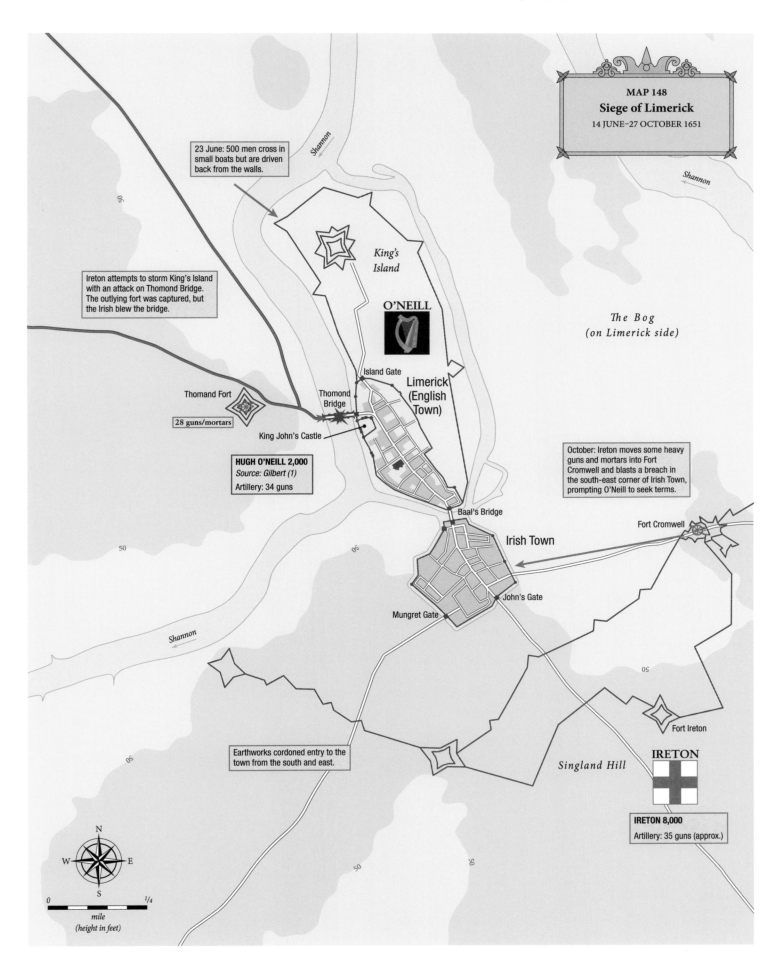

23 June: 500 men cross in small boats but are driven back from the walls.

Ireton attempts to storm King's Island with an attack on Thomond Bridge. The outlying fort was captured, but the Irish blew the bridge.

Shannon

King's Island

O'NEILL

The Bog
(on Limerick side)

Island Gate

Limerick
(English Town)

Thomand Fort

Thomond Bridge

28 guns/mortars

King John's Castle

HUGH O'NEILL 2,000
Source: Gilbert (1)
Artillery: 34 guns

October: Ireton moves some heavy guns and mortars into Fort Cromwell and blasts a breach in the south-east corner of Irish Town, prompting O'Neill to seek terms.

Baal's Bridge

Irish Town

Fort Cromwell

50

Shannon

John's Gate

Mungret Gate

50

Earthworks cordoned entry to the town from the south and east.

Fort Ireton

Singland Hill

IRETON

IRETON 8,000
Artillery: 35 guns (approx.)

N
W   E
S

0   1/4
mile
(height in feet)

were discussed. As siege gunners often boasted, there was nothing quite like a 47-pound iron ball to bring people to their senses.

On 27 October O'Neill surrendered Limerick. It had been a costly siege with nearly half the Irish garrison having perished, along with 2,000 of Ireton's men – mainly from disease. The death toll included Ireton himself, who passed away on 26 November, his body being repatriated for a state funeral on the same vessel that transported O'Neill for imprisonment.

The following year the Parliamentary commissioners began planning the settlement of the Irish lands. Coote captured Galway in May and Muskerry surrendered his forces in Munster the following month. In August, Parliament passed the Act of Settlement for Ireland, which declared the country to be part of the Commonwealth. Legislative power was transferred to London and executive power was divided between the Council of State and its appointed lord deputy in Ireland.

CHAPTER 42

THE INVASION OF SCOTLAND, JULY 1650 TO SEPTEMBER 1651

The 'Anti-Engagers' (otherwise known as Whigs or Whiggamores) were convinced that the disasters of 1648 were divine punishment for straying from the tenets of Presbyterian fundamentalism. The Whigs now reinstated full control over the Covenanter movement and, while they did not exclude opening negotiations with the new King, they made it clear that he must accept and embrace Presbyterianism across his three kingdoms and within his own household. Throughout 1649, the Covenanter army, under the command of David Leslie, had spent much of the year ruthlessly putting down Royalist uprisings from Inverness to Stirling. Despite this, they failed to extinguish the embers of Royalism and, in March 1650, capitalizing on continued unrest and instability in the Highlands, Montrose returned to Scotland from the Hague. He had collected a small mercenary army of Germans, Danes and Swedes and was well equipped with arms, ammunition and supplies. Despite losing much of his ammunition in a storm, he was able to supplement his army by some vigorous recruiting in the Scottish Isles. In April, when he crossed the Pentland Firth to the Scottish mainland, his army numbered over 1,000 men.

Seemingly unaware that Charles II had also opened negotiations with the Covenanters, Montrose moved to Inverness and linked up with the Mackenzies. He then marched south, capturing Dunbeath Castle en route, before heading south-west and setting up camp near Carbisdale, on the southern side of the Kyle of Sutherland. Here he waited for his allied clans to join him. News of Montrose's return soon reached Edinburgh and it was not long before Leslie was ordered north to remove the King's captain general once and for all. Having mustered a force at Brechin, he sent Colonel Strachan, with an advance guard of five troops of horse, to fix the renegade Royalist and his ad hoc band. In fact, Strachan went one further, and on 27 April he surprised and defeated Montrose's far larger force. A few days after the engagement he succeeded in cornering and capturing Montrose, who had tried to slip away across the moors. Montrose was taken to Edinburgh with no little ceremony. The junto was hell bent on making an example of him and wasted little time in sentencing James Graham, the Earl of Montrose, to be hanged. Hanging was deliberately chosen, for it was not the fate of a nobleman and soldier, but that of a criminal. It was carried out on 21 May at Mercat Cross on the Royal Mile, Edinburgh. Montrose's head was fixed on a spike at the Tolbooth in Edinburgh; his legs and arms were fixed to the gates of Stirling, Glasgow, Perth and Aberdeen.[1] A grizzly end to an extraordinary man.

Negotiations with Charles had been concluded at the Treaty of Breda on 1 May. The Covenanters agreed to raise an army on his behalf and he, albeit with reservations, agreed to take the Covenant. On 23 June Charles landed at Speymouth, while his army of 16,000 foot and 7,000 horse was being assembled further south under Leslie's command.[2] These events were no secret to the Council of State in London and, three days after Charles set foot on Scottish soil, they voted to send an army north in order to pre-emptively strike and protect England from another Scottish invasion.[3] It was Parliament's intention that Fairfax and Cromwell would jointly command the army, but the Rump had, for some time, been uneasy about Fairfax's resolve. His resignation on 26 June opened the door to Cromwell who had returned from Ireland a month earlier, having more than demonstrated the kind of steadfastness the Rump considered essential for the mission (see chapter 41). Two days later Cromwell set out for Newcastle, and by mid-July his army had grown to 16,000 men, consisting of eight cavalry and eight infantry regiments (commanded by Lambert and Monck respectively).[4] On 22 July he passed through Berwick and crossed into Scotland, having laid the political groundwork beforehand, in the guise of two public statements 'to the people of Scotland'.[5] A fleet of ships hugged the coast and shadowed the advance of the New Model Army.[6]

Although Leslie's army outnumbered that of Cromwell, his plan was not to engage the English army as they entered Scottish soil, but to draw them into the country as far as Leith, where they would be stopped at a fortified line of defences and, by so doing, the English lines of communication would be stretched and vulnerable. In addition, Leslie orchestrated a scorched earth policy along the English line of march, destroying crops and evacuating the population and livestock. Cromwell had made provision for this with supplies being carried by the fleet, but it did result in every soldier having to carry many days' rations upon his back, which slowed their advance and exhausted the men. They trudged along the Great North Road, reaching Dunbar on 26 July, where they were resupplied before moving on towards the Scottish capital. Clearing Haddington and Musselburgh (where Cromwell established his forward headquarters), the army arrived opposite Leslie's defence lines at Leith on the 29th. Cromwell then ordered the fleet to bombard the port and the defences. While four men-of-war in the Firth of Forth duly obliged, Cromwell conducted a full reconnaissance of the lines. He quickly appreciated their strength, and the size of Leslie's force, neither of which was particularly encouraging. Leslie clearly knew his business and Cromwell had his work cut out. With the Scottish left anchored on the Firth and his right on Edinburgh Castle, the only way around was through the Pentland Hills and away from the sea and his support and firepower.

---

2 Kenyon & Ohlmeyer, *Military History*, p. 65.

3 *CSPD -I*, vol. IX, dated 26 June 1650.

4 Gentles, *New Model Army*, p. 387.

5 Ibid.

6 To meet the costs of this large army and the increasing strength of the navy, Parliament passed a new Militia Act on 11 July. This fell mainly on property holders who were required to contribute proportionally to the escalating defence costs.

---

1 On 11 May 1661, after the Restoration, Montrose's embalmed heart and bones were buried at the High Kirk of St Giles in Edinburgh in an elaborate ceremony with fourteen noblemen bearing the coffin.

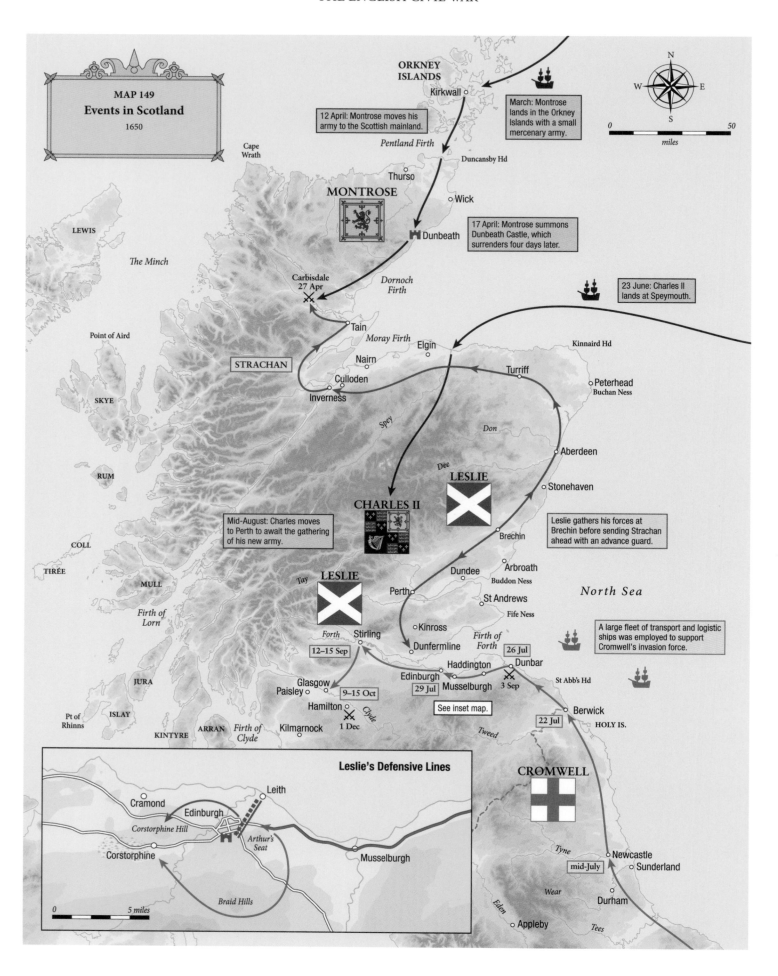

MAP 149
Events in Scotland
1650

ORKNEY ISLANDS

Kirkwall

12 April: Montrose moves his army to the Scottish mainland.

March: Montrose lands in the Orkney Islands with a small mercenary army.

Pentland Firth

Cape Wrath

Duncansby Hd

Thurso

MONTROSE

Wick

17 April: Montrose summons Dunbeath Castle, which surrenders four days later.

Dunbeath

LEWIS

The Minch

Carbisdale 27 Apr

Dornoch Firth

23 June: Charles II lands at Speymouth.

Point of Aird

Tain

Moray Firth

Elgin

Kinnaird Hd

STRACHAN

Nairn

Turriff

Peterhead

Buchan Ness

SKYE

Culloden

Inverness

Spey

Don

Aberdeen

Dee

LESLIE

RUM

Stonehaven

Leslie gathers his forces at Brechin before sending Strachan ahead with an advance guard.

COLL

CHARLES II

Brechin

Mid-August: Charles moves to Perth to await the gathering of his new army.

TIRÉE

Tay

Dundee

Arbroath

Buddon Ness

North Sea

MULL

LESLIE

Perth

St Andrews

Fife Ness

Firth of Lorn

Kinross

Dunfermline

Firth of Forth

A large fleet of transport and logistic ships was employed to support Cromwell's invasion force.

Forth Stirling

12–15 Sep

26 Jul

Dunbar

3 Sep

JURA

Glasgow

Paisley

9–15 Oct

Haddington

Edinburgh

29 Jul

Musselburgh

St Abb's Hd

Hamilton

Clyde

Berwick

22 Jul

HOLY IS.

Pt of Rhinns

ISLAY

ARRAN

Firth of Clyde

Kilmarnock

1 Dec

KINTYRE

Tweed

CROMWELL

Leslie's Defensive Lines

Leith

Cramond

Edinburgh

Corstorphine Hill

Corstorphine

Arthur's Seat

Musselburgh

Braid Hills

0   5 miles

Tyne

Newcastle

mid-July

Sunderland

Wear

Durham

Eden

Appleby

Tees

N

W   E

S

0   50
miles

Before first light on 30 July, Leslie sent 800 of his best cavalry out to give the New Model Army a Scottish welcome. They succeeded in breaking through the picket line and engaged a number of the English horse, before being driven back. Cromwell pondered his options, and with intelligence that food supplies were low in the city, he decided to try to entice Leslie from behind his defences by moving through the Pentlands and cutting him off from resupply from the west. On 20 August, Leslie moved a strong force to Corstorphine Hill to pre-empt such a move and to keep open the Stirling road. The two armies closed a week later but, once again, Leslie had chosen the ground well. The marshy area behind which he had positioned his force, and the many low dry-stone walls that crisscrossed the expanse, frustrated any attempt by Cromwell to instigate battle. Cromwell gave the order to pull back.

This setback, the appalling weather and the delay in victualling the force from the sea led, as Leslie had planned, to a corresponding collapse in morale among the soldiers of Cromwell's army.[7] Disease and desertion began to thin the English ranks. By the end of August, Cromwell was growing increasingly frustrated and, on the 31st, he gave orders for the army to fall back to Dunbar, where many of the sick were loaded on to the waiting naval transports. Cromwell's invading army had been reduced to 11,000 men. He realized that the invasion had failed and began planning to pull back towards Berwick. However, Cromwell's movement had enticed Leslie out from behind his defences; he followed the New Model Army towards Dunbar and positioned his Covenanter force atop Doon Hill, from where he dominated the Great North Road, Dunbar port and Cromwell's camps. He also sent a force south to cut the escape route at Copperspath. Cromwell had been outwitted at every turn and, at first, was at a loss as to how to proceed. He wrote, on 2 September, 'we are on an engagement very difficult… the enemy hath blocked-up our way at the Pass of Copperspath… he lieth so upon the hills that we know not how to come that way without great difficulty… and our lying here daily consumeth our men.'[8]

Cromwell's position certainly looked bleak but Leslie, uncharacteristically, was about to err. Watching from the top of Doon Hill the Scots could see the sick being loaded on board the ships and it appeared that the rest of the English army was destined to follow. Egged on by a number of Covenanter government officials, Leslie moved his army down from the safety of the heights and took up a position along Brox Burn with the aim of attacking the final elements of the army on the morn.[9] The foul weather drove many of the Scottish officers to seek shelter for the night in the few farmhouses that scattered the valley floor and, at about 2am on 3 September, General Holborne gave (somewhat extraordinarily) permission for the musketeers to extinguish their matches. The Scots had no inkling that they might be attacked. Because many of the officers had sought refuge from the weather, the Scottish commanders were seemingly oblivious to the reorganization that was taking place in the English lines on the other side of the burn. During the afternoon, as Leslie's men had taken up their new positions along Brox Burn, they had been closely monitored by the New Model Army's senior commanders. Cromwell and Lambert both saw the error of the Scottish deployment. On this constricted ground, with the end in the river protruding towards them and the high ground to their backs, the Scots could not turn their centre and

left in support of their right, if this were attacked. Through the night, under cover of the stormy weather, Cromwell and his officers readjusted the English force to be able to strike at the vulnerable Scottish right wing, just prior to the break of day, in order to maximize surprise. They succeeded in making the necessary readjustments but it took longer than hoped, 'the time of falling-on to be by break of day: but through some delays it proved not to be so; "not" till six o'clock in the morning'.[10]

Lambert led the vanguard, consisting of his own, Fleetwood's and Whalley's regiments of horse supported by Monck's brigade of infantry. As they began their advance in the half light, the Scottish suddenly realized what was going on and were desperately trying to organize their defences, but with many officers absent from their posts they were caught entirely unprepared. After a sharp fight the vanguard drove back the Scottish picket guarding the road. They then pushed on and engaged the main body of Scottish horse. Cromwell noted that they 'made a gallant resistance, and there was a very hot dispute at sword's point between our horse and theirs'.[11] After some time the infantry came up and moved towards Lumsden's battalia and 'did come seasonably in; and, at the push of pike, did repel the stoutest regiment the Enemy had there'.[12] Meanwhile, the Scottish infantry in the centre and left was being engaged and occupied by Okey's Dragoons and a number of field guns that had been left in their original position for that purpose. A few of the Scottish infantry were able to move to their right, but the majority were constrained, as Cromwell had foreseen. The other two English brigades of infantry now began to advance and, at the same time, Cromwell moved his last brigade and the two remaining cavalry regiments in the reserve to the seaward side of Broxmouth House. They crossed the burn unhindered, before turning right and into the unprotected flank and rear of the Scottish horse and foot.[13] It proved to be the decisive moment as Cromwell joyfully recorded: 'The best of the Enemy's horse being broken through and through in less than an hour's dispute, their whole Army being put into confusion, it became a total rout; our men having the chase and execution of them near eight miles.'[14]

Four thousand Scots died in the battle, and another 10,000 were taken prisoner. Dunbar was more than just a catastrophic military failure; it damaged the Covenanters politically and militarily, weakened the Royalist resurgence from its Scottish base and secured England's independence.[15] It also damaged Leslie's reputation, while significantly enhancing that of Cromwell. As Leslie fell back to Stirling, Cromwell marched into Edinburgh and took control of the city and the port at Leith. Edinburgh Castle held out for another few months until Christmas Eve, when the garrison surrendered, some suggest treacherously, by Walter Dundas. Immediately following the victory at Dunbar, and well aware that the battle for Scotland was far from over, Cromwell sent to London for reinforcements. He received more than 6,000 fresh soldiers over the next two months. He also set about trying to convert members of the Council of Estates with persuasion and prayers. He did not get far with the representatives in Stirling, but in Glasgow he was given a warmer reception, with many of the officers in the Western Association agreeing not to fight for Charles II.[16] However, by

---

7   The army was not provided tents until mid-August – Firth, *Dunbar*, p. 25 and Gardiner, *Commonwealth and Protectorate*, vol. I, p. 275.

8   Carlyle, *Cromwell's Letters*, vol. II, p. 30. This must have been penned in the morning, for by 4pm the situation had changed.

9   Douglas, *Cromwell's Scotch Campaigns*, p. 106, casts doubt on whether there were any commissioners or politicians anywhere near the battlefield.

10   Carlyle, op. cit., p. 44. First light was at about 5.30am.

11   Ibid.

12   Ibid.

13   Douglas, op. cit., p. 109.

14   Carlyle, op. cit., p. 44.

15   Kenyon & Ohlmeyer, op. cit., p. 66.

16   The Western Association included the lands of Renfrewshire, Ayrshire, Lanarkshire, Wigtown and Kirkcudbright – see map 2.

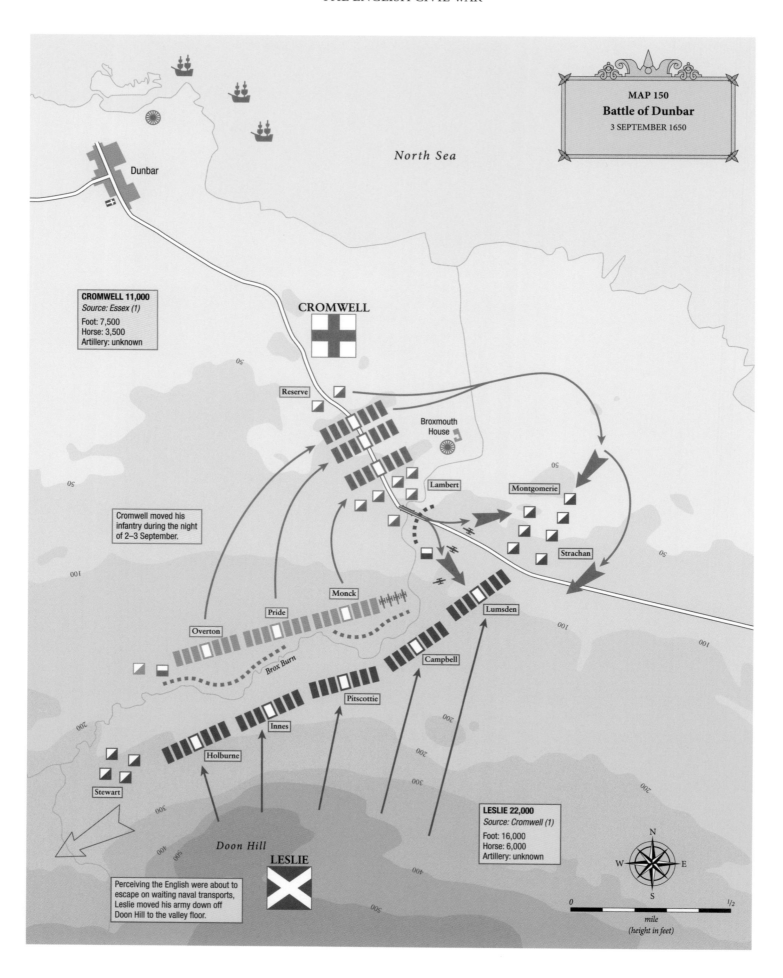

North Sea

Dunbar

MAP 150
Battle of Dunbar
3 SEPTEMBER 1650

CROMWELL 11,000
Source: Essex (1)
Foot: 7,500
Horse: 3,500
Artillery: unknown

CROMWELL

Reserve

Broxmouth House

Cromwell moved his infantry during the night of 2–3 September.

Lambert

Montgomerie

Strachan

Monck

Pride

Lumsden

Overton

Campbell

Brox Burn

Pitscottie

Innes

Holburne

Stewart

LESLIE 22,000
Source: Cromwell (1)
Foot: 16,000
Horse: 6,000
Artillery: unknown

Doon Hill

LESLIE

Perceiving the English were about to escape on waiting naval transports, Leslie moved his army down off Doon Hill to the valley floor.

N
W E
S

0   1/2
mile
(height in feet)

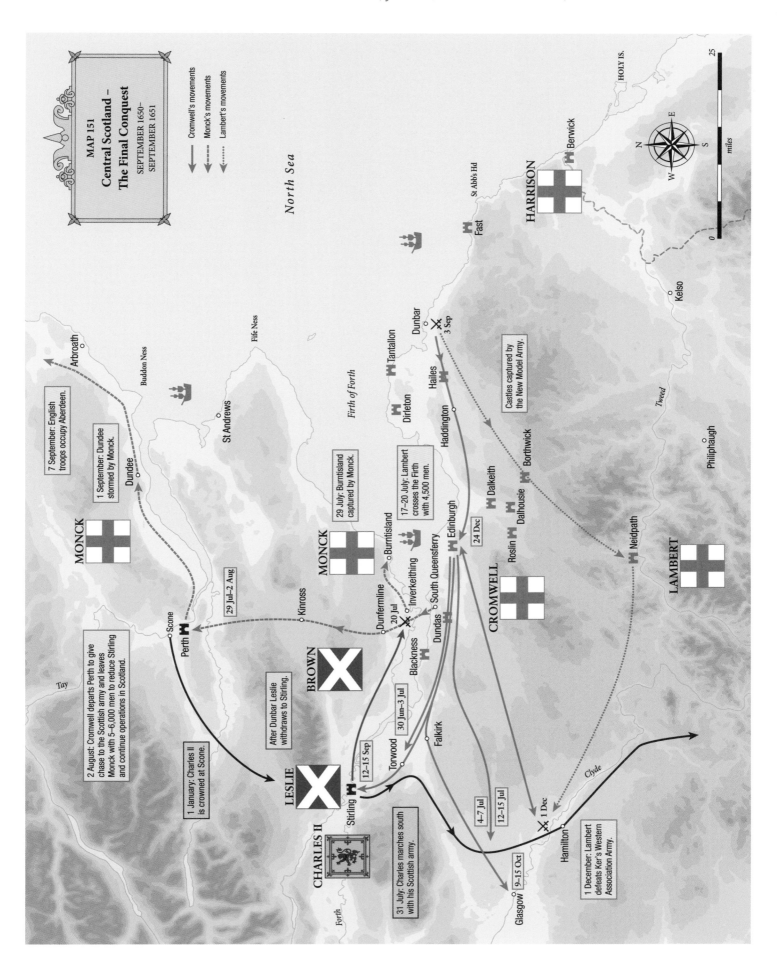

MAP 151
**Central Scotland –
The Final Conquest**
SEPTEMBER 1650–
SEPTEMBER 1651

Cromwell's movements
Monck's movements
Lambert's movements

North Sea

HOLY IS.

HARRISON

Berwick

St Abb's Hd

Fast

Kelso

Castles captured by
the New Model Army.

Tweed

7 September: English
troops occupy Aberdeen.

Arbroath

MONCK

1 September: Dundee
stormed by Monck.

Dundee

Buddon Ness

Fife Ness

Tantallon

Dunbar

3 Sep

Dirleton

Hailes

Haddington

Firth of Forth

St Andrews

29 July: Burntisland
captured by Monck.

MONCK

Dalkeith

Borthwick

Philiphaugh

17–20 July: Lambert
crosses the Firth
with 4,500 men.

Burntisland

Edinburgh

Roslin

Dalhousie

Neidpath

LAMBERT

2 August: Cromwell departs Perth to give
chase to the Scottish army and leaves
Monck with 5–6,000 men to reduce Stirling
and continue operations in Scotland.

Inverkeithing

Dunfermline

South Queensferry

24 Dec

CROMWELL

29 Jul–2 Aug

Kinross

20 Jul

Blackness

Dundas

Tay

Scone

Perth

BROWN

1 January: Charles II
is crowned at Scone.

After Dunbar Leslie
withdraws to Stirling.

30 Jun–3 Jul

Falkirk

Clyde

12–15 Sep

Torwood

4–7 Jul

12–15 Jul

1 Dec

1 December: Lambert
defeats Ker's Western
Association Army.

LESLIE

Stirling

CHARLES II

31 July: Charles
marches south
with his Scottish army.

9–15 Oct

Glasgow

Hamilton

Forth

N

E

W

S

0   25

miles

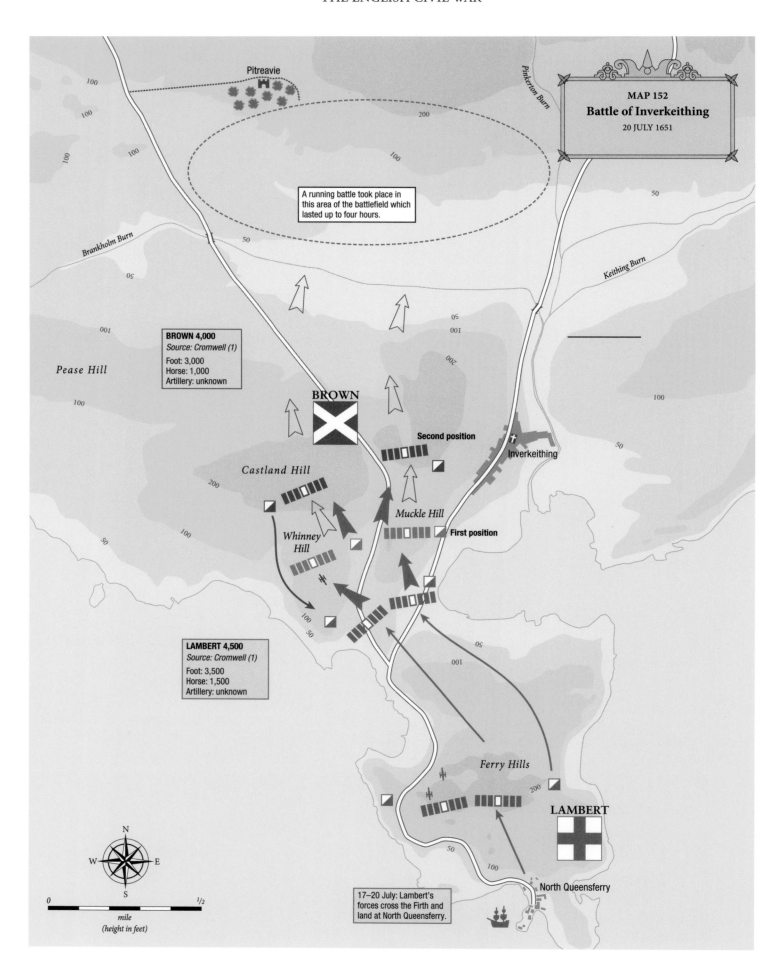

Pitreavie

100

100

100

100

200

100

A running battle took place in this area of the battlefield which lasted up to four hours.

Pinkerton Burn

MAP 152
Battle of Inverkeithing
20 JULY 1651

50

Brankholm Burn

50

50

Keithing Burn

50

50

100

BROWN 4,000
Source: Cromwell (1)
Foot: 3,000
Horse: 1,000
Artillery: unknown

200

100

Pease Hill

100

50

BROWN

Second position

50

Inverkeithing

100

Castland Hill

200

Muckle Hill

First position

Whinney Hill

100

100

50

LAMBERT 4,500
Source: Cromwell (1)
Foot: 3,500
Horse: 1,500
Artillery: unknown

50

100

Ferry Hills

200

LAMBERT

N
W E
S

0   1/2

mile
(height in feet)

50

100

North Queensferry

17–20 July: Lambert's forces cross the Firth and land at North Queensferry.

November Cromwell had tired of Scottish procrastination and he decided that military coercion was necessary to force their hands to a national settlement. But his rendezvous with Whalley and Lambert at Hamilton on 27 November misfired, and Cromwell returned to Edinburgh only for Lambert to appear at Hamilton on his own two days later. Lambert then clashed with the Western Association Covenanter army at Hamilton and, to all intents and purposes, destroyed it.

Once Edinburgh Castle had fallen, Cromwell 'controlled' everything in Scotland south of the Forth and Clyde. Through a combination of military action, political and religious coercion and espionage, Cromwell had significantly reduced the effectiveness and the credibility of the Covenanters.[17] Despite this, the final phase of the Scottish conquest did not commence in earnest for another six months. The inclement weather, two bouts of serious illness that incapacitated Cromwell, and the difficulty in flushing the Scots out to open battle, were the main reasons for this impasse. Within the ranks of the English army this delay, and the perennial problems with pay, did nothing for morale. Desertion and drunkenness prevailed. Nevertheless, more recruits arrived, and by June 1651, the size of the army exceeded 20,000 men. News that Leslie's, or more precisely Charles's army (by this time), were suffering from similar shortages and poor spirits reinforced Cromwell's determination to get on with the job. Charles had been crowned King of Scotland at Scone on 1 January. His coronation had helped heal rifts, overcome clan rivalries and curtail internecine squabbles, producing the only true Scottish army of the era containing troops from every shire if not every clan. The English threat had drawn the Scots together, but the union was fragile.

Cromwell's plan was to split his force, making an amphibious landing on the north of the Firth of Forth with 4,000 men, while keeping the balance of his army on the south side near Torwood, in front of the main Scottish defences on the main road to Stirling. The flat assault boats (designed to carry men, horses and cannon) had been procured to be built at Newcastle for the sum of 1,000 shillings and sanctioned by the Council of State on 9 December.[18] They arrived in dribs and drabs during the first few months of 1651 and were complete by June, but still Cromwell hesitated. Amphibious operations were risky, and he decided that, in the first instance, he should try to lure Leslie from his defensive lair. He advanced towards Stirling at the end of June and, when this failed, he made two attempts towards Glasgow in July. Leslie was not for turning, but the forays had served another purpose; they distracted Leslie's attention from the preparations to cross the Firth at Queensferry. On 17 July the first wave of 1,400 foot and some horses under Colonel Overton crossed and established a bridgehead at South Queensferry. The small Scottish garrison at Burntisland had witnessed the crossing and sent immediate word to Stirling. Two days later more men, horses and guns crossed under Lambert

and, by early on 20 July, there were nearly 4,500 men established on Ferry Hills above North Queensferry.

Meanwhile, Cromwell had marched back towards Stirling. His appearance may have delayed a Scottish counter-attack along the north bank of the Firth of Forth. It may also have prompted Leslie to despatch a smaller force than he would have hoped towards Fife. Sir John Brown hurried east with a body of 4,000 men and arrived on the hills west of Inverkeithing, from where he could see Lambert's force deployed with his infantry and guns in the centre and the cavalry on both wings. The two armies faced each other for some time. Brown was reluctant to give General Holbourne the order to attack and yield the high ground, while Lambert was reluctant to commence proceedings until all his force, including the balance of the cavalry, were landed and in position. In the interim, Brown decided to pull back to the higher ground of Castland Hill. Lambert saw the movement and decided to attack the Scottish rearguard. The Scots reeled to meet them and established a more formidable position atop Castland Hill straddling the road. Lambert's forces then deployed and expected to be attacked, but once again a long period of inactivity followed, with each side waiting for the other to make the first move. At about midday a report from Cromwell reached Lambert that Leslie was en route from Stirling with the Scottish army. Lambert could wait no longer.

The English advanced across the frontage. Brown led a cavalry counter-charge with the lancers using the slope on the Scottish right and broke the English cavalry on their left wing, but the English infantry were rampant and drove the Scots back, capturing Brown in the process.[19] The English cavalry on the right fared better and, after a short while, the entire Scottish force was fleeing for the lower slopes by Pitreavie Castle. It is unclear whether the Scottish cavalry covered the retreat of the infantry or whether the infantry left the cavalry to fight on alone. What is more certain is that a four-hour running battle ensued, during which 2,000 Scots were killed and another 500–600 taken prisoner.[20] English losses, according to their accounts, were almost negligible.[21] If Dunbar had been the tipping point, then Inverkeithing had been the decisive point in both Cromwell's conquest of Scotland and of the Covenanters' hold on the military reins. From now on Charles and the Scottish Royalists dictated plans and policy for the army. Cromwell's army, meanwhile, had returned to Edinburgh and over the course of the next week they crossed into Fife at Queensferry. However, instead of marching on the Scottish army, which had retired back to Stirling, Cromwell set off north to Perth. With their line of retreat into the Highlands blocked, Cromwell hoped the Scottish army would head south, where Thomas Harrison had been instructed to hold them until Cromwell returned to administer the *coup de grâce*. Cromwell's intuition served him well; the Scottish army did head south, but their destination was not Edinburgh but London.

17 Gentles, op. cit., p. 400.
18 *CSPD -I*, vol. IX, dated 9 December 1650.
19 Historic Scotland, *Battle of Inverkeithing*, p. 3.
20 Carlyle, op. cit., pp.137–9.
21 Gentles, op. cit., p. 403.

CHAPTER 43
WORCESTER, 1651: THE FINAL BATTLE

Charles's army, although only 12,000 strong, still posed a significant threat to stability in England. Cromwell wrote, on 4 August, 'I do apprehend that if he goes for England, being some few days march before us, it will trouble some men's thoughts; and may occasion some inconveniences; which I hope we are as deeply sensible of, and have been, and I trust shall be, as diligent to prevent, as any.'[1] Those 'men' were, of course, the Council of State and they had reacted, as early as 1 August, by ordering the militia commissioners in Norfolk, Suffolk, the Isle of Ely, Shropshire, Cheshire and Lancaster to raise a proportion out of the late militia of each county, to be taken into pay for three months.[2] Yorkshire, Derbyshire, Worcestershire and Nottinghamshire were fired up a few days later. These troops were to provide an interim defence against the Scots and guard against any Royalist insurrection in their counties until the New Model Army was back to administer the killer blow. Cromwell needed no new orders. He immediately despatched Lambert and Harrison (on separate routes – see map 153), each with 4,000 horse and dragoons, to catch up and keep contact with the Scots. He followed with the balance of 10,000 men, horses and guns. General Fleetwood's troops were also sent north from Reading and London to link up with Harrison. The plan was for the three forces to combine, channel and destroy the invading force, long before it reached London. In the capital itself, the trained bands mustered 14,000 men, who paraded at Tothill Fields for inspection by the speaker and other members of the Rump. The speed with which the Commonwealth had rallied a significant force in its defence was impressive.

Harrison and Lambert met at Haslemoor on 13 August and, two days later, having been reinforced with troops from Cheshire and Staffordshire, they were holding the bridge over the Mersey at Warrington. They began dismantling the bridge and erecting defences, but they had not long started when Charles's vanguard appeared, with the main body a few miles behind. Charles led the attack on the bridge himself and after a short skirmish Lambert decided to withdraw south. It was a curious decision, given that his force now outnumbered the Royalists by about a thousand men, and it clearly angered the Council of State, and led to suspicion about the motives and resilience of both Lambert and Harrison. That suspicion grew when, following the withdrawal, they failed to inflict any delay on the Royalists as they continued their southerly movement.[3] There is a suggestion that the commanders were under orders from Cromwell not to get embroiled in a major engagement, until the entire army was united.[4] This seems plausible. Cromwell had entered Yorkshire in the second week of August, but he appears to have been in no hurry. Perhaps his intention was to see which route or routes Charles would take before committing to a westerly movement.

Charles's earlier attempt to raise recruits in Lancashire had failed. James Stanley, the Earl of Derby, had been summoned from his hideout on the Isle

of Man to stir the county. He landed at Wyre Water on 16 August, with 300 men, and met with the King the following day, when he received his rather optimistic commission to raise a force of 6,000 infantry and over 1,000 horse. He returned to Warrington where, following a council of war, the enormity of the task was readily apparent. Cromwell had anticipated that Charles would try to capitalize on Royalist sympathies of the region, and had ordered Lambert to leave a small force under Colonel Lilburne in the area to counter any such attempts. On 25 August, Lilburne received intelligence that Derby was marching towards Preston. Outnumbered, he fell back, but his group was caught at Wigan and committed to battle. The better trained, equipped and disciplined Parliamentarian troops fought with great skill within the confines of the town and, after a short, sharp engagement, inflicted a total defeat on Derby's men. This action ended any hopes of a Royalist revival in Lancashire and denied Charles the recruits he so desperately needed.

On 22 August Cromwell entered Nottinghamshire on the same day that Charles entered Worcester. The garrison in the city, hopelessly outnumbered, retired south to Gloucester without a fight. It was now clear that Charles, having failed in Lancashire, was trying to recruit soldiers from the Severn valley and the Welsh Marches before making an attempt on London. Cromwell linked up with Lambert and Harrison at Warwick two days later, and moved towards Evesham, where he stayed for a few days, waiting for the Essex and Suffolk militia to arrive. When Fleetwood arrived with the militia, Cromwell's army stood at nearly 30,000 men. Charles had less than half that number, '10,000 Scots and about 2,000 English; and those too not excellently armed nor plentifully stored with ammunition'.[5] Charles's plan was to use the natural obstacles of the rivers Severn and Teme to limit Cromwell's options. He ordered the bridge to the south at Upton, and that to the north at Bewdley, to be destroyed and covered by fire.

In terms of defences, Worcester had changed considerably since the first action that had taken place at Powick in September 1642 (chapter 4). The city was walled, with a ditch that did not extend around the circumference, and access was via seven gates (see map 155). A number of redoubts and protruding bastions had been constructed in the 1640s, and the wall to the south had been extended and linked to the main defence at Fort Royal. The fort, however, suffered from a considerable weakness, being overlooked by the high ground of Perry Wood and Red Hill. A large building in the south of the city (known today as the Commandery) served as the Royalist headquarters.

Cromwell arrived on the outskirts of the city on 28 August. His priority was to defeat the Royalist army, lock, stock and barrel and prevent large numbers escaping west into Wales. He had no intention of getting embroiled in a lengthy and costly siege. Instead, he intended to entice the Royalist troops out into open battle. In order to achieve these aims, he needed to get

1 Carlyle, *Cromwell's Letters*, vol. II, pp. 137–9.
2 *CSPD -I*, vol. XVI, dated 1 August 1651.
3 Ibid., entries dated 16–23 August 1651.
4 Wanklyn, *The Warrior Generals*, p. 223.

5 Blount, *Boscobel*, p. 14. Cromwell estimated the force to be nearer 16,000 men – Carlyle, op. cit., p. 158.

large numbers of troops on the west bank of the River Severn, and quickly.[6] He despatched Lambert, with about 1,000 men, to seize the bridge at Upton, unaware that it had already been partially destroyed. The Royalist force at Upton was under the command of Edward Massey; he was a very capable officer but his sentinels at the bridge were about to let him down.[7] The Royalists had broken down part of the bridge, but a single plank had been left in place, and Lambert sent a forlorn hope of 18 dragoons forward to rush the bridge. They succeed in their endeavour and occupied a defensive position in the churchyard, directly opposite. They were quickly supported by some of Lambert's foot, who had forded the river, and the bridgehead was consolidated. They beat back Massey's men who tried to counter-attack, and Massey was badly injured in the process. Lambert was then able to repair the bridge, through which the large follow-up force of 11,000 men under Fleetwood passed in the early hours of 3 September.

As Fleetwood's force moved north, they were persistently attacked by Royalist skirmishers, who slowed their advance considerably. It was 2pm before his vanguard approached Powick village. They had been further encumbered by the boats and wooden planks they had brought with them in order to build a bridge of boats.[8] One officer recalled the endeavour:

> Upon Wednesday morning between 5 and 6 of the Clocke, we began to march from Upton, and by reason of some hindrances in our march, we reached not the Tame [Teme] river, till betweixt 2 and 3 in the afternoon: As soon as our boats came up, which was much about the same time, the Bridge was presently made over the Severn on the General's side [Cromwell on the east bank], and another over the River Tame on our side.[9]

Despite the fact that Massey, or at least his men, had fought a fighting withdrawal, it is difficult to piece together exactly what happened when Fleetwood's large force arrived south of Powick. He certainly divided his force, sending a group to Powick Bridge, most likely under his overall command. Robert Stapleton, a Roundhead officer, recalled that 'the right wing of Lieut-General Fleetwood's force came over the bridge of Teme, while the left wing disputed the bridge at Powick, which dispute lasted a long time and was very hot'.[10] What is less clear is just exactly what the Scottish were doing to counter this large force, about which they must have been aware for some considerable time. The only Royalist source recorded:

> … his Majesty discovered a body of the enemy's foot, about a thousand, with carriages of poles and planks… with intention to make a bridge. And immediately after… he gave order… to put the army in posture, and went himself in person out of the town where he found the parties already engaged near Powick, where the enemy were making two bridges of boats to pass a part of their army over the two rivers Severn and Teme, so to get to the other side of the town of Worcester.[11]

Stapleton concurs that the Royalists appear to have been taken by surprise:

> We were come as far as Poyick [Powick] half a mile on this side of the bridge with one Van[guard] before the enemy took alarm, which after they had taken, they drew down both their horse and foot from their leaguer at St. Jones, to oppose our passing over the bridges of boats.[12]

Across the second pontoon bridge, Cromwell personally led two regiments of foot and three of horse to support Fleetwood's men, who were, by now, pouring over the Teme bridge and driving back Pitscottie's Highland Brigade that had been sent to block the advance. Realizing the significance of this large flanking manoeuvre, Charles had sent his sergeant major of foot, General Robert Montgomery, to assume command of the west bank sector. While Montgomery remained in reserve with three regiments of cavalry and the balance of the infantry, he sent Keith's Regiment of Foot to the broken bridge north of Powick. The attacks across both bridges and into the fields of Lower Wick were ferocious and, at some stage, Cromwell ordered Lambert to bring reinforcements over to the west side of the Severn.[13]

At Powick bridge, Colonel Haines had his men wade the river and they soon established a bridgehead on the north bank, driving back Keith's Lowlanders in the process. The fighting was brutal. The Scots lined the hedges with great skill and courage but, after a time, were driven back by superior numbers. The terrain hindered the Scottish cavalry's attempts to drive back the Parliamentarian infantry. Cromwell recalled that 'we beat the enemy from hedge to hedge, till we beat him into Worcester'.[14] As both the Highland and Lowland Scots fell back on the west bank, Charles ordered an attack on Cromwell's forces on the high ground to the east of the city. He led the right wing and the Duke of Hamilton the left against Harrison's troops on Red Hill and Perry Wood. Stapleton, who was with the troops on Red Hill, recalled that 'the enemy rallying made a very bold sally out on this side of the town, and came with great bodies of horse and foot… they gave our men a very hot

6   Just how much of this was Cromwell's plan is unclear. Certainly, the Council of State had suggested an attack on both sides of the Severn as early as 27 August – *CSPD -I*, vol. XVI, dated 27 August 1651.

7   After denouncing the execution of Charles I, Massey came over to the Royalists as a leading representative of the English Presbyterians and joined the English contingent in Charles II's Scots-Royalist army.

8   It is not clear if they brought with them wherewithal to build both boat bridges. I calculate that the second bridge was constructed from boats/materials procured by Cromwell's engineers on the east bank.

9   Emminent (*sic*) officer of the army, *The fight at Worcester*, p. 1. There is considerable confusion about this operation and exactly where the boats/bridges were laid. It is generally accepted, based upon a letter from the Council of State to Admiral Blake written before news of the battle arrived in London, and Letchmere's diary (Captain Edmund Letchmere, *Calendar of his letters in the Worcester Record Office*) that the bridge from the east bank was above the confluence of the two rivers. Cromwell's post-battle letter is unclear, and Downing's letter (he was Cromwell's chief intelligence officer – the letter is in Cary, *Memorials of the Great Civil War*, vol. II) seems to support the above confluence position. But there are two other sources; namely Sam Wharton (*Account of the Battle of Worcester*) and Edmund Ludlow (Firth, *The Memoirs of Edmund Ludlow*), which, although not definitive, seem to indicate that the bridge across the Severn was below the confluence. It might be that Cromwell moved the crossing site, fearing that Fleetwood's attack had stalled, and laid the Severn bridge to the south in order to link up and reinforce the west bank force south of the Teme. To get a better idea of military bridging operations during the war, see Marsh, 'Military Bridging Operations During the Civil War', pp. 3–25. According to Atkin, the bridge across the Severn was 80 metres wide and that over the Teme 35 metres – Atkin, *Cromwell's Crowning Mercy*.

10   Stapleton, letter dated 3 September 1651, reproduced in Willis Bund, *Worcestershire*, p. 249.

11   Monkhouse (ed.), *State Papers Collected by Edward Earl of Clarendon*, vol II., pp. 362–3.

12   Stapleton, op. cit., p. 249.

13   It is unclear if he executed this order as he was concerned about the strength of Royalist forces on the east bank – see Firth (ed.), *Memoirs of Edmund Ludlow*, vol. I, pp. 280–1.

14   Cromwell, *Letter from the Lord General Cromwell*, p. 4.

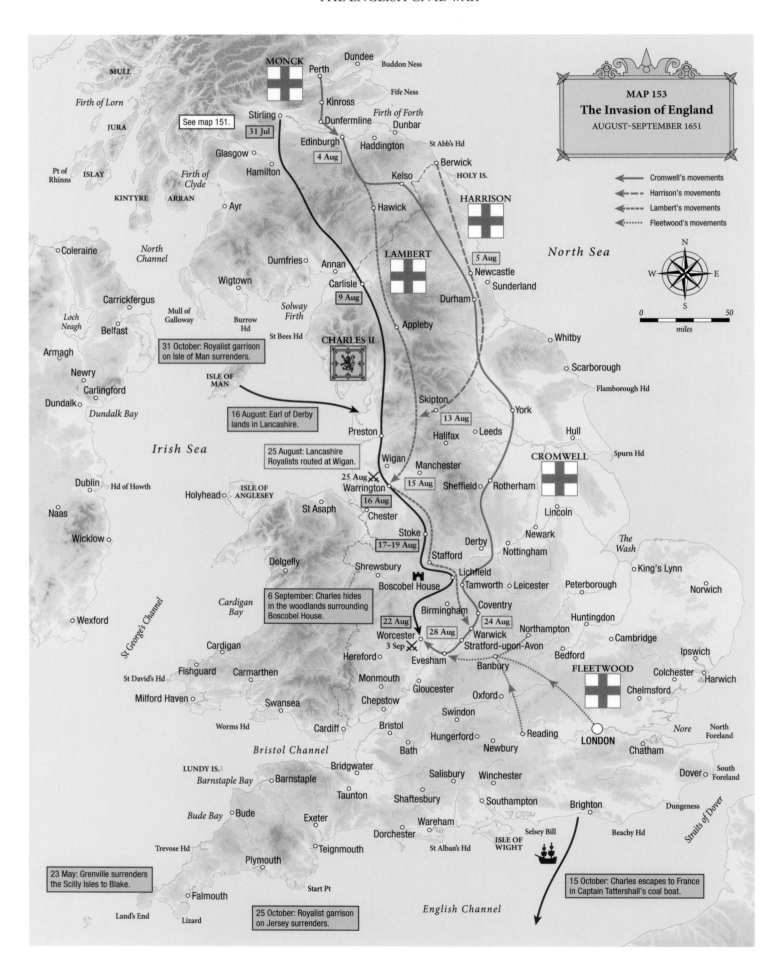

MULL

Firth of Lorn

JURA

Pt of
Rhinns   ISLAY

*Firth of
Clyde*

KINTYRE   ARRAN

Coleraine

*North
Channel*

Carrickfergus

*Loch
Neagh*

Belfast

Armagh

Newry

Carlingford

Dundalk

Dundalk Bay

Dublin   Hd of Howth

Irish Sea

Naas

Wicklow

Wexford

St George's Channel

MONCK   Perth   Dundee   Buddon Ness

Kinross   Fife Ness

Stirling   Dunfermline   *Firth of Forth*
    Edinburgh   Dunbar
See map 151.   4 Aug   Haddington   St Abb's Hd
31 Jul   Berwick
Glasgow   Kelso   HOLY IS.
Hamilton   Hawick   HARRISON
Ayr   North Sea
    Dumfries   Annan   5 Aug
    Carlisle   LAMBERT   Newcastle
    9 Aug   Sunderland
Wigtown   Durham
Mull of   Solway   9 Aug
Galloway   Firth   Whitby
Burrow
Hd   Appleby
St Bees Hd   Scarborough
CHARLES II
31 October: Royalist garrison   Flamborough Hd
on Isle of Man surrenders.   Skipton   York
ISLE OF   13 Aug
MAN   Leeds   Hull
16 August: Earl of Derby   Preston   Halifax   Spurn Hd
lands in Lancashire.   Wigan   Manchester   CROMWELL
25 August: Lancashire   25 Aug   Sheffield   Rotherham
Royalists routed at Wigan.   Warrington   15 Aug
Holyhead   ISLE OF   16 Aug   Lincoln
    ANGLESEY   Chester   *The
St Asaph   Newark   Wash*
    Stoke   Derby
Dolgelly   17–19 Aug   Nottingham   King's Lynn
    Shrewsbury   Stafford   Norwich
    Boscobel House   Lichfield   Leicester   Peterborough
*Cardigan   Tamworth
Bay*   Coventry   Huntingdon
6 September: Charles hides   Birmingham   24 Aug   Cambridge
in the woodlands surrounding   22 Aug   Warwick   Northampton
Boscobel House.   Worcester   Stratford-upon-Avon   Bedford   Ipswich
Cardigan   3 Sep   28 Aug   FLEETWOOD
    Evesham   Banbury   Colchester   Harwich
Hereford   Chelmsford
Fishguard   Carmarthen   Oxford   LONDON   North
St David's Hd   Monmouth   Gloucester   Swindon   Foreland
Milford Haven   Chepstow   Hungerford   Reading   Chatham
    Swansea   Cardiff   Bristol   Newbury
Worms Hd   Bath   Dover
Bristol Channel   Salisbury   Winchester   South
LUNDY IS.   Bridgwater   Foreland
Barnstaple Bay   Barnstaple   Southampton   Brighton   Dungeness
    Taunton   Shaftesbury   Straits of Dover
Bude Bay   Bude   ISLE OF   Selsey Bill   Beachy Hd
    Exeter   Wareham   WIGHT
Trevose Hd   Dorchester   St Alban's Hd
    Plymouth   Teignmouth   15 October: Charles escapes to France
23 May: Grenville surrenders   Start Pt   in Captain Tattershall's coal boat.
the Scilly Isles to Blake.
Falmouth   *English Channel*
Land's End   Lizard   25 October: Royalist garrison
    on Jersey surrenders.

MAP 153
The Invasion of England
AUGUST–SEPTEMBER 1651

N
W   E
S
0   50
miles

⟶ Cromwell's movements
⟵ - - Harrison's movements
⟵ - - Lambert's movements
⟵ · · · Fleetwood's movements

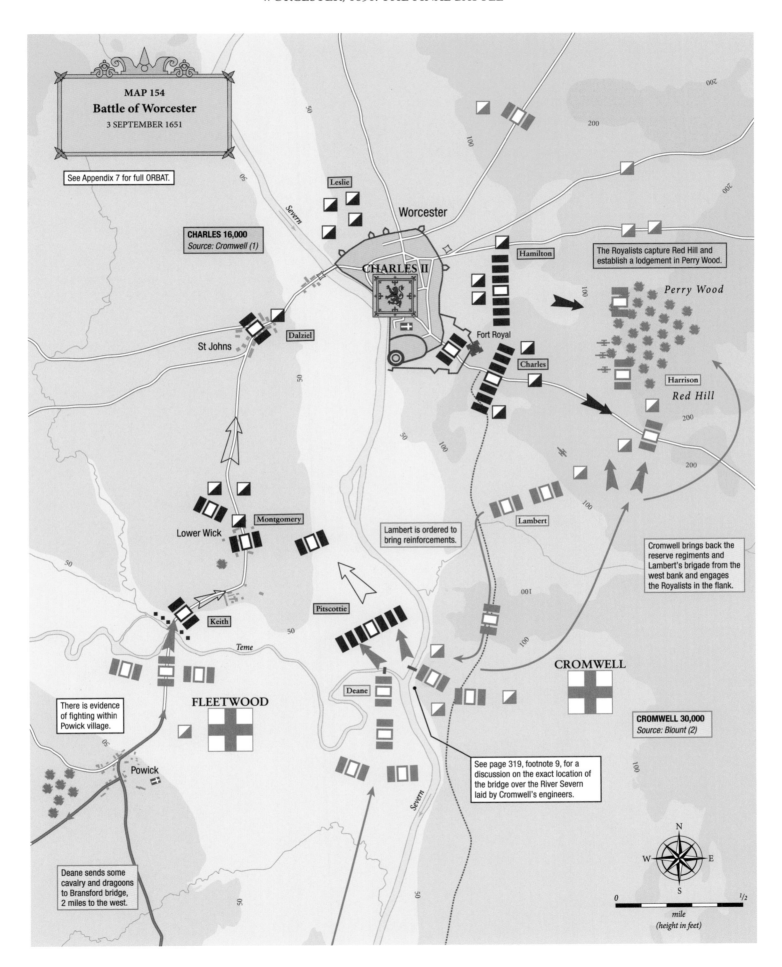

MAP 154
Battle of Worcester
3 SEPTEMBER 1651

See Appendix 7 for full ORBAT.

CHARLES 16,000
Source: Cromwell (1)

Leslie

Worcester

CHARLES II

The Royalists capture Red Hill and
establish a lodgement in Perry Wood.

Perry Wood

Hamilton

Dalziel

St Johns

Fort Royal

Charles

Harrison

Red Hill

Lambert

Montgomery

Lower Wick

Lambert is ordered to
bring reinforcements.

Cromwell brings back the
reserve regiments and
Lambert's brigade from the
west bank and engages
the Royalists in the flank.

Keith

Pitscottie

Teme

CROMWELL

Deane

There is evidence
of fighting within
Powick village.

FLEETWOOD

CROMWELL 30,000
Source: Blount (2)

Powick

See page 319, footnote 9, for a
discussion on the exact location of
the bridge over the River Severn
laid by Cromwell's engineers.

Deane sends some
cavalry and dragoons
to Bransford bridge,
2 miles to the west.

Severn

N
W   E
S

0   1/2
mile
(height in feet)

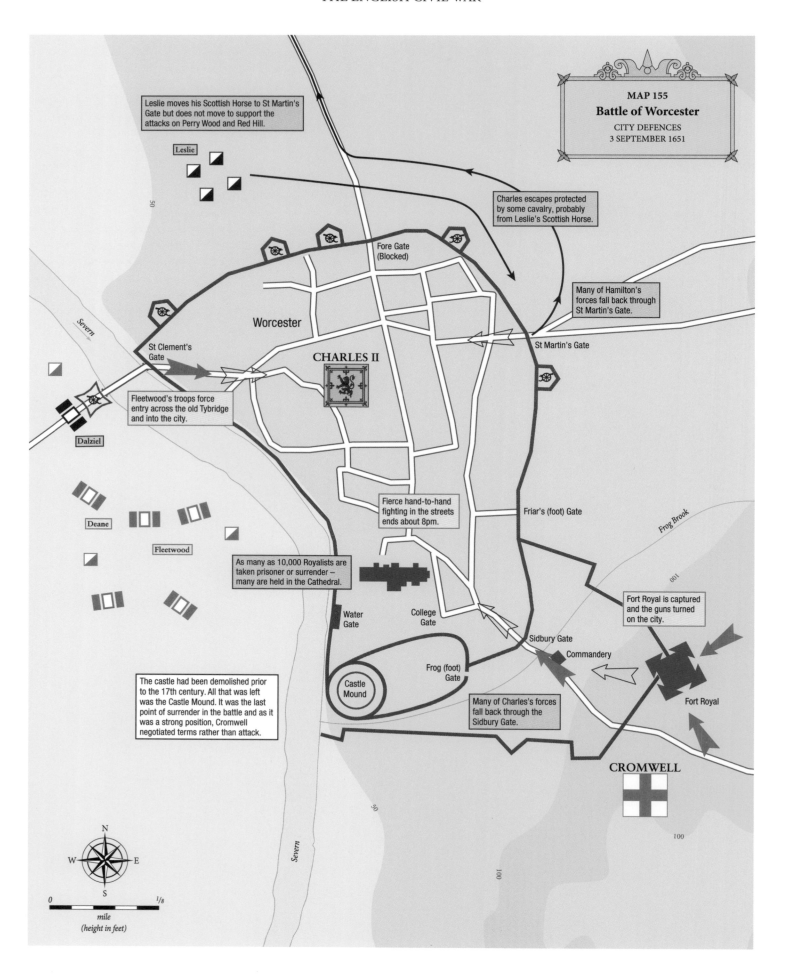

salute and put them to a little retreat'.[15] According to Thomas Blount, an English antiquarian and lexicographer of the period, 'his Majesty gave an incomparable example of valour to the rest by charging in person, which the Highlanders especially imitated in great measure, fighting with the but-ends of their muskets when their ammunition was spent'.[16]

The fight went on for nearly three hours and, by the end, the Royalists had taken Red Hill and had a lodgement in Perry Wood. With reports of these reverses, and with the Scots falling back on the west bank, Cromwell returned to the east bank. He brought with him the troops from the reserve, and those of Lambert, and moved north with speed. As he approached Red Hill, he sent a force around the rear of the feature to rally Harrison's men, who had fallen back and then attacked the King's force in the flank. It was the decisive action. The Royalists soon began to fall back. Charles tried to rally his men, but for the Scots it was now a matter of survival not victory. Cromwell recalled that 'we beat him totally and pursued him to the Royal Fort which we took… we [then] turned his own guns upon him'.[17]

The Essex militia had captured the Fort Royal, while the other infantry regiments poured into the narrow streets through Sidbury Gate. Bloody and bitter street fighting ensued, and many fled out of the city via St Martin's Gate. By 8pm the fighting within the city was all but over. There was some sporadic resistance, but a large number of men had surrendered and were imprisoned within the cathedral. Charles escaped with a small body of cavalry, but his army, as was Cromwell's plan, had ceased to exist. Nearly 10,000 were taken prisoner, almost 3,000 were slain and about the same number were fugitives.[18] Parliamentarian losses seem extraordinarily light at 200 men, if Cromwell's report is to be believed. That same report to the House concluded that his victory at Worcester, a battle that was to be his last and the last of the Wars of the Three Kingdoms, was 'a crowning mercy. Surely, if it be not such a one we shall have, if this provoke those that are concerned in it to thankfulness; and the Parliament to do the will of Him who hath done His will for it, and for the Nation.'[19] Charles escaped through the west Midlands, narrowly avoiding capture near Boscobel House, where he hid in a large oak tree, before heading to the South-West. He took a boat and escaped to France in October. The victory for the New Model Army, Cromwell and the Commonwealth was complete in every sense.

15 Stapleton, op. cit.

16 Blount, op. cit., p. 19.

17 Cromwell, op. cit.

18 Emminent (*sic*) officer of the army, op. cit., p. 3. Stapleton provides similar numbers.

19 Carlyle, op. cit., p. 158.

CHAPTER 44

THE INTERREGNUM, 1649–60

A week after the final battle at Worcester, Cromwell returned to London to a hero's welcome. The following month affairs in Scotland were settled by a 'Declaration', which was adopted by Parliament on 24 December. Earlier that month Cromwell had summoned a conference of army officers, lawyers and members of (the Rump) Parliament to discuss the settlement of the nation. Since the regicide and the establishment of a Commonwealth, the army, and it could be argued the nation, had been distracted from the matter of settlement by the need to resolve matters in Ireland and Scotland. Politically, however, the execution of Charles I had created more complications than solutions with regard to the future governance of the nation. The Rump Parliament was never intended to be a permanent body and, by 1653, its members were deemed to be feathering their nest, and the body, along with the Council of State, was disbanded. This left the nation under direct military rule by the Army Council. The Nominated Assembly filled the void from July to December 1653; it was then followed by another interim solution, which, in turn, was superseded by the founding of the Protectorate. The portfolio for the Protectorate was outlined in a constitutional paper, known as the 'Instrument of Government'. Cromwell was installed as the 'Lord Protector', a position he was to hold for five years. His death in 1658 threw the nation back into turmoil, rekindled opportunities for change among republicans and Presbyterians, and refocussed the Royalists' attempts at restoration.

In fact, as it turned out, Worcester was not the final battle of the nation's civil struggle. Throughout the 1650s insurgent activity continued in Ireland and there was a large-scale revolt in Scotland. The troubles in Scotland lasted 18 months, from 1653 to 1655, and required the deployment of many thousands of New Model Army troops. The exiled Charles II formed the Sealed Knot at the end of 1653, in order to coordinate covert Royalist activity in England, and to prepare the way for a general uprising against the Protectorate government.[1] There were some low-level uprisings in 1655 and 1657–58, but it was Sir George Booth's revolt in the north-west in 1659 that was a far more serious affair. It ended with the battle at Winnington Bridge on 19 August.

Throughout the 1650s the Commonwealth and Protectorate kept a standing army of over 30,000 men. This army surged on three occasions (1652, late 1654 and early 1655) to over 50,000.[2] Furthermore, the nation found itself at war with the Dutch (1652–54) and Spain (1654–56). The Dutch wars were deemed necessary in order to enforce the Navigation Ordinance of 1651, passed to control the access the Dutch had to English ports, in an attempt to abate the trade domination built up by the Dutch during the years of civil war. Although these were largely naval wars, England's military reputation, which had been largely ridiculed during the first half of the century and the Thirty Years' War (1618–48), began to flourish. This inevitably lessened Catholic support for Stuart restoration,

and did a great deal for Cromwell's reputation abroad. But the costs of maintaining this force, and an expanding navy, were fearfully expensive, and the necessary taxation damaged his standing domestically.

Christopher Hill, in his classic work *The World Turned Upside Down*, suggests that 'the gentry and merchants who had supported the Parliamentarian cause in the civil war expected to reconstruct the institutions of society as they wished, to impose their values'.[3] He goes on to propose that, had they not been prevented from doing this, England might have moved directly to something akin to the 1688 settlement without military dictatorship. Under the terms of the Instrument of Government a parliament was scheduled to meet in September 1654. The elections were, by the standards of the 17th century, free and fair, and the new House contained representatives from across the divide, including some Royalist sympathizers. Cromwell hoped they would implement the ordinances that he and the Council of State had drafted, but instead they challenged the right of the Protector to exercise civil and military authority. After five months he dissolved Parliament and introduced a system of direct military government, known as the 'rule of major generals'.

The generals in the 12 districts were granted unprecedented powers but they were not, in the main, local men from the area they now commanded, and this caused considerable unrest across the country.[4] The rule of the major generals challenged local independence, imposed local taxes and raised local troops – all without authority from the centre or reference to the local leaders and magistrates. Under the terms of the 'Instrument', Cromwell was required to summon a new Parliament every three years, but given the unpopularity of the military rule, Cromwell decided to execute this a year early in 1656. It was not his only reason for doing so. He needed money to finance both his domestic and foreign policy, in the same way that both James I and Charles I had earlier been caught between the devil and the deep sea. A point that would, no doubt, have amused Cromwell's many opponents. A number in this new legislature, and others in key appointments in public life, wished to see the Protectorate become essentially a civilian government. They formulated their views in a document known as the 'Humble Petition and Advice'. It laid out a new constitution which would replace the Instrument of Government and, *ipso facto*, the Army Council. Furthermore, it proposed a return to monarchy and that Cromwell should be king.

Cromwell had earlier spoken about the attractions of monarchy (in general) and rumours spread that he was seriously considering the proposal. This led to significant unrest among many army officers, who petitioned him to remain faithful to the 'good old cause'.[5] After considerable soul-searching and dialogue, Cromwell finally decided that was sage advice, and he rejected the crown, but his pontification had sown the seeds of doubt among many of his old comrades. Throughout this period, Cromwell was suffering from bouts of malaria, contracted during the Irish campaigns.

---

1   The Knot comprised six members: Lord Belasyse, Lord Loughborough, Sir William Compton, Sir Richard Willys, Colonel John Russell and Colonel Edward Villiers.

2   Kenyon & Ohlmeyer, *Military History*, p. 306.

3   Hill, *Upside Down*, p. 14.

4   Lynch, *Interregnum*, p. 52.

5   Ibid., p. 59.

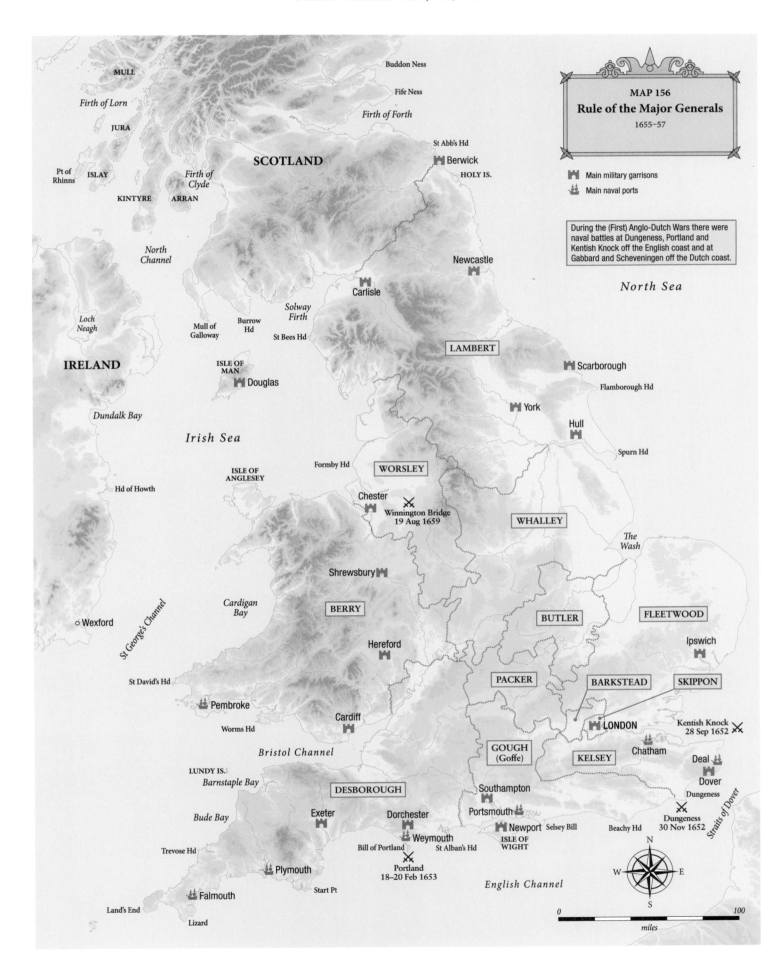

MULL

Firth of Lorn

JURA

Buddon Ness

Fife Ness

Firth of Forth

Pt of
Rhinns ISLAY

*Firth of
Clyde*

KINTYRE ARRAN

St Abb's Hd

Berwick

HOLY IS.

SCOTLAND

MAP 156
Rule of the Major Generals
1655–57

Main military garrisons

Main naval ports

During the (First) Anglo-Dutch Wars there were
naval battles at Dungeness, Portland and
Kentish Knock off the English coast and at
Gabbard and Scheveningen off the Dutch coast.

*North
Channel*

North Sea

Newcastle

Carlisle

*Loch
Neagh*

*Solway
Firth*

Mull of
Galloway

Burrow
Hd

St Bees Hd

LAMBERT

Scarborough

Flamborough Hd

IRELAND

ISLE OF
MAN

Douglas

Dundalk Bay

York

Hull

Irish Sea

Spurn Hd

Hd of Howth

ISLE OF
ANGLESEY

Formby Hd

WORSLEY

Chester

Winnington Bridge
19 Aug 1659

WHALLEY

*The
Wash*

Shrewsbury

*Cardigan
Bay*

BERRY

Hereford

BUTLER

FLEETWOOD

Ipswich

St George's Channel

Wexford

St David's Hd

PACKER

BARKSTEAD

SKIPPON

Pembroke

Cardiff

LONDON

Kentish Knock
28 Sep 1652

Worms Hd

Chatham

Bristol Channel

GOUGH
(Goffe)

KELSEY

Deal

Dover

Dungeness

LUNDY IS.

Barnstaple Bay

DESBOROUGH

Southampton

Portsmouth

Selsey Bill

Beachy Hd

Dungeness
30 Nov 1652

Bude Bay

Exeter

Dorchester

Newport

ISLE OF
WIGHT

Weymouth

Trevose Hd

Bill of Portland

St Alban's Hd

Portland
18–20 Feb 1653

Plymouth

Start Pt

English Channel

Falmouth

Land's End

Lizard

N
W   E
S

Straits of Dover

0   100
miles

By the time of his death, on 3 September 1658, stability within the three nations was as remote as it had ever been since the regicide, and the prospect of restoration growing by the year. Under the terms of the Humble Petition, Richard Cromwell duly succeeded his father, as both Lord Protector and Commander-in-Chief. Lacking the grass-roots-level support of the armed forces, he was soon urged to give up his post as their commander; he, in turn, turned towards civilian solutions. With arrears mounting and growing civil unrest, Richard was compelled to call another Parliament to seek funds, or the means to generate them.

The Presbyterian and Republican members clashed over command of the local militia, the latter keen to regain control of these forces at Parliamentary level. The army demanded that Parliament be disbanded, but Richard stalled and was eventually forced into a humiliating U-turn. With his authority in tatters, he resigned a few months later, but the Commonwealth took another ten months to die a slow, agonizing death. In April 1660, another Parliament made one last bid to save the republican cause, but the army was divided on the matter. Later in the month, both houses reconvened and debated the terms of the Declaration of Breda, issued by Charles II on 4 April. In this proclamation, Charles promised a general pardon for crimes committed during the English Civil War and the Interregnum, for all those who recognized him as the lawful king. The declaration also addressed the retention by the current owners of property purchased during the same period; religious toleration; and the payment of arrears to members of the army, and that the army would be recommissioned into service under the crown. On 8 May 1660 England was no longer a republic, but neither was it a return to the monarchy of the 1640s; government now resided with the King, the Lords and the Commons. On 29 May Charles II returned to London – God had changed his mind.

I beseech ye in the bowels of Christ, think that ye may be mistaken.

Oliver Cromwell

NOTES TO MAPS

MAP 12. Source: Ravell's 1749 Map from Dalton's *History of Drogheda* (Dublin, 1749) and reproduced from the map in Thomas D'Arcy's *Popular History of Ireland* (Dublin, 1908).

MAP 13. Sources: I. T. Smith's Foundation Plan of the Ancient Palace of Westminster, 1807, and the Floor Plan of the Houses of Parliament, *The Illustrated London News*, 30 September 1843 and Charles Barry's Plan of the Houses of Parliament and Offices, on the principal floor of the Palace of Westminster, dated 1852.

MAP 14. Source: From the plan of the Tower Liberties, surveyed in 1597 by Guilelmus Haiward and J. Gascoyne. A few changes were made in the early 17th century.

MAP 15. Sources: John Speed's map of Hull, *c*.1611, Wenceslas Hollar's map of Hull, *c*.1640, and a map of Kingston upon Hull, British Library Maps K. Top 44.32.

MAP 17. Source: Map of Worcester 1651 by Henry Seile, the King's Stationer, published 1660.

MAP 19. Sources: Foard, *History from the Field – The Edgehill Battlefield Survey* (Battlefields Trust, 2005); Harridence, *The Battle of Edgehill, 1642, Terrain Conjecture 2011*, updated Aug 2012. **Notes:** 1. See Appendix 1 for details and references of army strengths; 2. Young, *Edgehill 1642*.

MAP 23. Source: Roque, *A plan of the cities of London and Westminster, and borough of Southwark* (engraved by John Pine, 1746).

MAP 26. Source: The exact location of the battle is unclear. The version shown here is not the traditional position in Boconnoc park, but that proposed by English Heritage/The Battlefields Trust. The problem with this position is that preliminary digging in the area in 1999 to lay pipes revealed no evidence of a battle. However, deployments indicated are, therefore, the most *logical* until archaeological survey can prove otherwise.

MAP 28. Source: English Heritage Battlefield Report, Number 1000015 and The Battlefields Trust. **Note:** 1. Young, 'The Battle of Hopton Heath, 19th March 1643' in the *Journal of the Society for Army Historical Research*, XXXIII (1954).

MAP 32. Note: 1. Corbet, a primary source, states that Waller's force was a third the strength of Maurice's, but as a Parliamentarian supporter, his reliability is in question.

MAP 33. Source: J. A. Burt's Map of Reading during the siege of 1643, drawn in *c*.1896. The original is in the British Museum. **Notes:** 1. Eight regiments, including three from Fielding, Lunsford, Fitton, Salusbury, Bolle and Gerard; 2. Cavalry regiment was Thomas Aston's; 3. Artillery included 2x demi-culverin (iron), 1x saker-drake (brass), 8x 3-pounder (brass) and 1x bastard-falcon 2¼-inch (brass); 4. The exact number and type of siege guns is unrecorded. However, with access to the resources of the Tower of London, it is likely that it was a well-supplied train with good guns and siege materials. Clarendon, *History of the Rebellion*, vol. IV, p. 22.

MAP 35. Sources: Chadwyck-Healey (ed.), *Bellum Civile*; Coate, *Cornwall* and Barratt, *South-West*.

MAP 38. Source: Topographical details based on David Johnson's study in *Adwalton Moor 1643*.

MAP 40. Notes: 1. Essex, *Two letters from his excellencie Robert Earl of Essex*; 2. Only about 1,000 were on the field; 3. Warburton (ed.), *Memoirs of Prince Rupert*, vol. II., p. 204.

MAP 42. Source: Henry Bell's map of King's Lynn dated 1692: reproduced in Yaxley, *The Siege of King's Lynn 1643*. **Note:** 1. Ketton-Cremer, *Norfolk in the Civil War*, p. 208.

MAP 44. Notes: 1. Chadwyck-Healey (ed.), *Bellum Civile*; 2. I am unsure where Wroughton, *Battle of Lansdown*, has sourced this figure, but it is also used in the English Heritage Report. The five guns are mentioned in Waller's report.

MAP 45. Sources: Mapping: 1664 Joan Blau in *Atlas Major*, Blane's map of Wiltshire, 1681 and Andrews' and Dury's Map of Wiltshire, 1810. **Notes:** 1.

Byron's account of the battle; he inflates the number of horse in his summary; 2. There is no primary source listing the numbers of Royalist infantry in Devizes. Burne & Young's figure (*Great Civil War*) is a good estimate.

MAP 47. Sources: J. Speed's 1610 Map of Bristol; R. Walton's 1671 Map of the Famous Citie of Bristoll and Lynch, *King and Parliament*, p. 76 – general plan of Bristol during the civil war. **Notes:** 1. Lynch, *King & Parliament* and Ede-Barrett (ed.), *Storm of Bristol: De Gomme's Account*; 2. Fiennes, *A Relation made in the House of Commons*, p. 6.

MAP 48. Sources: John Speed's map of Hull, *c*.1611; Wenceslas Hollar's map of Hull, *c*.1640 and Map of Kingston upon Hull, British Library Maps K. Top 44.32. **Notes:** 1. Fairfax, *Short memorials of Thomas Lord Fairfax*.

MAP 49. Sources: The deployments are based on the traditional location of the battle (using G. Foard's analysis) and Betty Brammer's work *Winceby and the Battle*. Stuart Weston's *Battlefield Survey of the Battle of Winceby* casts considerable doubt on this traditional battle location, but is not able to definitively identify where the battle took place. His suggestion is also indicated on the map. **Notes:** 1. Widdrington's report captured by the Parliamentarians. Rushworth, *Historical Collections*, part 3, vol. II, pp. 268–70; 2. Dillingham, *The Parliament Scout*, Issue 13–20 October 1643. Also the English Heritage Battle Report.

MAP 52. Source: Based on the 1643 siege map of Plymouth, by Wenceslas Hollar. **Note:** 1. Anon, *Late siege of Plymouth*, supported by *Mercurius Aulicus* dated 10 September 1643.

MAP 54. Sources: John Speed's 1610 map of Gloucester, and the map in Day's *Gloucester & Newbury 1643*. **Note:** 1. Corbet, *Gloucester*. Day, op. cit., p. 17 – taking the guns deployed at Bristol as the approximated figure, plus details from the map.

MAP 55. Sources: John Roque's 1761 map of the 'County of Berkshire'. Baker's 1775 map of 'The Manor of Endborne'. Maps in Day, *Gloucester & Newbury 1643*. With the exception of Newbury Wash, the entire battlefield was tightly enclosed. **Note:** 1. See Day, op. cit., pp. 157–62 for analysis. Most historical accounts have not made any allowance for attrition since the start of the campaign.

MAP 60. Notes: 1. See main text for discussion on actual numbers; 2. This includes the 8,000 Newcastle brought from York, the 2,000 of Glemham's covering force but not the garrison.

MAP 61. Sources: J. Speed's 1610 Map of Newcastle; R. Beilby's 1788 Map of Newcastle and Gateshead. **Note:** 1. The exact location of the bridging operation is not known – that shown on the map is diagrammatic only.

MAP 64. Sources: Joan Blaeu's Map of Cheshire 1645–48; H. Moll's map of 1724. The defence works around Nantwich are based on research by the Nantwich Museum and from Transactions of the Historic Society of Cheshire and Lancashire. **Notes:** 1. Fairfax, *Short Memorials*; 2. Byron, in Carte, *A Collection of Original Letters*, and refined by Dore & Lowe, *The Battle of Nantwich*.

MAP 65. Sources: Clampe, *A Description of the Seidge of Newarke upon Trent* (1646), British Library (maps) 4670 (I). Period map depicting the Siege of Newark, held by the NCWC, possibly by the Royalist engineer Sir Bernard de Gomme; Royal Commission on Historical Monuments – Newark on Trent: The Civil War siegeworks. **Notes:** 1. Anon Eyewitness, *Rupert's raising of the siege*; 2. Reid, *King's Armies*.

MAP 68. Sources: *The Extract of a Survey of Cheriton Manor 1534* (HRO) 45M83/PZ2, *A Survey of Cheriton Manor 1602–04* (HRO) 53M67/1, and the *Sale by Parliamentary Trustees of Bishopric Lands in Tichborne*, 1649 (HRO) 11M59/BP/E/T1. These lists depict East Down and Cow Down as the only open heathland in the entire mapped area, including the ground on, and around, Hinton Ampner. **Notes:** 1. Walker *Historical Discourses*, p. 7. Another two regiments joined Hopton before battle; these have been included in the totals;

2. CSP-D dated 4 March 1644, which stipulates the size of Waller's army to which must be added Balfour's mounted brigade, which I estimate to have been 1,200 horse and 300 dragoons.

MAP 71. Sources: J. Speed's 1610 Map of Yorke; Braun & Hogenberg's 1617 Map and Archer's 1682 plan of York. An Inventory of the Historical Monuments in City of York, vol. II, *The Defences* (HMSO London, 1972). **Note:** 1. Wenham, *The Great and Close Siege of York 1644*.

MAP 72. Source: Firth, The English Historical Review, Vol. 13, No. 52 (Oct., 1898): *The Journal of Prince Rupert's Marches, 5 Sept. 1642 to 4 July 1646*, pp. 729–41.

MAP 73. Sources: The deployment is based on de Gomme's Map (in Firth), Young's *Marston Moor* and Tincey's *Marston Moor 1644*. Finer aspects of the terrain based upon Leadman, *The Battle of Marston Moor* (published in the *Yorkshire Archaeological and Topographical Journal*); Newman & Roberts, *Battle of the Five Armies*; Young's *Marston Moor*, the English Heritage Battlefield Report and Woolrych's *Decisive Battles of the English Civil War* (latter for ditch detail). **Note:** 1. Firth, *Marston Moor*, Transactions of the Royal Historical Society, vol. XII, pp. 17–79 (London, 1898). Using de Gomme's figures.

MAP 76. Source: Firth, The English Historical Review, vol. 13, no. 52 (Oct. 1898): *The Journal of Prince Rupert's Marches, 5 Sept. 1642 to 4 July 1646*, p. 737.

MAP 77. Sources: Toynbee & Young, *Cropredy Bridge 1644*, map facing p. 116; Coate, *Cornwall*, map p. 134.

MAP 78. Notes: 1. Symonds (Peachey, *Richard Symonds*, p. 11), recorded on 21 June: 6,000 foot and 4,000 or nearly 5,000 horse. However, Toynbee & Young, *Cropredy Bridge, 1644*, chapter 12 and Morris, *Battle of Cropredy Bridge*, pp. 14–19, have done a lot of work and dovetail with a figure of 9,500, including 4,000 horse; 2. There are no primary source account to confirm Waller's strength. Both sides were recorded as being equal in size. *Mercurius Aulicus*, Week 26, quotes a figure of 10,000 and *CSPD* dated 4 July 1644, refers to his army being 9,000 foot and 3,000 horse.

MAP 80. Notes: 1. Peachey, *Richard Symonds*, p. 18. Symonds states that Grenville's force was 8,000: I have divided this up to 5,500 foot and 2,500 horse; 2. Essex, *Lord Generall his quarters*, p. A2. He states 10,000 men. Ede-Borrett, *Lostwithiel 1644*, pp. 71–2 has a muster of the Parliamentarian horse at Tiverton in July, showing just over 3,000.

MAP 83. Sources: 1. Money, *Battles of Newbury*, p. 142. These are Cromwell's figures from his evidence against the Earl of Manchester; 2. Walker, *Historical Discourses*, p. 98. Figure for 30 September 1644.

MAP 87. Sources: Worton, *Battle of Montgomery* pp. 73–83 – note the contours on map on p. 74 are incorrect. Walters & Hunnisett, *English Civil War Battlefield of Montgomery*. J. Speed's map of Montgomeryshire (inset town map) 1610. **Note:** 1. Brereton, Myddleton, & Meldrum, *Letters from Sir William Brereton, Sir Thomas Middleton, Sir John Meldrum*. There is little disagreement with the numbers; Brereton stated that the Royalists had 4,000, while Myddleton stated 5,000.

MAP 91. Source: De Gomme's Plan of the Defences of Oxford, 1644.

MAP 92. Sources: *Transactions: The Leicestershire Archaeological and Historical Society*, vol. I, dated 1860; Fielding Johnson, *Ancient Leicester*. **Note:** 1. Temple, *An examination examined*, p. 3; 2. Tibbutt, *Samuel Luke*, p. 548.

MAP 94. Sources: Foard, *Naseby The Decisive Campaign*. Streeter's map of the battle in Sprigge, *Anglia Rediviva* and de Gomme's sketch map; **Note:** 1. The numbers on both sides at Naseby are contentious and have tended to be overstated. I am grateful to Martin Marix Evans who drew my attention to an article by David Blackmore, 'Counting the New Model Army'. Martin sums up the problems with, and possible solutions for, the numbers in his books *Naseby, English Civil War* (co-written) and *Triumph of the New Model Army*. In terms of artillery the Royalists had 12 guns (Fairfax, *Three letters*, report by Cromwell p. 2) but these are unlikely to have been on the field in time, and the New Model Army had 11 guns (Streeter's map) but there is evidence that these were not deployed in time.

MAP 98. Sources: English Heritage Battlefield Report: *Langport 1645*, dated 1995. However, the exact location of the battle remains subject to debate.

There is evidence that it might have been to the south on the Pibsbury road (the modern A372) and another version (proposed by Foard) positions the battle between the Pibsbury road and the version depicted on the map. **Note:** 1. Browne, *From Leicester to Langport*, p. 262.

MAP 99. Source: Sketch maps in Buchan, *Marquis of Montrose*.

MAP 104. Source: For the movement of Charles see Peachey (ed.), *Richard Symonds*.

MAP 106. Sources: J. Speed's 1610 Map of Bristol; R. Walton's 1671 *Map of the Famous Citie of Bristoll* and Lynch, *King and Parliament*, p. 76 – general plan of Bristol during the civil war. **Notes:** 1. Rupert, *A declaration of His Highness Prince Rupert*; 2. There are no sources providing the Parliamentarian strengths. I have used numbers from Langport in Browne, *From Leicester to Langport*.

MAP 107. Notes: 1. Godwin, *Civil War in Hampshire*, p. 346. Cromwell brought five guns and Dalbier had a battery; 2. Carlyle, *Oliver Cromwell's Letters*, vol. I, p. 213 – from his report of 300 prisoners and 100 slain.

MAP 109. Sources: John Speed's 1610 map of Chester and Joseph Hemingway's 1645 map of Chester, published in 1836. Maps in *A History of the County of Chester*, vol. V, Part 1, The City of Chester: General History and Topography (London, 2003).

MAP 110. Notes: 1. Peachey (ed.), *Richard Symonds* – Symonds lists the three brigades and Gerard's Horse; the figure of 3,500 is from Barratt, *The Siege of Chester and the Battle of Rowton Heath*; 2. Poyntz's post-battle account, enlarged upon by Colonel Parsons, who conveyed it to Parliament – Morris and Lawson, 'The Siege of Chester' in *The Journal of Chester & North Wales Archaeological and Historical Society* (Chester, 1923), Volume XXV.

MAP 113. Notes: 1. Carte, *Collection of Original Letters*, pp. 109–10; 2. Fairfax, *Sir Thomas Fairfax letter*.

MAP 114. Sources: Sutton Nicholl's 17th-century map of Exeter; John Roque's 1744 map of Exeter and Stoyle, *Deliverance to Destruction*.

MAP 116. Note: 1. Morgan, *Morgan Governor of Glocester's letter*.

MAP 117. Sources: Clampe, *A Description of the Seidge of Newarke upon Trent (1646)*; British Library (maps) 4670 (I): Period map depicting the Siege of Newark, held by the NCWC, possibly by the Royalist engineer, Sir Bernard de Gomme; Royal Commission on Historical Monuments – Newark on Trent: The Civil War siegeworks (London, 1964). **Note:** 1. Belasyse, *The reducing of Newark*.

MAP 118. Sources: De Gomme's Plan of the Defences of Oxford, 1644; Rallingson's Plan of the Defences of Oxford, 1648; Wood's copper-plate engraving of the Defences of Oxford, 1644 in Varley, *The Siege of Oxford*; Lattey, Parsons, & Philip, *A Contemporary Map of the Defences of Oxford in 1644* (Oxoniensia, 1936). **Note:** 1. Anon, *Rupert's marching out of Oxford*.

MAP 119. As for map 118.

MAP 123. Notes: 1. Anon, *A bloody fight at Black-Water in Ireland*; 2. Gardiner, *Great Civil War*, vol. III, p. 152.

MAP 126. Note: 1. Matthew, *A diary and relation of passages*, pp. 1–3.

MAP 127. Source: Officer of the Parliaments army, *Battell of Knocknones*. **Note:** 1. Inchiquin, *Lord Inchiquine in Munster in Ireland*, p. 2.

MAP 129. Source: A copy of the Map by George Virtue published in 1739. Much of the detail of the city comes from Wenceslas Hollar's plan of London from the mid-17th century. The depiction of the defence lines is not completely accurate.

MAP 130. Source: For Battle of St Fagans – Gaunt, *Civil War in Wales*, p. 69.

MAP 131. Source: John Speed's map of 1611. **Notes:** 1. T. W. Letter from Pembroke in Anon, *Sir Marmaduke Langdale*, p. A2; 2. Gardiner, *Great Civil War*, vol. IV, p. 118.

MAP 133. Source: A Map of Maidstone in 1650 from a written description by Nicholas Wall, Kent Archaeological Society. **Note:** 1. Rushworth, *Lord Fairfax's forces at Maidstone*, pp. 4–5. Dudley's numbers include the reinforcements from Aylesford.

MAP 134. Source: Keymer's Map from Anon, *A diary of the siege of Colchester*. **Notes:** 1. *A diary of the siege of Colchester*; 2. Townsend, *The Siege of Colchester*, pp. 11–12.

MAP 136. Note: 1. Bull and Seed, *Bloody Preston*, pp. 104–13.

MAP 137. Note: 1. Carlyle, *Cromwell's Letters*, vol. I, part IV, p. 29.

MAP 138. **Source:** Holmes (ed.), *The Sieges of Pontefract Castle 1644–1648* – frontispiece sketch. **Note:** 1. Paulden, *Pontefract Castle*, p. 9.

MAP 139. **Source:** Maps in Young, *Carisbrooke Castle* (English Heritage Guidebook, 2013).

MAP 142. **Sources:** John Speed's 1610 map of Dublin; the Down Survey from the 1650s which shows the Dublin defences; Herman Moll's map of Dublin, 1714, and John Rocque's very detailed maps from the 1750s. **Notes:** 1. Carte (ed.), *Collection of Original Letters*, vol. II, p. 396. His figures do not include the forces of Dillon to the north; 2. Cary, *Memorials of the Great Civil War*, vol. II, p. 161 and R. C., *The present condition of Dublin*, p. 2.

MAP 143. **Sources:** Ravell's 1749 Map from Dalton's *History of Drogheda* (Dublin, 1749) and the map in Thomas D'Arcy's *Popular History of Ireland* (Dublin, 1908). **Notes:** 1. Murphy, *Cromwell in Ireland*, from the muster rolls; 2. Carlyle, *Cromwell's Letters*, vol. I, p. 151.

MAP 145. **Note:** 1. Gardiner, *Commonwealth and Protectorate*, vol. I, p. 127.

MAP 146. **Sources:** Goubet's map, showing the line of town defences in 1690 and other references in *Clonmel Town Walls Conservation & Management Plan* (Dublin, 2009). **Notes:** 1. Carlyle, *Cromwell's Letters*, vol. I, p. 256; 2. McKeiver, *A New History of Cromwell's Irish Campaign*, p. 156. Due to the high levels of sickness in Cromwell's force it is difficult to be absolutely accurate with regard to the numbers of New Model Army troops before Clonmel.

MAP 148. **Source:** An old undated sketch of Limbrick *(sic)* Leaguer 1651 (on the internet). **Note:** 1. Gilbert, *Diaries of the proceedings of the forces in Ireland*, entry dated 29 October 1651.

MAP 154. **Notes:** 1. Carlyle, *Cromwell's Letters*, vol. II, p. 158. The figure for the Royalists is almost certainly too high – see appendix 7; 2. Blount, *Boscobel*, p. 14.

MAP 155. **Source:** T. Nash's map of Worcester as it stood fortified in September 1651, dated 1781 from an engraving made in 1660.

APPENDIX 1: ARMY STRENGTHS AND COMPOSITIONS, 1642

BATTLE OF EDGEHILL, 23 OCTOBER 1642

The Royalist Army

Command

Commander-in-chief: King Charles I

Lieutenant General: Patrick Ruthven, Earl of Forth (who replaced the Earl of Lindsey)

General of the Horse: Prince Rupert of the Rhine

Commissary General of Horse: Henry Wilmot

Sergeant Major General of Foot: Sir Jacob Astley

Major General of Dragoons: Sir Arthur Aston

Master of the Ordnance: Mountjoy Blount, Earl of Newport

Lieutenant of the Ordnance: Sir John Heydon

Right Wing of Royalist Horse: Prince Rupert, Front Line

Prince Rupert's Regiment of Horse – 7 troops, total 465 horse[1]

Prince of Wales' Regiment (Col Thomas Byron in command) – 8 troops, total 500 horse

Prince Maurice's Regiment – 4 troops, total 180 horse

King's Lifeguard – 2 troops, total 300 horse[2]

Right Wing of Royalist Horse: Prince Rupert, Second Line

Sir John Byron's Regiment – 6 troops, total 250 horse

Left Wing of Royalist Horse: Commissary General Wilmot, First Line

Henry Wilmot's Regiment – 6 troops, total 355 horse

Lord Grandison's Regiment – 4 troops, total 200 horse

Earl of Carnarvon's Regiment – 4 or 5 troops, total 200 horse

Left Wing of Royalist Horse: Commissary General Wilmot, Second Line

Lord Digby's Regiment – 3 or 4 troops, total 150 horse

Sir Thomas Aston's Regiment – 3 troops, total 150 horse

Dragoons – total of 800

Right – James Usher's Regiment – 3 troops

Left – Edward Grey's Regiment and Edmund Duncombe's Regiment – 3 troops each

Royalist Foot: Sir Jacob Astley, First Line

Charles Gerard's Brigade – 3 regiments, total 1,449

  Charles Gerard's Regiment (Gerard wounded)

  Sir Lewis Dyve's Regiment

  Sir Ralph Dutton's Regiment

Richard Fielding's Brigade – 5 regiments, total 2,456

  Richard Fielding's Regiment (Fielding taken prisoner)

  Sir Thomas Lunsford's Regiment (Lunsford taken prisoner)

  Richard Bolle's Regiment

  Sir Edward Fitton's Regiment

  Sir Edward Stradling's Regiment (Stradling taken prisoner)

Henry Wentworth's Brigade – 3 regiments, total 1,643

  Sir Gilbert Gerard's Regiment

  Sir Thomas Salusbury's Regiment

  Lord Molyneux's Regiment

Royalist Foot: Sir Jacob Astley, Second Line

John Belasyse's Brigade – 3 regiments, total 1,789

  John Belasyse's Regiment

  Thomas Blagge's Regiment

  Sir William Pennyman's Regiment

Sir Nicholas Byron's Brigade – 3 regiments, total 1,766

  King's Lifeguard of Foot

  Lord General's Regiment

  Sir John Beaumont's Regiment

Royalist Foot: Sir Jacob Astley, Reserve

Gentleman Pensioners (1 troop, 50 horse)

Artillery and Train

William Legge's firelocks provided protection to the Royalist artillery train that consisted of: 2x demi-cannon; 2x culverin; 3x (iron) demi-culverin; 1x saker; 1x minion; 2x 3-pdr guns; 6x falcons; 6x falconets; 3x robinets (source: Royal Ordnance Papers, vol. I., p. 153).

The Parliamentarian Army

Command

The pay warrants suggest that the Parliamentarian foot numbered about 9,700 without officers; 970 dragoons without officers; and cavalry about 2,700 without officers.

Captain General: Robert Devereux, Earl of Essex

General of the Horse: William Russell, Earl of Bedford

Lieutenant General of the Horse: Sir William Balfour

Commissary General of Horse: Sir James Ramsay

Sergeant Major General of Foot: Sir John Merrick (not present at Edgehill)

General of the Ordnance: John Mordaunt, Earl of Peterborough

Lieutenant General of the Ordnance: Philibert Emmanuel Du Bois

---

1 Numbers are estimates.

2 The King's Lifeguard joined the attack with Prince Rupert rather than staying in reserve.

Right Wing of Horse: Sir William Balfour[3]

The Lord General's Regiment – 7 troops, total 400 horse
Sir William Balfour's Regiment – 6 troops, total 300 horse
Lord Fielding's Regiment – 6 troops, total 300 horse

Left Wing of Horse: Sir James Ramsay

Approximately 24 troops of horse – total 1,560 horse, although other troops are known to have arrived on the field during the battle.[4] The regiments known to be on the field at the start include:

Sir William Waller's Regiment
Colonel Arthur Goodwin's Regiment
Sir James Ramsay's Regiment
Colonel Edwin Sandy's Regiment
Earl of Bedford's Regiment
Colonel John Urry's Regiment

Cavalry supporting the foot in the centre: Earl of Bedford – 4 troops, total 300 horse

Sir Philip Stapleton's troop of cuirassiers (Lord General's Lifeguard)
Captain Nathaniel Draper's troop of harquebusiers
Sir William Balfour's troop of cuirassiers
The Earl of Bedford's troop of cuirassiers

Dragoons on Right Wing

Col John Browne's Dragoons – 6 troops, total 537
Col Middleton's Dragoons – 6 troops, total 500
(Note: Wardlawe was not at Edgehill – Middleton's hastily assembled dragoon regiment was there.)

Parliamentarian Foot: Acting Sergeant Major General Thomas Ballard

Sir John Meldrum's Brigade (vanguard) – 4 regiments (possibly 5), total 2,650
Sir John Meldrum's Regiment
Lord Robartes' Regiment
Sir William Constable's Regiment
Sir William Fairfax's Regiment (may have been with Essex's Brigade)
Charles Essex's Brigade – 4 regiments, total 2,828
Sir Charles Essex's Regiment
Sir Henry Cholmley's Regiment
Lord Mandeville's Regiment
Lord Wharton's Regiment
Thomas Ballard's Brigade – 4 regiments, total 3,604
The Lord General's Regiment, Earl of Essex's
Lord Brooke's Regiment
Thomas Ballard's Regiment (300 commanded musketeers detached to left wing in the hedges)
Denzil Holles' Regiment (400 commanded musketeers detached to left wing among the horse)

Artillery

Colonel John Hampden's Regiment of Foot
Firelocks – unknown number under the command of captains Devereaux, Turnet and Tyndal.
The artillery train consisted of 41 pieces of ordnance: 4x 12-pdr guns, 5x demi-culverins, 5 Dutch sakers, 6x saker cuts/6-pdr guns, 21 3-pdr drakes and two mortars. The 12-pdr guns may not have been on the battlefield but two were captured at some stage.

Sources: Peacock, Rushworth Papers, Young (De Gomme's Plan), Scott/Turton & Gruber von Arni, Roberts/Tincey & BCW Project.

---

3 This accounts for approximately half the 75 (or so) cavalry troops in the Parliamentarian army. The total number of horse was between 2,000 and 2,300.
4 Troops known to have arrived late include: Oliver Cromwell's troop, John Fiennes' troop, Edward Kightley's troop, Alexander Douglas's (Duglis) troop and Lord Willoughby's Horse.

APPENDIX 2: ARMY STRENGTHS AND COMPOSITIONS, 1643

BATTLE OF BRADDOCK DOWN, 19 JANUARY 1643

The Royalist Army: 5,000 approximately

Command
Lord General: Lord Warwick Mohun
Lieutenant General of the Horse: Sir Ralph Hopton (*de facto* Commander-in-Chief)
Sergeant Major General of Foot: Colonel William Ashburnham
General of the Ordnance: Sir Nicholas Slanning
Commissary General: Sir John Berkeley
Secretary of the Army: Fuller
Provost Marshal: Crue
Captain of Carriages: Weekley
Quartermaster: Cory
Muster Master: Captain Spiser

Royalist Horse
Hopton's Troop
Stowell's Troop
Digby's Troop
Hawley's Troop

Royalist Dragoons
Hopton's Troop
Coswarth's Troop

Artillery
2 guns ('two little iron minion-drakes')

Royalist Foot
Grenville's Cornish Regiment
Slanning's Cornish Regiment
Trevanion's Cornish Regiment
Godolphin's Cornish Regiment
Lord Mohun's Cornish Regiment
Cornish Trained Bands
Cornish Posse Comitatus

The Parliamentarian Army: 4,000 approximately

Command
Commander: Lt General William Ruthven
(Other members of the army staff unknown)

Parliamentarian Horse
Boscawen's Troop
Drake's Troop
Earl's Troop
Gould's Troop
Halsey's Troop
Pym's Troop
Rouse's Troop
Thompson's Troop
Yeo's Troop

Parliamentarian Dragoons
Belfor's Troop

Parliamentarian Foot
Bamfield's Regiment
Buller's Cornish Regiment
Carew's Cornish Regiment
Calmady's Devon Regiment
Crocker's Devon Regiment
Pyne's Somerset Regiment
Strode's Somerset Regiment
Ruthin's Regiment (not sure if this unit was at the battle)

Artillery
None (the artillery train was yet to arrive and would be captured during the Royalist pursuit: 'four brass guns upon carriages (whereof two were 12 pounders, and one iron saker)'.

Sources: Braddock Down is one of the most poorly documented major battles of the Civil War. Most books give it no more than a passing mention (including Clarendon and Gardiner). Detailed primary information on the armies and numbers is almost non-existent. Therefore, much of this ORBAT is based on the work of later authors, particularly Stuart Peachey and Alan Turton. Peachey, *Battle of Braddock Down*.

BATTLE OF STRATTON, 16 MAY 1643

The Royalist Army: 3,200

Command

Lord General: Sir Ralph Hopton
Lieutenant General of the Horse: Sir John Digby
Sergeant Major General of Foot: Colonel Thomas Bassett
General of the Ordnance: Sir Nicholas Slanning
Commissary General: Sir John Berkeley
Secretary of the Army: ? Fuller
Provost Marshal: ? Crue
Captain of Carriages: ? Weekley
Quartermaster: ? Cory
Muster Master: Captain ? Spiser

Royalist Horse

Hopton's Troop
Stowell's Troop
Digby's Troop
Hawley's Troop

Royalist Dragoons

Hopton's Troop
Coswarth's Troop

Royalist Foot

First Assault Column (Sir Ralph Hopton, Lord Mohun)
  Lord Mohun's Cornish Regiment
Second Assault Column (Sir John Berkeley and Sir Bevil Grenville)
  Grenville's Cornish Regiment
Third Assault Column (Sir Nicholas Slanning and Colonel Trevanion)
  Slanning's Cornish Regiment
  Trevanion's Cornish Regiment
Fourth Assault Column (Colonel Thomas Bassett and Colonel William Godolphin)
  Godolphin's Cornish Regiment

Artillery

8 guns (divided equally among the four assault columns)

The Parliamentarian Army: 6,000

Command

Lord General: The Earl of Stamford
Sergeant Major General of Foot: James Chudleigh
Commissaries: Richard Clapp, Samuel Slade, Nicholas Worth
Carriage Master: Nicholas Ashford
Surgeon: Thomas Sandford
Provost Marshal: John Jessop
Pioneers: Captain Thomas Somerston (captured)

Parliamentarian Horse

Freeman's Troop (possibly one or two unidentified additional troops)

Parliamentarian Foot (known to have been present)

Merrick's Regiment
Wear's Devon Regiment
Rolle's Devon Trained Band Regiment

Parliamentarian Foot (possibly present)

W. Bamfield's Regiment
Sir John Bamfield's Devon Trained Band Regiment
Northcott's Devon Regiment
Russell's Devon Regiment

Artillery

14 guns ('thirteen pieces of brass ordnance and a brass mortar piece')

Sources: Compared to Braddock Down, Stratton is fairly well documented, in both primary and secondary sources. Hopton is particularly useful for detailing the Cornish army. Most secondary works rely heavily on Hopton, but rarely address the composition of the Parliamentarian army. Although the primary sources mention three Parliamentarian foot regiments and volunteer units, militia units, and trained bands, the remainder of their ORBAT is obscure. As with Braddock Down, we again have to rely upon the research of Stuart Peachey and Alan Turton. Peachey is the only author to have attempted an ORBAT for Stratton. Peachey, *The Battle of Stratton, 1643*.

BATTLE OF LANSDOWN, 5 JULY 1643

The Royalist Army: 6,300

Command

Lieutenant General of the Western Counties: William, Marquis of Hertford
Lieutenant General of the Horse: Prince Maurice
Field Marshal: Sir Ralph Hopton
General of the Horse: Robert, Earl of Carnarvon
Major General of Horse: Sir James Hamilton
Major General of Foot: Colonel Joseph Wagstaffe
Major General of Cornish Foot: Sir Thomas Bassett
General of Ordnance: James, Earl of Marlborough
Comptroller of the Ordnance: Captain Pope

Royalist Horse

Cornish Army Horse
  Sir Ralph Hopton's Regiment (?)
Marquis of Hertford's Horse
  Marquis of Hertford's Lifeguard
  Sir Humphrey Bennet's Regiment
  Lord Carnarvon's Regiment
  Marquis of Hertford's Regiment
  Prince Maurice's Regiment
  Sir George Vaughan's Regiment

Royalist Dragoons

Sir Ralph Hopton's Regiment (unsure)

Royalist Foot

Cornish Army Regiments
  Sir Bevil Grenville's Regiment
  William Godolphin's Regiment
  Lord Mohun's Regiment
  Sir Nicholas Slanning's Regiment
  John Trevanion's Regiment
Marquis of Hertford's Regiments
  Brutus Buck's Regiment
  Marquis of Hertford's Regiment
  Prince Maurice's Regiment

Artillery

16 guns

The Parliamentarian Army: 4,600

Command

Lord General: Sir William Waller
Lieutenant General of Horse: Sir Arthur Haselrig
Major General of Foot: Colonel James Carr
Comptroller of the Ordnance: Captain Robert Bower
Commissary General: John Haynes
Surgeon: James Bicknor

Parliamentarian Horse and Dragoons

Sir William Waller's Brigade
  Sir William Waller's Regiment
  Sir Arthur Haselrig's Regiment
  Robert Burghill's Regiment
  Sir William Waller's Regiment of Dragoons
Devon Horse
  Devon Horse (Sir William Gould)
  Nicholas Boscowan's Troop
  Thomas Drake's Troop
  William Gould's Troop
  Thomas Halsey's Troop
  Earl of Stamford's Troop
  George Thompson's Troop
  Wansey's Troop
  William Sandall's Troop of Dragoons
  Sandbagg's Troop of Dragoons
  Woodley's Troop of Dragoons
Gloucestershire Horse
  Edward Cooke's Troop
  Walter Parry's Troop
  Gifford's Troop
Somerset Horse (Richard Cole)
  Richard Cole's Troop
  Edward Popham's Troop
  William Strode's Troop (?)
  Thomas Council's Troop of Dragoons
  James Harrington's Troop of Dragoons

Parliamentarian Foot

Sir John Merrick's Regiment (2 companies?)
Tom Essex's Regiment
Horatio Carey's Gloucestershire Regiment (Sgt Maj J. Baker) (3 companies or less?)
Sir Robert Cooke's Gloucestershire Regiment
Thomas Stephen's Gloucestershire Regiment
Possibly present: William Strode's Somerset Regiment (3 companies?)

Artillery

7–8 brass guns and an unknown number of 'hammered guns' from Bristol

Sources: Lansdown is well documented, both in primary and secondary sources. Hopton provides us with the numbers of foot, horse and dragoons present on 4 June 1643, when the Cornish army joined with that of the Marquis of Hertford. He also gives the number of Royalist horse at Lansdown. Atkyns gives the total number of foot and horse at Lansdown for both Royalists and Parliamentarians (although for the latter it must be an overestimate), and the number of Parliamentarian dragoons present. Brigadier Young lists the foot and horse regiments in the Royalist army during May–July 1643, but this is not an ORBAT for Lansdown itself. Using Young's list, Wroughton provides an outline of the armies at Lansdown, but this is also not an ORBAT *per se*. By far the best source for the units present, and likely numbers, is Morris, who draws heavily on the extensive research of Peachey and Turton. Morris, *The Battles of Lansdown & Roundway 1643*.

BATTLE OF ROUNDWAY DOWN, 13 JULY 1643

The Royalist Army: 1,800 plus 2,500–3,000 foot inside Devizes

Western Army Command
Lieutenant General of the Western Counties: William, Marquis of Hertford
Lieutenant General of the Horse: Prince Maurice
Field Marshal: Sir Ralph Hopton
Major General of the Horse: Sir James Hamilton
Major General of Foot: Colonel Joseph Wagstaffe
Major General of Cornish Foot: Sir Thomas Bassett
General of Ordnance: James, Earl of Marlborough
Adjutant General: Major Atkyns
Comptroller of the Ordnance: Captain Pope

Royalist Western Army Horse and Dragoons (organized into a composite regiment under Prince Maurice, and attached to Wilmot's Brigade)
Marquis of Hertford's Lifeguard (1 troop)
Sir Humphrey Bennet's Regiment
Lord Carnarvon's Regiment
Marquis of Hertford's Regiment
Prince Maurice's Regiment
Sir George Vaughan's Regiment
Thomas Howard's Regiment (Lord Andover's) (?)
Sir James Hamilton's Regiment (?)
Sir Ralph Hopton's Regiment (?)
Sir Ralph Hopton's Regiment Dragoons (?)

Royalist Oxford Army Horse
Lieutenant General of the Horse: Henry Lord Wilmot
Forlorn Hope (300 men under Major Paul Smyth of Wilmot's Regiment)
Henry Lord Wilmot's Brigade
    Lord Wilmot's Regiment
    Lord Digby's Regiment
    Sir John Digby's Regiment
Sir John Byron's Brigade
    Sir John Byron's Regiment
    Thomas Morgan's Regiment
    Henry Sandy's Regiment
Ludovic Lindsay, Earl of Crawford's Brigade
    Earl of Crawford's Regiment
    James Long's Regiment

Royalist Western Army Foot
Cornish Army Regiments
    Sir Bevil Grenville's Regiment
    William Godolphin's Regiment
    Lord Mohun's Regiment
    Sir Nicholas Slanning's Regiment
    John Trevanion's Regiment
Marquis of Hertford's Regiments
    Brutus Buck's Regiment
    Marquis of Hertford's Regiment
    Prince Maurice's Regiment

Artillery
16 guns in Devizes and 2 light guns with Wilmot's Horse

The Parliamentarian Army: 5,000

Command
Lord General: Sir William Waller
Lieutenant General of Horse: Sir Arthur Haselrig
Major General of Foot: Colonel James Carr
Comptroller of the Ordnance: Captain Robert Bower
Commissary General: John Haynes
Quartermaster General of Foot: Sergeant Major Archibald Strachan
Surgeon: James Bicknor

Parliamentarian Horse and Dragoons
Sir William Waller's Brigade
    Sir William Waller's Regiment
    Sir Arthur Haselrig's Regiment
    Robert Burghill's Regiment
    Sir William Waller's Regiment of Dragoons
Devon Horse (Sir William Gould)
    Nicholas Boscowan's Troop
    Thomas Drake's Troop
    William Gould's Troop
    Thomas Halsey's Troop
    Earl of Stamford's Troop
    George Thompson's Troop
    Wansey's Troop
    William Sandall's Troop of Dragoons
    Sandbagg's Troop of Dragoons
    Woodley's Troop of Dragoons
Gloucestershire Horse (Edward Cooke)
    Edward Cooke's Troop
    Walter Parry's Troop
    Gifford's Troop
Somerset Horse (Richard Cole)
    Richard Cole's Troop
    Edward Popham's Troop
    Thomas Council's Troop of Dragoons
    James Harrington's Troop of Dragoons
Bristol Horse – Nathaniel Fiennes Regiment (at least 1 and up to 6 troops of horse and 1 troop of dragoons)
    Hercules Langrish's Troop
    Nathaniel Fiennes' Troop (?)
    Rawlins' Troop (?)
    Henry Vaughan's Troop (?)
    Thomas Essex's Troop (Lt John Cockein) (?)
    Alban Cox's Troop (?)
    Henry Oland's Troop of Dragoons (?)

Parliamentarian Foot
Sir John Merrick's Regiment (2 companies?)
Thomas Essex's Regiment
Horatio Carey's Gloucestershire Regiment (Sgt Maj J. Baker) (3 companies or less?)
Sir Robert Cooke's Gloucestershire Regiment

Thomas Stephen's Gloucestershire Regiment
Alexander Popham's Regiment (Bristol garrison) (6 companies)
Nathaniel Fiennes Regiment (Bristol garrison) (up to half?)

Artillery
7–8 brass guns

Sources: There is a single Parliamentarian primary account of Roundway Down, which provides little detail. However, we do have useful Royalist eyewitness accounts from Byron, Atkyns and Slingsby. Unfortunately, Hopton gives little detail on the battle itself, presumably because he was in Devizes recovering from serious wounds. As the most senior eyewitness, Byron's account is particularly useful, and he details the number of Parliamentarian regiments present and the overall totals of men. Of the secondary accounts, Morris (*Battle of Lansdown and Roundway Down*) offers good information on Waller's army at Roundway. For the Royalists, Brigadier Young, in an appendix to Atkyn's *Vindication*, provides a list of Wilmot's regiments at Roundway and identifies the brigade affiliation of all but two. His 1953 article on Roundway is also very useful and crucially includes Byron's account. His work with Burne provides more analysis: Burne & Young, *The Great Civil War, A Military History of the First Civil War 1642–1646*. Chris Scott's recently published book on Roundway, *The Most Heavy Stroke*, also provides a detailed ORBAT.

THE SIEGE AND STORMING OF BRISTOL, 26 JULY 1643

The Royalist Oxford Army

Command
General of Horse: Prince Rupert
Major General of Horse: Sir Arthur Aston
Colonel General of Foot: William Villiers, Lord Grandison
General of Ordnance: Bartholomew de la Roche
Engineer: Bernard de Gomme

Horse (the brigade breakdown is speculative)
Right Wing: Sir Arthur Aston
Left Wing: Charles Gerrard
Prince Rupert's Lifeguard of Horse (1 troop) (not brigaded)
Sir Arthur Aston's Brigade
  Lord Andover's Regiment
  Sir Arthur Aston's Regiment
  Lord Chandos' Regiment
  Sir George Vaughan's Regiment
  Colonel Samuel Sandy's Regiment
Colonel Charles Gerard's Brigade
  Colonel Thomas Dalton's Regiment
  Colonel William Eure's Regiment
  Colonel Charles Gerard's Regiment
  Lord Molyneux's Regiment
  The Queen's Lifeguard Regiment
  Sir Thomas Tyldesley's Regiment
Sir John Byron's Brigade
  Sir Thomas Aston's Regiment
  Sir John Byron's Regiment

Lord Digby's Regiment
Colonel Thomas Morgan's Regiment

Dragoons
Colonel Henry Washington's Regiment (formerly James Usher's) (7 troops)
Sir Robert Howard's Regiment (2 troops)

Royalist Foot
Lord Grandison's Tertia/Brigade
  The Lord General's (Earl of Forth's) Regiment
  Earl Rivers' Regiment
  Lord Molyneux's Regiment
  Sir Gilbert Gerard's Regiment
  Sir Ralph Dutton's Regiment
  Colonel John Owen's Regiment
Henry Wentworth's Tertia/Brigade
  Sir Jacob Astley's Regiment
  Sir Edward Fitton's Regiment
  Colonel Richard Bolles' Regiment
  Sir Richard Herbert's Regiment
John Belasyse's Tertia/Brigade
  Colonel John Belasyse's Regiment
  Sir Edward Stradling's Regiment
  Colonel Henry Lunsford's Regiment
  Sir Charles Lloyd's Regiment

Artillery
8 guns (2x 27-pdr demi-cannon, 2x 18-pdr whole culverins, 2x 12-pdr quarter cannon, 2x 6-pdr)

The Royalist Western Army

Command
Lieutenant General of the Army: Prince Maurice (actual commander); William, Marquis of Hertford (titular commander)
Field Marshal: Sir Ralph Hopton (incapacitated)
Lieutenant General of the Horse: Robert Dormer, Earl of Carnarvon
Sergeant Major General of the Horse: Ludovic Lindsay, Earl of Crawford
Major General of Foot: Colonel Joseph Wagstaffe
Major General of Cornish Foot: Sir Thomas Bassett

Royalist Horse and Dragoons
Marquis of Hertford's Lifeguard
Sir Humphrey Bennet's Regiment
Lord Carnarvon's Regiment
Marquis of Hertford's Regiment
Prince Maurice's Regiment
Sir George Vaughan's Regiment
Sir Ralph Hopton's Regiment (?)
Sir Ralph Hopton's Regiment Dragoons (?)

Royalist Foot
Brutus Buck's Tertia/Brigade
  Marquis of Hertford's Regiment
  Prince Maurice's Regiment
  Colonel Brutus Buck's Regiment

Sir Nicholas Slanning's Tertia/Brigade
    Sir Nicholas Slanning's Regiment (Cornish)
    Colonel John Trevanion's Regiment (Cornish)
    Lord Mohun's Regiment (Cornish)
Thomas Bassett's Tertia/Brigade
    Sir Bevil Grenville's Regiment (Colonel Sir John Grenville?) (Cornish)
    William Godolphin's Regiment (Cornish)

Artillery

16 guns

The Parliamentarian Army

Command

Bristol Garrison Commander: Colonel Nathaniel Fiennes
Master Gunner: Hazard

Parliamentarian Horse and Dragoons

Colonel Richard Cole's Somerset Regiment of Horse and Dragoons
Colonel Nathaniel Fiennes' Regiment of Horse and Dragoons (Bristol Garrison)
Colonel William Strode's Somerset Troop of Horse
Colonel (Alexander or Edward) Popham's Regiment of Dragoons (may have included a troop of horse)
Four troops of dragoons have been identified in Bristol during 1643: Captain Henry Oland's, Captain Thomas Council's, Captain James Harrington's and Captain Richard Whippey's. These served at various times with Cole's Regiment, Fiennes' Regiment and Popham's Regiment. It is unclear which regiment(s) they served under on 26 July 1643.

Parliamentarian Foot

Colonel Nathaniel Fiennes' Regiment (Bristol garrison) (at least half)
Colonel John Fiennes' Regiment (Bristol garrison) (all: 300–400 men)
Colonel Alexander Popham's Somerset Regiment (either half or remnants)
Colonel William Strode's Somerset Regiment (formerly Bath garrison; probably amalgamated with Nathaniel Fiennes' regiments)
Locally raised volunteers (militia), including:
City of Bristol Trained Bands
Bristol Volunteers (1 company; Captain John Birch)
Bristol Volunteers (1 company; Captain Bagnell)
In addition, probably remnants from:
Colonel Horatio Carey's Gloucestershire Regiment
Sir Robert Cooke's Gloucestershire Regiment
Colonel Tom Essex's Regiment
Colonel Edward Hungerford's Wiltshire Regiment (ex-Malmesbury garrison)
Colonel Thomas Stephen's Gloucestershire Regiment

Artillery

98–99 guns, excluding hammered iron pieces (4x demi-culverin, 19x sakers, 33x minions, 7x falcons, 11x falconets, 19x robinets, 4x murderers, 1x mortar)

Sources: de Gomme's account is the outstanding source for the Royalist armies. He lists all of the Royalist foot regiments, brigade structures and number and types of guns. Unfortunately, he does not include all the Royalist cavalry regiments, but from comparing the officers he mentions to other sources we can determine the regiments with a degree of certainty and offer a possible brigade structure. Peachey and Turton have conducted extensive primary research and are the best source for determining the composition and size of the Parliamentarian garrison. There is a lack of reliable primary data for both Royalist and Parliamentarian numbers present: Nathaniel Fiennes provided totals for the garrison, but these have been widely discredited. Nevertheless, thorough analysis of all sources does allow a range of totals to be offered for both sides, which are probably close to actuality. Peachey, *The Storming of Bristol 1643*; Ede-Borrett (ed.), *The Storm of Bristol, de Gomme's Account*.

FIRST BATTLE OF NEWBURY, 20 SEPTEMBER 1643

The Royalist Army: 12,000

Command

Commander-in-Chief: King Charles I
Lieutenant General: Patrick Ruthven, Earl of Forth
General of the Horse: Prince Rupert of the Rhine
Sergeant Major General of Foot: Sir Jacob Astley
Master of the Ordnance: Henry, Lord Percy
Lieutenant of the Ordnance: Sir John Heydon

Royalist Horse (the brigade breakdown is speculative)

Rupert's Brigade
    Prince Maurice's Regiment
    Prince Rupert's Lifeguard (1 troop)
    Prince Rupert's Regiment of Horse
    Prince of Wales's Horse
Lord Wilmot's Brigade
    Lord Wilmot's Regiment
    Lord Digby's Regiment
    Earl of Northampton's Regiment
    Lord General?
Charles Gerard's Brigade
    Dalton
    Colonel William Eure's Regiment
    C. Gerard
    Molyneaux
    The Queen's Regiment
    Tyldesley's
Sir John Byron's Brigade
    Sir Thomas Aston's Regiment
    Sir John Byron's Regiment
    Digby
    Colonel Thomas Morgan's Regiment (Morgan killed)
Earl of Carnarvon's Brigade
    Lord Andover's Regiment
    Sir Arthur Aston's Regiment
    The Earl of Carnarvon's Regiment (Carnarvon killed)
    Lord Chandos' Regiment
    Pye
    Vaughan
    Vavasour
Other Regiments
    The King's Lifeguard (2 troops)
    Sir Charles Lucas's Regiment

Royalist Foot
John Belasyse's Tertia/Brigade (1,800)
  Sir Jacob Astley's Regiment
  Colonel John Bolles' Regiment
  Sir Ralph Dutton's Regiment
  Sir Richard Herbert's Regiment
  Colonel John Owen's Regiment
  Colonel John Belasyse's Regiment
  Colonel B. Astley's Regiment
  Colonel Thomas Blagge's Regiment
  Sir Lewis Dyve's Regiment
  Earl Rivers' Regiment (in Donnington Castle)
Sir Gilbert Gerard's Tertia/Brigade
  Sir Gilbert Gerard's Regiment
  Sir Charles Lloyd's Regiment
  Lord Molyneux's Regiment
  Sir Edward Stradling's Regiment
  Northampton
  Vaughan
Sir Nicholas Byron's Tertia/Brigade
  Sir Edward Fitton's Regiment
  Lord General's (Earl of Forth's) Regiment
  The King's Lifeguard
  Composite Regiment drawn from C. Gerard's, Pennyman's, Percy's, Pinchbeck's, Sandy's, the Queen's Lifeguard and the Prince of Wales's
Sir William Vavasour's Tertia/Brigade
  Regiments from South Wales and Worcestershire
  Composite Regiment from Bassett, Mansell, Price, Vavasour and Williams
Independent Regiments
  Darcey's Regiment, composed of soldiers from Darcey's, Blackwell's, Eure's and Tyldesley's regiments
  Lisle's commanded musketeers

Artillery
19 guns (2x 24-pdr demi-cannon, 2x 15-pdr culverins, 3x 12-pdr, 7x 6-pdr, 1x 5-pdr saker and 4x 3-pdr)

The Parliamentarian Army: 13,000

Command
Lord General: Robert Devereux, Earl of Essex
Sergeant Major General of Foot: Philip Skippon
Cavalry commanders: Sir Philip Stapleton, Colonel John Middleton
General of the Ordnance: Sir John Merrick

Parliamentarian Horse
Right Wing: Sir Philip Stapleton's Brigade
  Earl of Essex's Lifeguard
  Earl of Essex's Regiment of Horse
  Colonel John Dalbier's Regiment
  Sir James Ramsay's Regiment
  Colonel Arthur Goodwin's Regiment
  Colonel Edmund Harvey's Regiment
  Colonel Richard Norton's Regiment
  Scoutmaster General Samuel Luke (three commanded troops of dragoons)
Left Wing: Colonel John Middleton's Brigade
  Colonel John Middleton's Regiment
  Lord Grey of Groby's Regiment
  Colonel James Sheffield's Regiment
  Sir John Meldrum's Regiment
  Earl of Denbigh's Regiment
  Colonel Hans Behre's Regiment

Dragoons
Captain Jeremiah Abercrombie's Company
Captain Cornelius Shibborne's Company

Parliamentarian Foot
Vanguard: Colonel Harry Barclay's Brigade
  Barclay's Regiment
  John Holmstead's Regiment
  Thomas Tyrell's Regiment
Vanguard: Colonel James Holborne's Brigade
  Holborne's Regiment
  Francis Thompson's Regiment
  George Langham's Regiment
Sergeant Major General Philip Skippon's Brigade
  Skippon's Regiment
  William Brooke's Regiment
  Henry Bulstrode's Regiment
Lord Robartes' Brigade
  Robartes' Regiment
  William Constable's Regiment
  Francis Martin's Regiment
The City Brigade: Sergeant Major General Randall Mainwaring
  Red Regiment, London Trained Bands
  Blue Regiment, London Trained Bands
  Red Auxiliaries, City of London
  Blue Auxiliaries, City of London
  Orange Auxiliaries, City of London
  Sergeant Major General Mainwaring's Regiment
  Sir William Springate's Regiment
Independent Regiments
  Earl of Essex's Regiment of Foot

Artillery
40 pieces (approximately)
About 20 light artillery pieces and drakes, and at least two demi-culverins (Essex's heaviest artillery had been left at Gloucester)

Source: Day, *Gloucester & Newbury*; see pp. 157–62 for analysis.

APPENDIX 3: ARMY STRENGTHS AND COMPOSITIONS, 1644

BATTLE OF NANTWICH, 25 JANUARY 1644

The Royalist Army: 3,300

Command

Field Marshal General of North Wales and those parts: John Lord Byron

Major General of Foot: Sir Michael Earnley (sick), replaced by Colonel Richard Gibson

Royalist Horse

Lord Byron's Regiment

Lord Molyneux's Regiment

Sir Thomas Tyldesley's Regiment (probably including Tyldesley's Dragoon Regiment)

John Marrow's Regiment (formerly Lord Cholmondeley's)

Sir Richard Willy's Regiment

Ralph Sneyd's Regiment (?)

Royalist Dragoons

Nathaniel Moyle's Troop ('Irish')

Radcliffe Duckenfield's Troop ('Irish')

Adam Pate's Troop ('Irish')

Royalist Foot

Irish Infantry

Sir Michael Earnley's Regiment

Richard Gibson's Regiment

Sir Fulk Hunke's Regiment

Sir Robert Byron's Regiment

The Lord General's Regiment (commanded by Major (Colonel?) Henry Warren)

Formerly Thomas Sandford's Firelocks (one company); possibly merged into a single company by the time of the battle

Francis Langley's Firelocks (one company)

English – present at battle, but probably played no part

Sir Thomas Tyldesley's Regiment

Sir Francis Gamull's Chester Trained Bands Regiment (detachment)

Lord Molyneux's Regiment

Artillery

6 guns; apart from a 'great brass piece' (probably a demi-culverin), the rest were 'smaller pieces'

The Parliamentarian Army: 4,800

Command

Lord General: Sir Thomas Fairfax

Unknown command: Sir William Brereton

Unknown command: Sir William Fairfax

Parliamentarian Foot

Cheshire Foot

Sir William Brereton's Regiment

Henry Mainwaring's Regiment

Duckenfield's Regiment

John Booth's Regiment

Allen's Regiment

Lancashire Foot

Richard Holland's Regiment

Ralph Assheton's Regiment

Sir William Constable's Regiment

Alexander Rigby's Regiment

Sir Thomas Mauleverer (foot or horse?)

John Bright's Regiment of Foot

3–4 Independent companies of foot

Parliamentarian Horse

Thomas Fairfax's Regiment of Horse

Sir William Brereton's Regiment of Horse

Sir William Fairfax's Regiment of Horse

John Lambert's Regiment of Horse

Hugh Bethel's Regiment

Copley's Horse (regiment or troop?)

Parliamentarian Dragoons

Thomas Morgan's Regiment

Artillery

An unknown number of guns, which seem to have played no part in the battle.

Sources: There are a number of useful primary accounts of the battle, including reports by both commanders, Sir Thomas Fairfax and Lord Byron. Malbron provides a list of Parliamentarian commanders from which an ORBAT can be constructed. Letters from Lord Byron and Thomas Byron give details of the Royalist foot engaged and their relative deployment. Fairfax gives numbers of Parliamentarian foot, horse and dragoons. However, the numbers of Royalist foot engaged is less clear and there is a major contradiction between the numbers given by Fairfax and Lord Byron. John Dixon is the foremost secondary source and goes some way to reconciling this issue. See Dore & Lowe, *The Battle of Nantwich*; Dixon, *The Business at Acton*.

BATTLE OF CHERITON, 29 MARCH 1644

The Royalist Army: 8,000–9,000

Command

Field Marshal General: Ralph, Lord Hopton

Lord General: Patrick Ruthven, Earl of Forth and Brentford

Lieutenant General of Horse: Lord John Stuart

Major General of Foot: Sir John Paulet

General of Ordnance: Colonel Richard Fielding
Commissary General: Sir John Smyth

Lord Hopton's Army: Horse
Stuart's Brigade
  Lord John Stuart's Regiment
  Sir Nicholas Crisp's Regiment
  Sir Edward Ford's Regiment
  Colonel Dutton Fleetwood's Regiment
  Sir William Clerke's Regiment
  Sir William Boteler's Regiment
Stawell's Brigade
  Ralph, Lord Hopton's Regiment
  Sir Edward Stawell's Regiment
  Colonel George Gunter's Regiment
  Sir Allen Apsley's Regiment
  Colonel Edmond Pierce's Regiment
  Marquess of Hertford's Regiment
Smyth's Brigade
  Sir Humphrey Bennet's Regiment
  Sir George Vaughan's Regiment
  Sir Edward Waldegrave's Regiment
  Colonel Andrew Lindsay's Regiment
  Sir John Smyth's Regiment

Lord Hopton's Army: Dragoons
Ralph, Lord Hopton's Regiment (probably a troop in Hopton's Regiment of Horse)

Lord Hopton's Army: Foot
Slingsby's Brigade
  Ralph, Lord Hopton's Regiment
  Colonel Walter Slingsby's Regiment
Apsley's Brigade
  Sir John Paulet's Regiment
  Sir Charles Vavasour's Regiment (Commanded by Sir Matthew Appleyard)
  Sir Allen Apsley's Regiment
Astley's Brigade
  John Talbot's Regiment
  Sir William Courtney's Regiment
  Sir Bernard Astley's Regiment
  Colonel Francis Cooke's Regiment
  Colonel Henry Shelley's Regiment

Lord Hopton's Army: Artillery
5 sakers and 4 robinets

Ruthven/Lord Forth's Contingent (attached from the Oxford Army): Horse
One brigade consisting of detachments from:
  The Queen's Regiment
  Lord Forth's Regiment
  Colonel Thomas Howard's Regiment
  Colonel Richard Neville's Regiment
  Prince Maurice's Regiment
  Colonel Richard Manning's Regiment

Ruthven/Lord Forth's Contingent: Dragoons
Lord Ogle's, *A true relation... 1645*, suggests that a detachment from the Queen's Regiment of Foot was present, mounted as dragoons.

Ruthven/Lord Forth's Contingent: Foot
Oxford Battalia (commanded by Sir Henry Bard)
  Sir Henry Bard's Regiment
  Sir Charles Gerard's Regiment
Reading Battalia (commanded by Colonel George Lisle) consisting of detachments from regiments in Reading garrison: regiments of colonels Sir Jacob Astley, Sir Thomas Blackwell, Sir Lewis Dyves, William Eure, Sir Theophilus Gilby, George Lisle, Charles Lloyd, Sir John Owen, Sir James Pennyman, John Stradling, Anthony Thelwell and Sir Henry Vaughan.

Artillery
Probably a total of 17 pieces (including 4 robinets, 5 saker drakes, 2 sakers)

The Parliamentarian Army: 10,000

Command
Major General: Sir William Waller
Lieutenant General of Horse (Western and Southern Associations): Sir Arthur Haselrig
Lieutenant General of Horse (Earl of Essex's Army): Sir William Balfour
Adjutant General of Horse: Captain John Fleming
Major General of Foot (Western and Southern Associations): Andrew Potley
Major General of Foot (London Trained Bands): Richard Browne
Lieutenant General of the Ordnance: James Wemyss
Comptroller of the Ordnance: Captain David Weymss
Wagon Master General: Henry Lloyd/Floyd
Commissary of Provisions: Nicholas Cowling

Parliamentarian Horse
Sir William Balfour's Brigade of Horse (attached from The Earl of Essex's Army)
  Sir William Balfour's Regiment (6 troops, including one Lifeguard Troop of Cuirassiers)
  Colonel John Middleton's Regiment (6 troops)
  Colonel John Meldrum's Regiment (6 troops)
  Colonel John Dalbier's Regiment (4 troops)
  Colonel Adam Cunningham's Mounted Foot (detachments from the foot regiments of Colonels Adam Cunningham, John Holmstead, Francis Thompson, Thomas Tyrell, Sir William Constable, Francis Martin and George Langham)
Western and Southern Association's Horse
  Sir William Waller's Regiment (11 troops, including Lifeguard Troop)
  Sir Arthur Haselrig's Regiment (7 troops)
  Colonel Jonas Vandruske's Regiment (6 troops)
  Colonel Richard Norton's Regiment (4 troops)
  Colonel George Thompson's Regiment (4 troops)
  Sir Michael Livesey's Regiment (5 troops, or according to one account, 4 horse troops plus a troop of dragoons)
  Colonel Edward Cooke's Regiment (4 troops)

Parliamentarian Dragoons
Sir William Waller's Regiment
Sir Michael Livesey's Dragoons

Parliamentarian Foot
Western and Southern Association's Foot (probably in two or more brigades)
  Sir William Waller's Regiment
  Sir Arthur Haselrig's Regiment
  Colonel Andrew Potley's Regiment
  Colonel Ralph Weldon's Regiment
  Detachment of Colonel Samuel Jones' Regiment
London Trained Bands Brigade of Foot (attached)
  Yellow Regiment London Trained Bands
  White Regiment London Trained Bands

Artillery
Total 26 light guns, including 4 barricadoes (multiple-barrelled guns), 4 'cases of drakes', and possibly some heavier guns
Lieutenant General James Wemyss' Trainguard Regiment of Foot (firelocks, up to 6 companies totalling about 200 men)

Sources: For the Royalist army, we have a simple statement by Hopton in *Bellum Civile* of the troops with Forth and the recruits he draws out of Winchester, along with the history of the campaign up to that point, to which we can add another contemporary reference from Lord Ogle, commander of Winchester, Slingsby's account and, of course, the Aldbourne Chase muster. There are four key sources for the strength of the Parliamentarian forces and the regiments present at Cheriton: Captain Harley's account of the muster at West Meon; Records of the Derby House Committee; Pay warrants for several of the regiments that may also have been present, at least in part; Strength returns for the horse in Balfour's Brigade prior to and after the battle.

Sources: Adair, *Cheriton 1644*; Adair, *Roundhead General*; L. Spring, *The Battle of Cheriton 1644*; Peachey (ed.), *Richard Symonds's diary*; Walker, *Historical Discourses*; Chadwyck-Healey, *Bellum Civile*.

BATTLE OF MARSTON MOOR, 2 JULY 1644

The Royalist Army: 18,000

The Army of Prince Rupert of the Rhine: Command
Lord General: Prince Rupert
Lieutenant General of the Horse: John, Lord Byron
Sergeant Major General of Foot: Henry Tillier

Royalist Horse
Prince Rupert's Lifeguard – H1
Prince Rupert's Regiment of Horse – H2
Lord Byron's Regiment of Horse – H3
Colonel Marcus Trevor's Regiment – H4
Sir John Hurry's Regiment - H5
Sir William Vaughan's Regiment – H6
Lord Molyneux's Regiment – H7
Sir Thomas Tyldesley's Regiment of Horse – H8
Rowland Eyre's Regiment – H9
Colonel John Frescheville's Regiment of Horse – H10
Colonel Thomas Leveson's Regiment – H11

Royalist Dragoons
Colonel Henry Washington – D1

Royalist Foot
Prince Rupert's Regiment of Foot – F1
Lord Byron's Regiment of Foot – F2
Henry Warren's Regiment – F3
Erneley's and Gibson's regiments brigaded together – F4
Henry Tillier's Regiment – F5
Robert Broughton's Regiment – F6
Sir Thomas Tyldesley's Regiment – F7
Edward Chisenall's Regiment – F8
Henry Cheater's Regiment – F9
Frescheville's, Eyre's and Millward's regiments brigaded together – F10

Artillery
25 pieces of artillery

The Royalist Army

The Army of the Marquis of Newcastle: Command
Lord General: William Cavendish, Marquis of Newcastle (Lord Eythin as military advisor)
Lieutenant General of the Horse: George Goring
Commissary General: George Porter
Sergeant Major General of the Foot: Sir Francis Mackworth

Royalist Horse
Sir Charles Lucas's Brigade – H12
Sir Richard Dacre's Brigade – H13
Sir William Blakiston's Brigade – H14
Sir Edward Widdrington's Brigade – H15
Samuel Tuke's Regiment – H16
Sir Francis Carnaby's Regiment – H17
Commissary General George Porter's Troop – not depicted on map
Marquis of Newcastle's lifeguard (Sir Thomas Metham) – not depicted on map

Royalist Foot
Grouped into 7 divisions – exact brigading unknown – F11
Sir Philip Byron's Regiment
Cuthbert Conyer's Regiment
Lord Eythin's Regiment
Sir John Gerlington's Regiment
John Hilton's Regiment
Sir Richard Hutton's Regiment
Richard Kirkebride's Regiment
Sir William Lambton's Regiment
John Lamplugh's Regiment
Sir Marmaduke Langdale's Regiment
Lord Mansfield's Regiment
Sir Thomas Metham's Regiment
Marquis of Newcastle's Regiment (the Whitecoats)
Sir Arthur Basset's Regiment
Sir Charles Slingsby's Regiment
Sir Richard Strickland's Regiment
Charles Towneley's Regiment
Lord Widdrington's Regiment

The York Garrison
Sir Thomas Glemham's Regiment
John Belasyse's Regiment
Sir Henry Slingsby's Regiment

The Allied Armies: 27,000

The Scottish Army of the Covenant: Command
Lord General: Alexander Leslie, Earl of Leven (senior Allied commander)
Lieutenant General of the Horse: David Leslie
Lieutenant General of the Foot: William Baillie
Sergeant Major General of the Foot: Sir James Lumsden
General of the Ordnance: Sir Alexander Hamilton

Scottish Horse
Grouped under the Earl of Eglington
   Earl of Leven's Regiment (Lord Balgonie) – H1
   Earl of Dalhousie's Regiment – H2
   Earl of Eglinton's Regiment – H3
Grouped under Major General David Leslie
   Major General David Leslie's Regiment – H4
   Earl of Balcarres' Regiment – H5
   Lord Kirkcudbright's Regiment – H6

Scottish Dragoons
Col Hugh Fraser – D1

Scottish Foot: Lieutenant General Baillie's Brigades
Earl of Crawford-Lindsay's Brigade
   The Fifeshire Regiment (Earl of Crawford-Lindsay) – F1
   The Midlothian Regiment (Viscount Maitland) – F2
Sir Alexander Hamilton's Brigade
   The Clydesdale Regiment (Sir Alexander Hamilton) – F3
   The Edinburgh Regiment (Colonel James Rae) – F4

Scottish Foot: Sergeant Major General Lumsden's Brigades
Earl of Loudon's Brigade
   The Loudon-Glasgow Regiment (Earl of Loudon) – F5
   The Tweed-dale Regiment (Earl of Buccleugh) – F6
Earl of Cassilis's Brigade
   The Kyle and Carrick Regiment (Earl of Cassilis) – F7
   The Nithsdale and Annandale Regiment (William Douglas of Kilhead) – F8
Earl of Dunfermline's Brigade
   The Fifeshire Regiment (Earl of Dunfermline) – F9
   The Strathearn Regiment (Lord Coupar) – F10
Lord Livingstone's Brigade
   The Stirlingshire Regiment (Lord Livingstone) – F11
   The Linlithgow and Tweed-dale Regiment (The Master of Yester) – F12
Viscount Dudhope's Brigade
   The Angus Regiment (Viscount Dudhope) – F13
   The Minister's Regiment (Sir Arthur Erskine of Scotscraig) – F14
   The Levied Regiment (Lord Sinclair) – F15

Artillery
Only the lighter guns were present at the battle: 8 brass demi-cannons, 1 brass culverin, 3 brass quarter-cannons, 9 iron demi-culverins and 48 brass demi-culverins.

Army of the Eastern Association

Command
Lord General: Edward Montagu, Earl of Manchester
Lieutenant General of the Horse: Oliver Cromwell
Sergeant Major General of the Foot: Lawrence Crawford
General of the Ordnance: Thomas Hammond

Eastern Association Horse
Lieutenant General Oliver Cromwell's Regiment (Lt Col Edward Whalley) – H7
Grouped under Bartholomew Vermuyden
   Earl of Manchester's Regiment (Col Algernon Sidney) – H8
   Bartholomew Vermuyden's Regiment – H9
   Colonel Charles Fleetwood's Regiment – H10

Eastern Association Dragoons
Lieutenant Colonel John Lilburne – D2

Eastern Association Foot
Grouped into one brigade of Manchester's (large) Regiment and two brigades under Lawrence Crawford and one brigade under – F16 to F18
   Earl of Manchester's Regiment (Lt Col Clifton) – F16
   Major General Crawford's Regiment (Lt Col Hamilton) – F17
   Sir Michael Hobart's Regiment - F17
   Colonel Francis Russell's Regiment – F18
   Colonel Edward Montagu's Regiment – F18
   Colonel John Pickering's Regiment – F18

Army of the Northern Association

Command
Lord General: Ferdinando, Lord Fairfax
Lieutenant General of the Horse: Sir Thomas Fairfax

Northern Association Horse (total 80 troops of horse)
First Line under Sir Thomas Fairfax – H11 to H14
   Lord Fairfax's Regiment
   Sir Thomas Fairfax's Regiment
   Charles Fairfax's Regiment
   Hugh Bethell's Regiment
Second Line under John Lambert – H15 to H18
   John Lambert's Regiment
   Lionel Copley's Regiment
   Francis Boynton's Regiment
   Sir Thomas Norcliff's Regiment

Northern Association Dragoons
Thomas Morgan – D3

Northern Association Foot (in three brigades)
Exact composition of brigades unknown; each brigade assumed to have two regiments – F19 to F21
Lord Fairfax's Regiment
John Bright's Regiment
Sir William Constable's Regiment
Francis Lascelles's Regiment
Robert Overton's Regiment
Ralph Ashton' Regiment
George Dodding's Regiment
Alexander Rigby's Regiment

Sources: There are good primary and secondary sources providing a breakdown of the troops present at Marston Moor. De Gomme's map, currently in the British Museum and most likely copied from an ORBAT drawn by Prince Rupert, gives a good idea of the Royalist regiments present and their place on the field. But it is impossible to provide a definitive list of those regiments because many units were, by this stage of the war, weak and small and thus brigaded together. This is particularly the case with Newcastle's Northern Army. Furthermore, the command and breakdown of these brigades or Tercios is unknown. For the allied armies the plan of the armies (now in the library at York Minster) provides an excellent basis as to the ORBAT and deployment. Sources: Young, P., *Marston Moor 1644, The Campaign and the Battle*; Barratt, J., *The Battle for York, Marston Moor 1644*; Tincey, J., *Marston Moor 1644* and Cooke, D., *The Road to Marston Moor*.

BATTLE OF CROPREDY BRIDGE, 29 JUNE 1644

The Royalist Army: 9,000

Command
King Charles I
Lord General: Patrick Ruthven, Earl of Forth and Brentford
Lieutenant General of the Horse: Henry, Lord Wilmot
Major General of Foot: Sir Jacob Astley
General of Ordnance: Henry, Baron Percy of Alnwick
Lieutenant General of Ordnance: Sir John Heydon

Royalist Horse
King's Lifeguard Troop (Lord Bernard Stuart)
Lord Henry Wilmot's Brigade
    Lord General, Lord Forth's Regiment
    Prince Maurice's Regiment
    Thomas Howard's Regiment
    Gerrard Croker's Regiment
James Compton, Earl of Northampton's Brigade
    Lord Wilmot's Regiment
    Earl of Northampton's Regiment
    Lord Percy's Regiment
    Thomas Weston's Regiment
Sir Thomas Wentworth, Earl of Cleveland's Brigade
    Earl of Cleveland's Regiment

Prince Charles's (Thomas, Lord Wentworth's) Regiment
    Richard Neville's Regiment
    Sir William Boteler's Regiment
    Sir William Clerke's Regiment
Sir Humphrey Bennet's Brigade
    Sir Humphrey Bennet's Regiment
    Sir George Vaughan's Regiment
    Sir Edward Waldegrave's Regiment
    Andrew Lindsey's Regiment
Bennet's or Wilmot's Brigades
    Sir Nicholas Crispe's Regiment
    Sir Edward Ford's Regiment
    Dutton Fleetwood's Regiment
    George Gunter's/Sir Allan Apsley's combined Regiment
    Sir Edmund Pierce's Regiment
    James Hamilton's Regiment

Royalist Dragoons
No regiments identified, but Royalist primary accounts refer to a party of dragoons being present.

Royalist Foot
First Tertia: Colonel Thomas Blagge
    King's Lifeguard Regiment
    Queen's Lifeguard Regiment
    Lord General's (Earl of Forth's) Regiment
    Sir Jacoby Astley's Regiment
    Sir Henry Bard's Regiment
    Duke of York's Regiment
    Sir James Pennyman's Regiment
    Lord Percy's Regiment
    Sir Lewis Dyve's Regiment
Second Tercia: Colonel George Lisle
    Charles Lloyd's Regiment
    George Lisle's Regiment
    Anthony Thelwall's Regiment
    Sir John Owen's Regiment
    William Eure's Regiment
    Sir Thomas Blackwall's Regiment
    Sir Theophilus Gilby's Regiment
    John Stradling's Regiment
    Sir Henry Vaughan's Regiment
Third Tercia: Sir Bernard Astley
    Lord Ralph Hopton's Regiment
    Sir Allen Apsley's Regiment
    John Talbot's Regiment
    Francis Cooke's Regiment
    Sir William Courtney's Regiment
    Sir Bernard Astley's Regiment
    Matthew Appleyard's Regiment
    Henry Shelley's Regiment
    Sir John Paulet's Regiment

Artillery
10–13 guns of various calibres, including a 'great mortar piece'

The Parliamentarian Army: 9,000

Command
Lord General: Sir William Waller
Lieutenant General of Horse: John Middleton
Major General of Foot: Christopher Potley
General of Ordnance: James Wemyss
Comptroller of the Ordnance: David Weymss or Henry Hazard
Adjutant General: Captain Butler
Commissary General: Nicholas Cowling
Quartermaster General: Jeremy Baines

Parliamentarian Horse
Sir William Waller's Lifeguard Troop (Edward Cooke's Regiment)
Sir William Waller's Regiment
Sir Arthur Haselrig's Regiment
Jonas Vandruske's Regiment
Edward Cooke's Regiment
'Kentish Horse' Regiment
Sir Michael Livesey's Regiment
William Purefoy's Regiment (detachment)
George Thompson's Regiment (two troops)
Attached Midlands Garrison forces:
   John Barker's Troop (Coventry garrison)
   Sir Samuel Luke's Regiment (Newport Pagnell garrison, detachment 80 men)
   Nathaniel Whetham's Regiment (Northampton garrison, 80 men)

Parliamentarian Dragoons
Sir William Waller's Regiment
'Kentish Dragoons' (detachment, 100 men)

Parliamentarian Foot
Southern Association
   Sir William Waller's Regiment
   Sir Arthur Haselrig's Regiment
   Christopher Potley's Regiment
   Ralph Weldon's Regiment
   Samuel Jones' Regiment (4 or 5 companies)
   James Wemyss' Firelock Regiment
London Trained Bands (The City Brigade), Major General Sir James Harrington
   Southwick White Auxiliaries Regiment
   Westminster Yellow Auxiliaries Regiment
   Tower Hamlets Regiment
Attached Midlands Garrison forces:
   John Barker's Regiment (Coventry garrison, detachment 200 men)
   Edward Massey's Regiment (Gloucester garrison, detachment 270 men)
   Nicholas Devereux's Regiment (Malmesbury garrison, detachment 100 men)
   Sir Samuel Luke's Regiment (Newport Pagnell garrison, detachment 200 men)
   Thomas Ayloffe's Regiment (Newport Pagnell garrison, detachment 200 men)
   Nathan Godfrey Bosseville's Regiment (Warwick garrison, detachment 340 men)
   Nathaniel Whetham's Regiment (Northampton garrison, detachment 100 men)

Artillery
27 guns (likely: 1x 12-pdr, 1 culverin, 3 demi-culverin, 1 demi-culverin drake, 7 saker/saker-drake, 3 minion, 5x 3-pdr, 6 baricadoes/cases of drakes)

Sources: There are a number of detailed primary accounts for the campaign and battle. Walker is particularly useful, listing the composition of Northampton's and Cleveland's Royalist brigades. The starting point for the Royalist foot is the invaluable record of the Aldbourne muster on 10 April 1644 by Richard Symonds, and his numbers for Royalist foot at Witney on 19 June. Toynbee and Young's book remains the best examination of the composition of the Royalist army, but their list of Parliamentarian regiments needs to be updated with Spring and Hall's more recent works. Sources: Toynbee, and P. Young, *Cropredy Bridge, 1644, The Campaign and the Battle*; Spring, *Waller's Army, The Regiments of Sir William Waller's Southern Association*.

BATTLE OF LOSTWITHIEL, 21 AUGUST–1 SEPTEMBER 1644

The Royalist Armies, 20,000 – The Royalist Oxford Army

Command
Captain General: King Charles I
Lord General: Patrick Ruthven, Earl of Forth and Brentford
Lieutenant General of the Horse: Henry, Lord Wilmot (until 8 August 1644), George, Lord Goring (from 8 August 1644)
Major General of Foot: Sir Jacob Astley
General of Ordnance: Henry, Baron Percy of Alnwick (until 14 August 1644), Ralph, Lord Hopton (from 14 August 1644)

The Royalist Oxford Army Horse
The King's Lifeguard of Horse (1 troop)
The Queen's Lifeguard of Horse (1 troop)
Prince Maurice's Lifeguard of Horse (1 troop)
Lord Ralph Hopton's Lifeguard of Horse (1 troop)
The Queen's Regiment
Sir Thomas Aston's Regiment
First Brigade: Lord Henry Wilmot
   Prince Maurice's Regiment
   Thomas Howard's Regiment
   Gerrard Croker's Regiment
   Lord Percy's Regiment
   Thomas Weston's Regiment
Second Brigade: James Compton, Earl of Northampton
   Lord Wilmot's Regiment
   Earl of Northampton's Regiment
   Lord General, Lord Forth's Regiment
Third Brigade: Sir Thomas Wentworth, Earl of Cleveland
   Earl of Cleveland's Regiment
   Colonel Thomas Culpepper's Regiment
   Sir Nicholas Crispe's Regiment (Lt Col John Luntly)
   Sir Edward Ford's Regiment
   Colonel John Fleetwood's Regiment
   Colonel James Hamilton's Regiment
   Colonel Richard Thornhill's Regiment

Fourth Brigade: Thomas, Lord Wentworth
  The Prince of Wales's Regiment
  Richard Neville's Regiment
  Sir William Boteler's Regiment
Fifth Brigade: Sir Humphrey Bennet's (not at Lostwithiel, but in the Saltash area)
  Sir Humphrey Bennet's Regiment
  Sir George Vaughan's Regiment
  Sir Edward Waldegrave's Regiment
  Colonel Andrew Lindsey's Regiment

The Royalist Oxford Army Foot

First Tertia/Brigade: Colonel Thomas Blagge
  The King's Lifeguard of Foot
  The Lord General's Regiment
  Sir Jacob Astley's Regiment
  Sir Henry Bard's Regiment
  The Duke of York's Regiment
  Sir James Pennyman's Regiment
  Henry, Lord Percy's Regiment
  Sir Lewis Dyve's Regiment
  The Queen's Lifeguard of Foot (detachment)?
Second Tertia/Brigade 'Reading Tertia': Colonel Charles Lloyd
  Colonel George Lisle's Regiment
  Colonel Charles Lloyd's Regiment
  Colonel Anthony Thelwell's Regiment
  Colonel John Owen's Regiment
  Colonel William Eure's Regiment
  Colonel Thomas Blackwall's Regiment
  Sir Theophilus Gilby's Regiment
  Colonel John Stradling's Regiment
  Sir Henry Vaughan's Regiment
Third Tertia/Brigade: Sir Bernard Astley
  Lord Hopton's Regiment of Foot
  Sir Allan Apsley's Regiment
  Colonel John Talbot's Regiment
  Colonel Francis Cooke's Regiment
  Sir William Courtney's Regiment
  Sir Bernard Astley's Regiment
  Colonel Matthew Appleyard's Regiment
  Sir John Paulet's Regiment
  Colonel Henry Shelley's Regiment
  Colonel Walter Slingsby's Regiment of Foot

Artillery

17 'pieces of cannon' of various calibres, including (or in addition to) leather guns

The Royalist Western Army

Command

General of the Western Army: Prince Maurice
General of Horse: Lieutenant General John Digby
General of Foot: Major General Sir Joseph Wagstaffe
General of Ordnance: Sir Francis Bassett

The Royalist Western Army Horse

The Western Army horse were probably organized in two or three unidentified brigades, comprising:
Colonel John Arundell's Regiment
Sir Thomas Bassett's Regiment
Colonel Nicholas Borlace's Regiment
Sir Henry Cary's Regiment
Sir John Digby's Regiment
Sir Edmund Fortescue's Regiment
Colonel Francis Hawley's Regiment
Sir Thomas Hele's Regiment
Colonel Thomas Monk's Regiment
Lord Paulet's Regiment
Sir John Stawell's Regiment
Colonel Giles Strangeway's Regiment
Colonel Thomas Stuckley's Regiment

The Royalist Western Army Foot

First Tertia/Brigade: Major General Sir Thomas Bassett (?)
  Sir Thomas Bassett's Regiment (Old Cornish)
  Sir John Grenville's Regiment (Old Cornish)
  Colonel Thomas St Aubyn's Regiment (Old Cornish)
  Sir William Godolphin's Regiment (Old Cornish)
Second Tertia/Brigade: Sir Henry Carey (?)
  Sir Henry Carey's Regiment
  Colonel John Digby's Regiment (Old Cornish)
  Colonel Richard Arundell's Regiment
Third Tertia/Brigade: Major General Sir Joseph Wagstaffe (?)
  Sir Richard Cholmley's Regiment
  'Irish' (detachment of 300 men from Lord Inchiquin's Irish Regiment)
  Colonel James Strangeway's Regiment
  Colonel Edmund Fortescue's Regiment
  Colonel Bullen Reymes' Regiment
  Sir John Hele's Regiment
  Sir John Ackland's Regiment (Prince of Wales' Regiment, 'The Tinners')
  Prince Maurice's Regiment (Lt Col Philip Champernon)
  Sir Richard Vivian's Cornish Trained Band Regiment

Artillery

11 'pieces of cannon'

Sir Richard Grenville's Command (technically part of the Western Army, but acting as an independent command)

Commander: Lieutenant General Sir Richard Grenville

Sir Richard Grenville's Horse

Sir Richard Grenville's Regiment
Sir Piers Edgecombe's Regiment
Horse of the Cornish Posse Comitatus (150 plus men commanded by Captain Mohun)

Sir Richard Grenville's Foot

Sir Richard Grenville's Regiment
Sir William Courtney's Regiment
Sir John Grenville's Cornish Trained Band Regiment of the Hundreds of Stratton and Lesnewth

Sir Piers Edgecombe's Cornish Trained Band Regiment
Foot of the Cornish Posse Comitatus (probably up to 500 men)

Artillery
5 drakes

The Parliamentarian Army: 10,000–11,000

Command
Lord General: Captain General Robert Devereux, Earl of Essex
Lord Marshal: John Lord Robartes
Lieutenant General of Horse: Sir William Balfour
Major General of Foot: Philip Skippon
General of Ordnance: Sir John Merrick
Commissary General: Nicholas Bond
Commissary General of Horse: Colonel Hans Behre
Commissary General of Musters of Horse: Edward Dodsworth
Commissary General for the Provisions of Horse and Draught Horses: Anthony Fastalfe
Quartermaster General: Colonel John Dalbier

Attached to Headquarters
Essex's Foot Guard: Captain Thomas Pudsey's Company of Halberdiers

Parliamentarian Horse (brigade structure unknown)
Essex's Lifeguard Troop (cuirassiers)
Earl of Essex's Regiment of Horse (Colonel Sir Philip Stapleton)
Lieutenant General Sir William Balfour's Regiment
Colonel Hans Behre's Regiment
Colonel John Dalbier's Regiment
Colonel James Sheffield's Regiment
Colonel Sir Robert Pye's Regiment
Colonel Edmund Harvey's (London) Regiment
Colonel Elizeus Leighton's (Plymouth) Regiment

Parliamentarian Dragoons
Captain Jeremiah Abercromby's Company (attached to Essex's horse regiment)
Colonel John Weare's Company

Parliamentarian Foot (brigade structure unknown)
The Earl of Essex's Regiment
Sir Philip Skippon's Regiment
John Lord Robartes' Regiment
Colonel Edward Aldrich's Regiment
Colonel Henry Barclay's Regiment
Colonel Richard Fortescue's Regiment
Colonel Thomas Tyrrell's Regiment
Colonel William Davies' Regiment
Northampton Foot Company
'Party of Foot' under Lieutenant Colonel Innis
London Trained Bands Brigade: Major General Christopher Whichcote
  The Green Regiment of the City Auxiliaries
  The Orange Regiment of the City Auxiliaries
Plymouth Foot (probably combined):

Colonel James Carr's Regiment (detachment under Lt Col Robert Moore)
Colonel Anthony Rouse's Regiment (detachment under Lt Col Robert Martin)
Newly raised in the West Country:
  Colonel John Weare's Regiment
  Colonel Alexander Popham's Regiment

Artillery
40–50 guns, including at least 3 demi-cannon, 9-pounders and 1 mortar

Attached to the Artillery Train
Pioneers:
  Captain Roe's Company
  Captain Hodgson's Company
  Captain Cheese's Company
  Captain Frodsham's Company
Firelocks:
  One company (unidentified)

Sources: The two outstanding primary sources are Richard Symonds' *Diary* (Peachey (ed)) and Edward Walker's *Historical Discourses*. To these must be added the Crediton muster for Maurice's army, first published in Peter Young's 1939 article on 'King Charles I's Army 1643–1645'. Symonds not only provides information on the Royalist armies, but also a July muster for Essex's horse. Simon Marsh's unpublished paper on Essex's army at Lostwithiel and Second Newbury is an invaluable source for the numbers of men in Essex's foot and horse regiments, based on surviving pay warrants. The only book published specifically on the campaign and battle is Ede-Borrett's *Lostwithiel 1644*, which includes all the major primary accounts. It also includes the only published order of battle, which has been updated in light of further primary information and analysis. Peachey (ed.), *Richard Symonds*; Walker, *Historical Discourses*; Ede-Borrett, *Lostwithiel 1644*; Marsh, '"This Disarmed Multitude": The Impact of the Lostwithiel Campaign on the Earl of Essex's Army and its Reconstruction for Second Newbury'.

SECOND BATTLE OF NEWBURY, 26–27 OCTOBER 1644

The Royalist Armies: 9,500

Oxford Army Command
Captain General: King Charles I
Lord General: Patrick Ruthven, Earl of Forth and Brentford
Lieutenant General of the Horse: George, Lord Goring
Major General of Foot: Sir Jacob Astley
General of Ordnance: Ralph, Lord Hopton
Quarter Master General: Sir Charles Lloyd

Western Army Command
General of the Western Army: Prince Maurice
General of Horse: Lieutenant General John Digby
General of Foot: Major General Sir Joseph Wagstaffe
General of Ordnance: Sir Francis Bassett

Right Wing of Horse and Foot (Sir Jacob Astley)

Detachment from Wentworth's Brigade of Horse (Oxford Army): Sir John Browne

- The Prince of Wales' (Thomas, Lord Wentworth's) Regiment of Horse
- Prince Rupert's Regiment of Dragoons (Sir Thomas Hooper)

Second Tertia/Brigade 'Reading Tertia' (Oxford Army): Colonel Sir George Lisle

- Colonel George Lisle's Regiment of Foot
- Colonel Charles Lloyd's Regiment of Foot
- Colonel Anthony Thelwell's Regiment of Foot
- Colonel John Owen's Regiment of Foot
- Colonel William Eure's Regiment of Foot
- Colonel Thomas Blackwall's Regiment of Foot
- Sir Theophilus Gilby's Regiment of Foot
- Colonel John Stradling's Regiment of Foot
- Sir Henry Vaughan's Regiment of Foot

Third Tertia/Brigade (Oxford Army): Sir Bernard Astley

- Lord Hopton's Regiment of Foot
- Sir Allan Apsley's Regiment
- Colonel John Talbot's Regiment
- Colonel Francis Cooke's Regiment
- Sir William Courtney's Regiment
- Sir Bernard Astley's Regiment
- Colonel Matthew Appleyard's Regiment
- Sir John Paulet's Regiment
- Colonel Henry Shelley's Regiment
- Colonel Walter Slingsby's Regiment of Foot

Central Body of Horse and Foot (King Charles I)

Sir Thomas Wentworth, Earl of Cleveland's Brigade of Horse (Oxford Army)

- Earl of Cleveland's Regiment of Horse
- Colonel Thomas Culpepper's Regiment of Horse
- Colonel John Fleetwood's Regiment of Horse (Lt Col John Stuart)
- Colonel James Hamilton's Regiment of Horse
- Colonel Richard Thornhill's Regiment of Horse

Thomas, Lord Wentworth's Brigade of Horse (Oxford Army)

- Colonel Richard Neville's Regiment of Horse
- Sir William Boteler's Regiment of Horse

Sir Humphrey Bennet's Brigade of Horse (Oxford Army)

- Sir Humphrey Bennet's Regiment of Horse
- Sir George Vaughan's Regiment of Horse
- Sir Edward Waldegrave's Regiment of Horse
- Colonel Andrew Lindsey's Regiment of Horse
- Sir Thomas Aston's Regiment of Horse (?)

Colonel Thomas Howard's Brigade of Horse (Oxford Army)

- Prince Maurice's Regiment of Horse
- Thomas Howard's Regiment of Horse
- Colonel Gerrard Croker's Regiment of Horse
- Sir Arthur Slingsby's (ex-Lord Percy's) Regiment of Horse
- Colonel Thomas Weston's Regiment of Horse

Unidentified Brigade of Horse (Ralph, Lord Hopton?) (Oxford Army)

- Lord Hopton's Lord Ralph Hopton's Lifeguard of Horse (1 troop)
- Lord Hopton's Regiment of Horse
- Marquis of Hertford's Regiment of Horse
- Colonel Francis Doddington's Regiment of Horse
- Sir Edward Ford's Regiment of Horse

Colonel Edward Pierce's Regiment of Horse

Colonel George Gunter's & Colonel Allan Apsley's Regiments of Horse

Unbrigaded Horse (Oxford Army)

- The King's Lifeguard Regiment of Horse (2 troops, the King's and Queen's)
- The Queen's Regiment of Horse

First Tertia/Brigade (Oxford Army) : Colonel Thomas Blagge

- The King's Lifeguard of Foot
- The Lord General's Regiment of Foot
- Sir Jacob Astley's Regiment of Foot
- Sir Henry Bard's Regiment of Foot
- Sir James Pennyman's Regiment of Foot
- Henry, Lord Percy's Regiment of Foot
- Colonel Thomas Blagge's Regiment of Foot (detachment)?
- The Queen's Lifeguard of Foot (detachment)?

Left Wing Horse and Foot (Prince Maurice)

The Western Horse (Western Army): A single brigade, comprising some of:

Colonel John Arundell's Regiment of Horse

Sir Thomas Bassett's Regiment of Horse

Colonel Nicholas Borlace's Regiment of Horse

Sir Henry Cary's Regiment of Horse

Sir John Digby's Regiment of Horse

Sir Edmund Fortescue's Regiment of Horse

Colonel Francis Hawley's Regiment of Horse

Sir Thomas Hele's Regiment of Horse

Colonel Thomas Monk's Regiment of Horse

Lord Paulet's Regiment of Horse

Sir John Stawell's Regiment of Horse

Colonel Thomas Stuckley's Regiment of Horse

Unbrigaded Horse (Western Army) – Prince Maurice's Lifeguard of Horse (1 Troop)

First Tertia/Brigade: Major General Sir Thomas Bassett (Western Army)

- Sir Thomas Bassett's Regiment of Foot (Old Cornish)
- Sir John Grenville's Regiment of Foot (Old Cornish)
- Colonel Thomas St Aubyn's Regiment of Foot (Old Cornish)
- Sir William Godolphin's Regiment of Foot (Old Cornish)

Second Tertia/Brigade: Sir Henry Carey (Western Army)

- Sir Henry Carey's Regiment of Foot
- Colonel John Digby's Regiment of Foot (Old Cornish)
- Colonel Richard Arundell's Regiment of Foot

Divided between the two tertias, brigading unknown (Western Army):

- Colonel Edmund Fortescue's Regiment of Foot
- Colonel Bullen Reymes' Regiment of Foot
- Sir John Hele's Regiment of Foot
- Sir John Ackland's Regiment of Foot (Prince of Wales' Regiment, 'The Tinners')
- Prince Maurice's Regiment of Foot (Lt Col Philip Champernon)

Artillery

32–33 guns unknown types/calibres

Donnington Castle Garrison (Oxford Army)

Earl of Rivers Regiment of Foot (Colonel Sir John Boys) (200)

Lt Col Sir John Boys Troop of Horse (25)

4 Cannon

The Parliamentarian Armies 19,000

Western Group Command
Major General: Sir William Waller
Lieutenant General of Horse: Sir Arthur Haselrig (Waller's Army)
Lieutenant General of Horse: Sir William Balfour (Earl of Essex's Army)
Major General of Foot: Phillip Skippon (Earl of Essex's Army)
Quartermaster General: Colonel John Dalbier (Earl of Essex's Army)
Commissary General of Horse: Colonel Hans Behre (Earl of Essex's Army)
Commissary General of Horse: Colonel Jonas Vandruske (Waller's Army)

Western Group Right Wing Horse and Foot
Sir William Balfour's Brigade (Earl of Essex's Army)
  Earl of Essex's Lifeguard Troop of Horse (cuirassiers)
  Earl of Essex's Regiment of Horse (Sir Philip Stapleton)
  Lieutenant General Sir William Balfour's Regiment of Horse
  Commissary General Hans Behre's Regiment of Horse
  Quarter Master General John Dalbier's Regiment of Horse
  Colonel Edmund Harvey's (London) Regiment of Horse
  Colonel James Sheffield's Regiment of Horse
  Colonel Sir Robert Pye's Regiment of Horse
  Earl of Manchester's Regiment of Horse (Manchester's army)
  Sir Philip Stapleton's Company of Dragoons
Sir Arthur Haselrig's Brigade (Waller's Army)
  Sir Arthur Haselrig's Regiment of Horse
  Colonel John Fiennes' Regiment of Horse
  Colonel John Fitzjames' Regiment of Horse
Lieutenant General John Middleton's Brigade (Waller's Army)
  Lieutenant General John Middleton's Regiment of Horse
  Colonel Edward Cooke's Regiment of Horse
  Major General James Holborne's Regiment of Dragoons
Waller's Army, brigading unknown
  Colonel Jonas Vandruske's Regiment of Horse
  Colonel George Thompson's Regiment of Horse
  Sir Michael Livesey's Regiment of Horse
  Colonel Alexander Popham's, or Colonel Francis Popham's Regiment of Horse
  Colonel William Strode's Regiment of Horse
  Sir Richard Onslow's Troop of Horse ('the Surrey Horse')
  Captain Nathan Butler's Company of Dragoons ('the Kentish Dragoons')
  Sir William Waller's Regiment of Foot (mounted as dragoons)
  Colonel Anthony Stapley's Regiment of Foot (detachment, mounted as dragoons)

Western Group Central Body Horse and Foot
Colonel Henry Barclay's Brigade (Earl of Essex's Army)
  Major General Phillip Skippon's Regiment of Foot
  Lord Robartes' Regiment of Foot
  Colonel Henry Barclay's Regiment of Foot
Colonel Edward Aldrich's Brigade (Earl of Essex's Army)
  Colonel Edward Aldrich's Regiment of Foot
  Colonel Adam Cunningham's Regiment of Foot
  Colonel William Davies' Regiment of Foot
  Colonel Thomas Tyrell's Regiment of Foot
London Trained Bands Brigade (Major General Sir James Harrington)
  The Red Regiment of Foot, City Trained Bands
  The Blue Regiment of Foot, City Trained Bands
  The Red Regiment of Foot, Westminster Trained Bands
  The Yellow Regiment of Foot, Tower Hamlets Auxiliaries.

Western Group Left Wing Horse and Foot
Lieutenant General Oliver Cromwell's Brigade (Manchester's Army)
  Lieutenant General Oliver Cromwell's Regiment of Horse
  Colonel Bartholomew Vermuyden's Regiment of Horse
  Sir William Waller's Regiment of Horse (Waller's Army)
  Unbrigaded Horse (Waller's Army) – Sir William Waller's Lifeguard Troop of Horse

Eastern Group Command
Major General: Edward Montagu, Earl of Manchester
Major General of Foot: Lawrence Crawford
Lieutenant General of Ordnance: Captain Thomas Hammond (Manchester's Army)
Quartermaster General: Major Henry Ireton
Scoutmaster General: Major Lionel Watson
Commissary General: William Harlakenden
Deputy Commissary General: James Standish
Adjutant General: Captain Walter Stirling
Wagon Master General: Richard Fennyer

Eastern Group Horse
Unknown Brigade
  Colonel Charles Fleetwood's Regiment of Horse
  Earl of Manchester's Regiment of Dragoons
Major General Brown's London Brigade of Horse
  Major General Brown's Regiment of Horse
  Colonel Richard Mainwaring's Regiment of Horse
  Colonel William Underwood's Regiment of Horse
Unbrigaded Horse
  Earl of Manchester's Lifeguard Troop of Horse
  Lieutenant General Edmund Ludlow's Regiment of Horse (Waller's Army)
  Colonel Richard Norton's Regiment of Horse (one troop, Waller's Army)

Eastern Group Foot
Major General Lawrence Crawford's Brigade
  Colonel Edward Montagu's Regiment of Foot
  Colonel John Pickering's Regiment of Foot
  Colonel Francis Russell's Regiment of Foot
Unknown Brigade
  Major General Lawrence Crawford's Regiment of Foot
  Sir Miles Hobart's Regiment of Foot
Unknown Brigade
  Sir Thomas Hoogan's Regiment of Foot
  Colonel Thomas Rainsborough's Regiment of Foot
  Colonel Valentine Walton's Regiment of Foot
Unbrigaded – Earl of Manchester's Regiment of Foot

Artillery
32-plus guns
Sources: Walker, *Historical Discourses*; Ede-Borrett, *The Royalist Army at the Second Battle of Newbury 27 October 1644*; Marsh, '"This Disarmed Multitude": The Impact of the Lostwithiel Campaign on the Earl of Essex's Army and its Reconstruction for Second Newbury'; Money, *The First and Second Battles of Newbury*; Scott, *The Battles of Newbury*.

APPENDIX 4: ARMY STRENGTHS AND COMPOSITIONS, 1645

THE BATTLE OF NASEBY, 14 JUNE 1645

The Royalist Army: 9,000–12,500

Command

Commander-in-Chief: King Charles I
Captain General: Prince Rupert of the Rhine
Sergeant Major General of Foot: Sir Jacob, Lord Astley

Royalist Horse

Prince Rupert's and Prince Maurice's Lifeguards – H1
Prince Rupert's Regiment of Horse – H2
The Queen's and Prince Maurice's Regiment of Horse – H3
The Earl of Northampton's Regiment – H4
Sir William Vaughan's Regiment – H5
The Northern Horse, three divisions under Sir Marmaduke Langdale – H6
The Northern Horse, one division under Sir William Blackiston – H7
Sir Horatio Carey's Regiment – H8
Colonel Thomas Howard's Divisions of Horse (two, maybe three) – H9
The Newark Horse – H10
The King's Lifeguard – H11
The King and Queen's Lifeguard of Horse – H12
Both wings of horse were each supported by 200 musketeers.

Royalist Foot

Sir Bernard Astley's Tertia of Foot
    The Duke of York's Regiment – F1
    Sir Edward Hopton's Regiment – F2
    Sir Richard Page's Battalion – F3
Sir Henry Bard's Tercia of Foot
    Sir Henry Bard's and Colonel Thomas's Regiments of Foot – F4
    Colonel Owen's and Colonel Gerard's Battalions – F5
Sir George Lisle's Tertia of Foot
    Sir George Lisle's and Colonel St George's Regiments – F6
    Colonel Smith's Battalion, the Shrewsbury Foot – F7
Reserve
    The King's Lifeguard of Foot – F8
    Prince Rupert's Regiment of Foot (the Bluecoats) – F9

Artillery

There is general agreement that the Royalist artillery did not make it to the battlefield, other than a few very light pieces. Twelve Royalist guns were captured after the battle from those that were en route to the field.

The Parliamentarian (New Model) Army: 15,200–17,000

Command

Captain General: Sir Thomas Fairfax
Lieutenant General of the Horse: Oliver Cromwell
Commissary General of Horse: Henry Ireton
Sergeant Major General of Foot: Philip Skippon
General of the Ordnance: Richard Deane

Parliamentarian Horse

Sir Thomas Fairfax's Regiment (Lifeguard) – H1
Sir Robert Pye's Regiment (1 division) – H2
Colonel Edward Whalley's Regiment – H3
Colonel Thomas Sheffield's Regiment – H4
Colonel John Fiennes' Regiment (1 division) – H5
Colonel Edward Rossiter's Regiment (1 division) – H6
The Associated Horse (East Anglia) – H7
Commissary General Henry Ireton's Regiment – H8
Colonel Bartholomew Vermuyden's Regiment – H9
Colonel John Butler's Regiment – H10
Colonel Nathaniel Rich's Regiment – H11
Colonel Charles Fleetwood's Regiment – H12
Eastern Association Horse (1 division) – H13
Colonel Okey's Dragoons - D1

Parliamentarian Foot

Sir Thomas Fairfax's Regiment – F1
Colonel Edward Montagu's Regiment – F2
Colonel John Pickering's Regiment – F3
Sir Hardress Waller's Regiment – F4
Sergeant Major General Philip Skippon's Regiment – F5
Colonel Edward Harley's Regiment (Lt Col Thomas Pride) – F6
Colonel Robert Hammond's Regiment – F7
Colonel Thomas Rainsborough's Regiment – F8
Reserve
Colonel Pride's Rearguard – F9

Artillery

14 guns approximately

Sources: The numbers on both sides at Naseby are contentious and have tended to be overstated. I am grateful to Martin Marix Evans who drew my attention to an article by David Blackmore, *Counting the New Model Army*. Martin sums up the problems with, and possible solutions for, the numbers in his books *Naseby, English Civil War* (co-written) and *Naseby 1645, Triumph of the New Model Army*. In terms of artillery the Royalists had 12 guns (Fairfax, Three letters, report by Cromwell, p. 2.) but these are unlikely to have been on the field in time, and the New Model Army had 11 guns (Streeter's map) but there is evidence that these were not deployed in time. Other Sources: Foard, *Naseby, The Decisive Campaign*. Young, *Naseby 1645*.

BATTLE OF LANGPORT, 10 JULY 1645

The Royalist Army: 4,000–4,500

Command
General of the West: Lord, George Goring
Major General of Horse: Sir John Digby
Lieutenant General of Horse: Thomas, Lord Wentworth
Major General of Foot: Joseph Wagstaffe
Commissary General: George Porter
Lieutenant General of Ordnance: Colonel Betridge

Royalist Horse & Dragoons (brigading unknown)
Ex-Oxford Army ('The Old Oxford Horse')
  Sir Thomas Aston's Regiment of Horse
  Earl of Cleveland's Regiment of Horse
  Sir Nicholas Crispe's Regiment of Horse
  Colonel Thomas Culpepper's Regiment of Horse
  Colonel John Fleetwood's Regiment of Horse (Lt Col John Stuart) (?)
  Colonel James Hamilton's Regiment of Horse
  Colonel Nathaniel Hevingham's Regiment of Horse (formerly Sir Edward Waldegrave's)
  Thomas Howard's Regiment of Horse (part)
  Lord General, Lord Forth's Regiment of Horse
  Colonel Richard Neville's Regiment of Horse
  Ames Pollard's (formerly Lord Wilmot's) Regiment of Horse
  Sir Arthur Slingsby's (formerly Lord Percy's) Regiment of Horse
  Colonel Richard Thornhill's Regiment of Horse
Ex-Prince Maurice's Western Army
  Lieutenant General John Digby's Regiment of Horse
  Sir John Stawell's Regiment of Horse
Other Horse – unbrigaded
  Lord Goring's Lifeguard
  Lord Goring's Regiment of Horse
  George Porter's Lifeguard
  Sir John Digby's Regiment of Horse
  Sir Allen Apsley's Regiment of Horse (Barnstaple garrison)
  Sir John Berkeley's Regiment of Horse (detachment?) (Exeter garrison)
  Sir William Courtney's Regiment of Horse
  Colonel Charles Finch's Regiment of Horse
  Sir Richard Grenville's Regiment of Horse (detachment?)
  Sir Ralph Hopton's Regiment of Horse (Bristol garrison)
  Colonel Robert Phelips's Regiment of Horse (Ilchester Garrison)
  Colonel Bertrand Rossin De La Plume's Regiment of Horse (French reformadoes?)
  Colonel Williams Slaughter's Regiment of Horse (South Wales)
  Colonel Samuel Tukes' Regiment of Horse (Duke of York's)
  Captain Berry's Troop of Dragoons

Royalist Foot (brigading unknown)
Ex-Sir Richard Grenville's Army ('The New Cornish Tertia')
  Sir Richard Grenville's Regiment of Foot
  Colonel John Arundell's Regiment of Foot
  Colonel Richard Arundell's Regiment of Foot
  Colonel Lewis Tremaine's Regiment of Foot
  Sir William Courtney's Regiment of Foot

Ex-Prince Maurice's Western Army
  Colonel John Digby's Regiment of Foot (Old Cornish)
  Sir Thomas Bassett's Regiment of Foot (Old Cornish)
  Colonel Thomas St Aubyn's Regiment of Foot (Old Cornish)
  Sir William Godolphin's Regiment of Foot (Old Cornish)
  Sir John Grenville's Regiment of Foot (Old Cornish)
  Colonel John Digby's Regiment of Foot
  Sir John Ackland's Regiment of Foot (Prince of Wales', 'The Tinners') (?)
  Colonel Sir Edmund Fortescue's Regiment of Foot (?)
  Colonel Bullen Reymes' Regiment of Foot (?)
  Sir John Hele's Regiment of Foot (?)
  Prince Maurice's Regiment of Foot (?)
Other Foot – unbrigaded
  Sir John Stawell's Regiment of Foot
  Sir Allen Apsley's Regiment of Foot
  Lord Hopton's Regiment of Foot
  Colonel John Coventry's Regiment of Foot (?)
  Colonel Ames Pollard's Regiment of Foot (?)
  Colonel Williams Slaughter's Regiment of Foot (South Wales)
  Colonel Matthew Wise's Regiment of Foot (South Wales)

Artillery
2 guns (small-calibre)

The Parliamentarian (New Model) Army: 10,600

Command
General: Sir Thomas Fairfax
Lieutenant General of Horse: Oliver Cromwell
Major General of Foot: Robert Hammond (?)
Commissary General of Horse: Henry Ireton
Lieutenant General of Ordnance: Thomas Hammond
Comptroller of the Ordnance: Captain Richard Deane
Scoutmaster General: Major Leonard Watson

Parliamentarian Horse (brigading unknown)
Sir Thomas Fairfax's Lifeguard Troop
Sir Thomas Fairfax's Regiment of Horse
Lieutenant General Oliver Cromwell's Regiment of Horse
Colonel John Butler's Regiment of Horse
Colonel Charles Fleetwood's Regiment of Horse
Colonel Nathaniel Rich's Regiment of Horse
Colonel Edward Whalley's Regiment of Horse

Parliamentarian Dragoons
Colonel John Okey's Regiment of Dragoons (1 troop)

Parliamentarian Foot
Colonel Ralph Weldon's Brigade
  Colonel Ralph Weldon's Regiment of Foot
  Colonel Richard Ingoldsby's Regiment of Foot
  Colonel Richard Fortescue's Regiment of Foot
  Colonel Philip Herbert's Regiment of Foot
Colonel Thomas Rainsborough's Brigade
  Colonel Robert Hammond's Regiment of Foot
  Colonel Thomas Rainsborough's Regiment of Foot
  Colonel Phillip Skippon's Regiment of Foot

Colonel Edward Montagu's Brigade
  Sir Hardress Waller's Regiment of Foot
  Sir Thomas Fairfax's Regiment of Foot (pikemen only)
  Colonel Edward Montagu's Regiment of Foot (pikemen only)
  Colonel John Pickering's Regiment of Foot (pikemen only)

Artillery
20-plus guns (at least 17 sakers and 3 drakes)
Trainguard: Captain Lieutenant Desborough (2 companies of firelocks) (?)
Sources: R. Bulstrode, *Memoirs and Reflections* (Whitlocke ed.); Anon, *An Exact and perfect relation of the proceedings of the army under the command of Sir Thomas Fairfax; Worthy Gentleman in Sir Thomas Fairfax His Army, A letter sent to the Right Honourable William Lenthall Esquire, Speaker to the Honourable House of Commons, Concerning the Routing of Colonel Goring's Army near Bridgewater;* Barratt, *The Battle of Langport 1645.*

BATTLE OF ROWTON HEATH, 24 SEPTEMBER 1645

The Royalist Army: 3,500 Horse and 1,600 Foot from the Chester garrison

Command
Captain General: King Charles I
Lieutenant General of the Horse: Lord Charles Gerrard
Major General of Foot: Sir Jacob Astley
Major General of Horse: Sir Marmaduke Langdale
Chester garrison: Lord John Byron

Royalist Horse
Unbrigaded Horse – The King's Lifeguard Regiment of Horse (4 troops, the King's, Queen's, Earl of Lichfield's, Sir Henry Stradling's)
Sir William Vaughan's Brigade of Horse
  Sir William Vaughan's Regiment of Horse
  The Queen's Regiment of Horse
  Prince Maurice's Regiment of Horse
  Earl of Northampton's Regiment of Horse
  Colonel Samuel Sandy's Regiment of Horse
  Colonel Thomas Weston's Regiment of Horse
Lord Charles Gerrard's Brigade of Horse
  Lord Charles Gerrard's Lifeguard Troop of Horse
  Lord Charles Gerrard's Regiment of Horse
  Colonel Randolph Egerton's Regiment of Horse
  Colonel Herbert Price's Regiment of Horse
  Colonel Roger Whitely's Regiment of Horse
  Colonel John Davalier's (Devalier) Regiment of Horse
  Colonel Johan Horther's (Hurter/Heiter) Regiment of Horse
  Colonel Henry Grady's Regiment of Horse
  Colonel Robert Werden's Regiment of Horse

The Northern Horse (Sir Marmaduke Langdale)
Sir Marmaduke Langdale's Brigade (Colonel Sir Phillip Monkton)
  Sir Marmaduke Langdale's Reformadoes (Lifeguard Troop of Horse)
  Sir Marmaduke Langdale's Regiment of Horse
  Sir Philip Monkton's Regiment of Horse
  Sir Francis Middleton's Regiment of Horse
  Sir Gamaliel Dudley's Regiment of Horse

Sir William Mason's Regiment of Horse
Sir William Bradshaw's Regiment of Horse
Colonel Francis Hungate's Regiment of Horse
Colonel John Sallcross' Regiment of Horse
Colonel Francis Malham's Regiment of Horse
Ex Sir John Girlington's Regiment of Horse
Sir William Blakiston's Brigade
  Sir William Blakiston's Regiment of Horse
  Sir Francis Anderson's Regiment of Horse
  Sir Francis Howard's Regiment of Horse
  Sir John Preston's Regiment of Horse
  Sir Edward Widdrington's Regiment of Horse
  Colonel Ralpht Mylott's Regiment of Horse
  Colonel John Forcer's Regiment of Horse
  Colonel John Errington's Regiment of Horse
  Colonel Francis Carnaby's Regiment of Horse
  Colonel John Smyth's Regiment of Horse
  Colonel Edward Grey's Regiment of Horse

Royalist Foot: Chester Garrison (Lord John Byron)
Sir Francis Gamull's Regiment of Foot
Colonel Roger Mostyn's Regiment of Foot
Colonel Hugh Wynne's Regiment of Foot
Sir Thomas Glemham's Regiment of Foot (remnants)
Lord John Byron's Regiment of Horse

Artillery
unknown

The Parliamentarian Army: 5,000

Command (Army of the Cheshire Committee)
Lieutenant General of Horse: Michael Jones
Major General of Foot: James Lothian

Cheshire Horse (elements probably from):
Sir William Brereton's Regiment of Horse
Colonel Prince's Shropshire Horse
Lieutenant Colonel Chidley Coote's Shropshire Horse

Cheshire Foot (elements probably from):
Sir William Brereton's Regiment of Foot (including Finch's and Gimbert's firelock (dragoons) companies)
Colonel George Booth's Regiment of Foot
Colonel Henry Brooke's Regiment of Foot
Colonel Robert Duckenfield's Regiment of Foot
Colonel John Leigh's Regiment of Foot
Colonel Henry Mainwaring's Regiment of Foot
Adjutant General Lothian's Company
John Booth's Foot
Colonel Bowyer's Staffordshire Foot
Unidentified Lancashire and Cheshire auxiliary companies

Command (Poyntz's Army)
Colonel General: Sydenham Poyntz
Quarter Master General: Lawrence Parsons

Horse

Sydenham Poyntz's Reformadoes (Lifeguard Troop of Horse)

Sydenham Poyntz's Regiment of Horse

Hugh Bethell's Regiment of Horse

Robert Lilburne's Regiment of Horse

Lawrence Parson's Regiment of Horse

Colonel Greaves' (Graves') Yorkshire Regiment of Horse (Northern Association)

Major Hawksworth Warwickshire Horse

Major Lydcot's Northamptonshire Horse (?)

Major Thomas Saunders' Derbyshire Horse (?)

Francis Thornhaugh's Nottinghamshire Regiment of Horse (?)

Edward Rossiter's Lincolnshire Regiment of Horse (?)

Artillery

At least 2 guns

Sources: Walker, *Unfortunate Success of his Majesty's Army*; Peachey (ed.), *Richard Symonds's diary of the marches*; Barratt, *The Siege of Chester and the Battle of Rowton Heath*; Barratt, *Great Siege of Chester*.

APPENDIX 5: ARMY STRENGTHS AND COMPOSITIONS, 1646

BATTLE OF STOW-ON-THE-WOLD, 21 MARCH 1646

The Royalist Army: 3,000

Command
Lord General: Jacob, Lord Astley
Lieutenant General of the Horse: Sir Charles Lucas

Royalist Horse (brigading unknown – remnants, detachments and reformadoes)
Prince Maurice's Regiment of Horse
Prince Maurice's Lifeguard Troop of Horse
Lord John Byron's Regiment of Horse
Lord Charles Gerard's Regiment of Horse
Vicomte Nicholas St Pol's Regiment of Horse
Sir William Vaughan's Regiment of Horse
Colonel Thomas Leveson's Regiment of Horse (Dudley Castle garrison) (?)
Sir John Pettus' Regiment of Horse
Henry Hastings, Lord Loughborough's Regiment of Horse
Thomas Weston's Regiment of Horse (?)

Royalist Foot (brigading unknown – remnants, detachments and reformadoes)
Prince Rupert's Lifeguard of Foot (firelocks)
Prince Maurice's Firelocks
Jacob, Lord Astley's Regiment of Foot
Henry Hastings, Lord Loughborough's Regiment of Foot
Lord Charles Gerard's Regiment of Foot
Henry Somerset, Marquis of Worcester's Regiment of Foot (Raglan Castle garrison) (?)
Sir Bernard Astley's Regiment of Foot
Sir Michael Earnley's Regiment of Foot (Irish – Bridgnorth garrison)
Sir Lewis Kirke's Regiment of Foot (Bridgnorth Castle garrison) (?)
Sir Charles Lloyd's Regiment of Foot (Bridgnorth garrison)
Sir Herbert Price's Regiment of Foot
Sir Samuel Sandy's Regiment of Foot (Worcester garrison)
Sir Michael Woodhouse's Regiment of Foot (Ludlow garrison)
Colonel Harvey Bagot's Regiment of Foot
Colonel Francis Billingsley's Regiment of Foot (Bridgnorth Town Regiment)
Colonel John Corbet's Regiment of Foot
Colonel Randolph Egerton's Regiment of Foot (Ludlow garrison)
Colonel Edward Gerard's Regiment of Foot
Colonel Ratcliffe Gerard's Regiment of Foot (Worcester garrison)
Colonel Thomas Leveson's Regiment of Foot (Dudley Castle garrison)
Colonel Anthony Thelwell's Regiment of Foot (?)
Colonel Henry Washington's Regiment of Foot (Worcester garrison)

Artillery
Unknown

The Parliamentarian Army: 3,600

Command
Colonel Thomas Morgan (Gloucester troops)
Colonel John Birch (Hereford troops)

Horse: Brereton's Brigade – Major General Sir William Brereton
Major Joseph Hawksworth's Warwickshire Horse (6 troops)
Major Joseph Swetenham's Derbyshire Horse (3 or 4 troops)
Leicestershire Horse (3 troops)
Firelocks (200 men mounted as dragoons)

Parliamentarian Foot
Gloucestershire Brigade – Colonel Thomas Morgan. Detachments probably from:
    Colonel Thomas Morgan's Regiment of Foot ('the Governor's Regiment')
    Colonel Charles Blunt's Regiment of Foot
    Colonel Nicholas Devereux's Regiment of Foot
    Gloucester Horse (? Troops)
Hereford Brigade – Colonel John Birch. Detachments probably from:
    Colonel John Birch's Regiment of Foot
    Colonel John Birch's Regiment of Horse .
Evesham Force – Colonel Edward Rouse. Detachment probably from:
    Colonel Edward Rouse's Regiment of Foot

Sources: *Morgan, Morgan Governor of Glocester's letter to the Honoble William Lenthal Esq; Speaker to the Honorable House of Commons*; Morgan, *A true relation by Colonell Morgan, in a letter of the totall routing of the Lord Ashley, by him and Sir William Brereton at Stow*; R. S., *A true and fuller relation of the battell fought at Stow in the Would, March 21, 1645*; Dore, *The Letter Books of William Brereton*; Webb (ed.), *Military Memoir of Colonel John Birch*; Barratt, *The Last Army*.

APPENDIX 6: ARMY STRENGTHS AND COMPOSITIONS, 1647–49

BATTLE OF PRESTON, 17 AUGUST 1648

Scottish/Royalist Army: 24,000

Scottish Command
Commander-in-Chief: James Duke of Hamilton
Lieutenant General: James Livingstone, Earl of Callendar
Lieutenant General of Horse: John Middleton
Adjutant General: William Baillie
General of Artillery: Alexander Hamilton

Horse: brigade structure unknown – Middleton's Command
Hamilton's Lifeguard
Barclay's Horse
College of Justice Regiment
Cranston's Horse
Crawford-Lindsay's Horse
Dalhousie's Horse
Dunfermline's Horse
Erroll's Horse
Forbes' Horse
Frendraught's Horse
Garthland's Horse
Home's Horse
Innes' Horse
Kenmure's Horse
Lanark's Horse
Lauderdale's Horse
Livingstone's Horse
Middleton's Troop
Earl Marischal's Horse
Montgomery's Horse
Sinclair's Horse
Traquair's Horse
William Hurry's Horse

Foot: brigade structure unknown – Baillie's Command
Marquis of Argyll's Regiment
Earl of Atholl's Regiment
William Baillie's Regiment
Lord Bargany's Regiment
Earl of Callendar's Regiment
Lord Carnegie's Regiment
Douglas's Regiment
Drummond of Mechanie's Regiment
Earl of Dumfries' Regiment
Frazer of Philorth's Regiment
Grey's Regiment
Hamilton's Regiment
Earl of Home's Regiment
Keith's Regiment

Maule's Regiment
Lord Roxborough's Regiment
Earl of Tullibardine's Regiment
Turner's Regiment
Lord Hay of Yester's Foot

Artillery
Hamilton's Command, 20 guns approximately
Monro's force: not at the battle; about 1,800 foot and just under 1,000 horse

English Command
Commander in Chief: Sir Marmaduke Langdale
Lieutenant General of Horse: Sir Philip Musgrave

Horse: Musgrave's Command, comprised from the following units:
Tyldesley's Horse
Strickland's Regiment
Wogan's Regiment
Denton's Regiment
Roscarick's Horse from the Appleby garrison

Foot: brigade structure unknown – Langdale's Command
Philip Musgrave's Regiment
Bellingham's Regiment
Curwen's Regiment
Edward Musgrave's Regiment
Huddleston's Regiment
Featherstone's Regiment
Chater's Regiment
Carleton's Regiment

Artillery
Approximately 20 field guns

Parliamentarian Army: 11,200

Command
Commander-in-Chief: Lieutenant General Oliver Cromwell
Commander of the Northern Association Army: Major General John Lambert

Horse: brigade structure unknown
New Model Army Horse
   Cromwell's Regiment
   Harrison's Regiment
   Twistelton's Regiment
   Thornhaugh's Regiment
   Scroope's Regiment
Northern Association Horse
   Lambert's Regiment
   Lilburne's Regiment

Lancashire Militia
   Rigby's Horse
   Shuttleworth's Regiment
   Rawlinson's Troop

Dragoons
Okey's Regiment

Foot: brigade structure unknown
New Model Army
   Fairfax's Regiment
   Deane's Regiment
   Pride's Regiment
   Overton's Regiment

Northern Association Foot
   Bright's Regiment
Lancashire Foot
   Ashton's Regiment
   Dodding's Regiment
   Standish's Regiment
   Rigby's Regiment
   Shuttleworth's Regiment

Artillery
Some garrison guns; numbers unknown

Source: Bull & Seed, *Bloody Preston.*

APPENDIX 7: ARMY STRENGTHS AND COMPOSITIONS, 1650–51

THE BATTLE OF DUNBAR, 3 SEPTEMBER 1650

The Scottish Army: 22,000

Command
Commander-in-Chief: General Alexander Leslie, Earl of Leven – he was not at the battle and had delegated field/tactical command to Leslie
Lieutenant General: David Leslie
(Major) General of the Horse: Robert Montgomerie
Commander of the Ordnance: James Wemyss

Scottish Horse: no formal brigade structure
Leven's Regiment
Leslie's Regiment
Montgomerie's Regiment
John Browne's Regiment
Thomas Craig of Riccarton's Regiment
Charles Arnott's Regiment
Archibald Strachan's Regiment
Master of Forbes' Regiment
Walter Scott's Regiment
James Halkett's Regiment
Lord Mauchline's Regiment
Lord Brechin's Regiment
Arthur Erskine of Scotscraig's Regiment
Robert Adair of Kinhilt's Regiment
William Stewart's Regiment
Earl of Cassillis' Regiment
Robert Halkett's Regiment
Gibby Carr's Regiment

Scottish Foot: brigade structure based on Reid (see Source)
James Lumsden's Brigade
  General of the Artillery's Regiment
  William Douglas of Kirkness' Regiment
  James Lumsden's Regiment
James Campbell of Lawyers' Brigade
  James Campbell of Lawyers' Regiment
  George Preston of Valleyfield's Regiment
  John Haldane of Gleneagles' Regiment
Colin Pitscottie's Brigade
  Colin Pitscottie's Regiment
  David Holme of Wedderburn's Regiment
  John Lindsay of Edzell's Regiment
John Innes' Brigade
  John Innes' Regiment
  John Forbes of Leslie's Regiment
  Master of Lovat's Regiment

James Holburne's Brigade
  George Buchanan of Buchannan's Regiment
  James Holburne's Regiment
  Alexander Stewart's (Edinburgh) Regiment

Artillery
32 guns

The New Model Army: 11,000

Command
Commander-in-Chief: General Oliver Cromwell
Lieutenant General: Charles Fleetwood
Major General of the Horse: John Lambert
Master of the Ordnance: unknown

Horse
John Lambert's Brigade
  Charles Fleetwood's Regiment
  John Lambert's Regiment
  Edward Whalley's Regiment
Robert Lilburne's Brigade
  Robert Lilburne's Regiment
  Francis Hacker's Regiment
  Philip Twistelton's Regiment
Lord General's Regiment – operated independently under Cromwell's direct command

Foot
George Monck's Brigade
  George Monck's Regiment
  John Malverer's Regiment
  George Fenwick's Regiment
Thomas Pride's Brigade
  Thomas Pride's Regiment
  Lord General's Regiment
  John Lambert's Regiment
Robert Overton's Brigade
  Alban Cox's Regiment
  William Daniel's Regiment
  Charles Fairfax's Regiment

Artillery
Unknown; one account suggests that he placed two small field pierces with each foot regiment – possibly, therefore, 18 guns

Source: Reid, *Dunbar 1650, Cromwell's most famous victory*.

THE BATTLE AT WORCESTER, 3 SEPTEMBER 1651

The Royalist (largely Scottish) Army: 16,000

Command

Commander-in-Chief: Charles II

Lieutenant General: William Hamilton, 2nd Duke of Hamilton (he may not have held any formal rank)

(Lieutenant) General of the Horse: David Leslie

Sergeant Major General of Foot: Robert Montgomerie

Master of the Ordnance: James Wemyss

The Duke of Buckingham commanded the English element of the force

Worcester Castle

Rothes' Foot

Drummond's Foot

Fort Royal

Forbes' Foot

Powick Bridge (north bank)

Keith's Foot (c.700 men)

Rivers Teme/Severn confluence (under the command of Major General Pitscottie)

Pitscottie's Foot

MacLeod's Foot

Neil MacNeil's Foot (fought on the right flank of the MacLeods)

Sleat's Foot

On West Bank near St John's (under the overall command of Major General Robert Montgomerie)

Dalziel's Foot

Three (additional) regiments of foot

Montgomerie's Horse?

Cranston's Horse

Dunfermline's Horse

Linlithgow's Horse

North of the City on the east bank (under the command of Lt Gen David Leslie)

Leslie's Horse

Brechin's Horse

Craig of Riccarton's Horse

Rothes' Horse

Inside the City (under the command of James Wemyss)

The General of Artillery's Regiment

East of the City

7th Cavalry Brigade (under the command of the Duke of Hamilton)
  Hamilton's Horse Troop
  Buckingham's Horse
  Homes' Horse (probably single troop)

Charles II's Brigade
  Lifeguard of Horse
  Lifeguard of Foot
4th Cavalry Brigade
  Middleton's Horse
  Erskine of Scotcraig's Horse
  Mercer of Aldie's Horse
6th Cavalry Brigade (under the command of Van Druschke)
  Van Druschke's Horse
  James Forbes' Horse
  Mauchline's Horse
  Innes' Horse
Unbrigaded: Hurry's Horse

Foot (brigade structure unknown):

Earl of Atholl's

Master of Banff's Foot (c.500 men)

Master of Caithness's Foot

Sir James Cambell of Lawer's Foot

Sir George Douglas of Kirkness's Foot

Colonel James Grant's Foot (c.300 men)

Master of Gray's Foot

Major General Holburne's Foot

Earl of Kellie's Foot (c.960 men)

Lord Kintail's Foot (c.980 men)

Colonel John Lindsay of Edzell's Foot

Colonel Harie Maule's Foot

Sir Giorgi Preston of Valleyfield's Foot

Colonel William Gordon of Rothiemay's Foot (c.400 men)

Colonel Henry Sinclair's Foot

Colonel Walter Forces of Tolquhon's Foot (c.600 men)

Lord George Spynie's Foot (c.560 men)

Other clans that were present that may have been allocated to other regiments or fought in clan groups

Frazer (c.800 men)

Gunn

MacGregor

MacKay

Mackenzie

MacKinnon

MacNab

The Parliamentarian Army (NMA indicates a New Model Army unit): 30,000

West bank (under the command of Major General Fleetwood)

Left column
  Cobbett's Foot (NMA)
  Haynes' Foot
  Mathew's Foot – reserve
  Fleetwood's Horse (NMA)
Right column (under the command of Major General Richard Deane)
  Gibbon's Foot (NMA)
  Marsh's Foot
  Blake's Foot (NMA)
  Lord Gray's Foot

Column to Bransford Bridge (under Twisleton's command)
   Twistleton's Horse (NMA)
   Kendrick's Dragoons
   Worcestershire Dragoons
Column to Bewdley (under Colonel Blundell's command)
   Worcestershire Dragoons
   Worcestershire Horse
   Rich's Horse (NMA – 2 troops)
   Barton's Horse

East Bank under the command of Cromwell

Reserve Assault Force (under Cromwell's direct command)
First Wave
   Lifeguard Horse (NMA)
   Cromwell's Horse (NMA)
   Ingoldsby's Horse (NMA)
   C. Fairfax's Foot (NMA)
Second Wave
   Goffe's Foot (NMA)
   Deane's Foot (NMA)

Red Hill/Perry Hill (under the command of generals Lambert and Harrison)
Pride's Foot (NMA)
Cooper's Foot (NMA)
Lambert's Foot (NMA)
Duckenfield's Foot (NMA)
Cheshire Militia – 3 regiments under colonels Bradshaw, Brooke and Croxton – brigaded under command of Duckenfield
Essex Militia – 3 regiments under colonels Cooke, Honywood and Mathews
Worcestershire Militia
Surrey Militia – part only
Whalley's Horse (NMA)
Tomlinson's Horse (NMA)
Harrison's Horse (NMA)
Lambert's Horse (NMA)
Saunders' Horse (NMA)
Desborough's Horse (NMA)
Rich's Horse (NMA)

Source: Atkin, *Cromwell's Crowning Mercy.*
The Royalist numbers at 16,000 are almost certainly too high but they are based on Cromwell's estimate. The (Royalist) prisoner of Chester's figure is 12,000. James Turner, who as a Royalist adjutant ought to have known, says upward of 9,000 infantry and 4,000 cavalry plus the artillery on leaving Scotland. Parliamentarian spies at Blore Heath, *c.*17 August, put them at 5,000–6,000 weak horse and 6,000–7,000 sickly foot.

GLOSSARY

Absolutism: The political doctrine and practice of unlimited, centralized authority and absolute sovereignty, as vested especially in a monarch or dictator. The divine right of kings asserted that kings derived their authority from God and could not therefore be held accountable for their actions by any earthly authority, such as a parliament.

Arminianism: Relates to the doctrines of Jacobus Arminius, a Dutch Protestant theologian who rejected the Calvinist doctrine of predestination and reprobation. His teachings had a considerable influence on Methodism.

Assembly of Divines: The Westminster Assembly of Divines was a council of theologians and members of the English Parliament appointed to restructure the Church of England. It met from 1643 to 1653.

Battalia: Battle array or deployment for an army and the components of an army. It is also sometimes referred to as a *tercio*.

Calvinism: The Protestant theological system of John Calvin, and his successors, which developed Luther's doctrine of 'justification by faith alone' and centres on the doctrine of *predestination*.

Canister: Small bullets (musket or carbine balls) packed in tin cases that fit the bore of an artillery gun.

Caracole: A cavalry manoeuvre designed to incorporate gunpowder weapons into cavalry tactics. Cavalry would advance in formation and as each rank came into range of their adversary, the cavalry troopers would turn their mount slightly to one side, discharge one pistol, then turn slightly to the other side to discharge another pistol at their target. The horsemen then retired to the back of the formation to reload, and repeated the manoeuvre.

Cavalier: Derives from the same Latin root as the French word 'chevalier' (as well as the Spanish word 'caballero'). It was first used by Roundheads as a term of abuse for the Royalist military supporters of the King.

Clubmen: Refers to a movement essentially based upon groups of civilians who wished to remain neutral during the war. Their aims were far from revolutionary, wanting to be left alone during the conflict for which they desired a political settlement, an end to indiscriminate taxation, and the preservation of episcopacy and Protestantism.

Commanded musketeers (or shot): Musketeers temporarily attached to other units (usually horse) to provide firepower and protection.

Commission of Array: A commission given by English sovereigns to officers or gentry in a given territory, to muster and array the inhabitants and to see them in a condition for war, or to put soldiers of a country in a condition for military service.

Committee of Both Kingdoms: Developed from Committee of Safety in February 1644 to jointly conduct the war after the Scots joined forces with Parliament.

Committee of Estates: The Committee of Estates governed Scotland during the Wars of the Three Kingdoms, when the Parliament of Scotland was not in sitting.

Corslet: A piece of defensive armour covering the body, consisting of a *gorget*, breast covering, back and *tassets*, full arms and gauntlets.

Counter-march: The first rank (of infantry of armed cavalry) would fire and counter-march to the rear in order to reload, while the second rank marched forward and fired before they counter-marched, and so on. This provided the basis of a continuous volley fire. See also *caracole*.

Covenanters: Refers to those part of a Scottish Presbyterian movement who, in 1638, signed the 'National Covenant' to uphold the Presbyterian religion in Scotland. They derive their name from the term 'covenant' after the covenant between God and the Israelites in the Old Testament.

Derby House: The name given to the Committee of Both Houses that had assumed responsibility for conducting the war from the Committee of Both Kingdoms. It was so called because it met at Derby House, the London home of the Earl of Derby.

Diggers: The Diggers were a group of Protestant radicals, sometimes seen as forerunners of modern anarchism, with roots in pantheism, agrarian utopianism and Georgism. Gerrard Winstanley's followers were known as True Levellers and later became known as Diggers, because of their attempts to farm on common land.

Engagement, the: An agreement made between some Scottish Covenanter commissioners and King Charles I in December 1647. It committed the King to experiment with Presbyterianism in England in return for military intervention in England by the Scots on his behalf. The result was the invasion of England in 1648 and the start of the Second Civil War.

Engagers: The Engagers were a faction of the Scottish Covenanters, who made 'The Engagement' with King Charles I in December 1647, while he was imprisoned in Carisbrooke Castle by the English Parliamentarians after his defeat in the First Civil War.

Episcopalianism: The advocating of government of a church by bishops.

Faggot: A long fascine or bundle of sticks bound together and used for filling in marshy ground or other obstacles and for strengthening the sides of embankments, ditches, or trenches

Firelock musket: A musket having a lock in which the priming is ignited by sparks struck from flint and steel. Otherwise called a 'flintlock musket'. See also *matchlock musket*.

Forlorn Hope: From the Dutch meaning 'lost troop' it means a group of soldiers chosen or volunteered to take the leading part in a military operation, such as an assault on a defended position, where the risk of casualties is high. It is mainly used in describing the group leading the assault at a siege but during the civil war it was also often used to mean the vanguard.

Gorget: A steel or leather collar designed to protect the throat. By the beginning of the 16th century, the gorget became fully developed as a component of plate armour in its own right.

Granadoe: A grenade.

Grape shot: A type of shot that was a mass of small metal balls or slugs, packed tightly into a canvas bag.

Harquebus (or arquebus): An early muzzle-loaded firearm, used in the 15th–17th centuries.

Huguenots: French Protestants who were inspired by the writings of John Calvin and endorsed the reformed tradition of Protestantism.

Iconoclasm: The rejection or destruction of religious images as heretical.

Ironsides: Parliamentarian cavalry, formed by Cromwell, who were an elite fighting unit within the New Model Army.

Junto: A political grouping or faction, especially in 17th- and 18th-century Britain.

Laudianism: An early 17th-century reform movement within the Church of England, promulgated by Archbishop William Laud and his supporters (Laudians). It rejected the *predestination* upheld by the previously dominant *Calvinism* in favour of free will, and hence the possibility of salvation.

Levellers: The Levellers were a radical group that developed during the first English Civil War. They were committed to popular sovereignty, extended suffrage, equality before the law and religious tolerance. During 1647 the Levellers allied themselves with radical factions in the New Model Army.

Lutheranism: A major branch of Protestant Christianity, which identifies with the theology of Martin Luther (1483–1546).

(The) Marches: The (Welsh) Marches is a medieval European term for any kind of borderland; in this case, an imprecisely defined area along and around the border between England and Wales. The precise meaning of the term has varied over time.

Matchlock musket: A form of gunlock in which the priming was ignited by a slow-burning match.

Matross: A semi-skilled gunner.

Mercurius Aulicus: An English Civil War weekly newspaper, supporting the Royalist cause, appearing on Sundays from January 1643 until January 1646.

Mercurius Civicus: (The City Mercury) An English Civil War weekly newspaper, supporting the Parliamentarian cause, appearing on Thursdays from 4 May 1643 to 10 December 1646. Published by John Wright and Thomas Bates.

ORBAT: Order of battle; the detail and breakdown of an army.

Parliamentarian: A supporter of Parliament in the English Civil War; a Roundhead.

Poll Axe: A weapon resembling a mason's lathing hammer, with a sharp little axe on one side and a hammer on the other.

Posse comitatus: The common-law or statute law authority of a county sheriff, or other law officer, to conscript any able-bodied man to assist him in keeping the peace or to pursue and arrest a felon.

Predestination: The belief that some people are chosen to be saved while others are destined for damnation. It was generally accepted theology within the Church of England in the late 16th century, largely to refute the Catholic standpoint that people could be saved by good works.

Presbyterianism: A form of Protestant Church government in which the Church is administered locally by the minister with a group of elected elders of equal rank, and regionally and nationally by representative courts of ministers and elders.

Protestantism: A form of Christian faith and practice which originated with the Protestant Reformation, a movement against what its followers considered to be errors in the Roman Catholic Church.

Puritanism: English Reformed Protestants who sought to 'purify' the Church of England from its 'Catholic' practices, maintaining that the Church of England was only partially reformed since the Reformation.

Ranters: The Ranters were an antinomian group that developed around the time of the English Commonwealth (1649–60). They rejected the church structure and common morality and argued that there was no need for social institutions like marriage, or sins like blasphemy. They were largely 'common people' and there is plenty of evidence that the movement was widespread throughout England, though they were poorly organized.

Reformado: An officer deprived of command by the reorganization or disbandment of his troops but retaining rank and receiving full or half pay.

Reformadoes: The term applied to reformed regiments, bodies of discharged officers, or those whose original regiments had been disbanded.

Reiter: Reiter or Schwarze Reiter ('black riders') were a type of light cavalry in 16th- and 17th-century Central Europe. Similar to the French Argoulets, they were recruited in northern Germany and used smaller, more agile horses.

Roundhead: A supporter of Parliament in the English Civil War; a Parliamentarian. It arose from the Puritans' custom of wearing their hair cut close round their heads, like apprentices, who shortened their hair to demonstrate their contempt for lovelocks.

Sconce (English): A small fort or earthwork defending a ford, pass, or castle gate.

Self-Denying Ordinance: A bill passed by the House of Commons on 19 December 1644, stipulating that no member of the House of Commons or the House of Lords could hold any command in the army or navy.

Swedish Feather or Swinefeather: A shortened version of the pike that was issued to musketeers to provide additional protection from cavalry (it was used in the same manner as the archer's stakes of the Hundred Years' War).

Targe: Old English word for shield.

Tassets: A piece of plate armour designed to protect the upper thighs.

Tenaille (archaic Tenalia): An advanced defensive work, in front of the main defences of a fortress, which takes its name from resemblance, real or imaginary, to the lip of a pair of pincers.

Tercio: A tercio was a powerful Spanish infantry division or brigade during the time of Hapsburg Spain. It was an all-arms formation consisting of an administrative unit and 10 or 12 companies of soldiers.

Wain: Wagon or cart.

BIBLIOGRAPHY

Note of dates: In 1582, the Gregorian calendar reform restored 1 January as New Year's Day. When the new calendar was put in use, the error accumulated in the 13 centuries since the Council of Nicaea was corrected by a deletion of ten days. The Julian calendar day Thursday, 4 October 1582 was followed by the first day of the Gregorian calendar, Friday, 15 October 1582. Most Catholic countries adopted the Gregorian calendar almost immediately, but it was only gradually adopted among Protestant countries. Britain did not adopt the reformed calendar until 1752. Therefore, some of the dates of battles which we refer to, using the Gregorian calendar, do not match those used at the time in Britain which still remained, during the period of the wars, on the Julian calendar.

Note: the bold text is used to identify the source title used in the footnotes.

BRITISH LIBRARY

Anon, *Joyfull newes from Plimouth* (London, 1643). Thomason /18:E.102[9].

Anon, *A true relation of the great and glorious victory through Gods providence, obtained by **Sir William Waller, Sir Arthur Haslerig** and others of the Parliament forces* (London, 1643). Thomason /11:E.60[12].

Anon, ***Hulls managing** of the kingdoms cause: or, A brief historicall relation of the severall plots and attempts against Kingston upon Hull* (London, 1644). Thomason /9:E.51[11].

Anon, *A brief and true Relation of the Siege and **Surrendering of King's Lyn** to the Earl of Manchester* (London, 1643). Thomason / 12:E.67[28].

Anon, *The **Round-heads remembrancer**: or, a true and particular relation of the great defeat given to the rebels by His Majesties good subjects of the county of Cornwall* (London,1643). Thomason /19:E.105[13].

Anon, *A true relation of the late fight betweene the right honourable the **Earle of Manchester's forces** and the Marquesse of Newcastle's forces on Wednesday the 11 day of this instant October, 1643* (London, 1643). Wing /240:E.71[5].

Anon, *A true narration of the most observable passages, in and at the **late siege of Plymouth**, from the fifteenth day of September 1643, until the twenty fifth of December following* (London, 1644). Thomason /6:E.31[15]. This is incorrectly attributed to the pen of Prince Maurice, but it is a narration written by a Parliamentarian.

Anon, *A true relation of the late expedition of His Excellency, Robert Earle of Essex, for the **relief of Gloucester*** (London, 1643). Wing / 240:E.70[10].

Anon Eyewitness, *His Highnesse Prince **Rupert's raising of the siege** at Newarke upon Trent, March 21. 1643* (1644). Thomason / 7:E.38[10].

Anon, *A **glorious victory obtained by Sr. Thomas Fairfax**, June, the 14 1645* (London, 1645). Thomason / 47:E.288[21].

Anon, *The **Kings forces totally routed by the Parliaments army*** (London, 1645). Thomason / 50:E.303[18].

Anon, *The **Articles of Exeter***. Wing / 1394:11.

Anon, ***Rupert's marching out of Oxford*** (London, 1646). Thomason / 55:E.341[17].

Anon, *Articles concluded & agreed on for the **surrender of Oxford & Farringdon** to His Excellency Sir Tho Fairfax* (London, 1646). Thomason / 55:E.341[15].

Anon, *A **bloody fight at Black-Water in Ireland*** (London, 1646). Thomason / 55:E.340[21].

Anon, *A **declaration from the Isle of Wight*** (London, 1648). Thomason / 68:E.435[14].

Anon, *A list of the prisoners taken, and those that were slain by Collonell **Horton in South-Wales*** (London, 1648). Thomason / 69:E.441[33].

Anon, ***Colonell Poyers forces in Wales** totally routed* (London, 1648). Thomason / 69:E.441[26].

Anon, *The Scots resolution, wherein, they express their intentions to come to **Sir Marmaduke Langdale*** (London, 1648). Wing / 2359:17.

Anon, *A **diary of the siege of Colchester** by the forces under the command of Generall Fairfax* (Colchester, 1648). Wing / 2512:06.

Anon, *A **letter from Holland**: being a true relation of all the proceedings of the Northern armies* (Holland, 1648). Thomason / 75:E.467[21].

Anon, *The **resolution of the Kings Majesties subjects** in the county of Cornwall* (London, 1648). Thomason / 72:E.456[18].

Anon, *An Exact and perfect relation of the proceedings of the **army under the command of Sir Thomas Fairfax**, from the sixth of this instant July to the eleventh of the same* (London, 1645). Wing / 316:10.

Archer, E., *A fuller relation of the great victory obtained… at **Alsford**, on Friday the 28 of March* (London, 1644). Wing / 45:03.

Ashe, S., *A continuation of **true intelligence from the English and Scottish forces** in the north* – Issue number: 5, Date 10 June–10 July 1644 (London, 1644). Thomason / 1:E.2[1].

Atkyns, R., *The **vindication of Richard Atkyns** Esquire* (London, 1669). Wing / 1877:11.

Balfour, W., *Sir **Willam Balfores letter** of March 30 1644 to His Excellency the Earl of Essex Lord Generall* (London, 1644). Thomason / 7:E.40[13].

Belasyse, J., *A letter to the Honoble William Lenthal Esq; Speaker to the Honorable House of Commons, from the commissioners imployed by the Parliament for the **reducing of Newark*** (London, 1646). Thomason / 54:E.330[23].

Bishop, G., *A more **particular and exact relation of the victory** obtained by the Parliaments forces under the command of Sir Thomas Fairfax* (London, 1645). Thomason / 47:E.288[38].

Blackwell, J., *A more exact relation of the **great defeat given to Goring's army** in the west; by the victorious Sr. Thomas Fairfax* (London, 1645). Thomason / 48:E.293[8].

Blount, T., ***Boscobel**, or, The compleat history of His Sacred Majesties most miraculous preservation after the Battle of Worcester, 3 Sept., 1651* (London, 1680). Wing / 836:14.

Bowles, E. (ed.), *A true relation of the late proceedings of the **Scottish army*** (London, 1644). Thomason / 6:E.33[17].

Brereton, W., Myddleton, T., and Meldrum, J., *__Letters from Sir William Brereton, Sir Thomas Middleton, Sir John Meldrum__ of the great victory, by God's providence, given them in raising the siege from before Mountgomery-castle* (London, 1644). Wing / 229:E.10[4].

Bury, *A briefe relation of the **siege at Newark*** (London, 1644). Thomason / 7:E.39[8].

Byron, J., *Sir **John Byron's Relation** to the secretary, of the last westerne action between the Lord Willmott and Sir William Waller on Thursday, July 13, 1643* (York, 1643). Wing / 131:14.

Carter, M., *A most true and exact relation of that as honourable as **unfortunate expedition of Kent, Essex, and Colchester*** (Colchester, 1650). Wing / 347:03.

Charles I, *The **Kings cabinet opened**: or, certain packets of secret letters & papers, written with the Kings own hand, and taken in his cabinet at Nasby-Field, June 14* (London, 1645). Wing / 2205:08.

Charles II, *A **great fight at Colchester** upon Tuesday night last, being the 25. of this instant July* (London, 1648). Thomason / 72:E.454[15].

Clampe, R., *A Description of the Seidge of Newarke upon Trent* (1646). British Library (maps) 4670 (I).

Coe, R., *__An exact diarie__. Or A breife relation of the progresse of Sir William Wallers army since the joyning of the London avxilliaries with his forces: which was the twelfth of May 1644. untill their returne homeward on Thursday the 11 of July following* (London, 1644). Thomason / 1:E.2[20].

Colonell in the Army, *A true relation* of the late fight betweene Sr. William Wallers forces and those sent from Oxford (London, 1643). Wing / 239:E.61[6].

Compton, James Earl of Northampton, *The battaile on Hopton-Heath in Staffordshire, March 19.* (Oxford, 1643). Thomason / 17:E.99[18].

Corbet, J., *A true and impartiall history of the military government of the citie of Gloucester* (London, 1647). 64:E.402[4].

Corbet, J., *An historicall relation of the military government of Gloucester* (London, 1645). Thomason / 50:E.306[8].

Cromwell, O., *A letter from the Lord General Cromwell*, touching the great victory obtained neer Worcester (London, 1651). Thomason / 98:E.641[5].

Digby, G., *A true and impartiall relation of the battaile betwixt, His Majesties Army, and that of the rebells neare Newbery in Berk-shire* (Oxford, 1643). Thomason / 12:E.69[10].

Dillingham, J. (ed.), *The Parliament scout Date: 1643–1645* (London). Thomason / 12:E.71[25].

D. R., *A great fight at Walmer Castle in the county of Kent* (London, 1648). Thomason / 71:E.451[21].

Ellis, T., *An exact and full relation of the last fight, between the Kings forces and Sir William Waller* (London, 1644). Thomason / 9:E.53[18].

Emminent (sic) officer of the army, *An exact and perfect relation of every particular of the fight at Worcester and ordering the battle on both sides of the river of Severne* (London, 1651). Wing / 66:14. Copy from: Yale University Library.

Essex, *The copie of a letter from the Lord Generall his quarters* (London, 1644). Thomason / 2:E.8[22].

Essex, *Two letters from his excellencie Robert Earl of Essex* (London, 1643). Thomason / 10:E.55[19].

Fairfax, F., *A letter from the Right Honourable Ferdinando Lord Fairfax, to His Excellency Robert Earle of Essex* (London, 1643). Thomason / 12:E.71[15].

Fairfax, T., *Three letters, from the Right Honourable Sir Thomas Fairfax, Lieut. Gen. Cromwell and the committee residing in the army* (London, 1645). Thomason / 47:E.288[27].

Fairfax, T., *The coppie of a letter from Sir Thomas Fairfax his quarters to the Parliament* (London, 1645). Thomason / 44:E.261[4].

Fairfax, T., *Sir Thomas Fairfax letter to the Honorable William Lenthal Esq; Speaker of the Honorable House of Commons* (London, 1646). Thomason / 53:E.324[15].

Fairfax, T., *A letter from His Excellency the Lord Fairfax to the House of Peers* (London, 1648). Thomason / 70:E.445[40].

Fiennes, N., *A relation made in the House of Commons, by Col: Nathaniel Fiennes, concerning the surrender of the city and castle of Bristoll, August 5 1643* (London, 1643). Thomason / 11:E.64[12].

Fiennes, N., *Colonell Fiennes letter to my lord general concerning Bristol, 22 August 1643* (London, 1643). Wing / 239:E.65[26].

Fiennes, N., *A most true Relation of the Battell fought by his Excellency and his Forces against the bloody Cavalliers. A Letter, Purporting the true relation of the Skirmish at Worcester* (London, 1642). Thomason / E.126[39].

Foster, H., *A true and exact relation of the marchings of the two regiments of the trained-bands of the city of London* (London, 1643). Wing/ 240:E.69[15].

Gentleman in Northampton, *A more exact and perfect relation of the great victory (by Gods providence) obtained by the Parliaments forces under command of Sir Tho. Fairfax in Naisby field, on Saturday 14. June 1645* (London, 1645). Thomason / 47:E.288[28].

Goode, W., *A particular relation of the severall removes, services, and successes of the Right Honorable the Earle of Manchesters army* (London, 1644). Thomason / 8:E.47[8].

Hamilton, *Bloody newes from the Scottish Army* (London, 1648). Thomason / 72:E.453[34].

H. T., *A glorious victorie obtained by Sir William Waller, and Sir William Balfoure, against the Lord Hoptons forces, neere Alsford, on Fryday last March 29* (London, 1644). Wing / 418:15.

Humbie, A., *A letter from Newcastle, to the Right Honourable the Lord High Chancellor of Scotland… Containing a relation of the taking of the town of Newcastle by storm* (London, 1644). Thomason / 3:E.14[8].

Ibbitson, R., *Perfect occurrences of every dayes journall in Parliament* (London 1647–49). Thomason / 83:E.533[15].

Inchiquin, Murrough O'Brien, *A true relation of a great victory obtained by the forces under the command of the Lord Inchiquine in Munster in Ireland, against the rebels under the command of Lord Taaff, Novemb. 13, 1647* (London, 1647). Thomason / 66:E.418[6].

Jones, *A letter from Captain Jones* (London, 1644). Thomason / 7:E.40[12].

Jones, M., *An exact and full relation of the great victory obtained against the rebels at Dungons-Hill in Ireland, August 8. 1647* (London, 1647). Thomason / 64:E.402[27].

Kightley, E., *A full and true relation of the great battle fought between the Kings army, and His Excellency, the Earle of Essex, upon the 23 of October last past* (London, 1642). Thomason / 22:E.126[13].

Langdale, M., *An impartiall relation of the late fight at Preston* (1648). Thomason / 74:E.464[42].

Laugharne, R., *A declaration by Major General Laughorn, and the rest of the forces joyned with him in Wales* (London, 1648). Thomason / 70:E.442[8].

Leslie, A., *A letter from Generall Leven, the Lord Fairfax, and the Earl of Manchester, to the committee of both kingdoms, and by them communicated to the Parliament* (Edinburgh, 1644). Wing / 1618:16.

Lilburne, J., *A more full relation of the great battell fought betweene Sir Tho: Fairfax, and Goring. on Thursday last* (London, 1645). Thomason / 48:E.293[3].

Lloyd, D., *Memoires of the lives, actions, sufferings & deaths of those noble, reverend, and excellent personages, that suffered by death, sequestration, decimation, or otherwise, for the Protestant religion, and the great principle thereof, allegiance to their soveraigne, in our late intestine wars, from the year 1637, to the year 1660* (London, 1667). Wing / 2127:14.

Matthew, R., *A diary and relation of passages in, and about Dublin: from the first of August, 1647. to the tenth of the same* (London, 1647). Wing / 2352:01.

Morgan, T., *Morgan Governor of Glocester's letter to the Honoble William Lenthal Esq; Speaker to the Honorable House of Commons* (London, 1646). Thomason / 54:E.329[7].

Morgan, T., *A true relation by Colonell Morgan, in a letter of the totall routing of the Lord Ashley, by him and Sir William Brereton at Stow* (London, 1646). Thomason / 54:E.329[8].

Mercurius Aulicus, Communicating the Intelligence and Affaires of the Court (January 1643–January 1646, Birkenhead, John & Heylyn, Peter). See glossary.

Mercurius Civicus, Londons intelligencer, or, Truth really imparted from thence to the whole kingdome to prevent misinformation (1643–46, Bates, Thomas & Wright, John). See glossary.

Numerous, *An exact and true relation of the dangerous and bloody fight, betweene His Majesties Army, and the Parliaments forces, neer Kyneton in the county of Warwicke, the 23 of this instant October* (London, 1642). Wing / 1758:48.

Officer of the Parliaments army, *A perfect narrative of the battell of Knocknones* (London, 1647). Thomason / 66:E.418[10].

Parliamentary Report, *An exact and true relation of the dangerous and bloody fight, betweene His Majesties Army, and the Parliaments forces, neer Kyneton in the county of Warwicke, the 23 of this instant October* (London, 1642). Wing / 1758:48.

Pye, R., *A more exact relation of the siege laid to the town of Leicester* (London, 1645). Thomason / 47:E.287[6].

Rainsborough, T., *A true relation of the storming Bristoll* (London, 1645). Thomason / 49:E.301[5].

R. B. and E. H., *A true relation of the sad passages, between the two armies in the west* (London, 1644). Thomason / 2:E.10[27].

R. C., *The present condition of Dublin in Ireland* (London, 1649). Thomason / 86:E.562[11].

R. S., *A true and fuller relation of the battell fought at Stow in the Would, March 21. 1645* (London, 1646). Wing / 2041:04.

Rupert, Prince, *A briefe relation of the siege at Newark* (London, 1644). Thomason / 7:E.39[8].

Rupert, Prince, *A declaration of His Highness Prince Rupert* (London, 1645). Thomason / 50:E.308[32].

Rushworth, J., *An ordinance of the Lords and Commons assembled in Parliament* (London 1645). Thomason / 47:E.288[26].

Rushworth, J., *The Fight between His Excellency **Lord Fairfax's forces at Maidstone** – A letter sent to the Honorable William Lenthal Esq; Speaker of the Honorable House of Commons* (London, 1648). Thomason / 70:E.445[37].

Smith, W., *A true and exact relation of the proceedings and **victorious successe of the ships** in the service of the King and Parliament* (London, 1644). Thomason / 8:E.42[14].

Stewart, W., *A **full relation of the late victory** obtained (through Gods providence) by the forces under the command of Generall Lesley, the Lord Fairfax, and the Earl of Manchester* (London, 1644). Thomason / 10:E.54[19].

Symmons, E., ***A vindication of King Charles**: or, A loyal subjects duty* (1648). Wing / 2179:01.

Temple, P., ***An examination examined*** (London 1645). Thomason / 50:E.303[13].

T. V., *A True relation of the late **battell neere Newbery*** (London, 1643). Wing / 240:E.69[2].

Watson, L., *A more **exact relation of the late battell neer York**; fought by the English and Scotch forces, against Prince Rupert and the Marquess of Newcastle* (London, 1644). Thomason / 1:E.2[14].

Weare, J., *The **apologie of Colonell John Were*** (London, 1644). Thomason / 4:E.21[34].

W. G., ***A just apologie** for an abused armie* (London, 1647). Thomason / 59:E.372[22].

Worthy Gentleman in Sir Thomas Fairfax His Army, *A letter sent to the Right Honourable William Lenthall Esquire, Speaker to the Honourable House of Commons, **Concerning the Routing of Colonel Goring's Army near Bridgewater*** (London, 1645). Thomason / 48:E.293[17].

W. R., *An exact relation of the last newes from the quarters of His Excellency, the **Lord Generall of the Scottish Army*** (London, 1644). Thomason / 7:E.37[3].

BRITISH MUSEUM

MS No. 6789 – Isaac Tullie: Narrative of the Siege of Carlisle.

MS 16370, f. 64, de Gomme, B., Order of his Majesty.

MS 27402, F. 82., Sir William Ogle, *A True Relation of My Lord Ogle's Engagements Before the Battle of Edgehill and After, Written by Himself About the Year 1645*.

NATIONAL ARCHIVES

NA SP28/145 f.60r – Artillery Train for New Model Army.

NA SP16/539/2 – ***A true relation of the passages that were in his Ex[cellen]cies army after such time as Colonel Were came into it**, p. f.195v.*

OXFORD UNIVERSITY/BODLEIAN LIBRARY

Atkinson, J. A., *Tracts relating to the **Civil War in Cheshire**, 1641–1659: including Sir George Booth's rising in that county* (Manchester, 1909). Printed for the Chetham Society xiv. Duke Humphries, R.Top 230 (ii,65).

Calendar of State Papers Domestic (***CSPD***): Charles I, 23 volumes (London, HMSO, 1888).

Calendar of State Papers Domestic (***CSPD -I***): Interregnum 1650, 13 volumes (London, 1876).

Chadwyck-Healey, C. E. H. (ed.), ***Bellum Civile**, Hopton's Narrative of his Campaign in the West (1642–1644)* (Somerset Record Society – London, 1902). Bodleian, Duke Humphries, R.Top 375(18).

*His Highness **Prince Rupert's Late Beating up** the Rebel's Quarters at Post-Comb and Chinner and his victory at Chalgrove Field on Sunday morning18 June 1643* (Oxford, 1643).

Paulden, T., ***Pontefract Castle**, An account how it was taken: and how General Rainsborough was surprised in his quarters at Doncaster, anno 1648* (London, 1702).

Portland MS, *Letter **Captain Robert Harley** to Colonel Edward Harley dated 12 April 1643 (covers the Battle of Cheriton), vol. III, pp. 106–10 (K3.550.29(3)).*

Walker, E., ***Historical discourses**, upon several occasions: viz. I. The happy progress and success of the arms of K. Charles I. of ever blessed memory, from the 30th of March, to the 23rd of November, 1644* (London, 1705). Ref:[16], 369 [1].

INTERNET SOURCES

BCW Project – http://bcw-project.org/

British History Online – http://www.british-history.ac.uk/search/series/rushworth-papers

BL – https://www.bl.uk/collection-items/autograph-manuscript-of-king-james-vi-and-is-basilikon-doron-or-the-kings-gift#

Wisconsin University – Ship Money:

http://faculty.history.wisc.edu/sommerville/123/123%20303%20Personal%20Rule.htm#Ship Money

http://research.ucc.ie/celt/document/E650001-001 Gilbert, J. T. (ed.), *Diaries of the proceedings of the forces in Ireland.*

SOURCES AVAILABLE ONLINE

Braddick J., ***War and Politics** in England and Wales, 1642–1646* (2014).

Corbet, J., *An historicall relation of the military government of **Gloucester**, from the beginning of the Civill Warre betweene King and Parliament, to the removall of Colonell Massie from that government to the command of the westerne forces* (London, 1645).

Everett Green, M. A. (ed.), ***Letters of Queen Henrietta Maria**, including her private correspondence with Charles the First* (London, 1857).

Gilbert, J. T. (ed.), ***Diaries of the proceedings of the forces in Ireland** under Sir Hardress Waller and the Lord Deputy Ireton, from 20th July, 1650, to 5th November, 1651, by officers in the Parliamentary Army in Ireland.*

Hampshire Record Office: *The Extract of a Survey of Cheriton Manor 1534 (HRO) 45M83/PZ2, A Survey of Cheriton Manor 1602-04 (HRO) 53M67/1 and the Sale by Parliamentary Trustees of Bishopric Lands in Tichborne, 1649 (HRO) 11M59/BP/E/T1.*

Ingram, M., *Naseby: What happened after the battle?* https://www.academia.edu/.

Parliamentary Report on the Battle of Edgehill: *A Relation of the Battel between his Majesty's Army and the Parliament's Forces, under the Command of the Earl of Essex, at Edghill near Keynton in the County of Warwick, Octob. the 23d, 1642, as it was communicated to the Speaker and Commons Assembled in Parliament, and by them Ordered to be Printed and Published.*

Peacey, J., *The **Revolution in Print*** (2014).

Phillips, J. E., *Memoirs of the **Civil War in Wales** and the Marches 1642–1649*, two volumes (London, 1874).

Royalist Papers, *A Relation of the Battel fought between Keynton and Edgehill, by His Majesty's Army and that of the Rebels* (Printed by his Majesty's Command at Oxford by Leonard Lichfield, Printer to the University, 1642).

Rushworth Papers, Private Passages of State, (Originally published by D Browne, London, 1721) – See Internet sources, **British History Online**.

MISCELLANEOUS SECONDARY SOURCES/ JOURNALS & PERIODICALS

*A History of the **County of Chester**, vol. V, Part 1, The City of Chester: General History and Topography* (London, 2003).

*A History of the **County of Stafford**, vol. 14, Lichfield.* (Originally published by Victoria County History, London, 1990).

*An Inventory of the **Historical Monuments in City of York**, vol. II, The Defences* (HMSO London, 1972).

Battle of Worcester Society, *The **Battle of Worcester**, a collection of essays on the history of the battle of Worcester, 1651* (Worcester, 2012).

Beardsley, W. F., *An Account of the battle of **Willoughby Field**, in the County of Nottingham* (Journal of the Leicestershire Architectural Society, 1908).

Blackmore, D., **Counting the New Model Army** (English Civil War Times No. 58, Partizan Press, 2003).

Browne, G. F., **From Leicester to Langport**, *1645* (Journal of the Royal United Services Institute XXXIX, 1895) pp. 253–67.

Bruce, J., *The Quarrel between the* **Earl of Manchester and Oliver Cromwell**, *an episode of the Civil War* (Camden Society, 1875).

Clonmel Town Walls Conservation & Management Plan (Dublin, 2009).

Cooper, J., and Elrington, E. R. (ed.), **A History of the County of Essex**, Volume 9 (London, 1994).

Day, J., Michael **Jones and the Defeat of Royalist Ireland** *1647-9*.

Dore, R. N., and Lowe, J., *The* **Battle of Nantwich** in *Transactions of the Historic Society of Cheshire and Lancashire* (1961).

Dunrobin Muniments, *a letter from the Battle of Hopton Heath* in the Staffordshire Record Society's volume for 1936, pp. 181–4.

Ede-Borrett, S., *The Royalist Army at the Second Battle of Newbury 27 October 1644*, JSAHR, Vol. 77 (1999).

Firth, C. H., The English Historical Review, Vol. 13, No. 52 (Oct., 1898). *The* **Journal of Prince Rupert's Marches**, *5 Sept. 1642 to 4 July 1646*, pp. 729–41.

Firth, C. H., **Marston Moor**, Transactions of the Royal Historical Society, vol. XII, pp. 17–79 (London, 1898).

Firth, C. H., *The Battle of* **Dunbar**, Transactions of the Royal Historical Society, New Series, Vol. 14, pp. 19–52 (Cambridge, 1900).

Historic Scotland, *The Inventory of Historic Battlefields* – **Battle of Inverkeithing** *II*, dated 14 December 2012.

Hyett, F. A., **The Last battle** *of the First Civil War*. Published by the Bristol and Gloucestershire Archaeological Society (Bristol, 1888).

Lattey, R. T., Parsons, E. J. S., and Philip I. G., A Contemporary Map of the Defences of Oxford in 1644. (Oxoniensia, 1936).

Leadman, A. D. H., **The Battle of Marston Moor**. Yorkshire Archaeological and Topographical Journal, vol. XI, pp. 289–347 (London, 1891).

Lester D., and Lester G., *The Military and Political Importance of the* **Battle of Chalgrove** *(1643)*. Oxoniensia, 80 (2015), pp. 27–40.

Lewis, D. E. (Doctoral Thesis), *The Office of Ordnance and the Parliamentarian land forces 1642–1648* (Loughborough, 1976).

Malbron, T., *Memorials of the Civil War in Cheshire and the Adjacent Counties, 1651*, Cowper MSS (J. Hall [ed], The Record Society of Lancashire and . Cheshire, 1889).

Marsh, S., **Military Bridging Operations During the Civil War**, Arquebusier Magazine, vol. XXXVI/I pp. 3–25.

Marsh, S., **Battalia** (e-journal of the Battlefields Trust) vol. I, December 2017, **Maidstone** 1648, pp. 42–58.

Marsh, S., 'This Disarmed Multitude': The Impact of the Lostwithiel Campaign on the Earl of Essex's Army and its Reconstruction for Second Newbury (unpublished, 2017).

Morris, R. H., and Lawson p. H., **The Siege of Chester** *1643–1646*. The Journal of Chester & North Wales Archaeological and Historical Society (Chester, 1923), Volume XXV.

Rigaud, G., **Lines formed round Oxford**, *with notices of the part taken by the university in behalf of the Royalist cause, between 1642 and 1646.* Archaeological journal of the Archaeological Institute of Great Britain and Ireland, vol. III, (London, 1851).

Robinson, G., *Equine Battering Rams? A Reassessment of Cavalry Charges in the English Civil War* pp. 718–731. The Journal of Military History, vol. 75, No. 3 dated July 2011.

Royal Commission on Historical Monuments – England. City of Oxford (London, 1939).

Royal Commission on Historical Monuments – Newark on Trent: The Civil War siegeworks (London, 1964).

Shaw, S., *The* **history and antiquities of Staffordshire**. *Compiled from the manuscripts of Huntbach, Loxdale, Bishop Lyttelton, and other collections of Dr. Wilkes. The Rev. T. Feilde, &c. &c. including Erdeswick's survey of the county; and the approved parts of Dr. Plot's natural history*, two volumes (London, 1798). Gale Document Number: CW3303537075.

Stevenson, J., and Cater, A., *The Raid on Chinnor and the* **Fight at Chalgrove Field**, *June 17 and 18 1643*. Oxoniensia, 38 (1973) pp. 346–56.

Terry, C. S., *Papers relating to the* **Army of the Solemn League and Covenant**, *1643–1647*, Scottish Historical Society, two volumes (Edinburgh, 1917).

Walters, M. and Hunnisett, K., *The* **English Civil War Battlefield of Montgomery** *– September 18th 1644,* archaeological assessment, Clwyd-Powys Archaeological Trust (Welshpool, 1995).

Young, C., *Carisbrooke Castle* (English Heritage Guidebook, 2013).

Young, P., *The Battle of* **Hopton Heath**, *19th March 1643,* in the Journal of the Society for Army Historical Research, XXXIII (1954).

Young, P., *King Charles I's Army of 1643–1645*, Journal of the Society for Army Historical Research, Vol. 18 (1939).

PRIMARY SOURCES

Barriffe, W., **Military Discipline**: *or the Yong Artillery Man Wherein is Discoursed and Showne the Postures Both of Musket and Pike* (London, 1635).

Bell, R., *Memorials the civil war: comprising the* **correspondence of the Fairfax family** *with the most distinguished personages engaged in that memorable contest* (London, 1849).

Binns, J., *Memoirs and Memorials of Sir Hugh* **Cholmley** *of Whitby, 1600–1657* (Yorkshire Archaeological Society, 2002).

Birch, J., **Military memoire Colonel John Birch**, *sometime governor of Hereford in the civil war between Charles I and the Parliament* (Campden Historical Society, 1873).

Bruce, J., **Charles I in 1646**, *The letters of King Charles I to Queen Henrietta Maria* (Campden Society, 1856).

Bulstrode, R., **Memoirs and Reflections** *upon the reign and government of King Charles I and King Charles II* (London, 1720).

Byron, J., **Account of the Siege of Chester**. Cheshire Sheaf, 4th series, No. 6, 1971.

Carlyle, T., *Oliver* **Cromwell's Letters** *and Speeches,* two volumes (London, 1907).

Carte, T. (ed.), *A* **Collection of Original Letters** *and Papers found among the Duke of Ormonde's Papers*, two volumes (London 1739).

Cary, H., **Memorials of the Great Civil War** *in England from 1646 to 1652*, two volumes (London, 1842).

Clarendon, E. H., *The* **history of the rebellion** *and civil wars in England: to which is added an historical view of the affairs of Ireland*, six volumes (Oxford, 1826).

Cruso, J., **Militarie Instructions for the Cavallrie** (Cambridge, 1632).

Dore, R. N., *The* **Letter Books of William Brereton**, two volumes (Stroud, 1990).

Ede-Borrett, S. (ed.), *The* **Storm of Bristol**: *De Gomme's Account* (1996).

Fairfax, T., **Short memorials** *of Thomas Lord Fairfax.* Published in the Yorkshire Archaeological and Topographical Journal, vol. VIII, pp. 199–258 (London, 1884).

Firth, C. H. (ed.), **Memoirs** *of the Life of William Cavendish* **Duke of Newcastle** (London, 1886).

Firth, C. H. (ed.), *The* **Memoirs of Edmund Ludlow**, *Lieutenant-General of The Horse in the Army of The Commonwealth of England 1625–1672*, three volumes (Oxford, 1894).

Fraser, J., **Chronicles of the Frasers**, *The Wardlaw Manuscript* (Edinburgh, 1905).

Hamper, W. (ed.), *The Life, Diary, And Correspondence of Sir* **William Dugdale**, *Knight, Sometime Garter Principal King of Arms* (London, 1827).

Harrington, J., *The* **Commonwealth of Oceana** (London, 1656).

Heath, J. A., **Chronicle of The Late Intestine War** *In The Three Kingdoms Of England, Scotland And Ireland With The Intervening Affairs Of Treaties and Other Occurrences Relating Thereunto* (London, 1676).

Hill, P. R. and Watkinson, J. M., *Major* **Sanderson's War**, *Diary of a Parliamentary Cavalry Officer* (Stroud, 2008).

Hollis, D., **Memoirs of Denzil Lord Hollis**, *from the year 1641 to 1648* (London, 1699).

Hutchinson, L. (ed.), *Memoirs of the* **Life of Colonel Hutchinson** (London, 1885).

Laing, D. (ed.), *the* **Letters and Journals of Robert Baillie**: *Principal of the University of Glasgow, 1637–1662*, three volumes (Edinburgh, 1841–2).

Letchmere, Captain Edmund, **Calendar of his letters in the Worcester Record Office** (Worcester 1692–1701). TRN/25

Lithgow, W., *An Experimental and Exact Relation upon that famous and renowned **Siege of Newcastle*** (Edinburgh, 1645).

Long, C. E. (ed.), ***Richard Symonds's diary of the marches*** *of the Royal Army* (Cambridge UP, 1997).

Marsh, S. (ed.), ***Train of Artillery*** *of the Earl of Essex: The accounts of Sir Edward Peyto, Lt. General of the Train of Artillery, October 1642–September 1643* (Romford, 2016).

May, T., ***History of Parliament of England*** (1647) and *A Breviary of the History of the Parliament of England* (1650).

McKenna, J. (ed.), *A Journal of the English Civil War. The **Letter Book** of Sir **William Brereton**, Spring 1646* (Jefferson, 2012).

Monkhouse, T. (ed.), ***State Papers Collected by Edward Earl of Clarendon***, three volumes (Oxford, 1773).

Norton, R., ***Of the Art of Great Artillery*** (London, 1624).

Norton, R., ***The Gunner*** (London, 1628).

Norton, R., ***The Gunner's Dialogue*** (London, 1643).

Nye, N., ***Art of Gunnery*** (London, 1647).

Parsons, D., *The Diary of Sir **Henry Slingsby**, Of Scriven* (London, 1836).

Peachey, S. (ed.), ***Richard Symonds*** *The Complete Military Diary* (Partizan Press, 1989).

Phillips, J. R., ***Memoirs of the Civil War in Wales*** *and the Marches 1642–1649, two volumes* (London, 1874).

Roy, I. (ed.), *Royal **Ordnance Papers***, two parts (Oxfordshire Record Society, 1969).

Rushworth, J., ***Historical collections***. *Containing the principal matters which happened from the meeting of the Parliament, November the 3rd 1640. to the end of the year 1644. Part Three in Two Volumes* (London, 1692).

Slingsby, H., and Hodgson, J., ***Original Memoirs, written during the Great Civil war***; *Being the life of Sir Henry Slingsby, and memoirs of Captain Hodgson* (Edinburgh, 1806).

Sprigge, J., ***Anglia Rediviva***; *England's recovery being the history of the motions, actions, and successes of the army under the immediate conduct of his excellency, Sir Thomas Fairfax, KT, Captain-General of all the Parliament's forces in England* (London, 1647 – this edition Oxford, 1854).

Tibbutt, H. G., *The letter books of Sir **Samuel Luke**, 1644–45, Parliamentary Governor of Newport Pagnell* (London HMSO, 1963).

Townsend, G. F., ***The Siege of Colchester*** *or an event of the Civil War, A.D. 1648* (Naval and Military Press Reprint).

Vicars, J., ***The burning-bush*** *not consumed: or, The fourth and last part of the parliamentarie-chronicle. Containing a full and faithfull continuation and exact narration of all the most materiall and most memorable proceedings of this renowned parliament... from August, 1644... to... July, 1646* (London, 1646).

Walker E., ***Historical discourses***, *upon several occasions* (London, 1705).

Warburton, E. (ed.), ***Memoirs of Prince Rupert*** *and the Cavaliers*, three volumes (London, 1849).

Ward, R., ***Anima'dversions of warre***: *or a military magazine of the truest rules, and ablest instructions, for the managing of warre* (London, 1639).

Webb, J. (ed.), ***Military Memoir of Colonel John Birch***, *written by Roe, his secretary* (Camden Society, New Series, vol. 7, 1873).

Weston, S., *Lincolnshire's lost Battlefield? A **Battlefield Survey of the Battle of Winceby**, 1643* (York University, 2013).

White, J., *A True Relation of a great and glorious victory through God's providence, obtained by Sir William Waller, Sir Arthur Haselrig... against Marquesse Hartford, Prince Maurice, Sir Ralph Hopton...* (London, 1643).

Whitlocke, R. H. (ed.), ***Memoirs***, *Biographical and Historical, of Bulstrode Whitelocke, Lord Commissioner of the Great Seal, and Ambassador at the Court of Sweden, at the Period of The Commonwealth* (London, 1860).

Wishart, G., ***Memoirs of James Graham Marquis of Montrose*** (Edinburgh, 1819).

SECONDARY SOURCES

Abram, A., *The Battle of **Montgomery** 1644* (Bristol, 1993).

Ackroyd, P., *The **History of England**, volume III, Civil War* (London, 2014).

Adair, J., *By the Sword Divided, Eyewitnesses of the English Civil War* (London, undated).

Adair, J., *A Life of **John Hampden** the Patriot* (London, 2003).

Adair, J., ***Roundhead General***: *the campaigns of Sir William Waller* (Thrupp, 1997).

Adair, J., ***Cheriton 1644*** (Kineton, 1973).

Adamson, J., *The **Noble Revolt**, The Overthrown of Charles I* (London, 2007).

Anderson, A., *The **Civil Wars** 1640–9* (London, 1995).

Andriette, E. A., ***Devon and Exeter*** *in the Civil War* (Newton Abbot, 1971).

Anon, ***An account of the siege of Chester***: *during the civil wars between king Charles I and his parliament* (Chester, 1790).

Ashley, M., *The English **Civil War*** (Stroud, 1974).

Ashley, M., ***The Battle of Naseby*** *and the Fall of King Charles I* (New York, 1992).

Ashton, R., *The English Civil War, **Conservatism and Revolution** 1603–1649* (London, 1978).

Atkin, M., ***Cromwell's Crowning Mercy***: *The Battle of Worcester 1651* (Stroud, 1998).

Atkin, M., ***Worcestershire Under Arms***: *An English County During the Civil Wars* (Barnsley, 2004).

Baker, A., *A Battlefield Atlas of the English Civil War* (London, 1986).

Barbary, J., *Puritan and Cavalier* (Harmondsworth, 1977).

Barnett, C., ***Britain and Her Army*** – *A military, political and social history of the British Army 1509–1970* (London, 1970).

Barratt, J., ***Cavalier Capital***, *Oxford in the English Civil War 1642–1646* (Solihull, 2015).

Barratt, J., ***Great Siege of Chester*** (Stroud, 2003).

Barratt, J., ***Sieges of the English Civil Wars*** (Barnsley, 2009).

Barratt, J., *The **Battle for York**, Marston Moor 1644* (Stroud, 2002).

Barratt, J., *The Civil War in the **South-West*** (Barnsley, 2005).

Barratt, J., *The **Battle of Nantwich** 1644* (Bristol, 1993).

Barratt, J., ***The Siege of Chester and the Battle of Rowton Heath*** *1645* (Bristol, 1994).

Barratt, J., *The **Battle of Langport** 1645* (Bristol, 1995).

Barratt, J., ***The Last Army*** – *The Battle of Stow-on-the Wold and the end of the Civil War in the Welsh Marches, 1646* (Solihull, 2018).

Barrès-Baker, M. C., ***The Siege of Reading***: *The Failure of the Earl of Essex's 1643 Spring Offensive* (EbookLib, 2004).

Barrès-Baker, M. C., ***The Siege of Reading***: *The Failure of the Earl of Essex's 1643 Spring Offensive* (Ottawa, 2007).

Bennett, M., *Traveller's Guide to the Battlefields of the English Civil War* (Exeter, 1990).

Bennett, M., *The English Civil War* (Hereford, 1992).

Bennett, M., *The English Civil War, A Historical Companion* (Stroud, 2004).

Bennett, M., *Cromwell at War, The Lord General and his Military Revolution* (London, 2017).

Black, J., *A **Military Revolution?** Military Change and European Society 1550–1800* (Basingstoke, 1991).

Brammer, B., ***Winceby*** *and the Battle* (Boston, 1994).

Broxap, E., *The Great Civil War in **Lancashire** (1642–1651)* (Manchester, 1910).

Buchan, J., *The **Marquis of Montrose*** (London, 1913).

Bull, S., ***The Furie of the Ordnance***, *Artillery in the English Civil Wars* (Woodbridge, 2008).

Bull, S., and Seed, S., ***Bloody Preston*** (Lancaster, 1998).

Burne, A. H., and Young, P., *The **Great Civil War**, A Military History of the First Civil War 1642–1646* (London, 1959).

Burne, A. H., *More **Battlefields of England*** (London, 2002).

Carlton, C., ***Going to the Wars***, *The Experience of the English Civil Wars, 1638–1651* (London, 1992).

Carruthers, B., *The English Civil Wars* (London, 2000).

Carte, T., *The life of **James, Duke of Ormond**; containing an account of the most remarkable affairs of his time, and particularly of Ireland under his government, five volumes* (Oxford, 1851).

Chandler, D. (ed.), *The Oxford Illustrated History of the British Army* (Oxford, 1994).

Childs, W. M., *The Story of the Town of **Reading*** (London, 1905).

Churchill, W., *History of the **English-Speaking** Peoples,* four volumes (London, 1956).

Clark, D., ***Marston Moor July 1644*** (Barnsley, 2004).

Clarke, J. S., ***The Life of James the second*** *King of England,* two volumes (London, 1816).

Coate, M., ***Cornwall in the Great Civil War*** *and Interregnum 1642–1660* (Truro, 1963).

Cobbett, W., *The **Parliamentary History of England** from the earliest period to the year 1803,* 36 volumes (London, 1807).

Coleman P., *Devizes in the Civil War* (Devizes, 1981).

Cooke, D., ***Yorkshire Sieges*** *of the Civil Wars* (Barnsley, 2011).

Cooke, D., ***The Road to Marston Moor*** (Barnsley, 2007).

Davies, N., ***The Isles*** (London, 1999).

Day, J., ***Gloucester & Newbury*** *1643, the turning point of the Civil War* (Barnsley, 2007).

Dixon, J., *The Business at Acton: The Battle of Nantwich, 25th January 1644 and the Civil War in Cheshire 1642–1646* (Nottingham, 2012).

Donagan, B., ***War in England*** *1642–1649* (Oxford University Press, 2008).

Douglas, W. S., ***Cromwell's Scotch Campaigns*** *1650–1651* (London, 1898).

Ede-Borrett, S., ***Lostwithiel 1644*** (Farnham, 2004).

Ellis, J., *To Walk in the Dark: **Military Intelligence** in the English Civil War, 1642–1646* (Stroud, 2011).

Evans, D., *Montgomery, 1644* (Powys, undated).

Fielding Johnson, T., *Glimpses of **Ancient Leicester** in Six Periods* (Leicester, 1891).

Firth, C. H., ***Cromwell's Army***: *a history of the English soldier during the Civil Wars, the Commonwealth and the Protectorate* (London, 1902).

Fletcher, A., *The **Outbreak of the Civil War*** (New York University Press, 1981).

Foard, G., ***Naseby, The Decisive Campaign*** (Whitstable, 1995).

Fortescue, J. W., *A **History of the British Army** 1645–1870,* twenty volumes (London, 1899–1920).

Franck, R., ***Northern Memoirs,*** *Calculated for the Meridian of Scotland* (Edinburgh, 1821).

Fraser, A., ***Cromwell,*** *Our Chief of Men* (London, 1973).

Gardiner, S. R., *History of England from the **Accession of James I** to the Outbreak of the Civil War, 1603–1642,* ten volumes (London, 1883–84).

Gardiner, S. R., *The History of the **Great Civil War***, four volumes (London, 1901).

Gardiner, S. R., *The History of the **Commonwealth and Protectorate** 1649–56,* four volumes (London, 1903).

Gaunt, P., *A Nation under Siege, The **Civil War in Wales** 1642–48* (London, 1991).

Gaunt P., ***The English Civil War – A Military History*** (London, 2017).

Gaunt, P., ***The English Civil Wars*** *1642–1651* (Oxford, 2003).

Gentles, I., *The **New Model Army** in England, Ireland and Scotland, 1645–1653* (Oxford, 1992).

Gilbert, J. T. (ed.), *History of the **Irish Confederation** and the War in Ireland 1641–1643,* 2 volumes (Dublin, 1882).

Gilbert, J. T. (ed.), *A contemporary **history of affairs in Ireland,** from 1641 to 1652,* seven volumes (Dublin, 1879).

Godwin, G. N., *The **Civil War in Hampshire** 1642–45* (Southampton, 1904).

Gordon, P., *A short abridgement of **Britane's distemper:** from the yeare of God M.DC.XXXIX. to M.DC.XLIX* (Aberdeen, 1844).

Griffin, S., *The Battle of **Aylesbury** 1642* (Bristol, 1998).

Guest, K. and D., *British Battles* (Leicester, 2002).

Haldane, A., *Portraits of the English Civil Wars* (London, 2017).

Hamilton, E., *The **Irish Rebellion** of 1641, with a history of events which led up to and succeeded it* (London, 1920).

Haverty, M., *The **History of Ireland,** Ancient & Modern* (Dublin, 1860).

Haythornthwaite, P., *The English Civil War 1642–1651, An **Illustrated Military History*** (Poole, 1983).

Henry, C., *English **Civil War Artillery** 1642–51* (Oxford, 2005).

Hibbert, C., *Cavaliers and Roundheads – The English at War 1642–1649* (London, 1994).

Hibbert, C., ***Charles I*** (London, 1968).

Hill, C., *The World Turned **Upside Down*** (Harmondsworth, 1972).

Hill, C., *The **Century of Revolution*** (London, 1980).

Hill, C., *The **English Revolution*** (London, 1955).

Hill, P. R. and Watkinson, J. M., *Major General **Lambert's Campaigns in the North,** 1648* (Barnsley, 2012).

Hobbes, T., *Behemoth, the history of the **causes of the Civil Wars** in England* (London, 1840).

Hogg, F. G., ***English Artillery*** *1326–1716* (London, 1963).

Hollings, J. F., ***The History of Leicester*** *During the Great Civil War* (Leicester, 1840).

Holmes, C., *The **Eastern Association** in the English Civil War* (Cambridge University Press, 1974).

Holmes, R. (ed.), ***The Sieges of Pontefract Castle 1644–1648*** (Naval and Military Press Reprint from 1887 original).

Hudson, R. (ed.), *The Grand Quarrel, Women's memoires of the English Civil War* (Stroud, 1993).

Hunt, T., *The English Civil War at First Hand* (London, 2002).

Hyde, E., *History of the **Great Rebellion*** (Oxford, 1839).

Irwin, M., *The Stranger Prince, The Story of Rupert of the Rhine* (London, 1937).

James, L., *The Battle of Torrington 1646* (Epsom, 2015).

Johnson, D., ***Adwalton Moor*** *1643, The Battle that changed the War* (Pickering, 2003).

Kenyon, J. P., *The **Civil Wars of England*** (London, 1988).

Kenyon, J., and Ohlmeyer, J., *The Civil Wars, A **Military History** of England, Scotland and Ireland 1638-1660* (Oxford University Press, 1998).

Ketton-Cremer, R. W., ***Norfolk in the Civil War,*** *A portrait of a society in conflict* (Connecticut, 1970).

Kishlansky, M. A., *The Rise of the New Model Army* (Cambridge University Press, 1979).

Kitson, F., *Old Ironsides, The Military Biography of Oliver Cromwell* (London, 2004).

Lenihan, P., ***Confederate Catholics*** *at War 1641–1649* (Cork University Press, 2001).

Lynch, J., *For **King & Parliament,** Bristol and the Civil War* (Stroud, 1999).

Lynch, M., *The **Interregnum** 1649–60* (London, 2002).

Macaulay, T. B., *The **History of England** from the Accession of James II,* four volumes (London, 1848–61).

Malbon, T., *Memorials of the Civil War in Cheshire and Adjacent Counties* (1889).

Manning, R. B., *An **Apprenticeship in Arms**: The Origins of the British Army 1585–1702* (Oxford University Press, 2006).

Marix Evans, M., *Naseby 1645, The **Triumph of the New Model Army*** (Oxford, 2007).

Marix Evans, M., Burton, P., and Westaway, M., ***Naseby, English Civil War – June 1645*** (Barnsley, 2002).

Marsh, S., '"This Disarmed Multitude": The Impact of the Lostwithiel Campaign on the Earl of Essex's Army and its Reconstruction for Second Newbury' in Jones, S. (ed.), *Home and Away: The British Experience of War 1618–1721,* pp. 44–66 (Warwick, 2018).

Marx, K., *Capital,* three volumes (Moscow 1986).

Matthews, R., *The **Sieges of Newark** 1643–46* (Epsom, 2013).

McKeiver, P., *A **New History of Cromwell's Irish Campaign*** (Didsbury, 2007).

McNicol, P., *The Sieges of **Kingston upon Hull,** 1642 and 1643* (Hull, 1987).

Meehan, C. P., *The **Confederation of Kilkenny*** (Dublin, 1846).

Miller, J., *The English Civil Wars, Roundheads, Cavaliers and the **Execution of the King*** (London, 2009).

Money, W., *The First and Second **Battles of Newbury** and the Siege of Donnington Castle during the Civil War A. D. 1643–6* (Second Edition, London, 1884).

Morrah, P., *Prince **Rupert of the Rhine*** (London, 1976).

Morrill, J., *The **Revolt of the Provinces,** Conservatives and Radicals in the English Civil War 1630–1650* (London, 1976).

Morris, R., *The **Battle of Lansdown and Roundway Down*** (Bristol, 1993).

Morris, R., *The **Battle of Cropredy Bridge** 1644* (Bristol, 1994).

Murdoch, A. D. (ed.) and Morland Simpson, H. F. (ed.), ***Marquis of Montrose 1639–1650*** *by The Rev. George Wishart* (London, 1893).

Murphy, D., ***Cromwell in Ireland,*** *A History of Cromwell's Irish Campaign* (Dublin, 1883).

Newman, P. R., *Atlas of the English Civil War* (Beckenham, 1985).

Newman, P. R., *The Battle of Marston Moor 1644* (Chichester, 1981).

Newman, P. R. and Roberts, P. R., *Marston Moor 1644, The Battle of Five Armies* (Pickering, 2003).

Ó Súilleabháin, S., *Alasdair Mac Colla McDonnell and the Battle of Knocknanuss* (Dublin, 2012).

Ollard, R., *This War without an Enemy* (London, 1976).

Parker, G., *The Military Revolution: Military Innovation and the Rise of the West, 1500–1800* (Cambridge, 1996).

Parry, R. H. (ed.), *The English Civil War and After 1642–1658* (London, 1970).

Peachey, S., *The Battle of Braddock Down, 1643* (Bristol, 1993).

Peachey, S., *The Battle of Stratton, 1643* (Bristol, 1993).

Peachey, S., *The Storming of Bristol* (Bristol, 1993).

Peachey, S., *The Sieges of Exeter 1642–43* (Bristol, 1995).

Peachey, S., and Turton, A., *Old Robin's Foot* (Partizan Press, 1987).

Peachey, S., and Turton, A., *The Fall of the West,* (eight volumes, Stuart Press, (Bristol 1993, 1994).

Peacock, E. (ed.), *The Army Lists of the Roundheads and Cavaliers* (Naval & Military Press Reprint).

Porter, S., *The Blast of War, Destruction in the English Civil Wars* (Stroud, 2011).

Porter, S., and Marsh, S., *The Battle for London* (Stroud, 2011).

Reeves, W., *A Study in Siegecraft, York 1644* (Bristol, 1994).

Reid, S., *All the King's Armies* (Stroud, 1998).

Reid, S., *Auldearn 1645, The Marquis of Montrose's Scottish Campaign* (Oxford, 2003).

Reid, S., *Dunbar 1650, Cromwell's most famous victory* (Oxford, 2004).

Reilly, T., *Cromwell, An Honourable Enemy* – *The untold story of the Cromwellian invasion of Ireland* (Kerry, 1999).

Roberts, K., *London and Liberty* (Partizan Press, 1987).

Roberts, K., *Pike and Shot Tactics 1590–1660* (Oxford, 2010).

Roberts, K., *First Newbury 1643* (Oxford, 2003).

Roberts, K., and Tincey, J., *Edgehill 1642* (Oxford, 2001).

Roberts, M., *The Military Revolution, 1560–1660.* First published in January 1955; reproduced in Rodgers, C. J. (ed.), *The Military Revolution Debate: Readings on the Military Transformation of Early Modern Europe* (Oxford, 1995).

Robertson, B., *Royalists at War in Scotland and Ireland 1638–1650* (Farnham, 2014).

Robertson, G., *The Tyrannicide Brief, the story of the men who sent Charles to the scaffold* (New York, 2005).

Rogers, H. C. B., *Artillery Through the Ages* (London, 1971).

Rogers, H. C. B., *Battles and Generals of the Civil wars 1642–1651* (London, 1968).

Royale, T., *Civil War, The Wars of the Three Kingdoms 1638–1660* (London, 2004).

Russell, C., *Causes of the English Civil War* (Oxford University Press, 1990).

Scott, C. L., *The Battles of Newbury, Crossroads of the English Civil War* (Barnsley, 2008).

Scott, C. L., *The Most Heavy Stroke, The Battle of Roundway Down 1643* (Warwick, 2018).

Scott, C. L., Turton, A., and Gruber von Arni, E., *Edgehill, The Battle Reinterpreted* (Barnsley, 2004).

Serdiville, R., *The Great Siege of Newcastle* (Stroud, 2011).

Skinner, T., *The Life of General Monk, Duke of Albemarle* (London, 1724).

Spalding, J. *The history of the troubles and memorable transactions in Scotland, from the year 1624 to 1645,* two volumes (Aberdeen, 1792).

Spence, T., *Skipton Castle in the Great Civil War 1642–1645* (Otley, 1991).

Spencer, C., *Prince Rupert, The Last Cavalier* (London, 2007).

Spicer, T., *The Battle of Worcester, 1651* (Manchester, 2002).

Spring, L., *The Regiments of the Eastern Association,* two volumes (Bristol, 1998).

Spring, L., *Waller's Army, The Regiments of Sir William Waller's Southern Association* (Bristol, 2007).

Spring, L., *The Battle of Cheriton* (Bristol, 1997).

Stevenson, D., *Revolution and Counter Revolution 1644–51* (Edinburgh, 1977).

Stevenson, D., *The Scottish Revolution 1637–44* (Edinburgh, 2011).

Stone, L., *Causes of the English Revolution* (London, 1972).

Stoyle, M., *Devon and the Civil War* (Exeter, 2001).

Stoyle, M., *Loyalty and Locality* (University of Exeter Press, 1994).

Stoyle, M., *From Deliverance to Destruction, Rebellion and Civil War in an English City* (University of Exeter Press, 1996).

Stubbs, S., *Reprobates, The Cavaliers of the English Civil War* (London, 2011).

Tallett, F., *War and Society in early-modern Europe, 1495–1715* (London, 1992).

Tawney, R. H., *Religion and the Rise of Capitalism* (1926).

Taylor, P. A. M. (ed.), *The Origins of the English Civil War, Conspiracy, Crusade or Class Conflict?* (Boston, 1960).

Terry, C. S., *The life and campaigns of Alexander Leslie, first earl of Leven* (London, 1899).

Thomson, G. M., *Warrior Prince, The Life of Prince Rupert of the Rhine* (London, 1976).

Tincey, J., *Marston Moor 1644* (Oxford, 2003).

Townsend, G. F., *The Siege of Colchester or an event of the Civil War A.D. 1648* (London, 1874).

Toynbee M., and Young, P., *Cropredy Bridge, 1644* (Kineton, 1970).

Trevor-Roper, H. R., *The Social Causes of the Great Rebellion* (London, 1957).

Tullie, I., *A Narrative of the Siege of Carlisle in 1644 and 1645* (Carlisle, 1840).

Underdown, D., *Revel, riot, and rebellion: popular politics and culture in England 1603–1660* (Oxford, 1985).

Varley, J., *The Siege of Oxford, An account of Oxford during the Civil War, 1642–1646* (Oxford, 1932)

Walker, E., *Brief Memorials of the Unfortunate Success of his Majesty's Army and Affairs in the Year 1645* (London, 1705).

Wanklyn, M., *Decisive Battles of the English Civil Wars* (Barnsley, 2014).

Wanklyn, M., *The Warrior Generals, Winning the British Civil Wars* (Yale University Press, 2010).

Wanklyn, M., *Reconstructing the New Model Army, Volume 1: Regimental Lists April 1645 to May 1649* (Solihull, 2015).

Warwick, P., *Memoirs of the Reign of Charles I* (London, 1702).

Washburn, J., *Bibliotheca Gloucestrensis: Collection of scarce and curious Tracts, relating to the County and City of Gloucester; Illustrative of, and Published during the Civil War* (London, 1825).

Waylen, J., *A history, military and municipal, of the ancient borough of the Devizes* (Devizes, 1859).

Wedgwood, C. V., *Montrose* (London, 1952).

Wedgwood, C. V., *The King's Peace 1637–1641* (London, 1974).

Wedgwood, C. V., *The King's War* (London, 1958).

Wenham, L. P., *The Great and Close Siege of York 1644* (York, 1994).

Willis Bund, J. W., *The Civil War in Worcestershire, 1642–1646 and the Scotch Invasion of 1651* (Worcester, 1905).

Wood, A. C., *Nottinghamshire in the Civil War* (Oxford, 1937).

Woolrych, A., *Battles of the English Civil War* (London, 1961).

Worden, B., *The English Civil Wars 1640–1660* (London, 2009).

Worden, B., *Roundhead Reputations, The English Civil Wars and the Passions of Posterity* (London, 2001).

Worton, J., *The Battle of Montgomery, 1644* (Solihull, 2016).

Worton, J., *To Settle the Crown, Waging Civil War in Shropshire 1642–1648* (Solihull, 2016).

Wroughton, J., *The Battle of Lansdown 1643* (Bath, 2008).

Yaxley, S., *The Siege of King's Lynn 1643* (Dereham, 1993).

Young, P., and Holmes, R., *The English Civil War* (Ware, 1974).

Young, P., *Edgehill 1642* (Moreton-in-Marsh, 1995).

Young, P., *Marston Moor 1644, The Campaign and the Battle* (Moreton-in-Marsh, 1997).

Young, P., *Naseby 1645, The Campaign and the Battle* (London, 1985).

ABOUT THE AUTHOR

Nicolas (Nick) Lipscombe MSc FRHistS served for 34 years in the British Army. He is an accomplished historian, author and lecturer. He was made a Fellow of the Royal Historical Society in 2016. He has concentrated on the Napoleonic Wars, and the Peninsular War in particular, but he is now working on projects associated with the English Civil War. He is a tutor at the University of Oxford, Department of Continuing Education and an active member of numerous historical societies.

His works include the award-winning *Peninsular War Atlas and Concise History, Wellington's Guns, Wellington Invades France*, the official *Waterloo* 200 Bicentenary compendium and, most recently, *Wellington's Eastern Front*.